Keyboarding & Formatting

COMPLETE COURSE
LESSONS 1-120

Microsoft® Word 2007

2e

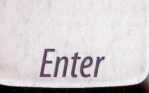

Enter

Susie H. VanHuss, Ph.D.
Distinguished Professor Emeritus
University of South Carolina

Connie M. Forde, Ph. D.
Department of Instructional
Systems, Leadership, and
Workforce Development
Mississippi State University

Donna L. Woo
Department Chair
Computer Information Systems
Cypress College
Cypress, California

SOUTH-WESTERN
CENGAGE Learning

Australia Brazil Japan Korea Mexico Singapore Spain United Kingdom United States

Printed in China by China Translation & Printing Services Limited

4 5 6 7 11 10

Photo Researcher: Terri Miller

Photography Manager: Deanna Ettinger

Cover Images: Grannan Graphic Design, Ltd.

Cover & Internal Designer: Grannan Graphic
Design, Ltd.

Art Director: Bethany Casey, Tippy McIntosh

Copyeditor: Gary Morris

Production Service: GGS Book Services

Sr. Manufacturing Coordinator: Charlene Taylor

Sr. Technology Project Editor: Mike Jackson

Manager of Technology, Editorial: Liz Prigge

Sr. Content Project Manager: Martha Conway

Marketing Coordinator: Kelley Gilreath

Marketing Manager: Valerie Lauer

Consulting Editor: Mary Todd, Todd Publishing
Services

Sr. Developmental Editor: Dave Lafferty

Acquisitions Editor: Jane Phelan

VP/Editor-in-Chief: Karen Schmohe

VP/Editorial Director: Jack W. Calhoun

**Keyboarding & Formatting Essentials,
Complete Course, Lessons 1-120,
Second Edition**
Susie VanHuss, Connie Forde, Donna Woo

© 2008, 2005 South-Western, a part of Cengage Learning

For product information and technology assistance, contact us at
Cengage Learning Academic Resource Center, 1-800-423-0563

For permission to use material from this text or product, submit all
requests online at **www.cengage.com/permissions**
Further permissions questions can be emailed to
permissionrequest@cengage.com

Microsoft is a registered trademark of Microsoft Corporation in the U.S.
and/or other countries.

The names of all products mentioned herein are used for identification
purposes only and may be trademarks or registered trademarks of their
respective owners. South-Western disclaims any affiliation, association,
connection with, sponsorship, or endorsement by such owners.

Student Edition ISBN-13: 978-0-538-97464-6
Student Edition ISBN-10: 0-538-97464-8
Data CD ISBN-13: 978-0-538-97463-9
Data CD ISBN-10: 0-538-97463-X
Student Edition with CD ISBN-13: 978-0-538-72980-2
Student Edition with CD ISBN-10: 0-538-72980-5

South-Western Cengage Learning
5191 Natorp Boulevard
Mason, OH 45040
USA

Cengage Learning products are represented in Canada by
Nelson Education, Ltd.

For your course and learning solutions, visit **school.cengage.com**

CONTENTS

Summary of Functions

FOCUS ON THE ESSENTIALS

Building a skill takes practice, and that's what you'll get with the *Keyboarding Essentials 2E* series. More timed writings, five supplemental keyboarding lessons using the keyboarding software, and technique drills throughout.

This versatile skill development program combines keying from the text and computer screen to provide well-rounded practice.

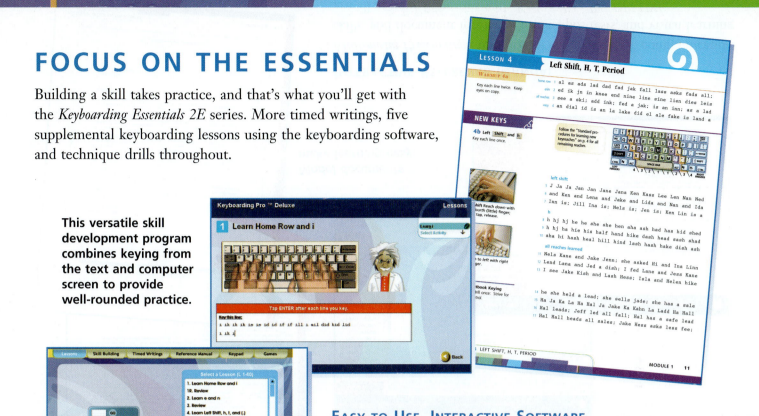

EASY-TO-USE, INTERACTIVE SOFTWARE

Keyboarding Pro DELUXE teaches keyboarding skills in the first 25 lessons and then checks the speed and accuracy of timed writings, drills, and formatting and accuracy in documents for lessons 26–120.

Keyboarding Pro 5 is also available for a keyboarding short course (Lessons 1–25).

Skill Builders provide numerous Technique Builders and Timed Writings to strengthen skill.

What's more, *Keyboarding Pro* includes 20 additional lessons with both speed and accuracy emphasis that challenge you at every level to improve. Five new assessments help place you at the right level of instruction.

FORMATTING USING MICROSOFT® WORD 2007

Keyboarding Essentials 2E teaches document formatting using the commands of *Microsoft Word 2007*. Defaults have changed with this new version of *Word* and so have the rules for formatting business documents. You'll also learn to create business documents using traditional *Word 2003* formats so you'll be prepared for any workplace situation.

Keyboarding Pro DELUXE software checks documents for accuracy of keystrokes and commands.

Text includes instructions to support Microsoft Word 2007 and offers many tips for a smooth transition into the new software.

UP-TO-DATE FORMATS

New formats are explained and illustrated with callouts for proper placement.

INTERACTIVE REFERENCE MANUAL

Multimedia Presentations reinforce *Word* commands, communication skills, and document formats. Pretests, posttests, and visual learning are all at your fingertips with *Keyboarding Pro DELUXE*.

Model documents make learning easy.

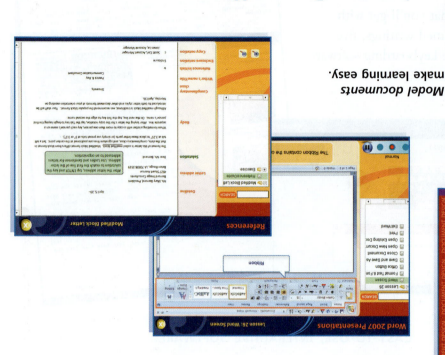

EXTRA PRACTICE FOR THE REAL WORLD

Communication Skills reinforce language arts skills such as proofreading, capitalization, and composition.

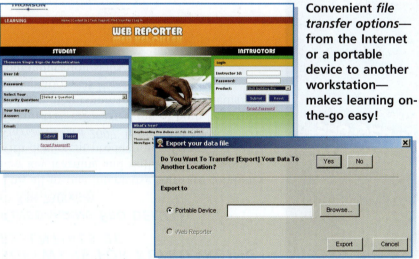

Drills reinforce new functions.

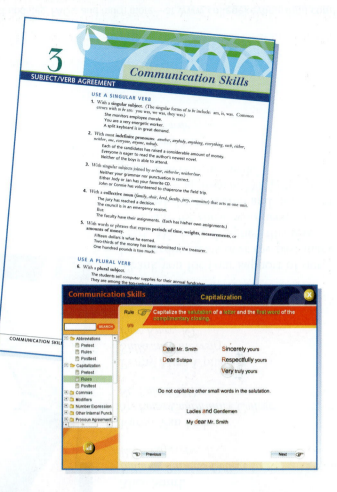

Convenient *file transfer options*—from the Internet or a portable device to another workstation—makes learning on-the-go easy!

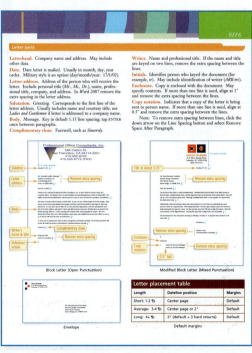

KEYBOARDING PRO DELUXE SOFTWARE

The enhanced *Web Reporter* for distance learning allows instructors to manage classes, create a grade book, and add comments to student reports. Students can view these comments online.

The *Reference Manual* provides easy access to model documents.

KEYBOARDING ESSENTIALS 2E

This comprehensive series offers 120 lessons in three different texts: Lessons 1–60 focus on basic keyboarding and formatting; Lessons 61–120 moves onto more advanced formatting and document processing; and the complete course offers all lessons in one convenient text.

SOFTWARE FOR KEYBOARDING ESSENTIALS 2E

KEYBOARDING PRO DELUXE
(0-538-73006-4)

This all-in-one interactive software combines new key learning and skill building lessons with document production software for *Microsoft Word 2007*. It includes error diagnostics, error checking of both keystrokes and common commands, and multimedia presentations of *Word* functions, communication skills, and document formats.

ALSO AVAILABLE

NEW! SKILL BUILDING PRO
(0-538-72991-0)

Developing speed and accuracy has never been easier or more fun. This fully integrated text and software program includes 60 lessons of instruction as well as self-paced writings, drill practices, timed writings with error diagnostics, games for building skill, and a word processor.

A WORD FROM THE AUTHORS

Thank you for your support of our keyboarding texts over the past many years. We have designed this text especially for those who need an essentials keyboarding and document formatting approach. We hope our series meets your needs.

Susie VanHuss
Connie Forde
Donna Woo

REVIEWERS

Debbie Franklin
Bryant & Stratton College
Orchard Park, NY

Jane E. McDowell
Columbus State Community College
Columbus, OH

Teresa Moore
Volunteer State Community College
Gallatin, TN

Vicki R. Robertson
Southwest Tennessee Community College
Memphis, TN

Alice Smith
Indiana Business College
West Lafayette, IN

Karen Van Dyke
St. Louis Community College
St. Louis, MO

Penny Mize Uphaus
Sullivan University
Fort Knox, KY

x

WELCOME TO KEYBOARDING PRO DELUXE

Keyboarding Pro DELUXE is an all-in-one Keyboarding and Document Processing software that builds on the popular *Keyboarding Pro 5*. This interactive software combines new key learning, skill building, and document processing using *Microsoft Word 2007*.

Keyboarding Pro DELUXE includes features such as new key learning; error diagnostics with related drill practice; engaging games; error checking of both keystroke accuracy and common *Word* commands; multimedia presentations on *Word 2007* commands, communication skills, and document formats. It includes 120 lessons. You may be using *Keyboarding Pro 5*, which includes the first 25 lessons of *Keyboarding Pro DELUXE* as well as skill building lessons for speed and accuracy, timed writings, and the numeric keypad lessons and drills.

HOW DO I GET STARTED?

Detailed information is given in the Student's User Guide packaged with your software.

Step 1: Begin by installing the software on your home computer.

Step 2: From the Start menu, select Programs, then South-Western Keyboarding, and click *Keyboarding Pro DELUXE* or *Keyboarding Pro 5*. The Log In dialog box appears. Select the New User button.

Step 3: The first time you use *Keyboarding Pro*, key your user information in the New Student dialog box to create a student record. Do this only once so that all lessons are stored in one file.

- To select the class in which you are enrolled, click the down arrow on the Class field.
- If your class will be online and you will be using the Web Reporter for managing files, enter a Class Code to easily send your files to your instructor using your browser. When your instructor provides you with the Class Code, copy and paste it into this field. To *copy* the Class Code, hold down the CTRL key and tap *C*; then paste it (CTRL + V) into the Class Code field. (**Note:** If this is an online course, the Class Code field will be active.)
- Notice that by default your student record is saved to C:\Program Files\ KeyboardingPro Deluxe\Students. If you will be saving to a network drive, click the Folder button and browse to identify the path. Click OK.

Step 4: The first time you enter *Keyboarding Pro*, you may be required to key a Skill Analysis to evaluate your current skill level.

The software and the textbook work together. In Lessons 1–25, the software will show you the new key locations and automatically provide a variety of drills. You'll key Textbook Keying exercises and Timed Writings from the book. In Lessons 26–120, you'll key all timings, documents, and tests from your textbook and use multimedia features to review related skills.

MAIN MENU

The Main menu provides the primary navigation. It includes tabs for selecting a lesson, a timed writing, and many other options. The first time you enter *Keyboarding Pro*, you may be required to key a Skill Analysis to evaluate your current skill level.

Lessons: The number of lessons available to you depends on the length of your course; typically you will see L1–25, Lessons 1–60, or Lessons 1–120. Results are reported in the Summary Report.

Skill Building: After you know the alphabetic keys (Lesson 10), use these 20 lessons to boost your keyboarding skill. Optional exercises are available for building your skill, including Technique Builders that correlate with supplementary skill building pages in the textbook and Drill Practices that recommend error-diagnostic drills to correct accuracy problems. Results are reported in the Skill Building Report.

Timed Writings: Most timed writings in the textbook are available for additional practice or measurement purposes. Error diagnostics tracks specific accuracy problems and then suggests drills by row, by finger, or by type to improve your accuracy (Lesson 26 and beyond). Your results are reported in the Timed Writing Report.

References: Multimedia presentations reinforce the commonly used *Word 2007* commands. Communication Skills review topics such as proofreading and word usage; a pretest and posttest will help you evaluate your progress. Document Formats illustrate and review common business document formats.

Keypad: You will learn the numeric keypad by touch and build your skill.

Each time you enter *Keyboarding Pro* after the first time, the Log In dialog box displays your name. Select your name and key your password. If you do not see your name, click the Folder button and locate the drive where your student record is located.

To transfer your student record from a portable device such as a flash drive, diskette, or other media, browse to identify the path. If you have sent your student record to the Web Reporter previously, you can update your current file from the Web.

NAVIGATION

The buttons at the bottom of the *Keyboarding Pro* main screen will help you execute common functions.

 Help answers questions about the screen you are on.

Word Processor enables you to create documents or take timings; it does not launch *Word 2007*.

Send File transmits your student record to your instructor. If you have enrolled in an online course (see step 2 on page ix), your student record will automatically be attached; you can select other files to send as well. You must be logged onto the Internet in order to send files.

Web Reports enables you to view reports online or view comments your instructor may have posted for you. When you get to the link, key your user information from step 2 on page ix.

 Log In allows you to transfer your student files to another location such as a portable device (flash drive or to the server) or to the Web Reporter.

Exit quits the program.

HOW DO I COMPLETE DOCUMENTS IN *WORD 2007?*

Beginning in Lesson 26, you will create business documents in *Word 2007*. When you choose a document that is created in *Word 2007*, the Document Options dialog box displays. The first time you key each document, the option *Begin new document* displays, which automatically launches *Word 2007*.

The Document toolbar displays in the upper-right corner. Click the Back button and the document saves automatically without checking it. Click the Check button when you have proofread the document for mistakes and previewed for placement.

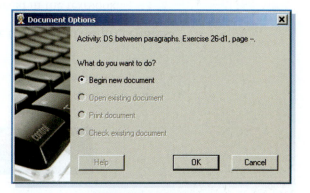

Back   Help

Check

The Document toolbar changes when the checked document is displayed. Click Display Error List to identify the types of mistakes you have made. The error number correlates to the numbered errors on the document. Use the Print command of *Word* if you wish to print the document. Close the document to return to the Lesson menu and continue with the rest of the lesson.

Help
Close the Document
Display Error List

To complete *Word* documents, follow these standard procedures:

1. Key and format the document as directed in the textbook.
2. Proofread for keying or formatting errors. Verify your document against the exercise in the textbook. Preview for placement.
3. Check the document when you are completely satisfied. The software will check the accuracy and display a checked version on screen. Mistakes will be counted above each paragraph and errors will be highlighted.
4. Select Display Error List for an explanation of each error.
5. Scroll to the bottom of the screen to view the report of errors, *gwam*, number of errors, etc.
6. Print the document using the *Word* Print command if desired.
7. Close the document from the *Keyboarding Pro DELUXE* toolbar.

If you wish to edit the document (make corrections), select it again from the Lesson menu. From the Document Options dialog box, choose *Open existing document*. Revise the document as desired and again proofread, preview, check, and close it.

WHAT ELSE SHOULD I KNOW?

Reports. Numerous reports are available by selecting Reports from the menu bar. The Summary Report includes a brief summary of each lesson completed. You can link to a specific lesson report from the Summary Report. The Skill Building Report includes the results of your progress on the Accuracy and Speed Lessons, Drill Practice, and more. The Timed Writing Report tracks the result of your last 20 timings and the best timings at each length. The Document and Production Test Report summarizes the results and grades on those completed.

- Keyboarding Pro ™ Deluxe
Reports   Help
Summary L1-25
Summary L26-120
Skill Building Report...
Timed Writings...
Cumulative Error Diagnostic...
Document and Production Test
Performance Graphs ▶
Certificate of Completion...

Web Reports. If you are enrolled in a course that is using the Web Reporter, click the Send File button to send your student report to your instructor.

WINDOWS VISTA

When you turn on your computer using *Windows Vista*, it may open to the *Welcome Center*, depending on whether the checkbox for *Run at startup* has been left selected. If the checkbox is de-selected, the "Logon screen" or the "Sign-on screen" immediately appears after booting. This screen lists any users who have been signed up to use the computer. Once a user is selected, you are prompted to enter your password. Enter the password, and the *desktop* appears, displaying an attractive picture. Like the top of a desk, this screen serves as a surface for your work. Your computer manufacturer may have chosen the picture, or you may have selected one during installation.

While the *Windows Vista* desktop looks relatively simple, it contains many sophisticated tools. We will be learning about some of the most important tasks that can be performed from this screen.

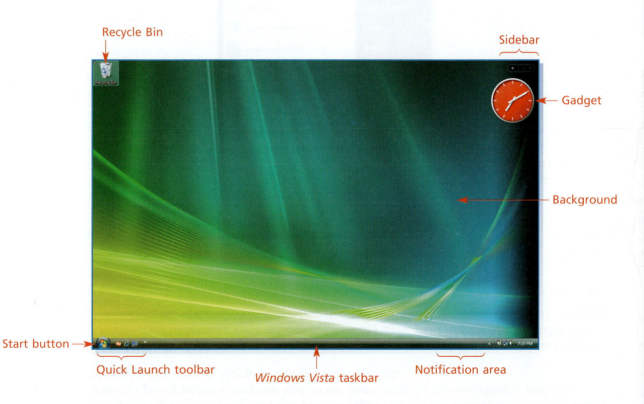

Recycle Bin

Sidebar

Gadget

Background

Start button

Quick Launch toolbar

Windows Vista taskbar

Notification area

The *taskbar* is located at the bottom of your screen. It shows which programs are running and allows you to switch to a different program. *Vista* shows a thumbnail sketch of running programs when you hold your mouse over a running program in the taskbar.

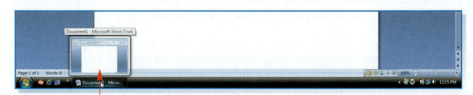

Thumbnail of *Microsoft Word*

Windows Vista

On the right side of the screen, *Sidebar* contains small programs called *gadgets*. *Vista* ships with several interesting gadgets including a clock, currency converter, calculator, and news headlines. You can add or remove gadgets from the *Sidebar*, and additional gadgets are available online.

The Start button is located at the bottom, left-hand corner of the screen. The Start button opens the Start menu, which acts as a gateway to your computer's programs, folders, and settings. Click it to open the Start menu. It is called a menu because it provides a list of choices.

The left pane of the Start menu contains the *pinned program list* and the Search results box. Pinned programs are programs that you use regularly, so *Vista* creates a shortcut to them. You can pin or unpin a program icon to the Start menu by right-clicking it and then choosing Pin to Start Menu or Remove from this list.

The right side of the Start menu contains shortcuts to many of *Vista's* predefined folders. Quick access to features such as Search, Control Panel, and Help are also available here. You can install updates, lock your computer, put it to sleep, restart it, shut it off, or switch users from here as well.

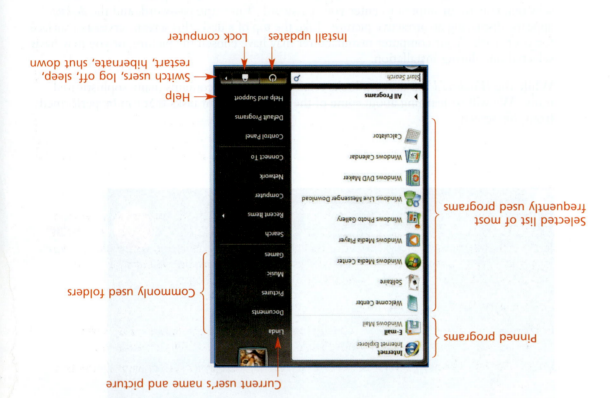

- Install updates
- Lock computer
- Switch users, log off, sleep, restart, hibernate, shut down
- Help
- Selected list of most frequently used programs
- Commonly used folders
- Pinned programs
- Current user's name and picture

GET HELP

The Help function in *Windows Vista* is quite extensive. You can also set an option in Help so that *Vista* connects to the Internet any time you search for help.

To access Help, click the Start button; then choose Help and Support. The fastest way to get help is to type a word or phrase in the Search box. You can also click the Browse Help button and then click an item in the index listing of subject headings that appears. Some subject headings contain Help topics within a subject heading. Click the Help topic to open it, and click the subheading to narrow your search.

If you don't find what you need using the Search box or the Browse Help button, you can access Windows Online Help and Support. If all else fails, you can contact a technical support professional via phone, e-mail, or live chat.

Tip: You can also tap F1 to access Help.

CUSTOMIZE THE DESKTOP

Once you begin using *Vista* on a regular basis, you may want to customize your desktop. One of the easiest ways to personalize *Vista* is to change the *desktop background* (formerly called the wallpaper). Change the desktop background if you have a favorite picture you have taken with your camera and want to use it as the background. *Windows Vista* also includes several sample desktop backgrounds that you may choose.

To change the background:

1. Right-click on an empty part of the desktop and choose Personalize. The Vista Personalize appearance and sounds dialog box appears (providing options to).
2. Click the Desktop Background link. The Choose a Desktop Background dialog box appears.
3. Click the down arrow to choose from different groups of pictures, or browse to locate the picture saved in another area. Click the desired picture to use as the desktop background.
4. Choose how you would like to position the picture (*Fit to screen*, *Tile*, or *Center*). Fit to screen covers the entire desktop; Tile repeats a small version of the picture over and over until it fills the entire desktop; Center places the picture in the middle of the desktop and a colored border fills any gaps.
5. Click OK.

Windows Vista allows you to customize your desktop in many other ways including adding a new gadget, controlling icons, changing the mouse pointer, or selecting a screen saver. You may wish to access the *Vista Help* feature to learn about these methods to personalize your desktop.

File Management

File management includes the process of creating and managing the electronic files on your computer. Using *Windows Vista*, you can perform many common file-related tasks, such as renaming, deleting files, or compressing files.

In this section, you will also learn to work with auxiliary drives, including CD/DVD and universal serial bus (USB) flash drives. USB flash drives vary in size and shape and can hold gigabytes of information. They are also called thumb drives, key chain drives, key drives, and memory keys. Data that needs to be used again in the future must be saved on a storage device such as a USB flash drive, CD/DVD, or hard drive.

UNDERSTAND THE FILE SYSTEM

As with paper files, it is important to establish a logical and easy-to-use computer file management procedure to organize files efficiently so that you can find them quickly and easily. The *Windows Vista* operating system provides a file management program, *Windows Explorer*, which helps you keep track of your files and folders.

USB flash drive

USE WINDOWS EXPLORER

From the desktop, *Windows Explorer* is used to perform many common file management tasks. *Windows Explorer* displays locations such as hard disk drives, CD or DVD drives, removable storage media, or network locations that are connected to your computer. You can also access an external device that might be connected to your computer, such as a digital camera. The figure below displays parts of the *Explorer* window.

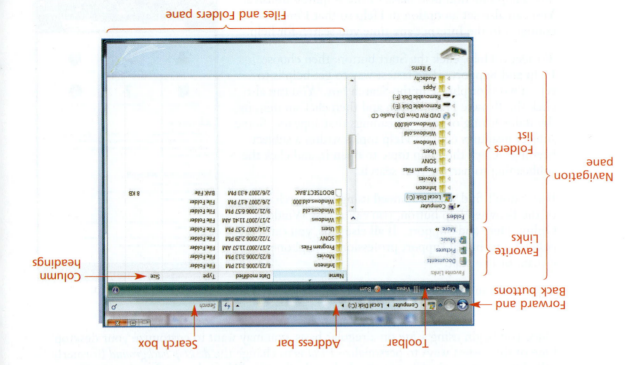

At the top of the *Explorer* window, the Address bar displays the currently viewed location as well as a series of links separated by arrows. It shows the path, including folders to arrive at the location displayed. You can click links within the Address bar to navigate to a different folder without closing the current folder window.

Use the Back and Forward buttons on the Address bar to navigate to other folders you have already opened without closing the current window. After you use the Address bar to change folders, for example, you can use the Back button to return to the original folder.

The Navigation pane is located on the left, and it displays the drives and the folders stored on each computer drive. View the files within a folder by clicking the folder.

The Search box searches for a file or subfolder stored in the current folder. The search begins as soon as you begin typing, so as you type *L*, for example, all the files that start with the letter *L* will appear in the folder's file list. Column headings change how the files in the file list are organized. You can sort or group files in the current view.

The toolbar performs common tasks, such as changing the appearance of your files and folders, copying files to a CD, or starting a digital picture slide show. The toolbar's buttons change to show only the commands that are useful. For example, if you click a picture file, the toolbar shows different buttons than it would if you clicked a music file.

The files display in the right pane, called the *Files and Folders pane*. The *Navigation pane* (displayed on the right) contains two parts: the *Favorite Links* (top part) and the *Folders* (the bottom part). The *Favorite Links* area lists places to which you want quick access. The *Folders* list shows a hierarchy of your computer. It displays the drives and folders on your computer.

To access *Windows Explorer*:

1. Right-click on the Start button and select Explore.
2. In the left Folders list, scroll down until you see the desired storage device drive or folder and click.

CHANGE VIEWS OF FILES AND FOLDERS

Clicking the Views button on the toolbar changes the way the file and folder icons are displayed. Each time you click the Views button, the folder window alternates from *List*, *Details*, *Tiles*, and *Large Icons*. Click the arrow next to the Views button and move the slider up or down to view and select one of the other view selections.

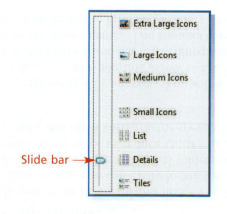

Slide bar ⟶

WORK WITH FILES AND FOLDERS

Folders are extremely important in organizing files. You will create and manage folders and the files within them so that you can easily locate them. A folder can store files; or in some cases, a folder is used to store additional folders where files are stored. This folder-in-a-folder organization helps to reduce clutter so you can find, navigate, and manage your files, folders, and disks with greater speed. Folders within folders are called subfolders.

All files and folders are represented by an icon. You will know that a folder contains another folder when it has the right-pointing arrow to the left of the folder icon. To "expand" or show the contents of a folder with a right-pointing open arrow, click the arrow icon to the left of the folder name. The triangle changes to a down-pointing solid triangle. Double-click a folder in the Files and Folders pane to open the folder.

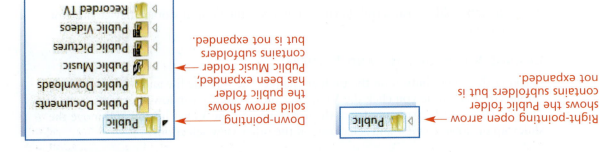

Right-pointing open arrow
shows the Public folder
contains subfolders but is
not expanded.

Down-pointing
solid arrow shows
the public folder
has been expanded;
Public Music folder
contains subfolders
but is not expanded.

To create a folder:

1. Access an *Explorer window* and display the contents of the desired storage device. Click the Organize drop-down arrow and choose New Folder.

2. A new folder displays with the name *New Folder*. The insertion point is blinking next to the highlighted words *New Folder*. Key the desired folder name and tap ENTER.

1. Access *Windows Explorer* and display the contents of your removable storage drive (or the location where you have been instructed to save your document files).

2. Create a folder named *Assignments*.

3. Open the *Assignments* folder, and create a subfolder named *Keyboarding*.

4. Access the contents of your storage drive in the Folders list. Expand the *Assignments* folder located on your storage drive and view its contents.

5. Open the *Assignments* folder. Within it, create a subfolder named *Accounting*.

6. Access Help and Support and use search to get help on *Create folder*. When the search results appear, choose *Create a new folder*. Read the information. Close Help.

7. The *Assignments* folder should be open. Create a subfolder called *Term Papers*.

8. Close *Windows Explorer*.

NAMING FILES

Good file organization begins with giving your folders and files names that are logical and easy to understand. In Drill 1, you created a folder named *Assignments*. You created a new folder within *Assignments* to separate Keyboarding assignments from your Accounting assignments.

In a later lesson, you will be creating a folder named *Module 3* to hold all work that you key in Module 3. You will save the files by the exercise name, such as *26-d1* (Lesson 26, document 1) or *26-d2*. A system like this makes finding files simple.

Filenames can be up to 260 characters long, but in practice you won't use filenames that long. In addition, *Vista* doesn't let you use any of these symbols in a filename: \ / : * ? " < > |

Rename Files or Folders

Occasionally, you may want to rename a file or folder.

To rename a file or folder:

1. Access an *Explorer* window and display the contents of your removable storage drive (or the location where you have been instructed to save your document files or folders).
2. Click the file or folder icon to be renamed.
3. Choose Organize on the toolbar.
4. Select Rename.
5. Key the new name and tap ENTER.

Tip: You can also right-click a file or folder icon, and then left-click Rename from the Shortcut menu. Key the new name, and tap ENTER.

Copy, Move, or Delete Files or Folders

Copy   Cut   Paste   Delete

Copy a file to leave it in its current location and make a duplicate of it in another location. The new location can be a network location, disk, CD, the desktop, or other storage location. *Cut* a file when you want to move a file. You actually paste the copy to a new location and automatically remove it from the original location. The pasted copy may be placed on the original disk or network location or on a separate location. *Delete* a file to remove a file from the location where it is stored. If the storage location is your hard disk, the file is moved to the *Recycle Bin*. If the storage location is a disk, CD, or network location, the file is permanently removed.

To copy a file or folder, highlight the file or folder icon in an *Explorer* window and choose Organize from the toolbar; then select Copy. Navigate to the desired location, choose Organize from the toolbar, and select Paste. Moving a file or folder is similar to copying, except once you highlight the file or folder icon in the *Explorer* window, you choose Organize from the toolbar and select Cut. View the desired location, choose Organize, and select Paste.

To delete a file or folder, highlight the file icon in the *Explorer* window, choose Organize from the toolbar, and then select Delete. A dialog box will display asking you to confirm the deletion. Choose Yes, and the file is deleted. When you delete a file or folder, it is not removed from storage immediately. It moves to the Recycle Bin until the Recycle Bin is emptied. This step gives you the opportunity to restore the file to its original location if you discover that it should not have been deleted.

To empty the Recycle Bin:

1. Access *Windows Explorer* and click the Recycle Bin icon.

   [Empty the Recycle Bin]

2. Choose Empty Recycle Bin from the toolbar.

3. Click Yes to confirm that you want to permanently delete the item(s).

Tip: To permanently delete a file or folder from your computer without first sending it to the Recycle Bin, click the filename and press SHIFT + DELETE.

DRILL 2 | COPY FOLDER FROM CD TO STORAGE DRIVE

1. Insert your data CD in the CD drive and insert your USB drive or other storage device.
2. Access *Windows Explorer* and display drives on your computer.
3. Click the CD drive icon.
4. Click the *File Management* folder.
5. Click Organize in the toolbar and select Copy.
6. Click the drive and folder in which you want to copy the *File Management* folder (in this case, Removable Disk E or wherever your USB drive resides).
7. Choose Organize on the toolbar and then select Paste. The folder contents remain on the CD and have also been copied to the new location. You should see the *File Management* folder on your USB drive.
8. Leave *Windows Explorer* open if you are continuing with Drill 3.

1. *Windows Explorer* should be open and displaying drives on your computer.

2. Navigate to the USB drive.

3. Expand the *File Management* folder.

4. Click once in the Files and Folders pane (right side) to select the file named *john doe*. Click Organize on the toolbar and choose Rename. Key **new john doe** and tap ENTER.

5. In the Files and Folders pane, click the *new john doe* file icon once. Choose Organize from the toolbar, and then select Delete. Confirm the deletion of this file from your storage device.

6. Expand the *File Management* folder. Highlight the *Assignment 1* file icon. Choose Organize from the toolbar, and select Cut. Access the *Assignments* folder on your storage drive. Choose Organize and then select Paste.

7. Use the procedures just described to move the file *term paper 1* to the *Term Papers* folder on your storage drive.

8. Use the procedures just described to move the file *keyboarding homework* to the *Keyboarding* folder on your storage drive.

9. Rename the *File Management* folder *Practice*.

10. Delete the *Assignments* folder and all its contents.

11. Close *Windows Explorer*.

Tip: You can also drag and drop files or folders to a new location when you are copying or moving.

It is very important to understand the file management capabilities of the *Vista Windows* operating system when using a computer for any task. Continue to learn about file management in *Vista* as you work through the drills and exercises in this book. Use Help when necessary.

KNOW YOUR COMPUTER

The numbered parts are found on most computers. The location of some parts will vary.

1. **CPU (Central Processing Unit):** Internal operating unit or "brain" of computer.

2. **CD-ROM drive:** Reads data from and writes data to a CD.

3. **Monitor:** Displays text and graphics on a screen.

4. **Mouse:** Used to input commands.

5. **Keyboard:** An arrangement of letter, figure, symbol, control, function, and editing keys and a numeric keypad.

© FRANKSITEMAN.COM 2007

KEYBOARD ARRANGEMENT

© FRANKSITEMAN.COM 2007

1. **Alphanumeric keys:** Letters, numbers, and symbols.

2. **Numeric keypad:** Keys at the right side of the keyboard used to enter numeric copy and perform calculations.

3. **Function (F) keys:** Used to execute commands, sometimes with other keys. Commands vary with software.

4. **Arrow keys:** Move insertion point up, down, left, or right.

5. **ESC (Escape):** Closes a software menu or dialog box.

6. **TAB:** Moves the insertion point to a preset position.

7. **CAPS LOCK:** Used to make all capital letters.

8. **SHIFT:** Makes capital letters and symbols shown at tops of number keys.

9. **CTRL (Control):** With other key(s), executes commands. Commands may vary with software.

10. **ALT (Alternate):** With other key(s), executes commands. Commands may vary with software.

11. **Space Bar:** Inserts a space in text.

12. **ENTER (return):** Moves insertion point to margin and down to next line. Also used to execute commands.

13. **DELETE:** Removes text to the right of insertion point.

14. **NUM LOCK:** Activates/ deactivates numeric keypad.

15. **INSERT:** Activates insert or typeover.

16. **BACKSPACE:** Deletes text to the left of insertion point.

Level
1

DEVELOPING KEYBOARDING SKILL

LEARNING OUTCOMES

Keyboarding

- To key the alphabetic and numeric keys by touch.
- To develop good keyboarding techniques.
- To key fluently—at least 25 words per minute.
- To develop reasonable accuracy.

Communication Skills

- To develop proofreading skills.
- To apply proofreaders' marks and revise text.

Writing 53

We are living in a wonderful period of history. This is a 12
time when historians are recording many exciting changes in our 25
world. The past two decades have shown that all inhabitants of 37
this planet must learn to exist together. We no longer are able 50
to isolate ourselves from other countries. The action of one 63
nation has a direct effect on nearly every other nation in the 75
world. We must quickly recognize and adjust to peaceful solutions. 89

| 1 | 2 | 3 | 4 | 5 | 6 | 7 | 8 | 9 | 10 | 11 | 12 | 13 |

Writing 54

Traffic jams, deadlines, problems at work, and squabbles at 4 | 2 | 52
home are some ways in which tension is created. When our tension 8 | 5 | 54
is about to reach the boiling point, what do people usually tell 13 | 8 | 57
us? In most cases, they urge us to relax. But relaxing is not 17 | 10 | 60
always easy to accomplish. We frequently think we cannot find the 21 | 13 | 62
time for this important part of our daily activity. 25 | 15 | 64

To understand how relaxation works for us, we must realize how 29 | 17 | 67
the stress of contemporary existence works against us. Developed 33 | 20 | 69
for survival in a challenging world, the human body reacts to a 38 | 23 | 72
crisis by getting ready for action. Whether we are preparing for a 42 | 25 | 75
timed writing or for an encounter in a dark street, our muscles 47 | 28 | 77
tighten and our blood pressure goes up. After years of this type 51 | 31 | 80
of response, we often find it difficult to relax when we want to. 55 | 33 | 83

Now think about the feeling which is the opposite of this tur- 59 | 36 | 85
moil. The pulse slows down, the breath comes slowly and calmly, 64 | 38 | 88
and the tension leaves the body. This is total relaxation. And if 68 | 41 | 90
it sounds good, consider how good it must actually feel. Our bod- 72 | 43 | 93
ies are already prepared to relax; it is an ability all indivi- 77 | 46 | 95
duals have within themselves. What we have to practice is how to 81 | 49 | 98
use this response. 82 | 49 | 99

| 3' | 1 | 2 | 3 | 4 |
| 5' | 1 | 2 | 3 |

Keyboarding Assessment/Placement

Warmup

1. Open *Keyboarding Pro*.
2. Go to the Word Processor by clicking the **WP**.
3. Key each line twice. Tap ENTER after each group of lines.
4. Close the document by clicking **X** in the upper-right corner.

alphabet Max quietly promised a very big gift for the jazz club next week. Zack worked on five great projects and quickly became the expert. Jack Meyer analyzed the data by answering five complex questions.

figures The invoice dated 9/28/07 was for $18,493.56; it is due 10/24/07. Our dinner on 6/25/08 cost $432.97 plus 18% tip totaling $510.90. The 3 invoices (#49875, #52604, and #137986) totaled $379,912.46.

easy Pam may go with me to town to work for the auditor if he is busy. Jan and six girls may go to the lake to sit on the dock and fish. My neighbor may tutor the eight girls on the theory and problems.

Timed Writing

1. From the main screen, click the Timed Writing tab.

Timed Writings

2. Choose 3' as the length. Choose *pretest* from the list of writings.
3. Tap TAB to begin. Key from the textbook.
4. Repeat the timing for 3'.
5. Your results will be displayed in the Timed Writing Report, which is available on the menu bar.

all letters

	gwam	1'	3'

Most businesses want to be seen as good citizens. Working with the arts is one way in which they can give back to the community in which they operate. It is easy to support the arts because most people believe that a vibrant arts program is key to the quality of life for local citizens. Quality of life is a major factor in recruiting new employees.

13 | 4
26 | 9
39 | 13
53 | 18
68 | 23
71 | 24

Most art groups are nonprofits that provide tax benefits to those who give to them. A business may give money, services, or products, or it may sponsor an event. Sponsoring an event is not the same as making a gift. The business receives a public relations benefit by having its name linked with the event, whereas a gift may have no obvious benefit. Both forms help the arts.

13 | 28
27 | 33
40 | 37
54 | 42
67 | 46
76 | 49

A business may also support the arts by buying and displaying art in its facilities. Some choose to use the art of local artists, while others buy high-quality art from well-known artists. The former helps to build a good local art community. The latter may bring recognition to the business for the quality of its artwork.

13 | 53
27 | 58
40 | 63
53 | 67
66 | 71

1'	1	2	3	4	5	6	7	8	9	10	11	12
3'		1			2			3			4	

Writing 51

	gwam	1'
Educated people have learned that they can find important		12
details just through the simple act of listening. The secret,		24
however, as is well known, is to listen with discretion. Our		37
usual ability to hear forces us to hear many thousands of noises,		50
while our amazing listening ability lets us select only what we		63
think is important from what is minutiae. Often our only contri-		75
bution is a question; and if our listening area is an exciting		88
television show, we are not required to reply.		98

| 1 | 2 | 3 | 4 | 5 | 6 | 7 | 8 | 9 | 10 | 11 | 12 | 13 |

Writing 52

	gwam	3'	5'
People spend far more time listening than they spend communi-	12	4	2
cating in any other way, but only a very few people have developed	26	9	5
good listening skills. There is a big difference between hearing	39	13	8
and listening. Hearing does not require major effort, but listen-	52	17	10
ing is hard work. One of the problems with listening is that we	65	22	13
can listen about three times faster than most people speak. We	78	26	16
are able to hear what the speaker is saying and still have extra	91	30	18
time for our minds to wander to other things.	100	33	20
An active listener utilizes the difference between the	11	37	22
listening and the speaking rates to make mental summaries of the	24	41	25
conversation. One way to listen actively is to try to anticipate	37	46	27
the next point that the individual will make. It is also impor-	50	50	30
tant to clarify in your own mind what is being said. Generally,	63	54	32
people try to assume too much. A good listener will let the per-	76	58	35
son explain in her or his words exactly what he or she would like	89	63	38
to say. Paraphrasing is a good way to confirm that the message is	102	67	40
understood.	104	68	41
A person who has developed good listening skills will not	12	72	43
interrupt the person who is speaking. The problem is that more	24	76	46
people prefer to speak than to listen. Sometimes it takes a con-	37	80	48
siderable amount of effort to give the person an opportunity to	50	85	51
get the message across. Showing that you are interested in what	63	89	53
is being said helps to put the speaker at ease. It is not enough	76	93	56
just to listen; you also have to look like you are listening. The	90	98	59
effective use of body language enhances listening.	100	101	61

1'	1	2	3	4	5	6	7	8	9	10	11	12	13
3'	1		2		3		4
5'	1		2		3

Alphabetic Keys

LEARNING OUTCOMES

- Key the alphabetic keys by touch.
- Key using proper techniques.
- Key at a rate of 14 *gwam* or more.

LESSON 1 — Home Row, Space Bar, Enter, I

1a
Home Row Position and Space Bar

1. Open *Keyboarding Pro* and create your student record.
2. Go to the Word Processor. (The WP will appear next to exercises keyed in the Word Processor in Lessons 1–25.)
3. Practice the steps at the right until you can place your hands in home-row position without watching.
4. Key the drills at the bottom of the page several times.
5. Continue to the next page; keep the document on your screen.

HOME ROW POSITION

1. Drop your hands to your side. Allow your fingers to curve naturally. Maintain this curve as you key.
2. Lightly place your left fingers over the **a s d f** and the right fingers over the **j k l ;**. You will feel a raised element on the *f* and *j* keys, which will help you keep your fingers on the home position. You are now in **home-row position**.

SPACE BAR AND ENTER

Tap the Space Bar, located at the bottom of the keyboard, with a down-and-in motion of the right thumb to space between words.

Enter   Reach with the fourth (little) finger of the right hand to ENTER. Tap it to return the insertion point to the left margin. This action creates a **hard return**. Use a hard return at the end of all drill lines. Quickly return to home position (over ;).

Key these lines

```
a  s  d  f  SPACE  j  k  l  ;  ENTER
a  s  d  f  SPACE  j  k  l  ;  ENTER
```

DRILL 27

NUMBER REVIEW
Key each line once at a comfortable rate; practice difficult lines.

1 On June 11 and July 11, 11 men and 11 women worked 11 hours each.
2 Al received Invoice 22RC22 on May 22 and paid $225.22 on June 22.
3 The 33 boys visited 3 girls at 3:30 p.m. on May 3 at 33 Oak Road.
4 The 44 men found 44 sections of 4' pipe required before 4:44 p.m.
5 On June 15, 55 women ran over 25 miles in 2 hours and 55 minutes.
6 The 66 players shot 6,666 free throws in 66 minutes and made 666.
7 The 7 rooms were 17' 7" wide and 7' 7" long with 17' 7" ceilings.
8 Those 8 coaches made 88 trips averaging 88 miles each in 88 days.
9 The 9 boys packed 9 boxes weighing 99 pounds in 9 hours on May 9.
10 Was the value listed at $10,000,000 or $20,000,000 on October 20?

| 1 | 2 | 3 | 4 | 5 | 6 | 7 | 8 | 9 | 10 | 11 | 12 | 13 |

KEYBOARDING PRO DELUXE   TIMED WRITINGS

Writing 50

A
all letters

gwam 3' | 5'

The kinds of leisure activities you choose constitute   4 | 2 | 62
your life style and, to a great extent, reflect your personality.   8 | 5 | 65
For example, if your daily activities are people oriented, you   12 | 7 | 67
may balance this by spending your free time alone. On the other   17 | 10 | 70
hand, if you would rather be with people most of the time, your   21 | 13 | 72
socialization needs may be very high. At the other end of the   25 | 15 | 75
scale are people who are engaged in machine-oriented work and   29 | 18 | 77
also enjoy spending leisure time alone. These people tend to be   33 | 20 | 80
rather quiet and reserved.   35 | 21 | 81

Every individual needs a certain amount of relaxation to   39 | 23 | 83
remain physically and mentally alert. However, what one person   43 | 26 | 86
finds relaxing may be just the opposite for another person. For   48 | 29 | 89
example, one person may like to read a good book; another may   52 | 31 | 91
find that reading causes nervousness and fatigue. The same holds   56 | 34 | 94
true for the person who enjoys sports. Studies have shown that   61 | 36 | 96
jogging may be quite good for a person who enjoys it but may be   65 | 39 | 99
detrimental to another person who does not enjoy it.   69 | 41 | 101

Experts have noted that the proper balance of leisure,   72 | 43 | 103
relaxation, and recreation is almost essential for individuals   76 | 46 | 106
who live and work in a highly automated world. This balance is   81 | 48 | 108
necessary if each person is to be productive in handling the   85 | 51 | 111
everyday pressure and stress of life. Because every person has   89 | 53 | 113
unique needs that are met in a variety of ways, one must properly   93 | 56 | 116
assess all of the day's activities if the maximum benefit is to   98 | 59 | 118
be gained from each day of life.   100 | 60 | 120

3' | 1 | 2 | 3 | 4 |
5' | 1 | 2 | 3 |

NEW KEYS

1b
Procedures for Learning New Keys

Apply these steps each time you learn a new key.

STANDARD PLAN | for Learning New Keyreaches

1. Find the new key on the illustrated keyboard. Then find it on your keyboard.
2. Watch your finger make the reach to the new key a few times. Keep other fingers curved in home position. For an upward reach, straighten the finger slightly; for a downward reach, curve the finger a bit more.
3. Repeat the drill until you can key it fluently.

1c Home Row **WP**

1. The Word Processor should be open.
2. Key lines 1-9 once. Tap ENTER once at the end of each line and twice to double-space (DS) between 2-line groups.
3. Keep the document on your screen.

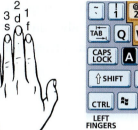

Tap Space Bar once.

```
1  fff  jjj  fjf  fff  jjj  fjf  fjf  jfj  jfj  fjf
2  ddd  kkk  dkd  ddd  kkk  dkd  dkd  kdk  kdk  dkd
```
Tap ENTER twice to DS
```
3  sss  lll  sls  sss  lll  sls  sls  lsl  lsl  sls
4  aaa  ;;;  a;a  aaa  ;;;  a;s  a;a  ;a;  ;a;  a;a
```
DS
```
5  ff  jj  ff  jj  fj  fj  fj  dd  kk  dd  kk  dk  dk  dk
6  ss  ll  ss  ll  sl  sl  sl  aa  ;;  aa  ;;  a;  a;  a;
```
DS
```
7  f  j  d  k  s  l  a  ;
8  ff  jj  dd  kk  ss  ll  aa  ;;
9  fff  jjj  ddd  kkk  sss  lll  aaa  jjj  ;;;
```

1d **i** **WP**

1. Apply the standard plan for learning the letter *i*.
2. Key lines 10–12 in the Word Processor. Keep fingers curved. Repeat until you can key it fluently.
3. Click **X** in the upper right corner of your screen to exit the Word Processor. You will be at the Main menu of *Keyboarding Pro*.

```
10  i ik ik ik is is id id if if ill i ail did kid lid
11  i ik aid ail did kid lid lids kids ill aid did ilk
12  id aid aids laid said ids lid skids kiss disk dial
```

DRILL 26

RESPONSE PATTERN
Key each line once;
DS between groups.

TIP

Combination response drills contain both word- and letter-response sequences. Use top speed for easy words and phrases and lower speed for words that are more difficult to key. (Key phrases marked with a line as a unit.)

1 it to the us me you so go now we my he two in can her by of do no
2 it is | it is the | is it | is it you | he can | can he | he can go | can he go
3 who is | who is it | is it you | you can go | can you go | you can go to it

4 car mail two you may just can lake ask sail sign his form her who
5 who can sail | you can sail | you may sign | can you sign | sign his form
6 sign the form | mail the form | sign and mail | sign and mail that form

7 it was | was it so | if she can go to | can he go to the | can she go to the
8 she can | she may not | she may not go | can you go to the | so we may go
9 sign the | sign the form | they may sign that | they may sign that form

Writing 49

all letters

gwam 3' 5'

An essential part of analyzing a career option is to determine the type and extent of education that are required for a selected career. A main factor to consider about an education is how long it will take to get the skills that are needed to compete successfully for a job. This factor includes any other training that may be essential at the outset of employment. Because jobs change, also assess how an educational program is structured to meet work changes.

Many people choose a career without considering how well they may be suited for it. For example, a person who is outgoing and enjoys being around people probably should not select a career that requires spending long hours working alone. A job that requires quick, forceful action to be taken probably should not be pursued by a person who is shy and contemplative. Just because one has an aptitude for a specific job does not mean he or she will be successful in that job. Thus, be sure to weigh individual personality traits before making a final career choice.

Money and inner satisfaction are the two leading reasons why most people work. For most persons, the need for money translates into food, shelter, and clothing. Once the basic needs of a person are met, satisfaction is the greatest motivator for working. To the average person, a job is satisfying if he or she enjoys the work, likes the people associated with the work, and feels a sense of pride in a job well done. Because you may not be the average person, analyze yourself to discover what will provide job satisfaction.

1e

Lesson 1 from Software

1. Read the information at the right. Then do Lesson 1 from *Keyboarding Pro*.

1. Select the Lessons tab. Select a lesson from the drop-down list or key the lesson number (Figure 1-1).

2. The first activity is displayed automatically. Follow the directions on screen. Key from the screen. The software will move automatically to the next activity.

Figure 1-1 Lesson Menu

Figure 1-2 Lesson 1: Learn Home Row and i

3. Key the Textbook Keying activity from the textbook (lines 13–18 below). Tap ESC or click the Stop button to end the activity.

4. Figure 1-3 shows the Lesson Report. A check mark next to the exercise indicates that it is completed.

5. To end the lesson, check with your instructor. You may do the following:
   - Print your Lesson Report, view the Performance Graph or send your student record to the Web Reporter.

6. From the Main menu, select the Exit button to quit the program. You may choose to transfer your file to another location.

Textbook Keying

1. Key each line once; do not key the numbers. Tap ENTER at the end of each line. Keep your eyes on the book.

2. Tap ESC or click the Stop button to end the activity.

```
13  a  a;  al  ak  aj  s  s;  sl  sk  sj  d  d;  dl  dk  dj
14  j  ja  js  jd  jf  k  ka  ks  kd  kf  l  la  ls  ld  lf
15  a;   sl  a;sl  dkfj  a;sl  dkfj  a;sldkfj  asdf  jk
16  a;   sl  a;sl  dk  fj  dkfj  a;sl  dkfj  fkds;a;  fj
17  f  ff  j  jj  d  dd  k  kk  s  ss  l  ll  a  aa  ;  ;;  fj
18  afj;  a  s  d  f  j  k  l  ;  asdf  jkl;  fdsa  jkl;
```

1f End the lesson

1. Follow steps 5 and 6 above to print the Lesson Report, send your files to the Web Reporter, and exit the software.

2. Clean up your work area.

Figure 1-3 Lesson Report Screen

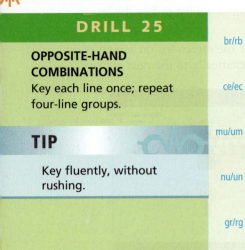

DRILL 25

OPPOSITE-HAND COMBINATIONS
Key each line once; repeat four-line groups.

TIP

Key fluently, without rushing.

br/rb
1 break barb brawn orbit brain carbon brakes barbecue brazen barber
2 Barbara Brady brought us a new brand of barbecue to eat at break.

ce/ec
3 cease decide cent collect cell direct cedar check center peck ice
4 Cecil recently received a check for his special barbecue recipes.

mu/um
5 mull dumb must human mud lumber mulch lump mumps slump music fume
6 Bum Muse must have dumped too much muddy mulch on the bumpy lawn.

nu/un
7 nut sun fun nurse gun sinus number punch nuzzle pound lunch until
8 Uncle Gunta, a nurse, was uneasy about numerous units unionizing.

gr/rg
9 grade merge grand purge great large grab organ green margins gray
10 Margo, our great grandmother, regrets merging those large groups.

ny/yn
11 Wayne any shyness many agony balcony Jayne lynx penny larynx myna
12 Wayne and Jayne fed many skinny myna birds on that sunny balcony

all letters

Writing 48

gwam   1' | 5'

	1'	5'
The job market today is quite different than it was a few	12	2
years ago. The fast track to management no longer exists.	24	5
Entry-level managers find that it is much more difficult to	36	7
obtain a promotion to a higher-level position in management than	49	10
it was just a few years ago. People who are in the market for	61	12
new jobs find very few management positions available. In fact,	74	15
many managers at all levels have a difficult time keeping their	87	17
current management positions. Two factors seem to contribute	99	20
heavily to the problem. The first factor is the trend toward	112	22
self-managed teams. The second factor is that as companies	124	25
downsize they often remove entire layers of management or an	136	27
entire division.	140	28
Layoffs are not new; but, what is new is that layoffs are	12	30
affecting white-collar workers as well as blue-collar workers.	24	33
Coping with job loss is a new and frustrating experience for many	38	35
managers. A person who has just lost a job will have concerns	50	38
about personal security and welfare, and the concerns are com-	63	40
pounded when families are involved. The problem, however, is	75	43
more than just an economic one. Job loss often damages an in-	87	45
dividual's sense of self-worth. An individual who does not have	100	48
a good self-concept will have a very hard time selling himself	112	50
or herself to a potential employer.	120	52

1'	1	2	3	4	5	6	7	8	9	10	11	12	13
5'			1			2				3			

WARMUP

Getting Started
1. Start *Keyboarding Pro*.
2. Select your name and key your password. Click OK.
3. Select Lesson 1R.
4. Key each exercise as directed in the software.

Fingers curved and upright

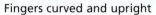

1Ra Textbook Keying
1. Key each line once. Tap ENTER twice to double space (DS) between 2-line groups.
2. Try to keep your eyes on the book the entire time you key.
3. Tap ESC or click Stop to end the exercise.

```
1   f  j  fjf  jj  fj  fj  jf  dd  kk  dd  kk  dk  dk  dk
2   s  ;  s;s  ;;  s;  s;  s;  aa  ;;  aa  ;;  a;  a;  a;
```
Tap ENTER twice to DS.
```
3  fj  dk  sl  a;  fjdksla;  jfkdls;a  ;a  ;s  kd  j
4  f  j  fjf  d  k  dkd  s  l  sls  a  ;  fj  dk  sl  a;a
```
DS
```
5  a;  al  ak  aj  s  s;  sl  sk  sj  d  d;  dl  dk  djd
6  ja  js  jd  jf  k  ka  ks  kd  kf  l  la  ls  ld  lfl
```

SKILL BUILDING

1Rb Keyboard Review
Key these lines from the software screen as directed.

```
7   f fa fad s sa sad f fa fall fall l la lad s sa sad
8   a as ask a ad add j ja jak f fa fall; ask; add jak

9   ik ki ki ik is if id il ij ia ij ik is if ji id ia
10  is il ill sill dill fill sid lid ail lid slid jail

11  if is il kid kids ill kid if kids; if a kid is ill
12  is id if ai aid jaks lid sid sis did ail; if lids;

13  a lass; ask dad; lads ask dad; a fall; fall salads
14  as a fad; ask a lad; a lass; all add; a kid; skids

15  as asks did disk ail fail sail ails jail sill silk
16  ask dad; dads said; is disk; kiss a lad; salad lid

17  aid a lad; if a kid is; a salad lid; kiss sad dads
18  as ad all ask jak lad fad kids ill kill fall disks
```

1Rc End the Lesson
1. Print the Lesson Report if directed by your instructor.
2. If necessary, transfer your student record to another location.
3. If instructed, select Send File to send your record to the Web Reporter.
4. Exit the software; clean up your work area.

DRILL 24

SPECIFIC ROWS
Key each line once;
DS between groups.

TIP

Reach to the first and third rows with a minimum of hand movement; keep hands quiet; don't bounce on the keys.

Rows 3, 2, 1

1 you we quip try pot peer your wire put quit wet trip power toy to
2 salad fad glad lass lag has gall lash gas lad had shall flag half
3 comb zone exam man carve bun oxen bank came next vent zoo van cab

4 we try to; you were; put up your; put it there; you quit; wipe it
5 Gail asked Sissy; what was said; had Jake left; Dana sold a flag
6 Zam came back; can Max fix my van? a brave man, Ben came in a cab

7 Peter or I will try to wire our popular reports to Porter or you.
8 Ada Glass said she is glad she had half a kale salad with Dallas.
9 Zack drove a van to minimize expenses; Ben and Max came in a cab.

Writing 47

Take two 3' or one 5' writing; key with fluency and control.

all letters

	gwam	3'	5'
Sports are very big business today; that is, those sports competi-	4	3	62
tions in which men participate are very big business. What about	9	5	65
sports for women? At the professional level, women have made real	13	8	67
progress in golf and tennis; they, as well as their sponsors, can	18	11	70
make big money in both of these events. The other sports for women	22	13	73
still are not considered to be major revenue sports. The future	26	16	75
may be much better, however, because sports for women at all levels	31	19	78
are gaining in popularity. Programs that are designed to help	35	21	81
young girls develop their athletic skills and interest are having	40	24	83
an impact. The result is that girls now expect to play for organ-	44	26	86
ized clubs as well as in school programs just as boys do. Club	48	29	88
sports often will lead to varsity teams.	51	31	90
Many people wonder how much impact the current emphasis on	55	33	92
gender equity will have on sports at the college level. Most	59	35	95
people agree that this new emphasis is very positive for women.	63	38	97
Some people feel, though, that it either has had or could have a	68	41	100
negative impact on sports for men. They believe that resources	72	43	103
that would have been spent on sports such as football, basketball,	77	46	105
and baseball for men are now being spent on the Olympic sports for	81	49	108
women. Overall, most people believe that both men and women who	85	51	111
have the ability to excel in an athletic event as well as in the	90	54	113
classroom should have the opportunity and should be encouraged to	94	56	116
do so. Success for both women and men is better than success for	98	59	118
either.	99	59	119

```
3' |    1    |    2    |    3    |    4    |
5' |      1      |      2      |      3      |
```

E and N

1. Open *Keyboarding Pro*.
2. Locate your student record.
3. Select Lesson 2.

```
1  ff dd ss aa ff dd ss aa jj kk ll ;; fj dk sl a; a;
2  fj dk sl a; fjdksla; a;sldkfj fj dk sl a; fjdksla;
3  aa ss dd ff jj kk ll ;; aa ss dd ff jj kk ll ;; a;
4  if a; as is; kids did; ask a sad lad; if a lass is
```

NEW KEYS

2b E and N

Key each line once; DS between groups.

e Reach *up* with *left second* finger.

n Reach *down* with *right first* finger.

e
```
5  e ed ed led led lea lea ale ale elf elf eke eke ed
6  e el el eel els elk elk lea leak ale kale led jell
7  e ale kale lea leak fee feel lea lead elf self eke
```

n
```
8  n nj nj an an and and fan fan and kin din fin land
9  n an fan in fin and land sand din fans sank an sin
10 n in ink sink inn kin skin an and land in din dink
```

all reaches learned
```
11 den end fen ken dean dens ales fend fens keen knee
12 if in need; feel ill; as an end; a lad and a lass;
13 and sand; a keen idea; as a sail sank; is in jail;
14 an idea; an end; a lake; a nail; a jade; a dean is
```

2c Textbook Keying
Key each line once; DS between groups.

```
15 if a lad;
16 is a sad fall
17 if a lass did ask
18 ask a lass; ask a lad
19 a;sldkfj a;sldkfj a;sldkfj
20 a; sl dk fj fj dk sl a; a;sldkfj
21 i ik ik if if is is kid skid did lid aid laid said
22 ik kid ail die fie did lie ill ilk silk skill skid
```

> Reach with little finger; tap **Enter** key quickly; return finger to home key.

TECHNIQUE TIP

Keep your eyes on the text-book copy.

DRILL 23

SPECIFIC FINGERS
Key each line once;
DS between groups.

1st
1 fun gray vent guy hunt brunt buy brunch much gun huge humor vying
2 buy them brunch; a hunting gun; Guy hunts for fun; try it for fun

2nd
3 cite decide kick cider creed kidded keen keep kit idea ice icicle
4 keen idea; kick it back; ice breaker; decide the issue; sip cider

3rd
5 low slow lax solo wax sold swell swollen wood wool load logs doll
6 wooden dolls; wax the floor; a slow boat; saw logs; pull the wool

4th
7 quip zap Zane zip pepper pay quiz zipper quizzes pad map nap jazz
8 zip the zipper; jazz at the plaza; Zane quipped; La Paz jazz band

KEYBOARDING PRO DELUXE   TIMED WRITINGS

Writing 46

gwam 3' 5'

1. Take three 1' writings on each paragraph.
2. Take a 5' or two 3' writings.

Option: Practice as a guided writing.

1/4'	1/2'	3/4'	1'
8	16	24	32
9	18	27	36
10	20	30	40
11	22	33	44
12	24	36	48
13	26	39	52
14	28	41	56
15	30	45	60
16	32	48	64
17	34	51	68
18	36	54	72

gwam

all letters

How much power is adequate? Is more power always better   4 | 2 | 50
than less power? People often raise the question in many differ-   8 | 5 | 52
ent instances. Regardless of the situation, most people seem to   12 | 7 | 55
seek more power. In jobs, power is often related to rank in an   17 | 10 | 57
organization, to the number of people reporting to a person, and   21 | 13 | 60
to the ability to spend money without having to ask someone with   25 | 15 | 63
more power. Most experts indicate that the power a person has   30 | 18 | 65
should closely match the responsibilities (not just duties and   34 | 20 | 68
tasks) for which he or she can be held accountable.   37 | 22 | 70

Questions about power are not limited to jobs and people.   41 | 25 | 72
Many people ask the question in reference to the amount of power   45 | 27 | 75
or speed a computer should have. Again, the response usually   50 | 30 | 77
implies that more is better. A better approach is to analyze how   54 | 32 | 80
the computer is to be used and then try to match power needs to   58 | 35 | 82
the types of applications. Most people are surprised to learn   62 | 37 | 85
that home computer buyers tend to buy more power than buyers in   67 | 40 | 87
offices. The primary reason is that the computers are used to   71 | 43 | 90
play games with extensive graphics, sound, and other media appli-   75 | 45 | 93
cations. Matching the needs of the software is the key.   79 | 47 | 95

3' | 1 | 2 | 3 | 4
5' | 1 | 2 | 3

2d Reinforcement
Key each line once; concentrate on what you are keying.

i

23 ik ik ik if is il ik id is if kid did lid aid ails
24 did lid aid; add a line; aid kids; ill kids; id is

n

25 nj nj nj an an and and end den ken in ink sin skin
26 jn din sand land nail sank and dank skin sans sink

e

27 el els elf elk lea lead fee feel sea seal ell jell
28 el eke ale jak lake elf els jaks kale eke els lake

all reaches

29 dine in an inn; fake jade; lend fans; as sand sank
30 in nine inns; if an end; need an idea; seek a fee;
31 if a lad; a jail; is silk; is ill; a dais; did aid
32 adds a line; and safe; asks a lass; sail in a lake

2e End the lesson
1. Print the Lesson Report.
2. If appropriate, send your student record to the Web Reporter.
3. Exit the software; clean up your work area.

WORKPLACE SUCCESS

Keyboarding: The Survival Skill

© CREATAS IMAGES/JUPITERIMAGES

Keyboarding is a valuable and necessary skill for everyone in this technological world. It is an expected tool for effective communication throughout one's life.

Students who resort to "hunting and pecking" to key their school assignments are constantly searching for the correct letter on the keyboard. Frustration abounds for students who wish to enter their research report into the computer, but do not have the touch keyboarding skills required to accomplish the task quickly and proficiently. Students who can key by touch are much more relaxed because they can keep their eyes on the screen and concentrate on text editing and composing.

Some people claim that voice-activated computers will replace the need for keyboarding. Voice activation currently works best in conjunction with keyboarding. The first draft of a document can be inputted using voice; the draft is then edited using the keyboard. Together, this process can greatly speed work performance.

DRILL 20

ADJACENT KEYS

Key each line once; repeat entire drill. DS between groups

Goal: To eliminate persistent errors on side-by-side keys.

as/sa	1	has sale fast salt was saw vast essay easy say past vast mast sap
	2	We saw Sam; Sal was sad; Susan has a cast; as Sam said; as I said
er/re	3	were there tree deer great three other her free red here pert are
	4	we were there; here we are; there were three; here are three deer
io/oi	5	point axiom prior choir lion boil toil billion soil action adjoin
	6	join a choir; prior to that action; millions in a nation rejoiced
op/po	7	polo drop loop post hope pole port rope slope power top pony stop
	8	rope the pony; drop the pole; power at the top; hope for the poor
rt/tr	9	trail alert train hurt tree shirt trap smart trim start tray dirt
	10	trim the tree; start the train; dirt on the shirt; alert the trio
ew/we	11	few we stew were pew went dew web sew wept crew wear brew wet new
	12	we were weak; few were weeping; the crew went west; we knew a few
gh/ui	13	sight quit laugh suit might ruin ghost guide ghastly guilt ghetto
	14	a ghastly suit; quit laughing; recruit the ghost; might be guilty

DRILL 21

OUTSIDE REACHES

Key each line once. DS between groups.

Goal: To key with a maximum of one error per line. (Letters are often omitted in outside reaches—concentrate.)

	1	tapioca actual against casual areas facial equally aware parallel
a/p	2	impower purpose people opposed compute pimple papyrus pope puppet
	3	Perhaps part of the chapter page openers can appear on red paper.
	4	class sash steps essential skills business discuss desks insisted
s/w	5	wow wayworn away awkward wrong awaits wildwood waterworks wayward
	6	The snow white swan swayed as the waves swept the swelling shore.
	7	hazard zip zero zeolite freezer zoom zealous z-axis zodiac sizing
z/l	8	likely indelibly, laurel finally leaflet regularly eloquently lily
	9	A New Zealand zoologist was amazed as a zebra guzzled the zinias.
	10	fax oxford exert excite examples xylan exercise oxygen exact taxi
x/?	11	When? Where? Which? For her? How much? What color? To whom?
	12	After examining the x-rays, why did Dr. Ax exempt an exploratory?

DRILL 22

ALPHABETIC SENTENCES

Key each line once with good rhythm. Keep fingers curved and upright over the keys. DS between groups.

1	Judge McQuoy will have prizes for their next big track meet.
2	Jack may provide some extra quiz problems for the new group.
3	Gary Quazet mended six copies of books and journals we have.
4	Jack quibbled with a garrulous expert on Zoave family names.
5	Jake will study sixty chapters on vitamins for the big quiz.
6	Max asked Quin to provide a jewel box for the glossy zircon.
7	This judge may quiz the Iowa clerks about extensive profits.
8	Meg Keys packed and flew to Venezia to acquire her next job.

LESSON 3 | Review

WARMUP 3a

Key each line at a steady pace; tap and release each key quickly. Key each line again at a faster pace.

© FRANKSITEMAN.COM 2007

home	1	ad ads lad fad dad as ask fa la lass jak jaks alas
n	2	an fan and land fan flan sans sand sank flank dank
i	3	is id ill dill if aid ail fail did kid ski lid ilk
all	4	ade alas nine else fife ken; jell ink jak inns if;

SKILL BUILDING

3b Rhythm Builder
Key each line twice.

Lines 5–8: Think and key words. Make the space part of the word.

Lines 9–12: Think and key phrases. Do not key the vertical rules separating the phrases.

easy words

5 if is as an ad el and did die eel fin fan elf lens
6 as ask and id kid and ade aid eel feel ilk skis an
7 ail fail aid did ken ale led an flan inn inns alas
8 eel eke nee kneel did kids kale sees lake elf fled

easy phrases

9 el el|id id|is is|eke eke|lee lee|ale ale|jill jill
10 is if|is a|is a|a disk|a disk|did ski|did ski|is a
11 sell a|sell a|sell a sled|fall fad|fall fad|did die
12 sees a lake|sees a lake|as a deal|sell a sled|all a a

3c Technique Practice
Key each 2-line group twice.

TECHNIQUE TIP

Reach with the little finger; tap Enter key quickly; return finger to home key.

home row: fingers curved and upright

13 jak lad as lass dad sad lads fad fall la ask ad as
14 asks add jaks dads a lass ads flak adds sad as lad

upward reaches: straighten fingers slightly; return quickly to home position

15 fed die led ail kea lei did ale fife silk leak lie
16 sea lid deal sine desk lie ale like life idea jail

double letters: don't hurry when stroking double letters

17 fee jell less add inn seek fall alee lass keel all
18 dill dell see fell eel less all add kiss seen sell

LESSON 3 REVIEW

MODULE 1   9

Writing 43: 85 gwam

	gwam	1'	3'

Business letters can be defined by their goals; for example, 12 | 4 | 60
a letter of inquiry, a reply letter, a promotion letter, a credit 25 | 8 | 65
letter, or other specialized letter. While you learn to compose 38 | 13 | 69
these letters, just keep each letter's individual goals always in 52 | 17 | 74
front of you. If you fix in your mind a theme, pattern, and 64 | 21 | 78
ideal for your writing, composing good business letters may 75 | 25 | 82
emerge as one of the best tricks in your bag. 85 | 28 | 85

Competent business writers know what they want to say—and 12 | 32 | 89
they say it with simplicity and clarity. Words are the utensils 25 | 37 | 93
they use to convey ideas or to convince others to accomplish some 38 | 41 | 98
action. The simple word and the short sentence usually are more 51 | 45 | 102
effective than the big word and the involved sentence. But don't 64 | 50 | 106
be afraid of the long or unusual word if it means exactly what 77 | 54 | 111
you intend to say in your business letter. 85 | 57 | 113

Writing 44: 90 gwam

	gwam	1'	3'

Although many of us are basically comfortable with sameness 12 | 4 | 64
and appear to dislike change, we actually prize variation. We 24 | 8 | 68
believe that we are each unique individuals, yet we know that we 38 | 12 | 72
are really only a little different; and we struggle to find 50 | 16 | 76
"sense of self" in how we think and act. Our cars, too, built 62 | 21 | 81
on assembly lines are basically identical; yet when we purchase 75 | 25 | 85
one, we choose model, color, size, and style which suits us 87 | 29 | 89
individually. 90 | 30 | 90

Also many people expect to find security by buying things 12 | 34 | 94
that are in keeping with society's "image" and "status." But 24 | 38 | 98
what we think of as "status" always changes. The wise buyer will 37 | 42 | 102
buy those items that give most in utility, comfort, and satisfac- 50 | 47 | 106
tion. Status should just be a thing we create in ourselves, not 63 | 51 | 111
a thing created for us. Common sense should guide us in making good 77 | 55 | 115
decisions—and if our "status" is increased thereby, well, why not? 90 | 60 | 120

Writing 45: 95 gwam

	gwam	1'

Normally, customers do not abandon a firm because of a mistake. 13
All firms will make mistakes at one time or another. The way a 26
problem is resolved is far more crucial than the fact that a 38
problem existed. More customers leave a firm and take their 50
business to a competitor because they get upset with an employee 63
than for any other reason. The key qualifications for a customer 76
service employee are superb human relations skills and knowledge 89
of the product or service. 95

1'	1	2	3	4	5	6	7	8	9	10	11	12	13
3'		1			2			3			4		

3d Textbook Keying

Key each line once; DS between groups of two lines.

TECHNIQUE TIP

Tap keys quickly.
Tap the Space Bar with down-and-in motion.
Tap Enter with a quick flick of the little finger.

LEFT FINGERS 4 \ 3 \ 2 \ 1 \ 1 \ 2 \ 3 \ 4 RIGHT FINGERS

reach review

19 ea sea lea seas deal leaf leak lead leas fleas keas
20 as ask lass ease as asks ask ask sass as alas seas

DS

21 sa sad sane sake sail sale sans safe sad said sand
22 le sled lead flee fled ale flea lei dale kale leaf

DS

23 jn jn nj nj in fan fin an; din ink sin and inn an;
24 de den end fen an an and and ken knee nee dean dee

phrases (think and key phrases)

25 and and land land el el elf elf self self ail nail
26 as as ask ask ad ad lad lad id id lid lid kid kids

27 if if|is is|jak jak|all all|did did|nan nan|elf elf
28 as a lad| ask dad| fed a jak| as all ask| sales fad

29 sell a lead|seal a deal|feel a leaf|if a jade sale
30 is a|is as if|a disk|aid all kids|did ski|is a silk

3e Timed Writing

1. Key lines 35–38 for 1'. If you finish before time is up, repeat the lines.
2. Practice the remaining lines in the game.
3. End your lesson.
4. Clean up your work area.

31 den end fen ken dean dens ales fend fens keen knee
d/e
32 a deed; a desk; a jade; an eel; a jade eel; a dean

33 an an in in and and en end end sane sane sand sand
n/a
34 a land; a dean; a fan; a fin; a sane end; end land

35 el eel eld elf sell self el dell fell elk els jell
e/n
36 in fin inn inks dine sink fine fins kind line lain

37 an and fan dean elan flan land lane lean sand sane
all reaches
38 sell a lead; sell a jade; seal a deal; feel a leaf

Writing 40: 70 *gwam*

	gwam	1'	3'

Foreign study and travel take extra time and effort, but **11** | 4 | 50
these two activities quickly help us to understand people. Much **24** | 8 | 55
can be learned from other cultures. Today, business must think **37** | 12 | 59
globally. Learning about the culture of others is not a luxury. **50** | 17 | 63
Even the owner of a small business realizes that he or she cannot **64** | 21 | 68
just focus on the domestic scene. **70** | 23 | 70

Many examples can be used to show how a local business may **11** | 27 | 74
be influenced by global competition. A hair stylist may be re- **24** | 31 | 78
quired to learn European styles because customers may want to try **38** | 36 | 83
a style just like they saw on their travels. Or salons may want **51** | 40 | 87
to offer other services such as facials that people have tried **63** | 44 | 91
while they were traveling abroad. **70** | 47 | 93

Writing 41: 75 *gwam*

	gwam	1'	3'

Getting a job interview is certainly a triumph for the job **12** | 4 | 54
seeker. Yet anxiety quickly sets in as the applicant becomes **24** | 8 | 58
aware of the competition. The same attention to details that was **37** | 12 | 62
used in writing the successful resume will also be needed for the **51** | 17 | 67
interview. Experts often say that the first four minutes are the **64** | 21 | 71
most crucial in making a strong impact on the interviewer. **75** | 25 | 75

First, people focus on what they see. Posture, eye contact, **12** | 29 | 79
facial expression, and gestures make up over half of the message. **26** | 33 | 84
Next, people focus on what they hear; enthusiasm, delivery, pace, **39** | 38 | 88
volume, and clarity are as vital as what is said. Finally, **51** | 42 | 92
people get to the actual words that are said. You can make a **63** | 49 | 96
good impression. But, realize, you have just four minutes. **75** | 50 | 100

Writing 42: 80 *gwam*

	gwam	1'	3'

Would a pitcher go to the mound without warming up? Would **12** | 4 | 57
a speaker go to the podium without practice? Of course not! These **25** | 8 | 62
experts have spent many long hours striving to do their best. **38** | 13 | 66
Similarly, the performance of business employees is rated. The **51** | 17 | 70
manager's evaluation will include a record of actual performance **64** | 21 | 75
and a list of new goals. A good mark in these areas will demand **77** | 26 | 79
much hard work. **80** | 27 | 80

Many work factors can be practiced to help one succeed on **12** | 30 | 84
the job. Class attendance and punctuality can be perfected by **24** | 35 | 88
students. Because work is expected to be correct, managers do **37** | 39 | 92
not assign zeros. Thus, students must learn to proofread their **49** | 43 | 96
work. A project must also be completed quickly. Students can **62** | 47 | 101
learn to organize work and time well and to find ways to do their **75** | 52 | 105
work smarter and faster. **80** | 53 | 107

1'	1	2	3	4	5	6	7	8	9	10	11	12	13
3'		1			2			3			4		

Left Shift, H, T, Period

WARMUP 4a

Key each line twice. Keep eyes on copy.

home row	1 al as ads lad dad fad jak fall lass asks fads all;
e/i/n	2 ed ik jn in knee end nine line sine lien dies leis
all reaches	3 see a ski; add ink; fed a jak; is an inn; as a lad
easy	4 an dial id is an la lake did el ale fake is land a

NEW KEYS

4b Left Shift and h
Key each line once.

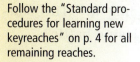
Follow the "Standard procedures for learning new keyreaches" on p. 4 for all remaining reaches.

left shift Reach *down* with *left fourth* (little) finger; shift, tap, release.

h Reach to *left* with *right first* finger.

left shift

5 J Ja Ja Jan Jan Jane Jana Ken Kass Lee Len Nan Ned
6 and Ken and Lena and Jake and Lida and Nan and Ida
7 Inn is; Jill Ina is; Nels is; Jen is; Ken Lin is a

h

8 h hj hj he he she she hen aha ash had has hid shed
9 h hj ha hie his half hand hike dash head sash shad
10 aha hi hash heal hill hind lash hash hake dish ash

all reaches learned

11 Nels Kane and Jake Jenn; she asked Hi and Ina Linn
12 Lend Lana and Jed a dish; I fed Lane and Jess Kane
13 I see Jake Kish and Lash Hess; Isla and Helen hike

4c Textbook Keying
Key the drill once: Strive for good control.

14 he she held a lead; she sells jade; she has a sale
15 Ha Ja Ka La Ha Hal Ja Jake Ka Kahn La Ladd Ha Hall
16 Hal leads; Jeff led all fall; Hal has a safe lead
17 Hal Hall heads all sales; Jake Hess asks less fee;

Writing 37: 55 gwam

A crucial life skill is the ability to put things in proper perspective. Individuals often fail to realize that many things are just not worth fighting about. A quick way to know whether an issue is worth fighting for is to look at the situation from a long-term perspective.

	1'	3'
	12	4	41
	25	8	45
	38	13	50
	51	17	54
	55	18	55

If you will care five or six years from now that you defended an issue, it is a principle worth defending. If you will not even remember, the situation does not justify the effort required for defending it. The odds of winning are also important. Why fight a losing battle?

11	22	59
24	26	63
36	31	67
49	35	72
55	37	74

Writing 38: 60 gwam

Why do we remember some things and forget others? Often, we associate loss of memory with aging or an illness such as Alzheimer's disease. However, the crux of the matter is that we all forget various things that we prefer to remember. We tend to remember things that mean something special to us.

12	4	44
24	8	48
37	12	52
50	17	57
60	20	60

For many people, recalling dates is a difficult task; yet they manage to remember dates of special occasions, such as anniversaries. Processing requires one not only to hear but to ponder and to understand what has just been said. We recall things that we say and do longer than things we hear and see.

12	24	64
25	28	68
36	33	72
49	37	77
60	40	80

Writing 39: 65 gwam

Humor is very important in our professional and our personal lives. Fortunately, we realize that many things can and do go wrong. If we can learn to laugh at ourselves and with other people, we will get through the terrible times. Adding a little extra laughter can help put the situation in proper perspective much quicker.

12	4	47
25	8	52
37	12	56
50	17	60
63	21	64
65	22	65

Maintaining our sense of humor lets us enjoy our positions to a greater degree. No one is perfect, and we cannot expect perfection from ourselves. However, the quality of our performance is greater when we do the things we like. We realize our prime time is devoted to work. Thus, it is important that we enjoy this time.

12	26	69
24	30	73
37	34	77
50	38	82
62	42	86
65	43	87

1'		1	2	3	4	5	6	7	8	9	10	11	12	13	
3'			1			2			3			4			

4d t and . (period)

Key each line once.

t Reach *up* with *left first* finger.

. (period) Reach *down* with *right third* finger.

t

18 t tf tf aft aft left fit fat fete tiff tie the tin

19 tf at at aft lit hit tide tilt tint sits skit this

20 hat kit let lit ate sit flat tilt thin tale tan at

. (period)

21 .1 .1 1.1 f1. f1. L. L. Neal and J. N. List hiked.

22 Hand J. H. Kass a fan. Jess did. I need an idea.

23 Jane said she has a tan dish; Jae and Lee need it.

all reaches learned

24 I did tell J. K. that Lt. Li had left. He is ill.

25 tie tan kit sit fit hit hat; the jet left at nine.

26 I see Lila and Ilene at tea. Jan Kane ate at ten.

SKILL BUILDING

4e Reinforcement
Key with control; concentrate as you practice the new reaches.

reach review

27 tf .1 hj ft ki de jh tf ik ed hj de ft ki 1. tf ik

28 elf eel left is sis fit till dens ink has delt ink

h/e

29 he he heed heed she she shelf shelf shed shed she

30 he has; he had; he led; he sleds; she fell; he is

i/t

31 it is if id did lit tide tide tile tile list list

32 it is; he hit it; he is ill; she is still; she is

shift

33 Hal and Nel; Jade dishes; Kale has half; Jed hides

34 Hi Ken; Helen and Jen hike; Jan has a jade; Ken is

enter

35 Nan had a sale.

36 He did see Hal.

37 Lee has a desk.

38 Ina hid a dish.

TECHNIQUE TIP

Tap Enter without pausing or looking up from the copy.

5   *Skill Builder*

1. Key a 1' writing on each paragraph.
2. Practice each ¶ in a set until you can complete it in 1' with no more than one error.
3. Take a 3' writing; strive to maintain your 1' rate.
4. Move onto the next set. Notice that each set progresses by 5 words.

all letters

Writing 34: 40 *gwam*

	gwam	1'	3'

"An ounce of prevention is worth a pound of cure" is really | 12 | 4 | 31
based on fact; still, many people comprehend this statement more | 25 | 8 | 35
for its quality as literature than on a practical, common-sense | 38 | 12 | 39
philosophy. | 40 | 13 | 40

Just take health, for example. We agonize over stiff costs | 12 | 17 | 44
we pay to recover from illnesses; but, on the other hand, we give | 25 | 22 | 48
little or no attention to health requirements for diet, exercise, | 38 | 26 | 53
and sleep. | 40 | 27 | 53

Writing 35: 45 *gwam*

	gwam	1'	3'

Problems with our environment show an odd lack of foresight. | 12 | 4 | 34
We just expect that whatever we may need to support life will be | 25 | 8 | 38
available. We rarely question our comforts, even though they may | 38 | 13 | 43
abuse our earth, water, and air. | 45 | 15 | 45

Optimism is an excellent virtue. It is comforting to think | 12 | 19 | 49
that, eventually, anything can be fixed. So why should we worry? | 25 | 23 | 53
A better idea, certainly, is to realize that we don't have to fix | 38 | 28 | 58
anything we have not yet broken. | 45 | 30 | 60

Writing 36: 50 *gwam*

	gwam	1'	3'

Recently, a friend of mine grumbled about how quickly papers | 12 | 4 | 37
accumulated on her desk; she never seemed able to reduce them to | 25 | 8 | 42
zero. She said some law seemed to be working that expanded the | 38 | 13 | 46
stack today by precisely the amount she reduced it yesterday. | 50 | 17 | 50

She should organize her papers and tend to them daily. Any | 12 | 21 | 54
paper that needs a look, a decision, and speedy, final action | 24 | 25 | 58
gets just that; any that needs closer attention is subject to a | 37 | 29 | 62
fixed completion schedule. Self-discipline is the key to order. | 50 | 33 | 67

1'	1	2	3	4	5	6	7	8	9	10	11	12	13
3'		1			2			3			4		

R, Right Shift, C, O

WARMUP 5a

Key each line twice.

home keys	1	a; ad add al all lad fad jak ask lass fall jak lad
t/h/i/n	2	the hit tin nit then this kith dint tine hint thin
left shift/.	3	I need ink. Li has an idea. Hit it. I see Kate.
all reaches	4	Jeff ate at ten; he left a salad dish in the sink.

NEW KEYS

5b r and Right Shift

Key each line once.

r Reach *up* with *left first* finger.

right shift Reach *down* with *right fourth* finger; shift, tap, release.

r

5 r rf rf riff riff fir fir rid ire jar air sir lair

6 rf rid ark ran rat are hare art rant tire dirt jar

7 rare dirk ajar lark rain kirk share hart rail tart

right shift

8 D D Dan Dan Dale Ti Sal Ted Ann Ed Alf Ada Sid Fan

9 and Sid and Dina and Allen and Eli and Dean and Ed

10 Ed Dana; Dee Falk; Tina Finn; Sal Alan; Anna Deeds

all reaches learned

11 Jane and Ann hiked in the sand; Asa set the tents.

12 a rake; a jar; a tree; a red fire; a fare; a rain;

13 Fred Derr and Rai Tira dined at the Tree Art Fair.

5c Textbook Keying
Key each line once; DS between groups of two lines.

14 ir ir ire fir first air fair fire tire rid sir

15 fir jar tar fir flit rill till list stir dirt fire

DS

16 Feral is ill. Dan reads. Dee and Ed Finn see Dere.

17 All is still as Sarah and I fish here in the rain.

DS

18 I still see a red ash tree that fell in the field.

19 Lana said she did sail her skiff in the dark lake.

Document 10

Cover Sheet

1. Prepare a cover page using the Conservative cover page style. Insert the name of the company and the name of the document. Delete the Subtitle text box. Delete the Abstract box.
2. Insert the logo below the horizontal line.
3. Insert your name and the current date.
4. Add a 3-point Green page border.
5. Check and close. (*120-d10*)

Document 11

Compose Memo

An entrepreneurship professor at your school, Dr. Lynn C. Matlock, teaches students how to write business plans. Several weeks ago, he offered to critique the business plan for you. Now that you have it complete, compose a memo to Dr. Matlock and ask him to critique it. Share your excitement about the plan and the expected success of Pommery Air. Ask if he could suggest improvements in the plan and if other items should be added to it. Attach the plan to your memo.

1. Use a template form of your choice; add the logo to it. *Keyboarding Pro DELUXE*: use *Word 2007*.
2. Edit your memo carefully.
3. Check and close. (*120-d11*)

Document 12

Internet Activity

Document 6 describes Pommery Air management as follows: Management emphasizes teamwork, empowerment, and productivity.

1. Search the Internet for articles about employee empowerment.
2. Write two or three paragraphs explaining why employee empowerment would be important for a company such as Pommery Air. Cite at least two articles used for information.
3. Edit carefully.
4. Check and close. (*120-d12*)

WORKPLACE SUCCESS

Employee Empowerment

Employee empowerment refers to allowing employees to participate actively in decision making relative to their jobs. Employees cannot truly be empowered unless they have the knowledge, skills, and ability to make good decisions that affect their jobs. Empowerment requires training and experience as well as a desire on the part of the individual employee to make contributions and decisions relative to the job being performed.

5d c and o

Key each line once.

c Reach *down* with *left second* finger.

o Reach *up* with right *third* finger.

c

20 c c cd cd cad cad can can tic ice sac cake cat sic
21 clad chic cite cheek clef sick lick kick dice rice
22 call acid hack jack lack lick cask crack clan cane

o

23 o ol ol old old of off odd ode or ore oar soar one
24 ol sol sold told dole do doe lo doll sol solo odor
25 onto door toil lotto soak fort hods foal roan load

all reaches learned

26 Carlo Rand can call Rocco; Cole can call Doc Cost.
27 Trina can ask Dina if Nick Corl has left; Joe did.
28 Case sent Carole a nice skirt; it fits Lorna Rich.

SKILL BUILDING

5e Keyboard Reinforcement

Key each line once; key at a steady pace. Strive for control.

TECHNIQUE TIP

Reach up without moving hands away from your body. Use quick keystrokes.

o/r
29 or or for for nor nor ore ore oar oar roe roe sore
30 a rose|her or|he or|he rode|or for|a door|her doll

i/t
31 is is tis tis it it fit fit tie tie this this lits
32 it is|it is|it is this|it is this|it sits|tie fits

e/n
33 en en end end ne ne need need ken ken kneel kneels
34 lend the|lend the|at the end|at the end|need their

c/o
35 ch ch check check ck ck hack lack jack co co cones
36 the cot|the cot|a dock|a dock|a jack|a jack|a cone

all reaches
37 Jack and Rona did frost nine of the cakes at last.
38 Jo can ice her drink if Tess can find her a flask.
39 Ask Jean to call Fisk at noon; he needs her notes.

Companies also use charter flights to take groups to conventions, meetings, and other business activities. Travel agencies often contract for charter flights between destinations on vacation packages.

Supplementary services. Meal and beverage services are frequently contracted, in addition to the transportation package. For example, box meals and cold drinks on the return flight after the game are usually a part of athletic charter flight packages. Equipment handling is also a part of the package. Tickets, convention packages, and other services provided usually are arranged through travel partners when they are included in a charter flight contract.

Market Analysis

The Midwest market was targeted first because of its population and central location. Another determining factor was the intense interest in and support of professional and college sports. Successful charters to games created demand from those institutions for their travel schedule. The most profitable section of the market stems from the athletic connections.

Emerging markets. An emerging market is being created by women's sports programs. This market is fueled by the gender equity emphasis in college athletics. Court decisions and athletic regulations focus on equal treatment of men's and women's sports. Other emerging markets are the resort (particularly tennis, golf, beach, and ski resorts) and casino charters that are arranged by the resorts to bring in customers at a relatively low cost.

Competition. Only one other charter air service in the Midwest competes in the same niche market in which Pommery competes with all jet service. Several smaller charter air service companies try to compete with relatively large turboprop aircraft.

Market expansion. The real challenge is to increase the size of this niche market through promotional activities and strategic alliances with travel partners. Pilot projects have produced promising results and are being evaluated as part of the growth strategy.

Pro Formas—2007–2009

Pro formas for 2007, 2008, and 2009 are based on the addition of two jet aircraft within the next 18 months. Revenue and expenses are in current dollars.

(Insert Pro Forma Statement of Income from 120-d8)

Ownership

Five million common shares have been authorized. Of the authorized shares, 2,802,654 shares have been issued. Common stock ownership is diverse as noted in the following groupings.

(Insert table from 120-d7)

TIP

Show gridlines if you need to adjust columns in the table.

Keyboarding Pro DELUXE users: Insert *120-d7* and *120-d8* files from the data CD.

LESSON 6

W, Comma, B, P

WARMUP 6a

Key each line twice; avoid pauses.

home row	1	ask a lad; a fall fad; had a salad; ask a sad jak;
o/t	2	to do it; to toil; as a tot; do a lot; he told her
c/r	3	cots are; has rocks; roll cot; is rich; has an arc
all reaches	4	Holt can see Dane at ten; Jill sees Frank at nine.

NEW KEYS

6b w and , (comma)

Key each line once.

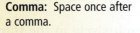

Comma: Space once after a comma.

w Reach *up* with *left third* finger.

, (comma) Reach *down* with *right second* finger.

w

5 w ws ws was was wan wit low win jaw wilt wink wolf
6 sw sw ws ow ow now now row row own own wow wow owe
7 to sew; to own; was rich; was in; is how; will now

, (comma)

8 k, k, k, irk, ilk, ask, oak, ark, lark, jak, rock,
9 skis, a dock, a fork, a lock, a fee, a tie, a fan,
10 Jo, Ed, Ted, and Dan saw Nan in a car lift; a kit

all reaches learned

11 Win, Lew, Drew, and Walt will walk to West Willow.
12 Ask Ho, Al, and Jared to read the code; it is new.
13 The window, we think, was closed; we felt no wind.

6c Textbook Keying

Key each line once.

14 walk wide sown wild town went jowl wait white down
15 a dock, a kit, a wick, a lock, a row, a cow, a fee
16 Joe lost to Ron; Fiji lost to Cara; Don lost to Al
17 Kane will win; Nan will win; Rio will win; Di wins
18 Walter is in Reno; Tia is in Tahoe; then to Hawaii

Business Plan

Pommery Air Service, Inc. (Pommery), since it was founded as a Delaware corporation in 2002, has operated as a niche player in the charter air segment of the airline.

Industry

Three distinct segments comprise the charter air service industry:

- Small local charter operations designed to provide point-to-point transportation for groups of fewer than 20 people in turboprop aircraft.
- Occasional charter flights provided by major passenger airlines.
- Small niche markets that target specific types of clientele.

Pommery operates exclusively in the third segment of the industry, offering contract charter flights and event charter flights. The overall charter air service industry is highly competitive. The most intensive competition exists in the other two segments of the charter air service. Pommery's Board of Directors and management agree that Pommery cannot and should not try to compete with the major passenger airlines for numerous reasons. They also agree that Pommery cannot compete with the small, local charter services because of the cost structure involved in providing jet air service exclusively.

The Service

Pommery provides event charter flights and contract charter flights throughout the United States. About 85 percent of the flights originate east of the Mississippi, and almost 65 percent of flights originate in the Midwest.

Event charter flights. These flights are called event charters because they exist to transport passengers to attend specific events that are occurring. The range of events spans from those that occur one time or once in a significant period of time to regularly scheduled events. Examples of one-time events include charters to attend Olympic events, Mardi Gras, or a world-class art exhibition or musical production.

Seasonal events are those that occur regularly during a specified period of time. Athletic events comprise a high percentage of seasonal events. Charter flights to a ski resort or to a nearby city on weekends during the season to watch professional football, basketball, or baseball games would be an example. The flight is made available to a number of participating travel partners who reserve a number of seats on these charter flights for their clientele.

Regularly scheduled charters include special packages (usually weekends) to fixed destinations such as Las Vegas, a Gulf Coast casino and resort, or a country music/golf weekend in Myrtle Beach. These events are generally marketed through participating travel partners.

Contract charter flights. Contract charter flights often overlap with event charter flights. The primary difference is that the contract charter flights are with specific organizations or individuals. For example, a contract may be issued with an athletic department to take its football team and band to a game. On the other hand, an event charter flight may go to the same football game with passengers from several travel partners and an alumni group.

6d b and p
Key each line once.

b Reach *down* with *left first* finger.

p Reach *up* with *right fourth* (little) finger.

b

19 bf bf bf biff fib fib bib bib boa boa fib fibs rob
20 bf bf bf ban ban bon bon bow bow be be rib rib sob
21 a dob, a cob, a crib, a lab, a slab, a bid, a bath

p

22 p; p; pa pa; pal pal pan pan pad par pen pep paper
23 pa pa; lap lap; nap nap; hep ape spa asp leap clap
24 a park, a pan, a pal, a pad, apt to pop, a pair of

all reaches learned

25 Barb and Bob wrapped a pepper in paper and ribbon.
26 Rip, Joann, and Dick were all closer to the flash.
27 Bo will be pleased to see Japan; he works in Oslo.

SKILL BUILDING

6e Keyboard Reinforcement
Key each line once; key at a steady pace.

reach review
28 ki kid did aid lie hj has has had sw saw wits will
29 de dell led sled jn an en end ant hand k, end, kin

s/w
30 ws ws lows now we shown win cow wow wire jowl when
31 Wes saw an owl in the willow tree in the old lane.

b/p
32 bf bf fib rob bid ;p p; pal pen pot nap hop cap bp
33 Rob has both pans in a bin at the back of the pen.

6f Speed Builder
Key each line twice. Work for fluency.

34 to do|can do|to bow|ask her|to nap|to work|is born
35 for this|if she|is now|did all|to see|or not|or if

all reaches
36 Dick owns a dock at this lake; he paid Ken for it.
37 Jane also kept a pair of owls, a hen, and a snake.

38 Blair soaks a bit of the corn, as he did in Japan.
39 I blend the cocoa in the bowl when I work for Leo.

Document 8

Table with Formulas

1. Create and key the four-column by ten-row table below beginning at approximately 2".

2. Merge row 1 and increase the row height to .45". Increase the row height for all other rows to .2". Key the title centered in 12-point caps and bold. Center the column headings in 12-point bold. Vertically center the text in all cells.

3. Right-align columns B, C, and D.

4. Write a formula to calculate Operating Profit/Loss. **Hint**: (Operating Revenue – Operating Expense).

5. Write a formula to calculate Net Income/(Loss). **Hint**: (Operating Profit – Non-Operating Expense).

6. Apply 15% grey shading to row 1 (White, Background 1, Darker 15%).

7. Change Operating Revenue for 2008 to $878,874,400. Recalculate the table.

8. Check and close. (*120-d8*)

POMMERY AIR PRO FORMA Statement of Income			
	2007	**2008**	**2009**
Operating Revenue	$844,438,400	$861,466,400	$878,874,400
Operating Expenses	41,144,600	53,190,000	68,898,400
Operating Profit/Loss			
Non-Operating Expense	671,200	709,800	1,673,600
Net Income/Loss			
Cost Per ASM	.1019	.0721	.0868
Yield	.1647	.1621	.1575
Operating Margin	7.4%	13.5%	12.6%

Document 9

Leftbound Report

1. Key the Pommery Business Plan, shown on the following pages, as a leftbound report.

2. Format the report as follows:

   a. Apply Title style to the title and Heading 1 style to side headings.

   b. Select the paragraph headings and apply Heading 2 style.

   c. Change the style of the two tables to Light List – Accent 1 so that they will be compatible with the document headings. Check to make sure that text is centered vertically in all cells and fits on one line. Make any adjustments needed in columns and redistribute the columns if necessary.

   d. Insert a next page section break at the beginning of the document for the table of contents in section 1.

   e. Number the table of contents ii at the bottom center.

3. Break the links to the header and footer in section 2, delete the number in the footer, and number the pages of the report at the top right beginning at 1. Do not print a page number on the first page.

4. Generate a table of contents on the blank page at the beginning of the report.

5. Check and close. (*120-d9*)

WARMUP 7a

Key each line twice; begin new lines promptly.

© FRANKSITEMAN.COM 2007

LEFT FINGERS 4 3 2 1 1 2 3 4 RIGHT FINGERS

all 1 We often can take the older jet to Paris and back.
home 2 a; sl dk fj a;sl dkfj ad as all ask fads adds asks
1st row 3 Ann Bascan and Cabal Naban nabbed a cab in Canada.
3rd row 4 Rip went to a water show with either Pippa or Pia.

SKILL BUILDING

7b Textbook Keying
Key each line once; DS between groups of three lines.

5 ws ws was was wan wan wit wit pew paw nap pop bawl
6 bf bf fb fb fob fob rib rib be be job job bat back
7 p; p; asp asp pan pan ap ap ca cap pa nap pop prow
DS

8 Barb and Bret took an old black robe and the boot.
9 Walt saw a wisp of white water renew ripe peppers.
10 Pat picked a black pepper for the picnic at Parks.

7c Textbook Keying
Key each line once; DS between groups of three lines

words 11 a an pan so sot la lap ah own do doe el elf to tot
phrases 12 if it|to do|it is|do so|for the|he works|if he bid
sentences 13 Jess ate all of the peas in the salad in the bowl.
DS

words 14 bow bowl pin pint for fork forks hen hens jak jaks
phrases 15 is for|did it|is the|we did a|and so|to see|or not
sentences 16 I hid the ace in a jar as a joke; I do not see it.
DS

TECHNIQUE TIP

words: key as a single unit rather than letter by letter;
phrases: say and key fluently;
sentences: work for fluency.

words 17 chap chaps flak flake flakes prow prowl work works
phrases 18 as for the|as for the|and to the|to see it|and did
sentences 19 As far as I know, he did not read all of the book.

Document 6

Continued

The Strategy

Pommery Air Service strives to become the dominant air charter service in the Midwest. Pommery's core competencies involve providing safe, high-quality jet air services that are cost effective. All other services provided are designed to facilitate and enhance the continual development of the core competencies.

To implement this strategy, Pommery Air Service must expand. Expansion requires the addition of two jet aircraft within the next year.

Document 7

Table with Formulas

1. Create and key the three-column by seven-row table shown below.
2. Merge cells in row 1. Use 14-point bold and center for the title. Use 12-point bold and center for the column headings and 11 point for the remainder of the table text.
3. Set decimal tabs for columns B and C.
4. Insert the following row between *Senior Officers* and *Business Community*.
   Outside Directors   651,700   23.3
5. Use the SUM function to total columns B and C.
6. Apply the Colorful List style.
7. Change the height of row 1 to .4". Change the height of all other rows to .3".
8. Center the text in each cell vertically.
9. Center the table vertically and horizontally.
10. Check and close. (*120-d7*)

POMMERY AIR STOCK OWNERSHIP		
Group	**Shares**	**% of Stock Issue**
Employees	584,268	20.9
Senior Officers	353,146	12.6
Business Community	640,000	22.8
Founder	571,540	20.4
Total		

7d Technique Practice

Key each set of lines once.

▼ Space once after a period following an abbreviation.

spacing: space *immediately* after each word

20 ad la as in if it lo no of oh he or so ok pi be we

21 an ace ads ale aha a fit oil a jak nor a bit a pew

22 ice ades born is fake to jail than it and the cows

spacing/shifting

23 Ask Jed. Dr. Han left at ten; Dr. Crowe, at nine.

24 I asked Jin if she had ice in a bowl; it can help.

25 Freda, not Jack, went to Spain. Joan likes Spain.

7e Using the Word Processor Timer

Exercises to be keyed in the Word Processor are identified with the Word Processor icon. Follow the instructions in the textbook and key from the textbook.

STANDARD PLAN | **for Using the Word Processor Timer**

You can check your speed in the Word Processor using the Timer.

1. In the Word Processor, click the Timer button on the status bar.
2. The Timer begins once you start to key and stops automatically. Do not tap ENTER at the end of a line. Wordwrap will cause the text to flow to the next line automatically.
3. To save the timing, click the File menu and Save as. Use your initals (*xx*), the exercise number, and number of the timing as the filename. Example: *xx-7f-t1* (your initials, exercise 7f, timing1).
4. Click the Timer button again to start a new timing.
5. Each new timing must be saved with its own name.

7f Timed Writing

1. Take two 1' writings. If you finish before time is up, begin again.
2. Do not tap ENTER at the ends of the lines.

Goal: 12 *gwam*.

	gwam
It is hard to fake a confident spirit. We will do	10
better work if we approach and finish a job and	20
know that we will do the best work we can and then	30
not fret.	32

| 1 | 2 | 3 | 4 | 5 | 6 | 7 | 8 | 9 | 10 |

7g Word Processor

1. In the Word Processor, key each line once for fluency. Do not save your work.
2. Set the Timer in the Word Processor for 30". Take two 30" writings on each line. Do not save the timings.

Goal: to reach the end of the line before time is up.

	gwam
26 Dan took her to the show.	12
27 Jan lent the bowl to the pros.	14
28 Hold the wrists low for this drill.	16
29 Jessie fit the black panel to the shelf.	18
30 Jake held a bit of cocoa and an apricot for Diane.	20
31 Dick and I fish for cod on the docks at Fish Lake.	20
32 Kent still held the dish and the cork in his hand.	20

| 1 | 2 | 3 | 4 | 5 | 6 | 7 | 8 | 9 | 10 |

Columns 2 and 3

Mission Statement

Pommery Air Service, Inc. is a company specializing in charter air flights. Pommery is headquartered in Chicago, Illinois. Its mission statement is as follows:

- Pommery provides its charter customers with safe, reliable jet transportation, quality service, and outstanding value.
- Pommery offers an environment for its employees that fosters teamwork and customer service and rewards integrity and productivity.
- Pommery delivers superior value to its shareholders.

The Company

Pommery Air Service, Inc., a Delaware corporation founded in January 2002, currently has a fleet of four 737 jet aircraft. Pommery provides air service to almost 60,000 passengers per month. The mix is almost equally divided among business trips, athletic functions, and leisure travel.

An experienced, highly competent management team leads Pommery Air Service. Senior management places major emphasis on teamwork, empowerment, and productivity. Employee stock options provide incentives to employees to focus on quality and profitability.

Pommery Air Service became profitable in its tenth month of existence and continues to be profitable. The company operates as a lean, efficient organization. Costs per available set mile (ASM) have dropped from 14 cents to 10 cents. Yield per revenue passenger mile increased from 12 cents to 16 cents.

The Market

Pommery Air Service provides charter flights to destinations throughout the United States. The primary market, however, is defined by the origination point rather than by the destination point. Approximately 65 percent of all flights originate in the Midwest. The secondary market by origination point is the West Coast.

The Services

Pommery Air Services provides two types of charter services: event charter flights and contract charter flights. Both event and contract charter flights include an array of services depending on the needs of the customer. The supplementary services available with both charter and event flights include meal and beverage services; local transportation; event tickets; side trips; conference facilities including logistical support; and a host of special activities.

G, Question Mark, X, U

WARMUP 8a

Key each line twice. Keep eyes on copy.

all 1 Dick will see Job at nine if Rach sees Pat at one.

w/b 2 As the wind blew, Bob Webber saw the window break.

p/, 3 Pat, Pippa, or Cap has prepared the proper papers.

all 4 Bo, Jose, and Will fed Lin; Jack had not paid her.

NEW KEYS

8b g and ?

Key each line once; repeat.

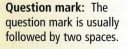

Question mark: The question mark is usually followed by two spaces.

g Reach to *right* with *left first* finger.

? Left SHIFT; reach *down* with *right fourth* finger.

g

5 g g gf gaff gag grog fog frog drag cog dig fig gig

6 gf go gall flag gels slag gala gale glad glee gals

7 golf flog gorge glen high logs gore ogle page grow

?

8 ? ?; ?; ? ? Who? When? Where? Who is? Who was?

9 Who is here? Was it he? Was it she? Did she go?

10 Did Geena? Did he? What is that? Was Jose here?

all reaches learned

11 Has Ginger lost her job? Was her April bill here?

12 Phil did not want the boats to get here this soon.

13 Loris Shin has been ill; Frank, a doctor, saw her.

8c Textbook Keying

Key each line once; DS between groups.

reach review

14 ws ws hj hj tf tf ol ol rf rf ed ed cd cd bf bf p;

15 wed bid has old hold rid heed heed car bed pot pot

g

16 gf gf gin gin rig ring go gone no nog sign got dog

17 to go|to go|go on|go in|go in|to go in|in the sign

TECHNIQUE TIP

Concentrate on correct reaches.

?

18 ?; ?;? who? when? where? how? what? who? It is I?

19 Is she? Is he? Did I lose Jo? Is Gal all right?

Document 5

Continued

Body of Letter:

A copy of the Pommery Air Service Business Plan is enclosed. Please review the plan carefully and be ready to vote on final approval at the Board meeting next Friday. Note that this item appears on the agenda sent to you last week.

If you have any questions prior to the meeting, please call me. All of the changes recommended by the Board at the last meeting have been implemented in the plan.

Document 6

Newsletter

1. Set a custom margin on all sides of .6."

2. Insert the clip art of the airplane used earlier in the logo. Size the clip art so that it is approximately 1½" wide by 1" high.

3. Use *WordArt* to key the banner heading **Pommery Facts**. Size the heading so that it is approximately 7" wide by 1" high.

4. Tap ENTER once. Position the insertion point above the hard return, and insert a 3-point Light Green line (bottom border).

5. Insert a continuous section break.

6. Use a three-column format with a line between columns. Set the width of the columns as follows: column 1: 1.78"; columns 2 and 3: 2.48".

7. Key **Pommery Air Service, Inc.** in 12-point bold. Key the remainder of the text in column 1 in 12 point font.

8. In column 2, change the Spacing After to 10 point. Key the text in columns 2 and 3, shown on the next two pages, in 10 point font. Apply Subtitle style and bold to each heading. Justify text. Position the bullets at the left margin of the column.

9. Preview and adjust the banner as necessary to make the newsletter attractive; fit it on one page.

10. Check and close. *(120-d6)*

Pommery Air Service, Inc.

Headquarters
1340 N. Astor Street
Chicago, IL 60610-2121

773-555-0142
Fax 773-555-0100

www.pommeryair.com

Mission Statement

Pommery Air Service, Inc. is a company specializing in charter air flights. Pommery is headquartered in Chicago, Illinois. Its mission statement is as follows:

- Pommery provides its charter customers with safe, reliable jet transportation, quality service, and outstanding value.
- Pommery offers an environment for its employees that fosters teamwork and customer service and rewards integrity and productivity.
- Pommery delivers superior value to its shareholders.

The Company

Pommery Air Service, Inc., a Delaware corporation founded in January 2002, currently has a fleet of four 737 jet aircraft. Pommery provides air service to almost 60,000 passengers per month. The mix is almost equally divided among business trips, athletic functions, and leisure travel.

An experienced, highly competent management team leads Pommery Air Service. Senior management places major emphasis on teamwork, empowerment, and productivity. Employee stock options provide incentives to employees to focus on quality and profitability.

Pommery Air Service became profitable in its tenth month of existence and continues to be profitable. The company operates as a lean, efficient organization. Costs per available seat mile (ASM) have dropped from 14 cents to 10 cents. Yield per revenue passenger mile increased from 12 cents to 16 cents.

The Market

Pommery Air Service provides charter flights to destinations throughout the United States. The primary market, however, is defined by the origination point rather than by the destination point. Approximately 65 percent of all flights originate in the Midwest. The secondary market by origination point is the West Coast.

The Services

Pommery Air Services provides two types of charter services: event charter flights and contract charter flights. Both event and contract charter flights include an array of services depending on the needs of the customer. The supplementary services available with both charter and event flights include meal and beverage services; local transportation; event tickets; side trips; conference facilities including logistical support; and a host of special activities.

The Strategy

Pommery Air Service strives to become the dominant air charter service in the Midwest. Pommery's core competencies involve providing safe, high-quality jet air services that are cost effective. All other services provided are designed to facilitate and enhance the continual development of the core competencies.

To implement this strategy, Pommery Air Service must expand. Expansion requires the addition of two jet aircraft within the next year.

Column 1

Pommery Air Service Inc.
Headquarters
1340 N. Astor Street
Chicago, IL 60610-2121

773-555-0142
Fax 773-555-0100

www.pommeryair.com

continued

8d x and u

Key each line once; repeat.

x Reach *down* with *left third* finger.

u Reach *up* with *right first* finger.

x

20 x x xs xs ox ox lox sox fox box ex hex lax hex fax
21 sx six sax sox ax fix cox wax hex box pox sex text
22 flax next flex axel pixel exit oxen taxi axis next

u

23 u uj uj jug jut just dust dud due sue use due duel
24 uj us cud but bun out sun nut gun hut hue put fuel
25 dual laud dusk suds fuss full tuna tutus duds full

all reaches learned

26 Paige Power liked the book; Josh can read it next.
27 Next we picked a bag for Jan; then she, Jan, left.
28 Is her June account due? Has Lou ruined her unit?

SKILL BUILDING

8e Reinforcement
Key each line once; work for control.

29 nut cue hut sun rug us six cut dug axe rag fox run
30 out of the sun|cut the action|a fox den|fun at six
31 That car is not junk; it can run in the next race.

32 etc. tax nick cure lack flex walls uncle clad hurt
33 lack the cash|not just luck|next in line|just once
34 June Dunn can send that next tax case to Rex Knox.

8f Timed Writing
Take two 1' timings. If time permits, continue to paragraph 2. Apply wordwrap.

TECHNIQUE TIP

Wordwrap: Text within a paragraph moves automatically to the next line. Tap ENTER only to begin a new paragraph.

| | | 4 | | | 8 | |
How a finished job will look often depends on how
| | 12 | | | 16 | | 20 |
we feel about our work as we do it. Attitude has
| | 24 | | | 28 | |
a definite effect on the end result of work we do.

Tap ENTER once

| | | 4 | | | 8 | |
When we are eager to begin a job, we relax and do
| | 12 | | | 16 | | 20 |
better work than if we start the job with an idea
| | 24 | | | 28 | |
that there is just nothing we can do to escape it.

Document 4

Fax

1. Open the *pommery air fax* template created in Job 3, and complete the fax using the following information.
2. Check and close. (*120-d4*)

To: Roberto Hernandez **From**: Student's Name
Fax Number: 773-555-0113 **Number of Pages**: 1
Telephone Number: 773-555-0199 **Date**: Current
Re: Charter Flights Delete the text for CC

Thank you for contacting Pommery Air regarding scheduling an event charter flight for your company. Pommery is the world's most comprehensive and efficient private jet company. With access to operators of the largest networks of luxury charter jets, we can arrange access to a private aircraft for any given flight to any destination in the United States on a moment's notice.

Visit our Web page to obtain an immediate charter quote. Simply fill in your origin, destination, and dates of travel. Our Trip Quote will produce a variety of aircraft available and prices based on your request.

Document 5

Mail Merge Letters

1. Open the *letterhead* template created in Job 2. Use mail merge to create a block letter with open punctuation. Save the main document as *merge letter*.
2. Refer to the next page for the body of the letter and below for the Board of Directors' names and addresses. Set up the data source with title, first name, and last name as separate fields. Use the field *position* for the job title. Save the data source as *data source*.
3. Supply necessary letter parts including the greeting line with *Dear Title Last Name* format. Use the current date; position it about 1" below the letterhead. Sign each letter from you with your title, **Administrative Assistant**.
4. Check and close. (*120-d5*)

Members of the Board of Directors:

Ms. Natalie Bass, Airline Consultant, RTA and Associates, 3829 Quincy Avenue, Denver, CO 80237-2756

Mr. Herman Davis, Chief Financial Officer, Financial Securities, Inc., 3979 El Mundo Street, Houston, TX 64506-2877

Ms. Betsy Burge, President, Associated Travel Services, 3958 Highland Drive, Sterling, CO 80751-1211

Mr. Joseph Perkins, Senior Vice President, River Industries, 7403 St. Andrews Drive, Dallas, TX 75205-2746

Dr. Kimberly Hess, Professor, Business Administration, Central University, 3744 Main Street, Oakdale, LA 71463-5811

LESSON 9

Q, M, V, Apostrophe

WARMUP 9a

Key each line twice.

all letters	1	Lex gripes about cold weather; Fred is not joking.
space bar	2	Is it Di, Jo, or Al? Ask Lt. Coe, Bill; he knows.
easy	3	I did rush a bushel of cut corn to the sick ducks.
easy	4	He is to go to the Tudor Isle of England on a bus.

NEW KEYS

9b q and m

Key each line once; repeat.

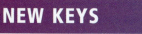

q Reach *up* with *left fourth* finger.

m Reach *down* with *right first* finger.

q

5 q qa qa quad quad quaff quant queen quo quit quick

6 qa qu qa quo quit quod quid quip quads quote quiet

7 quite quilts quart quill quakes quail quack quaint

m

8 m mj mj jam man malt mar max maw me mew men hem me

9 m mj ma am make male mane melt meat mist amen lame

10 malt meld hemp mimic tomb foam rams mama mire mind

all reaches learned

11 Quin had some quiet qualms about taming a macaque.

12 Jake Coxe had questions about a new floor program.

13 Max was quick to join the big reception for Lidia.

9c Textbook Keying

Key each line once for control. DS between groups of two lines.

m/x	14	me men ma am jam am lax, mix jam; the hem, six men
	15	Emma Max expressed an aim to make a mammoth model.

DS

q/u	16	qa qu aqua aqua quit quit quip quite pro quo squad
	17	Did Quin make a quick request to take the Qu exam?

DS

g/n	18	fg gn gun gun dig dig nag snag snag sign grab grab
	19	Georgia hung a sign in front of the union for Gib.

Document 1

Logo

1. In a new document window, change Spacing After to 0. Change line spacing to 1.0.

2. Draw a text box approximately 4½" wide by 1" high. Add Blue fill to the text box.

3. Insert clip art of an airplane similar to the one shown in the sample. Size the clip art to fit inside the text box.

4. Insert a text box approximately 2" wide by ½" high inside the first text box and to the right of the clip art. Use a script font such as Lucida Handwriting and add the following text in 14 point: **Pommery Air**.

5. Increase the size of the *P* and *A* to 20-point bold.

6. Add Light Green fill to the smaller text box.

7. Group the two text boxes. Move the insertion point to the end of the document, and tap ENTER until the insertion point is at approximately 1" on the Vertical Ruler.

8. Position the outside text box so that it is horizontally centered on the page.

9. Check and close. (*logo*)

Document 2

Letterhead

1. In a new document, insert the file *logo* (Insert/Text/Object/Text from File). (*Keyboarding Pro DELUXE* users: Insert the file *logo* from the data CD.)

2. Select the logo text box and position it at about .5". Center-align the text box.

3. Key the letterhead return address on one line and center it below the logo: **1340 N. Astor Street, Chicago, IL 60610-2121 | 773-555-0142 | www.pommeryair.com**

4. Insert a 3-point Light Green bottom border below the return address.

5. Non-*Keyboarding Pro DELUXE* users: Save the letterhead as a template.

6. Check and close. (*letterhead*)

Document 3

Fax Cover Sheet

Keyboarding Pro DELUXE users: Skip Document 3; go to Document 4.

1. Create a fax from the Equity Fax template in your Installed Templates.

2. Turn on Show/Hide. Move the insertion point to the *F* in the word *Fax*.

3. On the Layout tab, in the Tables group, click View Gridlines.

4. Delete the row containing the word *Fax*.

5. Move the insertion point above the table. From *letterhead* (Document 2), copy the entire letterhead, including the green line, and paste it above the table.

6. Delete the hard return immediately below the Light Green line.

7. Turn off the table gridlines.

8. Preview and save it as a template. Check and close. (*pommery air fax*)

9d

v and **'** (apostrophe)
Key each line once; repeat.

Apostrophe: The apostrophe shows (1) omission (as Rob't for Robert or it's for it is) or (2) possession when used with nouns (as Joe's hat).

v Reach *down* with *left first* finger.

' Reach to the right with the *right fourth* finger.

v

20 v vf vf vie vie via via vim vat vow vile vale vote
21 vf vf ave vet ova eve vie dive five live have lave
22 cove dove over aver vivas hive volt five java jive

' (apostrophe)

23 '; '; it's it's Rod's; it's Bo's hat; we'll do it.
24 We don't know if it's Lee's pen or Norma's pencil.
25 It's ten o'clock; I won't tell him that he's late.

all reaches learned

26 It's Viv's turn to drive Iva's van to Ava's house.
27 Qua, not Vi, took the jet; so did Cal. Didn't he?
28 Wasn't Fae Baxter a judge at the post garden show?

SKILL BUILDING

9e Reinforcement
Key each line once.

TECHNIQUE TIP

Keep your hands still as you reach to the third or bottom rows.

v/?
29 Viola said she has moved six times in five months.
30 Does Dave live on Vine Street? Must he leave now?

q/?
31 Did Viv vote? Can Paque move it? Could Val dive?
32 Didn't Raquel quit Carl Quent after their quarrel?

direct reach
33 Fred told Brice that the junior class must depart.
34 June and Hunt decided to go to that great musical.

double letter
35 Harriette will cook dinner for the swimming teams.
36 Bill's committee meets in an accounting classroom.

9f Timed Writing
Key the paragraph once for control. Key it again a little faster.

```
         •         4         •         8         •
We must be able to express our thoughts with ease
    12        •        16        •        20
if we desire to find success in the business world.
    •        24        •        28
It is there that sound ideas earn cash.
```

Pommery Air Service, Inc.

LEARNING OUTCOMES

- Integrate formatting and word processing skills.
- Build keyboarding skill.

LESSONS 117–120 > Business Plan

SKILL BUILDING

117–120a
Key two 5' timed writings.

all letters

	gwam	3'	5'

An effective job search requires very careful planning and a   3 | 2 | 42

lot of hard work. Major decisions must be made about the type of   8 | 5 | 45

job, the size and the type of business, and the geographic area. 13 | 8 | 48

Once all of these basic decisions have been made, then the com- 17 | 10 | 50

plex task of locating the ideal job can begin. Some jobs are 21 | 13 | 53

listed in what is known as the open job market. These positions 25 | 15 | 55

are listed with placement offices of schools, placement agencies, 30 | 18 | 58

and they are advertised in newspapers or journals. 33 | 20 | 60

The open market is not the only source of jobs, however. 37 | 22 | 62

Some experts believe that almost two-thirds of all jobs are in 41 | 25 | 65

what is sometimes called the hidden job market. Networking is 46 | 27 | 67

the primary way to learn about jobs in the hidden job market. 50 | 30 | 70

Employees of a company, instructors, and members of professional 54 | 32 | 72

associations are some of the best contacts to tap the hidden job 58 | 35 | 75

market. Much time and effort are required to tap these sources. 63 | 38 | 77

But the hidden market often produces the best results. 66 | 40 | 80

3' | 1 | 2 | 3 | 4
5' | 1 | 2 | 3

Z, Y, Quotation Mark, Tab

WARMUP 10a

Key each line twice.

all letters	1	Quill owed those back taxes after moving to Japan.
spacing	2	Didn't Vi, Sue, and Paul go? Someone did; I know.
q/v/m	3	Marv was quite quick to remove that mauve lacquer.
easy	4	Lana is a neighbor; she owns a lake and an island.

NEW KEYS

10b  z and y
Key each line once; repeat.

z Reach *down* with *left fourth* finger.

y Reach *up* with *right first* finger.

z

5 za za zap zap zing zig zag zoo zed zip zap zig zed
6 doze zeal zero haze jazz zone zinc zing size ozone
7 ooze maze doze zoom zarf zebus daze gaze faze adze

y

8 y yj yj jay jay hay hay lay nay say days eyes ayes
9 yj ye yet yen yes cry dry you rye sty your fry wry
10 ye yen bye yea coy yew dye yaw lye yap yak yon any

all reaches learned

11 Did you say Liz saw any yaks or zebus at your zoo?
12 Relax; Jake wouldn't acquire any favorable rights.
13 Has Mazie departed? Tex, Lu, and I will go alone.

10c Textbook Keying
Key each line once. DS between groups.

14 Cecilia brings my jumbo umbrella to every concert.

direct reach	15	John and Kim recently brought us an old art piece.
	16	I built a gray brick border around my herb garden.

DS

	17	sa ui hj gf mn vc ew uy re io as lk rt jk df op yu
adjacent reach	18	In Ms. Lopez' opinion, the opera was really great.
	19	Polly and I were joining Walker at the open house.

Pleading Form with Table List of Trial Exhibits

Keyboarding Pro DELUXE users: The form will open as a data file.

1. Use the Pleading form with 26 lines template to create the Table List of Trial Exhibits. Insert a table for the Exhibit Number section. Remove borders and underline column heads.

2. Continue to the next document. (*116-d1*)

LEE & DURAND, LLP
ATTORNEYS AT LAW
James W. Lee, Esquire
State Bar Number 202256
8578 Main Street, Suite 202
Huntington Beach, CA 92646-1801

Telephone: 714-555-0174

Attorneys for Plaintiffs

SUPERIOR COURT OF THE STATE OF CALIFORNIA

FOR THE COUNTY OF ORANGE

DONALD HURT, et. al., Plaintiffs, vs. SUSAN RECKLESS, et al., Defendants

Case No. 01 CC05144   PLAINTIFFS' LIST OF TRIAL EXHIBITS

Exhibit Number	Description		Date Identified	Date Admitted
1	City of Costa Mesa Police Department Accident Report dated February 15, 20--			

Dated this 19th day of June 20--

JAMES W. LEE

Attorney for Plaintiffs

116-d2

SOAP Note

1. Open, *111-d2.* Fill in the form with the following information: **Lucas, Steve; # 22653**; age **42**; allergies: **None known**; Meds: **Esomeprazole Magnesium**

2. T: **99.0**; P: **80**; R: **15**; B/P: **118/76**; C/O: **Pain left elbow**; Date: **4-10-xx**

3. Check and close. (*116-d2*)

S	Pt injured left elbow two days ago in fall from rollerblades. Complains of pain on outside of elbow, superficial.
O	No inflammation; slight hematoma; limited ROM on left elbow FLEXION.
A	Treatment: lateral epicondyle 15 minute hot pack every day for a week and help with passive ROM. Ask pt to apply a hot pack at home twice a day. Diagnosis: Lateral epicondylitis on left.
P	Pt will return twice a week to reduce pain and increase ROM.

CHECKPOINT →

Congratulations! You have successfully completed the lessons in Module 18. To check your understanding and for more practice, complete the objective assessment and performance assessment located on the textbook website at www.collegekeyboarding.com.

10d
" (quotation mark) and TAB

Key each line once; repeat.

TAB Reach *up* with *left fourth* finger.

" Shift; then reach to the right with the *right fourth* finger.

" (quotation mark)

20 "; "; " " "lingo" "bugs" "tennies" I like "malts."
21 "I am not," she said, "going." I just said, "Oh?"

tab key

22   The tab key is used for indenting paragraphs and aligning columns.
23   Tabs that are set by the software are called default tabs, which are usually a half inch.

SKILL BUILDING

10e Textbook Keying

Key lines 24–30 once. Tap TAB to indent each paragraph. Use wordwrap, tapping ENTER only at the end of each paragraph.

24   The expression "I give you my word," or put another
25 way, "Take my word for it," is just a way I can say, "I
26 prize my name; it clearly stands in back of my words."
27 I offer "honor" as collateral.
tab 28   Tap the tab key and begin the line without a pause to maintain fluency.
29   She said that this is the lot to be sent; I agreed with her.
30   Tap Tab before starting to key a timed writing so that the first line is indented.

10f Timed Writing

Take two 1' timings beginning with paragraph 1. If you finish before time is up, continue with paragraph 2. Use wordwrap.

Goal: 15 *gwam*

TECHNIQUE TIP

Wordwrap: Text within a paragraph moves automatically to the next line. Tap ENTER only to begin a new paragraph.

	gwam 1'
Tab → All of us work for progress, but it is not	8
always easy to analyze "progress." We work hard	18
for it; but, in spite of some really good efforts,	28
we may fail to receive just exactly the response we	39
want.	40
Tab → When this happens, as it does to all of us,	9
it is time to cease whatever we are doing, have	18
a quiet talk with ourselves, and face up to the	28
questions about our limited progress. How can we	38
do better?	40

| 1 | 2 | 3 | 4 | 5 | 6 | 7 | 8 | 9 | 10 |

alphabet	1	Di quickly won several junior prizes at the Foxburgh swim trials.
figures	2	From July 13 to 20, the extension numbers will be 45, 67, and 89.
shift/lock	3	Ms. Ing keyed the notations REGISTERED and CERTIFIED in ALL CAPS.
easy	4	Did he visit a city to handle the authentic enamel dish and bowl?

| 1 | 2 | 3 | 4 | 5 | 6 | 7 | 8 | 9 | 10 | 11 | 12 | 13 |

SKILL BUILDING

116b Timed Writing
Key one 3' timed writing and one 5' timed writing.

all letters

	gwam	3'	5'

Individuals who conduct interviews often make snap judg- 4 2 41
ments. In fact, the decision to hire or not to hire an applicant 8 5 43
is usually made in the first five minutes of the interview. The 12 7 46
rest of the time is used to verify that the decision made was the 17 10 49
correct one. The wisdom of making a decision so early should be 21 13 51
questioned. When a quickly made decision is analyzed, generally 25 15 54
the result is that the decision is influenced heavily by the 30 18 56
first impression the person makes. 32 10 58

You can learn to make a good first impression in an inter- 36 21 60
view; all you have to do is be on time, dress appropriately, 40 24 62
shake hands firmly, establish eye contact, relax, smile, and show 44 26 65
that you have excellent communication skills. Doing all of this 48 29 68
may seem very difficult, but it really is not. Making a good 53 32 70
impression requires careful planning and many hours of practice. 57 34 73
Practice gives you the confidence you need to be able to do the 61 37 75
things that make an excellent impression. 64 38 77

3' | 1 | 2 | 3 | 4 |
5' | 1 | 2 | 3 |

APPLICATIONS

116c

Assessment

→ Continue

✓ Check

With *Keyboarding Pro DELUXE*: When you complete a document, proofread it, check the spelling, and preview for placement. When you are completely satisfied, click the Continue button to move to the next document. Click the Check button when you are ready to error-check the test. Review and/or print the document analysis results.

Without *Keyboarding Pro DELUXE*: Key the documents in sequence. When time has been called, proofread all documents again and identify errors.

LESSON 11

Review

WARMUP 11a

Key each line twice (slowly, then faster).

alphabet 1 Zeb had Jewel quickly give him five or six points.

" (quote) 2 Can you spell "chaos," "bias," "bye," and "their"?

y 3 Ty Clay may envy you for any zany plays you write.

easy 4 Did he bid on the bicycle, or did he bid on a map?

| 1 | 2 | 3 | 4 | 5 | 6 | 7 | 8 | 9 | 10 |

SKILL BUILDING

11b
Keyboard Reinforcement
Key each line once; repeat the drill to increase fluency.

TECHNIQUE TIP

Work for smoothness, not speed.

5 za za zap az az maze zoo zip razz zed zax zoa zone
6 Liz Zahl saw Zoe feed the zebra in an Arizona zoo.

7 yj yj jy jy joy lay yaw say yes any yet my try you
8 Why do you say that today, Thursday, is my payday?

9 xs xs sax ox box fix hex ax lax fox taxi lox sixes
10 Roxy, you may ask Jay to fix any tax sets for you.

11 qa qa aqua quail quit quake quid equal quiet quart
12 Did Enrique quietly but quickly quell the quarrel?

13 fv fv five lives vow ova van eve avid vex vim void
14 Has Vivi, Vada, or Eva visited Vista Valley Farms?

11c Speed Builders
Key each balanced-hand line twice, as quickly as you can.

15 is to for do an may work so it but an with them am
16 am yam map aid zig yams ivy via vie quay cob amend

17 to do is for an may work so it but am an with them
18 for it|for it|to the|to the|do they|do they|do it

19 Pamela may go to the farm with Jan and a neighbor.
20 Rod and Ty may go by the lake if they go downtown.

| 1 | 2 | 3 | 4 | 5 | 6 | 7 | 8 | 9 | 10 |

115-d3

Compose Request for Reference

1. Select a former professor or employer and compose a letter requesting that he or she serve as a reference for you.
2. Edit the letter carefully.
3. Check and close. (*115-d3*)

115-d4

Thank-You Letter

1. Copy the letterhead you created in (*115-d1*) for Carrie Melby for this letter.
2. Key the letter shown below as a block letter with open punctuation, centered vertically on the page. Use Mr. Stanberry's address from *115-d1*.
3. Check and close. (*115-d4*)

Thank you for taking time to talk with me about the position as a junior graphic designer at *Forde Financial News*.

I appreciated the comprehensive tour and the information you provided about the Graphic Design Department. This group of professionals is very fortunate to be equipped with the most up-to-date hardware and software and an outstanding staff development program. Consequently, your subscribers are the real winners.

Mr. Stanberry, I would like the opportunity to work at *Forde Financial News* and to contribute to the popularity and success of this outstanding newspaper. I am eager to receive a call from you.

Sincerely | Carrie A. Melby

115-d5

Job Refusal Letter

1. Use Carrie Melby's letterhead and key the letter shown below. Use block style and open punctuation.
2. Check and close. (*115-d5*)

Mr. Miguel Mendoza | Director, Human Resources | Blackmon Development Corporation | 548 Poplar Street | Macon, GA 31201-2752. **Add salutation and closing lines for Carrie Melby.**

Yesterday I received your offer for a position as a management trainee in the Human Resources Department of Blackmon Development Corporation. Your offer is very interesting and very competitive. I also received an offer yesterday for a position as a junior graphics designer for a financial newspaper.

Although the position you offered is a very desirable one and I have considered it very carefully, it does not give me the opportunity to apply my graphic design and information technology skills immediately. Therefore, I have decided to accept the other position because it is more directly related to my long-term career goals.

I do appreciate Blackmon Development Corporation offering me a position and the many courtesies that were extended to me during my interview and visit to Macon. Blackmon Development Corporation is an excellent company, and I wish you much success in finding the right person for the position you have available.

115-d6

Job Acceptance Letter

1. You received an offer for the job you applied for in *115-d2*. Use your own personal letterhead and write an acceptance letter.
2. Confirm a starting salary that you think appropriate for the position and a starting date of one month from today.
3. Check and close. (*115-d6*)

11d Textbook Keying

Key each line once. Tap ENTER at the end of each line. DS between the groups of lines.

enter: key smoothly without looking at fingers

21 Make the return snappily

22 and with assurance; keep

23 your eyes on your source

24 data; maintain a smooth,

25 constant pace as you key.

DS

space bar: use down-and-in motion

26 us me it of he an by do go to us if or so am ah el

27 Have you a pen? If so, print "Free to any guest."

DS

caps lock: press to toggle it on or off

28 Use ALL CAPS for items such as TO, FROM, or SUBJECT.

29 Did Kristin mean Kansas City, MISSOURI, or KANSAS?

TECHNIQUE TIP

Tap [CAPS LOCK] to capitalize several letters. Tap it again to toggle [CAPS LOCK] off.

11e Timed Writing

1. Take two 2' timings on all paragraphs. If you finish before time is up, start over with paragraph 1. Use wordwrap. Key fluently but with control.
   Goal: 16 *wam*
2. End the lesson but do not exit the software.

To determine gross-words-a-minute (*gwam*) rate for 2':

Follow these steps if you are *not* using the Timer in the Word Processor.

1. Note the figure at the end of the last line completed.

2. For a partial line, note the figure on the scale direcly below the point at which you stopped keying.

3. Add these two figures to determine the total gross words a minute (*gwam*) you keyed.

		gwam	2'
Have we thought of communication as a kind		4	31
of war that we wage through each day?		8	35
When we think of it that way, good language		12	39
would seem to become our major line of attack.		17	44
Words become muscle; in a normal exchange or in		22	49
a quarrel, we do well to realize the power of words.		27	54

11f Enrichment

1. Click the Skill Building tab from the main menu and choose Technique Builder; select Drill 1a.

2. Key Drill 1a from page 31. Key each line once striving for good accuracy.

3. The results will be listed on the Skill Building Report.

THANK-YOU LETTER AFTER AN INTERVIEW

Good manners dictate that you should write a thank-you letter very soon after an interview—preferably the day of or the day after the interview. Many people do not write a thank-you letter; therefore writing one helps you to create a good impression. The thank-you letter can be a powerful tool because you know more about the job than you did when you applied. You can use it to reinforce your strengths and show specifically how they match the job requirements.

1. Begin with a warm, sincere thank you.
2. Reaffirm your interest in the position.
3. Point out several specific things that were of interest or that matched your strengths.

REQUEST FOR REFERENCE

Good strategy and good manners dictate that you ask for permission to use a person as a reference before you use their name by telephone, e-mail, or letter. Telephone and e-mail are better for individuals with whom you may have a current relationship. Letters are preferable for those with whom you have not had recent contact. If your name has changed, be sure to indicate your name at the time you were enrolled in classes with or employed by the person. Above all select references who will give you a good recommendation. Thank-you notes after the reference are a nice touch.

1. Introduce yourself and make the request.
2. Tactfully discuss the classes or work you did for the person, if appropriate.
3. Suggest that you will call to confirm the person's willingness to be a reference.

JOB ACCEPTANCE OR REFUSAL LETTERS

Most companies require a written acceptance of a job offer. It is much easier to write the acceptance letter than the refusal letter. Always decline a position gracefully. In the future, that company may have a position you would like to accept or may even become a customer or client.

Acceptance Letters

1. Express your delight in accepting the position.
2. Confirm specific details, such as salary and the starting date.
3. End on a friendly, optimistic note about your future with the company.

Refusal Letters

1. Begin with a buffer or neutral statement to cushion the bad news.
2. Present the reasons tactfully and let them lead to the decline.

End on a friendly note thanking the employer for considering you.

APPLICATIONS

115-d1
Application Letter

1. Design appropriate letterhead for the letter; position the letterhead in the header.
2. Key the letter shown on the previous page as a block letter with open punctuation. Position the date at about line 1.9".
3. Check and close. (*115-d1*)

115-d2
Compose Application Letter

1. Design appropriate personal letterhead. Use the same document theme as the resume you prepared for yourself in *113-d4*.
2. In *113-d3*, you searched for a job description for a position you would like to have. Compose an application letter for the position that you would like to have. Attach your resume. Check and close. (*115-d2*)

WARMUP 12a

Key each line twice (slowly, then faster).

alphabet 1 Jack won five quiz games; Brad will play him next.

q 2 Quin Racq quickly and quietly quelled the quarrel.

z 3 Zaret zipped along sizzling, zigzag Arizona roads.

easy 4 Did he hang the sign by the big bush at the lake?

| 1 | 2 | 3 | 4 | 5 | 6 | 7 | 8 | 9 | 10 |

SKILL BUILDING

12b New Key Review
Key each line once; DS between groups. Work for smoothness, not speed.

b/f 5 bf bf fab fab ball bib rf rf rib rib fibs bums bee

6 Did Buffy remember that he is a brass band member?

z/y 7 za za zag zig zip yj yj jay eye day lazy hazy zest

8 Liz amazed us with the zesty pizza on a lazy trip.

q/u 9 qa qa quo qt. quit quay quad quarm que uj jug quay

10 Where is Quito? Qatar? Boqueirao? Quebec? Quilmes?

v/m 11 vf vf valve five value mj mj ham mad mull mass vim

12 Vito, enter the words vim, vivace, and avar; save.

all 13 I faced defeat; only reserves saved my best crews.

14 In my opinion, I need to rest in my reserved seat.

all 15 Holly created a red poppy and deserves art awards.

16 My pump averages a faster rate; we get better oil.

12c Textbook Keying
Key each line once; DS between groups. Work for smooth, unhurried keying.

de/ed 17 ed fed led deed dell dead deal sled desk need seed

18 Dell dealt with the deed before the dire deadline.

ol/lo 19 old tolls doll solo look sole lost love cold stole

20 Old Ole looked for the long lost olive oil lotion.

op/po 21 pop top post rope pout port stop opal opera report

22 Stop to read the top opera opinion report to Opal.

we/ew 23 we few wet were went wears weather skews stew blew

24 Working women wear sweaters when weather dictates.

TECHNIQUE TIP

Keep fingers curved and body aligned properly.

Carrie A. Melby

1001 Hogan Street, Apartment 216A ▪ Mobile, AL 36617-1001 ▪ 334-555-0103 ▪ cmelby@cu.edu

Current date

Establish a point of contact if possible →

Mr. Coleman Stanberry
Managing Editor
Forde Financial News
840 Montclair Road
Birmingham, AL 35213-1943

Dear Mr. Stanberry

State the job you are applying for →

My bachelor's degree with double majors in graphic design and information technology and my graphic design work qualify me as a junior graphic designer for *Forde Financial News*.

Convey key qualifications →

As a result of my comprehensive four-year program, I am skilled in the latest office suite as well as the current versions of desktop publishing and graphics programs. In addition, my excellent research and writing skills played a very important role in the Cother University Design Award I received last month. Being able to locate the right resources and synthesize those data into useful information for your readers is a priority I understand well and have practiced in my positions at the Cother University Alumni Office and the Cother University Library.

State how the employer will benefit from your qualifications →

My technical and communication skills were applied as well as I worked as the assistant director and producer of the *Cother University Alumni News*. I understand well the importance of meeting deadlines and also producing a quality product within budget that will increase newspaper sales.

Request on interview →

After you have reviewed the enclosed resume as well as my graphic design samples located on my Web page at http://www.netdoor.com/~cmelby, I look forward to discussing my qualifications and career opportunities with you at *Forde Financial News*.

Sincerely

Carrie A. Melby

Enclosure

12d Textbook Keying

Key each line once; DS between groups of three lines. Concentrate and key with control.

TECHNIQUE TIP

Keep hands quiet; do not bounce. Keep fingers curved and upright.

```
25  a for we you is that be this will be a to and well
26  as our with I or a to by your form which all would
27  new year no order they so new but now year who may
                                                      DS
28  This is Lyn's only date to visit their great city.
29  I can send it to your office at any time you wish.
30  She kept the fox, owls, and fowl down by the lake.
                                                      DS
31  Harriette will cook dinner for the swimming teams.
32  Annette will call at noon to give us her comments.
33  Johnny was good at running and passing a football.
    |  1  |  2  |  3  |  4  |  5  |  6  |  7  |  8  |  9  |  10  |
```

12e Timed Writing

Key a 2' timing on both paragraphs. If you finish before time is up, start again with paragraph 1. Key fluently but not rushed. Repeat the timing again for 2'.

all letters

Goal: 16 *gwam*

Copy Difficulty

What factors determine whether copy is difficult or easy? Research shows that difficulty is influenced by syllables per word, characters per word, and percent of familiar words. Carefully controlling these three factors ensures that speed and accuracy scores are reliable—that is, increased scores reflect increased skill.

In Level 1, all timings are easy. Note "E" inside the triangle at left of the timing. Easy timings contain an average of 1.2 syllables per word, 5.1 characters per word, and 90 percent familiar words. Easy copy is suitable for the beginner who is mastering the keyboard.

```
                                                      gwam   2'
                •            4           •           8
        There should be no questions, no doubt, about     5  35
    •             12            •              16      •
the value of being able to key; it's just a matter       10  40
    20              •            24          •         28      •
of common sense that today a pencil is much too slow.    15  45
                •            4           •           8
        Let me explain.  Work is done on a keyboard     19  49
    •             12            •              16      •
three to six times faster than other writing and        24  54
    20              •            24          •         28
with a product that is a prize to read.  Don't you      29  59
    •
agree?                                                   30  60
    2' |    1    |    2    |    3    |    4    |    5    |
```

WARMUP 115a

Key each line, striving for control. Repeat if desired.

alphabet 1 Zane quickly talked with Baxter about five or six major programs.

numbers 2 My club has 1,827 members and is open from 6:30 a.m. to 9:45 p.m.

capital letters 3 Ty, Jo, Ann, Jan, Bo, Lee, Tom, and I are going to San Diego, CA.

fluency 4 Clancy and Makalaya may go downtown to visit with their neighbor.

DOCUMENT DESIGN

115b

APPLICATION LETTERS

The purpose of an application letter is to obtain an interview—not to get a job. Most organizations will not hire anyone on the basis of just a letter, resume, or application form. Application letters vary depending on how you learned of the position. It is important that the letter shows how your skills match the requirements of the job that is available. Design attractive personal letterhead for your application letter—never use a company's letterhead. Personal letterhead looks more professional than plain paper with a return address. Block style is generally preferred.

A good strategy for writing an application letter is to:

1. Establish a point of contact if possible.
2. Specify the job that you are seeking.
3. Convey your key qualifications.
4. Interpret your major qualifications in terms of employer benefit.
5. Request an interview.

If your resume is mailed or faxed, the letter serves as a cover. If your resume is transmitted electronically, the letter may have to be incorporated within an e-mail or as an attachment to the e-mail. Always follow the instructions provided by the organization.

Review Carrie Melby's application letter on the next page.

EMPLOYMENT LETTERS

A variety of documents are used in the employment process. Some of these documents relate to the prospective employer; others relate to the prospective employee. This lesson focuses on strategies for writing key employment documents that the prospective employee should write.

These letters include:

- Thank-you letters after interviews.
- Requests for references.
- Requests for transcripts or other records.
- Job acceptance or refusal letters.

Review the strategies for each of these letters on page 517.

Review

Key each line twice (slowly, then faster).

alphabet	1	Bev quickly hid two Japanese frogs in Mitzi's box.
shift	2	Jay Nadler, a Rotary Club member, wrote Mr. Coles.
, (comma)	3	Jay, Ed, and I paid for plates, knives, and forks.
easy	4	Did the amendment name a city auditor to the firm?

| 1 | 2 | 3 | 4 | 5 | 6 | 7 | 8 | 9 | 10 |

SKILL BUILDING

13b Textbook Keying
Key each line once; DS between groups of lines.
Key the text as suggested:

Lines 5–7: Key the words as a single unit.

Lines 8–10: Key the words letter by letter.

Lines 11–13: Vary your keying as your fingers find the right rhythm.

word-level response: key short, familiar words as units

5 is to for do an may work so it but an with them am
6 Did they mend the torn right half of their ensign?
7 Hand me the ivory tusk on the mantle by the bugle.

letter-level response: key more difficult words letter by letter

8 only state jolly zest oil verve join rate mop card
9 After defeat, look up; gaze in joy at a few stars.
10 We gazed at a plump beaver as it waded in my pool.

combination response: use variable speed; your fingers will let you feel the difference

11 it up so at for you may was but him work were they
12 It is up to you to get the best rate; do it right.
13 This is Lyn's only date to visit their great city.

| 1 | 2 | 3 | 4 | 5 | 6 | 7 | 8 | 9 | 10 |

13c
Keyboard Reinforcement
Key each line once; fingers well curved, wrists low.

p	14	Pat appears happy to pay for any supper I prepare.
x	15	Knox can relax; Alex gets a box of flax next week.
v	16	Vi, Ava, and Viv move ivy vines, leaves, or stems.
'	17	It's a question of whether they can't or won't go.
?	18	Did Jan go? Did she see Ray? Who paid? Did she?
.	19	Ms. E. K. Nu and Lt. B. A. Walz had the a.m. duty.
"	20	"Who are you?" he asked. "I am," I said, "Marie."
;	21	Find a car; try it; like it; work a price; buy it.

114-d1
Format Scannable Resume

1. Reformat the resume you prepared for Carrie Melby in *113-d1* as a scannable resume. Do not use a table or tabs. Remove slashes (/) and vertical bars (|). Tap ENTER twice to use about a 1.6" top margin. Use Calibri font.

2. Key a heading on the first line of the second page—position name on the left and Page 2 at the right margin. Tap the Space Bar to position the text at the right. See illustration below.

3. Check and close. (*114-d1*)

114-d2
Format Text-Only Resume

1. Open *114-d1* and change the margins to wide.

2. Move the second-page heading to the top of the page and re-position the page number at the right.

3. Non-*Keyboarding Pro DELUXE* users: Save as plain text; ignore the warning about losing formatting; click the Insert Line Breaks option; and then OK.

4. Check and close. (*114-d2*)

114-d3
Format Scannable Resume

1. Reformat your personal resume (*113-d4*) as a scannable resume.

2. Review your Summary of Achievements or Profile as well as other sections of your resume. Make sure it contains many keywords that accurately describe you and also that fit the description of the job you wish to obtain. If not, revise to include more keywords.

3. Check and close. (*114-d3*)

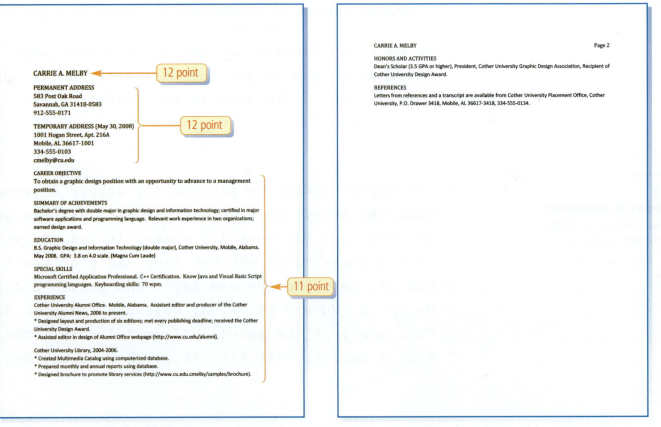

Scannable Resume

13d Textbook Keying

Troublesome Pairs: Key each line once; DS between groups.

TECHNIQUE TIP

Keep hands and arms still as you reach up to the third row and down to the first row.

t 22 at fat hat sat to tip the that they fast last slat
r 23 or red try ran run air era fair rid ride trip trap
t/r 24 A trainer sprained an arm trying to tame the bear.
                                                    DS

m 25 am me my mine jam man more most dome month minimum
n 26 no an now nine once net knee name ninth know never
m/n 27 Many men and women are important company managers.
                                                    DS

o 28 on or to not now one oil toil over only solo today
i 29 it is in tie did fix his sit like with insist will
o/i 30 Joni will consider obtaining options to buy coins.
                                                    DS

a 31 at an as art has and any case data haze tart smart
s 32 us as so say sat slap lass class just sassy simple
a/s 33 Disaster was averted as the steamer sailed to sea.
                                                    DS

e 34 we he ear the key her hear chef desire where there
i 35 it is in tie did fix his sit like with insist will
e/i 36 An expression of gratitude for service is desired.

13e Timed Writing

Key a 2' writing on both paragraphs. If you finish before time is up, start again with paragraph 1. Key fluently but not rushed. Repeat the timing again for 2'.

all letters

Goal: 16 *gwam*

                                                    gwam 2'

       •   4   •   8
    The questions of time use are vital ones; we   5
 •   12   •   16
miss so much just because we don't plan.   9
       •   4   •   8
    When we organize our days, we save time for   13
 •   12   •   16
those extra premium things we long to do.   17

2' | 1 | 2 | 3 | 4 | 5 |

KEYWORDS

One issue that must be discussed is keywords. Keywords typically are nouns. Generally, resumes are written in an action-oriented style, which means verbs are used rather than nouns. The more sophisticated applicant tracking systems will pick up verbs as well as nouns. However, some of the less sophisticated systems may not do so. Some experts in the area of writing resumes recommend putting a section of keywords at the beginning of the resume. Others think that this may do more harm than good. While the keyword section may get more initial "hits" in the software screening process, when individuals read the resume prior to inviting the individual in for an interview, the keyword section may have a negative effect.

Perhaps a good alternative is to work keywords carefully into each section of the resume. Perhaps the best advice is to use keywords only when they truly apply to you. Padding a resume is not a good approach. Preparing various styles of resumes and then tailoring each one to the specific company increases your chances of being successful in your job search.

The resumes that you formatted for Carrie A. Melby and yourself in Lesson 113 were designed to be printed. These resumes could also be attached to an e-mail and meet the criteria that some companies specify: Submit a *Word* file attached to an e-mail. The difference between a scannable resume and a text-only resume is that the scannable resume has very limited formatting and the text-only resume is just text. Often when a one-page resume is formatted as a scannable or text-only resume, it will become a two-page resume. In that case, key a heading on the second page.

TEN TIPS FOR FORMATTING SCANNABLE AND TEXT-ONLY RESUMES

Compare the following tips to the ones you found in your Internet search (*114c*).

1. Use a short line length—typically 80 or fewer characters for a text-only or online resume.
2. Use a sans serif True Type font such as Arial, Calibri, Consolas, or Courier.
3. Position your name on a line by itself at the top followed by your contact information; key a heading on the second page if a second page is needed.
4. Format section headings in uppercase.
5. Left-align all text including headings.
6. Avoid tabs, tables, bold, italic, underline, and graphics. Tap the Space Bar to position text.
7. Use hyphens, asterisks, or other symbols from the keyboard to replace bullets or serve as a section divider.
8. Print the scannable resume using a high-quality laser printer.
9. Use high-quality white or cream paper.
10. Proofread copy carefully; use checking tools. You can copy text to online resume builders or into an e-mail. Save the document first as a *Word* document; then change the margins to a short line of writing and also save it as a text file.

TIP

Use the tips shown at the right to prepare the three applications on the next page.

KEYBOARDING PRO DELUXE ➤ **Skill Building** **Technique Builder**

From the Skill Building tab, select Technique Builder and then the drill. Key each line once at a comfortable rate. Tap ENTER at the end of each line. Single-space the drill. Double-space between groups of lines. Concentrate and key accurately. Repeat if desired.

DRILL 1

Goal: reinforce key locations

Key each line once at a comfortable, constant rate.

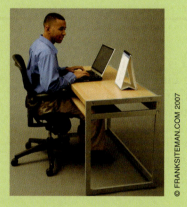

© FRANKSITEMAN.COM 2007

TECHNIQUE TIP

Keep
- your eyes on source copy
- your fingers curved, upright
- your wrists low but not touching
- your elbows hanging loosely
- your feet flat on the floor

Drill 1a

A We saw that Alan had an alabaster vase in Alabama.
B My rubber boat bobbed about in the bubbling brook.
C Ceci gave cups of cold cocoa to Rebecca and Rocco.
D Don's dad added a second deck to his old building.
E Even as Ellen edited her document, she ate dinner.
F Our firm in Buffalo has a staff of forty or fifty.
G Ginger is giving Greg the eggs she got from Helga.
H Hugh has eighty high, harsh lights he might flash.

Drill 1b

I Irik's lack of initiative is irritating his coach.
J Judge J. J. Jore rejected Jeane and Jack's jargon.
K As a lark, Kirk kicked back a rock at Kim's kayak.
L Lucille is silly; she still likes lemon lollipops.
M Milt Mumm hammered a homer in the Miami home game.
N Ken Linn has gone hunting; Stan can begin canning.
O Jon Soto rode off to Otsego in an old Morgan auto.
P Philip helped pay the prize as my puppy hopped up.
Q Quiet Raquel quit quoting at an exquisite marquee.

Drill 1c

R As Mrs. Kerr's motor roared, her red horse reared.
S Sissie lives in Mississippi; Lissa lives in Tulsa.
T Nat told Betty not to tattle on her little sister.
U Ula has a unique but prudish idea on unused units.
V Eva visited every vivid event for twelve evenings.
W We watched as wayworn wasps swarmed by the willow.
X Tex Cox waxed the next box for Xenia and Rex Knox.
Y Ty says you may stay with Fay for only sixty days.
Z Hazel is puzzled about the azure haze; Zack dozes.

INTERNET ACTIVITY

114c

Before you learn how to format electronic resumes, it is important to understand how the system that accepts and manages your resume works. This Internet activity is designed to help you gain a better understanding of the process that many companies use to recruit new employees.

1. Use the keywords *electronic resumes* and search for four or five articles on formatting electronic resumes.

2. Key the heading **Electronic Resumes** and then key a brief description of each of the various types of electronic resumes (online resume builder, *Word* document attached to e-mail, text-only resume, scannable resume, etc.) that you find listed in the articles.

3. Key the heading **Tips for Formatting an Electronic Resume** and use bullets or numbering to list at least eight or ten tips for formatting an electronic resume.

4. Use the keywords *applicant tracking system* and select one or two systems to see what they do and how they work. Take the tour or demo if the site offers one. Key the heading **Applicant Tracking Systems** and list the systems you previewed.

5. Check and close. (*114c*)

DOCUMENT DESIGN

114d

DESIGNING ELECTRONIC RESUMES

An electronic resume is simply a file containing a resume that is transmitted to the potential employer by e-mail, posting to a website, or pasting into the resume builder portion of an applicant tracking system (a software database that manages resumes). A scannable resume is a paper-based document that is transmitted to a potential employer, usually by regular or overnight mail services so that it can be scanned using OCR technology into the company applicant tracking system. Not all resumes scan accurately so it pays to learn as much as possible about the system that manages your resume. In fact, some companies request a "text-only" resume—meaning no formatting with tabs, a table, graphics, or text enhancements such as bold, color, or italic.

Checking the websites of many companies (of varying sizes) to see what information they provided about submitting a resume produced a wide range of alternatives. Many of them provided multiple alternatives, and size of the company was not always a good indicator of the company's preference. Here are some samples of what you may have found in your Internet search.

- Submit your resume by mail, *Word* document or PDF file attached to an e-mail; post to a specified website; or use our resume builder to submit online.
- All resumes must be submitted by attaching a *Word* document to an e-mail; we do not accept hand delivery, mail, or other resume submission methods.
- To apply for a position, use our resume builder to submit your information.
- Submit a text-only resume following instructions on this website.
- Contact information on the company's career page includes address, telephone, fax, and e-mail address—no indication of preferred way to receive information.

Note: The content of a resume does not change to make it an electronic or scannable resume; the format changes. A well-written resume can be reformatted to meet all of these styles.

DOCUMENT DESIGN DOCUMENT DESIGN DOCUMENT DESIG

DRILL 2

Goal: strengthen up and down reaches

Keep hands and wrists quiet; fingers well curved in home position; stretch fingers up from home or pull them palmward as needed.

home position
1 Hall left for Dallas; he is glad Jake fed his dog.
2 Ada had a glass flask; Jake had a sad jello salad.
3 Lana Hask had a sale; Gala shall add half a glass.

down reaches
4 Did my banker, Mr. Mavann, analyze my tax account?
5 Do they, Mr. Zack, expect a number of brave women?
6 Zach, check the menu; next, beckon the lazy valet.

up reaches
7 Prue truly lost the quote we wrote for our report.
8 Teresa quietly put her whole heart into her words.
9 There were two hilarious jokes in your quiet talk.

DRILL 3

Goal: strengthen individual finger reaches

first finger
1 Bob Mugho hunted for five minutes for your number.
2 Juan hit the bright green turf with his five iron.
3 The frigates and gunboats fought mightily in Java.

second finger
4 Dick said the ice on the creek had surely cracked.
5 Even as we picnicked, I decided we needed to diet.
6 Kim, not Mickey, had rice with chicken for dinner.

third/fourth finger
7 Pam saw Roz wax an aqua auto as Lex sipped a cola.
8 Wally will quickly spell Zeus, Apollo, and Xerxes.
9 Who saw Polly? Zoe Pax saw her; she is quiet now.

DRILL 4

Goal: strengthen special reaches

Emphasize smooth stroking. Avoid pauses, but do not reach for speed.

adjacent reaches
1 Falk knew well that her opinions of art were good.
2 Theresa answered her question; order was restored.
3 We join there and walk north to the western point.

direct reaches
4 Barb Nunn must hunt for my checks; she is in debt.
5 In June and December, Irvin hunts in Bryce Canyon.
6 We decided to carve a number of funny human faces.

double letters
7 Anne stopped off at school to see Bill Wiggs cook.
8 Edd has planned a small cookout for all the troop.
9 Keep adding to my assets all fees that will apply.

| 1 | 2 | 3 | 4 | 5 | 6 | 7 | 8 | 9 | 10 |

WARMUP 114a

Key each line, striving for control. Repeat if desired.

alphabet 1 Sandra quickly gave the boy a major prize for his excellent work.

figures 2 Invoice #758 for $294 is due 2/14/03 and #315 for $67 is due now.

double letters 3 Todd and Ann meet with a committee at noon to discuss all issues.

balanced hand 4 He may sign both of the forms for the amendment to the endowment.

| 1 | 2 | 3 | 4 | 5 | 6 | 7 | 8 | 9 | 10 | 11 | 12 | 13 |

SKILL BUILDING

114b Timed Writing
1. Key a 3' writing; work to increase speed.
2. Key a 5' timing; work for control.

all letters

	gwam	3'	5'
When you begin to think about applying for a job, one thing	4	3	37
that you will need to think carefully about is the list of references	9	5	40
that you will give to potential employers. How will you select the	14	8	43
individuals? First, each one should know you well. Second, each	18	11	46
should be able to offer information about aspects of your academic	22	13	48
work, job experience, or other attributes that might be of interest	27	16	51
to a potential employer. Third, can you predict if each of your	31	19	54
references will give you a stellar recommendation?	35	21	56
You can maximize the impact of your references by providing a	39	23	58
list of highly respected people whose judgment will be valued. At	44	26	61
the same time, you must take care not to damage your credibility by	48	29	64
adding people to your reference list who do not know you very well.	53	32	66
The time you spend selecting the right people will be an excellent	57	34	69
investment.	58	35	70

3'	1	2	3	4
5'	1	2	3	

WORKPLACE SUCCESS

Applicant Tracking Systems

© PHOTODISC / GETTY IMAGES

Many, if not most, medium- and large-size companies manage their job recruitment process by using an applicant tracking system. They request electronic resumes or scan paper-based resumes into their system using OCR technology. Once a resume has become a part of an applicant tracking system, the software then determines from a large number of resumes which ones will be selected for review by the potential employer. This process involves the use of keywords (usually nouns) to search a resume to see if it matches the keywords from the job description. The price of applicant tracking systems ranges from a few hundred dollars to hundreds of thousands of dollars, which is a strong indicator that the level of sophistication of the systems varies widely. The best way to format a resume often depends on the software being used by the company to which you want to submit a resume, which means that no one best way to format a resume exists. The best way you can format your resume is the way that produces the best results in the system of the company to which you are applying for a position.

DRILL 5

Goal: improve troublesome pairs

Use a controlled rate without pauses.

1 ad add did does dish down body dear dread dabs bad
d/k 2 kid ok kiss tuck wick risk rocks kayaks corks buck
3 Dirk asked Dick to kid Drake about the baked duck.

4 deed deal den led heed made needs delay he she her
e/i 5 kit kiss kiln kiwi kick kilt kind six ribs kill it
6 Abie had neither ice cream nor fried rice in Erie.

7 fib fob fab rib beg bug rob bad bar bed born table
b/v 8 vat vet gave five ever envy never visit weave ever
9 Did Harv key jibe or jive, TV or TB, robe or rove?

10 aft after lift gift sit tot the them tax tutu tyro
t/r 11 for far ere era risk rich rock rosy work were roof
12 In Toronto, Ruth told the truth about her artwork.

13 jug just jury judge juice unit hunt bonus quiz bug
u/y 14 jay joy lay you your only envy quay oily whey body
15 Willy usually does not buy your Yukon art in July.

DRILL 6

Goal: fluency

1 Dian may make cocoa for the girls when they visit.
2 Focus the lens for the right angle; fix the prism.
3 She may suspend work when she signs the torn form.
4 Augment their auto fuel in the keg by the autobus.
5 As usual, their robot did half turns to the right.
6 Pamela laughs as she signals to the big hairy dog.
7 Pay Vivian to fix the island for the eighty ducks.

DRILL 7

Goal: eyes on the copy

Option: In the Word Processor, set the Timer for Variable and then either 20" or 30". Choose a *gwam* goal that is two to three words higher than your best rate. Try to reach your goal.

	words	30"	20"
1 Did she make this turkey dish? **ENTER**		12	18
2 Blake and Laurie may go to Dubuque.		14	21
3 Signal for the oak sleigh to turn right.		16	24
4 I blame Susie; did she quench the only flame?		18	27
5 She turns the panel dials to make this robot work.		20	30

APPLICATIONS

113-d1

Resume

1. Key the model resume on the previous page. Use *Word 2007* defaults. Key all ZIP Codes and phone numbers using a non-breaking hyphen.

2. Use Title style for the name. For vertical divider line 1, use the shift of the backslash key. After the address, insert a horizontal line; format it using Blue, Accent 1.

3. Format the body as a two-column table; make the first column 1.5" wide. Tap ENTER to leave a blank line after each entry in the row. Use Cambria, uppercase, bold for the headings. Be sure to remove the bullets in the blank lines.

4. Check and close. (*113-d1*)

113-d2

Resume Planning Document

RESUME PLANNER

Carrie Melby used a planning document to map out her qualifications for a graphic design position. Use the *resume planner* in the data files to plan your resume.

1. Use *113-d1* as a model for headings and content; but adapt it to meet your needs and job objective.

2. Write a job objective that matches the type of position you would like to have.

3. Add headings that would assist you in showcasing your qualifications; delete headings that would not be helpful to you. You may change headings. For example, instead of using *Summary of Achievements*, some people might prefer to use *Profile*. The resume tells your story—use the style and the headings that best meet your needs.

4. Check and close. (*113-d2*)

Résumé Planner	
Résumé Heading	Key Your Information Here
Full name for identification section	
Permanent Address	
Temporary Address	
Career Objective	

113-d3

Job Search

Internet

1. Use the Internet to locate job listings in a city or area where you would like to live.

2. Key a list of two or three jobs that you would like to have. Key the URL so that you can locate the information again if you need to.

3. Either copy the advertisement or job description or print it for each job.

4. Match the job requirements to your qualifications; select the best match.

5. Check and close. (*113-d3*)

113-d4

Personal Resume

1. Use the information in your Resume Planner to prepare a resume for yourself. Create it to match the job you identified in *113-d3*. Use Copy and Paste to avoid rekeying the information.

2. Use the style illustrated in *113-d1*.

3. Try to keep the resume to one-page; if it goes to a second page, add a header with your name and the page number; do not show the header on the first page.

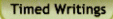
Timed Writings

Any timed writing in the book can be completed using the Timed Writing feature.

TO USE THE TIMED WRITING FEATURE:

1. Select the Timed Writing tab from the Main screen.
2. Scroll to select the timed writing.
3. Select the source and the timing length. For example,
   - Select Paragraph 1 and 1'. Key paragraph 1; if you finish before time is up, repeat the same paragraph.
   - Select Paragraph 2 and 1'. Key paragraph 2; repeat the same paragraph if you finish before time is up.
   - Select the Entire Writing and 2'. Try to maintain your 1' rate. If you finish before time is up, start over, beginning with paragraph 1.
4. Timings save automatically.
5. The Timed Writing Report displays the results of the last 20 timed writings and the best three timings at each speed.

Goal: build staying power

1. Key each paragraph as a 1' timing.
2. Key a 2' timing on both paragraphs.

all letters

Writing 1: 18 *gwam*   *gwam* 2'

    Why spend weeks with some problem when just a few quiet   6
minutes can help us to resolve it.   9
    If we don't take time to think through a problem, it will   15
swiftly begin to expand in size.   18

Writing 2: 20 *gwam*

    We push very hard in our quest for growth, and we all   5
think that only excellent growth will pay off.   10
    Believe it or not, one can actually work much too hard,   16
be much too zealous, and just miss the mark.   20

Writing 3: 22 *gwam*

    A business friend once explained to me why he was often   6
quite eager to be given some new project to work with.   11
    My friend said that each new project means he has to   16
organize and use the best of his knowledge and his skill.   22

Writing 4: 24 *gwam*

    Don't let new words get away from you. Learn how to spell   6
and pronounce new words and when and how finally to use them.   12
    A new word is a friend, but frequently more. New words   18
must be used lavishly to extend the size of your own word power.   24

2' | 1 | 2 | 3 | 4 | 5 | 6 |

Carrie A. Melby

Permanent Address: 583 Post Oak Road | Savannah, GA 31418-0583 | 912-555-0171 ← Calibri 11 point

Temporary Address (May 30, 2008): 1001 Hogan Street, Apt. 216A | Mobile, AL 36617-1001
334-555-0103 | cmelby@cu.edu

CAREER OBJECTIVE	To obtain a graphic design position with an opportunity to advance to a management position.
SUMMARY OF ACHIEVEMENTS	Bachelor's degree with double major in graphic design and information technology; certified in major software applications and programming language. Relevant work experience in two organizations; earned design award.
EDUCATION	B.S. Graphic Design and Information Technology (double major), Cother University, Mobile, Alabama. May 2008. GPA: 3.8/4.0. (Magna Cum Laude)
SPECIAL SKILLS	Microsoft Certified Application Professional. C++ Certification. Know Java and Visual Basic Script programming languages. Keyboarding skills: 70 wpm.
EXPERIENCE	Cother University Alumni Office. Mobile, Alabama. Assistant editor and producer of the Cother University Alumni News, 2006 to present.

- Designed layout/production of six editions; met every publishing deadline; received the Cother University Design Award.
- Assisted editor in design of Alumni Office webpage (http://www.cu.edu/alumni).

Cother University Library, 2004-2006.
- Created Multimedia Catalog using computerized database.
- Prepared monthly and annual reports using database.
- Designed brochure to promote library services (http://www.cu.edu.cmelby/samples/brochure).

HONORS AND ACTIVITIES	Dean's Scholar (3.5 GPA or higher), President, Cother University Graphic Design Association, Recipient of Cother University Design Award.
REFERENCES	Letters from references and a transcript are available from Cother University Placement Office, Cother University, P.O. Drawer 3418, Mobile, AL 36617-3418, 334-555-0134.

Cambria 11 point bold

Note: The dot above text represents two words.

Writing 5: 26 *gwam*

We usually get best results when we know where we are   5

going. Just setting a few goals will help us quietly see what   12

we are doing.   13

Goals can help measure whether we are moving at a good   19

rate or dozing along. You can expect a goal to help you find   25

good results.   26

Writing 6: 28 *gwam*

To win whatever prizes we want from life, we must plan to   6

move carefully from this goal to the next to get the maximum   12

result from our work.   14

If we really want to become skilled in keying, we must   19

come to see that this desire will require of us just a little   26

patience and hard work.   28

Writing 7: 30 *gwam*

Am I an individual person? I'm sure I am; still, in a   5

much, much bigger sense, other people have a major voice in   12

thoughts I think and actions I take.   15

Although we are each a unique person, we all work and   21

play in organized groups of people who do not expect us to   26

dismiss their rules of law and order.   30

2' | 1 | 2 | 3 | 4 | 5 | 6 |

FORMATTING RESUMES

A resume is a summary of your qualifications; it is the primary basis for the interviewer's decision to invite you for an interview. Prior to preparing a resume, complete a self-analysis, identifying your career goals and job qualifications. Most resumes contain some or all of the following information.

Identification: Your name, telephone numbers, address, e-mail address, and Internet address. Students may list a temporary and permanent address.

Career Objective: The type of position to let the employer know your specific career goal.

Summary of Achievements: A list of your most important achievements. Emphasize special or unique skills (foreign language, computer skills, etc.).

Education: Diplomas or degrees earned, schools attended, and dates. Include majors and grade-point averages when it is to your advantage to do so.

Experience: Job titles, employers, dates of employment, a brief description of the positions, and major achievements—not a listing of activities. Use active voice and concrete language; for example, "Handle an average of 200 customer orders per week." List information in the same order for each position.

Honors and Activities: Specific examples of leadership potential and commitment.

References: Information on how to obtain references. Usually a separate list of references is given to the interviewer upon request.

Carrie A. Melby

Permanent Address: 583 Post Oak Road | Savannah, GA 31418-0583 | 912-555-0171

Temporary Address (May 30, 2008): 1001 Hogan Street, Apt. 216A | Mobile, AL 36617-1001
334-555-0103 | cmelby@cu.edu

CAREER OBJECTIVE	To obtain a graphic design position with an opportunity to advance to a management position.
SUMMARY OF ACHIEVEMENTS	Bachelor's degree with double major in graphic design and information technology; certified in major software applications and programming language. Relevant work experience in two organizations; earned design award.
EDUCATION	B.S. Graphic Design and Information Technology (double major), Cother University, Mobile, Alabama. May 2008. GPA: 3.8/4.0. (Magna Cum Laude)
SPECIAL SKILLS	Microsoft Certified Application Professional. C++ Certification. Know Java and Visual Basic Script programming languages. Keyboarding skills: 70 wpm.
EXPERIENCE	Cother University Alumni Office. Mobile, Alabama. Assistant editor and producer of the Cother University Alumni News, 2006 to present. • Designed layout/production of six editions; met every publishing deadline; received the Cother University Design Award. • Assisted editor in design of Alumni Office webpage (http://www.cu.edu/alumni). Cother University Library, 2004-2006. • Created Multimedia Catalog using computerized database. • Prepared monthly and annual reports using database. • Designed brochure to promote library services (http://www.cu.edu.cmelby/samples/brochure).
HONORS AND ACTIVITIES	Dean's Scholar (3.5 GPA or higher), President, Cother University Graphic Design Association, Recipient of Cother University Design Award.
REFERENCES	Letters from references and a transcript are available from Cother University Placement Office, Cother University, P.O. Drawer 3418, Mobile, AL 36617-3418, 334-555-0134.

Items within the sections of the resume are arranged in reverse chronological order (most recent experiences listed first). Which section is presented first? From your self-analysis, you will determine which one of your qualifications is the strongest. If work experience is stronger than education, present this section first. A recent college graduate would present education first.

A major consideration in preparing an effective resume is the overall attractiveness of the resume. Use high-quality paper; print on a laser printer using effective layout design that will allow your resume to appear professionally created. However, do not overdo.

Figure and Symbol Keys

LEARNING OUTCOMES

- Key the numeric keys by touch.
- Use symbol keys correctly.
- Build keying speed and accuracy.
- Apply correct number expression.
- Apply proofreaders' marks.
- Apply basic Internet skills.

LESSON 14   1 and 8

WARMUP 14a

Key each line twice.

Line 2: Space once after a series of brief questions within a sentence.

alphabet 1   Jessie Quick believed the campaign frenzy would be exciting.
space bar 2   Was it Mary? Helen? Pam? It was a woman; I saw one of them.
3rd row 3   We were quietly prepped to write two letters to Portia York.
easy 4   Kale's neighbor works with a tutor when they visit downtown.

| 1 | 2 | 3 | 4 | 5 | 6 | 7 | 8 | 9 | 10 | 11 | 12 |

SKILL BUILDING

14b **Textbook Keying**

The words at the right are from the 100 most used words.

Key each line once; work for fluency.

Top 100 High-Frequency Words

5   a an it been copy for his this more no office please service
6   our service than the they up was work all any many thank had
7   business from I know made more not me new of some to program
8   such these two with your about and have like department year
9   by at on but do had in letter most now one please you should
10   their order like also appreciate that there gentlemen letter
11   be can each had information letter may make now only so that
12   them time use which am other been send to enclosed have will

Resumes

WARMUP 113a

Key each line, striving for control. Repeat if desired.

alphabet 1 Jacki might analyze the data by answering five complex questions.

figures 2 Memo 67 asks if Bill 35-48 is due on the 19th or the 20th of May.

shift 3 Plum trees on a hilly acre, in my opinion, create no vast estate.

easy 4 Did the foal buck? And did it cut the right elbow of the cowhand?

| 1 | 2 | 3 | 4 | 5 | 6 | 7 | 8 | 9 | 10 | 11 | 12 | 13 |

SKILL BUILDING

113b Textbook Keying

1. Key each line once, concentrating on good keying techniques. Tap ENTER twice after each 4-line group.
2. Repeat if time permits.

1st/2nd fingers
5 Did bedlam erupt when they arrived after my speech ended quickly?
6 Joyce bought me a new bright red jacket for my birthday tomorrow.
7 Did Rebecca make the needlepoint cushion for the club room couch?
8 Much to the concern of our teacher, I did my homework on the bus.

3rd/4th fingers
9 Zam saw six small poodle puppies playing in the meadow last week.
10 Paxton saw a lazy lizard on the old wooden oar at Pawley's Plaza.
11 Zam Velasquez sells squid in six stores near the pool at the zoo.
12 Paul quizzed a shop owner about a patchwork quilt we saw in Waco.

all fingers
13 Jarvis Zackery played quarterback with six teams before retiring.
14 Jan Weitzel made grave errors, but he quickly fixed the problems.
15 Quinn Zack wrote just six poems and a short story before leaving.
16 Maxey Czajka will quit swimming because he performed very poorly.

| 1 | 2 | 3 | 4 | 5 | 6 | 7 | 8 | 9 | 10 | 11 | 12 | 13 |

113c Timed Writing

1. Key a 1' writing on each paragraph; work to increase speed.
2. Key a 5' timing on all paragraphs.

all letters

	gwam	1'	5'

You can learn to make excellent presentations. People who · 13 · 3 · 42
master this skill have an advantage in moving up the corporate · 25 · 5 · 44
ladder. Whether you're making a presentation to your department or · 39 · 8 · 47
speaking in front of a large audience, you want to be a good speaker. · 53 · 11 · 50

Use simple words in a conversational style; you don't have to · 13 · 13 · 53
impress other people with your vocabulary. Listeners want to connect · 27 · 16 · 55
with you as a human being; they don't want to feel intimidated or · 41 · 19 · 58
lectured to. Avoid reading your presentation. A speaker who gets up · 55 · 22 · 61
and starts reading from a pile of papers will turn off the audience · 68 · 24 · 64
right away. Use note cards to remind yourself of the key points you · 82 · 27 · 66
want to cover. · 85 · 28 · 67

Include numbers and facts in your speech to give it some · 12 · 30 · 69
pizzazz. This also makes your speech more credible. Be careful · 25 · 33 · 72
not to include too many numbers as this can bore your audience very · 39 · 35 · 75
quickly. Finally, practice makes perfect. Jump at every opportunity · 53 · 38 · 77
you get to give a speech. · 58 · 39 · 78

1' | 1 | 2 | 3 | 4 | 5 | 6 | 7 | 8 | 9 | 10 | 11 | 12 | 13 |
5' | 1 | 2 | 3 |

14c ❚1❚ and ❚8❚

Key each line once.

Note: The digit "1" and the letter "I" have separate values on a computer keyboard. Do not interchange these characters.

1 Reach *up* with *left fourth* finger.

8 Reach *up* with *right second* finger.

Abbreviations: Do not space after a period within an abbreviation, as in Ph.D., U.S., C.O.D., a.m.

1

13 1 1a a1 1 1; 1 and a 1; 1 add 1; 1 aunt; 1 ace; 1 arm; 1 aye

14 1 and 11 and 111; 11 eggs; 11 vats; Set 11A; May 11; Item 11

15 The 11 aces of the 111th Corps each rated a salute at 1 p.m.

8

16 8 8k k8 8 8; 8 kits; ask 8; 8 kites; kick 8; 8 keys; spark 8

17 OK 88; 8 bags; 8 or 88; the 88th; 88 kegs; ask 88; order 888

18 Eight of the 88 cars score 8 or better on our Form 8 rating.

all figures learned

19 She did live at 818 Park, not 181 Park; or was it 181 Clark?

20 Put 1 with 8 to form 18; put 8 with 1 to form 81. Use 1881.

21 On May 1 at 8 a.m., 18 men and 18 women left Gate 8 for Rio.

14d Reinforcement

Key each line once; DS between groups. Repeat. Key with accuracy.

figures

22 Our 188 trucks moved 1881 tons on August 18 and December 18.

23 Send Mary 181 No. 188 panes for her home at 8118 Oak Street.

24 The 188 men in 8 boats left Docks 1 and 18 at 1 p.m., May 1.

25 pop was lap pass slaw wool solo swap Apollo wasp load plaque

26 Was Polly acquainted with the equipped jazz player in Texas?

27 The computer is a useful tool; it helps you to perform well.

14e Speed Builder

Key these lines in the game.

28 Did their form entitle them to the land?

29 Did the men in the field signal for us to go?

30 I may pay for the antique bowls when I go to town.

31 The auditor did the work right, so he risks no penalty.

32 The man by the big bush did signal us to turn down the lane.

| 1 | 2 | 3 | 4 | 5 | 6 | 7 | 8 | 9 | 10 | 11 | 12 |

Tests Administered

The Rorschach Technique

Roberts Apperception Test

Testing Behavior

Christopher Smith was tested while he was an inpatient at the Children's Unit at Oak Ridge Hospital. He is a friendly boy with short blond hair who is moderately overweight. He related to the examiner in a friendly and cooperative way. Eye contact was good. His speech and mannerisms were normal. The patient expressed himself well and had a good vocabulary. He appeared to enjoy the testing tasks and studied each stimuli card before responding. He described his responses well. His stories were fairly lengthy and had well-developed themes.

Testing Results

Personality testing suggests that mentally Christopher is very active, but his emotions are suppressed. There are indications of underlying depression and anger. Dissociation is also a probable defensive structure. He keeps experiences or memories dissociated so that he does not have to face or deal with them. They are potentially too overwhelming for him.

Christopher cannot keep memories and feelings detached all of the time; they occasionally break through and are likely to be acted out behaviorally. There may be periods of anger or aggressive outbursts or periods of despair or depression. The problems that Christopher experiences with anger may be apparent. His depression may be less frequently seen because he withdraws to wait it out or uses fantasy to escape from it. His feelings of depression may also be translated into anger.

Christopher does not experience an internal source of control for his actions. He expects others to control him or to punish him after the fact. He may take responsibility for aggressive episodes. He may tend to see these as "not me" and therefore minimize them. At times these events may be repressed or dissociated.

Summary and Recommendations

Personality testing suggests the use of repression and dissociation that prevent him from having to remember or relive past painful experiences. Repressed feelings of frustration may return to be acted out behaviorally. Christopher may tend to not take responsibility for his actions or may minimize them.

It may be important for the staff to assess, in an ongoing fashion, indications of the degree of personality fragmentation that Christopher experiences. Some exploration of whether or not he remembers past events that have been reported by other family members may assist with this.

Christopher needs to learn techniques of anger management. He should be taught to become aware of when he is beginning to become angry so that he can voluntarily learn to control his behavior. Christopher may have much difficulty learning to access the signs that he is beginning to become upset. He may need to practice a variety of techniques in order to control his behavior and then later resolve the problem verbally.

An additional focus should be on his relational skills. Assisting him in becoming sensitive to reading cues and the teaching of some empathy and conscious awareness would also help improve his functioning level.

5 and 0

Key each line twice.

For a series of capital letters, tap CAPS LOCK with the left little finger. Tap again to release.

alphabet 1 John Quigley packed the zinnias in twelve large, firm boxes.
1/8 2 Idle Motor 18 at 8 mph and Motor 81 at 8 mph; avoid Motor 1.
caps 3 Lily read BLITHE SPIRIT by Noel Coward. I read VANITY FAIR.
lock 4 Did they fix the problem of the torn panel and worn element?

| 1 | 2 | 3 | 4 | 5 | 6 | 7 | 8 | 9 | 10 | 11 | 12 |

15b

Technique Reinforcement
Reach up or down without moving your hands. Key each line once; repeat drill.

adjacent reaches

5 as oil red ask wet opt mop try tree open shred operas treaty
6 were pore dirt stew ruin faster onion alumni dreary mnemonic
7 The opened red hydrants were powerful, fast, and very dirty.

outside reaches

8 pop zap cap zag wasp equip lazy zippers queue opinion quartz
9 zest waste paper exist parquet azalea acquaint apollo apathy
10 The lazy wasp passed the potted azalea on the parquet floor.

NEW KEYS

15c 5 and 0

Key each line once.

5 Reach *up* with *left first* finger.

0 Reach *up* with *right fourth* finger.

5

11 5 5f f5 5 5; 5 fans; 5 feet; 5 figs; 5 fobs; 5 furs; 5 flaws
12 5 o'clock; 5 a.m.; 5 p.m.; is 55 or less; buy 55; 5 and 5 is
13 Call Line 555 if 5 fans or 5 bins arrive at Pier 5 by 5 p.m.

0

14 0 0; ;0 0 0; skip 0; plan 0; left 0; is below 0; I scored 0;
15 0 degrees; key 0 and 0; write 00 here; the total is 0 or 00;
16 She laughed at their 0 to 0 score; but ours was 0 to 0 also.

all figures learned

17 I keyed 550 pages for Invoice 05, or 50 more than we needed.
18 Pages 15 and 18 of the program listed 150, not 180, members.
19 On May 10, Rick drove 500 miles to New Mexico in car No. 08.

112-d2

Continued

Patient Name: Perez, Maria

Age: 16

Date of Testing: 6/25/20--

Reason for Referral

Maria Perez was referred for psychological testing by her inpatient psychiatrist, Douglas Martin, M.D. Description of personality dynamics was requested.

Tests Administered

Minnesota Multiphasic Personality Inventory (scored with adolescent norms)

Testing Behavior

Not observed

Testing Results

Test report is based solely on testing data. Profile configuration indicates a defensive attitude. This is likely to be a very ingrained defensiveness. Part of it may be an angry reaction to being in the hospital, but there is also a long-standing lack of self-awareness. She is likely to exhibit little psychological insight into herself.

She is denying feelings of depression or any kinds of physical problems. She sees herself as healthy and active. She denies problems with anger, anxiety, or depression. She may present herself as having no reason for being in the hospital or as in no need of help.

Others are likely to perceive her as defensive and very concrete and rigid in her thinking. She may be active, even hyperactive at times. She may appear easily irritable and react angrily to minor problems.

Summary and Recommendations

At the time Maria Perez took the test she appeared to be defensive and minimizing problems. On an ongoing basis she may have a lack of insight into her difficulties. Further testing may help describe her problems in more detail. She may lower her defensiveness so that she is more open to acknowledging and working on areas of difficulty as she adapts to the Unit and begins to feel more comfortable in the environment.

112-d3

Psychological Testing Report

1. Follow the steps in *112-d2* to create a Psychological Testing report for Christopher Smith.
2. Check and close. (*112-d3*)

Patient Name: Smith, Christopher

Age: 9

Date of Testing: 6/28/20--

Reason for Referral

Christopher Smith was referred for psychological testing by his inpatient psychiatrist, Linda Murillo, M.D. Description of personality dynamics with projective tests was requested.

continued

15d Textbook Keying
Key each line once; DS between 3-line groups.

improve figures

20 Read pages 5 and 8; duplicate page 18; omit pages 50 and 51.

21 We have Model 80 with 10 meters or Model 180 with 15 meters.

22 After May 18, French 050 meets in room 15 at 10 a.m. daily.

improve long reaches

23 Barb Abver saw a vibrant version of her brave venture on TV.

24 Call a woman or a man who will manage Minerva Manor in Nome.

25 We were quick to squirt a quantity of water at Quin and West.

15e Tab Review WP
1. Read the instructions to clear and set tabs.
2. Go to the Word Processor. Set a left tab at 4".
3. Practice the lines; tap TAB without watching your keyboard.

> **STANDARD PLAN** for Setting and Clearing Tabs in the Word Processor

Preset or default tabs are displayed on the Ruler. If necessary, display the Ruler in the Word Processor. (Choose the Show Ruler option on the Format menu.) Sometimes you will want to remove or clear existing tabs before setting new ones.

To clear and set tabs:
1. On the menu bar, click Format Tabs, and then Clear All Tabs.
2. To set tabs, select the type of tab you want to set (left, center, decimal, or right); enter the position and click Set.

Option: Click the tab button on the toolbar repeatedly to select the tab type. Then click the ruler where you want to set the tab.

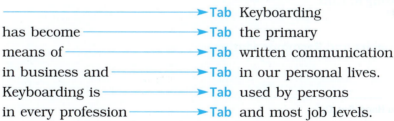

Set tab 4"

	→ Tab Keyboarding
has become	→ Tab the primary
means of	→ Tab written communication
in business and	→ Tab in our personal lives.
Keyboarding is	→ Tab used by persons
in every profession	→ Tab and most job levels.

15f Timed Writing
Take a 2' writing on both paragraphs. End the lesson; go to the Word Processor to complete 15e.

E

all letters

	gwam	2'	3'
I thought about Harry and how he had worked for me for		6	4
10 years; how daily at 8 he parked his worn car in the lot;		12	8
then, he left at 5. Every day was almost identical for him.		18	12
In a quiet way, he did his job well, asking for little		23	15
attention. So I never recognized his thirst for travel. I		29	19
didn't expect to find all of those maps near his workplace.		35	23

2'	1	2	3	4	5	6
3'	1	2	3	4		

PSYCHOLOGICAL TESTING

Patient Name:

Age:

Date of Testing:

Reason for Referral

Tests Administered

Testing Behavior

Testing Results

Summary and Recommendations

_____

Lydia Hong, Psy. D.
Licensed Psychologist

2 and 7

2 and 7

WARMUP 16a

Key each line twice.

alphabet 1 Perry might know I feel jinxed because I have missed a quiz.

figures 2 Channels 5 and 8, on from 10 to 11, said Luisa's IQ was 150.

caps lock 3 Ella Hill will see Chekhov's THE CHERRY ORCHARD on Czech TV.

easy 4 The big dog by the bush kept the ducks and hen in the field.

| 1 | 2 | 3 | 4 | 5 | 6 | 7 | 8 | 9 | 10 | 11 | 12 |

NEW KEYS

16b 2 and 7

Key each line once.

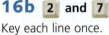

2 Reach *up* with *left third* finger.

7 Reach *up* with *right first* finger.

2

5 2 2s s2 2 2; has 2 sons; is 2 sizes; was 2 sites; has 2 skis

6 add 2 and 2; 2 sets of 2; catch 22; as 2 of the 22; 222 Main

7 Exactly at 2 on April 22, the 22nd Company left from Pier 2.

7

8 7 7j j7 7 7; 7 jets; 7 jeans; 7 jays; 7 jobs; 7 jars; 7 jaws

9 ask for 7; buy 7; 77 years; June 7; take any 7; deny 77 boys

10 From May 7 on, all 77 men will live at 777 East 77th Street.

all figures learned

11 I read 2 of the 72 books, Ellis read 7, and Han read all 72.

12 Tract 27 cites the date as 1850; Tract 170 says it was 1852.

13 You can take Flight 850 on January 12; I'll take Flight 705.

16c

Number Reinforcement
Key each line twice (slowly, then faster); DS between 2-line groups.

8/1 14 line 8; Book 1; No. 88; Seat 11; June 18; Cart 81; date 1881

2/7 15 take 2; July 7; buy 22; sell 77; mark 27; adds 72; Memo 2772

5/0 16 feed 5; bats 0; age 50; Ext. 55; File 50; 55 bags; band 5005

all 17 I work 18 visual signs with 20 turns of the 57 lenses to 70.

all 18 Did 17 boys fix the gears for 50 bicycles in 28 racks or 10?

LESSON 112

Preparing Medical Reports

WARMUP 112a

Key each line, striving for control. Repeat if desired.

alphabet	1	Dixon Krawczyk quit playing ball to save that time for a new job.
adjacent reach	2	As you said, the people's pool has a tree trunk as its wallpaper.
3rd/4th fingers	3	At a show at the zoo, Saxon squealed as the porpoise pups played.
easy	4	Did he use the endowment to pay for a visit to the city with Jan?

| 1 | 2 | 3 | 4 | 5 | 6 | 7 | 8 | 9 | 10 | 11 | 12 | 13 |

DOCUMENT DESIGN

112b

MEDICAL REPORT TEMPLATE

Formats may vary slightly at different medical facilities; however, all medical reports contain similar sections: the heading, body, and conclusion. The **heading** contains pertinent information necessary to identify the patient. The heading is keyed at the top of the report; some headings are quite lengthy and can take up to one-third of the first page. The **body** of the report contains the observations, testing results, and/or findings. The **conclusion** includes the diagnosis and recommendations. Save medical reports as template files so that they may be used as many times as necessary.

APPLICATIONS

112-d1

Medical Report Template

1. *Keyboarding Pro DELUXE*: In the open document, change the top margin to .6".

   Non-*Keyboarding Pro DELUXE* users: In a new document change the top margin to .6" and insert *111-d1*, the medical letterhead you created in Lesson 111. You will be creating the template for the psychological testing report shown on the next page.

2. Key the heading **PSYCHOLOGICAL TESTING** in all caps on approximately line 2.3" and apply Heading 1 style. Change the font to 18 point.

3. Key the side headings at the left margin and apply Heading 2 style to each. Tap ENTER twice after each heading.

4. Set a left underline tab at 3" for the physician's signature. Key the physician's name and title below the line. Apply the Strong style to the physician's name and title.

5. Non-*Keyboarding Pro DELUXE* users: Save as a template file.

6. Check and close. (*112-d1*)

112-d2

Psychological Testing Report

1. Non-*Keyboarding Pro DELUXE* users: Open a copy of the Psychological Testing template, *112-d1*.

2. Key the psychological testing report for Maria Perez shown on page 505.

3. Insert a header at the top of the second page that consists of the patient's name (last name first), the page number, and the date of the testing. For the page number, key the word **page** and then insert the page number. Choose Plain Number in the Current Position.

4. Format the report and delete extra returns as needed.

5. Check and close. (*112-d2*)

continued

16d Textbook Keying

Key each line once to review reaches; fingers curved and relaxed; wrists low. DS between groups.

3rd/4th
19 pop was lap pass slaw wool solo swap apollo wasp load plaque
20 Al's quote was, "I was dazzled by the jazz, pizza, and pool."

1st/2nd
21 bad fun nut kick dried night brick civic thick hutch believe
22 Kim may visit her friends in Germany if I give her a ticket.

3rd/1st
23 cry tube wine quit very curb exit crime ebony mention excite
24 To be invited, petition the six executive committee members.

16e Textbook Keying

Key each line once; DS between 3-line groups. Do not pause at the end of lines.

words: *think, say,* and *key* words

25 is do am lay cut pen dub may fob ale rap cot hay pay hem box
26 box wit man sir fish also hair giant rigor civic virus ivory
27 laugh sight flame audit formal social turkey bicycle problem

phrases: *think, say,* and *key* phrases

28 is it|is it|if it is|if it is|or by|or by|or me|or me|for us
29 and all|for pay|pay dues and|the pen|the pen box|the pen box
30 such forms|held both|work form|then wish|sign name|with them

easy sentences

31 The man is to do the work right; he then pays the neighbors.
32 Sign the forms to pay the eight men for the turkey and hams.
33 The antique ivory bicycle is a social problem for the chair.
| 1 | 2 | 3 | 4 | 5 | 6 | 7 | 8 | 9 | 10 | 11 | 12 |

TECHNIQUE TIP

Think and key the words and phrases as units rather than letter by letter.

16f Timed Writing

Take a 2' timing on both paragraphs. Repeat the timing.

gwam 2' | 3'

When choosing a password, do not use one you have already | 6 | 4
used. Change to a new one quite often, perhaps every two to | 12 | 8
four weeks. Be sure that you combine both letters and numbers. | 18 | 12

Know your password; do not write it on paper. If you must | 24 | 16
write it down, be sure it's not recognized. Don't let anyone | 30 | 20
see you key. Just turn your body or key a little extra. | 36 | 24

2' | 1 | 2 | 3 | 4 | 5 | 6
3' | 1 | 2 | 3 | 4

1. Open the template file *111-d2*.
2. Fill in the form with the information for Document 3. **Note:** *Pt* is the abbreviation for patient. Spell out the word *patient* when keying the notes.
3. Check and close. (*111-d3*)
4. Repeat the above steps for Document 4 (*111-d4*).
5. Check and close. (*111-d4*)

Field Names	Document 3	Document 4
Last Name	Jones	Pham
First Name	Sarah	Loriana
Patient No.	10680	31048
Age	20	27
Allergies	None	Bee stings
Meds	None	None
T	99.5	98.5
P	84	62
R	20	15
B/P	130/87	112/72
C/O	Cough	Pain in right knee
Date	6/9/--	6/21/--

DOCUMENT 3 SOAP NOTE BODY

S	Pt complains of cough and head congestion for the past 48 hours, shortness of breath, lethargy, and low appetite.
O	Pt coughing up green sputum. Lungs clear, ears clear. Lymph nodes enlarged bilateral neck. Bilateral tonsils enlarged. CXR-WNL, PPD negative. CBC—elevated white count.
A	Acute upper respiratory infection.
P	Pt is to take 333 Mg. E-Mycin, one tablet every 8 hours for one week. Increase fluids, increase rest. Pt is to remain off from work for 3 days. Recheck in one week or sooner, if needed.

DOCUMENT 4 SOAP NOTE BODY

S	Pt complains of pain in the right knee; tripped and fell 6/17/--.
O	Inflammation/hematoma on right anterior medial patella; decreased ROM right knee, with flexion, extension.
A	Diagnosis: Pre-patella bursitis. Treatment: R.I.C.E. on right patella anterior medial with ice pack twice a day for 4-6 weeks. Stay off right leg. ADL: rest knee; ice right anterior knee morn/night; elevate.
P	Stay off right leg. Rest; ice morn/night; elevate. Week 1: decrease pain; week 2: increase ROM.

WARMUP 17a

Key each line twice.

alphabet	1	Bob realized very quickly that jumping was excellent for us.
figures	2	Has each of the 18 clerks now corrected Item 501 on page 27?
shift keys	3	L. K. Coe, M.D., hopes Dr. Lopez can leave for Maine in May.
easy	4	The men paid their own firms for the eight big enamel signs.

NEW KEYS

17b 4 and 9

Key each line once.

4 Reach *up* with *left first* finger.

9 Reach *up* with *right third* finger.

4

5 4 4f f4 4 4 4; if 4 furs; off 4 floors; gaff 4 fish; 4 flags

6 44th floor; half of 44; 4 walked 44 flights; 4 girls; 4 boys

7 I order exactly 44 bagels, 4 cakes, and 4 pies before 4 a.m.

9

8 9 9l l9 9 9 9; fill 9 lugs; call 9 lads; Bill 9 lost; dial 9

9 also 9 oaks; roll 9 loaves; 9.9 degrees; sell 9 oaks; Hall 9

10 Just 9 couples, 9 men and 9 women, left at 9 on our Tour 99.

all figures learned

11 Memo 94 says 9 pads, 4 pens, and 4 ribbons were sent July 9.

12 Study Item 17 and Item 28 on page 40 and Item 59 on page 49.

13 Within 17 months he drove 85 miles, walked 29, and flew 490.

SKILL BUILDING

17c Textbook Keying
Key each line once.

14 My staff of *18* worked *11* hours a day from May *27* to June *12*.

15 There were *5* items tested by Inspector *7* at *4* p.m. on May *8*.

16 Please send her File *10* today at *8*; her access number is *97*.

17 Car *47* had its trial run. The qualifying speed was *198* mph.

18 The estimated score? *485*. Actual? *190*. Difference? *295*.

111-d1

Create Letterhead

LETTERHEAD GRAPHIC

1. Use WordArt (Insert, WordArt) to create the lettering in the company name, **Quality Care Medical Group**. Change the text wrapping to In Front of Text. Format the WordArt to make it attractive.

2. Search for *lines* in clip art. Choose a line that will complement your letterhead. Change the text wrapping of the line to In Front of Text.

3. Key the address in the letterhead. Format as needed.

   5252 Superior Road, Oak Park, IL 60301-7984
   708-555-0186
   fax 708-555-0188

4. Check and close. (*111-d1*)

111-d2

Create SOAP Note Form

Keyboarding Pro DELUXE users: The letterhead will open automatically.

1. Open *111-d1*.

2. Create a table for the patient's vital signs. Bold the text and change the row height to .4"; align text center left.

Last Name:		First Name:	
Patient No.	Age:	Allergies:	Meds:
T:	P:	R:	B/P:
C/O:		Date:	

3. Create a table for the SOAP notes. Make the letters *SOAP* 26 point and bold. Make each row height 1.25".

4. Modify the footer to make the tab at 3.25" a center underline tab. Place the physician's signature line in the footer. (See page 499.)

5. Preview the document and adjust vertical placement as needed.

6. Non-*Keyboarding Pro DELUXE* users: Save as a template so that you can use this form as many times as necessary.

7. Check and close. (*111-d2*)

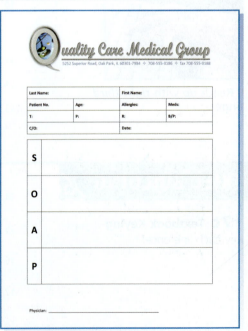

17d

Technique Reinforcement
Key smoothly; tap the keys at a brisk, steady pace.

first finger

19 buy them gray vent guy brunt buy brunch much give huge vying
20 Hagen, after her July triumph at tennis, may try volleyball.
21 Verna urges us to buy yet another of her beautiful rag rugs.

second finger

22 keen idea; kick it back; ice breaker; decide the issue; cite
23 Did Dick ask Cecelia, his sister, if she decided to like me?
24 Suddenly, Micki's bike skidded on the Cedar Street ice rink.

third/fourth finger

25 low slow lax solo wax zip zap quips quiz zipper prior icicle
26 Paula has always allowed us to relax at La Paz and at Quito.
27 Please ask Zale to explain who explores most aquatic slopes.

17e Timed Writing

Take a 2' timing on both paragraphs. Repeat the timing.

E

all letters

	gwam	2'	3'
We consider nature to be limited to those things, such		6	4
as air or trees, that we humans do not or cannot make.		11	7
For most of us, nature just exists, just is. We don't		17	11
question it or, perhaps, realize how vital it is to us.		22	15
Do I need nature, and does nature need me? I'm really		28	19
part of nature; thus, what happens to it happens to me.		33	22

2' | 1 | 2 | 3 | 4 | 5 | 6 |
3' | 1 | 2 | 3 | 4 |

17f Enrichment

TECHNIQUE TIP

Keep hands quiet and fingers well curved over the keys. Do not allow your fingers to bounce.

1. Click the Skill Building tab from the main menu and choose Technique Builder; select Drill 2.

2. Key Drill 2 from page 32. Key each line once striving for good accuracy.

3. The results will be listed on the Skill Building Report.

TEXT WRAPPING STYLE

PICTURE TOOLS/FORMAT/TEXT WRAPPING

Graphics that are inserted in a *Word* document are automatically inserted in line with the text. This does not allow the graphic to be moved around on the page. To create a better visual effect, you may need to move the graphics; you can do this by changing the text wrapping style of the graphic.

⬚	In Line with Text
⬚	Square
⬚	Tight
⬚	Behind Text
⬚	In Front of Text
⬚	Top and Bottom
⬚	Through

To change text wrapping:

1. Right-click the ClipArt, WordArt, or picture.
2. On the Format tab, under Picture Tools, choose Text Wrapping; then select the appropriate wrapping style.

PICTURE STYLES

PICTURE TOOLS/FORMAT/ /PICTURE STYLES/SELECT DESIRED STYLE

The Picture Styles group contains a variety of picture styles as well as border and picture effects that can be applied to a picture to change its shape, orientation, and appearance. Click the More button to display the entire gallery of picture styles.

To apply a picture style:

1. Click the picture to select it. Under Picture Tools, on the Format tab, in the Picture Styles group ❶, selected the style desired.
2. Select the More button ❷ to display more options.

❶ Picture Styles ❷

DRILL 1 CREATE LOGO

1. In a new document, change the top margins to .6" and set the side margins at 1". Turn on Show/Hide. Tap ENTER six times. Move the insertion point to the first ¶ on the page.

2. From the Insert tab, click WordArt. Select the WordArt style 8. Key a capital Q for the text. Click OK.

3. Right-click the WordArt and choose Format WordArt from the menu. In the Colors and Lines tab, click the Fill Color drop-list arrow and choose White, Background 1, Darker 35% (first column). In the Layout tab, change the Wrapping style to Behind Text.

4. In the Size tab, change the height to absolute 1.6". Place a check in the Lock aspect ratio box. Click OK.

5. Search for medical clip art on your computer. Insert a medical clip art that you would like to use in your logo. Change the height of the clip art to 1".

6. Select the picture and choose Picture Styles. Click the More drop list arrow and choose Metal Oval. Change the text wrapping to In Front of Text. Move the picture on top of the Q. Adjust size as needed to stretch it over the Q.

7. Check and close. (*111-drill1*)

3 and 6

WARMUP 18a

Key each line twice.

alphabet 1 Jim Kable won a second prize for his very quixotic drawings.
figures 2 If 57 of the 105 boys go on July 29, 48 of them will remain.
easy 3 With the usual bid, I paid for a quantity of big world maps.
| 1 | 2 | 3 | 4 | 5 | 6 | 7 | 8 | 9 | 10 | 11 | 12 |

NEW KEYS

18b 3 and 6

Key each line once.

3 Reach *up* with *left second* finger.

6 Reach *up* with *right first* finger.

Note: Ergonomic keyboard users will use *left first* finger to key 6.

3

4 3 3d d3 3 3; had 3 days; did 3 dives; led 3 dogs; add 3 dips
5 we 3 ride 3 cars; take 33 dials; read 3 copies; save 33 days
6 On July 3, 33 lights lit 33 stands holding 33 prize winners.

6

7 6 6j 6j 6 6; 6 jays; 6 jams; 6 jigs; 6 jibs; 6 jots; 6 jokes
8 only 6 high; on 66 units; reach 66 numbers; 6 yams or 6 jams
9 On May 6, Car 66 delivered 66 tons of No. 6 shale to Pier 6.

all figures learned

10 At 6 p.m., Channel 3 reported the August 6 score was 6 to 3.
11 Jean, do Items 28 and 6; Mika, 59 and 10; Kyle, 3, 4, and 7.
12 Cars 56 and 34 used Aisle 9; Cars 2 and 87 can use Aisle 10.

SKILL BUILDING

18c

Keyboard Reinforcement
Key each line once; DS between 3-line groups.

TECHNIQUE TIP

Make the long reaches without returning to the home row between reaches.

long reaches

13 ce cede cedar wreck nu nu nut punt nuisance my my amy mystic
14 ny ny any many company mu mu mull lumber mulch br br furbish
15 The absence of receiving my umbrella disturbed the musician.

number review

16 set 0; push 4; Car 00; score 44; jot 04; age 40; Billet 4004
17 April 5; lock 5; set 66; fill 55; hit 65; pick 56; adds 5665
18 Her grades are 93, 87, and 100; his included 82, 96, and 54.

110-d4

Continued

2. Key the Articles of Incorporation, shown below as the main document in the mail merge. Set a 3" top margin. Center the title in uppercase. Apply Heading 1 style.

3. Insert the fields shown on the previous page. Save the data file as *110-d4data*. Save the main document (*110-d4main*) again. Print a copy of the main document.

4. Merge the documents.

5. Check and close. (*110-d4final*)

3"

ARTICLES OF INCORPORATION

I

The name of this corporation is «Corporate_Name».

II

The purpose of the corporation is to engage in the profession of «Profession» and any other lawful activities (other than the banking or trust company business) not prohibited to a corporation engaging in such profession by applicable laws and regulations.

III

The corporation is a professional corporation within the meaning of Part 4, Division 3, Title I, California Corporation Code.

IV

The name and address in the State of California of this corporation's initial agent for service of process are:

    Name: «Name»

    Street Address: «Street_Address»

    City: «City»   California   ZIP Code: «ZIP_Code»

V

The corporation is authorized to issue only one class of stock; and the total number of shares which the corporation is authorized to issue is «Amount».

_____
                        David M. Smith, Incorporator

| Articles of Incorporation |

$ and - (hyphen), Number Expression

WARMUP 19a

Key each line twice.

alphabet 1	Why did the judge quiz poor Victor about his blank tax form?
figures 2	J. Boyd, Ph.D., changed Items 10, 57, 36, and 48 on page 92.
3rd row 3	To try the tea, we hope to tour the port prior to the party.
easy 4	Did he signal the authentic robot to do a turn to the right?

| 1 | 2 | 3 | 4 | 5 | 6 | 7 | 8 | 9 | 10 | 11 | 12 |

NEW KEYS

19b $ and -

Key each line once; DS between 2-line groups.

> - = hyphen
> -- = dash
> Do not space before or after a hyphen or a dash.

$ Shift; then reach *up* with *left first* finger.

- (hyphen) Reach *up* with *right fourth* finger.

$

5 $ $f f$ $ $; if $4; half $4; off $4; of $4; $4 fur; $4 flats
6 for $8; cost $9; log $3; grab $10; give Rolf $2; give Viv $4
7 Since she paid $45 for the item priced at $54, she saved $9.

- (hyphen)

8 - -; ;- - - -; up-to-date; co-op; father-in-law; four-square
9 pop-up foul; big-time job; snap-on bit; one- or two-hour ski
10 You need 6 signatures--half of the members--on the petition.

all symbols learned

11 I paid $10 for the low-cost disk; high-priced ones cost $40.
12 Le-An spent $20 for travel, $95 for books, and $38 for food.
13 Mr. Loft-Smit sold his boat for $467; he bought it for $176.

SKILL BUILDING

19c

Keyboard Reinforcement
Key each line once; repeat the drill.

e/d 14	Edie discreetly decided to deduct expenses in making a deed.
w/e 15	Working women wear warm wool sweaters when weather dictates.
r/e 16	We heard very rude remarks regarding her recent termination.
s/d 17	This seal's sudden misdeeds destroyed several goods on land.
v/b 18	Beverley voted by giving a bold beverage to every brave boy.

110-d1

Continued

necessary to the prosecution of this action, upon the ground that the witness is intimately involved with the defendant regarding the subject matter of this action and can provide testimony vital to plaintiff's case.

PLEASE TAKE FURTHER NOTICE that pursuant to the CPLR Rule 8829(a) you are required to serve upon the undersigned at least five (5) days before the return date of this motion any answering affidavits.

Tap ENTER.

4" left tab↓

TAB   KRAMMER, GONZALEZ, & NGUYEN
            Attorneys for Plaintiff
            55 Civic Center Drive
            Santa Ana, CA 92701-0485
            714-555-0110

Tap ENTER two times.
TO: (Recipient bookmark)

110-d2 and 110-d3

Insert Bookmarks

1. Open *110-d1* and insert the following information in each bookmark.
2. Check and close. (*110-d2* and *110-d3*)

> **NOTE**
>
> Addresses keyed within a paragraph will need to have a comma added after the state abbreviation.

Bookmark name	Document 2	Document 3
name	Linda Matsayama	Justin Lopez
position	President of Matsayama Tools Inc., a California Corporation	Marketing Director of Acme Tools, a privately owned company.
address	5200 Katella Avenue, Los Alamitos, CA 90720-6314	7901 Holder Street, Cypress, CA 90631-9215
residence	9342 Primrose Circle, Seal Beach, CA 90740-2875	3602 W. Third Street, Los Angeles, CA 90020-9215
mailing_address	LINDA MATSAYAMA 9342 Primrose Circle Seal Beach, CA 90740-2875	JUSTIN LOPEZ 3602 W. Third Street Los Angeles, CA 90020-9215

110-d4

Mail Merge Articles of Incorporation

1. Use mail merge to create and fill in the Articles of Incorporation. Start the mail merge by creating the main file, *110-d4main*.

Field Name	Entry 1	Entry 2
Corporate Name	Quality Care Medical Center	Gourmet Food Shops
Profession	providing medical care	providing retail sales
Name	Andrew Wainscott	Jeannette Smith
Street Address	5561 Golden Lantern Drive	1521 Mack Avenue
City	Laguna Niguel	Orange
ZIP Code	92677-1234	92865-2214
Amount	Ten Thousand (10,000)	Five Thousand (5,000)

continued

19d Textbook Keying

Key each line once, working for fluid, consistent stroking. Repeat at a faster speed.

easy words

19 am it go bus dye jam irk six sod tic yam ugh spa vow aid dug
20 he or by air big elf dog end fit and lay sue toe wit own got
21 six foe pen firm also body auto form down city kept make fog

easy phrases

22 it is|if the|and also|to me|the end|to us|if it|it is|to the
23 if it is|to the end|do you wish|to go to|for the end|to make
24 lay down|he or she|make me|by air|end of|by me|kept it|of me

easy sentences

25 Did the chap work to mend the torn right half of the ensign?
26 Blame me for their penchant for the antique chair and panel.
27 She bid by proxy for eighty bushels of a corn and rye blend.

COMMUNICATION

19e Textbook Keying

1. Study the rules and examples at the right.
2. Key the sample sentences 28–33.
3. Change figures to words as needed in sentences 34–36.

NUMBER EXPRESSION: SPELL OUT NUMBERS

1. **First word in a sentence.** Key numbers ten and lower as words unless they are part of a series of related numbers, any of which are over ten.

    Three of the four members were present.

    She wrote 12 stories and 2 plays in five years.

2. The **smaller of two adjacent numbers** as words.

    SolVir shipped six 24-ton engines.

3. **Isolated fractions and approximate numbers.** Key as words **large round numbers that can be expressed as one or two words.** Hyphenate fractions expressed as words.

    She completed one-fourth of the experiments.

    Val sent out three hundred invitations.

4. **Preceding "o'clock."**

    John's due at four o'clock. Pick him up at 4:15 p.m.

28 **Six** or **seven** older players were cut from the **37**-member team.
29 I have **2** of **14** coins I need to start my set.   Kristen has **9**.
30 Of **nine 24**-ton engines ordered, we shipped **six** last Tuesday.
31 Shelly has read just **one-half** of about **forty-five** documents.
32 The **six** boys sent well over **two hundred** printed invitations.
33 **One** or **two** of us will be on duty from **two** until **six** o'clock.
34 The meeting begins promptly at 9.   We plan 4 sessions.
35 The 3-person crew cleaned 6 stands, 12 tables, and 13 desks.
36 The 3rd meeting is at 3 o'clock on Friday, February 2.

To use the bookmarks:

1. In the document in which you inserted bookmarks, from the Home tab, in the Editing group, click the Find drop-list arrow and select Go To. The Find and Replace dialog box ❶ displays with the Go To tab selected.

2. In the Go to what pane, select Bookmark ❷.

3. Click the Enter bookmark name drop-list arrow and select the name of the bookmark ❸. Click the Go To button ❹.

4. Click Close. The insertion point displays at the position of the bookmark.

DRILL 2 — INSERT TEXT

1. Open *110-drill1*.

2. Use the Go To command to find each bookmark, and insert the text shown in the table at the right. Note that the bookmarks shown in uppercase should have the replacement text also keyed in uppercase.

3. Check and close. (*110-drill2*)

Go To the bookmark	Insert the following text
NAME	REBECCA PEREZ
NAME_AGAIN	REBECCA PEREZ
Address	One Main Street, Irvine, CA, 96203-4865
HUSBAND_NAME	MATEO PEREZ
HUSBAND_AGAIN	MATEO PEREZ
EXECUTOR	GREGORY LEON

APPLICATIONS

110-d1

Notice of Motion with Bookmarks

1. Key the first two lines below, then tap ENTER twice. Change to double space. Key the remaining Notice of Motion. Double-space the body and indent paragraphs 1".

2. Replace the text shown in parentheses (including the parentheses) with a bookmark.

3. Tap ENTER after the last paragraph and return to 1.15 line spacing. Set a left tab at 4" and key the attorney signature block; key the mailing address block (left aligned).

4. Check and close. (*110-d1*)

Index No. 12870

NOTICE OF MOTION

Tap ENTER two times.

    PLEASE TAKE NOTICE that upon the annexed affidavit of LOUISE TROMBLEY, sworn to the 23rd day of October, 20--, and upon all the papers and proceedings filed heretofore and had herein, the undersigned will move the Court at a Special Term to be held in and for the County of Orange, at the Courthouse in the City of Santa Ana, on the 15th day of November, 20--, at 10:30 o'clock in the forenoon, or as soon thereafter as counsel may be heard, for an order, pursuant to CPLR Section 7202(b) directing (Name bookmark), as (Position bookmark), of (Address bookmark), as an individual residing at (Residence bookmark), as a witness before trial, to submit to an oral examination at the offices of KRAMMER, GONZALEZ, & NGUYEN, 55 Civic Center Drive, Santa Ana, CA 92704-1288, on a day in December, 20--, to be fixed by this Court, concerning all matters material or

continued

LESSON 20

and /

WARMUP 20a

Key each line twice (slowly, then faster).

alphabet 1 Freda Jencks will have money to buy six quite large topazes.

symbols 2 I bought 10 ribbons and 45 disks from Cable-Han Co. for $78.

home row 3 Dallas sold jade flasks; Sal has a glass flask full of salt.

easy 4 He may cycle down to the field by the giant oak and cut hay.

NEW KEYS

20b # and /

Key each line once.

= number sign, pounds
/ = diagonal, slash

Shift; then reach *up* with *left second* finger.

/ Reach *down* with *right fourth* finger.

#

5 # #e e# # # #; had #3 dial; did #3 drop; set #3 down; Bid #3

6 leave #82; sold #20; Lyric #16; bale #34; load #53; Optic #7

7 Notice #333 says to load Car #33 with 33# of #3 grade shale.

/

8 / /; ;/ / / /; 1/2; 1/3; Mr./Mrs.; 1/5/09; 22 11/12; and/or;

9 to/from; /s/ William Smit; 2/10, n/30; his/her towels; 6 1/2

10 The numerals 1 5/8, 3 1/4, and 60 7/9 are "mixed fractions."

all symbols learned

11 Invoice #737 cites 15 2/3# of rye was shipped C.O.D. 4/6/09.

12 B-O-A Company's Check #50/5 for $87 paid for 15# of #3 wire.

13 Our Co-op List #20 states $40 for 16 1/2 crates of tomatoes.

SKILL BUILDING

20c

Keyboard Reinforcement
Key each line once; work for fluency.

Option: In the Word Processor, key 30" writings on both lines of a pair. Work to avoid pauses.

gwam 30"

14 She did the key work at the height of the problem. 20

15 Form #726 is the title to the island; she owns it. 20

16 The rock is a form of fuel; he did enrich it with coal. 22

17 The corn-and-turkey dish is a blend of turkey and corn. 22

18 It is right to work to end the social problems of the world. 24

19 If I sign it on 3/19, the form can aid us to pay the 40 men. 24

Notice of Motion

Articles of Incorporation

NEW FUNCTION

110d

USING BOOKMARKS

INSERT/LINKS/BOOKMARK

A bookmark marks a location in a document so that you can quickly move the insertion point to the location. If more than one bookmark is inserted into a document, you will need to give each bookmark a unique name. A bookmark name can include letters, numbers, and the underscore character. Do not include spaces in a bookmark name.

After bookmarks have been inserted in a document, you can use the Go To feature to move the insertion point to the specific bookmark. Bookmarks can be helpful when creating repetitive documents that contain variable information. **Note:** As a reminder to yourself, you may want to key a bookmark name in uppercase if the replacement text will also be keyed in uppercase.

To insert a bookmark:

1. Click the insertion point at the position where the bookmark is to be inserted. From the Insert tab, in the Links group, click Bookmark ① to display the Bookmark dialog box ②.

2. Key the name of the bookmark in the Bookmark name box ③.

3. Click the Add button ④. Repeat steps 1–3 for each bookmark to be inserted.

DRILL 1   **INSERT BOOKMARK**   BOOKMARK

1. Turn on Show/Hide.

2. Delete the text #1 bookmark. Create a bookmark named **NAME**.

3. Replace the text #2 bookmark with a bookmark named **NAME_AGAIN**. (Insert the underscore between words.)

4. Replace the text #3 bookmark with a bookmark named **Address**.

5. Replace the text #4 bookmark with a bookmark named **HUSBAND_NAME**.

6. Replace the text #5 bookmark with a bookmark named **HUSBAND_AGAIN**.

7. Replace the text #6 bookmark with a bookmark named **EXECUTOR**.

8. Check and close. (*110-drill1*)

COMMUNICATION

20d Textbook Keying: Number Usage Review

Key each line once. Decide whether the circled numbers should be keyed as figures or as words and make needed changes. Check your finished work with 19e, page 47.

20 Six or (7) older players were cut from the (37)-member team.

21 I have (2) of 14 coins I need to start my set. Kristen has (9).

22 Of (9) 24-ton engines ordered, we shipped (6) last Tuesday.

23 Shelly has read just (1) half of about (45) documents.

24 The (6) boys sent well over (200) printed invitations.

25 (1) or (2) of us will be on duty from (2) until (6) o'clock.

SKILL BUILDING

20e Timed Writing

WP

1. Take a 3' writing on both paragraphs. If you finish the timing before time is up, repeat the timing.
2. End the lesson but do not exit the software.
3. Go to the Word Processor, and follow the directions at the right to build your speed on each paragraph by 4 words.

STANDARD PLAN for Guided Writing Procedures

1. In the Word Processor, take a 1' writing on paragraph 1. Note your *gwam*.
2. Add four words to your 1' *gwam* to determine your goal rate.
3. Set the Timer for 1'. Set the Timer option to beep every 15".
4. From the table below, select from column 4 the speed nearest your goal rate. Note the 1/4' point at the left of that speed. Place a light check mark within the paragraphs at the 1/4' points.
5. Take two 1' guided writings on paragraphs 1 and 2. Do not save.
6. Turn the beeper off.

E

all letters

Goal: 16 *gwam*

1/4'	1/2'	3/4'	*gwam* 1'
4	8	12	16
5	10	15	20
6	12	18	24
7	14	21	28
8	16	24	32
9	18	27	36
10	20	30	40

gwam 2' | 3'

Some of us think that the best way to get attention is 6 | 4 | 35
to try a new style, or to look quixotic, or to be different 12 | 8 | 39
somehow. Perhaps we are looking for nothing much more than 18 | 12 | 43
acceptance from others of ourselves just the way we now are. 24 | 16 | 47

There is no question about it; we all want to look our 29 | 19 | 50
best to impress other people. How we achieve this may mean 35 | 23 | 54
trying some of this and that; but our basic objective is to 41 | 27 | 58
take our raw materials, you and me, and build up from there. 47 | 31 | 62

2' | 1 | 2 | 3 | 4 | 5 | 6
3' | 1 | 2 | 3 | 4

LESSON 110 | Preparing Legal Documents

WARMUP 110a

Key each line, striving for control. Repeat if desired.

1st row	1	Xavier bought the zebra costume for the masquerade party tonight.
home	2	A lass shall ask all lads; high fake fall fads shall fall faster.
3rd row	3	There is little gas left; use hay as fuel to heat the huge house.
balanced hand	4	I am busy, but I can make the formal amendment to the title form.

APPLICATIONS

110-b

Legal Terminology

1. Study the legal terms listed below, and then key the table at 2". Autofit contents.
2. Check and close. (*110b*)

Affidavit	Written statement of facts, made voluntarily and confirmed by the oath of the person making it, taken before an officer having authority to administer such oath and signed by the person making the statement.
Defendant	Person against whom the action is brought.
Jurisdiction	The name of the court hearing the case.
Order	A decision of the court made in writing and not included in a judgment or decree.
Plaintiff	Person bringing an action; party who claims to have been damaged or wronged.
Pleading	Court document that contains the claims and defenses of the parties of a lawsuit.
Testimony	A statement taken under oath that is used as evidence.

DOCUMENT DESIGN

110c

NOTICE OF MOTION AND ARTICLES OF INCORPORATION

A Notice of Motion and Articles of Incorporation are two routinely generated documents in a legal office. (See illustrations on next page and the full page model on page 498.) A Notice of Motion is an application for an Order addressed to the court. Some states require that the Notice of Motion be keyed on a pleading form; other states will have it keyed on plain paper as shown on the following page. Articles of Incorporation contain information regarding the name, address, and purpose of the company, as well as the share structure. Articles of Incorporation may differ for medical, nonprofit, professional, and municipal corporations.

Since these are documents that are routinely keyed in a legal office, they are often created as boilerplate documents. The data is inserted into the Notice of Motion by using the Bookmark and Go To features. Mail Merge is used to fill in the data in the Articles of Incorporation. A Notice of Motion uses default margins. Set a 3" top margin on the first page of the Articles of Incorporation to allow room for the Secretary of State to place a filing stamp in the upper-right corner. The signature line can be placed in the footer.

LESSON 21

% and !

WARMUP 21a

Key each line twice.

alphabet	1	Merry will have picked out a dozen quarts of jam for boxing.
fig/sym	2	Jane-Ann bought 16 7/8 yards of #240 cotton at $3.59 a yard.
1st row	3	Can't brave, zany Cave Club men/women next climb Mt. Zamban?
easy	4	Did she rush to cut six bushels of corn for the civic corps?

NEW KEYS

21b % and !

Key each line once.

> **% = percent sign:** Use % with business forms or where space is restricted; otherwise, use the word "percent."
>
> Space twice after the exclamation point!

% Shift; then reach *up* with *left first* finger.

SPACING TIP

- Do not space between a figure and the % or $ signs.
- Do not space before or after the dash.

%

5 % %f f% % %; off 5%; if 5%; of 5% fund; half 5%; taxes of 5%

6 7% rent; 3% tariff; 9% F.O.B.; 15% greater; 28% base; up 46%

7 Give discounts of 5% on rods, 50% on lures, and 75% on line.

! reach *up* with the *left fourth* finger

8 ! !a a! ! ! !; Eureka! Ha! No! Pull 10! Extra! America!

9 Listen to the call! Now! Ready! Get set! Go! Good show!

10 I want it now, not next week! I am sure to lose 50% or $19.

all symbols

11 The ad offers a 10% discount, but this notice says 15% less!

12 He got the job! With Clark's Supermarket! Please call Mom!

13 Bill #92-44 arrived very late from Zyclone; it was paid 7/4.

21c

Keyboard Reinforcement
Key each line once; work for fluency.

all symbols

14 As of 6/28, Jeri owes $31 for dinner and $27 for cab fare.

15 Invoice #20--it was dated 3/4--billed $17 less 15% discount.

16 He deducted 2% instead of 6%, a clear saving of 6% vs. 7%.

combination response

17 Look at my dismal grade in English; but I guess I earned it.

18 Kris started to blend a cocoa beverage for a shaken cowhand.

19 Jan may make a big profit if she owns the title to the land.

1	PLEASE TAKE FURTHER NOTICE that plaintiff Henry Hurt is required to
2	bring with him to the deposition the following records, documents, and
3	things:
4	
5	1. Any and all documents which substantiate the claim for property
6	damage.
7	
8	2. Any and all documents which substantiate the claim for loss of
9	earnings.
10	
11	3. All photographs which in any way relate to the subject matter of
12	this action.
13	*Dated this June 1, 20--*
14	*NEWTON & JOHNSON*
15	
16	
17	BARBARA M. JOHNSON
18	Attorney for Defendants JONATHAN MOVERS and LAUREL DELIVERIES
19	
20	
21	
22	
23	
24	
25	
26	

Notice of Deposition - 2

21d Textbook Keying

Key each line once; DS between groups; fingers curved, hands quiet. Repeat if time permits.

1st finger

20 by bar get fun van for inn art from gray hymn July true verb
21 brag human bring unfold hominy mighty report verify puny joy
22 You are brave to try bringing home the van in the bad storm.

2nd finger

23 ace ink did cad keyed deep seed kind Dick died kink like kid
24 cease decease decades kick secret check decide kidney evaded
25 Dedre likes the idea of ending dinner with cake for dessert.

3rd finger

26 oil sow six vex wax axe low old lox pool west loss wool slow
27 swallow swamp saw sew wood sax sexes loom stew excess school
28 Wes waxes floors and washes windows at low costs to schools.

4th finger

29 zap zip craze pop pup pan daze quote queen quiz pizza puzzle
30 zoo graze zipper panzer zebra quip partizan patronize appear
31 Czar Zane appears to be dazzled by the apple pizza and jazz.

21e WP

Speed Runs with Numbers

1. Set the Timer in the Word Processor for 1'.
2. Take two 1' writings; the last number you key when you stop is your approximate *gwam*. Do not save.

1 and 2 and 3 and 4 and 5 and 6 and 7 and 8 and 9 and 10 and
11 and 12 and 13 and 14 and 15 and 16 and 17 and 18 and 19
and 20 and 21 and 22 and 23 and 24 and 25 and 26 and 27 and

21f Timed Writing

1. Key a 2' writing. Repeat.
2. End the lesson but do not exit the software.
3. Go to the Word Processor and complete 21e.

all letters

Goal: 16 *gwam*

	gwam	1'	2'
Teams are the basic unit of performance for a firm.	11	5	42
They are not the solution to all of the organizational needs.	23	12	48
They will not solve all of the problems, but it is known	35	17	54
that a team can perform at a higher rate than other groups.	47	23	60
It is one of the best ways to support the changes needed for	59	30	66
a firm. The team must have time in order to make	71	36	72
a quality working plan.	74	37	74

1'	1	2	3	4	5	6	7	8	9	10	11	12
2'		1		2		3		4		5		6

```
 1  NEWTON & JOHNSON
    15 Civic Center Drive, Suite 200
 2  Santa Ana, CA 92701-3821

 3  Telephone:  714-555-0134

 4  Attorneys for Defendants
    JONATHAN MOVERS and
 5  LAUREL DELIVERIES

 6

 7

 8              SUPERIOR COURT OF THE STATE OF CALIFORNIA

 9                     FOR THE COUNTY OF ORANGE

10

11  HENRY HURT, et al.,                  )
                                         )
12          Plaintiff,                   )  Case No.: SO C 87321
                                         )
13      vs.                              )  NOTICE OF DEPOSITION AND REQUEST FOR
                                         )  PRODUCTION OF DOCUMENTS AT DEPOSITION
14  JONATHAN MOVERS, et. al.,            )
                                         )
15          Defendant.                   )
                                         )
16  _____

17  TO:   ALL PARTIES AND THEIR ATTORNEYS OF RECORD

18

19        PLEASE TAKE NOTICE that defendants will take the deposition of

20  plaintiff Henry Hurt on July 7, 20--, at 2:00 p.m., at the offices of

21  Newton & Johnson, 15 Civic Center Drive, Suite 200, Santa Ana, CA 92701-

22  3821, before a notary public authorized to administer oaths in the State

23  of California.  The deposition will continue from day today, excluding

24  Saturdays, Sundays, and holidays, until completed.

25  ///

26  ///


                          Notice of Deposition - 1
```

Notice of Deposition and Request for Production of Documents at Deposition

LESSON 22

(and) and Backspace Key

WARMUP 22a

Key each line twice.

alphabet 1 Avoid lazy punches; expert fighters jab with a quick motion.

fig/sym 2 Be-Low's Bill #483/7 was $96.90, not $102--they took 5% off.

caps lock 3 Report titles may be shown in ALL CAPS; as, BOLD WORD POWER.

easy 4 Do they blame me for their dismal social and civic problems?

| 1 | 2 | 3 | 4 | 5 | 6 | 7 | 8 | 9 | 10 | 11 | 12 |

NEW KEYS

22b

(and) (parentheses)

Key each line once.

( ) = parentheses
Parentheses indicate off-hand, aside, or explanatory messages.

(Shift; then reach *up* with the *right third* finger.

) Shift; then reach *up* with the *right fourth* finger.

5 ((l l((; (; Reach from l for the left parenthesis; as, ((.

6)); ;))); Reach from ; for the right parenthesis; as,)).

( )

7 Learn to use parentheses (plural) or parenthesis (singular).

8 The red (No. 34) and blue (No. 78) cars both won here (Rio).

9 We (Galen and I) dined (bagels) in our penthouse (the dorm).

all symbols learned

10 The jacket was $35 (thirty-five dollars)--the tie was extra.

11 Starting 10/29, you can sell Model #49 at a discount of 25%.

12 My size 8 1/2 shoe--a blue pump--was soiled (but not badly).

22c Textbook Keying

Key each line once, keeping eyes on copy.

13 Jana has one hard-to-get copy of her hot-off-the-press book.

14 An invoice said that "We give discounts of 10%, 5%, and 3%."

15 The company paid bill 3/17 on 5/2/09 and bill 4/1 on 3/6/08.

16 The catalog lists as out of stock Items #230, #710, and #13.

17 Elyn had $8; Sean, $9; and Cal, $7. The cash total was $24.

Keyboarding Pro DELUXE users: Pleadings will open automatically as a data file. You will not download templates.

To use the legal pleading template:

If saved to the hard drive:

1. From a new *Word* screen, click the Office button, and select New. The New Document dialog box displays.

2. Select My templates from the Templates pane. Select *Pleading form with 26 lines.dotx.* Click OK to display the template.

-or –

If saved to a flash drive:

1. From a new Word screen, click the Office button, select New, and select New from existing. Browse to your flash drive.

2. Click the down arrow next to Files of type and change to All Files. Select *Pleading form with 26 lines.dotx.* Click OK to display the template.

APPLICATIONS

109-d1

Download Pleading Template

Keyboarding Pro DELUXE users: Skip this exercise.

1. From a new *Word* screen, click the Office button and select New.

2. Search for the Legal Pleading on Microsoft Office Online.

3. Download the Pleading form with 26 lines.

4. Scroll through the document; then close it without saving it.

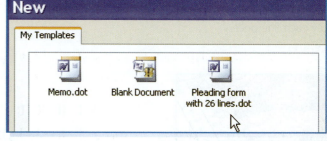

5. In a new *Word* screen, click the Office button and select New. Click My templates and select *Pleading form with 26 lines.dotx.* Save as a template. **Note:** If you are using a flash drive, select New from existing. Browse to your flash drive.

6. Check and close. (*109-d1*)

109-d2

Notice of Deposition and Request for Production of Documents at Deposition

A deposition is a testimony of a witness taken under oath in question-and-answer form. A deposition has the same legal effect as open court testimony.

1. Open *109-d1*, the template file you saved in Application 1. (*Keyboarding Pro DELUXE:* The pleadings template will open automatically.) Change the left margin to 1.25"; the right margin will remain at 1".

2. Key the document as shown on the next two pages. Align your text with the line numbers shown in the illustration. Text that is shown in uppercase should be keyed in uppercase.

3. Click on the bracketed text and key the new text.

4. Key / / / on lines 25 and 26; this shows that the lines were left blank by the writer. Key **Notice of Deposition** in the footer of the document.

5. Check and close. (*109-d2*)

continued

22d BACKSPACE Key

In the Word Processor, key the sentences using the BACKSPACE key to correct errors.

18 You should be interested in the special items on sale today.
19 If she is going with us, why don't we plan to leave now?
20 Do you desire to continue working on the memo in the future?
21 Did the firm or their neighbors own the autos with problems?
22 Juni, Vec, and Zeb had perfect grades on weekly query exams.
23 Jewel quickly explained to me the big fire hazards involved.

22e Timed Writing

1. Take a 3' timing on both paragraphs.
2. End the lesson; then go to the Word Processor and complete 22d and 22f.

E

all letters

	1'	3'
Most people will agree that we owe it to our children	10	4	28
to pass the planet on to them in better condition than we	22	7	32
found it. We must take extra steps just to make the quality	34	12	36
of living better.	38	13	37
If we do not change our ways quickly and stop damaging	11	16	41
our world, it will not be a good place to live. We can save	12	21	45
the ozone and wildlife and stop polluting the air and water.	35	25	49

1'	1	2	3	4	5	6	7	8	9	10	11	12
3'		1			2			3			4	

COMMUNICATION

22f Word Processor

1. Study the rules and examples at the right.
2. In the Word Processor, key the information below at the left margin. Tap ENTER as shown.
   Your name ENTER
   Current date ENTER
   Number Expression ENTER
3. Key the sample sentences 24–28. Backspace to correct errors.
4. Save the file as *xx-22f*.

NUMBER EXPRESSION: EXPRESS AS FIGURES

1. **Money amounts** and **percentages, even when appoximate**. Spell out cents and percent except in statistical copy.

   The 16 percent discount saved me $145; Bill, 95 cents.

2. **Round numbers expressed in millions or higher with their word modifier.**

   Ms. Ti contributed $3 million.

3. **House numbers** (except house number One) and street names over ten. If a street name is a number, separate it from the house number with a dash.

   1510 Easy Street   One West Ninth Avenue   1592--11th Street

4. **Date following a month.** A date preceding the month is expressed in figures followed by "rd" or "th."

   June 9, 2009   March 3   4th of July

5. **Numbers used with nouns.**

   Volume 1   Chapter 6

24 Ask **Group 1** to read **Chapter 6** of **Book 11** (**Shelf 19, Room 5**).
25 All **six** of us live at **One Bay Road**, not at **126--56th Street**.
26 At **9 a.m.** the owners decided to close from **12 noon** to **1 p.m.**
27 Ms. Vik leaves **June 9**; she returns the **14th or 15th of July**.
28 The **16 percent** discount saves **$115**.   A stamp costs **35 cents**.

Review the document on pages 492–493. The key identifying components of the legal pleading are described below. Each pleading begins with a **caption** to identify the action. The styles of captions vary, depending on the state; however, all captions include the **jurisdiction**—the name of the court that has authority to rule with reference to specific persons or subject matter. The name of the county and the state in which the court is located is usually included with the jurisdiction ❶.

The pleading also contains a **box**, which is formed with symbols. The box shows the names of the individuals or corporations involved in the lawsuit ❷. The **title** of the pleading is located to the right of the box ❸.

The name, address, and telephone number of the attorney originating the paper precedes the caption ❹. In some states, this information is placed at the end of the pleading.

The Microsoft Office Online website contains legal pleading forms that can be downloaded. The pleading forms are preformatted to include vertical rulings, line numbers, and the box.

NOTE

The Legal Pleading templates available from Microsoft are not *Word 2007* templates.

TO DOWNLOAD THE LEGAL PLEADING TEMPLATE:

OFFICE BUTTON/NEW

1. From a new *Word* screen, click the Office button and select New. The New Document dialog box displays ❶. Click in the center pane and key **Legal Pleading** in the Search Microsoft Office Online for a template text box ❷. Click the arrow to the right of the box ❸.

2. The search results display in the window. Choose Pleading form with 26 lines ❹. Click the Download button ❺. A dialog box will open to validate that you are running genuine Microsoft Office software. Click Continue.

3. The template displays on your screen and is ready for keying.

4. Once the template is downloaded, it is saved in My templates ❻ by default. Remember that in a classroom environment, however, you may need to save it to a flash drive or another location. **Note:** Refer to page 311 in Lesson 70 for a reminder on how to save a document as a template.

WARMUP 23a

Key each line twice.

alphabet 1 Roxy waved as she did quick flying jumps on the trapeze bar.
symbols   2 Ryan's--with an A-1 rating--sold Item #146 (for $10) on 2/7.
space bar 3 Mr. Fyn may go to Cape Cod on the bus, or he may go by auto.
easy   4 Susie is busy; may she halt the social work for the auditor?

| 1 | 2 | 3 | 4 | 5 | 6 | 7 | 8 | 9 | 10 | 11 | 12 |

NEW KEYS

23b & and : (colon)

Key each line once.

& = ampersand: The ampersand is used only as part of company names.

Colon: Space twice after a colon except when used within a number for time.

& Shift; then reach *up* with *right first* finger.

: (colon) Left shift; then tap key with *right fourth* finger.

& (ampersand)

5 & &j j& & & &; J & J; Haraj & Jay; Moroj & Jax; Torj & Jones
6 Nehru & Unger; Mumm & Just; Mann & Hart; Arch & Jones; M & J
7 Rhye & Knox represent us; Steb & Doy, Firm A; R & J, Firm B.

: (colon)

8 : :; :; : : :; as: for example: notice: To: From: Date:
9 in stock: 8:30; 7:45; Age: Experience: Read: Send: See:
10 Space twice after a colon, thus: To: No.:   Time: Carload:

all symbols learned

11 Consider these companies: J & R, Brand & Kay, Uper & Davis.
12 Memo #88-89 reads as follows: "Deduct 15% of $300, or $45."
13 Bill 32(5)--it got here quite late--from M & N was paid 7/3.

23c

Keyboard Reinforcement
Key each line twice; work for fluency.

double letters

14 Di Bennett was puzzled by drivers exceeding the speed limit.
15 Bill needs the office address; he will cut the grass at ten.
16 Todd saw the green car veer off the street near a tall tree.

figures and symbols

17 Invoice #84 for $672.91, plus $4.38 tax, was due on 5/19/08.
18 Do read Section 4, pages 60-74 and Section 9, pages 198-225.
19 Enter the following: (a) name, (b) address, and (c) tax ID.

Legal, Medical, and Employment Documents

LEARNING OUTCOMES

- Format legal office applications.
- Format medical office applications.
- Format employment application documents.

LESSON 109

Legal Pleadings

WARMUP 109a

Key each line, striving for control. Repeat if desired.

adjacent	1	Post your opinions on the Internet website prior to twelve today.
direct	2	In July, my azalea plant was placed in the center of Fred's deck.
1st/2nd	3	I went to the baseball game to see Ginger hit the first home run.
3rd/4th	4	Sal will keep the leopard suede skirt; it is back in style again.

DOCUMENT DESIGN

109b

PLEADING FORM

Legal documents that are presented for filing in court must follow specific guidelines and be keyed on pleading paper. Most documents today are keyed on standard 8.5" x 11" paper; some lawyers may still use legal size paper (8.5" x 14"). Legal documents contain a double ruling, from top to bottom, at the left margin; a single ruling displays at the right margin. Legal pleading forms contain line numbers in the left margin. The pleading form contains either 25, 26, 28, or 32 lines per page.

The margins for legal documents can be 1.25" on the left and 1" on the right. Some lawyers will use a 1.5" left margin and a .5" right margin. Top and bottom margins are usually 1".

23d Textbook Keying
Key each line once; work for fluency.

20 Jane may work with an auditing firm if she is paid to do so.
21 Pam and eight girls may go to the lake to work with the dog.
22 Clancy and Claudia did all the work to fix the sign problem.
23 Did Lea visit the Orlando land of enchantment or a neighbor?
24 Ana and Blanche made a map for a neighbor to go to the city.
25 Sidney may go to the lake to fish with worms from the docks.
26 Did the firm or the neighbors own the auto with the problem?

| 1 | 2 | 3 | 4 | 5 | 6 | 7 | 8 | 9 | 10 | 11 | 12 |

23e Timed Writing
Take a 3' timing on both paragraphs. Repeat.

all letters

	gwam	1'	3'
Is how you judge my work important? It is, of course;		11	4	26
I hope you recognize some basic merit in it. We all expect		23	8	30
to get credit for good work that we conclude.		32	11	33
I want approval for stands I take, things I write, and		11	14	36
work I complete. My efforts, by my work, show a picture of		23	18	41
me; thus, through my work, I am my own unique creation.		34	22	44

| 1' | 1 | 2 | 3 | 4 | 5 | 6 | 7 | 8 | 9 | 10 | 11 | 12 |
| 3' | | 1 | | | 2 | | | 3 | | | 4 | |

23f Edit Text
1. Read the information about proofreaders' marks.
2. In the Word Processor, key your name, class, and **23f** at the left margin. Then key lines 27–32, making the revisions as you key. Use the BACKSPACE key to correct errors.
3. Save as *xx-23f* and print.

Proofreaders' marks are used to identify mistakes in typed or printed text. Learn to apply these commonly used standard proofreaders' marks.

Symbol	Meaning	Symbol	Meaning
—	Italic	⊙ *sp*	Spell out
∼∼∼	Bold	¶	Paragraph
Cap or ≡	Capitalize	#	Add horizontal space
∧	Insert	/ or *lc*	Lowercase
⌒	Delete	⌒	Close up space
⊏	Move to left	∼	Transpose
⊐	Move to right	*stet*	Leave as originally written

27 We miss 50% in life's rewards by refusing to new try things.

28 do it now--today--then tomorrow's load will be 100%% lighter.

29 Satisfying work- whether it pays $40 or $400- is the pay off.

30 ⊏ Avoid mistakes: confusing a #3 has cost thousands.

31 Pleased most with a first-rate job is the person who did it.

32 My wife and/or me mother will except the certifi cate for me.

1. Prepare the following itinerary.
2. Position title at 2.0"; use Title and Subtitle style; set a tab with a hanging indent at 1.5" for the second column. **Hint:** Insert a nonbreaking space if necessary to keep a time (such as 9:28) on the same line with *a.m.* or *p.m.*
3. Check and close. (*108-d3*)

Itinerary for Tracy M. Westfield

July 14-17, 20--

Thursday, July 14	Boston to Bangor
8:15 a.m.	Leave Boston Airport on Coastline Flight 957 and arrive at Bangor Airport at 9:28 a.m.; Patriot Rental Car (Confirmation #218756).
10:30 a.m.	Meet with Rod Watson, Leigh Barber, Joe Coleman, and Mary Roszak of Round Rock Associates at their office—739 State Street, Bangor, Maine.
4:00 p.m.	Drive to Bar Harbor (approximately 40 miles), Cliff View Hotel, 29 Eden Street (Confirmation #S536017).
Friday, July 15	Bar Harbor
10:30 a.m.	Meet with Richard Odom, Bar Harbor Medical Supply—527 West Highway 3.
2:30 p.m.	Conference for Medical Supply Professionals, Cliff View Hotel.
5:00 p.m.	Conference ends; no events scheduled for evening.
Saturday, July 16	Bar Harbor
10:30 a.m.	Conference for Medical Supply Professionals, Cliff View Hotel.
12:30 p.m.	Conference ends; no events scheduled for afternoon.
7:30 p.m.	Conference Awards Banquet.
Sunday, July 17	Bar Harbor to Boston
1:30 p.m.	Drive to Bangor Airport.
3:30 p.m.	Depart on Coastline Flight 648; arrive at Boston Airport at 4:28 p.m.

CHECKPOINT ➡

Congratulations! You have successfully completed the lessons in Module 17. To check your understanding and for more practice, complete the objective assessment and performance assessment located on the textbook website at www.collegekeyboarding.com.

LESSON 24

Other Symbols

WARMUP 24a

Key each line twice.

alphabet 1 Pfc. Jim Kings covered each of the lazy boxers with a quilt.

figures 2 Do problems 6 to 29 on page 175 before class at 8:30, May 4.

" 3 They read the poems "September Rain" and "The Lower Branch."

easy 4 When did the busy girls fix the tight cowl of the ruby gown?

| 1 | 2 | 3 | 4 | 5 | 6 | 7 | 8 | 9 | 10 | 11 | 12 |

NEW KEYS

24b Textbook Keying

@ < > * + = [ ]

Key each pair of lines once;
DS between 2-line groups.

Become familiar with these symbols:

@   at

<   less than

>   greater than

*   asterisk

+   plus sign (use a hyphen for minus and x for "times")

=   equals

[ ]   left and right bracket

@ shift; reach *up* with *left third* finger to @

5 @ @s s@ @ @; 24 @ .15; 22 @ .35; sold 2 @ .87; were 12 @ .95

6 You may contact Luke @: LJP@rx.com or fax @ (602) 555-0101.

< shift; reach *down* with *right second* finger to <
> shift; reach *down* with *right third* finger to >

7 Can you prove "a > b"?   If 28 > 5, then 5a < x.   Is a < > b?

8 E-mail Al ajj@crewl.com and Matt mrw10@scxs.com by 9:30 p.m.

* shift; reach *up* with *right second* finger to *

9 * *k k8* * *; aurelis*; May 7*; both sides*; 250 km.**; aka*

10 Note each *; one * refers to page 29; ** refers to page 307.

+ shift; reach *up* with *right fourth* finger to +

11 + ;+ +; + + +; 2 + 2; A+ or B+; 70+ F. degrees; +xy over +y;

12 The question was 8 + 7 + 51; it should have been 8 + 7 + 15.

= reach *up* with *right fourth* finger to =

13 = =; = = =; = 4; If 14x = 28, x = 2; if 8x = 16, then x = 2.

14 Change this solution (where it says "= by") to = bx or = BX.

[ ] reach *up* with *right fourth* finger to [and]

15 Mr. Wing was named.   [That's John J. Wing, ex-senator.   Ed.]

16 We [Joseph and I] will be in Suite #349; call us @ 555-0102.

1. Key the action minutes shown below.

2. Position title at 2.5" and apply Title style to the title and Subtitle style to the subtitle.

3. Format the participants' names using hanging indent. Note that a signature line is not included.

4. Continue to the next document. (*108-d2*)

Investment Committee Meeting
Action Minutes—April 24, 20--

Presiding: Crystal Bingham

Participants: Todd Berkley, Jane Kennemur, Bert Radcliff, Julie Markham, Jerold Bradshaw, Chris Pruitt, and Sandy Westfield

Consultant: Bruce Diamond, Investment Evaluation Group (IEG)

Committee Chair Crystal Bingham called the meeting to order at 9:00 a.m., presented an overview of the meeting objectives, and introduced Bruce Diamond, who was representing our regular portfolio consultant, Fred Benjamin. She asked Bruce to summarize the results of the previous quarter. Bruce presented the written report including reports on domestic and international equity, fixed income, and alternative investments. He indicated that the portfolio results exceeded all benchmarks. The returns on the composite portfolio for the first quarter were 8.25 percent.

Jane Kennemur recommended that the portfolio structure be modified so that the core equity investments currently in index funds would be withdrawn and invested in actively managed funds. Bruce agreed that this move was prudent under market conditions. The committee concurred and requested that IEG complete the search for a core equity manager. Four managers need to be presented to the Committee before the final selection is made.

Jerold Bradshaw reported that the subcommittee reviewed the Investment Policy and recommended no changes. However, the change in the portfolio structure just approved would have to be incorporated in the policy. The updated policy will be sent to everybody.

James Wright reported that the Investment Oversight Committee had met monthly to monitor the investments carefully between Investment Committee meetings. The recommendation at each meeting during the past quarter had been to make no changes in the asset allocation of the portfolio or the investment managers. Monthly meetings have already been scheduled for the next quarter.

The meeting adjourned at 9:55 a.m.

24c Rhythm Builder
Key each line once.

double letters
17 feel pass mill good miss seem moons cliffs pools green spell
18 Assets are being offered in a stuffy room to two associates.

balanced hand
19 is if of to it go do to is do so if to to the it sign vie to
20 Pamela Fox may wish to go to town with Blanche if she works.

one hand
21 date face ere bat lip sew lion rear brag fact join eggs ever
22 get fewer on; after we look; as we agree; add debt; act fast

combination
23 was for|in the case of|they were|to down|mend it|but pony is
24 They were to be down in the fastest sleigh if you are right.

| 1 | 2 | 3 | 4 | 5 | 6 | 7 | 8 | 9 | 10 | 11 | 12 |

24d Edited Copy WP
1. In the Word Processor, key your name, class, and date at the left margin, each on a separate line.
2. Key each line, making the corrections marked with proofreaders' marks.
3. Correct errors using the BACKSPACE key.
4. Save as xx-24d.

25 Ask Group 1 to read Chater 6 of Book 11 (Shelf 19, Room 5).

26 All 6 of us live at One Bay road, not at 126-56th Street.

27 AT 9 a.m. the owners decided to close form 12 noon to 1 p.m.

28 Ms. Vik leaves June 9; she returns the 14th or 15th of July.

29 The 16 per cent discount saves $115. A stamp costs 35 cents.

30 Elin gave $300,000,000; our gift was only 75 cents.

24e Timed Writing
Take a 3' timing on both paragraphs. Repeat.

gwam 1' | 3'

Why don't we like change very much? Do you think that   11   4 26
just maybe we want to be lazy; to dodge new things; and, as   23   8 30
much as possible, not to make hard decisions?   32 11 33
We know change can and does extend new areas for us to   11 14 36
enjoy, areas we might never have known existed; and to stay 24 18 40
away from all change could curtail our quality of life.   34 22 44

| 1' | 1 | 2 | 3 | 4 | 5 | 6 | 7 | 8 | 9 | 10 | 11 | 12 |
| 3' | | 1 | | | 2 | | | 3 | | | 4 | |

24f Composition WP

1. In the Word Processor, open the file *xx-profile* that you created in Lesson 18.
2. Position the insertion point at the end of the last paragraph. Tap ENTER twice.
3. Key an additional paragraph that begins with the following sentence:
   Thank you for allowing me to introduce myself.
4. Finish the paragraph by adding two or more sentences that describe your progress and satisfaction with keyboarding.
5. Correct any mistakes you have made. Click Save to resave the document. Print.
6. Mark any mistakes you missed with proofreaders' marks. Revise the document, save, and reprint. Submit to your instructor.

APPLICATIONS

108c

Assessment

→ Continue

✓ Check

With *Keyboarding Pro DELUXE*: When you complete a document, proofread it, check the spelling, and preview for placement. When you are completely satisfied, click the Continue button to move to the next document. Click the Check button when you are ready to error-check the test. Review and/or print the document analysis results.

Without *Keyboarding Pro DELUXE*: Key the documents in sequence. When time has been called, proofread all documents again and identify errors.

108-d1

Agenda

1. Prepare the agenda shown below.
2. Position title at 2.0" and apply Title style; apply Subtitle style to the subtitle.
3. Set a right-align tab at 0.5" to align the times properly; then set a left-align tab at 1.0" and a right-align leader #2 tab at 6.5".
4. Because the agenda is short, do not remove the extra space after paragraphs for the subtopics in the agenda.
5. Continue to the next document. (*108-d1*)

Investment Committee Meeting

Agenda—April 24, 20--

9:00	Welcome...Crystal Bingham	
	Overview of Meeting Objectives	
9:10	Quarterly Performance Report......................Bruce Diamond	
	Equity—Domestic	
	Equity—International	
	Fixed Income	
	Alternative Investments	
9:35	Investment Policy Review ....Jerold Bradshaw	
9:45	Oversight Committee Review ....James Wright	
10:00	Adjourn	

WARMUP 25a

Key each line twice.

alphabet 1 My wife helped fix a frozen lock on Jacque's vegetable bins.

figures 2 Sherm moved from 823 West 150th Street to 9472--67th Street.

double letters 3 Will Scotty attempt to sell his accounting books to Elliott?

easy 4 It is a shame he used the endowment for a visit to the city.

| 1 | 2 | 3 | 4 | 5 | 6 | 7 | 8 | 9 | 10 | 11 | 12 |

25b Reach Review
Key each line once; repeat.

TECHNIQUE TIP

Keep arms and hands quiet as you practice the long reaches.

n/y 5 deny many canny tiny nymph puny any puny zany penny pony yen
6 Jenny Nyles saw many, many tiny nymphs flying near her pony.

b/r 7 bran barb brim curb brat garb bray verb brag garb bribe herb
8 Barb Barber can bring a bit of bran and herbs for her bread.

c/e 9 cede neck nice deck dice heck rice peck vice erect mice echo
10 Can Cecil erect a decent cedar deck?   He erects nice condos.

n/u 11 nun gnu bun nut pun numb sun nude tuna nub fun null unit gun
12 Eunice had enough ground nuts at lunch; Uncle Launce is fun.

25c Timed Writing
Key two 3' writings. Strive for accuracy.

all letters

Goal: 3', 19–27 *gwam*

gwam 3'

The term careers can mean many different things to   3 | 51
different people.   As you know, a career is much more than a   8 | 55
job.   It is the kind of work that a person has through life.   12 | 59
It includes the jobs a person has over time.   It also involves   16 | 63
how the work life affects the other parts of our life.   There   20 | 67
are as many types of careers as there are people.   23 | 71

Almost all people have a career of some kind.   A career   27 | 74
can help us to reach unique goals, such as to make a living   31 | 79
or to help others.   The kind of career you have will affect   35 | 83
your life in many ways.   For example, it can determine where   39 | 87
you live, the money you make, and how you feel about yourself.   44 | 91
A good choice can thus help you realize the life you want.   47 | 95

3' | 1 | 2 | 3 | 4 |

107-d1

Continued

Leading the Meeting

Much of the work for a meeting has been done by the time of the meeting. However, the leader can make a huge difference in the success of a meeting.

- Start the meeting on time even though some participants may not have arrived.
- Stick to the schedule and to the topics during the meeting.
- Make a concerted effort to involve everybody in the discussion.
- Jot notes down on the agenda, a whiteboard, a flip chart, or on notepaper so that you can prepare action minutes to distribute to participants.
- Work to reach consensus on issues rather that just voting on issues.
- If follow-up work needs to be done on any of the topics, make sure that the action item is assigned to someone and that a specific time for its completion is determined.
- Bring the meeting to a conclusion by summing up what has been accomplished and what still needs to be done, who will do it, and the time schedule.
- Try to end prior to the scheduled adjournment time if possible.

Following Up After the Meeting

Rarely is a meeting completed when it is adjourned. Usually follow-up activities must be accomplished.

- Prepare action minutes (or complete minutes, if required) and distribute to all participants and to others who may need the information.
- Communicate with those who have been assigned topics for future action and make sure they have the required information and deadlines.
- Make notes for future meetings based on the discussions of the meeting just completed.
- Assess the meeting to determine if the purposes were accomplished and try to determine how the meeting could be improved.

107-d2

Compose Memo

1. Compose a memo to your instructor from you with the subject **Guides for Effective Meetings**.
2. Tell your instructor that you have prepared the handout for the Management Seminar as requested and attach a copy. Write two or three paragraphs about the importance of learning to lead meetings effectively and what you learned from preparing this handout.
3. Edit and proofread your document carefully.
4. Check and close. (*107-d2*)

2 Skill Builder

KEYBOARDING PRO DELUXE

Skill Building   Technique Builder

Select the Skill Building tab from the Main menu and then Technique Builder. Select the drill and follow the directions in the book.

DRILL 8

OPPOSITE HAND REACHES
Key each line once and DS between groups of lines. Key at a controlled rate; concentrate on the reaches.

i/e

w/o

1 ik is fit it sit laid site like insist still wise coil light
2 ed he ear the fed egg led elf lake jade heat feet hear where
3 lie kite item five aide either quite linear imagine brighter
4 Imagine the aide eating the pears before the grieving tiger.
5 ws we way was few went wit law with weed were week gnaw when
6 ol on go hot old lot joy odd comb open tool upon money union
7 bow owl word wood worm worse tower brown toward wrote weapon
8 The workers lowered the brown swords toward the wood weapon.

DRILL 9

PROOFREADERS' MARKS
Key each line once and DS after each sentence. Correct the sentence as edited, making all hand-written corrections. Do not key the numbers.

≡ Capitalize
/ Change letter
⊂ Close up space
/ Delete
∧ Insert
lc Lowercase
Space
⋀ Transpose

1. When a writer create the preliminary version of a document, they are concentrating on conveying the intended ideas.
2. This ver sion of a preliminary document is called a rough.
3. After the draft is created, the Writer edits/refines the copy.
4. Sometimes proofreader's marks are used to edit the draft.
5. The changes will them be make to the original. editing
6. After the changes have been made, then the Writer reads the copy.
7. Edit ing and proofreading requires alot of time and effort.
8. An attitute of excellance is required to produce error-free message.

DRILL 10

PROOFREADING
Compare your sentences in Drill 9 with Drill 10. How did you do? Now key the paragraph for fluency. Concentrate on keying as accurately as possible.

When a writer creates the preliminary version of a document, he or she is concentrating on conveying ideas. This preliminary version is called a rough draft. After the draft is created, the writer edits or refines the copy. Proofreaders' marks are used to edit the rough draft. The editing changes will be made to the original. Then the writer reads the copy again. Editing requires a lot of time and effort. An attitude of excellence is required to produce an error-free message.

SKILL BUILDER 2   MODULE 2   60

Participants

Meetings often fail because the right people are not participants in the meeting. Follow these guides in determining who to invite to a metting:

- Invite people who are responsible for the topic or project being discussed.
- Include from the beginning, people who will have to do the work that is being discussed.
- Select people who have expertise about the topic and can contribute ideas.
- Invite only those people who absolutely need to participate–not those who it might be nice to have in the meeting.
- Give serious thought as to how you will get all participants involved in the discussion required for the meeting.

Meeting Materials

Appropriate materials should be prepared carefully and distributed prior to the meeting. Meetings are usual much shorter when participants have done their share of the preparation prior to the meeting.

- Prepare the agenda carefully indicating who will be responsible for leeding each item that is to be discussed.
- Ensure that the person responsible for presenting an item is aware of that responsibility and will be prepared to handle it.
- Prepare and distribute materials that are needed for the discussion of each item for enough in advance so that participants will have time to read and study the materials. Remind participants tactfully to review the materials prior to the meeting and be prepared to discuss the content.

Facilities and Equipment

Facilities and equipment can make significant contributions to a meeting. The number of people involved and the type of meeting should determine the type of facilities and equipment needed.

- Select a room that is large enough to accommodate the participants comfortably, but not so large that people are spread out too far apart.
- Pay particular attention to the layout of the room. For meetings requiring group discussion, a board room or hollow square setting facilitates discussion. If slides are to be shown, a classroom setting might be better.
- Control the temperature of the room if it is feasible to do so. An overly warm room is not conducive to a good meeting.
- Have the appropriate equipment available and test it prior to the meeting to ensure that if is working properly.
- Reserve facilities for recurring meetings for all meetings at one time.

Miscellaneous Items

In some cases, supplies, such as a notepad and pen, may be needed. For some meetings, such as a "working lunch," food and beverages are expected. These items should be ordered in advance.

continued

1' | 3'

ASSESS SKILL GROWTH:

1. Select the Timed Writing tab from the Main menu.

Timed Writings

2. Select the writing number such as Writing 8.
3. Select 3' as the length of the writing.
4. Repeat the timing if desired.

WORD PROCESSOR OPTION:

1. Key 1' writings on each paragraph of a timing. Note that paragraphs within a timing increase by two words.
   Goal: to complete each paragraph.
2. Key a 3' timing on the entire writing.

E

all letters

Writing 8

	1'	3'
Any of us whose target is to achieve success in our professional	13	4
lives will understand that we must learn how to work in harmony	26	8
with others whose paths may cross ours daily.	35	12
We will, unquestionably, work for, with, and beside people, just	13	16
as they will work for, with, and beside us. We will judge them,	26	20
as most certainly they are going to be judging us.	38	24
A lot of people realize the need for solid working relations and	13	28
have a rule that treats others as they, themselves, expect to be	26	33
treated. This seems to be a sound, practical idea for them.	40	37

Writing 9

	1'	3'
I spoke with one company visitor recently; and she was very much	13	4
impressed, she said, with the large amount of work she had noted	26	9
being finished by one of our front office workers.	36	12
I told her how we had just last week recognized this very person	13	16
for what he had done, for output, naturally, but also because of	26	21
its excellence. We know this person has that "magic touch."	38	25
This "magic touch" is the ability to do a fair amount of work in	13	29
a fair amount of time. It involves a desire to become ever more	26	34
efficient without losing quality--the "touch" all workers should	39	38
have.	40	38

Writing 10

	1'	3'
Isn't it great just to untangle and relax after you have keyed a	13	4
completed document? Complete, or just done? No document is	25	8
quite complete until it has left you and passed to the next step.	38	13
There are desirable things that must happen to a document before	13	17
you surrender it. It must be read carefully, first of all, for	26	22
meaning to find words that look right but aren't. Read word for	39	26
word.	40	26
Check all figures and exact data, like a date or time, with your	13	31
principal copy. Make sure format details are right. Only then,	26	35
print or remove the work and scrutinize to see how it might look	39	39
to a recipient.	42	40

1' | 1 | 2 | 3 | 4 | 5 | 6 | 7 | 8 | 9 | 10 | 11 | 12 | 13 |
3' | 1 | 2 | 3 | 4 |

107-d1

Seminar Handout

1. Use report format to prepare the following document that will be used as a handout in a management seminar. Use Title style for the title and Heading 1 style for the three main segments of meeting management. Use Heading 2 style for the subheadings under *Preparing for a Meeting*.

2. Read the copy carefully and correct errors as you key. Note that the copy has ten uncorrected errors in it.

3. Use a check mark for bulleted items.

4. Number pages at the upper right; do not show the number on the first page.

5. Prepare a cover page using Pinstripes from the Cover Page gallery. Use **Management Seminar** for the subtitle.

6. Check and close. (*107-d1*)

Guides for Effective Meetings

Employees of virtually all organizations participate in meetings at some point in there careers. Many employees at all levels will have the responsibility of leading meetings. Employes routinely complain about the time wasted in meetings and the manner in which meetings are conducted. Individuals who handle meetings effectively gain positive attention from participants and from managers. The time spent learning to manage meetings effectively is a very good career investment. Using negotiation and influencing skills are a critical part of most meetings.

Meeting management can be divided into three separate segments: preparing for the meeting, leading the meeting, and following up after the meeting. All three segments deserve careful attention. Neglecting any one of them can cause a meeting disaster. The following guide for each of these segments are designed to help you improve the quality of the meetings you lead.

Preparing for a Meeting

The preparation that is done prior to the meeting often determines the success of the meeting. Items that must be handled prior to the meeting relate to the schedule, participants, meeting materials, facilities and equipment, and other miscellaneous items. Most of these items are interrelated.

Schedule

Use the following points as a checklist for scheduling meetings:

- make sure the meeting is needed and the topics cannot be handled appropriately through an e-mail or telephone call.
- Determine how much time is needed and schedule at a time that participants are likely to be available. Be cognizant of the cost of time and try to minimize the time spent in meetings.
- Schedule recurring meetings for a long period of time, such as a year, so that participants will have it on their calendars and reserve the time.

continued

Writing 11

Anyone who expects some day to find an excellent job should 4 | 34
begin now to learn the value of accuracy. To be worth anything, 8 | 38
completed work must be correct, without question. Naturally, we 13 | 43
realize that the human aspect of the work equation always raises 17 | 47
the prospect of errors; but we should understand that those same 20 | 51
errors can be found and fixed. Every completed job should carry 26 | 56
at least one stamp; the stamp of pride in work that is exemplary. 30 | 60

Writing 12

No question about it: Many personal problems we face today 4 | 34
arise from the fact that we earthlings have never been very wise 8 | 38
consumers. We haven't consumed our natural resources well; as a 13 | 43
result, we have jeopardized much of our environment. We excused 17 | 47
our behavior because we thought that our stock of most resources 20 | 51
had no limit. So, finally, we are beginning to realize just how 26 | 56
indiscreet we were; and we are taking steps to rebuild our world. 30 | 60

Writing 13

When I see people in top jobs, I know I'm seeing people who 4 | 34
sell. I'm not just referring to employees who labor in a retail 8 | 38
outlet; I mean those people who put extra effort into convincing 13 | 43
others to recognize their best qualities. They, themselves, are 17 | 47
the commodity they sell; and their optimum tools are appearance, 20 | 51
language, and personality. They look great, they talk and write 26 | 56
well; and, with candid self-confidence, they meet you eye to eye. 30 | 60

3' | 1 | 2 | 3 | 4 |

LESSON 107

Meeting Management Guides

Key each line, striving for control. Repeat if desired.

alphabet 1 Paxton quoted Jay in an amazing article this week before leaving.

symbols 2 Take the 15% discount on the invoice (#4973280); then add 6% tax.

double letters 3 Bobby Lott feels that the meeting at noon will be cancelled soon.

fluency 4 Did Leigh visit the Land of Enchantment or a neighbor in Orlando?

| 1 | 2 | 3 | 4 | 5 | 6 | 7 | 8 | 9 | 10 | 11 | 12 | 13 |

SKILL BUILDING

107b Textbook Keying

1. Key each line once, concentrating on good keying techniques. Tap ENTER twice after each 2-line group.
2. Repeat if time permits.

adjacent key 5 Teresa and Erin's team chalked up a win against the guys at polo.

6 Brent said his opinion on the polo field was the same as Trent's.

direct reach 7 Cecilia decided that Hunter deserved the junior varsity position.

8 June decided to be brave and try the high jump at the track meet.

double letters 9 Jessie called to borrow an accounting book at noon from Lynnette.

10 The football team meeting will occur soon after the jazz concert.

WORKPLACE SUCCESS

Influencing Others

Effective leaders can influence others to do things even though they have no authority over them. The ability to influence others is a valuable career skill for upward job mobility.

There is no one right or wrong way to go about influencing others. However, effective leaders tend to use techniques that have common characteristics. Some examples are:

- They approach the situation from the perspective of the other person rather than from their own. They have learned how to use empathy effectively.
- They make the effort to show the benefits to the other person.
- They try to get agreement on the big concepts before getting into the details that bog people down.
- They use good human relations skills and make it easy for the other person to grant requests.

Participating in meetings with individuals from different departments provides an excellent opportunity to learn how to influence other people. A good way to get started is to observe leaders who are able to bring a group to a consensus even though the discussion might have begun with very diverse positions. Meetings provide an opportunity to demonstrate good communication skills, leadership skills, and good time management and organization skills as well as good negotiation skills.

Writing 14

What do you expect when you travel to a foreign country?   12 | 4
Quite a few people realize that one of the real joys of   23 | 8
traveling is to get a brief glimpse of how others think, work,   36 | 12
and live.   40 | 12

    The best way to enjoy a different culture is to learn as   11 | 16
much about it as you can before you leave home.   Then you can   24 | 20
concentrate on being a good guest rather than trying to find   36 | 24
local people who can meet your needs.   44 | 27

Writing 15

What do you enjoy doing in your free time?   Health experts   12 | 4
tell us that far too many people choose to be lazy rather than   24 | 8
to be active.   The result of that decision shows up in our   36 | 12
weight.   37 | 13

    Working to control what we weigh is not easy, and seldom   12 | 16
can it be done quickly.   However, it is quite important if our   24 | 21
weight exceeds what it should be.   Part of the problem results   37 | 25
from the amount and type of food we eat.   44 | 27

    If we want to look fit, we should include exercise as a   11 | 31
substantial part of our weight loss plan.   Walking at least   23 | 35
thirty minutes each day at a very fast rate can make a big   35 | 39
difference both in our appearance and in the way we feel.   47 | 42

Writing 16

Doing what we like to do is quite important; however,   10 | 4
liking what we have to do is equally important.   As you ponder   23 | 8
both of these concepts, you may feel that they are the same,   36 | 12
but they are not the same.   41 | 14

    If we could do only those things that we prefer to do, the   12 | 18
chances are that we would do them exceptionally well.   Generally,   25 | 22
we will take more pride in doing those things we like doing,   37 | 26
and we will not quit until we get them done right.   47 | 29

    We realize, though, that we cannot restrict the things   11 | 33
that we must do just to those that we want to do.   Therefore,   23 | 37
we need to build an interest in and an appreciation of all the   36 | 41
tasks that we must do in our positions.   44 | 44

1' | 1 | 2 | 3 | 4 | 5 | 6 | 7 | 8 | 9 | 10 | 11 | 12 |
3' | 1 | 2 | 3 | 4 |

106-d1

Continued

Mr. Bradley Tate
ATA Supplies, Inc.
2155 Mack Avenue
Los Angeles, CA 90055-2074
Russ
bradley.tate@atasupplies.com

Mr. Donald May
SDG, Inc.
9170 Glacier Drive
Selden, NY 11784-3579
Don
donald.may@sdg.com

Ms. Judith Olson
Trapp, Inc.
2593 Fifth Street
Dallas, TX 75221-4768
Judy
judith.olson@trapp.com

Ms. Elizabeth Roth
Ashcraft, Inc.
8265 Oregon Avenue
Arvada, CO 80002-3749
Liz
elizabeth.roth@ashcraft.com

106-d2

Name Badge Labels

1. Prepare name badge labels for all of the Customer Service Seminar participants.
2. Use the same format you used in *106-drill2*.
3. Select a name badge label of your choice from the Avery US Letter list.
4. Preview and print on plain paper.
5. Check and close. (*106-d2*)

106-d3

File Folder Labels

1. Prepare file folder labels for all of the Customer Service Seminar participants.
2. Use the same format you used in *106-drill3*.
3. Select a file folder label of your choice from the Avery US Letter list.
4. Preview and print on plain paper.
5. Check and close. (*106-d3*)

106-d4

Portfolio Labels for Handout Notebooks

1. Prepare labels to be used on handout notebooks for all of the Customer Service Seminar participants.
2. Select Avery 8464 from the Avery US Letter list.
3. Include the address block plus the e-mail address fields.
4. Format the label by placing a blank line between the address block and the e-mail address.
5. Preview and print on plain paper.
6. Check and close. (*106-d4*)

Writing 17

gwam 1' 3'

Many people like to say just how lucky a person is when | 11 | 4 | 29
he or she succeeds in doing something well. Does luck play a | 24 | 8 | 33
large role in success? In some cases, it might have a small | 36 | 12 | 37
effect. | 37 | 13 | 38

Being in the right place at the right time may help, but | 11 | 16 | 41
hard work may help far more than luck. Those who just wait for | 24 | 20 | 46
luck should not expect quick results and should realize luck | 36 | 24 | 50
may never come. | 39 | 26 | 51

| 1' | 1 | 2 | 3 | 4 | 5 | 6 | 7 | 8 | 9 | 10 | 11 | 12 |
| 3' | | 1 | | | 2 | | | 3 | | | 4 | |

Writing 18

gwam 1' 3'

New golfers must learn to zero in on just a few social | 11 | 4 | 39
rules. Do not talk, stand close, or move around when another | 23 | 8 | 44
person is hitting. Be ready to play when it is your turn. | 35 | 12 | 47

Take practice swings in an area away from other people. | 11 | 15 | 51
Let the group behind you play through if your group is slow. | 24 | 20 | 55
Do not rest on your club on the green when waiting your turn. | 36 | 23 | 59

Set your other clubs down off the green. Leave the green | 12 | 27 | 63
quickly when done; update your card on the next tee. Be sure | 24 | 31 | 67
to leave the course in good condition. Always have a good time. | 37 | 36 | 72

| 1' | 1 | 2 | 3 | 4 | 5 | 6 | 7 | 8 | 9 | 10 | 11 | 12 |
| 3' | | 1 | | | 2 | | | 3 | | | 4 | |

Writing 19

gwam 1' 3'

Do you know how to use time wisely? If you do, then its | 11 | 4 | 51
proper use can help you organize and run a business better. | 24 | 8 | 55
If you find that your daily problems tend to keep you from | 35 | 12 | 59
planning properly, then perhaps you are not using time well. | 48 | 16 | 63
You may find that you spend too much time on tasks that are | 60 | 20 | 67
not important. Plan your work to save valuable time. | 70 | 24 | 70

A firm that does not plan is liable to run into trouble. | 12 | 27 | 74
A small firm may have trouble planning. It is important | 23 | 31 | 78
to know just where the firm is headed. A firm may have a | 35 | 35 | 82
fear of learning things it would rather not know. To say | 46 | 39 | 86
that planning is easy would be absurd. It requires lots of | 58 | 43 | 90
thinking and planning to meet the expected needs of the firm. | 70 | 47 | 94

| 1' | 1 | 2 | 3 | 4 | 5 | 6 | 7 | 8 | 9 | 10 | 11 | 12 |
| 3' | | 1 | | | 2 | | | 3 | | | 4 | |

DRILL 2 — CREATE NAME BADGE LABELS

1. Use the same procedures and data source to create Name Badge labels.

2. In step 4 of To create labels on page 477, change the Product number to **5895 Name Badge**, and click OK.

3. In step 6, select Use an existing list, click Browse, and then select *106-drill1datasource* from the drive on which you stored it.

4. Click Next: Arrange your labels.

5. Click More items and use the fields: Nickname, First Name, Last Name, and Company Name.

6. Format the first label block as follows: Select the first label; click Center and Bold. Select Nickname and change font size to 36 point. Position the insertion point after *Nickname* and tap ENTER. Add a space between *First Name* and *Last Name* and tap ENTER after *Last Name*. Select name and company lines and change font to 18 point.

7. Update all labels and preview.

8. Check and close. (*106-drill2 name badge*)

DRILL 3 — CREATE FILE FOLDER LABELS

1. Use the same procedures and data source (*review labels*) to create file folder labels containing the last name followed by a comma and space and then the first name.

2. Use Product Number 5866 folder labels.

3. When you select the recipients from the *106-drill1datasource* data source, click the heading over *Last Name* and sort in ascending order so they will be in alphabetical order.

4. Check and close. (*106-drill3 folder*)

APPLICATION

106-d1

Address Labels

TIP

Make sure the label you select is large enough to accommodate the 1.15" spacing default of *Word 2007*. Select labels that use 8.5" x 11" paper to avoid printer issues.

1. Prepare labels for all participants in a Customer Service training program.

2. Use the information below to prepare a data source for address labels. The same data source will be used for name badges, file folder labels, and e-mail address; therefore, include all of the information in the data source when you prepare it.

3. Name the data source *customer service*. Select an address label of your choice from the Avery US Letter list.

4. Check and close. (*106-d1*)

Customer Service Seminar Participants

Mr. Alfred Carter
ATA Supplies, Inc.
2155 Mack Avenue
Los Angeles, CA 90055-2074
Al
alfred.carter@atasupplies.com

Ms. Pamela Cox
Ashcraft, Inc.
8265 Oregon Avenue
Arvada, CO 80002-3749
Pam
pamela.cox@ashcraft.com

Mr. Edward Nix
LeVan, Inc.
2896 Sky Way
Seattle, WA 98114-4342
Ed
edward.nix@levan.com

Ms. Janice Hill
SDG, Inc.
9170 Glacier Drive
Selden, NY 11784-3759
Jan
janice.hill@sdg.com

Mr. Russell Adams
Trapp, Inc.
2593 Fifth Street
Dallas, TX 75221-4768
Russ
russell.adams@trapp.com

Ms. Cynthia Busch
LeVan, Inc.
2896 Sky Way
Seattle, WA 98114-4342
Cyndi
cynthia.busch@levan.com

continued

Writing 20

	3'	5'

If asked, most people will agree that some people have far   4 | 2 | 21
more creative skills than others, and they will also say that   8 | 5 | 34
these skills are in great demand by most organizations. A follow-   12 | 7 | 37
up question is in order. Are you born with creative skills or   17 | 10 | 39
can you develop them? No easy answer to that question exists, but   21 | 13 | 42
it is worth spending a bit of time pondering.   24 | 15 | 44

If creative skills can be developed, then the next issue is   28 | 17 | 46
how can you develop these skills. One way is to approach each   32 | 19 | 49
task with a determination to solve the problem and a refusal to   37 | 22 | 51
accept failure. If the normal way of doing a job does not work,   41 | 25 | 54
just keep trying things never tried before until you reach a good   45 | 27 | 56
solution. This is called thinking outside the box.   49 | 29 | 58

```
3' |     1     |     2     |     3     |     4     |
5' |      1       |      2       |      3       |
```

Writing 21

	1'	3'

Figures are not as easy to key as many of the words we use.   12 | 4 | 36
Balanced-hand figures such as 16, 27, 38, 49, and 50, although   25 | 8 | 40
fairly easy, are slower to key because each one requires longer   37 | 12 | 44
reaches and uses more time per stroke.   45 | 16 | 46

Figures such as 12, 45, 67, and 90 are even more difficult   12 | 20 | 50
because they are next to one another and each uses just a single   25 | 25 | 54
hand to key. Because of their size, bigger numbers such as 178,   39 | 29 | 59
349, and 1,220 create extra speed losses.   45 | 32 | 61

```
1' | 1 | 2 | 3 | 4 | 5 | 6 | 7 | 8 | 9 | 10 | 11 | 12 | 13 |
3' |   1   |    2    |    3    |    4    |
```

SKILL TRANSFER

1. Set the timer for 2'. Take a 2' writing on paragraph 1.
2. Set the timer for 2'. Take a 2' writing on paragraph 2.
3. Take 2 or more 2' writings on the slower paragraph.

Writing 22

	1'	2'

Few people attain financial success without some kind of   11 | 6
planning. People who realize the value of prudent spending and   24 | 12
saving are those who set up a budget. A budget helps individ-   36 | 18
uals determine just how much they can spend and how much they   49 | 24
can save so that they will not squander their money recklessly.   61 | 31

Keeping records is a ~~crucial~~ *vital* part of *a* budget. ~~Complete~~ *A detailed*   12 | 6
records *of all* of income and expen~~ses~~ *ditures* over a period of ~~a number of~~ *several*   24 | 12
months ~~can~~ *will* help *to* determine what bills, ~~as water~~ *like utilities* or rent, are   37 | 18
fixed ~~static~~ and which are flexible. To get the most out of your   49 | 25
income, *focus* ~~pay~~ attention *on* ~~to~~ the items that you can ~~modify~~ *be changed*.   61 | 30

```
1' | 1 | 2 | 3 | 4 | 5 | 6 | 7 | 8 | 9 | 10 | 11 | 12 |
2' |   1   |   2   |   3   |   4   |   5   |   6   |
```

10. The Save Address List dialog box displays. Select the drive **15** to which you want to save your labels and then key the filename **16**, such as *review labels datasource*, in the File name box and click Save. (**Note:** If you do not select a drive, your file will be stored to the folder My Data Sources in the My Documents folder.)

11. Click OK and then click Next: Arrange your labels in the Mail Merge Wizard task pane.

12. Click Address block **17**; then click Update all labels **18**.

13. Click Next: Preview your labels in the Mail Merge Wizard task pane.

14. Click Next: Complete the merge; then click Print.

15. Print all records **19**.

DRILL 1   CREATE LABELS

1. Create address labels for the records shown below. Save the main document as *106-drilll1main*.

2. Use Avery US Letter labels, Product number 5962.

3. Customize fields to add Nickname and delete Address Line 2, Home Phone, Work Phone, and E-mail address.

4. Save the data source as *106-drill1datasource*; be sure to select the correct drive for your files.

5. Preview and print the labels on plain paper. (*106-drill1*)

Review Labels

Title	First Name	Last Name	Company Name	Address Line 1	City	State	ZIP Code	Nickname
Mr.	Reginald	McWhorter	Circle R, Inc.	1896 Lawndale Avenue	Salt Lake City	UT	84110-9365	Reggie
Ms.	Julie	Hartwell	Thomas General Hospital	2765 Sheridan Road	Chicago	IL	60650-7169	Julie
Dr.	Margaret	Wilson	Weeks Medical Center	957 W. Lake Drive	Milwaukee	WI	53221-2956	Peggy
Mr.	William	Bass	Marcus, Inc.	830 Birch Circle	Clinton	MS	39056-2864	Bill
Ms.	Rebecca	McGee	Circle R, Inc.	1896 Lawndale Avenue	Salt Lake City	UT	84110-9365	Becky
Mr.	Charles	Kapp	Marcus, Inc.	830 Birch Circle	Clinton	MS	39056-2864	Chuck
Dr.	Henry	Wise	Weeks Medical Center	957 W. Lake Drive	Milwaukee	WI	53221-2956	Hank
Ms.	Marjorie	Keene	Thomas General Hospital	2765 Sheridan Road	Chicago	IL	60650-7169	Margie

Internet Activities

Activity 1
Open Internet Explorer

KNOW YOUR BROWSER

The Internet is a global collection of computers linked together to share information. The World Wide Web is a part of the Internet that consists of website located on different computers around the world. A Web browser, such as Internet Explorer, is a program that allows you to "browse the Web." The browser enables you to find, load, view, and print Web pages.

To launch Internet Explorer:

1. Click the Start button on the taskbar to display the Start menu.
2. Point to All Programs, and then click Internet Explorer in the submenu.
3. The Internet Explorer menu bar displays.
   a. The Standard Buttons toolbar contains buttons for frequently used commands. If the toolbar is not visible on your screen, click View, Toolbars, Standard Buttons.
   b. The Address Bar displays the address of the current page. If the Address Bar is not visible on your screen, click View, Toolbars, Address Bar.

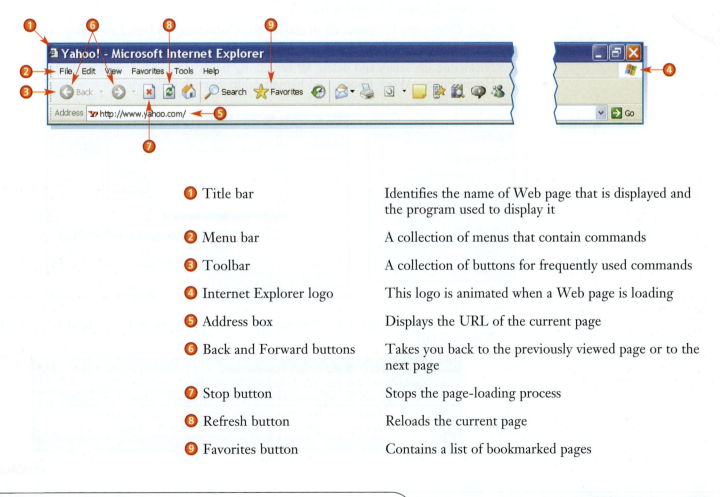

❶ Title bar	Identifies the name of Web page that is displayed and the program used to display it
❷ Menu bar	A collection of menus that contain commands
❸ Toolbar	A collection of buttons for frequently used commands
❹ Internet Explorer logo	This logo is animated when a Web page is loading
❺ Address box	Displays the URL of the current page
❻ Back and Forward buttons	Takes you back to the previously viewed page or to the next page
❼ Stop button	Stops the page-loading process
❽ Refresh button	Reloads the current page
❾ Favorites button	Contains a list of bookmarked pages

To create labels:

1. Select Labels ❶ as the document type.

2. Click Next located at the bottom of the task pane.

3. Select Change document layout ❷ and then click Label options ❸.

4. Select the Printer ❹, select the Label vendor ❺, the Product number ❻, and then click OK.

5. Then click Next: Select recipients at the bottom of the Mail Merge Wizard task pane.

6. Select either Use an existing list or Type a new list ❼ and then Create ❽ to display the New Address List dialog box ❾.

7. Click Customize Columns ❿ to display the Customize Address List dialog box.

8. Select fields not needed, such as Country or Region ⓫, and Rename ⓬, such as Nickname ⓭; select and delete ⓮ remaining fields not needed, such as Address Line 2, Home Phone, Work Phone, and E-mail Address; click OK.

9. Key the variables in the fields, tapping the TAB key to move from one field to the next; then click OK.

continued

DRILL 1

LAUNCH INTERNET EXPLORER

1. Launch Internet Explorer.

2. Locate the address box at the top of the screen. The address that currently displays in the box is your current home page; that is the page your browser goes to when you first open it.

3. Click your mouse in the address box to highlight the address. With the address highlighted, key the following address http://www.whitehouse.gov.

4. Tap ENTER. Notice the movement of the logo as the site is being located. If it takes a long time for the pages to load, you can click the Stop button to cancel the loading.

WEB ADDRESS

Each Web page has a unique address, which is commonly called the URL or Uniform Resource Locator. The URL is composed of one or more domains separated by periods. In the address, http://www.whitehouse.gov, the protocol is *http://*; the location of the website is *www.* (World Wide Web); the name of the website is *Whitehouse*; and the domain is *.gov* (U.S. government). Other domains include educational institution (.edu), commercial organizations (.com), military sites (.mil), and other organizations (.org).

DRILL 2

VISIT WEBSITES
1. Go to each of these websites.
2. Write the name of the Web page as it appears in the title bar.

1. http://www.house.gov _____
2. http://www.fbla.org _____
3. http://www.army.mil _____
4. http://www.news.com _____

DRILL 3

USE TOOLBAR BUTTONS

1. Open the following websites:

   http://www.cnn.com

   http://senate.gov

   http://nike.com

2. Click the Back button twice. The _____ website displays.

3. Click the Forward button once. The _____ website displays.

4. Print the active Web page.

LESSON 106

Labels and Name Badges

WARMUP 106a

Key each line, striving for control. Repeat if desired.

alphabet	1	Rex Patey quickly moved to a new zone just before the group came.
figures	2	Vi paid $19.50 for Seats 7 and 8; Pat paid $26 for Seats 3 and 4.
1st/2nd fingers	3	Guy tried to come to my rescue before going to work this morning.
easy	4	Jay and I may go with eight girls to fish on the docks by a lake.

| 1 | 2 | 3 | 4 | 5 | 6 | 7 | 8 | 9 | 10 | 11 | 12 | 13 |

DOCUMENT DESIGN

106b

LABELS

Label options exist for a variety of purposes, such as address labels, name badges, file folders, CD-Rom labels, and many others. Many of these labels are useful in managing meetings effectively. Because all of these labels can be created from the same data source, it is important to capture all of the data that is needed in the data source. In this lesson, you will use the same data source to prepare address labels, name badges, and file folder labels.

Name badges for meetings and conferences are printed in large type so that they can be read easily. The tone for the conference is usually set by the way the name is printed on the badge. If a meeting is designed to be informal and interactive, the name badge usually features the individual's first name or nickname with the full name below it. A more formal meeting would include the full name. Rarely is a courtesy title (Ms., Mr., Mrs., or Dr.) used on a name badge. Professional titles and company or organization information may be included.

FUNCTION REVIEW

106c

CREATE LABELS FOR MASS MAILING

MAILINGS/START MAIL MERGE/START MAIL MERGE

The mail merge process to create labels involves a series of five steps:

1. Select and set up the labels. The document used to do this is called the **label main document**.
2. Connect the labels to your address list, the data source used in the mail merge.
3. Edit the recipient list, choosing the ones to be included in the mail merge.
4. Add merge fields (placeholders) that will be filled with the information from your address list.
5. Preview and complete the merge.

Word contains a very helpful tool, the Mail Merge Wizard, to lead you through the mail merge process on a step-by-step basis. This approach is recommended until you become proficient at creating a mail merge.

To start the Mail Merge Wizard:

1. On the Mailings tab, in the Start Mail Merge group, click the Start Mail Merge button ❶.
2. Click Step by Step Mail Merge Wizard ❷ and follow the steps.

BOOKMARK A FAVORITE WEBSITE

Web pages that you display often can be added to a Favorites list. This will allow you to open the Favorites list and click the link to display the page you want; it saves you from having to key the Web address each time.

TO ADD WEB PAGE TO THE FAVORITES LIST:

1. Display the Web page on the screen.
2. Click Favorites on the Internet Explorer menu bar.
3. Select Add to Favorites from the drop-down menu. The Add Favorite dialog box displays.
4. The name of the Web page displays in the Name box. Click OK.

TO OPEN ONE OF YOUR FAVORITE PAGES:

1. Launch Internet Explorer.
2. Click the Favorites menu (or click the Favorites button to display the Favorites menu).
3. Select the page you want to open. As your list of favorite pages grows longer, you can organize it by moving pages into subfolders.

DRILL 4

VISIT WEBSITES

1. Open these websites and add them to your Favorites list.
   a. http://www.weather.com
   b. http://www.cnn.com
2. Use the Favorites list to go to the following websites to find answers to the questions below:
   a. The Weather Channel—What is today's temperature in your city? _____
   b. CNN—What is today's top news story? _____

 **Activity 2**
Set Up E-mail Addresses

ELECTRONIC MAIL

Electronic mail or **e-mail** refers to electronic messages sent by one computer user to another. To be able to send or receive e-mail, you must have an e-mail address, an e-mail program, and access to the Internet or an intranet (in-house network).

Many search engines such as Yahoo, Google, Excite, Lycos, and others provide free e-mail via their websites. These e-mail programs allow users to set up an e-mail address and then send and retrieve e-mail messages. To set up an account and obtain an e-mail address, the user must (1) consent to the terms to the agreement, (2) complete an online registration form, and (3) compose an e-mail name and password.

DRILL 1

SET UP E-MAIL

1. Click the Search button on the browser's toolbar.
2. Click a search engine that offers free e-mail.
3. Follow the directions to set up an e-mail account.

---

1. Format the title of this itinerary for **Travelle Gortman**; include **Technology Summit, June 1–3, 20--** as the subtitle. Use the same styles as *105-d1*.

2. Format the itinerary as a two-column table; adjust the width of the first column to 1.5". Bold the dates and locations. Tap ENTER at the end of each row to provide additional space between items. Remove the borders when you have completed the table.

3. Check and save. (*105-d2*)

Wednesday, June 1	**Mobile to Washington, D.C.**
7:00 a.m.	Leave Mobile on Flight 1475 and arrive in Atlanta at 7:35. Leave Atlanta on Freedom Flight 290 at 8:45 a.m. and arrive at Ronald Reagan Washington National Airport at 9:53; met by Executive Conference Service at baggage claim. ENTER
	Reservation on concierge level of the Hampton Hotel, 2300 Pennsylvania Avenue, NW (Confirmation #527918).
	Conference (preregistration confirmation #S-963248); see conference program for schedule.
8:30 p.m.	Dinner at Crystal's in Georgetown; reservations in your name for six (Anne Moore, Lee Roswell, Andy Cox, Leslie Kline, and Takisha Penn).
Thursday, June 2	**Washington, D.C.**
10:00 a.m.	Presentation in Ballroom A on the third floor of the Hampton Hotel.
12:30 p.m.	Lunch with Technology Summit Executive Committee in Terrace Room.
6:30 p.m.	Depart for performance at Kennedy Center followed by dinner at Marbelle Estate with Larry Newman, president of the Technology Summit.
Friday, June 3	**Washington D. C.**
1:00 p.m.	Depart for Ronald Reagan Washington National Airport (Executive Conference Service provides transportation).
2:45 p.m.	Leave on Freedom Flight 861 at 2:45 p.m. and arrive in Atlanta at 3:51. Leave Atlanta on Freedom Flight 1683 at 4:45 p.m. and arrive in Mobile at 5:28.

105-d3

Itinerary

1. Use the same format as you did for *105-d2* and prepare an itinerary for your trip to San Antonio. Use the information you collected from the Internet in *105c*.

2. Check and close. (*105-d3*)

Send E-mail Message

To send an e-mail message, you must have the address of the computer user you want to write. Business cards, letterheads, directories, etc., now include e-mail addresses. Often a telephone call is helpful in obtaining e-mail addresses. An e-mail address includes the user's login name followed by @ and the domain (sthomas@yahoo.com).

Creating an e-mail message is quite similar to preparing a memo. The e-mail header includes TO, FROM, and SUBJECT. Key the e-mail address of the recipient on the TO line, and compose a subject line that concisely describes the theme of your message. Your e-mail address will automatically display on the FROM line.

DRILL 2

1. Open the search engine used to set up your e-mail account. Click E-mail or Mail. (Terms will vary.)
2. Key your e-mail name and password when prompted.

E-mail Message 1

3. Key the e-mail address of your instructor or another student. Compose a brief message describing the weather in your city (from Activity 1, Drill 4). Include a descriptive subject line. Send the message.

E-mail Message 2

4. Key your e-mail address. The subject is **Journal Entry for March 29, 20--**. Compose a message to show your reflections on how keyboarding is useful to you. Share your progress in the course and your plan for improving this week. Send the message.

Respond to Messages

Replying to e-mail messages

Reading one's e-mail messages and responding promptly are important rules of netiquette (etiquette for the Internet). However, avoid responding too quickly to sensitive situations.

Forwarding e-mail messages

Received e-mail messages are often shared or forwarded to other e-mail users. Be sure to seek permission from the sender of the message before forwarding it to others.

DRILL 3

1. Open your e-mail account if it is not open.
2. Read your e-mail messages and respond immediately and appropriately to any e-mail messages received from your instructor or fellow students. Click Reply to answer the message.
3. Forward the e-mail message titled *Journal Entry for March 29, 20--* to your instructor.
4. Delete all read messages.

Attach a Document to an E-mail Message

Electronic files can be attached to an e-mail message and sent to another computer electronically. Recipients of attached documents can transfer these documents to their computers and then open them for use.

DRILL 4

1. Open your e-mail account if it is not open.
2. Create an e-mail message to your instructor that states your homework is attached. The subject line should include the specific homework assignment (**xx-profile**, for example).
3. Attach the file by clicking Attach (or the appropriate button; email programs may vary). Use the browser to locate the homework assignment.
4. Send the e-mail message with the attached file.

Itinerary for Susan C. Zachary

May 6 – 8, 20--

Set left tab and hanging indent

Monday, May 6   **Dallas to Denver**

9:25 a.m.   Leave Dallas Fort Worth International Airport on Skyway Flight 498 and arrive at Denver International Airport at 10:28 a.m.; Bronco Rental Car (Confirmation #492084); Mile High Hotel (Confirmation #360457), 3961 E. Louisiana Avenue (20 minutes).

12:30 p.m.   Luncheon meeting with Robert Jarworzky, Leigh Moreau, and Brad Matthews at Cherry Creek Eatery at 4827 Cherry Creek S. Drive.

3:00 p.m.   Tour of the Azure Manufacturing Plant; followed by meeting with the Quality Assurance Team. Transportation: picked up at hotel by Dave S. Roane. Dinner arranged by Azure. Return to hotel by 10:00 p.m.

Tuesday, May 7   **Lakewood**

8:30 a.m.   Drive to Lakewood (map in Lakewood file).

9:30 a.m.   Full-day meeting with Lakewood Pharmaceuticals.

6:00 p.m.   Dinner with Christopher Davis, President of Lakewood Pharmaceuticals and Karen Davis. Return to hotel by 9:30 p.m.

Wednesday, May 8   **Denver**

9:30 a.m.   Meeting with the Gentry Group at the Mile High Hotel, Conference Center Board Room.

12:00 noon   Lunch for the Gentry Group in Skyview Room.

2:45 p.m.   Leave for Denver International Airport.

3:55 p.m.   Leave Denver International Airport on Skyway Flight 639; arrive Dallas Fort Worth International Airport at 6:25 p.m.

Level

2

FORMATTING ESSENTIALS

LEARNING OUTCOMES

Keyboarding
- To key fluently using good keying techniques.
- To key about 40 words per minute with good accuracy.

Document Design Skills
- To format memos, e-mails, letters, reports, and tables appropriately.
- To apply basic design skills to newsletters and announcements.
- To enhance documents with basic graphics.

Word Processing Skills
- To learn the essential word processing commands.
- To create, edit, and format documents effectively.

Communication Skills
- To review and improve basic communication skills.
- To compose e-mails, memos, and other documents.
- To proofread effectively, apply proofreaders' marks, and revise text.

1. You plan to attend a Business Management Conference on May 1 – 4 at the Henry B. Gonzales Convention Center in San Antonio, Texas. Your expenses will be paid. Use the Internet to find the following information:

   - Round-trip flight to San Antonio from your city. Check cost and availability. Make a note of the airline, the schedule, and the rate. Try to arrive by noon on the first day and leave after noon on the last day.

   - A suitable hotel near the convention center. Check for availability and rates. Make a note of the hotel's address, telephone number, and rate.

   - Three restaurants that would be suitable for dinner. Make a note of the types of food and the address and telephone number of each.

2. Keep the information; you will use it later in this lesson.

ITINERARY

An itinerary is a detailed schedule prepared for individuals who are traveling or who are working away from their offices.   Normally when people are working in their offices, they have a variety of information available to them. When they are out of the office, a comprehensive itinerary provides a quick summary of all the logistical information needed to function effectively.   Itineraries for international travel typically require more information than for domestic travel. Types of information normally included in an itinerary include:

- Dates and times of meetings and events
- Transportation information—airline flight numbers and times, ticket information, passport or visa requirements, rental car or ground transportation
- Hotel information—name and address, confirmation number, special requests made
- Restaurant information—name and address, reservation information
- Meetings or appointments—individual and company names, times, addresses, transportation information if needed
- Leisure-time activities and information

Most organizations use a list-type format so that the information is easy to read. Fragments are generally used rather than complete sentences. The itinerary may be keyed setting tabs to align the information, or it may be keyed as a table. Position the heading between 1" and 2" from the top depending on the length of the document. Apply Title style. Apply Subtitle style to the second line of the heading.

Using tabs, set a left tab and a hanging indent at about 1.5" for the descriptive information. If you key the itinerary using a table, use a two-column table; adjust the width of the first column to about 1.5". Tap ENTER at the end of each row to add extra space. The borders may be removed from the table if desired.

1. Key the itinerary on the next page.
2. Position the title at about 1.4" and apply Title style; use Subtitle style for the second line.
3. On the line below the subtitle, set a left tab and a hanging indent at 1.5" for the second column.
4. Check and close. (105-d1)

The Transition—*Word 2003* to *Word 2007*

The transition from *Word 2003* to *Word 2007* will be significantly different for students, instructors, and for industry than the transition from previous versions of *Word* to new versions. Three factors account for the differences:

1. The user interface that replaces toolbars and menus with a ribbon is totally new.
2. The new XML default file format (.docx) is not backward compatible with previous versions of *Word*.
3. The formatting defaults have changed significantly from *Word 2003*.

USER INTERFACE

The Ribbon consists of three basic components:

1. Tabs are listed across the top of the Ribbon (Home, Insert, Page Layout, etc.). Each tab displays a different ribbon.
2. Groups are listed at the bottom of the Ribbon (Clipboard, Font, Paragraph, etc.) and contain a variety of related commands. The groups are different on each ribbon that is displayed by a tab.
3. Commands are the related functions that are located in each group.

The new user interface is easier to learn. The system is intuitive, and the use of groups facilitates the learning of related commands.

DEFAULT FILE FORMAT

The default file format presents a major challenge to industry during the transition period, but it is transparent to the user and is very simple to learn. The challenge to industry is that documents stored in previous formats will have to be converted to the new XML format. It also presents a problem when one organization sends a *Word 2007* document to an organization that is using a previous version of *Word*. Unless the document is stored in a 1997–2003 compatible format, the recipient will not be able to open the *Word 2007* document. Documents stored in a compatible format cannot be edited or use new features of *Word 2007* such as Smart Art. Since you are not likely to be sending documents from the classroom to other organizations, the default file format is not an issue.

Itineraries

WARMUP 105a

Key each line, striving for control. Repeat if desired

alphabet 1 Gayle just told them about five quick trips to Arizona next week.

figures 2 The system provides 168 majors to 39,475 students on 20 campuses.

direct reaches 3 Ned used their sled on cold days and my kite on warm summer days.

fluency 4 Sidney may go with us to the lake to fish with worms on the dock.

| 1 | 2 | 3 | 4 | 5 | 6 | 7 | 8 | 9 | 10 | 11 | 12 | 13 |

SKILL BUILDING

105b Timed Writing

1. Key one 3' writing, working at your control rate.
2. Key one 5' writing, working at your control rate.

all letters

	gwam	3'	5'

Most people today have become very health conscious. These 4 | 3 | 53
individuals worry about the bad effects of a diet that has far too 9 | 5 | 55
much fat and a lifestyle that does not include very much exercise. 13 | 8 | 58
However, many of those people never get past the stage of worrying. 18 | 11 | 61
Others just try to find a quick solution to the problem. They try 22 | 13 | 63
zany diets and easy exercise programs. The real solution is to get 27 | 16 | 66
in the habit of eating correctly and doing exercise on a regular 31 | 19 | 69
basis. The results are well worth the effort. 34 | 21 | 71

The combination of exercising on a regular basis and eating 39 | 23 | 73
properly produces much better results than either of these activities 43 | 26 | 76
can produce by itself. An effective diet includes food from all 48 | 29 | 79
of the major food groups. Eating food that has a very high 52 | 31 | 81
fiber content and a very low fat content can help to prevent a 56 | 34 | 84
number of diseases. Not eating a meal to save a few calories is 60 | 36 | 86
not a very good idea. A good exercise program has several important 65 | 39 | 89
characteristics. Each session lasts approximately twenty minutes 69 | 42 | 92
and occurs at least three times a week. Also, the activity should 74 | 44 | 94
be fast enough to increase your heart rate. Walking at a fast pace 78 | 47 | 97
is one of the best and one of the most desirable activities that 83 | 50 | 100
you can do. 83 | 50 | 100

3' | 1 | 2 | 3 | 4 |
5' | 1 | 2 | 3 |

FORMATTING DEFAULTS

The defaults of *Word 2007* and *Word 2003* differ significantly.

Default	Word 2007	Word 2003
Body font and size	Calibri (sans serif) 11 point	Times New Roman (serif) 12 point
Heading font	Cambria (sans serif) varied size	Arial (sans serif) varied sizes
Title style	Cambria, 26 point, dark blue, left align	Arial, 16 point, bold, centered
Margins	1" left, right, top, and bottom	1.25" left and right; 1" top and bottom
Line spacing	1.15	1.0
Space after paragraph	10 point	0
Document theme	Office ▪▪▪▪▪▪▪▪ Office	None

The new defaults—particularly the line spacing and the space after paragraph—produce documents that look different than traditional document formats. *Microsoft* emphasizes that the rationale for changing the defaults is to enhance both readability and the appearance of documents. The illustration on the left below shows how the date, letter address, and salutation of a letter would appear if traditional format guides were used with the *Word 2007* defaults. The illustration on the right shows how guides and defaults can be modified to produce an attractive letter format.

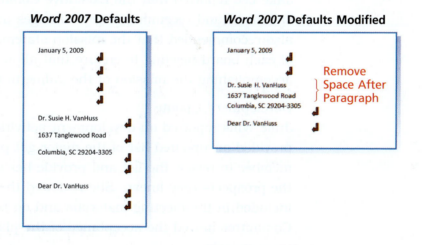

FORMATTING DECISIONS

Decisions regarding document formats require consideration of four elements: (1) attractiveness of the format, (2) readability of the format, (3) effective use of space on the page, and (4) efficiency in producing the document. Both documents formatted with *Word 2007* defaults and *Word 2003* defaults can meet these criteria. Employed students may find that they are creating documents using *Word 2007* in one setting and *Word 2003* traditional formats in the other.

In this textbook, you will prepare *Word 2007* documents using both formats to ease the transition from the traditional format to the new one. By using *Word 2003* style—a *Word 2007* style that emulates the defaults of *Word 2003*—you will learn to use the new features and at the same time produce traditional document formats. You will also learn to produce *Word 2007* document formats so that you are prepared for offices that have already made the transition to the new defaults. Full-page model documents are illustrated in both styles. The Reference Manual also provides illustrations of *Word 2007* formats and formats from previous versions of *Word*.

1. Key the following information to prepare minutes; then insert the data file *minutes* to complete the document.
2. Use the same format as *104-d1*.
3. Number pages as a right-aligned header; do not show number on the first page.
4. Add the signature line for **Mary Ott, Chair**. Remove the space after the line.
5. Check and close. (*104-d2*)

Palmetto Children's Home | Meeting of Board of Directors, May 20, 20--

The Board of Directors of Palmetto Children's Home met on May 20, 20-- at 8:00 a.m. in the Board Room. Mary Ott called the meeting to order and welcomed all participants.

Board members present were Allen Brown, Jeff Green, Steve Islam, Fred Jones, Jake Lee, Carol Marks, Mary Ott, Keith Price, Ann Ray, and Julie Wills. Staff members present were Nate Lipscomb, Wayne Simmons, Suzanne Reed, and Jack Washburn.

Mission Statement Review
Jake Lee reported that the Executive Committee reviewed the mission statement and recommended no changes in it. The Executive Committee also recommended that the mission statement be read at the beginning of each board meeting to ensure that all actions were focused on accomplishing the mission of the Palmetto Children's Home.

Development Update
Julie Wills reported on development activities since the last meeting. She provided an updated list of the major gift prospects and asked each board member to review the list and provide her with information about any of the prospects they knew. She reviewed the solicitation plan that was included in the meeting materials and on behalf of the Development Committee moved the acceptance of the plan. The motion was approved unanimously.

Financial Report
Jeff Green presented the actual revenues and expenditures year-to-date and compared them to the current budget. Revenues and expenditures were on target, and no budget revisions were recommended. He then reviewed the quarterly financial statements. The financial report was presented for information and no action was required until the audit report is presented.

Jeff Green then provided an update on the $6,000,000 proposed bond issue and moved on behalf of the Finance Committee that the transaction be finalized. The motion was approved unanimously.

Insert **minutes** here.

Word Processing Essentials

MODULE 3

LEARNING OUTCOMES

- Learn basic *Word 2007* commands.
- Create, save, and print documents.
- Apply text, paragraph, and page formats.
- Review documents and apply communication skills.
- Build keyboarding skills.

LESSON 26 › Learn Essential Functions

WARMUP 26a

Key each line, striving for control. Repeat if desired.

alphabet	1	Lorenz quietly exited just before the five, wet campers got back.
adjacent	2	I was sad that four people quit before our guys joined the choir.
direct	3	Brent must bring a great many golf umbrellas to sell to my group.
easy	4	Jane may go to visit the lake and fish with the girls. May I go?

SKILL BUILDING

26b Timed Writing
1. Key a 3' timed writing, working for speed.
2. Key a 3' timed writing, working for control.

all letters

	gwam	1'	3'
Many students find it quite difficult to juggle the things		12	4
they want to do with the things they ought to do. Too often the		25	8
things that they find the most tempting and desirable to do are just		39	13
distractions from doing things that need to be given priority.		51	17
The key is to set priorities and stick with them. Those who		12	21
organize their work and do the critical things first not only		25	25
accomplish more, they are the most likely to have sufficient time		38	30
to do the things that they enjoy doing as well.		47	33
Choosing friends wisely also helps you to stay on target.		12	37
Students who have friends with the same type of expectations as		25	41
they do usually help each other to meet their goals. They value		38	45
their time and try to use it well.		44	48

1'	1	2	3	4	5	6	7	8	9	10	11	12	13
3'		1			2			3			4		

Master Plan for Research Facilities

Planning and Data Analysis Meeting Minutes, February 15, 20--

The Master Plan for Research Facilities team met at 2:00 on February 15, 20-- in the Plaza Board Room. Team members present were Shirley Marshall, team leader; Chuck Taylor, president, Taylor Properties; Scott Johnson, architect; Jim Hendley, vice president for research; Toni Hess, provost; Andy Maxwell, chief financial officer; and Joyce Martin, chief executive officer, Foundations.

Work Session

Shirley Marshall opened the meeting and indicated that all team members were present. The team devoted the first half hour of the meeting to a working session designed to review a series of concepts relating the design of the Phase I building. Scott Johnson charted the pros and cons on each concept presented and will finalize the analysis that will guide the conceptual design of the Phase I building.

Project Goals and Process Review

Shirley Marshall reminded the team that the primary goal of this project was to complete the preliminary design work that Central University could use to develop state-of-the-art research laboratory and office facilities on the property designated as the research block. The team agreed that the highest and best use of the research block was for three separate buildings connected by an open plaza. All parking was moved from the research block to the block across the street on the east side. A 1,000-car parking deck was proposed for that site. All information collected to date has been processed and incorporated in the initial site plan options.

Site Plan Options

Chuck Taylor summarized the data collected and analyzed in the site evaluation. The topography of the site presents design challenges because there is a 50-foot difference in the highest and lowest points on the block. Slides detailing the four options were presented for the conceptual design of the facility. The team selected the horseshoe terrace as the preferred option, but recommended some modifications in the conceptual design.

Architectural Image Concepts

A series of architectural image concepts for the first building were critiqued. The feedback provided on the concepts will be used in preparing the building design to be presented at the next meeting.

After a general discussion on the progress on the project, the meeting was adjourned at 4:15 p.m. ↓2

Remove space after ⟶ _____

Shirley Marshall, Team Leader

WORD SCREEN

You are about to learn the leading word processing package available today. At the same time, you will continue to develop your keyboarding skills. You will use *Word*, an application of the *2007 Microsoft Office System©*, to create and format professional-looking documents. Most, if not all of you, will have completed the skill building activities on the previous page using *Keyboarding Pro DELUXE*.

Keyboarding Pro DELUXE users: If you are using *Keyboarding Pro DELUXE*, it will launch or open *Microsoft Word* automatically when you choose the first activity to be done in *Word*. See instructions on pages ix–xii.

Non-*Keyboarding Pro DELUXE* users: Start *Word* now.

1. Click the Start button at the bottom left corner of your screen and select *Word* from the programs listed.

2. You may also have an icon on your screen that you can double-click to launch *Word*.

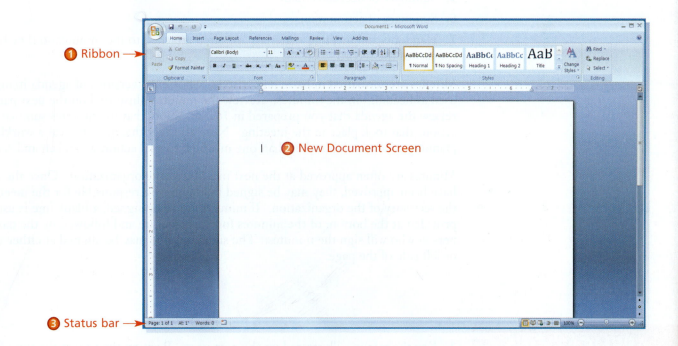

① Ribbon
② New Document Screen
③ Status bar

When you first use *Word*, you will note three distinct segments of the screen:

① The Ribbon containing the commands that you will use is located at the top of the screen.

② The New Document screen on which you will key your documents appears in the center of the screen.

③ The status bar, which gives information about the position in the document and enables you to view the document in different formats, is located at the bottom of the screen.

Study the entire screen on your computer for a few minutes; then you will work with the various segments.

MINUTES

Minutes provide a record of what occurred in a meeting. Two significantly different types of minutes may be prepared. Verbatim minutes provide a complete record of everything said in a meeting. Usually verbatim minutes are prepared only for very formal meetings or for meetings that have legal implications. Most organizations prefer to use minutes that capture the essential or very important information that needs to be recorded for future use. These minutes are often referred to as action minutes because they capture the decisions that are made and the actions that take place—such as assigning responsibilities to particular individuals and specifying deadlines for the responsibilities to be completed.

Typically minutes contain the following types of information:

1. Date, time, and place of the meeting
2. Name of the presiding officer or meeting leader
3. Names (may also include titles) of attendees
4. Meeting objectives
5. Summary of decisions made
6. Summary of action items
7. Handouts and meeting materials are often attached to the minutes so they become part of the record.

Minutes are formatted in basic report style. Shortened versions of agenda items are often used as headings in the minutes. Review the minutes illustrated on the next page; then review the agenda that you prepared in *103-d1*. Note that the minutes summarize the actions that took place in the meeting. Note also that this meeting was a working and planning type meeting rather than one in which formal action was taken and recorded.

Minutes are often approved at the next meeting of the organization. Once the minutes have been approved, they may be signed by the person responsible for the meeting or by the secretary of the organization. If minutes are to be signed, a blank line is usually provided at the bottom of the minutes for the signature and followed by the name of the person who will sign the minutes. The signature line may be aligned at either the right or left side of the page.

APPLICATIONS

104-d1

Minutes

1. Key the minutes illustrated on the next page. Position the title at the top of the page and apply Title style.
2. Key the subtitle and apply Subtitle style.
3. Apply Heading 3 style to all side headings.
4. At the bottom of the minutes, tap ENTER twice, set a left tab at 3.25", and use SHIFT + hyphen to key a signature line.
5. Remove the space after the signature line, and then key the name and title of the person who will sign the minutes.
6. Check and close. (*104-d1*)

KEY AND FORMAT TEXT AND PARAGRAPHS

In earlier lessons, you learned to key text using wordwrap. In this lesson and the next one, you will learn to format text and paragraphs.

- To begin a new paragraph, tap ENTER.
- To indent the first line of a paragraph to the first default tab, tap the TAB key.

| Insertion Point | To edit or format text, you must move the insertion point around with the mouse or use the arrow keys on the keyboard.

- To use the mouse, move the I-beam pointer to the desired position and click the left mouse button.

RIBBON BASICS

You key text using the keyboard. You format text using the commands contained on the **Ribbon**. The Ribbon has three basic components:

1 Tabs—located at the top of the Ribbon. Home, the first tab, has been selected.

Note that when you click a different tab, the options below the tab row change. Try clicking the Insert tab and the Page Layout tab. Note the types of activites that are included below each of these tabs. Click the Home tab again.

2 Groups—contain a number of related items. The names are positioned at the bottom of the Ribbon below each group. The group shown above is the *Font* group.

On the Home tab, the groups are Clipboard, Font, Paragraph, Styles, and Editing. These functions are commonly used while you are keying, formatting, and editing text.

3 Commands—the buttons, the boxes for keying information, and the menus that provide a choice of options. The command shown above is the *Font Color* command.

KEYBOARDING PRO DELUXE See References/Word Commands/Lesson 26

SELECT TEXT

To apply Font commands, you must first select the text to which you want to apply the command and then click that command.

- Click at the beginning of the text and drag the mouse over the text to select it.
- Double-clicking within a word will select that word.

To apply Paragraph commands, you must click in the paragraph or select it. **Note:** Each time you tap ENTER, *Word* begins a new paragraph.

LESSON 104 > Minutes

WARMUP 104a

Key each line, striving for control. Repeat if desired.

alphabet	1	Jeff and Gwen quickly analyzed the complex problem and solved it.
figures	2	Of the 20,473 square feet of office space, 16,598 is on Floor 16.
adjacent reaches	3	I saw her at an airport at a tropical resort leaving on a cruise.
easy	4	Andy and Blanche may make a map for a neighbor to go to the city.

| 1 | 2 | 3 | 4 | 5 | 6 | 7 | 8 | 9 | 10 | 11 | 12 | 13 |

SKILL BUILDING

104b Textbook Keying

1. Key each line once, concentrating on good keying techniques. Tap ENTER twice after each 2-line group.
2. Repeat if time permits.

adjacent key	5	Were other people as eager to participate as Guy and Junior were?
	6	Klara Bert has chalk on her hands; she stopped here to wash them.
direct reach	7	June and Hunter decided to bring that jumbo lunch for the group.
	8	Cecil and Kim sent my brother a nice kite for his fifth birthday.
one hand	9	Reece Lumpkin, in my opinion, deserved a red sweater as a reward.
	10	Jim agrees you'll get a greater reward only in a nonunion career.
balanced hand	11	Clement may blame us for the problems with the auditor if he can.
	12	Vickie or Rodney got a bicycle to go with a neighbor to the lake.

NEW FUNCTIONS

104c

INSERT TEXT FROM FILE

INSERT/TEXT/OBJECT/TEXT FROM FILE

Text that has been keyed and saved as a file can be inserted in other documents using the Insert Text from File command. This command is particularly useful in the preparation of long documents.

To insert text from a file:

1. Position the insertion point where you want to insert the file.
2. On the Insert menu, in the Text group, click Object.
3. Choose Text from File.

DRILL 1   TEXT FROM FILE   TEXT FROM FILE

1. In a new document, key the title **Repurposing Text**; then apply Title format.
2. Key the paragraph shown at the right.
3. On the line below the paragraph, insert *text from file* from your data files. (*104-drill1*)

Long documents such as minutes or reports may be keyed in sections as information becomes available and saved as separate files. Then the files can be inserted in the main document to complete it. Text used in previous documents can also be repurposed and used again in other documents.

1. Key your name in the New Document screen and tap ENTER.

2. Click the Home tab and hold the mouse over the items in the Font group to identify the command and note the short description of the function it performs. You will use some of these commands in the next drill.

3. Note that some of the commands such as *Font* and *Underline* have down arrows on the side of the command. Click the down arrow to see the menu of options that can be selected.

4. Click the Insert tab and the Page Layout tab and note the groups and commands that are located on these tabs.

5. Click the Home tab.

6. Leave the document open—keep it on your screen.

Note: If you need to leave this drill now, be sure to read the information on File Management on page 77 prior to exiting this drill and moving to the next activity. Otherwise, read the information that follows and continue with Drill 1 below.

HOME TAB COMMANDS

HOME TAB/FONT GROUP/FONT COMMANDS

TIP

Click the down arrow next to the font and the font size commands to select a different font and size. Also click the down arrow to select double underline.

The path (Home Tab/Font Group/Font Commands) including the tab, group, and commands is provided for most functions to assist you in locating them easily. To follow the path: Click the tab (Home); then look for the group label (Font) at the bottom of the ribbon, and select the command (Bold).

① Font ② Font Size ③ Grow the Font ④ Shrink the Font
⑤ Bold ⑥ Italic ⑦ Underline ⑧ Text Highlight Color ⑨ Font Color

1. In the open document below your name, key the phrases or sentences, including the information in parentheses shown below. Do not apply formats.

2. Select your name and highlight it in yellow.

3. Apply the formats shown in parentheses to each sentence or phrase. Remember to select the text before formatting it. If the command has a down arrow, click it to select the appropriate option.

4. Select Font Formats and click Shrink the Font twice; then click Grow the Font once.

5. Leave the document open—keep it on your screen.

Font Formats (Bold, Times New Roman, 16 point)

I read, *Learn to be Productive*, in the <u>Office Productivity Journal</u>. (Italic; then Underline)

The balance was <u>$45,750</u>; the loss was $12,398. (Double Underline; then red font color)

Compensation Committee Meeting

Agenda, August 12, 20--, 9:30 a.m. – 12:30 p.m.

Call to Order .... Ashley Wexford, Chair

Approval of Minutes, July 10, 20-- Meeting .... Ashley Wexford

Executive Session .... Committee

Review of Compensation Report and Recommendations .... Glenn Hanson, Consultant

    Review of current-year executive compensation based on targets

    Executive Incentive Plan goals for next year

    Executive compensation projections for next year

    Salary and benefits projection for next year

    Recommendations from CEO .... Mark Addison

Compensation Philosophy Statement .... Committee

Compensation Discussion and Analysis for Proxy Statement .... Olivia Matthews

Directors' Stock Plan Update .... Christopher Hay

Other Business .... Committee

Executive Session .... Committee

    Approval of CEO Compensation for Recommendation to the Board .... Committee

Adjournment

TIP

Read the information on file management carefully. The ability to manage files effectively is a very important career skill.

File management refers to saving documents in an organized manner so that they can be easily located and used again. Files may be managed by software or by the individual user. *Keyboarding Pro DELUXE* manages files automatically. It opens the appropriate document, saves, checks, and closes it. However, if you wish to use your word processing skills in other classes or in any situation other than your keyboarding class, you will have to learn how to manage your own files effectively.

An effective way to manage files is to create folders to store related documents. An important part of file management is naming files and folders effectively. For example, it is more effective to store all documents that relate to your English class in one folder and to your Economics class in a different folder than to store them all in one folder.

If you are not using *Keyboarding Pro DELUXE*, create a new folder for each module of the textbook. Documents for this module should be saved in a folder named *Module 3*. You are working in Lesson 26 on a document named Drill 1. Therefore a logical filename would be *26-drill1*. It is a short but easily identifiable name. You can store a file in a variety of locations, such as to a folder on your hard drive, a CD, a flash drive, a disk, a shared drive on a network, on the desktop, or to other removable storage media. Your instructor will indicate the location you should use for storing files in this class if you are not using *Keyboarding Pro DELUXE*.

If you are using *Keyboarding Pro DELUXE*, your software will save your file with the correct name. Note in the next activities that *Keyboarding Pro DELUXE* users follow different procedures for saving, closing, and opening documents than non-*Keyboarding Pro DELUXE* users.

OFFICE BUTTON

OFFICE BUTTON/COMMAND

The Office button located in the upper-left corner of the Ribbon provides you with all of the commands that you need to work with files. When you click the Office button, a menu drops down with the commands shown on the left and the most recently opened documents on the right.

Take a few minutes to review some of the options on the Office Button menu shown at the right. For example, you can create a new document, open an existing document, save a document, or print a document from this menu. Note that some of the options have arrows that display other functions. Click the arrow next to the Print icon and note the options.

	Recent Documents
New	1 master plan
Open	2 community park
Save	3 26-drill1
	4 Unbound report pages 1 2 and references p...
Save As ▶	5 Standard memo
	6 Leftbound report
Print ▶	7 Block letter (open punctuation)
	8 Standard memo with distribution list
Prepare ▶	9 Modified block letter (mixed punctuation)
	Cover Page
	Automatic table of contents

TIP

The Office button is available from all tabs on the ribbon.

Note: The normal path (tab/group/command) is not used because the Office button is available for all tabs on the Ribbon. Remember to click the Office button any time you are working with files—New, Open, Close, Save, Save As, or Print.

Set tabs

2"

Master Plan for Research Facilities

Planning and Data Analysis Meeting Agenda, February 15, 20--

2:00 – 2:30 Work Session—Design Options .... Team

2:30 – 2:50 Project Goals and Process Review .... Shirley Marshall

      Develop State-of-the-Art Research Laboratories and Offices

Left tab 1.0"   Develop Concept for "Highest and Best Use" for Research Block

      Create an Architectural Image for the Project

      Process to Date

        Needs Assessment   Remove extra space

Left tab 1.5"   Data Collection

        Site Evaluation

        Best Practices for Research Laboratories

2:50 – 3:20 Site Plan Options .... Chuck Taylor

      Site Evaluation Conclusions

      Options for Buildings on Block

        Central Courtyard   Remove extra space

        Dense Linear Design

        Horseshoe Terrace

        Perimeter Buildings with Central Parking

3:20 – 3:50 Architectural Image Concepts .... Scott Johnson

3:50 – 4:15 General Discussion .... Team

6.5" right leader tab

SAVE AND SAVE AS

OFFICE BUTTON/SAVE OR SAVE AS

You will use the Save and Save As commands on the Office Button menu to preserve your documents for future use. If you are saving a document for the first time, clicking either the Save or Save As button will display the Save As dialog box shown below.

To save a document:

1. Click the Office Button and then Save As to display the Save As dialog box.

2. In the Save As dialog box, click the arrow and select the location you wish to store your file. If you need to create a new folder, click the Create New Folder button on the right to display the New Folder dialog box.

3. Key the name of the folder in the Name box ❸ and click OK.

4. Key the name of the file in File name box ❹; leave the default Word Document in the Save as type box; and click Save ❺.

Once you have saved a document, you can just click the Save button and it will save the latest changes to the document in the same location with the same name. If you wish to make a copy of the document, click the Save As button and give the document a new name.

SAVE DOCUMENT USING KEYBOARDING PRO DELUXE

To save a document using *Keyboarding Pro DELUXE* without checking it, click the Back button. This option is normally used for work in progress.

To error-check a document and save it, click the Check button. Then review your results and close the window.

Note: For non-*Keyboarding Pro DELUXE* users, the filenames are shown in parentheses after all drills and documents.

DRILL 1 continued   **SAVE DOCUMENT USING WORD**

1. With Drill 1 open, click the Office button to display the File menu.

2. Click Save or Save As to display the Save As dialog box.

3. Select the location you wish to save the file.

4. Click the Create New Folder button and create a new folder named *Module 3*.

5. Key the filename **26-drill1** and click Save.

6. Leave the document open.

DOCUMENT DESIGN

103c

AGENDAS

The design of an agenda depends on the formality of the meeting and the customs and traditions of the organization. Both the format and the level of detail will vary depending on the organization.

Agendas generally have three or four components.

1. Heading providing information about the meeting
2. List of the topics to be discussed at the meeting
3. Name of the person or group responsible for leading the discussion of each topic
4. Amount of time allocated for the topic (optional)

Many organizations believe that allocating the specific time for each topic helps to keep the meeting on schedule and ensures that the amount of time allocated correlates with the importance of the topic. Other organizations believe that predicting the exact amount of time needed for a topic is difficult and may cut off important discussion or may extend unnecessary discussion simply because time is remaining.

Meeting materials may be attached to the agenda or may be distributed separately. If they are attached, they are usually indicated in parentheses next to the agenda item, e.g., (Attachment 1).

The format varies on the length of an agenda. Position the title of a short agenda at about 2". Position the title of a long agenda at 1" or 1.5" to fit the agenda on one page if possible.

Two different types of agendas are illustrated on the next two pages. The first agenda allocates time for each topic and is not as formal as the second. This type of agenda was used in a client meeting by an architectural firm planning the development of research laboratories on an entire block of city property.

The second agenda does not include time, but includes a formal call to order, approval of previous meeting minutes, and adjournment. This type of agenda was used by a Compensation Committee of a Board of Directors of a financial services organization.

103-d1

Agenda

1. Key the agenda shown on the next page. Position the title at approximately 2" and the subtitle directly below the title.
2. Set a left tab at 1" and a second left tab at 1.5"; then set a right leader tab (Style 2) at 6.5". Set tabs on the line below the subtitle.
3. Remove the extra space after the paragraph for the items positioned under main topics as illustrated.
4. Use an en dash to separate times (a space hyphen space will convert to an en dash.)
5. Check and close. (*103-d1*)

103-d2

Agenda

1. Key the agenda shown on page 467. Set tabs as marked. Remove the 1" tab.
2. In the subtitle, insert a hyphen with a space before and after it. *Word* will commant this to an en-dash.
3. Check and close. (*103-d2*)

CLOSE DOCUMENT

OFFICE BUTTON/CLOSE

You can close a document and leave *Word* open, or you can close a document and exit *Word*. If you have only one document open, and you click the Close button at the top right side of the screen, you will close the document and exit *Word*. If you have more than one document open, the Close button will close the document only.

To close a document and leave *Word* open:

1. Click the Office button ❶.
2. Click the Close button ❷ at the bottom of the menu.

NEW DOCUMENT

OFFICE BUTTON/NEW

The New button on the Office Button menu displays the New Document dialog box. Note the options that are available.

To create a new *Word* document:

1. Click the Office button ❶ to display the drop-down menu.
2. On the Office Button menu, click New ❷ to display the New Document dialog box.
3. Click the Blank Document button ❸; then click the Create button at the bottom of the dialog box.

DRILLS 1 AND 2 — CHECK DOCUMENT AND OPEN NEW DOCUMENT USING KEYBOARDING PRO DELUXE

1. Check the document and review the report; close the window.
2. On the Lesson menu, select the next activity 26-drill 2 to open it.
3. Key your name at the top of the document and tap ENTER.
4. Key the document name **26-drill2** and tap ENTER.
5. Key the following sentence:
   This is a new document I have created.
6. Check and close the document.

DRILLS 1 AND 2 — CLOSE DOCUMENT AND OPEN NEW DOCUMENT (NON-KEYBOARDING PRO DELUXE USERS)

1. Proofread the open document for errors.
2. Save and close *26-drill1*.
3. Open a new document.
4. Key your name on the first line and tap ENTER.
5. Key the document name **26-drill2** and tap ENTER.
6. Key the following sentence:
   This is a new document I have created.
7. Check, save, and, close the document (*26-drill2* in your *Module 3* folder).

Meeting Management

LEARNING OUTCOMES

- Build keyboarding skill.
- Format agendas.
- Format minutes.
- Format itineraries.
- Prepare labels and name badges.
- Prepare meeting management guides.

LESSON 103   Agendas

WARMUP 103a

Key each line, striving for control. Repeat if desired.

alphabet	1	Our unexpected freezing weather quickly killed Jo's mauve shrubs.
figures	2	Paula has moved from 8195 East 26 Street to 1730 West 148 Street.
double letters	3	Betty fooled Annabell by hitting a ball across the narrow valley.
easy	4	I fish for a quantity of smelt and may wish for aid to land them.

| 1 | 2 | 3 | 4 | 5 | 6 | 7 | 8 | 9 | 10 | 11 | 12 | 13 |

SKILL BUILDING

103b Timed Writing

Key two 3' timings; work for speed and try to increase your base rate.

all letters

	gwam	3'

For many years, readers who had examined carefully and chosen   4 | 51
a particular book had just one question to answer: Do you want   9 | 55
to purchase a hardcover or a paperback book? It was assumed that   13 | 60
books would be purchased from a retail outlet, such as a bookstore.   18 | 64
Currently books are being marketed and sold online. The book itself   22 | 69
is still printed on paper.   24 | 71

With the new technology that is on the market today, a third   29 | 75
alternative, the electronic or the so-called e-book, is emerging.   33 | 80
E-books are sold in digitized form. The book must be read from the   38 | 84
website on a computer or on a special device designed for reading   42 | 89
e-books. Some people, however, do not like to read from the computer.   47 | 93

3' | 1 | 2 | 3 | 4 |

OPEN AN EXISTING DOCUMENT

OFFICE BUTTON/OPEN

 ❶ On some occasions, you will want to use documents that you have previously prepared and saved.

Keyboarding Pro DELUXE users: To open a document that you have previously prepared, simply select that activity from the Lesson menu. If you are returning to a document you have already begun, then choose Open existing document. Non-*Keyboarding Pro DELUXE* users always follow *Word* directions.

TIP

If you have recently used the document you are opening, it will be listed in the Recent Documents on the Office Button menu. You can double-click the filename to open it.

To open an existing document:

1. Click the Office button to display the menu.

2. Click the Open button ❶ to display the Open dialog box.

3. Select the location where you saved the file. Click on the appropriate folder ❷, select the filename ❸, and click Open ❹. You may also double-click the filename to open it.

-or-

If you have recently worked with the document, double-click it on the list of Recent Documents ❺.

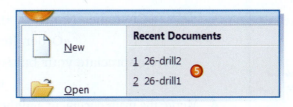

PRINT A DOCUMENT USING KEYBOARDING PRO DELUXE

Check the document; then print and close the checked document. If you wish to print a closed document, choose Print Document from the Document Options dialog box.

102-d2

Sort and Filter Mail Merge Document

 102-D2DATA

Prepare form letters for your patients who are 45 days delinquent on their payments.

1. Save a new document as *102-d2main*.
2. Prepare the form letter below as the main document. Use block letter style and open punctuation. Send a copy of this letter to **Justin Langberg**.
3. Choose the file *102-d2data* as the data source.
4. Sort the data source by ZIP Code in ascending order. Filter to select those patients whose Days Past Due field is greater than or equal to 45 days.
5. Merge the main document and the data source.
6. Continue to the next document. (*102-d2*)

February 23, 20--

«AddressBlock»

«GreetingLine»

Your unpaid balance of $«Unpaid_Balance» is now past due. We have requested payment from you on «No_Contacts_Made» occasions; however, we have received neither payment nor an explanation as to why payment has not been made.

Although we have no desire to cancel your credit privileges, we are forced to disallow any increase to your balance until payment of the past-due amount is paid. Future dental services for you and your family can be provided on a cash basis only.

Please call me at 305-555-0135 and make arrangements for paying your overdue amount. If we do not hear from you regarding a revised payment schedule, please pay $«Minimum_Payment», a minimum payment. This payment must be received by March 20.

Sincerely | Paul Vanzandt | Office Manager | xx

102-d3

Mailing Labels

 102-D3DATA

Prepare cards for the individuals who have ordered bakery goods from your organization.

1. Save a new document as *102-d3main*. Use the file *102-d3data* as the data source.
2. Prepare the note card below (Avery US Letter 3259) as the main document.
3. Include the fields shown. Key each item on a separate line. Format the card attractively. Sort by Delivery Date in ascending order.

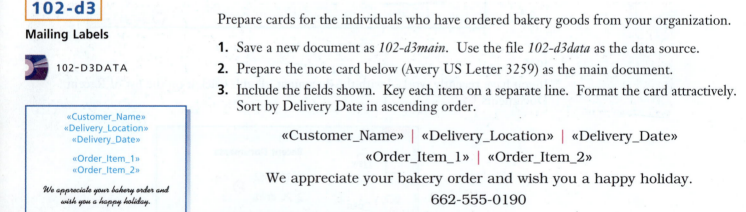

«Customer_Name» | «Delivery_Location» | «Delivery_Date»

«Order_Item_1» | «Order_Item_2»

We appreciate your bakery order and wish you a happy holiday.

662-555-0190

4. Merge the main document and the data source.
5. Save the test and close it. (*102-d3*)

CHECKPOINT ➡

Congratulations! You have successfully completed the lessons in Module 16. To check your understanding and for more practice, complete the objective assessment and performance assessment located on the textbook website at www.collegekeyboarding.com.

PRINT AND PRINT PREVIEW

OFFICE BUTTON/PRINT

The menu from the Office button is used for previewing and printing documents as well as for saving documents. Hold the mouse over the arrow next to the Print button ❶ and note that the right side of the menu displays three options to preview or print your document.

Print ❷ displays the Print dialog box, which allows you to select the printer you want to use, the number of copies, and other options.

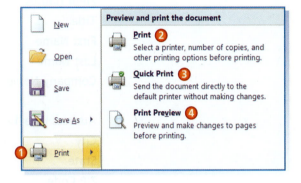

Quick Print ❸ prints one copy directly to the default printer.

Print Preview ❹ displays the document exactly like it will look printed. Once you have previewed a document, you must click the Close Print Preview button to return to your document. Note you can also Print from the Print Preview toolbar.

To print one copy of a document on the default printer:

1. On the Office Button menu, click the arrow next to Print ❶.
2. Select Quick Print ❸.

To preview a document:

1. On the Office Button menu, point to Print or click the arrow next to Print ❶.
2. Click Print Preview ❹ to display both the document as it will look printed and the Print Preview toolbar.

3. Note some of the options available:
   a. View one or two pages of a document ❺ at one time.
   b. Zoom ❻ in closer or out wider.
   c. Print ❼ from this toolbar.
   d. Close Print Preview ❽ to return to your document.

102-d1

Prepare the main document and data source for a form letter to participants of a summer workshop. You will need to edit your data source after you create it.

1. Save a new document as *102-d1main*.

2. Create the data source. Save it as *102-d1data*.

Field names	Record 1	Record 2	Record 3
Title	Mr.	Ms.	Ms.
First Name	Phillip	Anele	Anna
Last Name	Lancaster	Nyiri	Skelton
Company Name	Fulton High School	Curtis Middle School	Curtis Middle School
Address Line 1	35 Wallace Circle	16060 Aspen Road	16060 Aspen Road
City	Norfolk	Richmond	Richmond
State	VA	VA	VA
ZIP Code	23501-5126	27173-3844	27173-3844
Date	June 15–16	June 23–24	June 23–24
Room	204	205	205

3. Move Ms. Skelton to the June 15–16 workshop. Change Mr. Lancaster's address to 89 Castle Road.

4. Key the main document (mixed punctuation style) and insert the merge fields in it. Add notations as needed. Save the changes. Be sure the date updates automatically.

5. Merge the main document and the data source.

6. Continue to the next document. (*102-d1*)

Date

«AddressBlock»

Dear «First_Name»:

I am delighted that you will be attending the Principles and Applications of Web Design Workshop on «Date» at Braswell Community College. Please arrive at Room «Room» of the Harper-Kock Union Building at 8 a.m. for registration and a brief orientation.

As the workshop title indicates, the objectives include learning principles of Web design and applying these principles in realistic exercises. The first day is filled with outstanding assignments highlighting important principles of Web design. During the second day, you will team with one of your colleagues to plan and design impressive Web pages for «Company_Name». Do take time before coming to the workshop to locate materials from your office that you will need to create these Web pages.

Directions to Hathorn Hall, the residence hall designated for summer workshop participants, are enclosed. You may check in at Hathorn from 8 a.m. to 10 p.m. Housing payments can be made at the residence hall.

«First_Name», should you have any questions about the workshop, please call me at 555-0134. I look forward to your being a part of our workshop series.

Sincerely | Jane D. Gunter | Workshop Coordinator

1. Open Drill 1 (*26-drill1*); key **Drill 3** on the line below the last line of text.
2. Preview the document; then close Print Preview.
3. *Keyboarding Pro DELUXE* users: Use *Keyboarding Pro DELUXE* to print the document.
4. Click the Office button to display the menu again. Use Quick Print to print one copy of the document using the default printer.
5. Non *Keyboarding Pro DELUXE* users: Save the document with a new name and close it. Use the filename that is shown in parentheses. (*26-drill4*)

EXIT WORD

1. Display the Microsoft Office menu button and click the Exit *Word* button at the lower right side of the menu.

X **E**xit Word

-or-

2. Click the Close button at the top right of the screen.

APPLICATIONS

26-d1

Create a New Document

1. Key your name on the first line and then key **26-d1** on the next line.
2. Key the following sentences using the *Word 2007* defaults; then apply the font formats as they appear in the sentences. Do not apply the formats until you have keyed all sentences. Tap ENTER after each sentence.

> **TIP**
>
> Text appearing in bold within directions is keyed (e.g. **26-d1**). Do not format the text in bold unless specified.

I have changed the font on this sentence to Times New Roman, 12-point type.

This sentence has Gray-25% highlighting.

Our loss this year was $63,946; last year our net profit was $175,820.

This sentence illustrates the use of **bold**, *italic*, and single underline.

Grow this sentence to 16 point; then shrink this part to 10 point.

3. Preview, proofread, and print the document.
4. Check and close. (*26-d1*)
5. Exit *Keyboarding Pro DELUXE* or *Word*.

Reminder: Non-*Keyboarding Pro DELUXE* users must open a document for each activity. After you have completed an activity, proofread, preview, print, save the document with the name provided in parentheses, and close the document.

WARMUP 102a

Key each line, striving for control. Repeat if desired.

alphabet 1 Zan saw Jeffrey exit the park very quickly with a mean black dog.

figures 2 The stock price has increased 24.50 points to 189.75 in 36 weeks.

double letters 3 Pattie and Tripp meet at the swimming pool after football drills.

easy 4 Did the firm or their neighbor own the auto with signal problems?

| 1 | 2 | 3 | 4 | 5 | 6 | 7 | 8 | 9 | 10 | 11 | 12 | 13 |

SKILL BUILDING

102b Timed Writing
Key two 3' timed writings.

gwam   3'   5'

Most people today have become very health conscious. These	4	2	52
individuals worry about the bad effects of a diet that has	8	5	55
far too much fat and a lifestyle that does not include very much	13	8	57
exercise. However, many of those people never get past the stage	17	10	60
of worrying. Others just try to find a quick solution to the	21	13	63
problem. They try zany diets and easy exercise programs. The	25	15	65
real solution is to get in the habit of eating correctly and doing	30	18	68
exercise on a regular basis. The results are well worth the effort.	34	21	70
The combination of exercising on a regular basis and eating	38	23	73
properly produces much better results than either of these activi-	43	26	76
ties can produce by itself. An effective diet includes food from	47	28	78
all of the major food groups. Eating food that has a very high	51	31	81
fiber content and a very low fat content can help to prevent a	56	33	83
number of diseases. Not eating a meal to save a few calories is	60	36	86
not a very good idea. A good exercise program has several important	65	39	89
characteristics. Each session lasts approximately twenty minutes	69	41	91
and occurs at least three times a week. Also, the activity should	73	44	94
be fast enough to increase your heart rate. Walking at a fast pace	78	47	97
is one of the best and one of the most desirable activities that	82	49	99
you can do.	83	50	100

3' | 1 | 2 | 3 | 4 |
5' | 1 | 2 | 3 |

APPLICATIONS

102c

Assessment

Continue

Check

With *Keyboarding Pro DELUXE*: When you complete a document, proofread it, check the spelling, and preview for placement. When you are completely satisfied, click the Continue button to move to the next document. Click the Check button when you are ready to error-check the test. Review and/or print the document analysis results.

Without *Keyboarding Pro DELUXE*: Key the documents in sequence. When time has been called, proofread all documents again and identify errors.

LESSON 27

Formatting Essentials

Key each line, striving for control. Repeat if desired.

alphabet	1	Alex, a smart student, saw five zebras quickly jump a high fence.
figure	2	Kyoko mailed Invoices 73981 and 67358 on 4/15/2006 at 4:29 today.
double letters	3	Jarrett cheerfully killed millions of bugs near the pool at noon.
easy	4	Jane may go to visit the lake and fish with the girls? May I go?

NEW FUNCTIONS

27b

PARAGRAPH FORMATS

HOME/PARAGRAPH/COMMAND

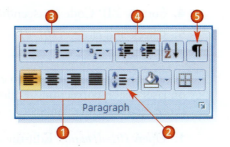

In Lesson 26, you worked with formats in the Font group on the Home tab. In this lesson you will work with some of the formats in the Paragraph group on the Home tab. Note that some of the commands are clustered together in this group.

① **Alignment commands**—Align Left, Center, Align Right, and Justify—specify how text lines up.

② **Line Spacing**—determines the amount of space between lines of text.

③ **Bullets and Numbering**—formats for lists of information.

④ **Decrease and Increase Indent**—moves all lines of a paragraph to the right or the left.

⑤ **Show/Hide**—displays paragraph markings and other nonprinting characters.

Paragraph formats apply to an entire paragraph. Each time you tap ENTER, *Word* inserts a paragraph mark and starts a new paragraph. Thus, a paragraph may consist of a partial line or of several lines. You must be able to see where paragraphs begin and end to format them.

SHOW/HIDE

HOME/PARAGRAPH/SHOW/HIDE

Turning on the Show/Hide button displays all nonprinting characters such as paragraph markers (¶) or spaces (..). The Show/Hide button appears highlighted when it is active. Nonprinting characters can be turned off by clicking the Show/Hide button again.

The Holland Eye Center invites you to attend a special seminar sponsored for our patients who are potential candidates for laser vision correction. This seminar held at our clinic on «Date» at 7 p.m. will feature a panel of doctors and patients and a live laser vision correction procedure. A question/answer period will also provide an opportunity to have all your questions answered by these laser vision correction experts. You will also have an opportunity to enter your name in a drawing for a complimentary laser vision correction procedure to be presented at the close of the seminar.

Would you like to join the millions of people who have chosen laser vision correction and be free of the daily hassles of glasses and contact lenses? Get started today by completing the enclosed reservation card indicating you will attend the seminar on «Date» and learn for yourself the details of laser vision correction.

Sincerely | Edward S. Vickery, M.D. | xx | Enclosure

4. Sort by ZIP Code in ascending order. Merge the data source and the main document.

5. Check and close. (*101-d1*)

101-d2

Edit Data Source

Several changes require you to edit the data source for the patients invited to the seminar on laser vision correction. Follow the directions below to make the edits and to print only those records with changes.

1. Open *101-d1main*. Edit the data source as follows:
   - Invite Dr. Jantz to the February 25 seminar.
   - Ms. Wiseman's new address is **235 N. Fifth Street, Omak, WA 98841-4958**.

2. Add two new records for the February 25 seminar.

   Mrs. Darlene Chism   Mr. James Lee
   830 Yorkville Street   332 Matilda Road
   Tonasket, WA 98855-0495   Omak, WA 98841-1230

3. Filter to select records of patients invited to the February 25 seminar. Merge to a new document.

4. Check and close. (*101-d2*)

101-d3

Envelopes

Prepare envelopes for all the patients invited to the laser vision correction seminar. **Reminder:** Clear the filter used in *101-d2* above.

1. Prepare envelopes for the records stored in the data source *101-d1data*.

2. Sort by ZIP Code in ascending order.

3. Check and close. (*101-d3*)

101-d4

Name Badges

All the patients you invited to the laser vision correction seminar have agreed to attend. Prepare name badges for their use at the seminar.

1. Prepare name badges (Avery 5095) for the records stored in the data source *101-d1data*. Include the first name and last name fields on the name badge. Sort by last name in ascending order. Format attractively (e.g., font, size, alignment, etc.).

2. Check and close. (*101-d4*)

ALIGNMENT

HOME/PARAGRAPH/ALIGN TEXT LEFT, CENTER, ALIGN TEXT RIGHT, OR JUSTIFY

DISCOVER

Enhanced Tool Tips
Position the mouse pointer over a command to display the name of the function, a description of it, and the keyboard shortcut to apply (if available).

B *I* U ▾ abc x₂ x² Aa ▾

Font

Bold (Ctrl+B)

Make the selected text bold.

① **Align Text Left**—all lines begin at left margin.

② **Center**—all lines are centered.

③ **Align Text Right**—all lines are aligned at the right margin.

④ **Justify**—all lines are aligned at both the left and right margins.

To apply alignment formats:

1. Turn on Show/Hide.
2. Click in a single paragraph or select multiple paragraphs to which a format is to be applied.
3. Click the format to be applied.

③ Student's·Name¶

② PARAGRAPH·FORMATS¶

① Note·that·my·name·has·Align·Text·Right·format·applied·to·it.··The·title· has·Center·format·applied.··This·paragraph·uses·the·default·Align·Text· Left·format.¶

④ This·last·paragraph·is·formatted·using·Justify.··Justify·aligns·text·at·both· margins.··Additional·space·is·added·to·force·the·text·to·align·evenly·at· the·right·margin.··The·only·line·in·a·justified·paragraph·that·may·not·end· at·the·right·margin·is·the·last·line·of·the·paragraph.¶

DRILL 1   ALIGN PARAGRAPHS

1. Key your name and tap ENTER.
2. Click the Home tab and hold the mouse over each command in the Paragraph group to identify the command and note the description of the function it performs.
3. Some commands such as Line Spacing and Bullets have down arrows next to the command. Click the arrow to see the options that can be selected.
4. Key the document shown above. Your name replaces *Student's Name*.
5. Format the title in uppercase, bold, 14-point Cambria font.
6. Format the document with the alignments shown. The red numbers illustrate alignment styles. Do not key them.
7. Preview, check, and close. (*27-drill1*)

DRILL 3 — MERGE LABELS

1. Follow the directions provided on the previous page to prepare address labels for the data source file *98-drill1data*.

2. Check and save. (*101-drill3*) **Reminder:** Resave the main document *101-drill3labels* after all steps of the Step by Step Mail Merge Wizard have been completed.

DRILL 4 — MERGE LABELS

1. Prepare file folder labels (5066-File Folder) for the records stored *98-d1data*, the data source file you created in Lesson 98. Open a new document and save it as *101-drill4labels*.

2. Sort by last name in ascending order.

3. From the More Items list, select the following merge fields. Select both lines and remove extra space between the lines.

   «Last_Name» «First_Name» «Title»
   «Company_Name»

4. Check and close. (*101-drill4*)

APPLICATIONS

101-d1

MAIL MERGE

The Holland Eye Center is hosting two seminars to inform their patients about laser vision correction. Prepare the form letters for the records shown below.

1. Save a new document as *101-d1main*.

2. Create the data source. Save as *101-d1data*.

Field names	Record 1	Record 2	Record 3
Title	Mr.	Dr.	Ms.
First Name	Angelo	Karen	Mary
Last Name	Seay	Jantz	Wiseman
Address Line 1	P.O. Box 88	137 Sonoma Drive	539 Swoope Avenue
City	Tonasket	Omak	Tonasket
State	WA	WA	WA
ZIP Code	98855-3847	98841-9681	98855-2039
Date	January 31	January 31	February 25

3. Key the main document and insert the merge fields in it. Use open punctuation. Save the changes.

«AddressBlock»

«GreetingLine»

Do you ever imagine being able to see the alarm clock when you wake up? Do you ever imagine no more hassles of daily contact lens maintenance? Perhaps you may have imagined playing your favorite sport with complete peripheral vision—no fogging or slipping glasses. Millions of people across the world have chosen laser vision correction as an alternative to glasses and contact lenses. They now are enjoying these freedoms that you have only imagined.

continued

BULLETS AND NUMBERING

HOME/PARAGRAPH/BULLETS AND NUMBERING

Numbering is used for lists of items that are in sequence, whereas bullets are used for an unordered listing. Bullets can be converted to numbers by selecting the list and choosing numbers or vice versa. Different styles are available for both bullets and numbers.

To apply Bullets and Numbering:

1. Key the list.
2. Select the list and click either the Bullets or Numbering command.

To select a different format for Bullets and Numbering:

1. Click the down arrow on either the Bullets or the Numbering command to display the library of styles.
2. Select the desired style.

<table>
<tr><td colspan="2">**DRILL 2**</td><td colspan="2">**APPLY BULLETS AND NUMBERING**</td></tr>
</table>

1. Key the two lists shown below before applying formats; use default spacing.

2. Apply Square bullets to the first list below the heading Favorite Puppies. Bold the headings.

3. Apply numbers to the list below the heading *Pet Nutrition*; select the first option from the Numbering Library.

4. Preview the document; check and close it. (*27-drill2*)

Favorite Puppies
Cairn Terrier
Cavalier King Charles Spaniel
Shih Tzu

Pet Nutrition
Consult your veternarian and select the proper type of food.
Monitor portions carefully.
Provide appropriate treats.

1. Follow the directions provided on the previous page to prepare envelopes for the data source *98-drill1data*.

2. Merge the main document and the data source.

3. Check and close. (*101-drill1*)

1. Prepare envelopes for the records stored in data source *98-d1data*. Open a new document and save as *101-d2Envelope*. From the More items list, select the following merge fields and arrange as shown here:

   Title First Name Last Name
   Company Name
   Address Line 1
   City, State ZIP Code

2. Sort by ZIP Code in ascending order.

3. Check and close. (*101-drill2*)

MERGE LABELS

MAILINGS/START MAIL MERGE/START MAIL MERGE

Labels designed for printers are available in all sizes and for many purposes, including file folder labels, mailing labels, name badges, and business cards. The data source is often used for merging letters, registration forms, envelopes, and numerous types of labels. Merging labels is very similar to merging envelopes.

To create labels:

1. Open a new document and save with an appropriate filename. (For Drill 3, save it as *101-drill3main*.)

2. From the Mailings tab, in the Start Mail Merge group, click Start Mail Merge. Click Step by Step Merge Wizard.

3. Under Select document type, choose Labels. Then click Next: Starting document.

4. Under Select starting document, choose Change document layout.

5. Under Change document layout, click Label options. Choose Avery US Letter from the label vendor list and 5160-Address from the product number list. Click OK. Click Next: Select recipients.

6. Under Select recipients, click Use an existing list. Under Use an existing list, click Browse. From the appropriate disk drive, select *98-drill1data*. The Mail Merge Recipients dialog box displays the records. Click OK. Click Arrange your labels.

7. Under Arrange your labels, click <<Address Block>>. Remove the extra spacing between the address lines. (Click More Items to select the merge fields individually for the address block.) Resave the main document. (*101-drill3main*)

8. Under Replicate labels, click Update all labels to replicate the <<AddressBlock>> merge field on each label on the page. Click Next.

9. From Preview your labels, click the navigation buttons to preview envelopes if needed. (If changes in the data source are needed, click Edit Recipient List.) Click Next: Preview your labels.

10. From Complete the merge, click Edit individual labels. Click All; then OK. The merged labels will appear on the screen.

LINE SPACING OPTIONS

HOME/PARAGRAPH/LINE SPACING

The default line spacing for *Word 2007* is 1.15. Note the options that are displayed by clicking the down arrow on the Line Spacing button. Previous versions used 1.0 as single spacing (SS) and 2.0 as double spacing (DS). The 1.15 default is treated the same as single-spacing; it just allows a little more space between lines of type. The default amount of space after each paragraph is 10 points. Note that you can remove space before or after a paragraph.

	1.0
✓	1.15
	1.5
	2.0
	2.5
	3.0
	Line Spacing Options...
≣	Add Space Before Paragraph
≣	Remove Space After Paragraph

To change line spacing:

1. Position the insertion point in the paragraph whose spacing you wish to change.
2. Click the Line Spacing command and select the desired spacing.

Note the differences between 1.15 spacing ❶, 1.0 spacing ❷, and 2.0 spacing shown below ❸. Also note the amount of space (10 points) after paragraphs ❹.

❶ These first two paragraphs are keyed using the default spacing of 1.15. The extra space between the lines makes text easier to read.

10 points ❹

❶ Note that tapping enter to move to the next paragraph adds additional space between the paragraphs. The amount of space added is 10 points.

❷ Note in this paragraph and in the fourth paragraph shown below that the spacing has been changed to single spacing or 1.0 spacing.

❷ The lines of text are closer together. More text can be placed on one page when single spacing is used to format a document.

❸ The fifth and sixth paragraphs are keyed using double spacing or

2.0 spacing. When double spacing is used, paragraphs are indented.

10 points ❹

❸ The use of double spacing is likely to decline since the default

provides enough space between the lines to enhance reading.

LESSON 101

Merge with Envelopes and Labels

WARMUP 101a

Key each line, striving for control. Repeat if desired.

alphabet 1 Jacky was given a bronze plaque for the extra work he did for me.

fig/sym 2 Order 12 pairs of #43 skis at $75.59 each for a total of $919.08.

3rd/4th fingers 3 Zane, Sally, and Max quit polo to swim six laps and work puzzles.

easy 4 Claudia and I do handiwork at both the downtown and lake chapels.

| 1 | 2 | 3 | 4 | 5 | 6 | 7 | 8 | 9 | 10 | 11 | 12 | 13 |

NEW FUNCTIONS

101b

MERGE ENVELOPES

MAILINGS/START MAIL MERGE/START MAIL MERGE

Envelopes can be merged from the data source. When printing envelopes, you will need to know the type of envelope feeder your printer uses. In this lesson, you will create #10 landscape envelopes (standard business envelope).

To create envelopes:

1. Open a new document and save it with an appropriate name, e.g., *101-drill1envelope*.

2. From the Mailings tab, in the Start Mail Merge group, click Start Mail Merge. Click Step by Step Merge Wizard.

3. Under Select document type, choose Envelopes. Click Next: Starting document.

4. Under Select starting document, click Change document layout. Click Next: Select recipients.

5. Under Change document layout, click Envelope options. The Envelope Options dialog box displays. The Size 10 envelope is the default. Click OK. Then click Next: Select recipients.

6. Under Select recipients, click Use an existing list. Under Use an existing list, choose Browse. From the appropriate disk drive, select *98-drill1data*, the data source created in Lesson 98. The Mail Merge Recipients dialog box displays the records. Click OK. Then click Next: Arrange your envelopes.

7. In the envelope document that displays on the screen, click the insertion point in the letter address area. Under Arrange your envelope, choose <<Address Block>>. Resave the main document. Click Next: Preview your envelopes.

8. Under Preview the envelopes, click Next: Complete the merge.

9. Under Complete the merge, click Edit individual envelopes. Click All; then OK. Merged envelopes will appear as a new document with a page break between each.

REMOVE SPACE AFTER PARAGRAPH

HOME/PARAGRAPH/LINE SPACING

 1 Sometimes it is desirable to remove the extra space after a paragraph to give copy a more traditional appearance. The spacing options provide an easy way to remove space after a paragraph.

| Line Spacing Options... |
| Add Space Before Paragraph |
| Remove Space After Paragraph **2** |

TIP

Always display Show/Hide to format paragraphs.

To remove space after a paragraph:

1. Position the insertion point at the end of the paragraph you wish to remove the spacing after.

2. Click the Line Spacing command **1** and then Remove Space After Paragraph **2**.

DRILL 3   **APPLY LINE SPACING**

1. Key the six paragraphs illustrated on the previous page; then format by applying the same line spacing and space after paragraph illustrated. The red numbers guide you to the proper alignment. Do not key the numbers.

2. Position the insertion point at the end of the second-to-last paragraph and remove the space after the paragraph.

3. Preview the document and check and close it. (*27-drill3*)

CLIPBOARD GROUP

HOME/CLIPBOARD/CUT, PASTE, OR COPY

 The Clipboard group on the Home tab provides very useful editing functions. The Clipboard is a feature used to store multiple items that have been cut or copied so that they can be used in other locations. You will work with the Clipboard more extensively in later lessons. An overview of the four editing commands follows.

Cut—removes the selected text from its current location.

Paste—positions the text that was cut in another location.

Copy—makes an additional copy of the selected text.

Format Painter—enables you to copy the format of one paragraph to another.

To cut, paste, and copy text:

1. To cut text, select the text and click the Cut command to remove the text from its current location and place it on the Clipboard.

2. To paste the text, place the insertion point where the text is to be pasted and click the Paste command.

3. To copy text, select the text to be copied and click the Copy command to leave it in its current position and make a copy of it.

4. Position the insertion point where the text is to be pasted and click the Paste command.

100-d1

Edit Data Source and Merge Letters

1. Open *98-d1main*. Edit the data source as follows:
2. Add two new records. Print the selected records.

Ms. Brenda Andres	Mr. Juan Seuffer
Gifts and More	Kubly and Ross Associates
1456 W. 18 Street	356 Airline Road
Starkville, MS 39759-1456	West Point, MS 39773-0356
Oktibbeha County	Clay County

3. Add **Representative** as a new field.
4. Edit the records with the following data:

Record	Representative
Quarrels	Beth Stevens
Bouchillon	Kelly Cancienne
Vang	Patrick Konscak
Andres	Wade Sanford
Seuffer	Jennifer Fleming

5. Edit the writer's name and title in the closing lines. Delete **Hunter Nyiri, Director** and insert the merge field **Representative**. Add the word Representative as the writer's title on the same line.
6. Sort by last name in ascending order and merge to a new document.
7. Check and close. (*100-d1*) (**Reminder:** Save the main document, *98-d1main*.)

100-d2

Filter Data Source

1. With *98-d1main* open, filter the data source to select records in Oktibbeha County.
2. Merge to a new document.
3. Check and close. (*100-d2*)

100-d3

Directory

1. Prepare the main document and data source for a Stock Portfolio. Choose directory as the document type. Name the main document **100-d3directory**.
2. Create a data source with these fields: Symbol, Name, Industry, and Trade. Search the Internet for current stock information for five stocks. One useful site is http://finance.yahoo.com. Key the following as the first stock entry.
Symbol: **WMT**; Name: **Wal-Mart**; Industry: **Discount, Variety Store**; and Trade: **46.20**.
3. Arrange the directory as follows. Set left tabs at .5" and 2" and right tab at 5.5".

    Name
         Symbol   Industry   Trade

4. Sort by name in ascending order and merge. Add the title **Directory of Stocks** at the top of document; apply the Title style.
5. Check and close. (*100-d3*)

DRILL 4   CUT, COPY, AND PASTE

1. In a new document, key your name and tap ENTER.
2. Key the document name **27-drill4**, and tap ENTER.
3. Key only the first and second sentences below.
4. Select *quickly* in the first sentence and cut it; then click between *graphics* and *by* and paste it.

5. Select the text in the second sentence and click Copy. Click at the end of the sentence and tap ENTER; then click Paste.
6. Edit the third sentence, which you have just copied, to add the text shown in the third sentence shown below.
7. Check the document and close it. (*27-drill4*)

The Cut and Paste functions enable you to quickly move text, pictures, or other graphics by cutting from one location and pasting in another location.

The Copy function enables you to duplicate text, pictures, or other graphics in another location.

The Copy function enables you to duplicate text, pictures, or other graphics in another location in the same document or in a different document.

FORMAT PAINTER

HOME/CLIPBOARD/FORMAT PAINTER

The Format Painter can be used to copy a format from one paragraph to another paragraph or to multiple paragraphs.

To copy a paragraph format to a single paragraph:

1. Click in the paragraph that has the desired format.
2. Click the Format Painter.
3. Click in the paragraph to copy the desired format.

To copy a paragraph format to multiple paragraphs:

1. Double-click the Format Painter to keep it turned on.
2. Click in the paragraphs to copy the desired format to each paragraph.
3. Click Format Painter to turn it off or tap ESC.

DRILL 5   FORMAT PAINTER

1. In a new document, key your name, and tap ENTER.
2. Key the document name **27-drill5**, and tap ENTER twice.
3. Key the title, **SERENDIPITY**, and tap ENTER.
4. Turn on Show/Hide (Home/Paragraph/Show/Hide) and key the paragraphs on the following page; tap ENTER after each paragraph.
5. Click your name and right-align it. Click Format Painter once; then click the document name.
6. Select the second paragraph below the title, apply double line spacing (2.0), Times New Roman, 12-point font, and tap TAB to indent the paragraph.

7. With the insertion point in paragraph 2, click Format Painter once; then click paragraph 1.
8. With the insertion point still in paragraph 1, double-click Format Painter; then click paragraph 3.
9. Click paragraph 4 and then turn off Format Painter.
10. Remove the extra space after the first three paragraphs.
11. Preview, check, and close the document. (*27-drill5*)

FILTER RECORDS

MAILINGS/START MAIL MERGE/EDIT RECIPIENT LIST

Filtering records before merging the main document and the data source allows you to select a specific set of records to merge. For example, you can create a target mailing to individuals in a specific state or ZIP Code area.

To filter data records:

1. On the Mailings tab, in the Start Mail Merge group, click Select Recipients. Click Use an Existing List. Locate the data source and click Open. Then, from the Start Mail Merge group, on the Mailings tab, click Edit Recipient List.

2. From the Refine recipient list, in the Mail Merge Recipients dialog box, click Filter.

3. From the Filter and Sort dialog box, select the Filter Records tab ❶.

4. Choose the appropriate data field ❷ (e.g., State); click a comparison phrase ❸ (e.g., Equal to); and key the text or data you will use for the comparison ❹ (e.g., IL). Click OK. **Note:** Click down arrow for comparison and note the comparison phrases.

5. Note the records displaying in the Mail Merge Recipients dialog box to determine if you have filtered correctly. Click OK.

Reminder: Click the Clear All button in the Filter and Sort dialog box to remove filters before using the main document again to ensure all records will merge.

DRILL 5 — FILTER DATA RECORDS

1. Open *98-drill1main* and filter as follows:

   Field: State

   Comparison Phrase: Equal to

   Compare to: Illinois (IL)

2. Merge to a new document.

3. Check and close. (*100-drill5*)

DRILL 6 — FILTER DATA RECORDS

1. With *98-drill1main* open, clear filters used in Drill 5.

2. Filter to select records of speakers who live in Chicago and are scheduled to speak at 8:30 a.m.

3. **Hint:** Because both conditions must be met, select *And* then key the requirements for the second condition.

4. Merge to a new document.

5. Check and close. (*100-drill6*)

Serendipity, a new homework research tool from Information Technology Company, is available to subscribers of the major online services via the World Wide Web.

Offered as a subscription service for college students, Serendipity is a collection of thousands of articles from major encyclopedias, reference books, journals, and Internet sources combined into a searchable database. The database is updated daily.

Serendipity puts an electronic library right at students' fingertips. The program offers two browse and search capabilities. Users can find articles by entering searches in simple question format or by selecting key words that identify related articles.

For more information, call 800-555-0174 or send an e-mail to lab@serendipity.com. Special discounts are available for entire classes to use the service.

QUICK ACCESS TOOLBAR

TIP

The Quick Access toolbar is available from all tabs on the Ribbon.

The Quick Access toolbar is located to the right of the Office button in the upper-left corner of the screen. It contains icons for three frequently used commands: Save, Undo, and Redo. In the last lesson, you used the Save command but you accessed it by clicking the Office Button menu. The Quick Access toolbar provides a shortcut or one-click option for these frequently used commands.

❶ **Save** preserves the current version of a document or displays the Save As dialog box to save a new document.

❷ **Undo** reverses the most recent action you have taken (such as inserting or deleting text or removing formats). The down arrow displays a list of the commands that you can undo. Selecting an item on the list will undo all items above it on the list.

❸ **Redo** reverses the last *Undo*; it can be used several times to redo the past several actions.

Note that the Quick Access toolbar can be customized by clicking the down arrow at the end of the toolbar. Customizing means that you can place additional commands that you use frequently on this toolbar. You will learn to add commands and use them in later lessons.

KEYBOARDING PRO DELUXE See References/Word commands/Lesson 27

To sort records by multiple fields:

MAILINGS/START MAIL MERGE/EDIT RECIPIENT LIST

1. On the Mailings tab, in the Start Mail Merge group, click Select Recipients. Click Use Existing List. Locate the data source and click Open. Then, from the Start Mail Merge group, on the Mailings tab, click Edit Recipient List. Under the Refine recipient list section in the Mail Merge Recipients dialog box, click Sort.

2. From the Filter and Sort dialog box, select the Sort Records tab ❶.

3. Click the down arrow beside Sort by ❷ and select the first field to be sorted in the multiple sort.

4. Click the down arrow beside Then by ❸ and select the second field, and so forth. Click OK.

DRILL 2   SORT IN ASCENDING ORDER

1. Open *98-drill1main*. Sort by ZIP Code in ascending order and merge to a new document.

2. Close *98-drill1main* without saving.

3. Check and close. (*100-drill2*)

DRILL 3   SORT IN DESCENDING ORDER

1. Open *98-drill1main*. Sort by ZIP Code in descending order and merge to a new document.

2. Close *98-drill1main* without saving.

3. Check and close. (*100-drill3*)

DRILL 4   MULTIPLE SORT

1. Open *98-drill1main*. Sort in descending order first by state, then by city, and then by last name.

2. Merge to a new document.

3. Close *98-drill1main* without saving.

4. Check and close. (*100-drill4*)

1. In a new document, key your name and tap ENTER. Then key the document name, **27-drill6**, and tap ENTER.

2. Key sentence 1; then apply bold and underline to *Undo/Redo*. Undo the underline in sentence 1.

3. Key sentences 2 and 3; then apply bold to *Undo* in sentence 2 and *Redo* in sentence 3. Then apply italic to both.

4. Remove italic in both sentences 2 and 3.

5. Click in your name and then center-align it.

6. Use Undo to remove the center-align; then use Redo to go back to center-align. Then center-align the document name.

7. *Keyboarding Pro DELUXE* users: Preview, check, and close.

8. Non-*Keyboarding Pro DELUXE* users: Preview your document and then use the Quick Access toolbar to save it. (*27-drill6*)

Keying and formatting changes can be reversed easily by using the Undo/Redo commands.

If you make a change, one click of the Undo command can reverse the change.

If you undo a change and decide that you want to keep the change as it was originally made, you can go back to the original change by clicking the Redo command.

MINI TOOLBAR

The Mini Toolbar

The Mini toolbar provides a shortcut to apply frequently used text and paragraph formatting commands. When you select text, the Mini toolbar appears in a very light or faded view. To darken the Mini toolbar, point the mouse cursor at it. You can click a command from this bar to apply a format.

To use the Mini toolbar:

1. Select text to which you want to apply a commonly used format.

2. Point the mouse at the Mini toolbar when it appears in a faded view.

3. Click the command(s) that you want to apply when the Mini toolbar darkens.

1. Key the title and paragraph shown below.

2. Select the title, *THE MINI TOOLBAR*; when the toolbar appears, point toward it to darken it; then apply bold, Times New Roman font, 14 point, and center-align.

3. Select *Mini toolbar* in line 1 of the paragraph and apply italic; do the same in line 3.

4. Preview, check, and close. (*27-drill7*)

THE MINI TOOLBAR

The Mini toolbar provides a quick and easy way to apply formatting commands while you are keying or after you have keyed a document. Note that both font and paragraph formatting commands are included on the Mini toolbar.

1. Open *98-drill1main*.
2. Add Fax Number as a new field after the ZIP Code field.
3. Update the records with the following fax numbers:

   Ms. Hershbarger 708-555-0188

   Dr. Hodnett 414-555-0194

   Mr. Zuber 708-555-0169

4. Change Ms. Hershbarger's address to **206 Fourth Avenue, Chicago, IL 60650-0206.**
5. When prompted, save changes to *98-drill1data*.
6. Close the main document without saving. (*98-drill1main*)

SORT DATA RECORDS

MAILINGS/START MAIL MERGE/EDIT RECIPIENTS LIST

Sorting records determines the order in which the records are merged. You might sort records by ZIP Code, last name, or city. Occasionally, a multiple sort is needed to sort first by one field and then a second field, and so forth. For example, merged names for badges or registration letters might be sorted first by state, then by city, and then by last name. Records are sorted in either ascending order (A to Z *or* 1, 2, etc.) or descending order (Z to A *or* 100, 99, etc.).

To sort records by one field:

1. Open the main document. On the Mailings tab, in the Start Mail Merge group, click Edit Recipient List. The Mail Merge Recipients dialog box displays.
2. Click the column heading of the field to be sorted to display the data (such as Last Name) in ascending order ❶. Click again to display in descending order. Click OK.

Note: You may also click the down arrow by each field ❷ and select Sort Ascending or Sort Descending.

To merge, in the Finish group, click the Finish & Merge button. Click one of the merge options.

© PHOTODISC GREEN/GETTY IMAGES

Most companies develop standard office procedures (SOPs) because they save time and enhance office productivity. Procedures range from the way mail is picked up to the handling of almost any activity that might occur.

SOPs also apply to document production. Many companies use standard formats as well to ensure a consistent appearance for all documents. You are already using SOPs in your keyboarding class.

- Open a new document for each drill or document that you prepare. *Keyboarding Pro DELUXE* users: Select the next activity to open a new document.

- Turn on Show/Hide to assist in formatting paragraphs.

- Proofread, preview, and print documents when they have been completed.

- *Keyboarding Pro DELUXE* users: Check the document; then print the checked document and close it.

- Non-*Keyboarding Pro DELUXE* users save documents using the name that is in parentheses after the last direction in a drill or application and close them.

SOPs are procedures that you are expected to do without being told to do each time you prepare a document. You will learn to use many other SOPs that apply to documents.

APPLICATIONS

27-d1

Formatting Title, Headings, and Paragraphs

1. In a new document, key all paragraphs below and on the next page using default font, size, and spacing.
2. Position the insertion point at the beginning of the title ❶ and tap ENTER three times. Apply bold, 14-point Arial font, and center-align the title.
3. Apply bold and 12-point Arial font to all side headings ❷.
4. Key your name on the line below the last line of the document and right-align it. Key the document's filename, **27-d1**, on the line below your name and right-align it.
5. Preview, proofread, check, print, and close the document. (*27-d1*)

❶ STANDARD OPERATING PROCEDURES

Many companies develop standard operating procedures (SOPs) for virtually every phase of their business. When standard operating procedures are mentioned, most people think of a manufacturing or service business and are surprised to learn that standard operating procedures apply to management and office administration as well. Most companies have SOPs for producing documents in their offices for several reasons.

continued

EDIT DATA SOURCE

MAILINGS/START MAIL MERGE/EDIT RECIPIENT LIST

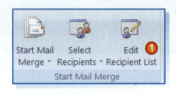

Sometimes you will need to edit the data source (list of variables) by changing individual records or revising the fields for all records.

To edit records:

1. You must be in the main document. On the Mailings tab, in the Start Mail Merge group, click Select Recipients.

2. Locate the data source and click Open. On the Mailings tab, in the Start Mail Merge group, click Edit Recipient List **1**. The Mail Merge Recipients dialog box displays.

3. In the Data Source box, click the data source **2**, e.g., *100-drill1data*. Click Edit **3**. The Edit Data Source dialog box displays.

4. Click in the desired entry or click Find **4** to locate a record quickly. Make the desired changes.

5. Click New Entry **5** to add a new record or click Delete Entry **6** to delete a record. Click OK.

Changes to fields are made by editing the data source. Once the change is made, all of the records are revised.

To edit fields:

1. Click the Customize Columns button in the Edit Data Source dialog box. Edit as follows:

   a. Add new field: Click the Add button; key the field name. Use the move buttons to position correctly. (**Reminder:** Be sure to update the main document by inserting the new merge field.)

   b. Delete field: Select the field to be deleted. Click the Delete button.

   c. Rename field: Select the field to be renamed. Click the Rename button. Key new name.

2. Save your main document to update your data source.

② Quality Control

SOPs ensure that company image is consistent throughout the organization. Guides are presented for using and protecting the logo, standard colors may be specified, and document formats are standardized.

② Training Tools

New and experienced employees both want to do a good job. SOPs provide an excellent training tool to ensure that all employees do their work accurately and meet company expectations consistently. Most employees do not like to be told repeatedly what to do. Having a set of guides to follow enables them to work independently and still meet quality standards.

② Productivity Enhancement and Cost Reduction

Documents are very expensive to produce. SOPs are designed to be efficient, and efficiency translates to cost savings.

27-d2

Editing and Applying Formats

1. Open *27-d1*; turn on Show/Hide.
2. Select the first paragraph below the title; (do not select the ¶ mark) apply Times New Roman 12-point font from the Mini toolbar. Change the line spacing to double spacing (2.0), tap tab to indent it, and remove spacing after the paragraph.
3. Use Format Painter to apply this format to each paragraph following a side heading.
4. Apply Times New Roman 12 point to your name and the document name and change document name to *27-d2*.
5. In the first sentence under *Training Tools*, use Cut and Paste to move *both* to the beginning of the sentence so that it reads: *Both new and experienced employees....*
6. Preview, proofread, check, print, and close the document. (*27-d2*)

WARMUP 100a

Key each line, striving for control. Repeat if desired.

alphabet	1	Dubuque's next track meet will have prizes given by forty judges.
fig/sym	2	Interest in 2000 climbed $346 (as the rates rose from 7% to 20%).
double letters	3	Ann and Buzz will carry my bookkeeping supplies to Judd's office.
easy	4	The auditor may laugh, but the penalty for chaotic work is rigid.

| 1 | 2 | 3 | 4 | 5 | 6 | 7 | 8 | 9 | 10 | 11 | 12 | 13 |

SKILL BUILDING

100b Textbook Keying

1. Key each line once, concentrating on good keying techniques. Tap ENTER twice after each 3-line group.
2. Repeat if time permits.

	5	Jimmy gave Molly a great uphill race; a brass moon pin was given.
one hand words	6	Kit, as we debated, you join my webcast created on poll opinions.
	7	Mom, join Johnny at a great café as we eat carved beef on bread.
	8	Four sleepy toddlers begged for the wiggle, squiggle worm riddle.
double letter	9	According to Miss Dillwood's syllabus, tardiness is unacceptable.
	10	Nothing feels as cool as a summer breeze when in a swimming pool.
	11	While four puppets talked, the group sat quietly with their pals.
third row	12	Quite powerful in the first day of trial, the lawyers slept well.
	13	The quilts were prepared for three people hurt at the house fire.

NEW FUNCTIONS

100c

MAILINGS TAB

After all the steps of the Mail Merge Wizard are completed, you may want to edit your data source. To do this, you may reopen the Mail Merge Wizard (Mailings/Start Mail Merge/Start Mail Merge/Step by Step Mail Merge Wizard) or use the Mail Merge ribbon by clicking on the Mailings tab.

Use the Insert Address Block ❶, the Insert Greeting Line ❷, and Insert Merge Field ❸ buttons to create the placeholders for the merge fields in the main document. The Edit Recipient List button ❹ is used to edit the data source, while the Finish & Merge button ❺ is used to complete the merge.

KEYBOARDING PRO DELUXE   See References/Word Commands/Lesson 100

Ribbon Essentials

WARMUP 28a

Key each line, striving for control. Repeat if desired.

alphabet 1 Beatriz joked quietly and played with five or six cute young men.

figure 2 I fed 28 men, 30 women, 19 girls, 25 boys, 17 babies, and 4 dogs.

one hand 3 Jimmy saw him carve a great pumpkin; John deserved better awards.

balanced hand 4 Jamale Rodney, a neighbor, and Sydney may go to the lake by auto.

SKILL BUILDING

28b Textbook Keying
Key each line once, concentrating on using good keying techniques; tap ENTER twice after each 2-line group.

one hand 5 A few treats were served as reserve seats were set up on a stage.

6 In my opinion, a few trees on a hilly acre created a vast estate.

balanced hand 7 Pam and Jake did go to visit the big island and may fish for cod.

8 Ken may visit the men he met at the ancient chapel on the island.

1/2 fingers 9 Kimberly tried to grab the bar, but she missed and hurt her hand.

10 My name is Frankie, but I prefer to be called Fran by my friends.

3/4 fingers 11 Zola and Polly saw us play polo at Maxwell Plaza; we won a prize.

12 Zack quickly swam past all six boys at a zoo pool on Saxony Land.

28c Timed Writing
1. Key a 3' timed writing, working for speed.
2. Key a 3' timed writing, working for control.

LA

all letters

	gwam	1'	3'
Learning new software can be fun, but it often requires much		12	4
hard work. However, if you are willing to work hard, in a short period		26	9
of time, you can learn important skills.		35	12
If you accept change easily, you are more likely to learn new		12	16
things quickly. A person who avoids change has just about the		25	20
same chance of learning new software as a lazy person.		36	24
Working smart might be just as important as working hard.		12	28
Help is easy to use if you will take the time to explore the resources		26	33
that are provided in your software.		33	35

1' | 1 | 2 | 3 | 4 | 5 | 6 | 7 | 8 | 9 | 10 | 11 | 12 | 13 |
3' | 1 | 2 | 3 | 4 |

99-d1

Mail Merge

Prepare the main document and data source for a form letter to new members of the Jefferson City Chamber of Commerce.

1. Save a new document as *99-d1main*.

2. Create the data source. Customize the address list to include the fields shown below.

3. Enter the following data for each of the three records. Save the data source as *99-d1data*.

Field names	Record 1	Record 2	Record 3
Title	Mr.	Ms.	Dr.
First Name	Dennis	Catherine	Stephanie
Last Name	Lamar	Bradberry	Wade
Company Name	Lamar Office Products, Inc.	ITC, Inc.	Jefferson City Medical Clinic
Address Line 1	P.O. Box 983	100 Jones Road	P.O. Box 3832
City	Jefferson City	Jefferson City	Jefferson City
State	MO	MO	MO
ZIP Code	65101-0983	65111-4757	65101-3832

4. Key the main document (open punctuation) and insert the merge fields in the main document. Edit spacing after the paragraph in the Address Block field. Save the changes.

Thank you for your continued support of the Jefferson City Chamber of Commerce. Your generous contributions made 2008 a great year for the Jefferson City Chamber. The enclosed *Annual Report* outlines just a few of our accomplishments.

A new membership decal and plaque for your business are enclosed. Please display those proudly on your car and in a prominent place in your business. We encourage you to promote the Chamber to fellow business colleagues and friends.

<<Title>> <<Last Name>>, again, we thank you for your support and invite you to join us the first Friday of each month at the Chamber Business Hour. Because we rotate locations among business members, be sure to watch the monthly newsletter for the specific location.

Sincerely | Your Name, Director | Jefferson City Chamber of Commerce | Enclosures

5. Merge the data source and the main document.

6. Check and close. (*99-d1*)

99-d2

Mail Merge

1. Consider the various form letters that are often used by businesses or organizations. Decide upon one effective use of form letters.

2. Save a new document as *99-d2main*.

3. Create the data source. Save as *99-d2data*.

4. Key the main document and insert the merge fields in the main document.

5. Merge the data source and the main document.

6. Check and close. (*99-d2*)

DATE AND TIME
INSERT/TEXT/DATE & TIME

28d

① 🗓 Date & Time   One of the most frequently used commands on the Insert tab is the Date & Time command. Most business documents are dated.

TIP

Remember to proofread and preview each document as a SOP. You will not be reminded to do this.

To insert the date and/or time:

1. Position the insertion point where you wish to insert the date or time.

2. On the Insert menu in the Text group, click the Date & Time command ① to display the Date and Time dialog box.

Date and Time   ? ✕

Available formats: Language:

4/20/2009   English (U.S.)
Monday, April 20, 2009
② April 20, 2009
4/20/09
2009-04-20
20-Apr-09
4.20.2009
Apr. 20, 09
20 April 2009
April 09
Apr-09
4/20/2009 3:35 PM
4/20/2009 3:35:50 PM
③ 3:35 PM
3:35:50 PM
15:35
15:35:50

④ ☐ Update automatically

Default...   OK   Cancel

3. Select the desired date format (April 20, 2009) ② or time format (3:35 PM) ③. In this textbook, assume mm/dd/yyyy format (April 20, 2009) is the default format for the date. Use this default unless the directions specify to use a different format.

4. Leave Update automatically ④ blank unless you want it to update each time the document is opened. Click OK.

DRILL 1   INSERT DATE AND TIME

1. In a new document, key your name and right-align it; then tap ENTER.

2. Insert the date in the month/day/year format highlighted above and tap ENTER. Note that the date is right aligned.

3. Insert the time in hour/minute format. Tap ENTER.

4. Key the text shown below. Left-align the text.

5. Check the document and close it. (*28-drill1*)

The date shown above illustrates common business format. The time format also illustrates common business format; however, some businesses prefer to use lowercase (p.m.) for time format. The 4/20/2009 3:35 PM format is often used in tables or with statistical material.

LESSON 99 | Mail Merge Applications

WARMUP 99a

Key each line, striving for control. Repeat if desired.

alphabet	1	Mickey bought six lavender azaleas and quite a few nice junipers.
fig/sym	2	We gave a 15% discount on 3 invoices (#28574, #6973, and #12095).
3rd & 4th fingers	3	Pam was quick to zap Dex about a poor sample that was on display.
easy	4	Jan and six girls may go to the lake to sit on the dock and fish.

| 1 | 2 | 3 | 4 | 5 | 6 | 7 | 8 | 9 | 10 | 11 | 12 | 13 |

SKILL BUILDING

99b Timed Writing

1. Key a 1' writing on each paragraph. Work to increase speed.
2. Key a 3' timing on both paragraphs.

all letters

A

	gwam	1'	3'

What do you think about when you hear individuals being · 11 · 4
called student athletes? Many people think only of the very · 23 · 8
visible football or basketball players who attract a lot of · 35 · 12
attention and often get special treatment on campus. Few people · 48 · 16
think about the large numbers of young men and women who put in · 61 · 20
long hours working and training to be the very best they can be · 74 · 25
in a wide variety of sports. These students may never receive · 86 · 29
any type of recognition in the news media, and they do not · 98 · 33
attract large crowds to watch them perform. They frequently · 110 · 37
excel in both academic and athletic performance. · 120 · 40

What does a student athlete in one of the less visible · 11 · 44
sports with very little opportunity to become a professional · 25 · 48
athlete gain from the significant investment of time and ef- · 35 · 52
fort in a sport? To be successful in a sport, a student must · 48 · 56
be organized, be an effective time manager, and have self- · 57 · 60
confidence. An athlete learns that teamwork, ethical conduct, · 72 · 64
and hard work are a major part of success in any type of en- · 84 · 68
deavor. The skills do not apply just to sports; they also apply · 97 · 72
to jobs and to life. Most important of all, these individuals · 109 · 77
are doing what they really enjoy doing. · 117 · 79

| 1' | 1 | 2 | 3 | 4 | 5 | 6 | 7 | 8 | 9 | 10 | 11 | 12 | 13 |
| 3' | | 1 | | | 2 | | | 3 | | | 4 | | |

MARGINS

PAGE LAYOUT/PAGE SETUP/MARGINS

 Margins are the distance between the edge of the paper and the print. The default margins for *Word 2007* are 1" at the top, bottom, right, and left. Note that the default margins are called Normal. If you want to fit more information on a page, you might select Narrow margins. Or if you have a limited amount of information, you might select Wide margins. You could select Office 2003 Default or set a custom style to format leftbound reports.

To change margins:

1. From the Page Layout tab in the Page Setup Group, click the down arrow on the Margins command ❶ to display the gallery of margins options.

2. Click the desired margins option ❷.

★	**Last Custom Setting** Top: 1" Left: 1.5"		Bottom: 1" Right: 1"	
	Normal Top: 1" Left: 1"		Bottom: 1" Right: 1"	
	Narrow Top: 0.5" Left: 0.5"		Bottom: 0.5" Right: 0.5"	
	Moderate Top: 1" Left: 0.75"		Bottom: 1" Right: 0.75"	
	Wide Top: 1" Left: 2"		Bottom: 1" Right: 2"	
	Mirrored Top: 1" Inside: 1.25"		Bottom: 1" Outside: 1"	
	Office 2003 Default Top: 1" Left: 1.25"		Bottom: 1" Right: 1.25"	
Custom Margins...				

DRILL 2   CHANGE MARGINS

1. Open *28-drill1*. In *Keyboarding Pro DELUXE*, select Drill 2 from the Lesson menu; *28-drill1* will open automatically. Click Margins and then click Narrow. Note how the appearance of the document changes.

2. Click Wide margins and note the difference in appearance.

3. Click Office 2003 default. Note that 1.25" side margins make very little difference in document appearance than the 1.0" side margins of *Word 2007*.

4. Check and close. (*28-drill2*)

INDENT

PAGE LAYOUT/PARAGRAPH/INDENT

The Indent command indents all lines in the paragraph to the same point. Text can be indented from both the left and right sides. Remember that the TAB key only indents the first line.

To indent text:

1. Click the Indent command.

2. Click the up arrows on both the left and right side to increase them to .5".

DRILL 3   INDENT TEXT

1. In a new document, key your name on the first line and right-align it.

2. Insert the date on the line below using the default format (mm/dd/yyyy).

3. Tap ENTER twice and key the title, **EFFECTIVE FORMATTING**. Center it and tap ENTER.

4. Apply Justify and key all text shown on the next page. Do not make any other format changes until all text has been keyed.

5. Apply Times New Roman, bold, 14-point font to the title.

6. Click in the second paragraph and indent it .5" on both the left and right sides.

7. Check and close. (*28-drill3*)

4. Key the main document below and insert the merge fields in the main document. Use open punctuation. Save the changes. **Reminder:** The date should update automatically.

Date

«AddressBlock»

«GreetingLine»

Thank you for submitting your proposal for enacting a more culturally diverse employment program for city workers to the American Studies Association.

The American Studies Association continually strives to work with city governments in three counties to provide work environments that value diversity. The goal, of course, is to employ persons who reflect differences in age, lifestyle, and interests. Different people solve problems differently, and that leads to better decisions.

You may be contacted, «Title» «Last_Name», to represent «County» County on the special Council for Managing Diversity that is being established in our three-county region. Again, thank you for letting us know what you are doing to ensure diversity at «Company_Name».

Sincerely | Hunter Nyiri, Director | xx

5. Merge the data source and the main document.

6. Check and close. (*98-d1*)

98-d2

Mail Merge

1. Decide on a form letter that would be useful to you personally or to your class. Secure the names and addresses of the recipients of the form letter.

2. Save a new document as *98-d2main*.

3. Create the data source. Save as *98-d2data*.

4. Key the main document and insert the merge fields in the main document.

5. Merge the data source and the main document.

6. Check and close. (*98-d2*)

WORKPLACE SUCCESS

Multicultural Skills

What is your multicultural quotient? Companies are seeking employees who have multicultural awareness, knowledge, and skills. These valuable employees are aware that their attitudes, beliefs, assumptions, etc., do affect how they work with others who are of different cultures. These employees are very knowledgeable of the many aspects of these cultures, including history, practices, and values. They also have developed skills that are needed to interact effectively with those of different cultures. One skill might be learning the language of that culture.

Spend some time in this module increasing your own multicultural literacy. Develop an awareness, knowledge, and skills in another culture.

Good formatting produces a document with a professional image and helps to make a good first impression. However, appearance is only one of many reasons to format documents effectively. My instructor said:

Indent   Effective formatting improves the readability of a document. It also adds structure and makes the document easier to understand. In addition, the format can be used to indicate which ideas are more important than other ideas.   Indent

My textbook makes many of the same points that my instructor made. It emphasizes that formatting documents appropriately is an important part of communicating effectively. Although the default formats of Word 2003 and those of Word 2007 are quite different, you can format documents effectively using the defaults of either software version.

RULER

Some commands are easier to use if the Vertical and Horizontal Rulers are displayed. If your ruler is not displayed, click the View Ruler button at the top of the scroll bars on the top right side of the screen. The Ruler will display. The Ruler can be displayed from any of the Command tabs at the top of the ribbon (Home, Insert, Page Layout, etc.). The numbers on the Horizontal Ruler indicate the distance in inches from the left margin.

❶ **Line of writing**—the white area of the Ruler.

❷ **Indent markers**—the markers at each end of the line of writing.

❸ **Tab alignment marker**—the *L* at the left side of the rule is the Left tab alignment marker. Clicking the Tab Alignment marker will cause the tab to change to other types of tabs.

In the last drill, you indented text from both the right and left sides by using the Indent command. You can also indent text by dragging the markers at each end of the line of writing.

Note that the Indent markers on the line of writing shown on the Ruler below have moved in .5" on each side.

KEYBOARDING PRO DELUXE ➤ See References/Word commands/Lesson 28

6. On the Quick Access toolbar, click Save to update the changes you have made to the file *98-drill1main*.

7. Click Next: Preview your letters.

Step 5: Preview your letters

1. Remove the extra spacing between the lines of the letter address 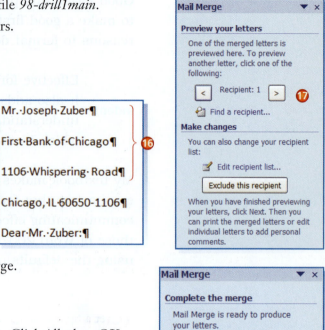 16 .

2. Click on the navigation buttons 17 to preview each of your letters. **Tip:** Should you need to edit one of the letters, click Edit Recipient List and make the necessary changes to the data source file.

Mr.·Joseph·Zuber¶

First·Bank·of·Chicago¶

1106·Whispering·Road¶

Chicago,·IL·60650-1106¶

Dear·Mr.·Zuber:¶

3. Click Next: Complete the merge.

Step 6: Complete the merge

1. Click Edit individual letters 18 . Click All; then OK. The merge letters will appear on the screen as a new document with a page break between each letter.

2. Check and close. (*98-drill1*)

APPLICATIONS

98-d1
Mail Merge

1. Save a new document as *98-d1main*.

2. Create the data source. Customize the address list to include the fields shown below.

3. Key the following data for each of the three records. Save the data source as *98-d1data*.

Field names	Record 1	Record 2	Record 3
Title	Mrs.	Mr.	Ms.
First Name	Jessica	Allen	Paje
Last Name	Quarrels	Bouchillon	Vang
Company Name	Hendrix Plastics	Magnolia Chemicals	Faulkner Florists
Address Line 1	5689 Old Vinton Road	538 Hill Street	885 N. Third Street
City	Starkville	Columbus	West Point
State	MS	MS	MS
ZIP Code	39759-5689	39701-0538	39773-0885
County	Oktibbeha	Lowndes	Clay

continued

TABS

Document tabs can be set and cleared on the Horizontal Ruler. The small gray lines below each half-inch position are the default tab stops. The Tab Alignment button at the left edge of the Ruler indicates the type of tab. Tabs can be set in a document to align text vertically.

Word has five types of tabs.

L	❶ Left Tab	Aligns text at the left.
⊥	❷ Center Tab	Aligns text evenly on both sides of the tab stop.
⅃	❸ Right Tab	Aligns text at the right.
⊥	Decimal Tab	Aligns numbers at the decimal point.
	Bar Tab	Aligns text to the right of a vertical bar.

Alignment button →

To set a tab: Click the Alignment button, select desired type, and then click Horizontal Ruler where you want to set the tab.

To delete a tab: Click the tab marker on the Ruler, and drag it straight down.

To move a tab: Click the tab marker on the Ruler, and drag it to the new location.

DRILL 4	SET AND MOVE TABS

1. On the Horizontal Ruler, set a left tab at 1", a center tab at 3.25", and a right tab at 5.5". (See ruler above.)

2. Key the first three lines of the drill below. Tap TAB at the beginning of each line. Tap ENTER twice after the third line.

3. Drag the left tab to 1.5" and the right tab to 5". Key the last three lines; note they will not align with the first three lines as shown in the illustration.

4. Check and close. (*28-drill4*)

	Left Tab 1"	Center Tab 3.25"	Right Tab 5.5"
(Tap TAB)	Largest player	324	Offensive tackle
	Average	255.5	Team
	Smallest player	165	Punter

Reset Tabs	Left Tab 1.5"	Center Tab 3.25"	Right Tab 5"
(Tap TAB)	Tallest player	6'6"	Tight end
	Average	6'	Team
	Shortest player	5'10"	Running back

4. In the Mail Merge task pane, in the far right pane, click Greeting Line (or on the Mailings tab, in the Write & Insert Fields group, click the Greeting Line). The Insert Greeting Line dialog box displays. Click the down arrow to the right of the comma and select the colon . Click OK. Tap ENTER one time and continue keying the letter until you reach the merge field code for Speech.

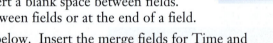

5. Insert the merge field for additional fields, such as Speech:

   a. Click More Items from the right pane (or click the Insert Merge Field button on the Write & Insert Fields group).

   b. Select Speech, click Insert, and then click Close. **Tip:** When necessary, tap the Space Bar to insert a blank space between fields. Insert punctuation as necessary between fields or at the end of a field.

   c. Continue keying the letter shown below. Insert the merge fields for Time and Room at the appropriate places.

   (Date Code) (Enter 2 times)

   «AddressBlock» (Enter 1 time)

   «GreetingLine» (Enter 1 time)

   Thank you for agreeing to present your paper titled «Speech» at the International Conference on Technology to be held at the Omni Hotel in San Francisco on May 12. Your presentation is scheduled for «Time» in the «Room». You may expect approximately 100 participants.

   You are also invited to be our special guest at the annual awards luncheon on Friday at 11:45 a.m. in the Grand Ballroom. Your conference registration materials and a luncheon ticket will be held for you at the hotel registration desk. If you need assistance when you arrive at the hotel, please call conference headquarters at ext. 7532.

   «Title» «Last_Name», we look forward to your presentation and to your outstanding contribution to our program.

   Sincerely, (Enter 2 times) | Jacqueline VonKohn

   Program Coordinator | xx

28-d1

Heading, Date, Tabs

1. Tap ENTER three times; then key the title. Insert the date on the next line as a subheading using day/month/date/year format.

2. Tap ENTER and key the first paragraph using Times New Roman, 12-point font.

3. Set a left tab at 1", a center tab at 3.25", and a right tab at 5.5".

4. Key the remainder of the document.

5. Format the title and the date as indicated.

6. Check and close. (28-d1)

Arial, 14 point bold center ⟶ **Preseason Starting Lineup**

Times New Roman 12 point bold, center ⟶ *Current Date*

The head coach named the preseason starting lineup today. She said that the positions were very competitive and might not be the same when the season started.

Set tabs ⟶

Power forward	6'1"	Shawna Kulchar
Small forward	6'	Larissa Perovic
Center	6'3"	Olga Gortman
Shooting guard	5'10"	Tonisha Burgess
Point guard	5'9"	Sara Penn

28-d2

Heading, Indent, Date

1. Tap ENTER three times; then key the entire document shown below.

2. Indent the second paragraph .5" from the left and right sides.

3. Insert the date and time right-aligned on the line below the last paragraph; use 00/00/0000 00:00 PM format.

4. Check and close. (28-d2)

Weekly Report (Cambria, 16-point bold)

The head football coach spoke with reporters at his weekly news conference. He was asked about the summer workout program and seemed to be very frustrated with some of his student-athletes. The coach said:

Summer workouts are voluntary programs, and it is against the rules to require student-athletes to participate. However, the workouts are a good way to judge the commitment level of your players. Some of our players are very committed and are very likely to get playing time. Others are lazy, and it is doubtful they will be ready to play when the season begins.

In response to a reporter's question, he indicated only about a dozen of the 85 scholarship players did not show up regularly. The goal of the program is to improve conditioning and lessen the likelihood of injuries.

6. The Save Address List dialog box displays. Enter a filename (*98-drill1data*) in the File name box and click Save. **Note:** By default, data files are saved to the folder My Data Sources under the My Documents folder. In the Save in box, choose the appropriate folder for saving this file.

7. The Mail Merge Recipients dialog box now displays and shows the variables in table format. Click OK ⑫.

Note: To move within the Mail Merge Recipients dialog box, click the desired row. Use the scroll bar to navigate in the record. With a long recipient list, click Find recipient to search for the desired recipient.

8. Click Next: Write your letter from the Mail Merge task pane.

Step 4: Write your letter

1. Begin keying the main document at approximately 2". Insert the date as a field (Insert/Text/Date & Time; click the Update automatically box). Tap ENTER two times.

2. Click Address block ⑬ from the right pane (or click the Address Block button from the Write & Insert Fields group on the Mailings tab). The Insert Address Block dialog box displays. Click OK ⑭ to accept the default settings for recipient's name, company name, and address.

3. Tap ENTER one time.

Editing Essentials

WARMUP 29a

Key each line, striving for control. Repeat if desired.

alphabet	1	JoQuin and Zola packed five large boxes for their weekly meeting.
fig/symbol	2	I bought 48 crabs, 50# of shrimp, and 26 fish ($1,397 @ 10% off).
double letters	3	All planning committees have four dinner meetings with key staff.
easy	4	Bud got the tub of big worms to go to the dock to fish with them.

SKILL BUILDING

29b Textbook Keying
Key each line once, concentrating on using good keying techniques. Tap ENTER twice after each 3-line group.

Direct reach words, phrases, and sentences

5 hung deck jump cent slope decide hunt serve polo brave cedar pump

6 no way | in tune | many times | jump in | funny times | gold plated | in sync

7 June and Cecil browsed in craft shops and found many funny gifts.

Adjacent reach words, phrases, and sentences

8 were pop safe sad quick column tree drew opinion excite guy point

9 we are | boil over | are we | few rewards | short trek | where are we going

10 Bert said he tries to shop where we can buy gas, oil, and treats.

29c Textbook Keying
Key each line once, striving for fluency.

11 Ken may go to the big lake to fish for sockeye and dig for clams.

12 Jan may go with us to visit the ancient chapel on the big island.

13 Their goal is to fix the bicycle or dismantle it to fit in a box.

14 A cow roams the cornfield, and fox, quail, and duck also roam it.

15 A neighbor bid by proxy for eighty bushels of corn and rye blend.

NEW FUNCTIONS

29d

NAVIGATE AND VIEW A DOCUMENT

The document window displays only a portion of a page at one time. The keyboard, mouse, and scroll bars can be used to move quickly through a document to view it.

Keyboard options—press CTRL + HOME to go to the beginning of a document and CTRL + END to move to the end of the document. The Page Up and Page Dn keys can also be used to move through a document.

Mouse—use the scroll bars to move through the document. Scrolling does not change the position of the insertion point; it only changes your view of the document. You must click in the text to change the position of the insertion point.

3. The New Address List dialog box displays.

4. In the New Address List dialog box, click Customize Columns 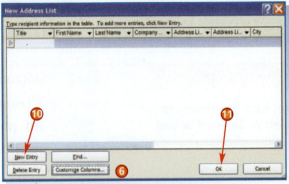 to edit the default field names provided in the Wizard. The Customize Address List dialog box displays.

   a. To delete a field name, select the field and click Delete 7. Click Yes to confirm the deletion of each field. For this drill, delete Address Line 2, Country or Region, Home Phone, Work Phone, and E-mail Address.

   b. To add a field name, click Add 8. The Add Field dialog box displays. Add three fields: Time, Room, and Speech.

   c. To position the new fields correctly, select the field to be moved. Click Move Up or Move Down 9 as appropriate. Move the field names so they are positioned as shown at the right. Click OK.

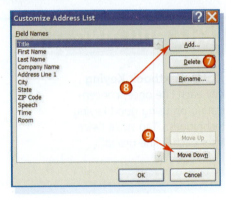

5. Key the variables for Record 1 in the New Address List dialog box. Click New Entry 10 to begin a new record, and key variables for Record 2. Repeat for Record 3. Click OK 11 after keying all of the records.

Field names	Record 1	Record 2	Record 3
Title	Ms.	Dr.	Mr.
First Name	Alison	Lisa	Joseph
Last Name	Hershbarger	Hodnett	Zuber
Company Name	Hershbarger & Ward Attorneys	Columbia Hospital	First Bank of Chicago
Address Line 1	844 Locksley Way	303 Park Circle Road	1106 Whispering Pines Road
City	Salt Lake City	Milwaukee	Chicago
State	UT	WI	IL
ZIP Code	84110-0844	53221-0303	60650-1106
Speech	"Copyright Issues in the Digital Age"	"Creating Interactive Presentations"	"Creating a Web Presence for Your Organization"
Time	8:30 a.m.	9:30 a.m.	10:30 a.m.
Room	Colonnade Room	Diplomat Room	Laurel Suite

SCROLL BAR AND VIEWS

The vertical and horizontal scroll bars are located on the lower-right side of the screen.

Scroll Bar

View buttons   Slider

To move through a document:

- Click above or below the scroll bar. -or-
- Click the bar and drag it to the desired position. -or-
- Click the up and down arrows.

Slider—used to zoom in and out on a document. Note that the Slider is positioned in the center of the bar, which shows text at 100% of its actual size.

To view smaller or larger versions of text:

1. To view a larger version of a segment of text, move the Slider toward the right or the positive (+) side. The text will be larger, but you see a smaller segment of it.

2. To see more of the document at one time, move the Slider toward the left or the negative (–) side. If you move the Slider to about 50%, you can probably see two full pages of a document.

Views—display document in different formats. The view that is selected when you save and close a document will be the view that displays when that document is opened again. Views can be accessed by clicking the view on the status bar or the View tab.

1. **Print Layout**—this shows the document as it will look when it is printed.

2. **Full Screen Reading**—this view uses the full screen to display the document. To return to the Normal view, click Close ❻ at the top right side of the screen.

3. **Web Layout**—shows the document as it will appear on the Web.

4. **Master Document Tools**—displays the document in outline format.

5. **Draft**—displays the document without graphics and formatting.

KEYBOARDING PRO DELUXE See References/Word commands/Lesson 29

DRILL 1   NAVIGATING AND VIEWING A DOCUMENT

1. In the open document (*27-d1*), move to the last line; select the document name, and replace it with *29-drill1*.

2. Use the keyboard to move up and down through the document. Press CTRL + END to move to the end of the document; then press CTRL + HOME to go to the beginning of it.

3. Use the mouse, the scroll bar, and the up and down arrows to move in the document.

4. Move the Slider to the left to 50% and view the document; then move it to 200% and view the document.

5. Move the Slider back to the center at 100%.

6. Click each View button and check the document in that view; leave the document in Print Layout view.

7. Check and close. (*29-drill1*).

Keyboarding Pro DELUXE users: Complete all mail merge drills and documents in Word 2007.

MAIL MERGE WIZARD

MAILINGS/START MAIL MERGE/START MAIL MERGE

The Mail Merge Wizard is a straightforward way to produce merged documents such as the form letters you will create in this lesson.

To start the Mail Merge Wizard:

1. Open a new document and save it with a meaningful name, e.g., *98-drill1main*.
2. From the Mailings tab, in the Start Mail Merge group, click Start Mail Merge ❶. A list of mail merge options displays.
3. Click Step by Step Mail Merge Wizard ❷.

📄	Letters
📧	E-Mail Messages
✉	Envelopes...
🏷	Labels...
📋	Directory
W	Normal Word Document
📄	Step by Step Mail Merge Wizard... ❷

☀ **KEYBOARDING PRO DELUXE** ➤ See References/Word Commands/Lesson 98

DRILL 1   MAIL MERGE WIZARD

1. Follow steps 1–3 above to start the Mail Merge Wizard. In step 1, save the blank document as *98-drill1main*.

2. There are six steps in the Mail Merge Wizard that follow. To move from one step to the next, click Next located at the bottom of the pane.

Step 1: Select document type

1. Choose Letters ❶ (or the type of document you will use for the main document).
2. Click Next: Starting document to go to step 2 of the Wizard ❷.

Step 2: Choose Next: Starting document.

1. Click Use the current document ❸ to create a new form letter in the active window. (Or choose Start from a *Word* template, or choose Start from existing document to use a form letter you have already created.)
2. Click Next: Select recipients. **Note:** You may click Previous: Select document type to return to the previous step.

Step 3: Select recipients

1. Click Type a new list ❹ because the data source does not yet exist. (Choose Select from *Outlook* contacts to use the *Outlook* address book, or choose Use an existing list to use a file that you created previously.)
2. Under Type a new list, click Create ❺ to display the New Address List dialog box.

Mail Merge ▼ ✕

Select document type
What type of document are you working on?
- ◉ Letters ❶
- ○ E-mail messages
- ○ Envelopes
- ○ Labels
- ○ Directory

Letters
Send letters to a group of people. You can personalize the letter that each person receives.
Click Next to continue.

Step 1 of 6
➡ Next: Starting document ❷

Mail Merge ▼ ✕

Select starting document
How do you want to set up your letters?
- ◉ Use the current document
- ○ Start from a template ❸
- ○ Start from existing document

Use the current document
Start from the document shown here and use the Mail Merge wizard to add recipient information.

Mail Merge ▼ ✕

Select recipients
- ○ Use an existing list
- ○ Select from Outlook contacts
- ◉ Type a new list ❹

Type a new list
Type the names and addresses of recipients.
📇 Create... ❺

SPELLING AND GRAMMAR OPTIONS

Three options are available for detecting errors in your documents.

axtual (spelling or keying)

It are to late. (Grammar and contextual)

1. Color-coded squiggly lines appear in your text as you key. Red indicates spelling or keying errors, green indicates grammar errors, and blue indicates contextual errors such as using *to* for *two* or *too*. Correct these errors as you key.

2. The Grammar and Spelling status is shown in the status bar at the bottom of the screen. The pen shows it is still checking. The ✗ indicates the document has errors. The ✓ indicates the document is error free.

ABC ✓ Spelling & Grammar

3. On the Review tab click Spelling & Grammar to display the Spelling and Grammar dialog box. You can either click Ignore Once or Change to correct the error. This feature is generally used to check the entire document at once. Note that many errors you make keying are corrected automatically by a function called AutoCorrect.

Spelling and Grammar: English (U.S.)

Not in Dictionary:
Axtual

Ignore Once
Ignore All
Add to Dictionary

Suggestions:
Actual

Change
Change All
AutoCorrect

☑ Check grammar

Options...   Undo   Cancel

HELP

 Help is installed on your computer when *Office 2007* is installed and more extensive help can also be accessed from *Office Online*.

To access *Word* Help:

1. Tap the **F1** key.

   -or-

2. Click the **Help** button ❶ at the top right of the screen.

3. In the *Word* Help search box ❷, key the topic on which you need help.

4. To access Help if you are not connected to the Internet, click the down arrow on Search ❸ and click Word Help under Content from this computer ❹.

MAIL MERGE

Creating personal form letters, printing labels, and addressing envelopes to a large number of individuals are tasks done easily using the mail merge feature. **Mail merge** is creating a new (merged) document by combining information from two other documents—the main document and the data source.

The **main document** contains the text and graphics that remain the same for each version of the merged document. Within the main document, **merge fields** are inserted as placeholders in locations where you want to merge names, addresses, and other variable information that comes from the data source file.

The **data source** is a file that contains the names, addresses, and other variables to be merged with the main document. All the variables for one individual person are called a **record**. The separate variables for each record are called **fields**.

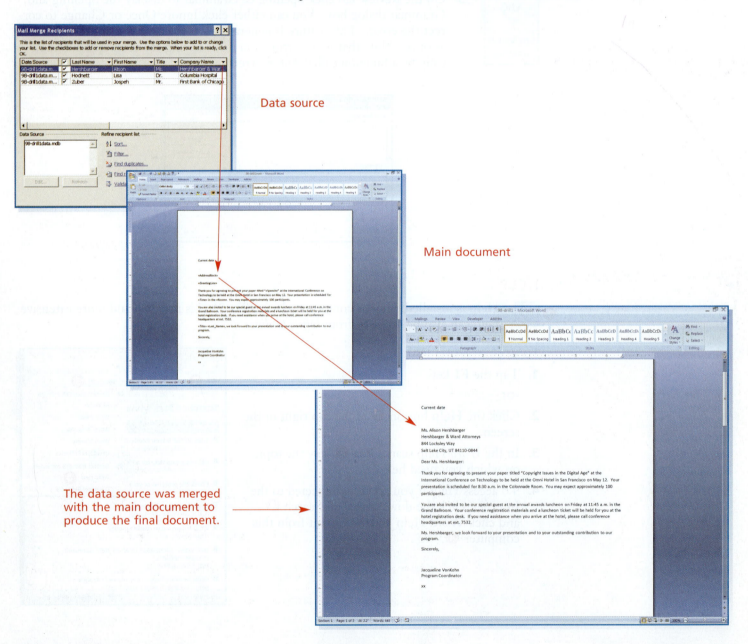

Data source

Main document

The data source was merged with the main document to produce the final document.

1. Key the paragraphs, filling in the information indicated.
2. Print the document; proofread it and mark any corrections needed using proofreaders' marks.
3. Correct the document. (*29-drill2*)

Review proofreaders' marks in Lesson 23, page 55.

My name is (*student's name*). I am a (*class level*) at (*school*) located on (*street*) in (*city, state*). In addition to (*name of this course*), I am also enrolled in (*names of other courses; modify sentence if you are not enrolled in any other courses*). My instructor in this course is (*title and name*).

The reason I enrolled in this course is (*complete sentence*). What I like most about this course is (*complete sentence*). What I like least about this course is (*complete sentence*).

1. Key the ten sentences (tap ENTER after each sentence) and the following paragraph shown below. Make the edits indicated by the proofreaders' marks. Use Help if needed.
2. Proofread and correct any errors.
3. Use Spelling and Grammar. Check and close. (*29-drill3*)

DISCOVER

Insert/Delete—to insert text, click in the document at the point you wish to insert text and key the text.

To delete text, select the text and tap the DELETE key.

Do you assess your writing skills as average, great, or mediocre?

You should also ask your instructor about your writing skills. *to assess*

Your instructor ~~will know~~ *may teach you* how to ~~greatly~~ improve your writing skills.

Do you ~~always~~ *take the time to* edit and proofread carefully things that you write?

few people who do not bother to edit there work are good writers.

Learning to edit effective*ly* may be just as important as writing well.

Another question to ~~ask~~ *answer* is: how important are writing skills?

Good writing skills are needed to be successful in ~~most~~ *many* careers. *reat*

You can improve your writing skills by making it a priority. *to do so*

Judge your writing ~~only if~~ *after* you have proofread and edited your work.

Take the time to carefully evaluate your completed work. *stet* Is the copy formatted attractively? Does it read ~~good~~ *well*? have your corrected all grammar and spelling errors? If your work does not impress you, it will not impress any one else.

Mass Mailings

LEARNING OUTCOMES

- Merge form letters.
- Merge envelopes and labels.
- Edit the data source.
- Sort and filter records.

LESSON 98

Mail Merge

WARMUP 98a

Key each line, striving for control. Repeat if desired.

adjacent keys
1 Ty was going to see the trio perform at a junior college theater.
2 My class was starting to talk about tilling the soil in Freeport.

fig/sym
3 My mileage is 28,475 on 2 front tires and 39,610 on 2 rear tires.
4 Mark paid $230.49 plus 6% tax for 1.75# of pate & 1/8# of caviar.

fluency
5 The Orlando auditor did a formal audit of the firm on the island.
6 Jane may work as a tutor for eight girls; Ty may also tutor them.

| 1 | 2 | 3 | 4 | 5 | 6 | 7 | 8 | 9 | 10 | 11 | 12 | 13 |

SKILL BUILDING

98b Textbook Keying

1. Key each line once, concentrating on good keying techniques. Tap ENTER twice after each 2-line group.
2. Repeat if time permits.

balanced hand
7 pens turn fur slam pay rifle worn pan duck ham lap slap burn girl
8 Andy Clancy, a neighbor, may visit at the lake and at the island.

one hand
9 read ploy create kiln crate plum were pony cats jump severe hump
10 Phillip, as you are aware, was a reader on deferred estate cases.

combination
11 did you we spent pony street busy jump held severe pant exert due
12 Were profits better when we were on Main Street than Duck Street?

| 1 | 2 | 3 | 4 | 5 | 6 | 7 | 8 | 9 | 10 | 11 | 12 | 13 |

---

1. Key the document below, making all edits indicated by the proofreaders' marks on the copy. Use the editing tools you have learned in this module. Use Help if needed.

2. Center the title, **STANDARD OPERATING PROCEDURES** and subtitle, **Document Production**; apply Cambria bold font to both; use 14 point for the title and 12 point for the subtitle.

3. Proofread; check spelling and grammar; correct errors; check and close. (*29-d1*)

Following standard operating procedures designed for this ~~K~~eyboarding *lc* ~~C~~ourse will enhance productivity and eliminate the need to repeat directions for each activity. These procedures will also ensure that documents are prepared in a consistent manner, and managed *the files are* appropriately.

Use Cambria, 11 point Bold → Procedures for *Keyboarding Pro DELUXE* Users

Change bullet format to round
- Select an activity to open a new ~~word~~ document or a data file.

- Use the Back and Check buttons to ~~easily~~ manage your files.

Use Cambria, 11 point Bold → Procedures for Non-*Keyboarding Pro DELUXE* Users

Change bullet format to round
- Prepare a folder for each module with the ~~name of the~~ module to store all documents for that module.

- Save each document with the lesson number and drill or application name (*29-drill1* or *29-d1*).

- Open a data file as soon as you see a CD icon plus **a** filename (*fitness*) and save it immediately with the drill or application name in which it is used.

Use Cambria, 11 point Bold → Procedures for Both *Keyboarding Pro DELUXE* and Non-*Keyboarding Pro DELUXE* Users

Change numbers to bullets
1. Preview, proofread, and print each document as soon as you complete it.

2. Prepare an envelope ~~when~~ **for each letter** you key ~~a letter~~.

3. Add your reference initials at the bottom of each letter or memo that does not have your name as the signature.

4. Add an Enclosure or Attachment notation if the document ~~contains one~~. **refers to materials being enclosed or attached**

97-d3

Announcement with Picture

 ANDY2

1. Prepare an announcement to be posted. Use narrow margins, landscape orientation, and Cambria 48-point font.
2. Insert the picture and crop it as shown on the right; apply Double Frame, Black style.
3. Key the text shown. Preview and adjust size if needed.
4. Continue to the next document. (*97-d3*)

Lost Pet Named

Andy

Honey-Colored

Cairn Terrier

Tanglewood Neighborhood

$500 Reward

Call Pat at 555-0189

97-d4

News Release

 PPFE NEWS RELEASE

1. In the open document, prepare the following news release for immediate release.
2. Check the test and close. (*97-d4*)

CELEBRATION TO BENEFIT SCHOOLS

OKEMOS, MI—The Okemos Chapter of Parents' Partnership for Education will hold its annual Celebration of the Arts, Friday from 7:30 to 11:30 p.m. at the Talbert Hotel.

Participants will have an opportunity to enjoy an hors d'oeuvres buffet, see excellent musical and dramatic entertainment by students at Okemos Schools, view award-winning student artwork, and bid on artwork by locally and nationally known artists. An annual fundraising event for the Okemos Chapter of Parents' Partnership for Education, Celebration of the Arts serves several key purposes, according to organizers.

"The Celebration of the Arts provides an opportunity to showcase the superior quality of talent that is being nurtured in the Okemos Schools," said Chapter President Sherry Sinago. "It also provides an evening when people of the community can come together to socialize and share their support of the schools of Okemos. Also, this event enables our chapter to raise funds to carry out projects for the next school year," Sinago added.

The annual Celebration of the Arts is open to the public. Reservations may be made by calling 555-0134. Tickets will also be available at the door.

CHECKPOINT ➡ Congratulations! You have successfully completed the lessons in Module 15. To check your understanding and for more practice, complete the objective assessment and performance assessment located on the textbook website at www.collegekeyboarding.com.

LESSON 30 — Assessment

WARMUP 30a

Key each line, striving for control. Repeat if desired.

alphabet	1	Gay expected to solve the jigsaw puzzle more quickly than before.
figures	2	Jane opened Rooms 16, 20, and 39 and locked Rooms 48, 53, and 57.
shift	3	Ted and I spent April in San Juan and May in St. Paul, Minnesota.
easy	4	The island is the shape of a big sleigh. Jamal got clams for us.

SKILL BUILDING

30b Timed Writing
Key two 3' timed writings.

all letters

	gwam	3'
I have an interesting story or two that will transport you to	4	53
faraway places, to meet people you have never known, to see	8	57
things you have never seen, to experience things available only to	13	61
a select few. I can help you master appropriate skills you desire	17	66
and need; I can inspire you, excite you, instruct you, challenge	22	70
you, and entertain you. I answer your questions. I work with you	26	75
to realize a talent, to express a thought, and to determine just who	31	79
and what you really are and want to be. I help you to understand	35	84
words, to write, and to read. I help you to discover the mysteries	40	88
of the past and the secrets of the future. I am your library. I hope	44	93
I shall see you regularly. You are very likely to find me online.	49	97

3' | 1 | 2 | 3 | 4 |

APPLICATIONS

30c

Assessment

→ Continue

✓ Check

With *Keyboarding Pro DELUXE*: When you complete a document, proofread it, check the spelling, and preview for placement. When you are completely satisfied, click the Continue button to move to the next document. Click the Check button when you are ready to error-check the test. Review and/or print the document analysis results.

Without *Keyboarding Pro DELUXE*: Key the documents in sequence. When time has been called, proofread all documents again and identify errors.

Pediatric News

PACIFIC NEWPORT MEDICAL GROUP

Hepatitis B Vaccine

Hepatitis B is most commonly contracted in the teenage and adult years. It is highly recommended that all pre-teens and teenagers be vaccinated with the series of three Hepatitis B vaccines. The three shots are administered over a six-month period.

Hepatitis B can affect anyone—in fact, it is estimated that one in ten adults may acquire Hepatitis B at some time unless immunized. The most serious complications of Hepatitis B are a deterioration of liver function and development of liver cancer.

The vaccine is safe and has no side effects. We can administer the MMR or tetanus booster (if they are due) at the same time as the Hepatitis vaccine.

Insurance Coverage

All health insurance policies are required to cover your child's *well child care* visits as immunizations. Most insurance policies cover the cost of one *well child care* visit each year.

Pediatric Asthma

The number of cases of asthma in children under 18 years of age was reported as 2.7 million during this past year. At least one child with asthma was reported by 4.3 percent of households.

Similar to an overly sensitive car alarm, the cells that line the lungs of adults and children with asthma are often set off by the smallest disturbance. The trigger may be a bit of pollen, cat dander, dust, tobacco smoke, or some other pollutant. It may also be a draft of cold air, the common cold virus, or even the demands of exercise.

Physical Exam for School Entry

Call now to set up an appointment for a physical exam if your child will be entering kindergarten or first grade this year. We recommend vision and hearing screenings before school entry. The number of appointments allocated for physical exams each day is limited, so call in advance to reserve your time.

30-d1

Rough Draft

1. Tap ENTER three times; use double spacing and Wide margins.
2. Key the title, **YOU ARE WHAT YOU EAT** and apply Arial 14-point bold format, and center-align. Use Times New Roman 12-point font for the remainder of the document.
3. Key the document, making all edits. Tab to indent paragraphs as you key.
4. Set a right-align tab at 4"; key your name below the last line of the document; insert the date using standard business format directly below your name.
5. Remove the extra spacing after paragraphs including your name.
6. Proofread; use spelling and grammar; correct all errors; continue with next document. (*30-d1*)

A speaker said, "you are what you eat". the speaker didnot mean to imply that fast food make fast people, or that an hearty meal makes a person heart, or even that good food manes a person good? On the other hand, though, a healthfull diet does indeed make person healthier; and good health effects many things including performance, energy level, and attitude. Learning what to include in a healthful diet is the 1st step. The 2nd step is developing the discipline to apply that knowledge. The results are wellworth the effort. IN fact, good health may be one of the most often over looked treasures within human existance.

30-d2

Tabs

1. Tap ENTER three times. Key title centered; apply Cambria 16 point, bold font. Insert date directly below; apply Cambria 12 point, bold font.
2. Format remainder of document using default Calibri 11 point. Bold the headings *Name* and *Description*. Set a left tab at .5" and a right tab at 6.0". See tip at left.
3. Check the test and close. (*30-d2*)

Internet Groups on Campus
Current date

Name	Description
webdes	Web page design topics
biz	Business administration majors
bioeng	Biomedical engineers
sprtmg	Sports management
marband	Marching band

CHECKPOINT ➡

Congratulations! You have successfully completed the lessons in Module 3. To check your understanding and for more practice, complete the objective assessment and performance assessment located on the textbook website at http://www.collegekeyboarding.com.

97-d1

SmartArt Graphics

FONT GROUP

QUICK ACCESS TOOLBAR

MINI TOOLBAR

1. Format a new document using landscape orientation and Solstice document theme.
2. Key the title and apply Title style; tap ENTER twice.
3. Insert Vertical Picture List from SmartArt graphics; expand the graphic across the line of writing.
4. Insert the pictures with the appropriate text; click the pictures of the toolbars and drag the height as shown so they will not be out of proportion. Key text shown below.
5. Preview and adjust pictures if necessary.
6. Continue to the next document. *(97-1)*

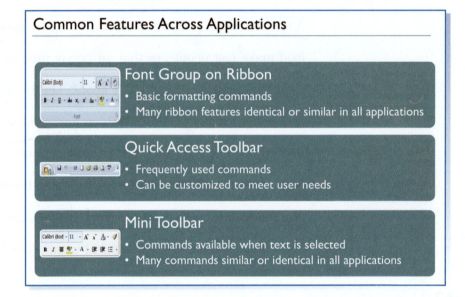

97-d2

Newsletter

1. Use Concourse document theme and Narrow margins for the newsletter shown on the next page.
2. Insert title as WordArt style 1; apply Shape fill Turquoise, Accent 1, Lighter 60% and 3-D effect 2. Expand the banner across the line of writing.
3. Use Shapes to insert a 3-point weight line. The shape outline should be Turquoise, Accent 1, Darker 25%—the same as the Heading 1 style.
4. Key the subheading and apply Heading 1 style; remove space after the paragraph; convert to uppercase.
5. Draw another line from Shapes; format the shape weight at 1 point, and position it below the subheading.
6. Key the newsletter as a one-column document; apply Heading 1 style to all headings and remove space after the paragraph on all headings.
7. Select the newsletter text and apply two-column format.
8. Using **medicine** as a keyword, search clip art for a clip with a child in it; insert the clip.
9. Use Tight Text Wrapping and position it in the center; format the picture with a metal frame; size it so that the newsletter fits on one page.
10. Continue to next document. *(97-d2)*

3

Skill Builder

LESSON A

KEYBOARDING PRO DELUXE | **SKILL BUILDING/ACCURACY EMPHASIS**

1. Select the Skill Building tab, Accuracy Emphasis, and then Assessment 1.

2. Key the timing from the screen for 3'; work for control.

3. Complete Lesson A or the first lesson you have not completed in either Speed Emphasis or Accuracy Emphasis as suggested by the software.

4. Your results will be summarized in the Skill Building Report.

KEYBOARDING PRO DELUXE | **TIMED WRITINGS**

Writing 23

1. Key a 1' writing on each paragraph. (Remember to change the source in the Timed Writing Settings dialog box.) Compare your *gwam* on the two paragraphs.
2. Key additional 1' writings on the slower paragraph.

	gwam	1'	3'

There are many qualities which cause good employees to stand out in a group. In the first place, they keep their minds on the task at hand. Also, they often think about the work they do and how it relates to the total efforts of the project. They keep their eyes, ears, and minds open to new ideas.

	1'	3'
	12	6
	25	13
	38	19
	52	26
	60	30

Second, good workers may be classed as those who work at a steady pace. Far too many people work by bits and pieces. They begin one thing, but then they allow themselves to be easily taken away from the work at hand. A lot of people are good starters, but many less of them are also good finishers.

	1'	3'
	13	6
	25	13
	39	19
	52	26
	60	30

1'	1	2	3	4	5	6	7	8	9	10	11	12	13
3'		1			2			3			4		

Key each line once, striving for control. Repeat if desired.

alphabet   1   Jack Voxall was amazed by the quiet response of the big audience.

fig/sym   2   Our #3865 clocks will cost K & B $12.97 each (less 40% discount).

shift   3   In May, Lynn, Sonia, and Jason left for Italy, Spain, and Turkey.

easy   4   It is the duty of a civic auditor to aid a city to make a profit.

| 1 | 2 | 3 | 4 | 5 | 6 | 7 | 8 | 9 | 10 | 11 | 12 | 13 |

SKILL BUILDING

97b Timed Writing
1. Key one 3' writing and one 5' writing; work for control.

all letters

	gwam	3'	5'

Do you wish to acquire a new automobile in the near future?   4   3
If so, you should consider whether buying or leasing is the best   9   5
alternative for you. The primary difference between leasing and   13   8
buying is that a purchased automobile belongs to you. A leased   17   10
automobile is available for your use for a specific period of time   22   13
and for a specific number of miles, but the leasing company owns it.   26   16

To make a good decision, you should analyze both alternatives   31   19
very carefully. Before you even think of costs, you need to consider   36   21
how you use a car. Leased cars limit mileage per month significantly   40   24
and excess mileage charges are quite high. Are you likely to change   45   27
your mind and want to terminate the lease earlier? The cost is   49   29
significant.   50   30

Justifying the cost is critical. Typically, if you compare   54   33
leasing an automobile for three years or less to financing an   58   35
automobile over the same time period, the leasing payment will be   63   38
less expensive. However, at the end of the lease you must return or   67   40
buy the automobile, which can be expensive. If you have financed it,   72   43
you own it and can do whatever you desire with it.   75   45

3' | 1 | 2 | 3 | 4 |
5' | 1 | 2 | 3 |

APPLICATIONS

97c

Assessment

Continue

Check

With *Keyboarding Pro DELUXE*: When you complete a document, proofread it, check the spelling, and preview for placement. When you are completely satisfied, click the Continue button to move to the next document. Click the Check button when you are ready to error-check the test. Review and/or print the document analysis results.

Without *Keyboarding Pro DELUXE*: Key the documents in sequence. When time has been called, proofread all documents again and identify errors.

LESSON B

KEYBOARDING PRO DELUXE   **SKILL BUILDING/ACCURACY EMPHASIS**

1. Select the Skill Building tab and choose either Speed Emphasis or Accuracy Emphasis as recommended in Assessment 1. Complete Lesson B.
2. Your results will be summarized in the Skill Building Report.

KEYBOARDING PRO DELUXE   **SKILL BUILDING/TECHNIQUE BUILDER**

DRILL 11

BALANCED-HAND COMBINATIONS
Key each line once, working for fluency. DS between groups.

1 to today stocks into ti times sitting until ur urges further tour
2 en entire trend dozen or order support editor nd and mandate land
3 he healthy check ache th these brother both an annual change plan
4 nt into continue want of office softer roof is issue poison basis

5 My brother urged the editor to have an annual health check today.
6 The manager will support the change to order our stock annually.
7 The time for the land tour will not change until further notice.
8 Did the letter mention her position or performance in the office?

KEYBOARDING PRO DELUXE   **TIMED WRITINGS**

1. Key a 1' writing on each paragraph. Compare your *gwam*.
2. Key additional 1' writings on the slower paragraph.

Writing 24

	gwam	1'	3'
Most of us, at some time, have had a valid reason to complain—		12	6
about a defective product, poor service, or perhaps being tired of		26	13
talking to voice mail. Many of us feel that complaining, however,		39	20
to a firm is an exercise in futility and don't bother to express		52	26
our dissatisfaction. We just write it off to experience and		64	32
continue to be ripped off.		70	35
Today, more than at anytime in the past consumers are taking some		12	6
steps to let their feelings be known—and with a great amount of		25	13
success. As a result, firms are becoming more responsive to		38	19
the needs of the consumer. complaints from customers alert firms		51	26
to produce or service defect and there by cause action to be taken		65	33
for their benefit.		70	35

1' | 1 | 2 | 3 | 4 | 5 | 6 | 7 | 8 | 9 | 10 | 11 | 12 | 13 |
3' | | 1 | | 2 | | 3 | | 4 |

SKILL BUILDER 3   MODULE 3   107

96-d3

Continued

KANOZA SCHOLARS PROGRAM ANNOUNCED

MEMPHIS, TN—Kanoza Corporation announced that the Kanoza family has established the Kanoza Scholars Foundation with a $25 million endowment and will begin the Kanoza Scholars program immediately. The Foundation will give 30 scholarships each year to outstanding graduating seniors from high schools throughout the ten-state region in which the company operates. Any senior from Alabama, Arkansas, Florida, Georgia, Kentucky, Louisiana, Mississippi, North Carolina, South Carolina, and Tennessee is eligible to apply to become a Kanoza Scholar.

The 10 top students will be designated as Kanoza All South Scholars, and the remaining 20 students will be designated as Kanoza Scholars. Kanoza All South Scholars receive $10,000 per year for four years for a total scholarship value of $40,000. Kanoza Scholars receive $7,500 per year for four years for a total scholarship value of $30,000. The Kanoza Scholars Foundation will provide scholarships at a value of $250,000 in Year 1, $500,000 in Year 2, $750,000 in Year 3, and $1 million in Year 4 and each year thereafter.

Criteria for determining scholarship winners include academic achievement (rank in class, grade point average, and scores on standardized tests), demonstrated leadership, and community service. Students who have overcome adversity to excel may be given additional consideration. A computer program selects 10 semifinalists from each state, and a panelist of business and education leaders who also serve as role models select the 30 finalists. The 70 semifinalists who do not receive scholarships are given $1,000 each to use for educational purposes.

The Kanoza All South Selection Panel—a group of leaders selected from across the region—will interview the 30 finalists and select the 10 Kanoza All South Scholars. The remaining 20 finalists are named Kanoza Scholars. An exciting program is planned for the expense-paid, three-day visit to Memphis for the 30 finalists hosted by executives of Kanoza Corporation.

A mentoring program has been set up by Kanoza Corporation across the ten-state region. Selected executives and managers have already completed the *Kanoza Effective Mentoring* training program and have committed to serve as a mentor for one or more students. The All South Scholars will be mentored by the senior executive team. Each mentor has committed to meeting with the assigned scholarship recipients a minimum of twice each semester and to maintaining telephone and e-mail contact on a regular basis.

Foundation resources have been designated to cover travel, meals, and other expenses necessary to make the mentoring program effective. In addition, all Kanoza Scholars will have the opportunity to participate in one or two selected company training programs each year that are offered during the summer or at times when their institutions are not in session. Kanoza Scholars will also be given priority for all company field projects and internships.

LESSON C

SKILL BUILDING/ACCURACY EMPHASIS

Select the Skill Building tab, the appropriate emphasis, and then Lesson C. Your results will be summarized in the Skill Building Report.

SKILL BUILDING/TECHNIQUE BUILDER

DRILL 12

BALANCED-HAND
Key each line once for fluency; DS between groups.

1 an anyone brand spans th their father eighth he head sheets niche
2 en enters depends been nd end handle fund or original sport color
3 ur urban turns assure to took factory photo ti titles satin still
4 ic ice bicycle chic it item position profit ng angle danger doing

5 I want the info in the file on the profits from the chic bicycle.
6 The original of the color photo she took of the factory is there.
7 Assure them that anyone can turn onto the road to the urban area.
8 The color of the title sheet depends on the photos and the funds.

TIMED WRITINGS

1. Take a 1' writing on each paragraph.
2. Take a 3' writing on both paragraphs.

Writing 25

	gwam	1'	3'
Practicing basic health rules will result in good body condition.		14	5
Proper diet is a way to achieve good health. Eat a variety of foods each		28	9
day, including some fruit, vegetables, cereal products, and foods rich		42	14
in protein, to be sure that you keep a balance. Another part of a good		57	19
health plan is physical activity, such as running.		67	22
Running has become popular in this country. A long run is a big		13	27
challenge to many males and females to determine just how far they		26	31
can go in a given time, or the time they require to cover a measured		40	36
distance. Long runs of fifty or one hundred miles are on measured		53	40
courses with refreshments available every few miles. Daily training is		67	45
necessary in order to maximize endurance.		76	48

```
1' |  1  |  2  |  3  |  4  |  5  |  6  |  7  |  8  |  9  | 10  | 11  | 12  | 13  |
3' |      1      |       2       |       3       |       4       |
```

96-d1

News Release Form

1. Prepare the news release form shown below.

2. From Shapes, draw a hexagon at the top, left side; size it 1.5" high and 2" wide; add **Kanoza Corporation** on two lines to the hexagon. Apply white font color to the text; grow the text as large as will fit in the hexagon; format the hexagon using Colored Fill White Outline Accent 2.

3. From Shapes, draw a text box to the right side of the hexagon; size it 1.2" high and 5.5" wide. Key the text shown below. Use 16-point bold text for the company name. Insert the date and check Update Automatically.

Kanoza Corporation

5 spaces   1986 Briarwood Circle   5 spaces

Memphis, TN 38116-1986

901-555-0132   Barbara.Hatten@kanozacorp.com   901-555-0148 Fax

NEWS RELEASE   **Contact Person:** Barbara Hatten

Insert Current date

For Release:

4. Bold *News Release*, *Contact Person*, and *For Release*.

5. Check and close. (*96-d1*)

96-d2

News Release

1. Open *96-d1*. Prepare the following news release.

2. Check and close. (*96-d2*)

Insert current date

For Release: Immediately

KANOZA MOVES HEADQUARTERS

MEMPHIS, TN—The Kanoza Corporation announced today that it is consolidating its statewide offices and moving its headquarters to Memphis. The company has leased space in the Davenport Building until its Churchill Tower can be built.

Kanoza employs 785 people. Of the 785 employees, 300 are expected to transfer to Memphis. During the next 15 months, Kanoza expects to hire 500 employees in sales, administrative support, accounting, engineering, architectural, and management areas.

Kanoza develops projects throughout the South. Its primary focus is commercial real estate development. Kanoza has already developed 3 shopping centers in the Hammond area and 25 in the state.

###

96-d3

Two-Page News Release

1. Open *96-d1*. Prepare the news release on the next page. For the release date, use one week from today.

2. Add an odd-page footer on page 1 with the text: **-more-**. Use the first option (blank) and center the footer. Add the even-page header Puzzle on page 2. Key **Kanoza Scholars Program** as the document title.

3. Preview the footer and header.

4. Check and close. (*96-d3*)

LESSON D

SKILL BUILDING/ACCURACY EMPHASIS

Select the Skill Building tab; choose the appropriate emphasis and then Lesson D.

SKILL BUILDING/TECHNIQUE BUILDER

DRILL 13

ADJACENT KEY REVIEW
Key each line once; strive for accuracy. DS between groups.

1 nm many enmity solemn kl inkling weekly pickle oi oil invoice join
2 iu stadium medium genius lk milk talk walks uy buy buyer soliloquy
3 mn alumni hymn number column sd Thursday wisdom df mindful handful
4 me mention comment same fo found perform info le letter flew files

5 The buyer sent his weekly invoices for oil to the group on Thursday.
6 Mindful of the alumni, the choirs sang a hymn prior to my soliloquy.
7 An inmate, a fogger, and a genius joined the weekly talks on Monday.
8 They were to join in the talk shows to assess regions of the Yukon.

TIMED WRITINGS

1. Take a 1' writing on each paragraph.
2. Take a 3' writing on both paragraphs.

Writing 26

	gwam	1'	3'
All people, in spite of their eating habits, have two major needs		13	4
that must be met by their food. They need food that provides a		26	9
source of energy, and they need food that will fill the skeletal and		40	13
operating needs of their bodies. Carbohydrates, fats, and protein		53	18
form a major portion of the diet. Vitamins and minerals are also		66	22
necessary for excellent health.		72	24
Carbohydrates make up a major source of our energy needs.		12	28
Fats also serve as a source of energy and act as defense against		25	32
cold and trauma. Proteins are changed to amino acids, which are		38	37
the building units of the body. These, in turn, are utilized to make		52	41
most body tissue. Minerals are required to control many body		64	45
functions, and vitamins are used for normal growth and aid against		77	50
disease.		84	52

```
1' |  1  |  2  |  3  |  4  |  5  |  6  |  7  |  8  |  9  | 10  | 11  | 12  | 13  |
3' |        1        |        2        |        3        |        4        |
```

alphabet 1 Joyce Wexford left my squad after giving back the disputed prize.

figures 2 Reply to items 4, 5, and 6 on page 39 and 1, 7, and 8 on page 20.

double letters 3 A committee supplied food and coffee for the Mississippi meeting.

easy 4 In Dubuque, they may work the field for the profit paid for corn.

| 1 | 2 | 3 | 4 | 5 | 6 | 7 | 8 | 9 | 10 | 11 | 12 | 13 |

DOCUMENT DESIGN

96b

NEWS RELEASE

A news release conveys information an organization wishes to publish. Organizations prepare news releases to send to newspapers, radio stations, television stations, and other media outlets. News releases that make preparing the story easy save news writers time and are more likely to get published provided the information contained in the release is newsworthy. Often, space limits prevent news media from publishing all of the information provided. Therefore, a good news release states the most important information first and the least important information last so that it can be cut or shortened from the end.

Most organizations prepare news releases on specially prepared forms (often called *mastheads*) for news releases or on letterhead. The form includes the date the news can be released and contact information in case the writer wishes to verify information. It also includes a short subject line that could serve as a heading. Use ### or -30- to indicate the end of the news release.

Two-Page News Release

If a release is two pages long, add an odd-page (page 1) footer with the word *more* centered to indicate that the release continues on the next page. On the second page, add an even-page (page 2) header (often called a *slug line*) with a very short heading followed by a vertical bar or forward slash and the page number or an appropriate built-in header.

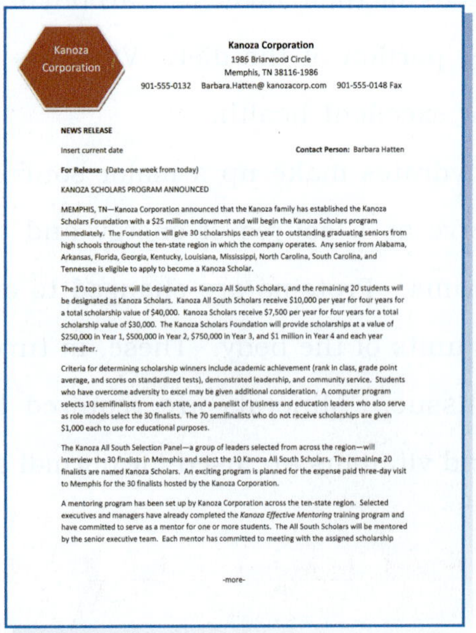

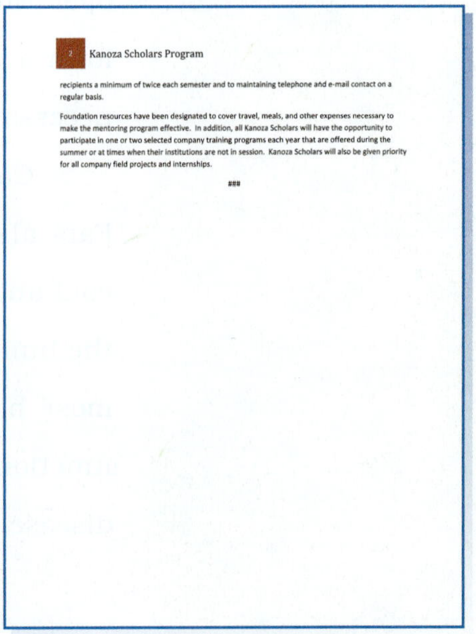

LESSON E

KEYBOARDING PRO DELUXE **SKILL BUILDING/ACCURACY EMPHASIS**

Select the Skill Building tab; choose the appropriate emphasis and then Lesson E.

KEYBOARDING PRO DELUXE **SKILL BUILDING/TECHNIQUE BUILDER**

DRILL 14

WORD BEGINNINGS
Key each line once, working for accuracy. DS between groups.

br
1 bright brown bramble bread breath breezes brought brother broiler
2 In February my brother brought brown bread and beans from Boston.

exe
3 exercises exert executives exemplify exemption executed exemplary
4 They exert extreme effort executing exercises in exemplary style.

bt
5 doubt subtle obtains obtrusion subtracts indebtedness undoubtedly
6 Extreme debt will cause more than subtle doubt among my creditors.

ny
7 tiny funny company nymph penny nylon many anyone phony any brainy
8 Anyone as brainy and funny as Penny is an asset to their company.

KEYBOARDING PRO DELUXE **TIMED WRITINGS**

1. Take a 1' writing on each paragraph.
2. Take a 3' writing on both paragraphs.

Writing 27

	gwam	1'	3'
Many people believe that an ounce of prevention is worth a pound		13	4
of cure. Care of your heart can help you prevent serious physical		26	9
problems. The human heart is the most important pump ever		38	13
developed. It constantly pushes blood through the body tissues. But		51	17
the layers of muscle that make up the heart must be kept in proper		65	22
working order. Exercise can help this muscle to remain in good		77	26
condition.		80	27
Another important way of keeping a healthy heart is just to avoid		13	31
habits which are considered detrimental to the body. Food that is high		27	36
in cholesterol is not a good choice. Also, use of tobacco has quite a		41	40
bad effect on the function of the heart. You can minimize your chances		56	45
of heart trouble by avoiding these bad health habits.		66	49

```
1' | 1 | 2 | 3 | 4 | 5 | 6 | 7 | 8 | 9 | 10 | 11 | 12 | 13 |
3' |    1    |     2     |     3     |     4     |
```

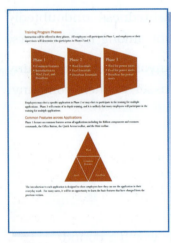

Outlook is not included in the regular training plan because all employees are part of the e-mail system using *Outlook*. When the system is converted to *Outlook 2007*, all employees will be provided with an online guide designed specifically for our company and will participate in a one-hour training program on the new features. Then a more comprehensive program will be offered to those wanting additional training.

Training Plan Approach

Most employees use a minimum of two applications in addition to using *Outlook* for e-mail, and a significant number of employees use three applications. Typically, employees use one application at a production level and other applications at the light-to-average level. Therefore, the training plan is designed to meet the varying needs of all employees.

Training Program Phases

Instruction will be offered in three phases. All employees will participate in Phase 1, and employees or their supervisors will determine who participates in Phases 2 and 3. (Insert SmartArt graphic 2)

Phase 1	Phase 2	Phase 3
• Common Features • Introduction to *Word, Excel*, and *PowerPoint*	• *Word* Essentials • *Excel* Essentials • *PowerPoint* Essentials	• *Word* for power users • *Excel* for power users • *PowerPoint* for power users

Employees may select a specific application in Phase 2 or may elect to participate in the training for multiple applications. Phase 3 will consist of in-depth training, and it is unlikely that many employees will participate in the training for multiple applications.

Common Features Across Applications

Phase 1 focuses on common features across all applications including the Ribbon components and common commands, the Office button, the Quick Access toolbar, and the Mini toolbar. (Insert SmartArt graphic 3)

Top: *Word*   Center: Common Features

Lower left: *Excel*   Lower right: *PowerPoint*

The introduction to each application is designed to show employees how they can use the application in their everyday work. For many users, it will be an opportunity to learn the basic features that have changed from the previous version.

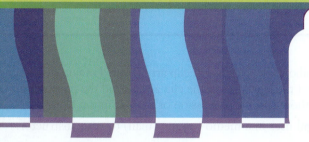

Business Correspondence Essentials

MODULE 4

LESSON 31 — Memos and E-mail

WARMUP 31a

Key each line, striving for control. Repeat if desired.

alphabet	1	I quickly explained to two managers the grave hazards of the job.
figures	2	All channels—16, 25, 30, and 74—reported the score was 19 to 8.
shift	3	Maxi and Kay Pascal expect to be in breezy South Mexico in April.
easy	4	Did the man fight a duel, or did he go to a chapel to sign a vow?

| 1 | 2 | 3 | 4 | 5 | 6 | 7 | 8 | 9 | 10 | 11 | 12 | 13 |

SKILL BUILDING

31b Timed Writing
1. Key a 3' timed writing, working for speed.
2. Key a 3' timed writing, working for control.

all letters

gwam 3'

Hard work is required for job success. Set high goals and — 4 | 43
devote time to the exact things that will help you succeed. Work — 8 | 47
hard each day and realize you must be willing to make sacrifices. — 13 | 51

Avoid being like the loser who says, "It may be possible, but — 17 | 55
it's too difficult." Take on the attitude of the winner who says, — 21 | 59
"It may be difficult, but it's possible." Count on working hard. — 26 | 64

Also, seek mentors to pilot you in your long road to success. — 30 | 69
They will encourage you and will challenge you to reach for higher — 34 | 73
dreams even when you are very happy with where you are. — 39 | 77

| 1' | 1 | 2 | 3 | 4 | 5 | 6 | 7 | 8 | 9 | 10 | 11 | 12 | 13 |
| 3' | | 1 | | 2 | | 3 | | 4 | | | | | |

LESSON 95

Report with SmartArt Graphics

WARMUP 95a

Key each line, striving for control. Repeat if desired.

alphabet 1 Express mail requested at zone twelve gave finish to a rocky job.

figures 2 Check the area codes 304, 593, 281, and 763 before dialing calls.

combination 3 Typing business letters using a simple format is often suggested.

direct reaches 4 My cousin Ed brought my brown mums to school to delight me again.

| 1 | 2 | 3 | 4 | 5 | 6 | 7 | 8 | 9 | 10 | 11 | 12 | 13 |

INTERNET ACTIVITY

95b
Legal Use of Clip Art

1. Search the Internet for information about the legal use of clip art provided in your *Microsoft Office 2007* software. Determine what the legal uses of the clip art are and the purposes for which you cannot use the clip art without specific permission or a subscription fee.

2. Summarize both the legal and illegal uses in a memo (or an e-mail) to your instructor.

3. Check and close. (*95b*)

APPLICATION

95-d1
Report with SmartArt Graphics

1. Key the following unbound report; use Equity document theme. Apply italic to all software names. Number pages using a plain number at the top right side of the page; do not show the number on the first page.

2. Position title at 2" and apply Title style. Apply Heading 1 style for the first two headings and Heading 2 style for the last two headings.

3. Use the following SmartArt graphics:
   First graphic—Segmented Process
   Second graphic—Trapezoid List
   Third graphic—Segmented Pyramid

4. Center and size all SmartArt graphics with 2.5" height and 5.5" width.

5. Make sure headings stay with the following text.

6. Check and close. (*95-d1*)

Training Plan for *Office 2007* Deployment

The Training Department was charged with developing a training plan for the company-wide deployment of *Office 2007*. To determine the level of training needed, a survey was used to determine which applications employees used and how extensively each employee used each application.

Applications and Usage

The applications with the highest usage were *Word*, *Outlook*, *Excel*, and *PowerPoint*. *Word* and *Outlook* were used by virtually all employees. Users were categorized into two groups: light-to-average users and production or very heavy users as shown in the following chart. [Insert SmartArt graphic 1]

	Word	
Light-to-Average Use 55%		Production Use 45%
	Excel	
Light-to-Average Use 40%		Production Use 25%
	PowerPoint	
Light-to-Average Use 35%		Production Use 20%

VERTICAL PAGE POSITION

When formatting documents, the user must decide on the vertical page position of the document. The default top margin for *Word 2007* is 1". Often users will simply tap the ENTER key to move the document lower on the page. Later in this module you will learn the Center Page command to center a document vertically on the page.

Two methods are often used to determine the vertical position of text.

VERTICAL RULER

The Vertical Ruler is displayed at the far left of the screen. If your ruler is not displayed, click the View Ruler button at the top of the scroll bars on the top right side of the screen. The ruler will display.

The blue area at the top of the ruler is the 1" top margin. The white area or the writing area begins at 0" and extends 9". The blue area at the bottom of the rule is the 1" bottom margin. To begin a document at approximately 2", you would tap ENTER three times until the insertion point is positioned at about the 1" marker on the Vertical Ruler.

STATUS LINE

Refer to the status line located at the bottom of the screen. The vertical page position does not display by default in *Word 2007*. To display it, right-click on the status line and click Vertical Page Position. The vertical page position now appears at the bottom left side on the status line.

| Page: 1 of 1   At: 2" |

DRILL 1 — VERTICAL PAGE POSITION

1. In a new document, display the vertical page position on the status line.

2. Tap the ENTER key three times to position the insertion point at about 1.5" on the ruler bar.

3. Insert the current date.

4. Check that the date prints approximately 2" from the top of the page, or at 2" on the status bar.

5. Check and close. (*31-drill1*)

REMOVE SPACE AFTER PARAGRAPH

HOME/LINE SPACING

 By this point you realize that *Word 2007* automatically adds extra white space (10 points) after the ENTER key is tapped. The white space between paragraphs is greater than the white spacing between the lines within the paragraph. The extra white space between paragraphs makes the text easier to read and saves the user time in only tapping the ENTER key once between paragraphs ❶.

However, on some occasions, it is necessary to remove the space added after a paragraph ❷. Remember that your software defines a paragraph when the ENTER key is tapped. The document design in Module 4 for interoffice memos and business letters will include several instances when the extra spacing adds unnecessary white space and consumes too many lines. Study the two examples shown below.

❶ Default Spacing

Daniel J. Lippincott

Business Manager

❷ Extra Spacing Removed

Daniel J. Lippincott
Business Manager

Healthy Heart Trails

The county, the Coastal University Foundation, and the Healthy Heart Foundation announced today a joint venture to build and interconnect a series of walking and bike trails throughout the coastal area.

Healthy Heart Study

Last week the Healthy Heart Foundation released the findings of a significant study showing that exercise, diet, and not smoking are the major controllable factors that lead to a healthy heart. Factors such as heredity cannot be controlled. The study included both males and females aged 25 to 65.

Individuals over 45 are more likely to have heart problems, but the number of young people experiencing heart problems is increasing. Scientists believe that the increasing number of heart problems experienced by younger adults stems from a combination of diet, smoking, and leading a sedentary lifestyle.

Just Take a Walk

The study showed that women especially benefited from just taking a walk. Those who walked an average of two to three hours a week were more than 30 percent less likely to have heart problems than those who did no exercise. Those who walked briskly for five or more hours a week were more than 40 percent less likely to have heart problems.

Make Exercising Fun

The key to a successful exercise program is to enjoy it. Most people who find exercise boring or painful do not continue the program long enough to accomplish the desired benefits. Interesting walking routes take the boredom out of the exercise.

The Bike Trail

The proposed bike trail will feature over 100 miles of packed surface, coquina, and boardwalk bike paths along the coast for those who enjoy biking. The bike trail is designed so that riders can take short loops (1 to 10 miles) or go on extended rides for the entire trail.

Walking Trails

A leading nature trails designer has been retained to design environmentally sensitive trails that are both interesting and educational. The initial Healthy Heart Trails project features six trails ranging from one to five miles long. Each trail features a different type of educational node—ranging from endangered species such as red cockaded woodpeckers and loggerhead turtle nests to sustainability exhibits and pond restoration projects to enhance the habitat for waterfowl.

Healthy Heart Trails Project			
Project Component	Primary Sponsor	Estimated Time	Estimated Cost
Trail design and layout	Coastal University Foundation	4–6 weeks	$ 22,500
Highway work at trailhead	County	6–8 weeks	30,000
Parking lot at entrance	Coastal University Foundation	3–4 weeks	26,000
Visitor's center	Healthy Heart Foundation	6–8 months	100,000
Walking trails	Coastal Univ./Healthy Heart	6–8 months	80,000
Bike trail	County	2 years	400,000
Total Project	All	2 years	$658,500

TIP

Remember to proofread and preview each document for placement. You will not be reminded to do this.

To remove space after paragraph:

1. Select the desired lines. Remember you are removing space after a paragraph (or when the ENTER key is tapped).
2. From the Home tab, on the Paragraph group, click the down arrow by the Line Spacing button. Select Remove Space After Paragraph.

1.0
✓ 1.15
1.5
2.0
2.5
3.0
More...
⤒ Add Space Before Paragraph
⤓ Remove Space After Paragraph

KEYBOARDING PRO DELUXE › See References/Word commands/Lesson 31

DRILL 2 — REMOVE SPACE AFTER PARAGRAPH

1. Key the lines, tapping TAB to indent each name.

Distribution List:
    Allen Bejahan
    Janet James   ❶
    Terry Johnson
    Ray Lightfoot

2. Select the first four lines. ❶
3. Apply the Line Spacing option to remove space after paragraph.
4. Check and close. (*31-drill2*)

COMMUNICATION ✳

31d

PROOFREAD AND FINALIZE A DOCUMENT

Before documents are complete, they must be proofread carefully for accuracy. Error-free documents send the message that you are detail oriented and capable. Apply these procedures when processing all documents:

1. Use Spelling and Grammar to check spelling when you have completed the document.
2. Proofread the document on screen to be sure that it makes sense.
3. Preview the document, and check the overall appearance.
4. Save the document, and then print it.
5. Compare the document to the source copy (textbook), and check that text has not been omitted or added. Revise, save, and print if necessary.

DRILL 3 — DATA FILES AND PROOFREAD A DOCUMENT — PROOFREAD

1. The CD ROM in the back of your book contains extra files you will use in this course. These files, known as data files, are organized by module. A CD icon appears with the drill or application heading when a data file is used, and the data filename appears as well.
2. Non *Keyboarding Pro DELUXE* Users: Ask your instructor how to access these files, or install the files on the hard drive following the instructions on the CD-ROM.

When the files are installed, locate the data path or folder where these files are stored. *Keyboarding Pro DELUXE* users: The data file will open automatically when you access the activity.

3. Open the data file *proofread*.
4. Apply steps 1-4 of the proofreading procedures discussed in **31d** above.
5. Apply step 5; the source copy is the paragraph shown above in **31d**.
6. Check and close. (*31-drill3*)

LESSON 94

Newsletter with Columns and Graphics

WARMUP 94a

Key each line, striving for control. Repeat if desired.

alphabet 1 Who enjoyed traveling to Mexico after buying a quick dozen picks?

figures 2 Send mail to ZIP Code 48279 in January and 56031 before November.

1st/2nd fingers 3 Assessment is a term used by educators when they are testing you.

adjacent reaches 4 Sara stopped here, where her ruined art was stored for the month.

| 1 | 2 | 3 | 4 | 5 | 6 | 7 | 8 | 9 | 10 | 11 | 12 | 13 |

SKILL BUILDING

94b Timed Writing

1. Key two 1' timed writings; work to increase speed on each.
2. Key a 3' timed writing; work for control.

	gwam	1'	3'
What do you like to do on a lazy, sunny weekend afternoon in		12	4
spring or summer? Some people may prefer a quiet afternoon of		25	8
watching television, while other people may want to wash the car		38	13
or work in their gardens. Many others, however, agree that the		51	17
very best way to enjoy a spring or summer afternoon is to attend		64	21
a college or professional baseball game. In fact, that choice is		77	26
so popular that the game is often said to be our national sport.		90	30
Many people even hope for extra innings to extend the fun. Over		103	34
the years, most baseball fans have shown excellent sportsmanship.		116	39
However, today many people are concerned that the bad behavior of		130	43
a few individuals may spoil the game for others.		139	46

1' | 1 | 2 | 3 | 4 | 5 | 6 | 7 | 8 | 9 | 10 | 11 | 12 | 13 |
3' | 1 | 2 | 3 | 4 |

APPLICATION

94-d1

Newsletter with Columns and Graphics

TIP

Keywords for clips:
1. *Medicine or heart medicine*
2. *Trails*–look for females
3. *Bicycle*
4. *Trails*–look for wooded trails

1. Key the newsletter text shown on the next page as a one-column document using narrow margins. Begin at about 2". Key the table on the second page. Use the default Office theme.

2. Insert WordArt above the first paragraph for the title, **Healthy Heart Trails**. Extend the banner across the line of writing and increase the height as well. Use WordArt style 22 and Red fill with Blue shape outline.

3. Select and format the text into three equal columns with a line between each.

4. Format headings using Heading 3 style; apply dropped caps to the first letter of each paragraph.

5. Select appropriate clip art for four locations. Use Tight Text Wrapping for each clip; position and size clips appropriately. Check to see that words are not divided when each clip is inserted. Adjust position or size to prevent word division.

6. Use Table design Medium Grid 3 – Accent 1. Format the table as shown.

7. Adjust column widths so that the information in each cell will fit on one line; change the text in column 2, row 7 to read: **Coastal University/Healthy Heart Foundation**.

8. Preview and make necessary adjustments.

9. Check and close. (*94-d1*)

In Module 3 you learned a variety of basic word processing functions. Now you are ready to apply these skills in formatting business documents. Two formatting approaches will be introduced in this textbook—the new document approach for *Word 2007* users and the traditional document approach for *Word 2003* users. Why are two document formatting approaches needed? The answer is simple—the defaults of *Word 2003* and *Word 2007* are vastly different. Our goal is to prepare you for the entry into industry—whether your employer supports the traditional defaults of *Word 2003* or the new defaults of *Word 2007*. As industry transitions to the new interface, the *Word 2007* document formats will be widely used and accepted. In instances where the formatting differences are minor, the new document approach for *Word 2007* users will be taught. For example, memos will be formatted with the new document approach. In Module 4 you will learn both approaches to formatting letters.

MEMORANDUMS

Messages sent to employees within an organization are called **memorandums** (memos for short). Memos may be printed on plain paper or on letterhead. Often a memo is sent electronically. It can either be in the form of an e-mail or as an attachment to an e-mail. Memos were designed to be documents that stayed within a company. However, e-mail is changing the role of memos. Study the full-page illustration of a memo on the following page.

To format a memo:

1. Tap ENTER three times to position the first line of the heading at about 2".

2. Format the memo headings in bold and uppercase. Turn off bold and uppercase, and tap TAB once or twice after each heading to align the information. Generally, courtesy titles (Mr., Ms., etc.) are not used; however, if the memo is formal, the receiver's name may include a title.

3. Use the 1.15 default line spacing. Tap ENTER once after each paragraph.

4. Add reference initials one line below the body if the memo is keyed by someone other than the sender. Do not include initials when keying your own memo.

5. Items clipped or stapled to the memo are noted as attachments; items included in an envelope are enclosures. Key these notations one line below the reference initials.

To format a distribution list:

When memos are sent to more than one person, list their names after TO. Generally the names are listed in alphabetical order; some organizations, however, list the names in order of rank. For readability, key the names on separate lines. When sending the memo to many people, refer to a distribution list at the end of the memo. Example: *TO: Task Force Members—Distribution Below*. Indent the names on the distribution list to the first tab. Remove the extra spacing between the list of names.

If you have any questions about these policies, please call me at any time.

xx

Distribution:
    Allen Bejahan
    Janet James   Remove Space After Paragraph
    Terry Johnson
    Ray Lightfoot

93-d3

Letterhead in Header

1. Create a letterhead for World-Wide Travel Services, LLC. Position the letterhead in the header.

2. Search clip art for a clip representative of a globe. Use Square Text Wrapping for the clip and align it on the left side.

3. Center the address shown below to the right of the clip. The text color should complement the colors in the clip.

4. Check and close. (*93-d3*)

World-Wide Travel Services, Inc.

3975 Buckingham Road

Annapolis, MD 21403-6820

Telephone: 410-555-0146 ↓ Fax: 410-555-0183 ⟵ 3 spaces

www.world-widetravelservices.com

93-d4

Personal Letterhead in Header

1. Use WordArt to create a letterhead for yourself. Use WordArt Style 6 with Orange Accent 6 color and position it in a header at the left. Key your initials as the text.

2. Key your full name, street address, city, state, ZIP Code, telephone number, fax number, and e-mail address as shown below. Apply Orange, Accent 6, and Darker 50% color.

3. Check and close. (93-d4)

93-d5

Personal Letterhead

1. Create the same letterhead for yourself as you did in *93-d4*, but do not position it in the header.

2. Change the WordArt style and the color of the letterhead to a different style and color of your choice. The illustration below is a sample only—use your own preferences.

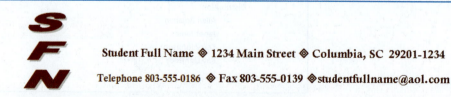

(Tap ENTER three times)

Sterling

2"

**1195 Singing Cactus Avenue
Tucson, AZ 85701-0947**

TO: Students ↓ 1

FROM: Roger C. Westfield ↓ 1

DATE: Insert current date ↓ 1

SUBJECT: A New Perspective on Memos ↓ 1

Your instructor has asked that I prepare a memo for you describing the changing role of memos and the importance of formatting memos effectively. Sterling uses its logo and company name on the top of its memos. First, you will learn to prepare memos on plain paper. Later you will learn to use templates for them. A template is a stored document format that would contain the company logo and name as well as the memo headings. ↓ 1

The format does not differ regardless of whether plain paper or a template is used. The headings are positioned about 2" from the top of the paper, and default side margins are used. Headings are keyed in uppercase and bold; tap the Enter key once after each heading. The body is single-spaced with a blank line between each paragraph. Notations such as reference initials, enclosures, or copies are keyed one blank line below the body. Some companies adopt slightly different styles; however, this style is very commonly used. ↓ 1

Often a memo is sent electronically. It can either be in the form of an e-mail or as an attachment to an e-mail. Memos were designed to be documents that stayed within a company. However, e-mail is changing the role of memos. E-mails, even though they are formatted as memos, are frequently sent outside of companies. Some companies use e-mail to deliver a document but attach a letter or a memo to it. ↓ 1

xx

Memo Format

93-d1

Announcement

1. Format the announcement using landscape orientation and Verve document theme.
2. Insert clip art appropriate for Valentine's Day at the top left side of the document; format it with Tight Text Wrapping. Align it at the left and size it about 2.5" wide.
3. Add **Parents' Night Out** in WordArt. Use a style and color that is compatible with the clip art. Expand the WordArt from the clip art to the right margin.
4. Key the heading directly below the WordArt and apply Heading 2 style. Center it and grow the font to fill the space from the clip art to the right margin.
5. Key the announcement text using 16-point font justified alignment.
6. Check and close. (*93-d1*)

Saturday, February 14, is Valentine's Day. Make it special!

The Student Chapter of the Early Childhood Education Association (ECEA) invites you to enjoy an evening without worrying about your children and to support the ECEA Scholarship Fund at the same time. The ECEA in cooperation with the University Child Development and Research Center is offering a fun night out for your children while you have a Valentine celebration without them. Your children will enjoy games, movies, crafts, snacks, and a variety of adventures.

The University Child Development and Research Center accommodates up to 100 children in age ranges from 6 weeks to 12 years old. College students preparing to be early childhood educators will provide the babysitting services for the evening. Our faculty advisor will supervise the event, and a minimum of two college students will be available for each ten children. Drop your children off at six o'clock and pick them up at eleven o'clock. The rate for the evening is $25 for your first child and $10 for each additional child.

93-d2

Announcement

1. Prepare the following announcement to be posted for the Fourth of July celebration.
2. Use narrow margins and landscape orientation.
3. Select clip art appropriate for the announcement that will be posted and sized about 2.5" high.
4. Use WordArt for the title; add a Shadow Style 1 Effect, and select appropriate fill and outline colors. Expand the title across the line of writing.
5. Key the text justified and with the first letter as a drop cap; grow the font to fill the space available on one page.
6. Check and close. (*93-d2*)

Fourth of July Celebration

Pack your lawn chairs or blankets and bring the entire family to join your friends and neighbors for the annual Fourth of July celebration at City Park. Music and festivities begin at 7:30 and end with a spectacular fireworks display at 10:30.

ELECTRONIC MAIL (E-MAIL)

Electronic mail (or e-mail) is a message sent by one computer user to another computer user. E-mail was originally designed as an informal, personal way of communicating. However, it is now used extensively in business. For business use, e-mail should not be casual or informal.

Business writers compose e-mail messages in two ways. First, the writer may compose the entire communication (or message) in the body of the e-mail. Second, the writer may compose a brief e-mail message and then attach electronic documents to it. Distribution of electronic documents via e-mail is a common business practice; these electronic documents include many types of document formats, e.g., memos, letters, reports, contracts, worksheets, and presentations. It is important for the business writer to recognize the importance of attractive and acceptable formats of all documents, including e-mail messages.

Using e-mail requires an e-mail program, an e-mail address, and access to the Internet. If you cannot meet these requirements, format all e-mail in this text as memos.

Address e-mail carefully. Key and check the address of the recipient ❶ and always supply a subject line ❷. Also, key the e-mail address of anyone who should receive a copy of the e-mail ❸.

Format the body ❹ of an e-mail single-spaced; double-space between paragraphs. Do not indent paragraphs. Limit the use of bold, italics, and uppercase. For business use, avoid abbreviations and emoticons (e.g., BTW for *by the way* or :-) for *wink*).

Attach electronic documents ❺ to an e-mail message using the attachment feature ❻ of the e-mail program. The attached file can then be opened and edited by the recipient.

Keyboarding Pro DELUXE: Complete all e-mails as memos.

Announcements and Letterheads

WARMUP 93a

Key each line, striving for control. Repeat if desired.

alphabet	1	Judging each issue will quickly prove the magazine's flexibility.
figures	2	Check the inventory for items #782, #936, #351, and #405 at noon.
double letters	3	The little bookkeeper from Mississippi keeps all books for Tammy.
balanced hand	4	Rodney and a neighbor may go with me to visit the ancient chapel.

| 1 | 2 | 3 | 4 | 5 | 6 | 7 | 8 | 9 | 10 | 11 | 12 | 13 |

SKILL BUILDING

93b Textbook Keying

1. Key each line once, concentrating on good keying techniques. Tap ENTER twice after each 6-line group.
2. Repeat if time permits.

one-hand lines

5 my wax jump dress pink fast limp crease hunk brace pool extra bat

6 link grace plump trace junk zebra you zest yolk vested opinion ax

7 tax only race join target union regret puppy graze hulk fewer him

8 My mom bragged after Holly, a stewardess, saw my best test grade.

9 In my opinion, Rebecca deserves a few extra rewards; Phil agrees.

10 Jimmy gave Phillip a great red sweater at a bazaar in West Texas.

balanced-hand lines

11 duck quake lake rigor prism proxy fix usual turkey right quake of

12 skeptic quantity problem mangy dogs handle ivory elbow cubicle six

13 augment burlap formal dismay kept mentor rigor social visit world

14 Claudia and Henry may work to fix a big problem with the bicycle.

15 Jane and Kent may want to go with a neighbor to the lake to fish.

16 The city auditor, Jake Hand, may fix the problems with the audit.

| 1 | 2 | 3 | 4 | 5 | 6 | 7 | 8 | 9 | 10 | 11 | 12 | 13 |

DOCUMENT DESIGN

93c

DESIGN ANNOUNCEMENTS AND LETTERHEAD

The design of an announcement may vary depending on whether the announcement is being posted so that it can be read as people walk by or whether it is sent directly to individuals. If the announcement is posted, landscape orientation and a large font are normally used to make it easier to read from a distance. Graphics may be used to enhance announcements.

An attractive letterhead can be designed using clip art, pictures, shapes, WordArt and text formatting. Try to fit the letterhead into approximately 1.5" of space; use part of the top margin if necessary. Position the letterhead in a header if the letter is to be centered. If the letter is to be distributed electronically and read online, do not position the letterhead in a header.

31-d1

Memo

— DISCOVER

Undo Automatic Capitalization	
Stop Auto-capitalizing First Letter of Sentences	
Control AutoCorrect Options...	

1. Read the memo illustrated on page 115 carefully. Key this memo; do not key the memo letterhead. Begin the heading at approximately 2".

2. Use the Date and Time feature to insert the current date.

3. If the first letter of your reference initials is automatically capitalized, point to the initial until the AutoCorrect Options button appears. Click the button; then choose Undo Automatic Capitalization.

4. Proofread the memo carefully and make any changes that are necessary.

5. Check and close. (*31-d1*)

31-d2

**Memo with
Distribution List**

1. Key the memo with a distribution list shown below. Remove the space after the paragraph when formatting the distribution list at the bottom of the memo.

2. Check and close. (*31-d2*)

TO: Manufacturing Team—Distribution Below

FROM: Mei-Ling Yee, Administrative Assistant

DATE: April 14, 2008

SUBJECT: Enrichment Seminars

As was stated by Robert Beloz in the January newsletter, *Focus for the New Year*, Foscari & Associates will be offering a series of enrichment seminars for its employees in the year ahead. If you have suggestions for seminars that would be beneficial to your team, please let me know.

We are proud to announce our first seminar offering, *First Aid and CPR*, on May 16 and 17. The seminar will be offered from 1 p.m. to 5 p.m. in the Staff Lounge. Participants will be awarded CPR certificates from the American Heart Association upon successful completion of this eight-hour course. If you are interested in taking this seminar, please call me at ext. 702 or send me an e-mail message by April 25.

You will want to mark your calendar today for this important seminar.

xx

Distribution:
> Eddie Barnett
> Steve Lewis
> Dinah Rice

31-d3

E-mail

Follow these directions for completing all e-mail applications in this text:

Without Internet access: Complete all documents as memos. Key an attachment notation if appropriate.

With an e-mail address: Complete the documents in your software and send them.

With Internet acccess but no e-mail address: Your instructor will assist you in setting up a free e-mail account and address.

1. Prepare an e-mail to your instructor using the subject line **CPR Certification Required**. Attach the file *31-d2* to the e-mail.

2. Print and send the e-mail or key it as a memo. Check and close. (*31-d3*)

Please review the attached memo from Mei-Ling Yee announcing the date for the *First Aid and CPR* seminar. All team members not certified in CPR are required to attend this seminar.

Crown Lake News and Views

Current date

Newsletter Staff

Eric Burge
  Editor

Nancy Suggs
Christopher Hess
Anne Reynolds
  Associate Editors

Wayne Martin
  Editorial Assistant

Crown Lake News and Views is a weekly newsletter compiled by the staff of the Human Resources Department, and it is sent to all employees.

New Development Project

Crown Lake won the bid to develop and construct the new multimillion dollar Business Center adjacent to Metro Airport. Connie McClure, one of the three senior project managers, has been named as the Business Center project manager. The project is expected to take more than two years to complete. Approximately fifty new permanent employees will be hired to work on this project. All jobs will be posted within the next two weeks. The recruiting referral program is in effect for all jobs. You can earn a $100 bonus for each individual you recommend who is hired and remains with Crown Lake for at least six months. You may pick up your recruiting referral forms in the Personnel Office.

Blood Drive Reminder

The Crown Lake quarterly blood drive is set for next Friday in the Wellness Center. The Community Blood Bank needs all types of blood to replace the supplies sent to the islands during the recent disaster caused by Hurricane Lana. Employees in all divisions are being asked to participate this quarter because of the current supply crisis. All three donation sites will be used. Several volunteers will be needed to staff the two additional sites. The regular division rotation will resume next quarter.

Lee Daye Honored

The Community Foundation honored Lee Daye of the Marketing Department with the Eagle Award for outstanding service this year. The Eagle Award is  presented each year to three citizens who have made a significant impact on the lives of others. The Community Foundation recognized Lee for his work with underprivileged children, the Community Relations Task Force, the Abolish Domestic Violence Center, and the Community Transitional Housing Project. Congratulations, Lee. You made a difference in the lives of many citizens in our community. Your award was richly deserved.

New Training Program

The pilot test of the new Team Effectiveness training program was completed last month, and the results were excellent. Thanks to all of you who participated in the development and testing of the program. Your input is vital to its success. The training schedule will be announced shortly.

31-d4

**Memo with
Distribution List**

TIP

Key a dash as two hyphens, with no space before or after it. *Word* usually converts this to a solid line called an em-dash.

1. Key the memo below. Remove the space after the paragraph when formatting the distribution list at the bottom of the memo.
2. Check and close. (*31-d4*)

TO: Safety Officers—Distribution Below | FROM: Louis Cross | DATE: May 10, 2008 | SUBJECT: Safety Seminar

Mark your calendar for the *Safety Practices and Accident Prevention* seminar scheduled for June 2, 2008, from 9:00 a.m. to 4:30 p.m. The seminar will be held at the Kellogg Center.

New OSHA regulations will be presented at this seminar, so it is extremely important for you as a safety officer to be in attendance. The seminar will be conducted by OSHA employees and professors from the local university.

xx

Distribution:
    Lori Baker, Production
    George Markell, Maintenance
    Henry Otter, Human Resources

31-d5

E-mail

1. Prepare the e-mail below to your instructor; copy a classmate. Attach the file *31-d1*.
2. Print and send the e-mail or key it as a memo. Check and close. (*31-d5*)

Subject: Preparing E-mails

The guides that Sterling Design Consultants prepared for memos are good advice for preparing business e-mails as well. I have attached a copy of the memo from Mr. Westfield for your review.

Be sure to proofread and edit e-mails carefully. Making e-mails error free is as important as making any other document error free.

31-d6

Memo or E-mail

1. Determine your instructor's preferred method of communication for receiving the information below. If the preference is a memo, key as a memo. If the preference is e-mail, prepare the information as an e-mail.
2. Key the appropriate information in the memo heading. Use **Contact Information** as the subject of the memo.
3. Key your contact information where indicated.
4. Print and send the e-mail. Check and close. (*31-d6*)

The contact information that you requested for your keyboarding class database is shown below:

Name: → **Tap the TAB key twice so the contact
information will be aligned.**

Address:

Home Phone:

Cell Phone:

E-mail Address:

92-d2

Newsletter with Clip Art

LITTER

1. Replace the keyed heading using WordArt style 10 with Dark Red fill. Extend the heading to span the line of writing.

2. Select the text, and format it using three equal-width columns.

3. Add four or five clips to the newsletter. Search for clip art that is appropriate for the content, and insert each at an appropriate place. For example, the following keywords would produce appropriate clips: *lakes, mountains, litter, tourist,* and *picnic.*

4. Format the clip art with Tight Text Wrapping and drag the clips to a size that fits easily in the column width with text wrapped to the right of the clip. You may also add a clip that takes the entire width of the column. Add a watermark using the *Draft 2* style, as shown at the right.

5. Preview the document, remove the watermark, and adjust clips if necessary.

6. Check and close. (*92-d2*)

92-d3

Newsletter with Unequal Columns

BUSINESS CENTER

1. Key the newsletter shown on the next page as a one-column document; apply Opulent document theme, Heading 2 style, and narrow margins. Remove the space after the paragraph between the staff names and positions as illustrated on the next page.

2. Position the title at about 1"; use WordArt style 16; adjust the banner to span the line of writing if necessary.

3. Select the text of the newsletter and format it with three unequal columns. Insert lines between the columns. Use the following setting in the Columns dialog box:

   Column 1: 1.5"

   Space between columns: .3"

   Columns 2 and 3: 2.7"

4. Insert a column break (Page Layout/Breaks/Column) after the information about *Crown Lake News and Views* and before *New Development Project.*

5. Insert the *business center* picture from the data files; use Tight Text Wrapping and size and position it as shown on the next page.

6. Insert an *Eagle* from the clip art gallery; use Tight Text Wrapping and size and position it as shown on the next page. Insert it after the Eagle Award has been mentioned.

7. Check and close. (*92-d3*)

Block Letter Format

Key each line, striving for control. Repeat if desired.

alphabet	1	Extra awards given by my employer amazed Jo, the file clerk.
figures	2	I will be on vacation June 4-7, October 3, 5, 8, and December 6-9.
shift	3	Sue, May, Al, Tom, and Jo will meet us at the Pick and Save store.
easy	4	Ask the girl to copy the letter for all the workers in the office.

| 1 | 2 | 3 | 4 | 5 | 6 | 7 | 8 | 9 | 10 | 11 | 12 | 13 |

NEW FUNCTIONS

32b

AUTOMATIC CURRENT DATE

The automatic current date is another easy way to enter the current date.

1. Key the first four characters of the current month. The current month will display.
2. Tap the ENTER key to accept the date.
3. Tap the SPACEBAR to display the remainder of the current date.

DRILL 1   AUTOMATIC DATE

1. In a new blank document, key the first four characters of the current month, e.g., Octo for October.

2. Tap the ENTER key and then the SPACEBAR.
3. Check and close. (32-drill1)

DIALOG BOX LAUNCHER

HOME/FONT GROUP/DIALOG BOX LAUNCHER

In some cases, more options than the ones displayed in a specific group may be needed. To access these options, click the Dialog Box Launcher ❶, the small diagonal arrow in the lower-right corner of the group. For example, when you click the Dialog Box Launcher for the Font group, the Font dialog box displays ❷.

DRILL 2   EXPLORE DIALOG BOX LAUNCHER

1. Open a new blank document.
2. On the Home tab, in the Font group, click the Dialog Box Launcher. Click Cancel to close the dialog box. Repeat step 2 for the Paragraph and Styles groups.

3. On the Page Layout tab, in the Page Setup group, click the Dialog Box Launcher.
4. On the References tab, in the Footnotes group, click the Dialog Box Launcher. Close the dialog box and the exercise.

1. Select the heading, apply Cambria 48-point Dark Red color, and center it.
2. Select all of the text and apply three-column format.
3. Insert a continuous section break at the end of the text to balance the columns.
4. Add a *Draft 2* watermark.
5. Check and close. (*92-drill5*)

To format columns of unequal width:

1. On the Page Layout tab, in the Page Setup group, click the down arrow on Columns.
2. Select More Columns to display the Columns dialog box ❶.
3. Select the number of columns ❷.
4. Remove the check from Equal column width ❸.
5. Check Line between to add a line between columns ❹.
6. Use the up and down arrows ❺ to increase or decrease the width of each column that you want to change. Click OK.

Are You a Litter Bug?

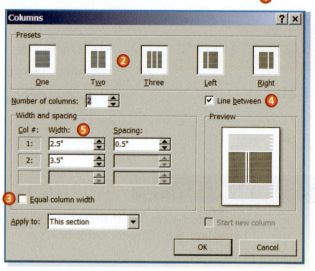

1. Select the heading, apply Corbel 48-point Green color, and center it.
2. Select all of the text to be formatted in columns, and click More Columns on the Columns gallery; select two columns.
3. Remove the check from Equal column width. Insert a line between columns.
4. Insert a continuous section break to balance the columns.
5. Reduce the width of column 1 to 2.5"; column 2 automatically increases to 3.5".
6. Check and close. (*92-drill6*)

APPLICATIONS

92-d1

SmartArt Graphic

1. Apply Oriel document theme.
2. Key the title **Job Experience Hierarchy**, and apply Title style.
3. Insert a Vertical Chevron List from SmartArt graphics and key the text shown below.

1 ▪ Relevant job experience in the field
  ▪ Intern/co-op in field
2 ▪ Temporary/part-time job in field
  ▪ Intern/co-op in related area
3 ▪ Temporary/part-time job in related area
  ▪ Unrelated job experience

4. Check and close. (*92-d1*)

CENTER PAGE

PAGE LAYOUT/PAGE SETUP/DIALOG BOX LAUNCHER

Page Setup

The Center Page command centers a document vertically on the page. Should extra hard returns (¶) appear at the beginning or end of a document, these are also considered to be part of the document. Be careful to delete extra hard returns before centering a page.

To center a page vertically:

1. Position the insertion point on the page to be centered.
2. From the Page Layout tab on the Page Setup group, click the Dialog Box Launcher ①. The Page Setup dialog box displays.
3. Click the Layout tab ②.
4. Click the Vertical alignment down arrow. Select Center ③.
5. Click OK.

KEYBOARDING PRO DELUXE ▶ See References/Word commands/Lesson 32

DRILL 3 CENTER PAGE

1. Key your first and last name in a new document and center-align it.

2. Center the page. Verify that your name now displays at about 4.5" on the Vertical Ruler. Allowing for the 1" top margin, your name would print at about 5.5" or the exact center of an 8½" x 11" sheet of paper.

3. Check and close the document. (32-drill3)

DOCUMENT DESIGN

32c

BUSINESS LETTERS

Business letters are used to communicate with persons outside of the business. Business letters carry two messages: the tone and content, and the appearance of the document. Appearance is important because it creates the critical first impression. Stationery, use of standard letter parts, and placement should convey that the writer is intelligent, informed, and detail minded.

STATIONERY

Letters should be printed on high-quality (about 24-pound) letterhead stationery. Standard size for letterhead is 8½" × 11". Envelopes should match the letterhead in quality and color.

WATERMARK

PAGE LAYOUT/PAGE BACKGROUND/WATERMARK

Page Background ❶

A watermark consists of text or a picture that appears in a light version behind document text. Some of the commonly used watermarks are *confidential*, *draft*, or *urgent*.

To add a watermark:

1. On the Page layout tab in the Page Background group, click Watermark ❶.

2. Select the watermark ❷, such as *Sample 1*, to be added from the Gallery.

3. The watermark can be seen on the printed document and also in Print Layout View and Full Screen Reading View.

DRILL 4   WATERMARK

1. Open *91-drill3*.
2. Apply Aspect document theme.
3. Insert the *Sample 1* watermark.

4. Add a ½-point box page border.
5. Apply Orange, Accent 1 color to the page border.
6. Check and close. (*92-drill4*)

REVIEW FUNCTIONS

92c Columns

COLUMNS

PAGE LAYOUT/PAGE SETUP/COLUMNS

Text is generally formatted using one column; that is, the text extends from the left margin to the right margin. However, text may also be formatted in multiple columns. Newsletters are usually formatted in columns similar to newspapers. These documents typically are designed with headings spanning the columns (called *banners* or *mastheads*). Text flows down one column to the top of the next one. Columns may be of equal or unequal width.

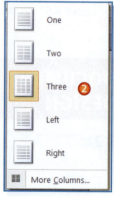

To create columns of equal width:

1. On the Page Layout tab, in the Page Setup group, click the down arrow on Columns ❶.

2. Select the number of columns ❷ you want the document to have.

3. If you wish columns to be balanced or end at approximately the same point, insert a continuous section break at the end of the last line of text (Page Layout/Breaks/Continuous).

Note: Column format may be applied before or after keying text. If columns are set before text is keyed, use Print Layout View to check the appearance of the text. Generally, column formats are easier to apply after keying text.

To format a banner or masthead:

1. Select the text to be included in the banner, click the Columns button, and select one column.

2. Format the banner as desired.

Are You a Litter Bug?

BUSINESS LETTER FORMATS IN TRANSITION

With *Word 2007* and its new defaults, it is likely that two letter formats will be used until the transition of all users to the new interface. Study the two letters below to note the appearance of the letter keyed in *Word 2007* with its defaults and a letter keyed in the traditional format with *Word 2003* defaults.

E-Market, Group
10 East Rivercenter Boulevard
Covington, KY 41016-8765

Current date

Mr. Eric Seymour
Professional Office Consultants
1782 Laurel Canyon Road
Sunnyvale, CA 94085-9087

Dear Mr. Seymour

Have you heard your friends and colleagues talk about obtaining real-time stock quotes, real-time account balances and positions, NASDAQ Level II quotes, or extended-hours trading? If so, then they are among the many serious investors who have opened an account with E-Market Firm.

We are confident that the best decisions are informed decisions that are made in a very timely manner. E-Market Firm has an online help desk that provides information for all levels of investors, from beginners to the experienced serious trader. You can learn basic tactics for investing in the stock market, avoiding common mistakes, and picking up some advanced strategies.

To stay on top of the market and your investments, please visit our online investing website at http:www.emarketfirm.com to learn more about our banking and brokerage services and to access our online help desk. E-Market Firm is the premier site for online investing.

Sincerely

Emily Zumwalt
Marketing Manager

xx

New Business Letter Format

E-Market, Group
10 East Rivercenter Boulevard
Covington, KY 41016-8765

Current date

Mr. Eric Seymour
Professional Office Consultants
1782 Laurel Canyon Road
Sunnyvale, CA 94085-9087

Dear Mr. Seymour

Have you heard your friends and colleagues talk about obtaining real-time stock quotes, real-time account balances and positions, NASDAQ Level II quotes, or extended-hours trading? If so, then they are among the many serious investors who have opened an account with E-Market Firm.

We are confident that the best decisions are informed decisions that are made in a very timely manner. E-Market Firm has an online help desk that provides information for all levels of investors, from beginners to the experienced serious trader. You can learn basic tactics for investing in the stock market, avoiding common mistakes, and picking up some advanced strategies.

To stay on top of the market and your investments, please visit our online investing website at http://www.emarketfirm.com to learn more about our banking and brokerage services and to access our online help desk. E-Market Firm is the premier site for online investing.

Sincerely

Emily Zumwalt
Marketing Manager

xx

Traditional Business Letter Format

SMARTART

INSERT/ILLUSTRATIONS/SMARTART

SmartArt provides a gallery of graphics that enable you to present data in graphic form. It is very easy to create sophisticated graphics using SmartArt. Seven different types of graphics are included in the SmartArt gallery. You can format and change colors as you did with clip art and WordArt. Note the list at the left of the design shown below.

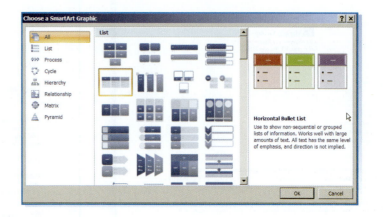

To create a SmartArt graphic:

1. On the Insert tab, in the Illustrations group, click SmartArt ①.

2. Select the graphic to be inserted from the gallery that displays, such as a Horizontal Bullet List ②; click OK.

3. Select text in the heading placeholder ③, and key the heading in each box.

4. Select the text in the bulleted items placeholder ④, and key the text.

5. To change colors, click in the graphic and select Design under SmartArt tools; click Change Colors.

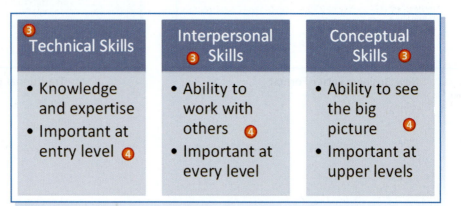

DRILL 3   SMARTART

1. Insert a Horizontal Bullet List graphic from the SmartArt gallery.

2. Click in each of the text boxes, and key the text shown in the illustration above.

3. Note that the text adjusts its size to fit in the box.

4. Click in the graphic, select Design, and then click change colors; select Colorful.

5. Check and close. (*92-drill3*)

LETTER PARTS AND BLOCK LETTER FORMAT

Businesspeople expect to see standard letter parts arranged in the proper sequence. Letters consist of three main parts: the opening lines to the receiver (letter address and salutation), the body or message, and the writer's closing lines. Standard letter parts and the required spacing using the defaults of *Word 2007* are explained below and illustrated on the following page.

Block letter style is a typical business letter format in which all letter parts are keyed at the left margin. For most letters, use open punctuation, which requires no punctuation after the salutation or the complimentary closing.

Communication Specialists, Inc.

3840 Cedar Mill Parkway
Athens, GA 30606-4384

Current date ↓2

Mr. Marcus Cavenaugh
Pomeroy Financial Services   **Remove extra space**
149 Research Park Road
LaGrange, GA 30240-0140 ↓1

Dear Mr. Cavenaugh ↓1

The new user interface offered with *Word 2007* as well as the new defaults are the center of business conversations across the globe. New terminology such as ribbons, galleries, Office button, mini toolbar, and contextual tabs require new learning by those who upgrade to *Word 2007*. Furthermore, the new defaults in line spacing (1.15) and 10 point after a paragraph are only two changes that offer new challenges in document layout. ↓1

Our staff of experts at Communication Specialists, Inc. understands your company's document layout needs as you communicate with your clients, your board of directors, your employees, and other business entities. We also realize that decisions regarding document formats require consideration of four elements: (1) attractiveness of the format, (2) readability of the format, (3) effective use of space on the page, and (4) efficiency in producing the format. Changes in *Word 2007* provide new opportunities for designing documents that portray the excellent image of your company. ↓1

We encourage you to call our office at 706-555-0138 to set up a meeting with our communication experts to discuss our comprehensive training program. This program is carefully designed to teach efficient use of the software, but most importantly our experts will teach your staff how to create the most attractive and efficient layout for each business document. ↓1

Mr. Cavenaugh, we understand your desire to distribute documents that include the design and appeal of contemporary office technology. We look forward to discussing your design needs with you. ↓1

Sincerely ↓2

Carole Gonzalez   **Remove extra space**
Communication Manager ↓1

xx

Block Letter Style with Open Punctuation

Letterhead: Preprinted stationery that includes the company name, logo, address, and other optional information such as telephone number and fax number.

Dateline: Date the letter is prepared. Position at about 2" (tap ENTER three times) or use the Center Page command. Be sure to begin at least 0.5" below the letterhead.

Letter address: Complete address of the letter recipient. Begin two lines below the date (tap ENTER twice).

Generally include receiver's name, company name, street address, city, state (one space after state), and ZIP Code. Include a personal title, e.g., Mr., Ms., Dr. Remove the added space between the lines of the letter address.

Salutation (or greeting): Begin one line below the letter address (tap ENTER once). Include courtesy title with person's name, e.g., Dear Mr. Smith. Use *Ladies and Gentlemen* when addressing a company.

Body: Begin one line below the salutation.

Use the 1.15 default line spacing; tap ENTER once between paragraphs. **Complimentary closing:** Begin one line below the body. Capitalize only the first letter of the closing.

Writer's name and title: Begin two lines below the complimentary closing (tap ENTER twice).

Include a personal title to designate gender only when the writer's name is not gender specific, such as Pat or Chris, or when initials are used, such J. A. Moe.

Key the title on the first line with the name or separately on the second line, whichever gives better balance. Use a comma to separate name and title if on one line. If two lines are used, remove the added space between the two lines.

Reference initials: Begin one line below the writer's name and title. Key reference initials, e.g., **xx** in lowercase. Replace *xx* with your initials.

CROP AND FRAME WITH PICTURE STYLES

PICTURE TOOLS/FORMAT/SIZE/CROP/AND FORMAT/PICTURE STYLES/ SELECT DESIRED STYLE

Many tools are provided to enhance the quality of a picture. Some of the formatting and editing tools are color correction, brightness, cropping, and framing. Cropping refers to cutting off unwanted parts of the picture.

To crop and frame a picture:

1. Click the picture to select it.
2. Under Picture Tools **1**, click the Format tab.
3. Use Text Wrapping style and position as desired.
4. On the Format tab, under Picture Tools, click the Crop button **2** to display the Crop handles **3** on the corners and center of the four borders of the picture.

5. Drag the handles on the borders of areas you want to crop. In this picture, the center bottom handle was used to crop from the bottom: the line **4** shows where the picture is being cropped. It also needs to be cropped on the left side and very slightly on the right.

6. On the Format tab, under Picture Tools, in the Picture Styles group, click the style **5** desired to frame the picture.

DRILL 2 · FORMAT PICTURE · HOUSE

1. Insert the data file *house*. Format it using Square Text Wrapping and position it at the top center.
2. Crop the picture on the bottom, left, and right sides as shown on the left.
3. Apply Metal Rounded Rectangle to frame the picture.
4. Preview and adjust cropping if needed.
5. Check and close. (*92-drill2*)

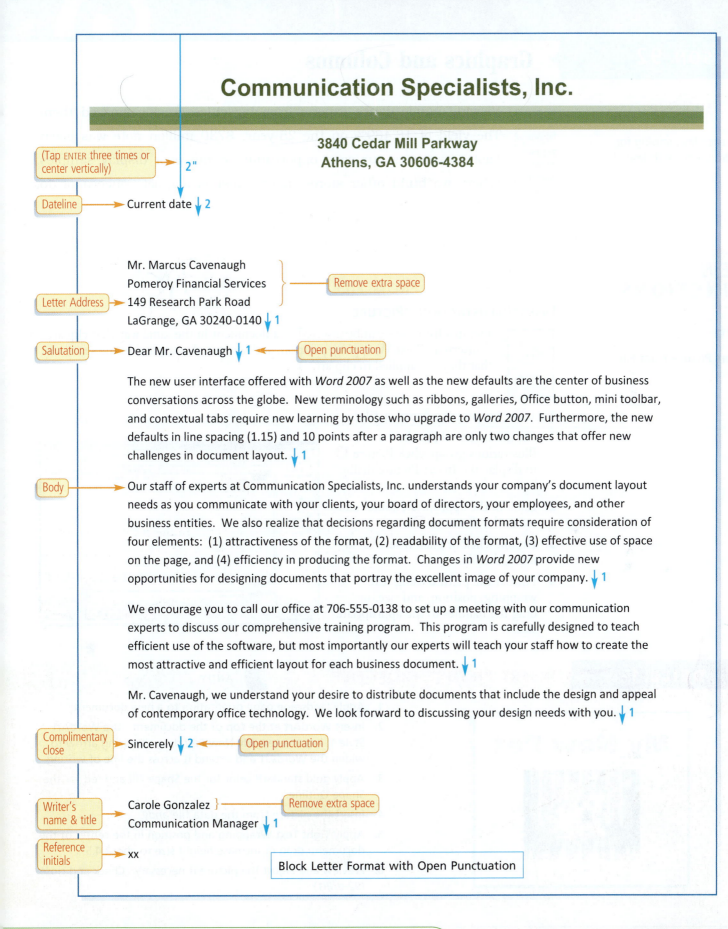

Communication Specialists, Inc.

3840 Cedar Mill Parkway
Athens, GA 30606-4384

(Tap ENTER three times or center vertically) → 2"

Dateline → Current date ↓2

Letter Address →
Mr. Marcus Cavenaugh
Pomeroy Financial Services ⟩ Remove extra space
149 Research Park Road
LaGrange, GA 30240-0140 ↓1

Salutation → Dear Mr. Cavenaugh ↓1 ← Open punctuation

The new user interface offered with *Word 2007* as well as the new defaults are the center of business conversations across the globe. New terminology such as ribbons, galleries, Office button, mini toolbar, and contextual tabs require new learning by those who upgrade to *Word 2007*. Furthermore, the new defaults in line spacing (1.15) and 10 points after a paragraph are only two changes that offer new challenges in document layout. ↓1

Body →
Our staff of experts at Communication Specialists, Inc. understands your company's document layout needs as you communicate with your clients, your board of directors, your employees, and other business entities. We also realize that decisions regarding document formats require consideration of four elements: (1) attractiveness of the format, (2) readability of the format, (3) effective use of space on the page, and (4) efficiency in producing the format. Changes in *Word 2007* provide new opportunities for designing documents that portray the excellent image of your company. ↓1

We encourage you to call our office at 706-555-0138 to set up a meeting with our communication experts to discuss our comprehensive training program. This program is carefully designed to teach efficient use of the software, but most importantly our experts will teach your staff how to create the most attractive and efficient layout for each business document. ↓1

Mr. Cavenaugh, we understand your desire to distribute documents that include the design and appeal of contemporary office technology. We look forward to discussing your design needs with you. ↓1

Complimentary close → Sincerely ↓2 ← Open punctuation

Writer's name & title →
Carole Gonzalez ⟩ Remove extra space
Communication Manager ↓1

Reference initials → xx

Block Letter Format with Open Punctuation

LESSON 92 | Graphics and Columns

WARMUP 92a

Key each line, striving for control. Repeat if desired.

alphabet	1	Viewing jungle dance experts from big cities quickly amazed them.
fig/sym	2	The yield of 18.469% on the 25-year, $730 million note was given.
3rd/4th fingers	3	Last spring was our good opportunity to zap poor display samples.
adjacent reaches	4	Where we build other stores in the west is a quiet concern of Jo.

| 1 | 2 | 3 | 4 | 5 | 6 | 7 | 8 | 9 | 10 | 11 | 12 | 13 |

NEW FUNCTIONS

92b

Insert Picture from File

INSERT PICTURE FROM FILE

INSERT/ILLUSTRATIONS/PICTURE

Pictures from files can be inserted in a document in the same way that clip art is inserted. Text Wrapping, position, and size are also applied in the same way that they are applied to clip art.

To insert a picture from a file:

1. On the Insert tab, in the Illustrations group, click Picture ① to display the Insert Picture dialog box.

2. Look in the appropriate folder and select the filename ②.

3. Double-click or click Insert ③ to insert the file.

4. Format the picture using text wrapping, position, and size, or drag the handles to the appropriate size.

DRILL 1 | INSERT PICTURE FROM FILE — ANDY

My New Pet

1. Apply landscape page orientation to a new document.

2. Insert WordArt at the top of the document. Use WordArt Style 1; key the text **My New Pet**; drag the sizing arrow to widen the WordArt and extend it across the line of writing.

3. Apply gold standard color for the Shape Fill and red for the Shape Outline.

4. Insert the picture from the data file *andy*.

5. Apply Tight Text Wrapping and position in the center of the document: drag or increase height size to about 4.5".

6. Preview and adjust the picture if necessary. Check and close. (*92-drill1*)

32-d1

Block Letter

1. Key the model letter on page 123 in block format with open punctuation. Assume you are using letterhead stationery.

2. Tap ENTER to position the dateline at about 2". Insert the current date using the Automatic Date feature.

3. Include your reference initials. If the first letter of your initials is automatically capitalized, point to the initial until the AutoCorrect Options button appears, click the button, and then choose Undo Automatic Capitalization.

4. Follow the proofreading procedures outlined in Lesson 31. Be sure to remove the added space in the letter address and between the writer's name and title. Use Show/Hide to view paragraph markers to confirm that you have correct spacing between letter parts.

5. Check and close. (*32-d1*)

32-d2

Block Letter

1. Key the letter below in block format with open punctuation. Insert the date using the automatic date.

2. Add your reference initials in lowercase letters. Remove extra space in the letter address and the writer's name and title.

3. Check and close. (*32-d2*)

Current date

Ms. Alice Ottoman
Premiere Properties, Inc.
52 Ocean Drive
Newport Beach, CA 92660-8293

Dear Ms. Ottoman

Is your website growing your real estate market as well as you would like? Internet Solutions invites you to take a look at our advanced strategies for marketing your properties on the World Wide Web. For example, we can create 360-degree panoramic pictures for your website. You can give your clients a virtual spin of the living room, kitchen, and every room in the house.

Call today for a demonstration of this remarkable technology and talk with our designers about other innovative website marketing strategies. Give your clients a better visual understanding of the property layout and more valuable information for decision making—something your competition does not have.

Sincerely

LeeAnn Rodgers
Marketing Manager

xx

91-d1

WordArt and Clip Art

1. In a new document, insert WordArt at approximately 2"; use the second WordArt style (#8) in the second row of the gallery of styles.

2. Key **Adoption Agreement**. Select WordArt and expand the size so that it spans the line of writing from the left margin to the right margin.

3. Use **dog** or **cat** as the keyword and search clip art for an appropriate clip. Insert the clip of your choice.

4. Use Text Wrapping Style In line with text; select position at the center top; drag the clip below the WordArt title. Size the picture about 2.5" high.

5. Key the information below. Apply a dropped cap to the first letter of the paragraph.

6. Insert a decorative checkbox from the Symbols using a Wingdings font for the list of the checked items.

7. Allow space for a signature and add a signature line that spans the line of writing using a right underline tab.

8. Check and close. (*91-d1*)

Adoption of a pet can be extremely rewarding. However, it is important to remember that adoption is a privilege that requires the new owner to take appropriate care of the pet. Read the five items checked below that contain the specific requirements for the adoption of a pet. Your signature below the five checked items obligates you to follow all of these guides.

☑ I agree to take my new pet to the veterinarian within five days of adoption.

☑ I will provide appropriate food, fresh water, and shelter for my pet.

☑ I will exercise my pet daily.

☑ I will spay or neuter my pet within six months.

☑ I will not sell my pet.

Signature _____

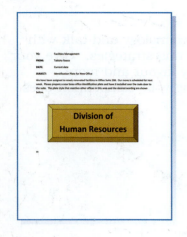

91-d2

Memo

1. Key the following memo:

   TO: Facilities Management | FROM: Takisha Reece | DATE: Current | SUBJECT: Identification Plate for New Office

   We have been assigned to newly renovated facilities in Office Suite 208. Our move is scheduled for next week. Please prepare a new brass office identification plate and have it installed over the main door to the suite. The plate style that matches other offices in this area and the desired wording are shown below.

2. From the Basic Shapes category, insert a Bevel shape. Size it about 2" by 5"; add text to the shape by right-clicking it and selecting Add Text.

3. Key **Division of Human Resources** on two lines; remove space after the paragraph on the first line. Apply Bold and grow the font until it fills the shape. Apply a gold standard color fill to the shape.

4. Check and close. (*91-d2*)

32-d3

Block Letter and Center Page

1. Open *32-d2*.
2. Replace the letter address with the one below, using proper format.

   Ms. Andrea Virzi, J. P. Personnel Services, 2351 West Ravina Drive, Atlanta, GA 30346-9105.
3. Supply the correct salutation. Turn on Show/Hide (¶). Delete the hard returns above the dateline. Center the page vertically; preview to check placement. Note that a short letter looks more attractive centered vertically than positioned at 2.0".
4. Check and close. (*32-d3*)

32-d4

Block Letter and Center Page

1. Read the *Workplace Success* feature shown below.
2. In a new blank document, compose a letter to your instructor responding to this feature article. Follow the outline below to compose your letter.

   ¶1 Inform your teacher that you have read the feature article on organizational skills. Include a personal reaction to the information in the article.

   ¶2 Discuss your rating on the eight items listed below.

   ¶3 Discuss one organizational skill that you will work on this week. Explain your plan of action to improve this skill. **Note:** You may list something that is not included in the feature article.
3. Format the letter as a block letter with open punctuation in the new document format used by *Word 2007* users. Align the page at vertical center. Turn on Show/Hide (¶) to check that no hard returns are entered before the date or at the end of the letter. Refer to the model letter on page 123 to ensure all letter parts are used appropriately. Use your name as the writer's name; use *Student* as the writer's title. Reference initials are not needed since you are the writer of the message.
4. Check and close. (*32-d4*)

WORKPLACE SUCCESS

Organizational Skills

© RON CHAPPLE/THINKSTOCK IMAGES/JUPITERIMAGES

Well-organized employees accomplish daily tasks in a timely manner, avoid stress, and impress their employers and coworkers. Following simple daily time management practices reaps benefits and often even a promotion. How would you rate yourself on the following time management practices?

1. Prioritize tasks to be done each day and the amount of time needed to complete each task. Assign tasks to a specific time on the calendar.
2. Set designated times to answer e-mail and return phone calls.
3. Place calendar/planner on desk in location for easy access to add notes and see priority items.
4. Record notes, phone numbers, addresses in calendar and not on post-it notes.
5. Place phone, notepad, and pen on desk for easy reach.
6. Keep reference books in a designated location—not on the desk.
7. File any materials for which you no longer need immediate access.
8. Prepare folders for pending items, projects, and reading, and file those materials away instead of keeping them piled on the desktop.

WORDART

INSERT/TEXT/WORDART

WordArt provides a gallery of text styles that can be used to create decorative text. WordArt is frequently used for banner heads on documents such as newsletters or on items posted. The gallery of WordArt styles is accessed from the WordArt button, in the Text group, on the Insert tab. The text can be enlarged and formatted in a variety of ways.

To insert WordArt:

1. From the Insert tab, in the Text group, click the WordArt button ❶ to display the gallery of WordArt styles ❷.

2. Click the desired WordArt Style to display the Edit WordArt Text dialog box ❸. Note the Style name displays when you hover the mouse over a style.

3. Select *Your Text Here* and key the desired text ❹; then click OK to display your text in WordArt.

To format WordArt:

1. Select the text to display the WordArt format tools ❺.

2. Under WordArt tools, on the Format tab, in the WordArt Styles group, click Shape Fill ❻ to change the color of the fill or to add effects such as gradient, texture, or pattern.

3. Click Shape Outline ❼ to change the color or weight of the border.

4. Click Shadow Effects ❽ to add a shadow to a shape.

DRILL 5   **WORDART**

1. Create the WordArt heading, **Sample Banner**, shown below; use Style 1 in the WordArt Gallery.

2. Format using Blue Accent 1 Lighter than 40% Shape Fill.

3. Format using Blue, Accent 1, Darker 50% Shape Outline and a line weight of 2¼ points.

4. Format with Shadow Style 5 effect.

5. Click the banner and drag the sizing arrow at the corner until the banner covers the line of writing.

6. Check and close. (*91-drill5*)

Block Letter with Envelope

WARMUP 33a

Key each line, striving for control. Repeat if desired.

1st finger
1 My 456 heavy brown jugs have nothing in them; fill them by May 7.
2 The 57 bins are numbered 1 to 57; Bins 5, 6, 45, and 57 are full.

2nd finger
3 Ed decided to crate 38 pieces of cedar decking from the old dock.
4 Mike, who was 38 in December, likes a piece of ice in cold cider.

3rd finger
5 Polly made 29 points on the quiz; Wex 10 points. Did they pass?
6 Sall saw Ezra pass 200 pizza pans to Sean, who fixed 20 of them.

| 1 | 2 | 3 | 4 | 5 | 6 | 7 | 8 | 9 | 10 | 11 | 12 | 13 |

SKILL BUILDING

33b Timed Writing
1. Key a 3' timed writing, working for speed.
2. Key a 3' timed writing, working for control.

all letters

	gwam	3'
So now you are operating a keyboard and don't you find it	4	38
amazing that your fingers, working with very little visual help,	8	43
move easily and quickly from one key to the next, helping you to	13	47
change words into ideas and sentences. You just decide what you	17	51
want to say and the format in which you want to say it, and your	21	56
keyboard will carry out your order exactly as you enter it. One	26	60
operator said lately that she sometimes wonders just who is most	30	64
responsible for the completed product—the person or the machine.	34	69

3' | 1 | 2 | 3 | 4 | 5 |

COMMUNICATION

33c

LETTER ADDRESSES AND SALUTATIONS

The salutation, or greeting, consists of the person's personal title (*Mr.*, *Ms.*, or *Mrs.*) or professional title (*Dr.*, *Professor*, *Senator*, *Honorable*), and the person's last name. Do not use a first name unless you have a personal relationship. The salutation should agree in number with the addressee. If the letter is addressed to more than one person, the salutation is plural.

	Receiver	Salutation
To individuals	Dr. Alexander Gray	Dear Dr. Gray
	Dr. and Mrs. Thompson	Dear Dr. and Mrs. Thompson
To organizations	TMP Electronics, Inc.	Ladies and Gentlemen
Name unknown	Advertising Manager	Dear Advertising Manager

DRILL 1   COMPOSE SALUTATIONS

1. In a new blank document, key the appropriate salutation for each letter recipient. (Do not key the letters *a* through *f*.)
2. Check and close. (*33-drill1*)

a. Mr. Thomas Green
b. Dr. John Watson
c. Phillips Insurance Company
d. Mr. and Mrs. Reginald Worthington
e. Senator Constance Wells
f. Smith College Board of Directors

To size clip art:

PICTURE TOOLS/FORMAT/SIZE/HEIGHT OR WIDTH

- Click the clip art to select it. On the Format tab, under Picture Tools, in the Size group, click Height and reduce the size to the desired amount, such as 1.5". The width reduces proportionately.

  - or -

- Click the clip art to select it. Hover the mouse over the handle on the lower-right corner. When it turns into a double-headed arrow, drag it up and to the left to reduce the size or down and to the right to increase the size.

DRILL 3   SIZE CLIP ART

1. Open *91-drill2*.
2. Click the clip art, and drag the clip down and to the right to enlarge it slightly.
3. With the clip art selected, on the Format tab, under Picture Tools, in the Size group, click the down arrow next to

Height and reduce the height to 1.5". Note that it reduces the width to 1".

4. Check and close. (*91-drill3*)

NEW FUNCTIONS

91e Drop Cap

DROP CAP

INSERT/TEXT/DROP CAP

A drop cap is a large version of the initial letter of a paragraph. Two options are available for positioning the large letter—within the text or in the margin. The options are accessed by clicking the down arrow on the Drop Cap button from the Insert tab in the Text group. Drop caps work better in paragraphs with several lines of text.

To apply a drop cap:

1. Select the letter to be enlarged and dropped; then on the Insert tab, in the Text group, click Drop Cap ❶.
2. Click either the Dropped or In margin option ❷.

To remove a drop cap:

1. Select the Dropped Cap; then on the Insert tab, in the Text group, click Drop Cap.
2. Click None ❸.

DRILL 4   DROP CAP   OFFICERS

1. Select the first letter of each officer shown in bold on the document and apply a drop cap using the In margin option.
2. Preview the document and remove all drop caps added in the margin.

3. Select the first letter of each officer and apply the Dropped option.
4. On the Page Layout tab, apply the Civic document theme. Note the difference the font style makes.
5. Check and close. (*91-drill4*).

NEW FUNCTIONS

ENVELOPES

MAILINGS/CREATE/ENVELOPES

33d

The Envelopes feature can insert the delivery address automatically if a letter is displayed; postage can even be added if special software is installed. The default is a size 10 envelope ($4^1/_8$" by $9^1/_2$"); other sizes are available by clicking the Options button on the Envelopes tab.

> **IMAGE MAKERS**
> 5131 Moss Springs Road
> Columbia, SC 29209-4768
>
>
>   Mr. Eric Seymour
>   Professional Office Consultants
>   1782 Laurel Canyon Road
>   Sunnyvale, CA 94085-9087

To generate an envelope:

1. Display the letter you have created and select the letter address.

2. On the Mailings tab in the Create group, click Envelopes ❶. The mailing address is automatically displayed in the Delivery address box. (To create an envelope without a letter, key the address in the Delivery address box.)

3. If you are using business envelopes with a preprinted return address (assume you are), click the Return address Omit box ❷. To include a return address, do not check the Omit box; click in the Return address box and key the return address.

4. Click Print to print the envelope or click Add to Document to add the envelope to the top of the document containing the letter ❸.

DRILL 2   CREATE ENVELOPE

1. Open *32-d1*.
2. Create and attach an envelope to the letter.

3. Your instructor may have you print envelopes on plain paper.
4. Check and close. (*33-drill2*)

DRILL 3   CREATE ENVELOPE

1. In a new blank document, go to the Envelopes and Labels dialog box without keying a letter address.
2. Key the following letter address in the envelope dialog box.

    Ms. Joyce Bohn, Treasurer
    Citizens for the Environment
    1888 Hutchins Avenue
    Seattle, WA 98111-1888

3. Add the envelope to the document.
4. Check and close. (*33-drill3*).

CLIP ART

INSERT/ILLUSTRATIONS/CLIP ART

 Clip art consists of a gallery of graphic images that can be added to your document. Clip art is organized into collections in the Clip Organizer to make searching easier.

To insert clip art:

1. On the Insert tab, in the Illustrations group, click Clip Art ❶.

2. In the Clip Art task pane, in the Search for box, key the name (**koala bear**) or category (**animals**) of the clip you wish to locate ❷.

3. In the Results should be box, you can search for all types of media or for clip art ❸.

4. Click the down arrow on the clip you wish to insert and select insert ❹.

To wrap text around a clip and position the clip:

PICTURE TOOLS/FORMAT/ARRANGE/TEXT WRAPPING/POSITION

1. Click the clip art to select it. On the Format tab, under Picture Tools, in the Arrange group, click the down arrow next to Text Wrapping ❶.

2. Select the desired Text Wrapping option such as Square ❷.

3. On the Format tab, under Picture Tools, in the Arrange group, click Position ❸, and then select the desired position from the gallery of options ❹.

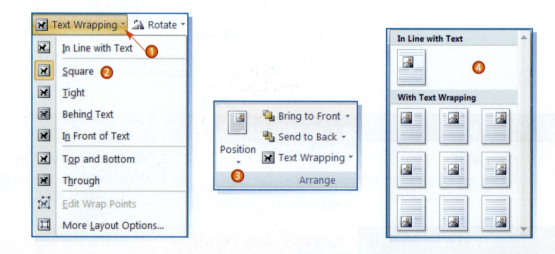

| DRILL 2 | CLIP ART | | KOALA BEAR |

1. Search for *animals* in the Clip Art task pane; select a clip of a koala bear and insert it in the open document.

2. Click the clip art, and then click the down arrow on Text Wrapping and choose the Square Text Wrapping option.

3. Click the down arrow on Position, and then select the position with the illustration at the top left with Square Text Wrapping.

4. Check and close. (*91-drill2*)

33-d1
Single Envelope

1. Key a single envelope to the following address. Include your address as the return address.
2. Check and close. *(33-d1)*

> Mr. Jacob Gillespie
> 1783 West Rockhill Road
> Bartlett, TN 38133-1783

33-d2
Block Letter and Envelope

1. Key the following letter in the block style with open punctuation. Begin the date at about 2". Remember to remove the extra space in the letter address.
2. Check the letter placement.
3. Select the letter address and create an envelope for the letter.
4. Check and close. *(33-d2)*

April 4, 2008 | Mrs. Rose Shikamuru | 55 Lawrence Street |Topeka, KS 66607-6657 | Dear Mrs. Shikamuru

Thank you for your recent letter asking about employment opportunities with our company. We are happy to inform you that Mr. Edward Ybarra, our recruiting representative, will be on your campus on April 23, 24, 25, and 26 to interview students who are interested in our company.

We suggest that you talk soon with your student placement office, as all appointments with Mr. Ybarra will be made through that office. Please bring with you the application questionnaire the office provides.

Within a few days, we will send you a company brochure with information about our salary, bonus, and retirement plans. You will want to visit our website at http://www.skylermotors.com to find facts about our company mission and accomplishments as well as learn about the beautiful community in which we are located. We believe a close study of this information will convince you, as it has many others, that our company builds futures as well as small motors.

If there is any way we can help you, please e-mail me at mbragg@skylermotors.com.

Sincerely | Myrtle K. Bragg | Human Services Director | xx

33-d3
Block Letter and Envelope

1. Key the letter at the top of the next page in block style with open punctuation. Center the letter vertically on the page.
2. Add an envelope to the letter.
3. Check and close. *(33-d3)*

SHAPES

INSERT/ILLUSTRATIONS/SHAPES

Shapes are often called drawing tools because the shapes are drawn by dragging the mouse at the point you want them to be positioned. Shapes can be drawn to any size desired. They can be formatted using shape styles or manually by changing the color, effects, or border. Shapes are selected from a gallery of shapes that are accessed from the down arrow on the Shapes button. Recently used shapes appear at the top of the gallery. Shapes are organized in categories for ease in locating them. Holding the mouse over a shape will display its name.

To insert and format shapes:

1. On the Insert tab, in the Illustrations group, click the down arrow on the Shapes button **1** to display the gallery of shapes **2**. Click the shape you wish to insert, and drag the mouse where you wish to position it.

2. To format a shape, click the shape to select it and then under Drawing Tools click the Format tab **3**.

3. To apply a shape style, select one of the styles shown or click the More button **4** in the Shapes Styles group and select the desired style.

4. Click any of the following options to format a shape manually: Shape Fill, Shape Outline, Change Shape, Shadow Effects, or 3-D Effects **5**.

DRILL 1   SHAPES

1. Draw the four shapes (Smiley Face, Striped Right Arrow, Five-Point Star, and Bevel) shown below; position them as shown.

2. Click the Star. In the Shape Styles group, on the Format tab, under Drawing Tools, select the Colored Fill, White Outline - Accent 6 shape style.

3. Click the Smiley Face, and in the Shape Outline, click Red from the Standard Colors; then click Shape Fill and select Yellow from the Standard Colors.

4. Click the Striped Right Arrow, and in the Shadow Effects, click Shadow Style 1.

5. Right-click in the Bevel, click Add Text, and key your name. Select your name, and on the Mini toolbar that appears, grow the font until it fills the top of the Bevel. If your name appears on two lines, shrink the font.

6. With the Bevel selected, click the Shape Fill arrow and select the last color on the Dark Red color theme.

7. Compare your shapes to the ones shown below.

8. Check and close. (*91-drill1*)

33-d3

Continued

Current date | Mr. Trace L. Brecken | 4487 Ingram Street | Corpus Christi, TX 78409-8907 | Dear Mr. Brecken

We have received the package you sent us in which you returned goods from a recent order you gave us. Your refund check, plus return postage, will be mailed to you in a few days.

We are sorry, of course, that you did not find this merchandise personally satisfactory. It is our goal to please all of our customers, and we are always disappointed if we fail.

Please give us an opportunity to try again. We stand behind our merchandise, and that is our guarantee of good service.

Sincerely | Margret Bredewig | Customer Service Department | xx

---

33-d4

Rough Draft Block Letter and Envelope

1. Key the following letter in block letter style. Add an appropriate salutation and other missing letter parts.
2. Center the page vertically. Create an envelope and add to the letter. Check and close. *(33-d4)*
3. Study the illustration in the Reference Guide on folding and inserting letters in an envelope. Fold the letter to insert in the envelope.

Mr. John Crane
5760 Sky Way
Seattle, WA 98108-0321

Would you like to invest in a company that will provide you with a 180% return on your investment? Consider investing in a ~~company~~ firm that specializes in importing and exporting with China. China's gross domestic product (GDP) is expected to be over a trillion dollars.

(bold & italic) Ameri-Chinois has made a significant number of business arrangements with key organizations in China to source goods and to participate in global two-way trade. Trade between China and ~~other countries~~ the rest of the world is expected to grow over 20% this year. China's exports are expected to rise to $244 billion in the year 2009. Imports ~~will~~ are expected to grow to $207 billion.

Please contact Lawrence Chen at Century Investments to learn how you can be an investor in the growing company of Ameri-Chinois. The current price is $0.52; the targeted price is $9.00 per share. Call today! 555-0134

Sincerely

Lawrence Chen, Agent

91c Timed Writing
1. Key three 1' timings; work for speed and try to increase your base rate by eight words.
2. Key one 3' timing writing.

A

all letters

Many people find that creative thinking can be nurtured with effort.   One way to do this is to find multiple solutions to a problem.   Alternatives to a problem should be sought out when there seems to be just one possible solution as well as when a solution has already been found and analyzed.   The more ideas generated, the more options there may be.   If a person can quickly identify the options that are available and experiment with them, then possibly he or she can come up with several other options.   This approach fosters new ideas and stimulates the creative thinking process.

	13	4	44
	26	9	49
	39	13	53
	53	18	57
	65	22	62
	78	26	66
	91	30	70
	104	35	75
	117	39	79
	120	40	80

```
1' | 1 | 2 | 3 | 4 | 5 | 6 | 7 | 8 | 9 | 10 | 11 | 12 | 13 | 14 |
3'        1            2            3            4
```

WORKPLACE SUCCESS

Role Models and Mentors

Role models and mentors are very different, but both can be helpful to young people beginning their careers. Role models are individuals who are admired and emulated by others for whom they are, the positions they hold, the behavior they exhibit, or specific skills they have. Role models may be positive, or they may be negative. Many young people look up to athletes, and some athletes are outstanding role models who exhibit exemplary behavior, while others may be highly successful in their athletic pursuits but exhibit behavior that should not be emulated.

   In the workplace, it is wise to have many role models selected because of specific traits that are outstanding. One person may be excellent at conducting meetings; another may command attention delivering presentations. You can learn from many male and female role models. A role model does not even have to know that she or he is serving as your role model.

   Mentors take a more active role in a person's career. Mentors agree to work with an individual counseling and coaching him or her. In addition, behind the scenes they may be strong advocates of the individuals they are mentoring. Mentors can work directly with the individual being mentored, or they can be total outsiders. Relying on mentors too heavily can have negative implications— especially if the mentor falls out of favor in the company. Having more than one mentor is helpful.

© PHOTODISC / GETTY IMAGES

Modified Block Letter Format

Key each line, striving for control. Repeat if desired.

alphabet	1	Buddy Jackson is saving the door prize money for wax and lacquer.
figures	2	I have fed 47 hens, 25 geese, 10 ducks, 39 lambs, and 68 kittens.
one hand	3	You imply Jon Case exaggerated my opinion on a decrease in rates.
easy	4	I shall make hand signals to the widow with the auditory problem.

| 1 | 2 | 3 | 4 | 5 | 6 | 7 | 8 | 9 | 10 | 11 | 12 | 13 |

SKILL BUILDING

34b Textbook Keying
Key each line once, concentrating on using good keying techniques; tap ENTER twice after each 2-line group.

Balanced-hand words, phrases, and sentences

5 am an by do go he if is it me or ox or so for and big the six spa
6 but cod dot dug eye end wit vie yam make also city work gage them

7 is it|is it|is it he|is it he|for it|for it|paid for it|it is she
8 of it|pay due|pay for|paid me|paid them|also make|such as|may end

9 Sue and Bob may go to the zoo, and he or she may pay for the gas.
10 Jim was sad; Ted saw him as we sat on my bed; we saw him get gas.

| 1 | 2 | 3 | 4 | 5 | 6 | 7 | 8 | 9 | 10 | 11 | 12 | 13 |

FUNCTION REVIEW

34c

TABS

PAGE LAYOUT/PARAGRAPH

Tabs are used to indent paragraphs and to align text vertically. You will recall from Lesson 28 that default tab stops are set at every half-inch position. Take a moment to look at the Horizontal Ruler to identify the small gray lines below each half-inch position.

In Lesson 34 you will set a tab stop at the center of the page (3.25") to key the date and closing lines of a letter formatted in the modified block style. Once you have set a tab stop, all default tabs to the left of the newly set tab are automatically cleared. Therefore, if other tabs are needed, simply choose the desired tab alignment by clicking the Alignment button at the far left of the Horizontal Ruler. Then click the Horizontal Ruler where the desired tab is to be set.

DRILL 1 — SET TABS

1. In a new blank document, set a left tab at 3.25". Key the date at 3.25" and tap the ENTER key twice. **Note:** All default tabs to the left of the newly set tab have been automatically cleared.

2. Set a left tab at 1". Key the following lines and tap the ENTER key once. Remove the space between the items.

    Enclosures: Promissory Note
                 Amortization Schedule

3. Set a left tab at 0.5". Key the following lines. Remove the space between the lines. Undo automatic capitalization in the first line.

    c   Ashley Nobles
         Ethan Vilella

4. Check and close. (*34-drill1*)

Graphic Enhancements

LEARNING OUTCOMES

- Build keyboarding skill.
- Use Shapes, Clip Art, Drop Cap, WordArt, Watermark, and SmartArt.
- Format newsletters in columns.
- Format news releases.

LESSON 91   ## Graphics

WARMUP 91a

Key each line, striving for control. Repeat if desired.

alphabet	1	Gwen and Jackie both analyzed our five complex physics questions.
fig/sym	2	Room #1507 is 42'6" long and 38'9" wide; it can accommodate them.
home row	3	Jake said Sally and Klaus gladly did all I asked the staff to do.
fluency	4	Claudia and Clement may go with their neighbor to fish for smelt.

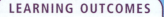

| 1 | 2 | 3 | 4 | 5 | 6 | 7 | 8 | 9 | 10 | 11 | 12 | 13 |

SKILL BUILDING

91b **Textbook Keying**

1. Key each line once, concentrating on good keying techniques. Tap ENTER twice after each 2-line group.
2. Repeat if time permits.

adjacent reaches	5	West said he was going to talk to my class prior to playing polo.
	6	Terry may join us at the new building to do the class assignment.
direct reaches	7	Hunt, my youngest brother, had a wreck because his brakes failed.
	8	June and my great friend decided to hunt for shells for two days.
1st/2nd fingers	9	Ginger and Gretchen recently found three cute bunnies in my yard.
	10	Buddy brought my younger brother that very nice gift this summer.
3rd/4th fingers	11	Alexa was at the zoo with six polo players who quit playing polo.
	12	Plaxwell Zoo owns quite a few polar bears that are quite popular.

MODIFIED BLOCK FORMAT

In the modified block format, the date line and the closing lines begin at the center point of the page. All other guidelines for the block letter style are applied to the modified block letter. Remember to remove the extra spacing between the letter address and other short lines. Review the model modified block letter on the next page.

NATIONAL
ASSOCIATION OF
INFORMATION
PROCESSING
PROFESSIONALS

February 6, 2008

Mr. Justin Novarini
7490 Oregon Avenue
Arvada, CO 80002-8765

Dear Mr. Novarini: ◄—— **Mixed punctuation**

Please consider this personal invitation to join the National Association of Information Processing Professionals (NAIPP). Membership is offered to the top 25 percent of the graduating class. NAIPP is a nonprofit organization comprised of technical professionals who are striving to stay current in their field. Member benefits include:

Career Development Opportunities—Resume preparation services, job search program, 120-day internship in many cities, and access to our online job bulletin board.

Professional Benefits—Industry standard skill testing, discounts on continuing education courses at colleges and universities, recertification programs, publications, medical insurance, financial planning programs, and free international travel services.

Sign on to our website at http://www.naipp.org to learn about many more benefits. A parking pass and discount coupons for the Multimedia Symposium on February 27 are enclosed.

Sincerely, ◄—— **Mixed punctuation**

Jolene Ryder, President
NAIPP Board of Directors

xx

Enclosures: Parking Pass
               Discount Coupons

c   Adam Vassel
     Bethany Corbin

**Modified Block Letter Format
with Mixed Punctuation**

Dateline:

- Position at about 2.0" or use the Center Page command.
- Begin at least 0.5" below the letterhead.
- Set a left tab at 3.25". Determine the position of the tab by subtracting the side margin from the center of the paper.

$$
\begin{array}{ll}
4.25" & \text{Center of the paper} \\
-\ 1.00" & \text{Margin} \\
\hline
3.25" & \text{Tab setting}
\end{array}
$$

Complimentary closing: Begin keying at 3.25".

Writer's name and title: Begin keying at 3.25".

MIXED PUNCTUATION STYLE

Although most letters are formatted with open punctuation, some businesses prefer mixed punctuation. To format a letter using mixed punctuation, key a colon after the salutation and a comma after the complimentary closing.

Dear Dr. Hathorn:

Sincerely,

Mixed Punctuation

ADDITIONAL LETTER PARTS

In Lesson 32 you learned the standard letter parts. Optional parts are listed below.

Enclosure notations: If an item is included with a letter, key an enclosure notation one line below the reference initials. Tap TAB to align the enclosures at 1.0".

Left tab at 1.0" ——

Enclosures: Check #831
               Order form

Enclosures: 2

Copy notation: A copy notation (c) indicates that a copy of the document has been sent to the person(s) listed. Key the copy notation one blank line below the reference initials or enclosure notation (if used). Tap TAB to align the names at 0.5". If necessary, click Undo Automatic Capitalization after keying the copy notation to lowercase the letter *c*.

Left tab at 0.5" ——

c   Larry Qualls
     Wendy Mullins

Level 4

DESIGNING SPECIALIZED DOCUMENTS

LEARNING OUTCOMES

Document Design Skills

- To display graphics attractively in newsletters, letterheads, and announcements.
- To produce mass mailings effectively using mail merge.
- To format agendas, minutes, badges, and itineraries attractively.
- To format legal, medical, and employment documents appropriately.

Word Processing Skills

- To apply graphics, merge, and other commonly used word processing functions.

Communication Skills

- To produce error-free documents.

Keyboarding

- To improve keyboarding speed and accuracy.

NATIONAL
ASSOCIATION OF
INFORMATION
PROCESSING
PROFESSIONALS

2" ← (Tap ENTER three times or center vertically)

Tab at 3.25" → February 6, 2008 ↓2

Mr. Justin Novarini
7490 Oregon Avenue
Arvada, CO 80002-8765 ↓1

Mixed punctuation → Dear Mr. Novarini: ↓1

Please consider this personal invitation to join the National Association of Information Processing Professionals (NAIPP). Membership is offered to the top 25 percent of the graduating class. NAIPP is a nonprofit organization comprised of technical professionals who are striving to stay current in their field. Member benefits include: ↓1

Career Development Opportunities—Resume preparation services, job search program, 120-day internship in many cities, and access to our online job bulletin board. ↓1

Professional Benefits—Industry standard skill testing, discounts on continuing education courses at colleges and universities, recertification programs, publications, medical insurance, financial planning programs, and free international travel services. ↓1

Sign on to our website at http://www.naipp.org to learn about many more benefits. A parking pass and discount coupons for the Multimedia Symposium on February 27 are enclosed. ↓1

Mixed punctuation → Sincerely, ↓2

Jolene Ryder, President
NAIPP Board of Directors ↓1

xx ↓1

Tab at 1"

Enclosures: Parking Pass
                Discount Coupons

c   Adam Vassel
        Bethany Corbin

Tab at 0.5"

Modified Block Letter Format
with Mixed Punctuation

90-d2

Personal Financial Statement

Use the following information to prepare a personal financial statement for **Tonisba C. Marcus, 3947 Keatley Avenue, Huntington, WV 25755-9603**.

1. Select the document theme of your choice, but use the same format as you did for *88-d1* on page 403. Set the following tabs: .25" left tab; 4.0" left leader tab, and a decimal tab at 5" and 6.25".

2. Include the following assets: cash, $1,025; savings, $2,486; and automobile, $14,675. Show the total assets of $18,186.

3. Include the following liabilities: credit cards, $1,000; automobile loan, $4,279. Show the total liabilities of $5,279.

4. Show the net worth of $12, 907.

5. Continue to the next document. (*90-d2*)

90-d3

Balance Sheet

1. Use the following information to prepare a balance sheet with the heading: **Saluda Gift Shop | Balance Sheet | As of December 31, 20--**. Use the same format as you did for *88-d3* on page 405, except position the heading at 2". Set the following tabs: 0.25" left tab, 4.5" decimal tab, and 6.25" decimal tab.

2. Check and close. (*90-d3*)

Assets

4.5" decimal tab

Current Assets
.25" Cash and equivalents $104,268
　　Receivables   26,493   6.25" decimal tab
　　Inventory   12,730
　　Total Current Assets $143,491

Long-Term Assets
　　Furniture and fixtures $14,862
　　Equipment   12,793
　　Total Long-Term Assets $27,655

Total Assets $171,146

Liabilities and Equity

Liabilities
　　Accounts payable $14,378
　　Accrued expenses   1,604
　　Total Liabilities $15,982

Equity
　　Owner's equity $155,164

Total Liabilities and Equity $171,146

CHECKPOINT ➡ Congratulations! You have successfully completed the lessons in Module 14. To check your understanding and for more practice, complete the objective assessment and performance assessment located on the textbook website at www.collegekeyboarding.com.

34-d1
Modified Block Letter

1. Open a new document and set a left tab at 3.25". Tap TAB and key the date at about 2.0".

2. Key the letter on page 132 in new modified block letter format with *Word 2007* defaults and use mixed punctuation. Remove extra spacing in letter address, enclosure notation, and copy notation.

3. Before keying the enclosure notation, set a left tab at 1.0". Before keying the copy notation, set a left tab at 0.5".

4. Preview the placement of the letter, check, and close. (*34-d1*)

34-d2
Modified Block Letter

1. Key the following letter in modified block letter style with mixed punctuation. Add an appropriate salutation, a complimentary closing, and any other missing letter parts. Send a copy of this letter to your instructor and a classmate. The writer is Mary Fleming-Davis, Marketing Manager.

2. Center the letter vertically.

3. Check and close. (*34-d2*)

Ms. Abbie Welborn
One Stop Printing Co.
501 Madison Road
Cincinnati, OH 45227-6398

Do you know that more and more people are opting to go on a shopping spree on the Internet rather than the mall? Businesses, ranging from small mom-and-pop stores to global multinational corporations, are setting up shop on the Web if they have not already.

Consumers expect businesses to have a website. Those companies that do not have a presence on the Web will most likely give their business to their competitors.

E-Business, Inc. has helped hundreds of businesses nationwide establish their business on the Internet. May we help integrate your online and offline sales strategies? Call us today at 555-0100 and arrange for one of our outstanding consultants to analyze your e-commerce strategies to increase your volume.

34-d3
Compose Modified Block Letter

1. Compose a letter to a businessperson in your area requesting that your keyboarding class complete a service project for that business. Format the letter as a new modified block letter with *Word 2007*; use mixed punctuation. Follow the outline below to compose your letter.

   ¶1 Introduce yourself as a keyboarding student at your college. Explain that the keyboarding course is designed to teach students various business formats. List some of the formats.

   ¶2 Explain that the class is offering keyboarding services for a three-week period so that students can learn to apply formatting skills in an authentic environment. Explain that a class office manager will accept the project assignments, and all members will format, proofread, and print the documents on company letterhead.

   ¶3 Close by asking the businessperson to call your teacher to discuss the many mutual benefits of the project. Provide a telephone number and e-mail address.

2. Check and close. (*34-d3*)

90c

Assessment

 Continue

Check

With *Keyboarding Pro DELUXE*: When you complete a document, proofread it, check the spelling, and preview for placement. When you are completely satisfied, click the Continue button to move to the next document. Click the Check button when you are ready to error-check the test. Review and/or print the document analysis results.

Without *Keyboarding Pro DELUXE*: Key the documents in sequence. When time has been called, proofread all documents again and identify errors.

90-d1

Printed Form

Use the information below to prepare a printed reservation form to be mailed with the Central University Soccer Camp brochure.

1. Use Flow document theme and Title style for the heading, **Central University Soccer Camp Reservation**; position it at about 1.7". Shrink heading font to fit on one line.
2. Apply Heading 1 style for the side headings, *Camper Information* and *Camp Options*; and Heading 2 style for the *Regular* and *Premier* Camp options. Tap ENTER twice after the first heading to allow room for handwriting.
3. Set a 6.5" underline right tab.
4. Add a 1-point Box page border that is Blue, Accent 1 in color.
5. Continue to the next document. (*90-d1*)

Camper Information

Full Name _____

Date of Birth _____

Name of Parent _____

Street Address _____

City, State, and ZIP Code _____

Area Code and Telephone Number _____

E-mail _____

Gender: ☐ Boy ☐ Girl

T-Shirt Size: ☐ Small ☐ Medium ☐ Large ☐ X-Large

Camp Options

Regular Camp for Boys and Girls Ages 6–15

☐ Half-day; June 23–27; $99

☐ Full-day; July 11–15; $199

Premier Residential Camp for Boys and Girls Ages 10–18

☐ Boys; June 12–16; $400

☐ Girls; June 18–22; $400

Note: Checks must be received 10 days before the camp begins to hold your reservation.

Traditional Letter Format

Key each line, striving for control. Repeat if desired.

alphabet	1	Jacky Few's strange, quiet behavior amazed and perplexed even us.
figures	2	Dial Extension 1480 or 2760 for a copy of the 3-page 95-cent book.
double letters	3	Ann will see that Edd accepts an assignment in the school office.
easy	4	If I burn the signs, the odor of enamel may make a toxic problem.

| 1 | 2 | 3 | 4 | 5 | 6 | 7 | 8 | 9 | 10 | 11 | 12 | 13 |

SKILL BUILDING

35b Textbook Keying
1. Key each line once, concentrating on using good keying techniques; tap ENTER twice after each 2-line group.
2. Repeat the drill if time permits.

adjacent reaches	5	The people were sad as the poor relish was opened and poured out.
	6	Sophia moved west with her new silk dress and poor walking shoes.
direct reaches	7	Freddy stated that hurricanes are much greater in number in June.
	8	Many juniors decide to work free to add experience to the resume.
balanced hand	9	The eight ducks lay down at the end of right field for cozy naps.
	10	Kala is to go to the formal town social with Henry and the girls.

NEW FUNCTIONS

35c

STYLES

AaBbCcDd
¶ Normal

The Styles feature enables you to apply a group of formats automatically to a document. A new *Word* document opens with approximately 18 styles attached to it. These styles include Normal, Heading 1, Heading 2, Heading 3, Heading 4, and Title. You will learn more about applying these styles in Module 5.

The Normal style is the default style that is automatically applied when a new *Word* document is opened. The Normal default style in *Word 2003* and *Word 2007* differ in a number of ways; however, the following differences affect formatting letters.

Word 2007 Defaults	Word 2003 Defaults
1.15 line spacing	1.0 line spacing
10-point spacing after the paragraph	0 spacing after the paragraph
11-point font size	12-point font size
Calibri font	Times New Roman font
1.0 left and right margins	1.25" left and right margins

To format a letter in the traditional format using *Word 2007* software, change to the *Word 2003* style. The key *Word 2003* style defaults are 1.0 line spacing, 0 spacing after the paragraph, and 12-point font size. Change the font to Times New Roman. Although the side margins do not change to the *Word 2003* default of 1.25", keep the 1.0" side margins.

KEYBOARDING PRO DELUXE ▶ See References/Word commands/Lesson 35

Key each line once, striving for control. Repeat if desired.

alphabet 1 A huge crowd went from Jackson Square to the lively Plaza by six.

fig/sym 2 Our meal was very expensive—$137.95 + 18% tip ($24.85) = $162.80.

direct reaches 3 Celia and June are great friends who swam long hours for my team.

fluency 4 Jamale may own the bicycle, but a neighbor owns the antique auto.

| 1 | 2 | 3 | 4 | 5 | 6 | 7 | 8 | 9 | 10 | 11 | 12 | 13 |

SKILL BUILDING

90b **Timed Writing**
Key two 5' timed writings; strive for control.

all letters

gwam 3' | 5'

Most people find it amazing that mobile telephones can create a number of etiquette and safety problems. The use of hand-held, mobile telephones has increased dramatically in the past few years. Just because a mobile telephone can be taken almost anywhere does not mean that it is appropriate to use it in any place it can be carried. Common sense and good manners seem to have been forgotten when it comes to using a mobile telephone.

The major safety hazard of using a hand-held telephone results from its use in moving automobiles. A significant percentage of all accidents is the result of drivers being distracted. Of all the distractions reported, the most frequent are those that occur while a driver is holding a telephone in one hand and trying to drive at the same time. A hands-free telephone is not as dangerous, but it can still cause a driver to be distracted.

The etiquette problem is the result of a person speaking on a telephone in a place that disturbs another person. Either the individual doing this just does not care or does not realize how rude he or she is being to another person. It is not unusual to see signs that prohibit the use of a mobile telephone in meeting rooms, restaurants, movie theaters, concert halls, and a number of other places. What is most shocking is that these signs are necessary. Except in rare cases, a telephone should not be used in these places. What has happened to basic courtesy?

gwam	3'	5'
	4	3
	9	5
	13	8
	18	11
	22	13
	26	16
	29	18
	33	20
	38	23
	42	25
	47	28
	51	31
	56	33
	59	35
	63	38
	67	40
	71	43
	76	45
	80	48
	84	51
	88	53
	93	56
	96	58

3' | 1 | 2 | 3 | 4 |
5' | 1 | 2 | 3 |

TO CHANGE TO WORD 2003 STYLE:

HOME/STYLES/CHANGE STYLES

1. From the Home tab, click the Change Styles button ❶.
2. Click Style Set ❷.
3. Click Word 2003 ❸. The line spacing is now 1.0; the space after paragraph is 0; the font size is 12; and the side margins remain at 1.0".

DRILL 1   CHANGE STYLES

1. From the Home tab, on the Styles group, click Change Styles. Click Style Set and *Word 2003*.

2. Click on the Home tab and note the 12-point Calibri font.

3. Click on the Line Spacing button and note the 1.0 line spacing.

4. Click the Paragraph Dialog Box Launcher and note the 0 spacing after the paragraph.

5. From the Page Layout tab, click Margins and note the Normal 1" left and right margins.

6. Close the document without saving.

DOCUMENT DESIGN

35d

LETTER PARTS AND TRADITIONAL LETTER FORMAT

The traditional letter format is keyed using the defaults of *Word 2003*. To restore these defaults, apply the *Word 2003* style and change the font to Times New Roman. Because the space after the paragraph is now 0, more spacing is needed when using the *Word 2003* style. The required spacing using the traditional format is explained below and illustrated on the following page. All other formatting you have learned concerning the block and modified block format remains the same.

Changes:

Apply *Word 2003* style and change font to Times New Roman.

Date: Position at about 2" (tap ENTER six times) or use the Center Page command.

Letter address: Three blank lines below the date (tap ENTER four times).

Salutation: Double-space below the letter address (tap ENTER twice).

Body: Double-space below the salutation. Single-space paragraphs and double-space between paragraphs (tap ENTER twice).

Complimentary close: Double-space below the body.

Writer's name and title: Three blank lines below the complimentary closing (tap ENTER four times).

Reference initials: Double-space below the writer's name and title.

Enclosures: Double-space below the reference initials.

Copy notation: Double-space below the enclosure notation if included.

E-Market, Group
10 East Rivercenter Boulevard
Covington, KY 41016-8765

Current date

Mr. Eric Seymour
Professional Office Consultants
1782 Laurel Canyon Road
Sunnyvale, CA 94085-9087

Dear Mr. Seymour

Have you heard your friends and colleagues talk about obtaining real-time stock quotes, real-time account balances and positions, NASDAQ Level II quotes, or extended-hours trading? If so, then they are among the many serious investors who have opened an account with E-Market Firm.

We are confident that the best decisions are informed decisions that are made in a timely manner. E-Market Firm has an online help desk that provides information for all levels of investors, from beginners to the experienced serious trader. You can learn basic tactics for investing in the stock market, avoiding common mistakes, and picking up some advanced strategies.

To stay on top of the market and your investments, please visit our online investing website at www.emarketfirm.com to learn more about our banking and brokerage services and to access our online help desk. E-Market Firm is the premier site for online investing.

Sincerely

Emily Zumwalt
Marketing Manager

xx

Central University Foundation
Operational Budget for Unrestricted Funds
For Fiscal Year 20--

4.5" decimal tab

Estimated Revenue

.5" left tab

Investment income	$1,025,000
Annual fund—unrestricted portion	485,000
Unrestricted gifts	1,275,500
Unrestricted endowment income	487,300
Endowment assessment income	1,720,000

6.5" decimal tab

Total Revenues	$4,992,800

Projected Expenditures

Academic Expenditures

Scholarships	$1,075,325
Graduate fellowships	448,950
Distinguished professor supplements	484,975
Administrative officer supplements	135,000
Faculty research awards	25,000
Faculty teaching awards	25,000
Graduate and undergraduate student awards	25,000
Faculty recruitment and retention	1,050,000

5.5" decimal tab

Total Academic Expenditures	$3,269,250

Fundraising and Marketing Expenditures

Marketing	$145,000
Gift acquisition and announcement costs	85,000
Fundraising support	260,725
Total Fundraising and Marketing Expenditures	$490,725

Operational Expenditures

Foundation operations	$775,250
Board Expenditures	35,000
Total Operational Expenditures	$810,250

Total Projected Expenditures	$4,570,225
Excess Revenues over Expenditures[1]	$422,575

---

[1] Excess revenues are available as contingencies for this budget year. If they are not needed, excess revenues are added to the reserves for future use.

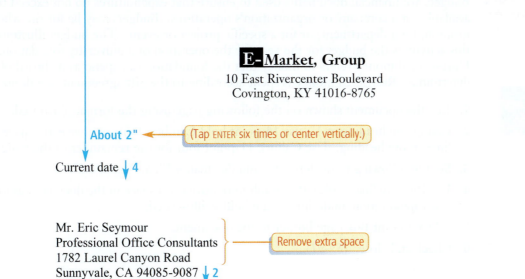

E- Market, Group

10 East Rivercenter Boulevard
Covington, KY 41016-8765

About 2" ← (Tap ENTER six times or center vertically.)

Current date ↓ 4

Mr. Eric Seymour
Professional Office Consultants } ← Remove extra space
1782 Laurel Canyon Road
Sunnyvale, CA 94085-9087 ↓ 2

Dear Mr. Seymour ↓ 2

Have you heard your friends and colleagues talk about obtaining real-time stock quotes, real-time account balances and positions, NASDAQ Level II quotes, or extended-hours trading? If so, then they are among the many serious investors who have opened an account with E-Market Firm. ↓ 2

We are confident that the best decisions are informed decisions that are made in a very timely manner. E-Market Firm has an online help desk that provides information for all levels of investors, from beginners to the experienced serious trader. You can learn basic tactics for investing in the stock market, avoiding common mistakes, and picking up some advanced strategies. ↓ 2

To stay on top of the market and your investments, please visit our online investing website at http://www.emarketfirm.com to learn more about our banking and brokerage services and to access our online help desk. E-Market Firm is the premier site for online investing. ↓ 2

Sincerely ↓ 4

Emily Zumwalt } ──── Remove extra space
Marketing Manager ↓ 2

xx

Traditional Block Letter Format
(Word 2003)

89-d1

Operational Budget

Budgets are financial documents used to ensure that expenditures do not exceed the money available for a company or organization's operations. Budgets may be for the whole organization, for a department, or for a specific project or event. The budget illustrated for this activity is the budget for the year for the operation of a university foundation. Unrestricted money refers to money that the foundation can spend as its board of directors determines. Restricted money is spent according to the gift agreement of a donor.

1. Key the document shown on the following page using the format illustrated.
2. Center the heading at 1"; use 14-point bold Cambria font; remove extra space after lines in the heading. Use Calibri, 11-point font for the remainder of the budget.
3. Set the following tabs—left: .5"; and decimal: 4.5", 5.5", and 6.5".
4. Use Remove Space After Paragraph to remove extra space in the document as illustrated. Use capitalization, underlining, and bold as illustrated.
5. Add a ½ point Box page border to the document.
6. Check and close. (*89-d1*)

89-d2

Project Budget

Use the following information to prepare a budget for the project described below.

1. Position the heading at 2"; use the same heading style as *89-d1*; heading information: **Professional Development Seminars, Inc./Effective Presentations Seminar/ current date**.
2. Use the same tab settings and format including spacing and page border as *89-d1*.
3. Key the document using the capitalization and bolding shown below.
4. Check and close. (*89-d2*)

Estimated Revenue
Number of participants projected	18		
Revenue per participant		$495	
Total Revenue Projected			$8,910

Projected Expenditures

Fixed Costs
Instructor fees	$1,600		
Instructor expenses	150		
Training room/equipment rental	650		
Program marketing material	450		
Advertising and promotional costs	800		
Overhead allocation	400		
Coaches/mentors	<u>400</u>		
Total Fixed Costs		$4,450	

Variable Costs
Seminar training manual ($15 each)	$270		
Meals/breaks ($30 each)	540		
Parking/other fees ($5 each)	<u>90</u>		
Total Variable Costs		<u>$900</u>	

Total Projected Expenditures			$5,350

Projected Profit			<u>$3,560</u>

35-d1

Block Letter in Traditional Format

1. Change the style set to *Word 2003* style and change the font to Times New Roman. Remember the spacing after the paragraph is now 0, the line spacing is 1.0, and the font size is 12.

2. Key the model letter on page 136 in block format with open punctuation in the traditional format.

3. Tap ENTER six times to position the date line at about 2". Insert the current date using the Automatic Date feature. Tap ENTER four times after the date and the complimentary closing. Tap ENTER twice after each paragraph.

4. Refer to the model letter for correct spacing between all letter parts. Use Show/Hide to view paragraph markers to confirm correct spacing between letter parts.

5. Check and close. (*35-d1*)

35-d2

Modified Block Letter in Traditional Format

1. Key the letter below in modified block format with mixed punctuation in the traditional format using the *Word 2003* style. Change font to Times New Roman.

2. Supply appropriate letter parts. Use the Center Page command to center the letter vertically.

3. Check and close. (*35-d2*)

February 1, 2008

Mr. Thomas Prescott, President
Prescott Financial Services
3054 North Kenswick Circle
Birmingham, AL 35242-3054

Two unique and focused word processing training programs are ready for your review. Since our initial meeting with your managers, a comprehensive needs assessment of training needs was conducted, and appropriate instructional materials have been designed and piloted.

The need for two levels of users—proficient and power—necessitated the design of two focused training programs. Employees who use word processing frequently but who use only a limited number of functions will complete the proficient-level training program. Those employees who must have an advanced level of expertise in the word processing software and troubleshoot software problems will complete the power-level training program.

We appreciate this opportunity to design these training programs and look forward to discussing them with you at our meeting on February 15.

Sincerely

Landon Maybury
Training Director

LESSON 89 Budget

WARMUP 89a

Key each line once, striving for control. Repeat if desired.

alphabet	1	Zack and Jimmy explored a quaint town and bought five neat gifts.
fig/sym	2	They got discounts (25% and 10%) on gifts priced $1,389 and $476.
adjacent reaches	3	We were going to walk to a new polo field with three junior guys.
fluency	4	Pamela and Jakken may go to town with a neighbor and eight girls.

| 1 | 2 | 3 | 4 | 5 | 6 | 7 | 8 | 9 | 10 | 11 | 12 | 13 |

SKILL BUILDING

89b Textbook Keying
1. Key each line once, concentrating on good keying techniques. Tap ENTER twice after each 3-line group.
2. Repeat if time permits.

direct reaches	5	red much brief hunt bred zany check jump decrease music many brat
	6	polo excel munch brake junk swim wreck lunch curve kick dazed bed
	7	Cec and Kim enjoy a great hunting trip in June after school ends.
adjacent reaches	8	were guy sad junior tree trio fast point rest joint walk gas join
	9	opt crew going port backlog poster web suit few folder buy porter
	10	Porter saw two important guys after we walked past Union Station.
double letters	11	bell look deed glass upper inn odd committee cabbage effect inner
	12	add spell pool happy jazz mass scurry connect office fall setting
	13	Debbie Desselle called a committee meeting at noon at the office.

| 1 | 2 | 3 | 4 | 5 | 6 | 7 | 8 | 9 | 10 | 11 | 12 | 13 |

COMMUNICATION

89c Internet and E-mail

WORKPLACE SUCCESS

This lesson focuses on budgets, which are very common business analysis tools. Many individuals talk about their personal budgets, but most people do not formally establish a budget and then compare their expenditures to their budget on a regular basis. A number of budgeting tools for specialized groups are available on the Internet. One very useful and easy-to-use tool is a budget calculator. Many budget calculators are available for college students.

1. Use a search engine such as Google to find budget calculators that are applicable to college students. Use *education budget calculators* as the keywords.

2. Review the budget calculators and select one that matches your situation.

3. Fill in the data to prepare a budget using your own personal data. This is for your use. You do not need to share your personal data with others.

4. Compose a memo (or an e-mail) to your instructor providing the website addresses (URLs) of three budget calculators you found. Tell your instructor which site you used for your budget and explain why you felt it was best suited to your needs.

5. Edit the memo carefully.

6. Check and close. (*89c*)

Option: You may want to do this document as an e-mail.

LESSON 36 ▸ Correspondence Review

WARMUP 36a

Key each line, striving for control. Repeat if desired.

alphabet	1	Perhaps Max realized jet flights can quickly whisk us to Bolivia.
fig/symbol	2	Send 24 Solex Cubes, Catalog #95-0, price $6.78, before April 30.
1st finger	3	The boy of just 6 or 7 years of age ran through the mango groves.
easy	4	The auditor did sign the form and name me to chair a small panel.

| 1 | 2 | 3 | 4 | 5 | 6 | 7 | 8 | 9 | 10 | 11 | 12 | 13 |

NEW FUNCTIONS

36b

MODIFYING TABS

Tabs can be added or moved in existing documents. When adding tabs to an existing document, you must first select all portions of the document where the new tab(s) will be applied; then set the additional tab(s). When moving a tab, first select all the text that will be affected. If you fail to select all the text, then only the tab that your insertion point is on will be moved.

DRILL 1 — ADDING TAB TO EXISTING DOCUMENT

1. Open *33-d4*.
2. Select the entire letter by pressing CTRL + A.
   Alternate method: Point to the left of any text until a right-pointing arrow displays; then triple-click.
3. Set a left tab at 3.25".
4. Tab the appropriate lines to format this letter in modified block letter format.
5. Check and close. (*36-drill1*)

DRILL 2 — MOVING A TAB

1. Open *36-drill1*.
2 Select the entire letter.
3. Drag the tab on the ruler from 3.25" to 3.0".
4. Check and close. (*36-drill2*)

APPLICATIONS

36-d1
Edit Letter

1. Open *33-d2*, a block letter keyed in Lesson 33.
2. Set a tab at the center of the page. Make the necessary changes to change this letter to a modified block letter with mixed punctuation.
3. Edit the first sentence of paragraph 3 as follows:

   A company brochure with information about our salary, bonus, and retirement plans is enclosed.

4. Add an enclosure notation.
5. Check and close. (*36-d1*)

Pat's Promotions, Inc. (at 1")
Balance Sheet
As of December 31, 20--

Assets

Current Assets   4.5" decimal tab
.25" left tab → Cash and equivalents $326,175
                 Receivables   198,403   6.25" decimal tab
                 Inventory   283,476
                 Prepaid expenses   102,964
                 Total Current Assets $911,018

Long-Term Assets
                 Building and equipment (depreciated) $209,685
                 Furniture and fixtures   117,482
                 Total Long-Term Assets $327,167

Total Assets $1,238,185

Liabilities and Equity

Current Liabilities
                 Accounts payable $158,964
                 Short-term debt   84,623
                 Accrued expenses   42,701
                 Total Current Liabilities $286,288

Long-Term Liabilities
                 Long-term debt $103,728
                 Other liabilities   98,605
                 Total Long-Term Liabilities $202,333

                 Total Liabilities $488,621

Equity
                 Owner's equity $390,476
                 Retained earnings   359,088
                 Total Equity $749,564

Total Liabilities and Equity $1,238,185

36-d2

Memo with Tab

1. Key the following memo in correct format.
2. After keying the second paragraph, tap ENTER once. From the ruler bar, set a left tab at 2.5", and key the last several lines.
3. Check and close. (*36-d2*)

TO: All Sunwood Employees

FROM: Julie Patel, Human Resources Director

DATE: Insert current date

SUBJECT: Eric Kershaw Hospitalized

We were notified by Eric Kershaw's family that he was admitted into the hospital this past weekend. They expect that he will be hospitalized for another ten days. Visitations and phone calls are limited, but cards and notes are welcome.

A plant is being sent to Eric from the Sunwood staff. Stop by our office before Wednesday if you wish to sign the card. If you would like to send your own "Get Well Wishes" to Eric, send them to:

Remove space ——
Eric Kershaw
County General Hospital
Room 401
P.O. Box 13947
Atlanta, GA 38209-4751

36-d3

Modified Block Letter and Envelope

1. Format the letter in the modified block format with mixed punctuation. Insert the current date. Position the letter attractively on the page. Remove extra spacing as necessary.
2. Supply the correct salutation and other necessary letter parts. Add an enclosure notation and a copy notation to **Laura Aimes, Sales Representative**. Set a left tab at 0.5" for keying the copy notation.
3. Create an envelope and add to the letter.
4. Preview for letter placement, check, and close. (*36-d3*)

Ms. Mukta Bhakta
9845 Buckingham Road
Annapolis, MD 21403-0314

Thank you for your recent inquiry about our wireless pet fence. The Hilton Pet Fence was developed to assist many pet owners like you who desire the safety of their pets without the barrier of a traditional fence.

Hilton Pet Fence also provides a customer support service to assist you in training your pet and a technical support team for providing technical assistance. For additional information, please call:

Customer and Technical Support
Telephone: 555-0112
9:00 a.m.-5:00 p.m., Monday-Friday, Eastern Time

Please look over the enclosed brochure. I will call you within the next two weeks to discuss any additional questions you may have.

Alexander Zampich | Marketing Manager

88-d3

Balance Sheet

Financial documents are used to show the financial condition of a business. Common financial documents include the balance sheet, income statement, and statement of cash flows. Financial statements can be formatted as a document using tabs to position columns of numbers, as a table, or as a spreadsheet. In this lesson, a balance sheet is illustrated. Documents are formatted by setting tabs. No single standard exists to determine which entries in a balance sheet are capitalized or have bold applied to them. Some businesses prefer to capitalize all major words in each entry; others prefer the style illustrated. Some prefer to bold all entries that begin at the left margin; others prefer to emphasize the total lines by applying bold to them as illustrated. Within a business, the format used for financial documents should be consistent.

1. Key the document shown on the following page using the format illustrated.
2. Center the heading using 14-point bold font. Remove extra space after the first two lines.
3. Set the following tabs: .25" left tab, 4.5" decimal tab, and a 6.25" decimal tab.
4. Use capitalization, underlining, and bold as illustrated. Remove the extra space after paragraphs in the groups of information as shown.
5. Add a ½ point Box page border to the document.
6. Verify numbers against the source document (textbook).
7. Check and close. (*88-d3*)

88-d4

Balance Sheet

1. Use the same format and all headings as in *88-d3* to prepare a balance sheet for The Pet Place as of December 31, 20--.
2. Substitute the following numbers for the various categories; total the amounts to determine the figures to be shown in the second column of the balance sheet.

Cash and equivalents	$125,000
Receivables	102,450
Inventory	150,975
Prepaid expenses	58,932
Building and equipment (depreciated)	183,206
Furniture and fixtures	98,065
Accounts payable	92,351
Short-term debt	23,074
Accrued expenses	18,649
Long-term debt	46,824
Other liabilities	12,706
Owner's equity	285,014
Retained earnings	240,010

3. Proofread and verify all numbers.
4. Check and close. (*88-d4*)

36-d4

Block Letter/Traditional and Envelope

1. Key the letter shown below in block letter style with open punctuation. Format in the traditional format; apply the *Word 2003* style and change font to Times New Roman. Insert the current date. Supply an appropriate salutation. Remove extra spacing as necessary.
2. Center the letter vertically on the page.
3. Send a copy to **Phillip Gilbert** and **Leigh Browning**. Add an envelope.
4. Check and close. (*36-d5*)

AMASTA Company, Inc. | 902 Greenridge Drive | Reno, NV 89505-5552

We sell your digital recorders and have since you introduced them. Several of our customers now tell us they are unable to follow the directions on the coupon. They explain that there is no company logo on the box to return to you as you requested.

What steps should we take? A copy of the coupon is enclosed, as is a digital recorder box. Please read the coupon, examine the box, and then let me know your plans for extricating us from this problem.

Sincerely | John J. Long | Sales Manager | Enclosures

36-d5

Move Tab

1. Open *36-d2*.
2. Select the last five lines of the memo (not including your reference initials).
3. Move the tab from position 2.5" to 3.0". This moves the last five lines to 3.0".
4. Check and close. (*36-d5*)

36-d6

E-mail

1. Compose an e-mail to your instructor using the subject line **Module 4 Quiz**. Key each question shown below and key your response to the question. Do not tap the ENTER key after the question; just space and key your answer.

   1. What are the two letter styles learned in Module 4?
   2. When formatting using the traditional format, what style is applied to the *Word 2007* document?
   3. What is the tab setting for the modified block letter style?
   4. Which letter parts are keyed at the tab you must set when keying a modified block letter?
   5. Distinguish between open punctuation and mixed punctuation.
   6. If a letter is addressed to a company, what is the appropriate salutation?
   7. What four items are included in the heading of a memo?

2. Print and send the e-mail. If you cannot send it, key it as a memo.
3. Check and close. (*36-d6*)

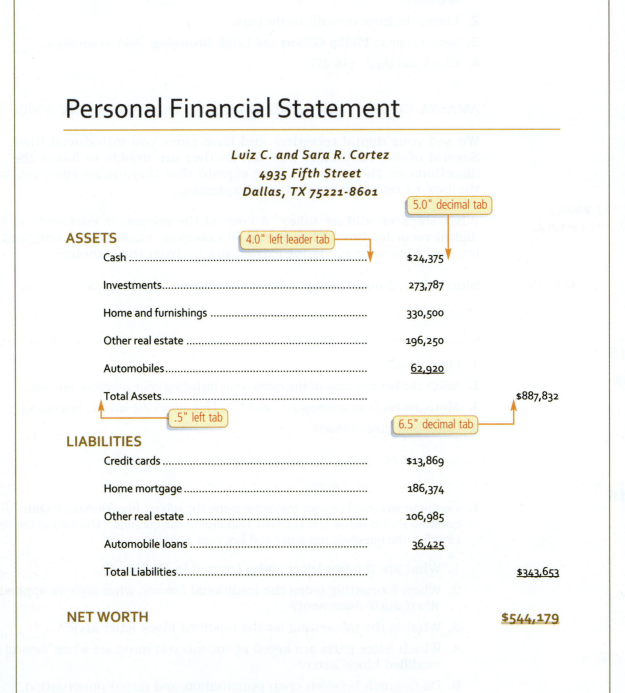

Personal Financial Statement

Luiz C. and Sara R. Cortez
4935 Fifth Street
Dallas, TX 75221-8601

5.0" decimal tab

ASSETS

4.0" left leader tab

Cash	$24,375
Investments..	273,787
Home and furnishings	330,500
Other real estate	196,250
Automobiles...	62,920
Total Assets...	$887,832

.5" left tab

6.5" decimal tab

LIABILITIES

Credit cards	$13,869
Home mortgage	186,374
Other real estate	106,985
Automobile loans	36,425
Total Liabilities...	$343,653

NET WORTH

$544,179

Key each line, striving for control. Repeat if desired.

alphabet	1	Johnny Willcox printed five dozen banquet tickets for my meeting.
fig/symbol	2	Our check #389 for $21,460—dated 1/15/08—was sent to O'Neil & Co.
1st finger	3	It is true Greg acted bravely during the severe storm that night.
easy	4	In the land of enchantment, the fox and the lamb lie by the bush.

| 1 | 2 | 3 | 4 | 5 | 6 | 7 | 8 | 9 | 10 | 11 | 12 | 13 |

SKILL BUILDING

37b Timed Writing
Key two 3' timed writings.

all letters

	gwam	3'
Many young people are quite surprised to learn that either	4	48
lunch or dinner is included as part of a job interview. Most of	8	52
them think of this part of the interview as a friendly gesture from	13	56
the organization.	15	58
The meal is not provided just to be nice to the person. The	18	62
organization expects to use that function to observe the social	22	66
skills of the person and to determine if he or she might be effective	27	71
doing business in that type of setting.	30	73
What does this mean to you if you are preparing for a job	33	77
interview? The time spent reading about and learning to use good	38	81
social skills pays off not only during the interview but also after	42	86
you accept the job.	44	87

3' | 1 | 2 | 3 | 4 |

APPLICATIONS

37c

Assessment

Continue

Check

With *Keyboarding Pro DELUXE*: When you complete a document, proofread it, check the spelling, and preview for placement. When you are completely satisfied, click the Continue button to move to the next document. Click the Check button when you are ready to error-check the test. Review and/or print the document analysis results.

Without *Keyboarding Pro DELUXE*: Key the documents in sequence. When time has been called, proofread all documents again and identify errors.

88-d1

Personal Financial Statement

Personal financial statements are often used when individuals apply for loans or other types of credit. Financial documents are usually formatted in tabular form with leaders so that the data is easily readable. If the information in a financial document is complicated and contains multiple columns, the document may be formatted as a table or a spreadsheet. The financial documents in this lesson are representative of those used by individuals and as such are relatively simple. Therefore, they are formatted using tabs and leaders. Note also that the style illustrated uses built-in headings and color and is less traditional than the accounting statements typically used by businesses. Some individuals may prefer to use a standard 14-point black font for headings.

1. Key the document shown on the following page using the *Module* document theme and the format illustrated.

2. Position the title at about 2"; apply Title style.

3. Apply Subtitle style to the name and address; also apply bold, Gold, Accent 1, Darker 50% color, and center them. Remove the extra space after the first two lines.

4. Apply Heading 1 style and uppercase to the three side headings.

5. Set the following tabs: 0.5" left tab, 4.0" left leader tab, 5.0" decimal tab, and 6.5" decimal tab. Underline as shown.

6. Apply a box, .25" page border using the Gold, Accent 1, Darker 50% color.

7. Check and close. (*88-d1*)

88-d2

Personal Financial Statement

Use the following information to prepare a personal financial statement for **Hayden S. Robinson, 3549 Woodview Drive, Las Cruces, NM 88012-9367**. Use the same general format as *88-d1* for this financial statement; however, select the Metro document theme.

1. Include the following assets: checking account, $1,975; savings account, $40,639; automobile, $28,910; apartment furnishings, $7,190; and art collection, $8,240. Show the total amount of assets.

2. Include the following liabilities: credit cards, $1,290; automobile loan, $2,073; college tuition loan, $6,539; and a personal loan, $1,496. Show the total amount of liabilities.

3. Determine the net worth by subtracting the total liabilities from the total assets; double-underline the net worth.

4. Add a page border to the document.

5. Check and close. (*88-d2*)

Memo with Distribution List

1. Key the memo to **Continuing Education Committee—Distribution List Below**. The memo is from **Alberto Valenzuela**. The date is April 3, 20--. The subject line is **May Seminar**.

2. The distribution list is as follows: John Patterson, Facilities Manager; Shawna Thompson, Regional Manager; Ed Vandenberg, Advertising Manager.

3. Continue to next document. (37-d1)

	gwam
I have invited Lynda A. Brewer, Ph.D., Earlham	33
College, Richmond, Indiana, to be our seminar	42
leader on Friday afternoon, May 10.	50
Dr. Brewer, a well-known psychologist who has	59
spent a lot of time researching and writing in the	69
field of ergonomics, will address "Stress Management."	80
Please make arrangements for rooms, speaker accom-	90
modations, staff notification, and refreshments.	100
I will send you Dr. Brewer's vita for use in pre-	110
paring news releases.	114
	closing lines 139

37-d2

Block Letter

1. Key the letter below in the block letter style using *Word 2007* defaults; use open punctuation. Add an appropriate salutation. Send a copy of the letter to **Olivia Cavenaugh**. Center the letter vertically on the page.

2. Add an envelope to the document.

3. Continue to next document. (37-d2).

	words
Current date	Mr. John J. Long, Sales Manager	The Record Store	9822	11
Trevor Avenue	Anaheim, CA 92805-5885	22

With your letter came our turn to be perplexed, and we apologize. When · 36
we had our refund coupons printed, we had just completed a total redesign · 51
program for our product boxes. We had detachable logos put on the · 65
outside of the boxes, which could be peeled off and placed on a coupon. · 79

We had not anticipated that our distributors would use back inventories · 94
with our promotion. The cassettes you sold were not packaged in our new · 108
boxes; therefore, there were no logos on them. · 118

I'm sorry you or your customers were inconvenienced. In the future, · 131
simply ask your customers to send us their sales slips, and we will honor · 146
them with refunds until your supply of older containers is depleted. · 160

Sincerely yours | Bruna Wertz | Sales and Promotions Dept. | xx · 173

37-d3

Modified Block Letter/Traditional Format

1. Key *37-d2* above in the traditional modified block letter format with mixed punctuation.

2. Check the test and close. (37-d3)

CHECKPOINT →

Congratulations! You have successfully completed the lessons in Module 4. To check your understanding and for more practice, complete the objective assessment and performance assessment located on the textbook website at www.collegekeyboarding.com.

Financial Documents

WARMUP 88a

Key each line, striving for control. Repeat if desired.

alphabet 1 Mickey bought six lavender azaleas and quite a few nice junipers.

figures 2 We gave a 15% discount on 3 invoices (#28574, #6973, and #12095).

shift key 3 Li, Jan, Al, and Carl went with Rod, Kay, and Oki to see Big Sky.

fluency 4 Jan and six girls may go to the lake to sit on the dock and fish.

| 1 | 2 | 3 | 4 | 5 | 6 | 7 | 8 | 9 | 10 | 11 | 12 | 13 |

SKILL BUILDING

88b Textbook Keying

1. Key each line once, concentrating on good keying techniques. Tap ENTER twice after each 3-line group.
2. Repeat if time permits.

1st and 2nd fingers

5 Gunther kicked the ball, but Ty recovered it in front of the net.

6 Cynthia tried to get that kitten from Hunter but did not succeed.

7 Freddie just gave a friend that nice ring for her fifth birthday.

3rd and 4th fingers

8 Alex quit polo; he waxes and polishes his old car and plays jazz.

9 Zack will ask six questions that will stump all six polo players.

10 Quinn will fix an old radio so Paul can play popular jazz loudly.

double letters

11 Bennett is accused of allocating too many dollars to his hobbies.

12 Anna and Judd will attend swimming class at noon at the new pool.

13 Darrell ate apples, made calls, and fell asleep in Anne's office.

88c Timed Writing

1. Key one 1' timing on each paragraph; work for speed.
2. Key one 3' timed writing on all paragraphs.

all letters

	gwam	1'	3'

Financial analysis tools range from very simple to quite complex. 14 | 5 | 58
One thing that both the simple and the complex tools share is that 28 | 9 | 63
they require the collection of valid data before they can be used to 41 | 14 | 67
analyze options in the decision-making process. 51 | 17 | 71

You might ask, just how can I ensure that I am using valid data? 14 | 22 | 75
Several factors must be considered. The data must be applicable to 28 | 26 | 80
solving the problem. The data must come from a reliable source. In 41 | 31 | 84
addition, it must be entered in the financial analysis tools 54 | 35 | 89
correctly. Keying errors occur quite often. 62 | 38 | 92

In addition to using the appropriate financial analysis tools, 14 | 42 | 96
good logic must always be used. The best tools will not work 26 | 47 | 100
correctly if the logic used is faulty. A problem should be carefully 40 | 51 | 105
thought out before any tools are used. 47 | 54 | 107

1'	1	2	3	4	5	6	7	8	9	10	11	12	13	14
3'		1		2		3		4		5	
5'		1		2		3	

CAPITALIZATION GUIDES

CAPITALIZE:

1. **First word of a sentence and of a direct quotation.**

   We were tolerating instead of managing diversity.
   The speaker said, "We must value diversity, not merely recognize it."

2. **Proper nouns**—specific persons, places, or things.

   Common nouns: continent, river, car, street
   Proper nouns: Asia, Mississippi, Buick, State Street
   Exception: Capitalize a title of high distinction even when it does not refer to a specific person (e.g., President of the United States).

3. **Derivatives** of proper nouns and capitalize **geographical** names.

   Derivatives: American history, German food, English accent, Ohio Valley
   Proper nouns: Tampa, Florida, Mount Rushmore

4. **A personal or professional title** when it precedes the name; capitalize a title of high distinction without a name.

   Title: Lieutenant Kahn, Mayor Walsh, Doctor Welby
   High distinction: the President of the United States

5. **Days of the week, months of the year, holidays, periods of history, and historic events.**

   Monday, June 8, Labor Day, Renaissance

6. **Specific parts of the country** but not compass points that show direction.

   Midwest   the South   northwest of town   the Middle East

7. **Family relationships** when used with a person's name.

   Aunt Carol   my mother   Uncle Mark

8. **A noun preceding a figure** except for common nouns such as line, page, and sentence.

   Unit 1   Section 2   page 2   verse 7   line 2

9. **First and main words of side headings, titles of books, and works of art.**
   Do not capitalize words of four or fewer letters that are conjunctions, prepositions, or articles.

   Computers in the News   Raiders of the Lost Ark

10. **Names of organizations and specific departments** within the writer's organization.

    Girl Scouts   our Sales Department

11. **The salutation of a letter and the first word of the complimentary closing.**

    Dear Mr. Bush   Ladies and Gentlemen: Sincerely yours,
    Very cordially yours,

Professional Development Seminars, Inc.

Seminar Breakeven Analysis

Program: *Effective Presentations*

Number of Days: *2*

Fixed Costs	Amount	Total Costs
Instructor fees	*$1,600*	
Instructor expenses	*150*	
Training room/equipment rental	*650*	
Program marketing material	*450*	
Advertising and promotional costs	*800*	
Overhead allocation	*400*	
Coaches/mentors	*400*	
Total Fixed Costs		*$4,450*
Variable Costs	**Per Participant**	
Seminar training manual	*15*	
Meals/breaks	*30*	
Parking/other fees	*5*	
Total Variable Costs	*$50 X 10*	*$500*
Total Costs		*$4,950*
Revenue Per Participant	*$495 X 10*	*$4,950*
Breakeven Level		*10*

DRILL 1

CAPITALIZATION

1. Review the rules and examples on the previous page.
2. Key the sentences, correcting all capitalization errors. Use the Numbering command to number each item.
3. Check and close. (*capitalize-drill1*)

1. according to one study, the largest ethnic minority group online is hispanics.
2. the american author mark twain said, "always do right; this will gratify some people and astonish the rest."
3. the grand canyon was formed by the colorado river cutting into the high-plateau region of northwestern arizona.
4. the president of russia is elected by popular vote.
5. the hubble space telescope is a cooperative project of the european space agency and the national aeronautics and space administration.
6. the train left north station at 6:45 this morning.
7. the trademark cyberprivacy prevention act would make it illegal for individuals to purchase domains solely for resale and profit.
8. consumers spent $7 billion online between november 1 and december 31, 2008, compared to $3.1 billion for the same period in 2007.
9. new students should attend an orientation session on wednesday, august 15, at 8 a.m. in room 252 of the perry building.
10. the summer book list includes *where the red fern grows* and *the mystery of the missing baseball.*

DRILL 2

CAPITALIZATION

CAPITALIZE2

1. Follow the specific directions provided in the data file. Remember to use the correct proofreaders' marks:

   Capitalize   sincerely

   lc Lowercase   My *lc* Dear Sir

2. Check and close. (*capitalize-drill2*)
3. Submit the rough draft and final copy to your instructor.

DRILL 3

CAPITALIZATION OF LETTER PARTS

1. Key the letter parts, using correct capitalization. Tap ENTER once after each item.
2. Check and close. (*capitalize-drill3*)

1. dear mr. petroilli
2. ladies and gentlemen
3. dear senator kuknais
4. very sincerely yours
5. dear reverend Schmidt
6. very truly yours
7. cordially yours
8. dear mr. fong and miss landow
9. respectfully yours
10. sincerely
11. dear mr. and mrs. Green
12. dear service manager

DRILL 4

CAPITALIZATION

CAPITALIZE4

1. This file includes a field for selecting the correct answer. You will simply select the correct answer. Follow the specific directions provided in the data file.
2. Check and close. (*capitalize-drill4*)

87-d1

Breakeven Analysis Form

Keyboarding Pro DELUXE users: Close the software and do 87-d1 and 87-d2 in *Word*.

CUSTOM FORMS

Custom forms are forms that are tailored to the specific needs of a business, a department, or an individual. The form illustrated on the next page is an example of a form that uses breakeven analysis to determine how many seminar participants must be enrolled in a program for it to break even. The analysis focuses on two types of costs for conducting a seminar—fixed costs and variable costs. Fixed costs are expenditures that must be made regardless of the number of participants. Variable costs are dependent on the number of participants enrolled in the program.

Review the form on the next page. Note that this form is designed to be used each time a seminar is conducted. The type of seminar and the number of times it is offered are immaterial. The same form can be used to do the breakeven analysis multiple times. Note also that the blank lines in the form are available to further customize the form—they are used to include special costs that might apply to some programs but not others.

1. Use a table to design and key the form shown on the next page. Do not include the handwritten information that will be added to the form for a specific seminar.

2. Use these styles:
   a. Title and Subtitle style centered
   b. Row height .3"
   c. Center text vertically in the cells
   d. Set decimal tabs in columns B and C
   e. Equity document theme
   f. Use the theme heading font and apply 14 point bold and the regular body text font
   g. .25" (add color of border from solution) border.

3. Save the form as a *Word* template so that it can be reused and completed in *Word*. Refer to page 311 in Lesson 70 for a reminder on how to save a document as a template.

4. Check and close. (*87-d1 breakeven analysis*)

87-d2

Complete Breakeven Analysis Form

1. Open the *Breakeven Analysis* template.

2. Use the handwritten information on the next page to complete the form.

3. Check the form to make sure all information has been added.

4. Check and close. (*87-d2*)

Report Essentials

LEARNING OUTCOMES

- Format two-page reports using *Word 2007* format and traditional format.
- Format reference pages and title pages.
- Indent long quotations and bibliography entries appropriately.
- Insert page numbers.
- Apply styles.
- Apply bullets and numbers.
- Insert and edit footnotes.

LESSON 38 — Unbound Report

WARMUP 38a

Key each line, striving for control. Repeat if desired.

alphabet	1	Dave Cagney alphabetized items for next week's quarterly journal.
figures	2	Close Rooms 4, 18, and 20 from 3 until 9 on July 7; open Room 56.
up reaches	3	Toy & Wurt's note for $635 (see our page 78) was paid October 29.
easy	4	The auditor is due by eight, and he may lend a hand to the panel.

| 1 | 2 | 3 | 4 | 5 | 6 | 7 | 8 | 9 | 10 | 11 | 12 | 13 |

SKILL BUILDING

38b Timed Writing

1. Key a 1' timed writing on each paragraph; work to increase speed.
2. Key a 3' timed writing on both paragraphs.

all letters

	gwam	1'	3'
Have simple things such as saying please, may I help you, and		12	4
thank you gone out of style? We begin to wonder when we observe		25	8
front-line workers interact with customers today. Often their bad		39	13
attitudes shout that the customer is a bother and not important. But		52	17
we know there would be no business without the customer. So what		66	22
can be done to prove to customers that they really are king?		79	26
First, require that all your staff train in good customer		12	30
service. Here they must come to realize that their jobs exist for		25	35
the customer. Also, be sure workers feel that they can talk to		38	39
their bosses about any problem. You do not want workers to talk		51	43
about lack of breaks or schedules in front of customers. Clients		64	48
must always feel that they are kings and should never be ignored.		77	52

| 1' | 1 | 2 | 3 | 4 | 5 | 6 | 7 | 8 | 9 | 10 | 11 | 12 | 13 |
| 3' | | 1 | | 2 | | 3 | | 4 | | | | | |

Custom Forms

Key each line, striving for control. Repeat if desired.

alphabet	1	Jack Meyer analyzed the data by answering five complex questions.
fig/sym	2	On May 15, my ZIP Code will change from 23989-4016 to 23643-8705.
1st/2nd fingers	3	June Hunter may try to give Trudy a new multicolored kite to fly.
fluency	4	Pamela may risk half of the profit they make to bid on an island.

| 1 | 2 | 3 | 4 | 5 | 6 | 7 | 8 | 9 | 10 | 11 | 12 | 13 |

SKILL BUILDING

87b **Timed Writing**
1. Key two 1' timed writings on each paragraph; work for speed.
2. Key one 3' timed writing on both paragraphs.

all letters

	gwam	1'	3'
Forms provide both a productive and an effective way to collect	14	5	48
data. Designing an effective form often does not happen quickly, but	28	9	52
the time spent can be justified quite easily. The time spent creating	42	14	57
a form is productive because once the form has been finished, it can	56	19	62
be used multiple times.	60	20	63
Forms provide an effective way of collecting data because they	14	25	68
add structure. Forms can be set up so that the data is organized in	27	29	72
exactly the way the designer wants to collect it. Analyzing data can	41	34	77
be simplified by the way in which the form is structured. Information	56	39	82
is also much easier to tabulate from data on a well-designed form.	69	43	86

1'	1	2	3	4	5	6	7	8	9	10	11	12	13	14
3'		1			2			3			4			5	
5'			1				2				3				

WORKPLACE SUCCESS

Effective Decision Making

© DIGITAL VISION / GETTY IMAGES

In an earlier *Workplace Success* feature, you learned that setting goals and learning how to make good decisions are critical elements of self-management. In this *Workplace Success* feature, the focus is on learning to have the appropriate quantitative as well as qualitative data on which to base decisions. The ability to use quantitative tools effectively is a critical decision-making skill.

Many financial tools are available to enhance decision making. Two very important tools are breakeven analysis and budgets. Managers need to be able to analyze a project before undertaking it to determine if the revenue from the project will cover the costs of doing it. Budgets are another example of a financial tool that is used to control expenditures and ensure that they do not exceed the money available for projects or for the general operation of a business.

STYLES

HOME/STYLES/QUICK STYLES

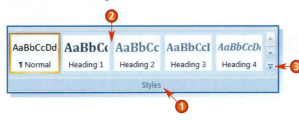

The **Styles** feature enables you to apply a group of formats automatically to a document. A new *Word* document opens with approximately 18 styles attached to it. These styles include Normal, Heading 1, Heading 2, Heading 3, Heading 4, and Title. Normal is the default style of 11-point Calibri, left alignment, 1.15 spacing, and no indent. Text that you key is formatted in the Normal style unless you apply another style.

Styles include both character and paragraph styles. The attributes listed in the Font group on the Home ribbon and on the Font dialog box make up the text formats. **Text formats** apply to a single character or characters that are selected. To apply character styles using the Font group, select the characters to be formatted and apply the desired font.

Paragraph styles include both the character style and other formats that affect paragraph appearance such as line spacing, bullets, numbering, and tab stops.

To apply paragraph styles:

1. Select the text to which you want to apply a style.
2. On the Home tab in the Styles group ❶, choose a desired style shown in the Quick Styles gallery ❷.
3. If the desired tab does not display, click the More button ❸ to expand the Quick Styles gallery.
4. Select the desired style from the expanded list of styles ❹.

KEYBOARDING PRO DELUXE ▸ See References/Word commands/Lesson 38

DRILL 1   STYLES   SCHEDULE

1. In the open document, select the title on the first line. Apply the Title style. Click the More button to select this style. Add your name.
2. Select the subtitle on the second line. Apply the Subtitle style.
3. Select *Monday*; apply the Heading 1 style. **Hint:** Click the scroll buttons to the right of the Styles buttons to move in the styles list.
4. Repeat step 3 for the remaining days of the week and the heading *Extracurricular Activities*.
5. Check and close. (*38-drill1*)

Professional Development Seminars, Inc.

Planning and Conducting Effective Meetings

April 28-30, 20--
The Inn at Central University
Columbia, SC 29201-7459

7.5" right underline tab

Company/Organization Name: _____

Mailing Address: _____

_____

First Team Member
Name: _____

Telephone:_____ E-mail _____

Second Team Member
Name: _____

Telephone:_____ E-mail _____

Third Team Member
Name: _____

Telephone:_____ E-mail _____

Seminar Registration Fees:
Individual: $350; Team of Two: $600; Team of Three: $850

6" left tab

$ _____

☐ Check or purchase order payable to PDS, Inc.

PO# _____

4" left underline tab

Charge my ☐ MasterCard ☐ Visa ☐ American Express

7.5" left underline tab

Card Number: _____ Expiration Date_____

Print name as it appears on card: _____

Mail or fax to: Jennifer Jameson (TAB) Fax: 803-555-0178
                         Professional Development Seminars, Inc.
                         3947 County Line Road
                         Columbia, SC 29201-3947

2" left tab

UNBOUND REPORT FORMAT

Reports prepared without binders are called unbound reports. Unbound reports may be attached with a staple or paper clip in the upper-left corner. Study the illustration below to learn to format a one-page unbound report. A full-page model of another report is shown on the following page.

2"

Trends for Business Dress ❶

Casual dress in the workplace has become widely accepted. According to a national study conducted by Schoen Associates, a majority of the companies surveyed allowed employees to dress casually one day a week, usually Fridays. Fifty-eight percent of office workers surveyed were allowed to dress casually for work every day, and 92 percent of the offices allowed employees to dress casually occasionally.

Decline in Trend ❷
The trend to dress casually may be shifting, however. Although a large number of companies are allowing casual attire every day or only on Fridays, a current survey revealed a decline of 10 percent in 2007 when compared to the same survey conducted in 2006. Some experts predict the new trend for business dress codes will be a dressup day every week. What accounts for this decline in companies permitting casual dress? Several reasons may include:

❸
1. Confusion about what business casual is, with employees slipping into dressing too casually (work jeans, faded tee-shirts, old sneakers, and improperly fitting clothing).
2. Casual dress does not portray the adopted corporate image of the company.
3. Employees are realizing that promotion decisions are affected by a professional appearance.

Guidelines for Business Dress
Companies are employing image consultants to teach employees what is appropriate business casual and to plan the best business attire to project the corporate image. Erica Gilreath, the author of *Casual Dress*, a guidebook on business casual, provides excellent advice on how to dress casually and still command the power needed for business success. She offers the following advice to professionals:

❸
- Do not wear any clothing that is designed for recreational or sports activities, e.g., cargo pants or pants with elastic waist.
- Invest the time in pressing khakis and shirts or pay for professional dry cleaning. Wrinkled clothing does not enhance one's credibility.
- Do not wear sneakers.
- Be sure clothing fits properly. Avoid baggy clothes or clothes that are too tight.

In summary, energetic employees working to climb the corporate ladder will need to plan their dress carefully. If business casual is appropriate, it is best to consult the experts on business casual to ensure a professional image.

Margins: Use the preset default top, side, and bottom margins.

Font size: Use the 11-point default font size.

Spacing: Use the default 1.15 line spacing for all reports.

Title: ❶

- Position at about 2". (Tap ENTER three times.)
- Capitalize the first letter of all main words.
- Tap ENTER once after heading.
- Apply the Title style; this style is 26-point Cambria font with a bottom border.

Side heading: ❷

- Key side headings at the left margin.
- Capitalize the first letter of all main words.
- Apply Heading 1 style; this style is 14-point Cambria font.
- Tap ENTER once after heading.

Enumerated items: ❸

- Use the default .25" indentation for numbers and bullets.
- Tap ENTER once after each item.

Page numbers:

- First page is not numbered.
- Second and succeeding pages are numbered in the upper-right corner in the header position (0.5").

DOCUMENT DESIGN DOCUMENT DESIGN DOCUMENT DESIGN DOCUMENT DESIGN DOCUMENT DESIGN DOCUMENT

86-d1

Fill-in Form

1. Use the information below to prepare a form.

2. Select the Aspect document theme and position the title at 2"; apply Title style.

3. Key the instructional paragraph and shade it Orange, Accent 1, Lighter 40%. Justify the paragraph and tap ENTER twice.

4. Set a 6.5" right underline tab for the first three lines of the form and key them.

5. Set left underline tabs at 3.5" and 4.5" for the City, State, ZIP Code line and key it.

6. Clear the 3.5" left underline tab and key the *Major* and *College* line. Tap ENTER twice; then clear all tabs.

7. Set .5", 3", and 3.5" left tabs and key the remaining information. Use Heading 2 for the headings and a box symbol from the Wingdings font.

8. Add a 3-point dark box page border of your choice.

9. Check and close. (*86-d1*)

Drawing for $1,000 Scholarship

The Athletics Department appreciates student attendance at all basketball games. To thank students for their strong support of the women's basketball program, the Athletics Department will hold a drawing for a $1,000 scholarship at the conclusion of each conference game in January. Only one form per student may be entered at each game, and the winner must be present at the conclusion of the game to receive the scholarship.

3.5" left underline tab   6.5" right underline tab

Name _____

Telephone _____

Street Address _____

City _____ State _____ ZIP Code _____

Major_____ College _____

4.5" left underline tab

Class   Grade Point Average

☐ Freshman   ☐ 3.75 or higher

☐ Sophomore   ☐ 2.75–3.74

☐ Junior   ☐ 2.0–2.74

☐ Senior   ☐ Less than 2.0

.5" left tab   3" left tab   3.5" left tab

86-d2

Fill-in Form

1. Format the form on the next page; position title at about 1.2"; use Title and Subtitle format; apply Heading 2 to side headings. Set narrow margins.

2. Set tabs as indicated; remove extra space in right-aligned information and address.

3. Apply a dark blue, 3-point box page border; use triple border with heavy line between single lines.

4. Check and close. (*86-d2*)

TIP

After keying the information for the first team member, copy it for the next two.

Electronic Mail Guidelines Title Style

Title →

Electronic mail, a widely used communication channel, clearly has three major advantages—time effectiveness, distance effectiveness, and cost effectiveness. To reap full benefit from this popular and convenient communication medium, follow the basic guidelines regarding the creation and use of e-mail.

Side Heading →

E-mail Composition Heading 1 Style

Although perceived as informal documents, e-mail messages are business records. Therefore, follow these effective communication guidelines. Write clear, concise sentences, avoiding clichés, redundancies, and wordiness. Break the message into logical paragraphs, sequencing in an appropriate order. White space is important in e-mail messages as well as printed documents, so be sure to add extra space between paragraphs.

1"   1"

Spell-check e-mail messages carefully, and verify punctuation and content accuracy. Do limit e-mail messages to one idea per message, and preferably limit to one screen. To ensure your e-mail message is opened, always include a subject line that clearly defines the e-mail message.

E-mail Practices

Although many people are using e-mail, some do not use it as their preferred method of communication and may check it infrequently. To accomplish tasks more effectively, be aware of individuals' preferred channels of communication and use those channels. Understand that your preferred channel of communication is not always that of the person to whom you must communicate.

Consider an e-mail message the property of the sender, and forward only with permission. Some senders include a note in the signature line that reminds recipients not to forward e-mail without getting permission.

BORDERS AND SHADING
PAGE LAYOUT/PAGE BACKGROUND/PAGE BORDERS

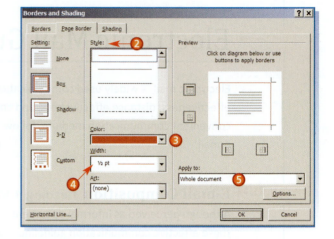

① Page Borders

Borders can be applied to pages, paragraphs, or selected text. Shading can also be applied. You can add page borders to all pages in a document, to the first page only, or to sections of a document. A variety of options can be applied to page borders, such as line style, color, and line width.

To apply page borders:

1. On the Page Layout tab, in the Page Background group, click Page Borders ①.

2. Make sure the Page Border tab is active in the Borders and Shading dialog box.

3. Choose the desired line style ②, color ③, and width ④.

4. Apply to the whole document or to the first page or to the section desired ⑤; click OK.

To apply paragraph borders:

1. Repeat step 1 above and then click the Borders tab.

2. Choose the desired line style, line color, and line width.

3. Click Apply to Paragraph and click OK.

To apply shading:

1. Repeat step 1 above and then click the Shading tab.

2. Choose the desired fill and pattern and click OK.

DRILL 2 — BORDERS AND SHADING

1. Open *86-drill1* and add the text shown below at the top of the form. Position the paragraph at 2".

2. Tap ENTER twice after the paragraph.

3. Apply a Red Accent 2, triple line, ½-point wide border to the paragraph.

4. Apply Red, Accent 2, Lighter 40% solid shading.

5. Add a ½ point wide page box border to the form. Use the darkest color in the same theme color (Red, Accent 2, Darker 50%).

6. Check and close. (*86-drill2*)

Please complete this form and return it to Lynn Martinez, manager of Employee Records in the Human Resources Department, by December 5. All records must be updated and entered into the new records management system, which will be effective January 1.

38-d1

Unbound Report

1. Key the model report on the previous page. Tap ENTER three times to position the title at about 2". Use default side margins. **Hint:** To stop the word *e-mail* at the end of the first paragraph from breaking onto two lines, use a nonbreaking hyphen. (Use the keyboard shortcut SHIFT + CTRL + _.) Use Help if necessary.

2. Capitalize the first letter of all main words in the title; tap ENTER once after the heading. Then select the heading and apply the Title style.

3. Select the side heading and apply the Heading 1 style. Tap ENTER once after the side heading.

4. Check and close. (*38-d1*)

38-d2

Edit Unbound Report

EDIT

1. In the open report, position the title at approximately 2". Apply Title style.

2. Correct the capitalization of the side headings; apply Heading 1 style.

3. Make other edits shown in the report. Refer to proofreaders' marks on page 55.

4. Key and format the side heading *Adding White Space*; then key the last paragraph of the report.

5. Check and close. (*38-d2*)

	words
Who Can Design a Better Brochure?	7
Producing a brochure with a professional appearance	17
requires careful creativity and planning. Not every one is	29
an accomplished paste-up artist who is capable of creating	41
a complex piece of printed art, but most skilled computer	50
users can create an attractive layout for a basic brochure.	62
Working with blocks	66
Work with copy and illustration in blocks. Type body	76
of text copy, leaving plenty of space for illustrations and	87
headlines. The blocks should then be arranged in a orderly	99
and eye-appealing manner.	101
Using a small a small size type is not recommended. *(or font)*	112
In most cases, use a font that is 11 point or larger to	122
make the document easy to read. Copy that is arranged in	133
more than one column is also more attractive. Try not to key	143
copy across the full width of a page. Preferably break the	147
page into smaller columns of copy and intersperse with photos or	160
illustrations.	163

UNDERLINE TABS

HOME/PARAGRAPH/PARAGRAPH DIALOG BOX LAUNCHER/TABS

86e

Tabs...

The Tab button on the bottom left side of the Paragraph dialog box is used to display the Tabs dialog box, which enables you to set various types of leaders including the underline tab, which is useful in forms development.

To set underline tabs:

1. On the Home tab, in the Paragraph group, click the Paragraph Dialog Box Launcher to display the Paragraph dialog box.

2. Click the Tabs button at the lower-left corner of the dialog box to display the Tabs dialog box.

3. In the Tab stop position box **❶**, key the position at which you want to set the underline tab.

4. In the Alignment options, click Right **❷**.

5. In the Leader options **❸**, click 4 _____ (underline); then click the Set button and OK.

Note: When you need to set other underline tab options, set them at the point in which you will use them. Do not preset all the tabs.

Tabs ? ×

Tab stop position: ❶
6" ❶

Default tab stops:
0.5"

6"

Tab stops to be cleared:
3", 3.5"

Alignment
○ Left   ○ Center   ⦿ Right
○ Decimal   ○ Bar   ❷

Leader
○ 1 None   ○ 2 ....   ○ 3 --------
⦿ 4 _____ ❸

Set   Clear   Clear All

OK   Cancel

DRILL 1   FORM WITH UNDERLINE TABS

1. Format the form shown below. Set a right underline tab at 6.5" for the first two lines.

2. On the third line of the form, set a right underline tab at 3" and a left tab at 3.5". (The right underline tab at 6.5" is still set.)

3. Check and close. (86-drill1)

Right underline tab 6.5" ——

Employee Name _____

Title _____

Reports to _____ Date _____

Review Period from _____ to _____

Right underline tab 3" ——   —— **Left tab 3.5"**

38-d2

Continued

Choosing a typeface	167
Typeface refers to the style of printing on the page.	178
Matching the style or "feeling" of the type with the purpose	190
of the finished product is very important. For example,	202
you would not ~~want to~~ use a gothic or "old style" typeface	215
to promote a modern, high tech product. Consider the bold-	227
ness or lightness of the style, the readability factor, and	233
the decorativeness or simplicity. Mixing more than three	251
different typefaces on a page should also be avoided. Vary	271
the type sizes to give the effect of different type styles.	275
Bold and italics can also be added for emphasis and vari-	286
ety, especially when only one type style is being used.	297

Handwritten edits: "a layout" "include" "of" inserted; "and" inserted before "the readability factor"; paragraph mark (¶) before "Mixing"; "ital." italics marking; "o" and "s" edits near "type styles."

Adding White Space

Desktop publishing experts claim a novice is easily recognized by a dense document filled with text and graphics and very little white space. This document appears busy, difficult, and unappealing to the eye of the reader. To add white space to a document, use left alignment, which leaves a ragged right edge. Adjust paragraph spacing before and after a paragraph to modify white space. Finally, increase margins around the page as well as between columns to create a more attractive document.

WORKPLACE SUCCESS

Integrity

Integrity is synonymous to the word *honesty* and is confronted by employees in the workplace daily. Think about these rather common situations where integrity is clearly a choice:

- Arriving at work ten minutes late and then drinking coffee and chatting with co-workers for ten more minutes
- Talking with relatives and friends throughout the day
- Leaving work early regularly for personal reasons
- Presenting a report to the supervisor as original work without crediting the proper individuals for thoughts and ideas in the report
- Presenting a report that was completed at the last minute and that includes facts and figures that have not been verified as accurate

Module 5 presents appropriate standards for citing references used in a report. As a student, practice integrity in documenting sources. Avoid what may be considered the easy way—copying text from the Internet and pasting it in a *Word* document. In all situations, ask the question, "Am I being honest?"

86c Timed Writing

1. Key one 1' timing on each paragraph, striving for speed.
2. Key one 3' or 5' timed writing on all paragraphs.

all letters

	gwam	1'	3'	5'
Americans tend to have a different view of vacation than		12	4	2
citizens of many other countries. In this country, companies usually		26	9	5
provide employees with a maximum of two or three weeks of vacation		40	13	8
each year. Many companies wait to award the second week of vacation		54	18	11
until employees have five years of tenure with them. Those who earn		67	22	13
more than three weeks of vacation typically do so by staying with the		81	27	16
same company for many years.		87	29	17

In many other countries, the case is quite different. Employees typically receive four to six weeks of vacation each year. It is also awarded much earlier in their tenure with the company. Vacation is thought of as just another benefit that has value to the company as well as to the employee. Employees often spend a whole month on holiday as they call vacation time.

14	34	20
27	38	23
41	43	26
54	47	28
68	52	31
75	54	32

While some individuals think how wonderful and luxurious it would be to have extra days or weeks of vacation, the fact is that a large percentage of Americans do not take the vacation time they are allotted by their companies. The American culture is such that many employees feel they cannot be away from their positions for more than two weeks at one time.

13	58	35
26	63	38
40	67	40
53	72	43
66	76	46
73	78	47

1'	1	2	3	4	5	6	7	8	9	10	11	12	13	14
3'	1		2		3		4		5
5'	1		2		3

DOCUMENT DESIGN

86d

PRINTED FORMS

The forms that you will work with in this lesson are forms designed in *Word* that will be printed and filled out in handwriting. Many practical uses exist for printed forms. Printed forms are frequently used for summarizing data, making reservations, and at events such as training seminars and registration for conferences. The forms are printed and handed out at the site for participants to complete.

Printed forms are relatively easy to design using the underline tab. However, they can also include boxes that can be checked. These boxes are available on the Symbol and Wingdings fonts. Usually boxes to be checked are used when the person filling out the form has to make a choice among several items such as the credit card that will be used.

Forms can also be designed for completion in *Word*. The person who creates a form is generally referred to as the designer, and the person who completes the form is usually referred to as the user. Tables are an effective way of preparing forms and saving them as templates to be completed in *Word*. Fill-in forms with fields that users complete in *Word* are often designed centrally and are posted on servers for completion. To create these types of forms, you would have to display the Developer tab on the Ribbon, which is beyond the scope of this module. For more information on this topic, search *Help for Forms that Users Complete in Word*.

DOCUMENT DESIGN   DOCUMENT DESIGN

Unbound Report with Title Page

Key each line, striving for control. Repeat if desired.

alphabet 1 The explorer questioned Jack's amazing story about the lava flow.

figure/sym 2 I cashed Cartek & Bunter's $2,679 check (Check #3480) on June 15.

1st/2nd fingers 3 Hugh tried to go with Katrina, but he did not have time to do so.

easy 4 The eighty firms may pay for a formal audit of their field works.

| 1 | 2 | 3 | 4 | 5 | 6 | 7 | 8 | 9 | 10 | 11 | 12 | 13 |

SKILL BUILDING

39b Textbook Keying

1. Key each line once, concentrating on using good keying techniques; tap ENTER twice after each 3-line group.
2. Repeat the drill if time permits.

t 5 it cat pat to top thin at tilt jolt tuft mitt flat test tent felt

r 6 fur bur try roar soar ram trap rare ripe true rear tort corral

t/r 7 The track star was triumphant in both the third and fourth heats.

m 8 me mine memo mimic named clam month maximum mummy summer remember

n 9 no snow ton none nine ninety noun mini mind minnow kennel evening

m/n 10 Men and women in management roles maximize time during commuting.

o 11 of one odd coil book oink cool polo crop soap yoyo option noodle

i 12 in it if did idea bike fix site with fill ilium indigo initiative

o/i 13 To know if you rock while giving a speech, stand on a foil sheet.

a 14 an as am is ask arm pass task team haze value salsa manage animal

s 15 so as sip spy must shape class shawl sister system second synergy

a/s 16 Assistants must find names and addresses for a class action suit.

e 17 he we me she they seal feel green there energy desire screensaver

i 18 is it in icon kite site tired unit limit feline service invisible

e/i 19 Initial triage services are limited to solely emergency patients.

TIP

Keep hands and arms still as you reach up to the third row and down to the first row.

39c Timed Writing

Key two 1' timed writings; work to increase speed.

all letters

gwam 1'

The value of an education has been discussed many times with a   13
great deal of zest. The value of an education is often assessed in   26
terms of costs and benefits to the taxpayer. It is also judged in   39
terms of changes in the ones taking part in this process. Acquiring   53
gains in knowledge, skill, and attitudes is often thought to be a vital   67
part of a good education.   72

1' | 1 | 2 | 3 | 4 | 5 | 6 | 7 | 8 | 9 | 10 | 11 | 12 | 13 |

Forms and Financial Documents

LEARNING OUTCOMES

- Create forms to be printed.
- Format financial documents.
- Build keyboarding skill.

LESSON 86

Printed Forms

WARMUP 86a

Key each line, striving for control. Repeat if desired.

alphabet	1	Benji Vazquez was prepared for the very difficult marketing exam.
fig/sym	2	About 25% of my team (1,460) earned an average salary of $39,627.
adjacent reaches	3	Ty was the guy people wanted in government; he responded quickly.
fluency	4	My neighbor may tutor the eight girls on the theory and problems.

| 1 | 2 | 3 | 4 | 5 | 6 | 7 | 8 | 9 | 10 | 11 | 12 | 13 |

SKILL BUILDING

86b Textbook Keying

1. Key each line once, concentrating on good keying techniques. Tap ENTER twice after each 3-line group.
2. Repeat if time permits.

	5	Jake Hass left; his dad was sad; Dallas's sales had fallen badly.
home row	6	Kala was glad Alyssa sold a glass flask at a gala sale in Dallas.
	7	Jack Hall's dad was in Dallas at a glass sale; a sad lad saw him.

	8	Zan relaxed in a cab, but Xavier fixed a van and drove back home.
first row	9	Max, Zam, and a local man saw an amazing cave on a long bus ride.
	10	Janna came back home six times to visit the bat caves at the zoo.

	11	We wrote Terry to try to get a quote; Perry tried to get a quote.
third row	12	Perry peeped at Terry's quote; were you there with Perry or Pete?
	13	Terry or Peter saw Perry at the polo tryout; you were there, too.

BULLETS AND NUMBERING

HOME/PARAGRAPH/BULLETS OR NUMBERING

39d

❶ Numbered and bulleted lists are commonly used to emphasize information in reports, newspapers, magazine articles, and overhead presentations. Use numbered items if the list requires a sequence of steps or points. Use bullets or symbols if the list contains an unordered listing. *Word* automatically inserts the next number in a sequence if you manually key a number. *Word* also automatically removes the extra space after the paragraph in a bulleted or numbered list. Note the spacing in the illustrations shown below.

- Word processing
- Spreadsheet
- Database
- Presentation
- Desktop publishing

1. Preheat oven to 350°.
2. Cream butter and sugar; add eggs.
3. Add flour.

To create bullets or numbers:

1. Key the list without bullets or numbers. Then select the list to be bulleted or numbered.
2. From the Home tab in the Paragraph group, click the Bullets or Numbering button ❶.
3. To add or remove bullets or numbers, click the Bullets or Numbering button.
4. To convert bullets to numbers or vice versa, select the items to change and click either the Bullets or Numbering button.

DRILL 1   BULLETS

1. Key the text below as a single list; do not key the bullets.
2. Apply bullets to the list by selecting the text to be bulleted and clicking the Bullets button.
3. Convert the bullets to numbers. Select the bulleted items and click the Numbering button.
4. Add **Roll Call** as the second item.
5. Delete the number before *Next Meeting*.
6. Check and close. (*39-drill1*)

- Call to Order
- Reading and Approval of the Minutes
- Announcements
- Treasurer's Report
- Membership Committee Report
- Unfinished Business
- New Business
- Adjournment
- Next Meeting: November 3, 20--

ATASCOCITA TECHNOLOGIES Top Five Sales Leaders for 20--		Sales			
Employee	ID	Hardware	Software	Services	Total
Rodriquez, Gabriela	RM29375	1,059,104.75	484,305.25	250,583.38	
Darnell, Tyler	CM39840	974,986.50	683,927.00	305,974.20	
Anderson, Taylor	RM28470	875,890.00	590,564.72	208,837.50	
Denzel, Travis	RM39873	850,987.75	550,725.00	210,845.50	
Smithfield, Xavier	CM39487	1,224,987.00	501,947.00	310,734.25	
Totals					

85-d3

Write Formula in Table

1. Key and format the table shown below. Format the title with 14-point Cambria bold font and the subtitle with 12-point bold font. Increase height to .8".

2. Write the formula to subtract expenses from income to calculate gross profits and complete column D. Then complete the total row at the bottom.

3. Use decimal tabs to format the three columns with numbers. Use the two-decimal number format. Gross profits and totals should be formatted with a $.

4. Apply Medium Grid 3 – Accent 6 table style. In the Table Style Options, check Total Row.

5. Center-align the title and subtitle. Check to see that all headings are bold.

6. Check the test and close it. *(85-d3)*

Klienwood, Inc. Income Summary			
Quarter	Income	Expenses	Gross Profits
First	$248,888.00	$174,937.00	
Second	263,478.00	178,350.00	
Third	245,927.00	168,934.00	
Fourth	236,452.00	152,805.00	
Total			

CHECKPOINT →

Congratulations! You have successfully completed the lessons in Module 13. To check your understanding and for more practice, complete the objective assessment and performance assessment located on the textbook website at www.collegekeyboarding.com.

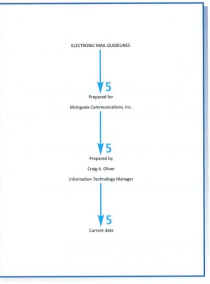

Traditional Title Page

COVER PAGE

INSERT/PAGES/COVER PAGE

Reports often include a cover or title page that identifies the report to the reader. As the name implies, the cover page is positioned on top of the report and provides an attractive cover for it. Traditionally a title page includes the title of the report, the name and title of the individual or the organization for which the report was prepared, the name and title of the writer, and the date the report was completed. The illustration at the left shows the traditional title page. Each line is center aligned. Allow nearly equal space between parts of the page (tap ENTER about five times).

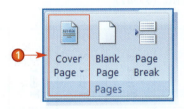

Word offers the Cover Page feature, which inserts a fully formatted cover page. You may choose from a variety of attractively formatted covers. Study the illustration of a cover page created using the Cover Page feature below. Remember, this only illustrates one specific style; you have many others from which to choose.

To create a cover page:

1. From the Insert tab in the Pages group, click Cover Page ❶. A gallery of cover pages displays.
2. Click the scroll arrows to determine the desired style ❷.
3. Select the desired style ❸. The cover page opens as a *Word* document.
4. Select *Type the document title* ❹ and key the report title. Repeat for all other items located in the template. **Note:** A blank page follows the cover page for keying the report.

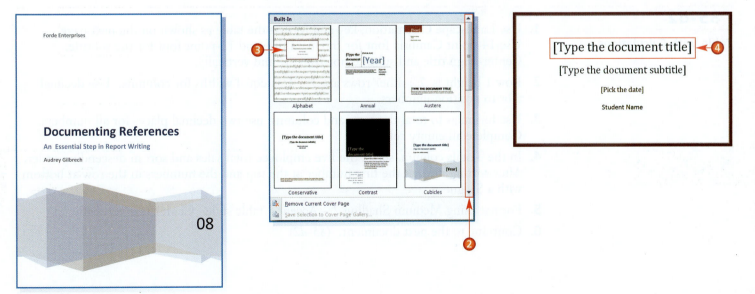

Cover Page, *Word 2007*

85-d1

Change Text Orientation in Table

1. Key and format the table shown below.
2. Row height: row 1 – 1"; all other rows – .3".
3. Column width: column B – 1.5"; all other columns .75".
4. Format text direction of column heads as shown; use 12-point Cambria bold font.
5. Use the AVERAGE(LEFT) function and #, ##0 number format for student averages; leave last two cells blank.
6. Use the MAX(ABOVE) function to calculate highest score and MIN(ABOVE) to calculate lowest score.
7. Merge cells in column A; use Cambria font and grow font as large as will fit on one line; apply bold.
8. Apply Medium Shading 1 – Accent 1 table style.
9. Center-align main headings and column heads (vertically and horizontally).
10. Left-align and center vertically text below *Student* column head. Center-align text in all cells below column heads for tests and student average.
11. Continue to the next document. (*85-d1*)

TIP

Do not merge the first column until you have made all row height adjustments.

Entrepreneurship	Student	Test 1	Test 2	Test 3	Test 4	Test 5	Student Average
	Fair, C.	86	88	82	92	86	
	Jeansonne, E.	95	94	95	92	94	
	Martin, D.	72	80	78	84	82	
	McMillan, J.	94	90	92	94	90	
	Quattlebaum, B.	74	76	72	68	70	
	Highest Score on Test						
	Lowest Score on Test						

85-d2

Table with Calculations

1. Use Landscape Orientation; key and format the table as shown on the next page. Use 14-point Cambria font for the main title and 12-point font for the subtitle. Center-align title and subtitle horizontally and vertically.
2. Row 1 height is .7"; other rows are 3". Use equal widths for columns. Use decimal tabs to position numbers.
3. Use formulas to total the rows and columns; use two decimal places for all numbers. Complete all empty cells.
4. In the Totals column, select the five employee total sales and sort in descending order. After sorting, format the first number at the top and the numbers in the row at bottom with a $ sign.
5. Format using Medium Shading 2 – Accent 3 table style. Center text vertically.
6. Continue to the next document. (*85-d2*)

continued

1. Create a cover page using the Cover Page feature. Select the Alphabet style in the Built-In category.
2. Click *[Type the document title]* and key **Updates for Document Processing**.
3. Key **Word 2007** as the document subtitle.
4. Key **Jun Yoshino** as the author name.
5. Click *[Pick the date]*, select the down arrow, and select a date.
6. Check and close the document. (*39-drill2*)

APPLICATIONS

39-d1
Unbound Report

1. Key the unbound report that follows. Position the title at approximately 2".
2. Add bullets to the three items.
3. Check and close. (*39-d1*)

Credible and Acceptable Reporting

Although its contents are of ultimate importance, a finished report's look is of almost equal importance. If it is to achieve the goal for which it was written, every report, whether it serves a business or academic purpose, should be acceptable from every point of view.

Citations, for Example

No matter which format is used for citations, a good writer knows citations are inserted for the reader's benefit; therefore, anything the writer does to ease their use will be appreciated and will work on the writer's behalf. Standard procedures, such as those stated below, make readers comfortable.

- Italicize titles of complete publications.
- Use quotation marks with parts of publications.
- Months and certain locational words may be abbreviated.

And the Final Report

The final report should have an attractive, easy-to-read look. The report should meet the criteria for spacing, citations, and binding that have been established for its preparation. Such criteria are set up by institutional decree, by generally accepted standards, or by subject demands. A writer should discover limits within which he or she must write and observe those limits with care.

In Conclusion

Giving the report a professional appearance calls for skill and patience from a writer. First impressions count when preparing reports. Poorly presented materials are not read, or at least not read with an agreeable attitude.

39-d2
Cover Page

1. Create a cover page using the Cover Page feature. Select the Alphabet style from the Built-In category of cover pages.
2. Key the report title from *39-d1* as the document title. Key **For All Management Employees** as the document subtitle.
3. Key **Dana Olmstead, Division Manager** as the author's name and title.
4. Check and close the document. (*39-d2*).

Key each line, striving for control. Repeat if desired.

alphabet 1 Jacqueline Katz made extra money by singing with the five groups.

figures 2 I sold 27 roses, 10 irises, 68 lilies, 54 tulips, and 39 orchids.

space bar 3 If she may go with me to a lake, I may do all of the work and go.

easy 4 The girls got the bicycle at the land of enchantment at the lake.

| 1 | 2 | 3 | 4 | 5 | 6 | 7 | 8 | 9 | 10 | 11 | 12 | 13 |

SKILL BUILDING

85b **Timed Writing**
Key two 3' writings, working for control.

all letters

gwam 3'

Employees who work together as a team are more effective   4
than those who work solo. This concept is known as synergy.   8
Synergy simply means that the joint action exceeds the sum of   12
individual actions. The results are not just in the quantity of   16
work; major gains in quality result when people work together as   21
a team. Teamwork is critical for success.   24

What characterizes an excellent team member? An excellent   28
team member understands the goals of the team and will place team   32
values above her or his individual objectives. An excellent team   36
member helps to determine the most effective way to reach the   40
goals that were set by the group and will help to make each   44
decision that affects the group. Above all, an excellent team   49
member will support a decision made by the team. Each member   53
must understand her or his role and respect the roles of others.   57
Every member of a team must share in both victory and defeat.   61

3' | 1 | 2 | 3 | 4 |

APPLICATIONS

85c

Assessment

→ Continue

✓ Check

With *Keyboarding Pro DELUXE*: When you complete a document, proofread it, check the spelling, and preview for placement. When you are completely satisfied, click the Continue button to move to the next document. Click the Check button when you are ready to error-check the test. Review and/or print the document analysis results.

Without *Keyboarding Pro DELUXE*: Key the documents in sequence. When time has been called, proofread all documents again and identify errors.

Multiple-Page Report

Key each line, striving for control. Repeat if desired.

alphabet	1	Jayne Cox puzzled over workbooks that were required for geometry.
figures	2	Edit pages 308 and 415 in Book A; pages 17, 29, and 60 in Book B.
shift	3	THE LAKES TODAY, published in Akron, Ohio, comes in June or July.

SKILL BUILDING

40b Textbook Keying

1. Key each line once, concentrating on using good keying techniques; tap ENTER twice after each 4-line group.
2. Repeat the drill if time permits.

n/u	5	nun nut unbolt null unable nudge under nurture thunder numb shunt
	6	Uncle Hunter runs with me to hide under the bed when it thunders.
c/e	7	ecru cell echo ceil check cedar pecan celery secret receive price
	8	Once Cecilia checked prices for acceptable and special offerings.
b/r	9	brag barb brown carbon brain marble break herb brace gerbil brick
	10	Bradley will try to break the unbroken brown brood mare bareback.
n/y	11	many bunny irony grainy granny sunny phony rainy runny zany funny
	12	Aunt Nanny says rainy days are for funny movies and many candies.

COMMUNICATION

40c Proofreading

Check your understanding of the unbound report by completing Drills 1 and 2 below. Refer to pages 147–148 if you have questions.

DRILL 1 — FORMAT KNOWLEDGE

Key each line at the right, choosing the correct choice shown in parentheses. Use the numbering feature to number each statement. Check and close. (*40-drill1*)

1. The title that appears on the first page of a report is keyed approximately (1", 2") from the top of the page.
2. The title is keyed at the (center, left margin.)
3. The title is formatted using the (Heading 1, Title) style; the font size of the title is (14 point, 26 point).
4. Side headings are keyed at the (center, left margin); the font size of side headings is (12 point, 14 point).
5. Side margins of an unbound report are (default or 1", 1.5").

DRILL 2 — PROOFREAD FOR CONSISTENCY — ASSOCIATIONS & ASSOCIATIONSKEY

Keyboarding Pro DELUXE: Before selecting Drill 2 from the menu, open *Word 2007*. Then open and print the data file **associationskey** from the data CD in the back of your book using *Word 2007*. Continue with step 2 as usual.

1. Open **associationskey** from the data files and print; close this file.

2. Open **associations** and print. Proofread this report and mark any formats that are not consistent with the solution printed in step 1. Use proofreaders' marks.
3. Correct the errors you marked. Print.
4. Submit the edited copy and the final copy to your instructor.
5. Check and close. (*40-drill2*)

1. Key the title **Single Life Unrestricted Gift Annuity Rate**, position it at 2", and apply Title style. Bold all column headings.

2. Key and format the table shown below. Format columns A, B, D, E, G, and H 1" wide and shade row 1 Dark Blue Text 2; format the text in white; format columns C and F .3" wide; merge the cells in columns C and the cells in columns F and shade each column with Blue Accent 1 – Lighter 60%. Apply double borders to the outside of the table and to the divider columns.

3. Check and close. (*84-d2*)

Age	Percentage		Age	Percentage		Age	Percentage
75	7.0		80	8.0		85	10.0
76	7.2		81	8.3		86	10.1
77	7.5		82	8.6		87	10.2
78	7.6		83	8.9		88	10.6
79	7.8		84	9.4		89 or older	11.2

84-d3

Table with Landscape Orientation

DISCOVER

On the Page Layout tab, in the Page Setup group, click Orientation. Choose Portrait or Landscape to change page orientation.

1. Use Landscape Orientation, Module document theme, and Title style.

2. Use the information below to create a seven-column, six-row table.

3. Center all column heads vertically and horizontally; apply bold. Change the text direction to vertical for the headings in columns D, E, and F.

4. Column widths: A – 1.8", B – 1.7", C – 1.2", D – .4", E – .9", F – 1.1", G – 2".

5. Row heights: row 1 – 1", rows 2 through 6 – .4"

6. Left-align and center vertically all text in rows 2–6.

7. Sort column A in alphabetical order.

8. Apply Medium Shading 2 – Accent 1 table style.

9. Check and close. (*84-d3*)

Title: Prospect List for the Tanglewood Southwest Development

Column heads: Name | Street Address | City | State | ZIP Code | Telephone Number | E-mail

Price, James and Mary | 237 Hope Road | Columbia | SC | 29223-2803 | 803-555-0187 | jprice@priceauto.com

Barker, Richard and Jill | 1515 Damon Drive | Florence | SC | 29505-3109 | 843-555-0192 | barker@crosscreek.com

Newton, Mark and Sally | 105 Wilderness Lane | Greenville | SC | 29607-1746 | 864-555-0133 | snewton@baycross.com

Edwards, Keith and Jan | 263 Oakwood Drive | Lexington | SC | 29073-9171 | 803-555-0174 | kedwards@emscboats.com

Hixson, Daniel and Ruth | 154 Gray Fox Court | West Columbia | SC | 29169-3722 | 803-555-0160 | jameson@rctfinance.com

PAGE NUMBERS

INSERT/HEADER AND FOOTER/PAGE NUMBER

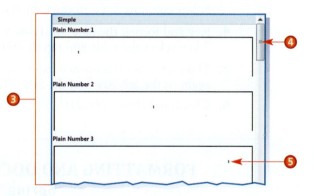

The Page Number command automatically inserts the correct page number on each page. Page numbers may be positioned automatically in the header position (0.5" at top of page) or in the footer position (bottom of the page). To prevent the number from printing on the first page, you will modify the layout.

To insert page numbers:

1. On the Insert tab, in the Header and Footer group, click the down arrow on the Page Number button ❶.

2. Click Top of Page ❷. A gallery of page number styles displays ❸.

3. Click the down scroll arrow to browse the various styles ❹. Click Plain Number 3 from the gallery ❺. The page number displays in the header position at the top right.

To remove the page number from the first page:

DESIGN/OPTIONS/DIFFERENT FIRST PAGE

On the Design tab, from the Options group, click Different First Page ❻. The page number does not display on the first page.

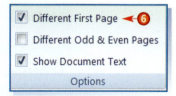

LINE AND PAGE BREAKS

HOME/PARAGRAPH/DIALOG BOX LAUNCHER

Pagination or breaking pages at the appropriate location can easily be controlled using two features: Widow/Orphan control and Keep with next.

Widow/Orphan control prevents a single line of a paragraph from printing at the bottom or top of a page. A check mark displays in this option box indicating that Widow/Orphan control is "on" (the default).

Keep with next prevents a page break from occurring between two paragraphs. Use this feature to keep a side heading from being left alone at the bottom of a page.

84e

1. Search the Internet for articles that deal with creativity in business.

2. Look specifically for tips on how to become more creative.

3. Develop a list of at least ten tips for becoming more creative. Select items that would help you become more knowledgeable about creativity if you were interviewing at a company that listed it as one of the major attributes being sought in new employees.

4. Edit your list carefully and format it attractively.

5. Check and close. (*84e*)

6. Compose an e-mail to your instructor describing a few key points you learned about creativity, and attach your list of tips for becoming more creative.

APPLICATIONS ◖

84-d1

Table with Vertical Text Headings

1. Open *83-d2*, and make the changes shown below in the table.

2. Select the headings for Tests 1–4, and click text direction to change it to vertical text that reads from the bottom up.

3. Click in the Test 4 column and add two columns to the right; adjust columns A and H so that all text is on one line if it is not already. Drag the borders of the four test columns to make them smaller so that your table will not extend off the right side. Select columns B–G; in the Cell Size group, click Distribute Columns.

4. Key and format the data for Tests 5 and 6 shown below; compute the average for both. Then select the table and tap the F9 key to update the fields in the table.

5. Make any adjustments needed in the format of the table. You may have to apply bold again to the last row and the last column after updating the fields.

6. Check and close. (*84-d1*)

FORMATTING AND DOCUMENT PROCESSING
Spring, 20--

Student	Test 1	Test 2	Test 3	Test 4	Test 5	Test 6	Highest Score
Culberson, J.	74	82	76	88	76	78	**88**
Maxwell, M.	93	99	89	97	95	94	**99**
Roquefort, B.	88	78	92	84	86	86	**92**
Westbrook, A.	90	88	84	94	88	96	**96**
Average Per Test	**86**	**87**	**85**	**91**			**91**

To use Keep with next:

1. Select the side heading and at least two lines of the paragraph that follows it.

2. On the Home tab, in the Paragraph group, click the Paragraph Dialog Box Launcher. The Paragraph dialog box displays.

3. From the Line and Page Breaks tab **1**, select Keep with next **2**.

4. Click OK. The side heading moves to the next page.

KEYBOARDING PRO DELUXE   See References/Word commands/Lesson 40

DRILL 3   **PAGE BREAKS AND PAGE NUMBERS**   KEEP WITH NEXT

1. Add page numbers positioned at the top of page at the right. Use Plain Number 3 as the default style. Do not print a page number on the first page.

2. Select the side heading at the bottom of the page along with the entire address and the first line with a time note.

3. Apply the Keep with next command so the side heading moves to page 2.

4. Preview to verify that the page number appears on page 2 only and that the side heading appears on page 2.

5. Check and close. *(40-drill3)*

DOCUMENT DESIGN

MULTIPLE-PAGE REPORT

In Lesson 38 you learned to format a one-page unbound report. Because reports are often longer than one page, you will learn in Lesson 40 to format a multiple-page report. When a multiple-page report is created, page numbers are required on all pages except the first. Study the illustration below noting specifically the position of page numbers. Review the callouts as well to reinforce your understanding of report formats.

To format a multiple-page report:

1. Insert page numbers at the upper-right corner in the header position (0.5").

2. Suppress the page number on the first page.

3. Protect side headings that may be separated from the related paragraph with the Keep with next feature. **Note:** The Keep with next feature is turned on automatically when styles are applied to a side heading.

TEXT ORIENTATION

TABLE TOOLS/LAYOUT/ALIGNMENT/TEXT DIRECTION

Text is traditionally displayed horizontally in a table cell. At times, it is preferable to display the text vertically in a cell. Typically, text is displayed vertically when a number of narrow columns are included in a table. The Text Direction command is used to rotate text to the desired direction.

To change the text direction in a cell:

1. Position the insertion point in the cell in which you want to change the text direction.
2. On the Layout tab, under Table Tools, in the Alignment group, click Text Direction ❶ until the text displays in the desired direction. Note that text can be positioned vertically reading from top to bottom or from bottom to top.
3. With the insertion point in the cell that you changed text direction, on the Layout tab, under Table Tools, in the Alignment group, click the direction in which you want the text aligned in the cell ❷.
4. Repeat steps 1–3 in each cell that you want to change text direction and align the text.

DRILL 1 — TEXT ORIENTATION

1. Key the title **Fall Semester Enrollments**; position it at 2" and apply Title style.
2. Insert an eight-column, seven-row table.
3. Click the first cell of the first row; then on the Layout tab, under Table Tools, in the Cell Size group, change the width of the first column to 2" and the height of the first row to 1". Select the remaining seven columns and click Distribute Columns to distribute them equally.
4. Key the table as shown below.
5. With row 1 of columns B–H selected, click the Text Direction command until you have vertical text read from the bottom up, and then click the Align Bottom Center button.
6. In row 1 of column A, center the text vertically and horizontally; left–align rows 2–7 of column A; right–align rows 2–7 of columns B–H.
7. Complete the total row by using the SUM ABOVE command and the Total column by using the SUM LEFT command. **Note:** If you work from the bottom cell up in the Total column, the default on the formula will be SUM LEFT.
8. Check and close. (*84-drill1*)

College	Freshman	Sophomore	Junior	Senior	Graduate Masters	Graduate Doctorate	Total
Business Administration	3,975	3,498	2,800	2,450	1,250	120	
Arts and Sciences	4,105	3,692	2,750	2,368	1,240	140	
Engineering	1,400	1,258	1,075	950	345	60	
Nursing	1,000	964	905	850	40	22	
Education	1,863	1,702	1,568	1,396	438	175	
Total							

40-d1

Multiple-Page Report

WRITING

☀ ── **DISCOVER**

Insert file—Position insertion point where file is to be inserted. On the Insert tab, click Object in the Text group. Select Create from File; choose the desired file; click Insert; and click OK.

1. Key the unbound report that follows. Do not indent paragraphs. Position the title at approximately 2".

2. Insert the data file *writing* below the second paragraph. (**Note:** Be sure to position the insertion point where you want the text to appear before inserting the file.)

3. Format the first side heading *Research* correctly. Check the remaining three side headings for proper format.

4. Revise the side headings to make them parallel with *Research* (gramatically consistent).

5. Insert page numbers; do not print the page number on page 1.

6. Preview the document to verify page numbers and that side headings are not left alone at the bottom of the page.

7. Check and close the document. (*40-d1*)

Learn to Win at Writing

Being able to communicate effectively continues to be one of the most demanded work skills. Today's high demand for clear, concise, and logical communication makes it impossible for an employee to excuse himself or herself from writing by saying, "I'm just not a writer," or "I can't write."

Realizing you need to improve your writing skills is the first step to enhancing them. Then you must apply a systemized approach to writing as detailed in this report.

Insert the data file writing here.

The effective writer understands the importance of using technology to create an attractive document that adheres to correct style rules. Review the list below to determine your use of technology in the report writing process.

- Number preliminary pages of the report with small Roman numerals at the bottom center of the page.
- Number the report with Arabic numbers in the upper-right corner.
- Create attractive headers or footers that contain helpful information for the reader.
- Suppress headers, footers, and page numbering on the title page and on the first page of the report.
- Invoke the Widow/Orphan control feature to ensure that no lines display alone at the bottom or top of a page.
- Use the Keep with next command to keep side headings from appearing alone at the bottom of the page.
- Format references using the hanging indent feature.
- Use typographic or special symbols to enhance the report.

continued

LESSON 84

Change Text Orientation

WARMUP 84a

Key each line, striving for control. Repeat if desired.

alphabet 1 Quin or Jack asked five big boys to play harder to maximize wins.

adjacent 2 Porter was hoping to buy a treat quickly for the new polo player.

direct reach 3 June and Cecilia braved the cold and visited their young friends.

fluency 4 The apricot clamshell memento is authentic; it's handiwork by Ty.

SKILL BUILDING

84b Textbook Keying
1. Key each line once, concentrating on good keying techniques. Tap ENTER twice after each 3-line group.
2. Repeat if time permits.

5 readers secrets dessert degrade cataracts abstracts basted create

left hand 6 barge adage beverages scarce assist trait area tea fast are dress

7 waves fatal taste zest craze star tear drawers garage grade trees

8 union poplin hookup hominy minimum onion link plump pool pink lip

right hand 9 million opinion pupil imply jolly knoll lymph yolk upon no nil on

10 nymph him hop hip ink mommy joy pin ply nip oil in poll oh pip my

11 work yams worn tutor vile slang shrug clams bogus slept me trains

both hands 12 blend sighs sign forks amend angle aisle visitor window if posted

13 tuck yield fowl cork duels roams tyrant clan soap rifle so jumped

| 1 | 2 | 3 | 4 | 5 | 6 | 7 | 8 | 9 | 10 | 11 | 12 | 13 |

gwam 3'

84c Timed Writing
Key two 3' writings, working for control.

all letters

Has anyone ever said to you that you should dress for success? 5
If you are planning to go to a job interview, this advice is 9
excellent, and you should follow it very carefully.   Dressing 13
appropriately will help you to make a good first impression.   Men 17
should wear a good-quality business suit, or at least a blazer.   A 22
clean shirt, preferably white, a nice tie, clean dark shoes, and dark 26
socks will complete the professional look.   Women should project a 31
very professional image.   A dark business suit with a medium-length 35
skirt is very appropriate.   A blouse in a pleasant color will also 40
help to make a very good impression. 42

Both men and women should pay very close attention to all aspects 47
of good grooming.   The interviewer expects to see potential employees 52
with clean, well-styled hair and clean, short fingernails.   The 56
interviewer will also check to see that good manners are displayed. 60
The additional effort that it takes to make a good first impression at 65
an interview may be one of the best investments that a person could 70
ever make in his or her future. 72

3' | 1 | 2 | 3 | 4 |

40-d1

Continued

Writers also take advantage of the online thesaurus for choosing the most appropriate word and the spelling and grammar features to ensure spelling and grammar correctness. Additionally, electronic desk references and style manuals are just a click away.

Finally, all the report needs is the title page. Effective writers know that it pays dividends to create a custom title page that truly reflects the quality of the report that it covers. Use page borders and shading as well as graphics to create an attractive title page.

Two simple steps followed in a systematic order will assist you in your goal to learn to win at writing. Knowing the approach is the first step; the second step is to practice, practice, practice.

40-d2

Title Page

1. Create a title page for the unbound report prepared in *40-d1*. Use the Cover Page feature.
2. Key the following information:

   Document title: **Learn to Win at Writing**

   Document subtitle: **For XYZ Employees**

   Author name: **Jennifer Schoenholtz, Office Manager**
3. Check and close. (*40-d2*)

1. Key the table shown below. Expand column A so that all entries will fit on one line. Select columns B through E and distribute columns equally.

2. Select the student names in column A and sort alphabetically in ascending order.

3. Use the =AVERAGE(ABOVE) Paste function to complete the average per test. Use #, ##0 format to round the average.

4. Use the =MAX(LEFT) Paste function to complete the highest score column including the Average Per Test cell.

5. Apply Medium Grid 1 – Accent 5 table style. In the Table Style Options group, deselect the First Column, and select Last Column and Total Row.

6. Format title using 14-point Cambria bold font; format the subtitle using the same attributes except 12-point font.

7. Increase row 1 height to .8" and center vertically and horizontally; increase other rows to .3".

8. Select the first column and align left and center vertically; select all other columns and center vertically and horizontally.

9. Bold all headings.

10. Preview and make any adjustments necessary. Check and close. *(83-d2)*

FORMATTING AND DOCUMENT PROCESSING Spring, 20--					
Student	**Test 1**	**Test 2**	**Test 3**	**Test 4**	**Highest Score**
Roquefort, B.	88	78	92	84	
Culberson, J.	74	82	76	88	
Maxwell, M.	93	99	89	97	
Westbrook, A.	90	88	84	94	
Average Per Test					

WORKPLACE SUCCESS

Creativity

Read the career pages on company websites and you will notice very quickly that numerous companies indicate that one of the key attributes they seek in new employees is creativity. Many questions surface when creativity is mentioned: What is creativity? Who is creative? Do you have to be born creative or can you develop creativity? One search using the keyword *creativity* produced more than 65 million responses. No consensus exists on a definition of creativity. To many, creative people are artists, musicians, architects, and people in similar occupations. However, businesses that list creativity as an attribute they seek in new employees are not looking for that type of employee. Many people describe creative people as those who can generate new or different ideas. Other people believe that creative people can take current unrelated ideas and connect them to make them useful or different. Many businesses believe that creativity can be developed and that many, if not most, of their employees can be creative.

Leftbound Report with Long Quotations

Key each line, striving for control. Repeat if desired.

alphabet	1	Jacki might analyze the data by answering five complex questions.
figures	2	Memo 67 asks if the report on Bill 35-48 is due on the 19th or the 20th.
shift	3	Plum trees on a hilly acre, in my opinion, create no vast estate.
easy	4	Did the foal buck? And did it cut the left elbow of the cowhand?

SKILL BUILDING

41b Textbook Keying
1. Key each line once, concentrating on using good keying techniques; tap ENTER twice after each 3-line group.
2. Repeat if time permits.

	5	you yes yelp year yield yellow yule yours symbol pray grassy money
y/t	6	to at tent triek treat trestle tribute thirty match matter clutter
	7	Timothy printed a symbol, yacht, and yellowjacket for Mr. Forsyst.
	8	got get giggle gargle gargoyle gangway engage eagle magic peg piggy
g/h	9	he she her head harp hay heavy hearth homograph hyena high height
	10	Gail Hughes, a researcher, charted the height and weight of Hugh.

| 1 | 2 | 3 | 4 | 5 | 6 | 7 | 8 | 9 | 10 | 11 | 12 | 13 |

REVIEW FUNCTIONS

41c

MARGINS

PAGE LAYOUT/PAGE SETUP/MARGINS

Margins are the distance between the edge of the paper and the print. The default settings are 1" side margins and 1" top and bottom margins. Default margins stay in effect until you change them.

To set margins not listed in the gallery:

1. From the Page Layout tab, in the Page Setup group, click Margins and then click Custom Margins ❶. The Page Setup dialog box displays.

Office 2003 Default			
Top:	1"	Bottom:	1"
Left:	1.25"	Right:	1.25"

❶ → Custom Margins...

2. From the Margins tab ❷, click the up or down arrows to increase or decrease the default settings ❸.

3. Apply margins to the Whole document ❹ unless directed otherwise.

4. Click OK.

PASTE FUNCTION

TABLE TOOLS/LAYOUT/DATA/FORMULA

Additional mathematical functions are available in the Paste Function box on the Formula dialog box. You have already worked with SUM, which is one of the Paste functions. The Paste functions use prewritten formulas that save you from writing formulas. You can use directions such as ABOVE, BELOW, LEFT, or RIGHT with the Paste functions just as you did with SUM. Some of the Paste functions you will work with include:

AVERAGE()	Calculates the average of the numbers in the cells indicated in parentheses such as cell above or to the left of the current cell.
MAX()	Locates the highest number in the cells indicated in parentheses such as cell above or to the left of the current cell.
MIN()	Locates the lowest number in the cells indicated in parentheses such as cell above or to the left of the current cell.
COUNT()	Counts the number of numeric values in the cells indicated in parentheses such as cell above or to the left of the current cell.

Note that these functions save time in large tables. In small tables, it is easy to find the highest and lowest numbers or to count the numbers in the range.

To use the paste function:

1. Place the insertion point in the cell where the calculation should be made.
2. Under Table Tools, on the Layout tab, in the Data group, click Formula.
3. If necessary, delete the existing formula (but not the = sign).
4. Click the Paste function drop list arrow.
5. Choose the new function such as AVERAGE, and then key the cell references between the parentheses or the direction (LEFT, RIGHT, ABOVE) to which the function should apply. Click OK.

Formula   ? ✕

Formula:

=AVERAGE(ABOVE)

Number format:

$#,##0.00;($#,##0.00)

Paste function:

AVERAGE
COUNT
DEFINED
FALSE
IF
INT
MAX
MIN

Paste bookmark:

OK   Cancel

The thrust to use e-mail almost exclusively is causing a tremendous challenge for both e-mail recipients and companies.

> With the convenience of electronic mail resulting in its widespread use, many users are forsaking other forms of communication—face-to-face, telephone (including voice mail), and printed documents. Now companies are challenged to create clear e-mail policies and to implement employee training on effective use of e-mail. (Ashford, 2008, 2)

Indent

Communication experts have identified problems that may occur as a result of misusing e-mail. Two important problems include information overload (too many messages) and inappropriate form of communication.

DOCUMENT DESIGN

REPORT DOCUMENTATION

Reports must include the sources of all information used in the report. Documentation gives credit for published material, whether electronic or printed, that is quoted or closely paraphrased by the writer. The writer may document sources by using footnotes, endnotes, or internal citations. In this module, you will use internal citations and footnotes.

At the end of the report, the writer provides the reader with a complete alphabetical listing of all references. This allows the interested reader to locate the original source. You will learn to format a reference list in Lesson 42.

INTERNAL CITATIONS

Internal citations are an easy and practical method of documentation. The last name of the author(s), the publication date, and the page numbers(s) of the cited material are shown in parentheses within the body of the report (Crawford, 2008, 134). This information cues a reader to the name Crawford in the reference list included at the end of the report. When the author's name is used in the text to introduce the quotation, only the year of publication and the page numbers appear in parentheses: "Crawford (2008, 134) said that...."

Short, direct quotations of three lines or fewer are enclosed within quotation marks. Long quotations of four lines or more are indented 0.5" from the left margin.

If a portion of the text that is referenced is omitted, use an ellipsis (…) to show the omission. An ellipsis is three periods, each preceded and followed by a space. If a period occurs at the end of a sentence, include the period or punctuation.

According to Estes (2008, 29), "Successful businesses have long known the importance of good verbal communication."

Short Quotation

Probably no successful enterprise exists that does not rely for its success upon the ability of its members to communicate:

> Make no mistake, both written and verbal communication are the stuff upon which success is built in all types of organizations…. Both forms deserve careful study by any business that wants to grow. Successful businesspeople must read, write, speak, and listen with skill. Often professional development in these areas is needed. (Schaefer, 2008, 28)

Long Quotation

1. Open *82-d1*. Note that the first column has a header (*College*) in a merged cell.

2. In the first column, select the text in the rows below the heading.

3. Under Table Tools, on the Layout tab, in the Data group, click Sort, Ascending, and No Header row. Click OK. Check to see that the text under *College* is sorted alphabetically.

4. Check and close. (*83-drill2*)

FORMULAS

TABLE TOOLS/LAYOUT/DATA/FORMULA

Word can perform basic mathematical calculations such as addition, subtraction, multiplication, and division when numbers are keyed in a table. *Word* inserts a field representing the formula rather than the actual answer, so if the numbers used in the formula are changed, the answer will recalculate. While *Word* is excellent for working with basic formulas, more complex calculations are better performed in a spreadsheet, such as *Excel*.

You can specify the format in which your answer is to be displayed. For example, if you are calculating money amounts, you can choose to have the answer display with two decimal places, with or without a dollar sign, and with or without commas.

USING THE SUM FUNCTION

TABLE TOOLS/LAYOUT/DATA/FORMULA

SUM is the default formula that appears if you click a cell below a column of numbers or to the right of a row of numbers. If you click a cell below a column of numbers, =SUM(ABOVE) appears in the dialog box as the formula. If you click a cell at the right of a row of numbers, =SUM(LEFT) appears in the dialog box as the formula.

To total a column or a row of numbers:

1. Position the insertion point in the cell that is to contain the answer.

2. Under Table Tools, on the Layout tab, in the Data group, click Formula. Note that the SUM formula—either ABOVE or LEFT depending on if you clicked below a column or at the end of a row—appears in the Formula box.

3. Click the down arrow by Number format and select the desired number format. Click OK.

Formula	? X
Formula:	
=SUM(ABOVE)	
Number format:	
#,##0	▼
Paste function:	Paste bookmark:
	▼
	OK Cancel

1. Open *82-drill1* and add a row at the bottom of the table.

2. Key **Total** in column A, and then click column B.

3. Under Table Tools, on the Layout tab, in the Data group, click Formula. Note that the formula =SUM(ABOVE) is entered in the Formula box.

4. Click the down arrow on Number Format and select the first option—#,##0 (whole numbers with commas). Click OK. Notice the total appears in the cell.

5. With the insertion point in the bottom row, under Table Tools, on the Design tab, in the Table Style Options group, select Total Row. Note the format that is added to the row.

6. Check and close. (*83-drill3*)

2"

Documentation in Report Writing

Preparing a thorough and convincing report requires excellent research, organization, and composition skills as well as extensive knowledge of documenting referenced materials. The purpose of this report is to present the importance of documenting a report with credible references and the techniques for creating accurate citations.

Documenting with References

For a report to be credible and accepted by its readers, a thorough review of related literature is essential. This background information is an important part of the report and provides believability of the writer and of the report. When sharing this literature in the body of the report, the writer understands the following basic principles of report documentation:

1½"

1"

- All ideas of others must be cited so that credit is given appropriately.
- The reader will need to be able to locate the material using the information included in the reference citation.
- Format rules apply to ideas stated as direct quotations and ideas that are paraphrased.
- Use the citations and bibliographic features of contemporary word processing software to assist to apply manuscript styles appropriately.
- A thorough list of references adds integrity to the report and to its author.

Good writers learn quickly how to evaluate the many printed and electronic references that have been located to support the theme of their reports. Those references judged acceptable are then cited in the report. Writer John Millsaps (2008, 12) shares this simple advice:

Indented Long Quotation →

> Today writers can locate a vast number of references in very little time. Electronic databases and Internet Web pages are very easy to locate and provide a multitude of information. The novice writer will be quick to include all these references in a report without verifying their credibility. Just as writers verify the value of printed sources, experienced writers check electronic sources as well.

Using a Style Manual

Three popular style manuals are the *MLA Handbook*, *The Chicago Manual of Style*, and the *Publication Manual of the American Psychological Association*. After selecting a style, carefully study the acceptable formats for citing books, magazines, newspapers, brochures, online

82-d2

Table

The table shown below has similar characteristics to the one you prepared in *82-d1*.

1. Key and format the table appropriately; apply table guides presented in this module.
2. Select the style, row height, and other formats of your choice.
3. Check and close. (*82-d2*)

OUTPATIENT PROSPECTIVE PAYMENT SYSTEM Unadjusted National Medicare Reimbursement				
Description	**Code**		**Insurance**	
	CPT	**APC**	**Medicare**	**Coinsurance**
Immobilization	77341	0303	71.08	69.28
Basic Dosimetry	77300	0304	388.52	498.26
Daily IMRT Treatment	60174	0302	7,625.19	8,662.14
Continuing Physics	77336	0311	270.48	253.26

82-d3

Memo with Table

WEXMARK MEMO

1. Key the following memo with a table on the Wexmark memo form.
2. Insert the table after the first paragraph; format it as shown in the illustration using AutoFit contents; apply .3" row height and Medium Shading 2 – Accent 2 style. On the Layout tab, under Table Tools, click Properties. Then in the Text wrapping section, click Around. Click OK.
3. Check and close. (*82-d3*)

Parents | Lynn Marshall | May 15, 20-- | Tuition

The Board of Directors has reviewed our financial statements, the proposed budget for next year, and our current tuition plan. Although we have tried to maintain tuition at the current rate, it is not possible to do so. Our costs for utilities, food, supplies, and gasoline for the buses have increased substantially. Therefore, we have applied a 2.5% increase in tuition for next year. The following table summarizes our new weekly rates.

Age Group	Single-Child Rate	Multi-Child Rate
Infant/Toddler	$168	$145
Preschool 2	153	133
Preschool 3	140	130
Preschool 4	137	128
Preschool 5	135	125

The new rates take effect on July 1 and will be guaranteed not to change for one full year. The Children's Center will continue to accept credit cards and personal checks as it has always done. Tuition may be paid weekly, monthly, and annually.

If you wish to pay the annual tuition at one time prior to July 1, you may pay the current rates rather than these new rates with the 2.5% increase shown in the table. If you have any questions about tuition or other financial issues, please check with our business manager at the Children's Center.

We look forward to seeing all of you at the annual picnic next week.

LESSON 42 ▸ Report with Reference Page

WARMUP 42a

Key each line, striving for control. Repeat if desired.

alphabet	1	Two exit signs jut quietly above the beams of a razed skyscraper.
figures	2	Send 345 of the 789 sets now; send the others on August 1 and 26.
direct reach	3	I obtain many junk pieces dumped by Marvyn at my service centers.
easy	4	Enrique may fish for cod by the dock; he also may risk a penalty.

| 1 | 2 | 3 | 4 | 5 | 6 | 7 | 8 | 9 | 10 | 11 | 12 | 13 |

SKILL BUILDING

42b Timed Writing
1. Key a 1' timed writing on each paragraph; work to increase speed.
2. Key a 3' timed writing on all paragraphs.

LA

all letters

	gwam	1'	3'
Does a relationship exist between confidence and success? If		12	4	42
you think it does, you will find that many people agree with you.		26	9	46
However, it is very hard to judge just how strong the bond is.		38	13	50
When people are confident they can do a job, they are very		12	17	54
likely to continue working on that task until they complete it		24	21	58
correctly. If they are not confident, they give up much quicker.		38	25	63
People who are confident they can do something tend to enjoy		12	29	67
doing it more than those who lack confidence. They realize that		25	34	71
they do better work when they are happy with what they do.		37	37	75

1' | 1 | 2 | 3 | 4 | 5 | 6 | 7 | 8 | 9 | 10 | 11 | 12 | 13 |
3' | 1 | 2 | 3 | 4 |

NEW FUNCTIONS

42c

HANGING INDENT

Hanging indent places the first line of a paragraph at the left margin and indents all other lines to the first tab. It is commonly used to format bibliography entries, glossaries, and lists. Hanging indent can be applied before text is keyed or after.

To create a hanging indent:
1. From the Horizontal Ruler, click the hanging indent marker ❶.
2. Drag the Hanging Indent marker ❷ to the position where the indent is to begin.
3. Key the paragraph. The second and subsequent lines are indented beginning at the marker. (**Shortcut:** CTRL + T, then key the paragraph; or select the paragraphs to be formatted as hanging indents and press CTRL + T.)

DRILL 1	HANGING INDENT

1. Drag the Hanging Indent marker to 0.5" to the right; then key the references on the following page.
2. Turn Hanging Indent off by dragging the Hanging Indent marker back to the left margin.
3. Check and close the document. (*42-drill1*)

1. In a new blank document, create the table shown below.

2. Distribute the columns evenly; left-align column heads; then center vertically and bold them.

3. Insert one row between rows 3 and 4; then insert two rows above row 1.

4. Insert a column between columns B and C. Key the column head: **Manager**.

5. In the row above the column headings, merge the cells into one cell. Then delete the top row.

6. Key the following heading in row 1: **Regional Equipment Sales Leaders for First Quarter**. Increase the height to .5" Apply 14-point Cambria bold font and center vertically and horizontally.

7. Select the remaining rows and increase the height to .3". Left-align and vertically center text in columns A, C, and D. Center horizontally and vertically the text in column B.

8. Key the following managers' names in column C that you added:

   Sydney Moore
   Todd Bradshaw
   Anna Mendoza
   Lee Jung

9. Add **Hailey Maxwell** with **2,196,753** sales in the **Northeast** region in the blank row between Gause and McNab.

10. AutoFit the table to the contents.

11. Apply Light List – Accent 2 table style; remove bold from the first column; reapply bold to the column heading. Center the table horizontally.

12. Preview the table and double-check to ensure that you applied all formats as directed.

13. Check and close. (*82-drill1*)

Employee	Sales $	Region
Roger Shaw	2,678,915	South
Amanda Gause	2,496,025	Midwest
Taylor McNab	1,373,986	West

DECIMAL TABS

You have been using the Align Text Right button to right-align the numbers in a column. Columns A and C show the numbers right-aligned using a decimal tab. Using the Align Text Right button produces the result shown in column B below. Setting a decimal tab allows you to keep the numbers right-aligned and make them appear centered in the column. Note with whole numbers you could also set a right-align tab in column C.

Numbers with Decimals	Align-Right Function	Decimal Tab
8.5	5,694,573	560
25.40	10,358,905	1,475
275.925	158,384,296	18,964

1. Key the text below.
2. Place the insertion point after the first set of goals. Insert a manual page break.
3. Continue keying page 2.

4. Use the Page Number command to insert a number at the top of the page. Use Plain Number 3 as the default style. Do not print number on the first page.
5. Check and close. *(42-drill4)*

Goal 1: Membership Development

Objective: To increase membership.

Indent → **Plan**

    A. Review and evaluate membership benefits.
    B. Study avenues for additional membership benefits.

← **Insert page break.**

Goal 2: Staff Development

Objective: To enhance performance and motivation of staff.

Indent → **Plan**

    A. Review and evaluate previous staff development programs.
    B. Survey staff to determine needs.
    C. Implement relevant staff development programs.

DOCUMENT DESIGN

REFERENCE PAGE

References cited in the report are listed at the end of the report in alphabetical order by authors' last names. The reference list may be titled References or Bibliography; apply the Title style to the reference page title.

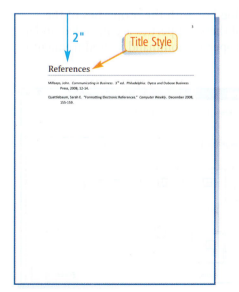

Become familiar with the three types of references listed below:

1. A book reference includes the name of the author (last name first), work (italicized), city of publication, publisher, and copyright date.

2. A magazine reference shows the name of the author (last name first), article (in quotation marks), magazine title (italicized), date of publication, and page references.

3. A reference retrieved electronically includes the author (inverted), article (in quotation marks), publication (italicized), publication information, Internet address, and date the document was retrieved or accessed (in parentheses).

Begin the list of references on a new page by inserting a manual page break at the end of the report. Begin the title of the reference page at approximately 2" from the top of the page (same as the first page of the report). Number the reference page at the top right of the page. References are keyed in the hanging indent format; tap ENTER once between references.

LESSON 82 — Review, Edit, and Format Tables

LESSON 82

WARMUP 82a

Key each line, striving for control. Repeat if desired.

alphabet	1	Jacob Vassar quickly analyzed data before doing the complex work.
figures	2	Call me at 803-555-0167 when you have opened rooms 2498 and 2476.
fig/sym	3	I bought items #42 and #54 for $39.87 (25% discount) on 10/16/09.
fluency	4	Did their neighbor go by auto to the lake? If so, it is a shame.

REVIEW FUNCTION

82b

FORMAT TABLES

TABLE TOOLS/LAYOUT

Once you have created a table, a variety of table tools are available on the Layout tab that can be used to change the structure and format of the table. Review the following options for formatting a table.

To change the structure or format of a table:

1. Click in a table to display the Table Tools tab.
2. Under the Table Tools tab, click Layout to display a ribbon that enables you to change the structure or format of the table.

ADD OR DELETE ROWS AND COLUMNS

TABLE TOOLS/LAYOUT/ROWS & COLUMNS

Table structure can be changed in many ways—one common way is to add or delete rows or columns to an existing table.

To add or delete rows or columns:

1. To insert a row, click the row that you wish to insert a row above or below. On the Layout tab, in the Rows & Columns group, click Insert Above or Insert Below **①**.
2. To insert a column, click the column to the left or right of which you wish to insert it. Click Insert Left or click Insert Right **②**.
3. To delete a column or row, click it; then click Delete **③** and select the desired option **④**.

MERGE OR SPLIT CELLS

TABLE TOOLS/LAYOUT/MERGE/MERGE CELLS OR SPLIT CELLS

Multiple cells can be merged to form one cell, or a single cell can be split into multiple rows or columns.

To merge or split cells:

1. Select cells that you wish to merge, and on the Layout tab, under Table Tools, in the Merge group, click Merge Cells.
2. Click in the cell to be split. On the Layout tab, under Table Tools, in the Merge group, click Split Cells.
3. Click the up and down arrows to select the desired number of columns or row.

42-d2

Continued

Guidelines for Business Dress

Companies are employing image consultants to teach employees what is appropriate business casual and to plan the best business attire to project the corporate image. Erica Gilreath (2008), the author of *Casual Dress*, a guidebook on business casual, provides excellent advice on how to dress casually and still command the power needed for business success. She presents the following advice to professionals:

- Do not wear any clothing that is designed for recreational or sports activities, e.g., cargo pants or pants with elastic waist.

- Invest the time in pressing khakis and shirts or pay the price for professional dry cleaning. Wrinkled clothing does not enhance one's credibility.

- Do not wear sneakers.

- Be sure clothing fits properly. Avoid baggy clothes or clothes that are too tight.

In summary, energetic employees working to climb the corporate ladder will need to plan their dress carefully. If business casual is appropriate, it is best to consult the experts on business casual to ensure a professional image.

References

Gilreath, Erica. "Dressing Casually with Power." http://www.casualdress.com (accessed March 23, 2008).

Monaghan, Margaret. "Business Dress Codes May Be Shifting." *Business Executive*. April 2008, 34-35.

Sutphin, Rachel. "Your Business Wardrobe Decisions Are Important Decisions." *Business Management Journal*. January 2007, 10-12.

Tartt, Kelsey. "Companies Support Business Casual Dress." *Management Success*. June 2005, 23-25.

42-d3

Title Page

1. Prepare a title page for the unbound report completed in *42-d2*. Use the Cover Page feature to create the title page. Choose the Alphabet style from the Built-In category of the Cover Page gallery.

2. Key the following information:

   Document title: Refer to title of *42-d2*.

   Document subtitle: **For All Employees**

   Author name: **Your name, Image Consultant**

3. Check and close. (*42-d3*)

To add, change, or remove a table style:

1. To add a table style, click the table; then under Table Tools, click Design. In the Table Styles group, click the desired style.

2. To remove a style, click the table; then under Table Tools, click Design. In the Table Styles group, under the gallery of styles, click Clear.

3. To change table style options, click the table; then under Table Tools, click Design. In the Table Style Options group, click the option you wish to change.

☑ Header Row	☑ First Column
☐ Total Row	☐ Last Column
☑ Banded Rows	☐ Banded Columns
Table Style Options	

DRILL 2   SHADING AND BORDERS

1. Open *81-drill1*.
2. Click in the table and apply Olive Green, Accent 3, Lighter 40% shading to the first row. Center and bold the headings.
3. Center column B.
4. Select the table and remove all borders.
5. Check and close. (*81-drill2*)

DRILL 3   TABLE STYLES

1. Open *81-drill1*.
2. Click in the table and hold your mouse over several of the styles to preview the way it would look.
3. Apply a new style. Apply Medium Shading 2 – Accent 3 table style.
4. In the Table Style Options group, remove the check from the Header Row and First Column boxes; preview the table.
5. Click Header Row and First Column to add the checks back.
6. Check and close. (*81-drill3*)

APPLICATIONS

81-d1
Table with Shading and Borders

1. Key the heading **LAUREL CANYON ENTERPRISES** at 2". Center it and apply 14-point Cambria bold font; then create the table shown below.
2. Bold and center the column headings; use the default body font. Apply Red, Accent 2, Darker 50% shading. Align columns according to the table guidelines.
3. Click Inside Borders to deselect it and remove the inside borders.
4. Check and close. (*81-d1*)

Employee	I.D.	Hardware	Software
Alexander, J.	R492	$105,134,384	$1,868,553,280
Courtenay, W.	R856	79,364,091	1,384,219,500
Holsonback, E.	C845	27,386,427	1,098,237,260
Palombo, L.	K511	44,296,101	971,360,515
Rajeh, C.	M451	82,665,900	1,052,564,100
Talbert, S.	P053	82,091,433	985,201,500

FOOTNOTES

REFERENCES/FOOTNOTES/INSERT FOOTNOTE

References cited in a report are often indicated within the text by a superscript number (...story.[1]) and a corresponding footnote with full information at the bottom of the same page where the reference was cited.

Word automatically numbers footnotes sequentially with Arabic numerals (1, 2, 3), positions them at the left margin, and applies 10-point type. A footnote is positioned the same as the paragraph of the report. In a single-spaced or 1.15 line spacing report, the paragraphs and the footnotes are not indented. However, if the report is double-spaced and paragraphs indented, tap the TAB key to indent the footnote 0.5" from the left margin.

A footnote divider line is automatically added above the first footnote on each page. Tap the ENTER key once to add one blank line between footnotes.

2

Payton Devaul set the school record for points in a game—50.[1] He holds six statewide records. This makes him one of the top ten athletes in the school's history.[2] He expects to receive a basketball scholarship at an outstanding university.[3]

7

6 [1] Marshall Baker, *High School Athletic Records* (Seattle: Sports Press, 2007), p. 41.

[2] Lori Guo-Patterson, "Top Ten Athletes," *The Sports Journal*, Spring 2008, http://www.tsj.edu/athletes/topten.htm (accessed June 25, 2008).

[3] Payton Devaul, pdevaul@mail.com "Basketball Scholarship," January 9, 2008, e-mail to Kirk Stennis (accessed April 15, 2008).

To insert and edit footnotes:

REFERENCES/FOOTNOTES/INSERT FOOTNOTE

1. Switch to Print Layout view if not in Print Layout View **1**.

2. Position the insertion point in the document where the footnote reference is to be inserted **2**.

3. Click the References tab **3**.

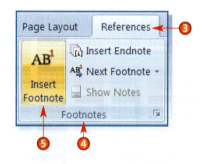

4. Choose the Footnotes group **4**.

5. Click Insert Footnote **5**.

6. The reference number and the insertion point appear at the bottom of the page. Key the footnote **6**.

7. Click anywhere above the footnote divider line to return to the document **7**.

To edit a footnote, click in the footnote at the bottom of the page and make the revision. To delete a footnote, select the reference number in the text and tap DELETE.

1. Create a three-column, four-row table using either of the methods listed on the previous page.
2. Key the table as shown below; make sure the text fits on one line in each row. Begin the table at 2" but do not format.

3. Check and close. (*81-drill1*)

Agent	Sales	Office
Charlene McGee	$3,986,203	Lakeshore Boulevard
Reginald Talbert	$2,692,476	Lexington Heights
Lynn Hawkins	$1,978,328	Center City

FORMAT TABLES

TABLE TOOLS/DESIGN

Once you have created a table, a variety of table tools are available under the Design and Layout tabs. These tools are used to change both the structure and the appearance of the table.

To change the appearance of a table:

1. Click in the table to display the Table Tools tab.
2. Under the Table Tools tab, click Design to display a ribbon that enables you to apply shading, borders, or styles. Review the following design options.

SHADE COLUMNS OR ROWS

TABLE TOOLS/DESIGN/TABLE STYLES/SHADING

 Shading adds emphasis to cells. Frequently, column heading rows or rows with totals are shaded.

To shade cells, rows, or columns:

1. To shade a cell, click it. Under Table Tools, on the Design tab, click Shading to display the color palette. Click the desired color.
2. To shade a row or a column, click to the far left of a row or above a column to select it. Under Table Tools, on the Design tab, click Shading to display the color palette. Click the desired color.

To remove the shading:

3. To remove shading, click the cell or select the row or column. Under Table Tools, on the Design tab, click Shading to display the color palette. Click No Color.

43-d1

Leftbound Report with Footnotes

1. Key the leftbound report shown below and on the next page. Format the title and side headings with the appropriate style.
2. Insert the two footnotes as marked in the report.
3. Key the items in the bulleted list and then apply the bullets.
4. Indent the long quotation 0.5" from the left margin.
5. Insert page numbers appropriately.
6. Check and close the document. (*43-d1*)

Planning a Successful Presentation

Presenters realize the need to prepare for a successful presentation. Two areas of extensive preparation are the development of a thorough audience analysis and a well-defined presentation purpose.

Audience Analysis

The presenter must conduct a thorough audience analysis before developing the presentation. The profile of the audience includes the following demographics.[1]

- Age and gender
- Education
- Ethnic group
- Marital status
- Geographic location
- Group membership

Interviews with program planners and organization leaders will provide insight into the needs, desires, and expectations of the audience. This information makes the difference in preparing a presentation that is well received by the audience.

Purpose of the Presentation

After analyzing the audience profile, the presenter has a clear focus on the needs of the audience and then writes a well-defined purpose of the presentation. Isabella Carrabbua, a well-known writer, states:

Long Quotation — With a clear focus, the presenter confidently conducts research and organizes a presentation that is on target. The presenter remembers to state the purpose in the introduction of the presentation to assist the audience in understanding the well-defined direction of the presentation. In the conclusion of the presentation, the speaker often will remind the audience of the purpose.[2]

KEYBOARDING PRO DELUXE ▶ See References/Word commands/Lesson 43

continued

DOCUMENT DESIGN

81c

TABLES

A table is used to align text, numbers, and graphics in a document.

Tables consist of columns and rows of data—alphabetic, numeric, or graphic.

Columns are vertical lists of information labeled alphabetically from left to right.

Rows are horizontal lists of information labeled numerically from top to bottom. The intersection of a column and a row form a **cell**. Each cell has its own address consisting of the column letter and the row number (cell A1).

TABLE FORMAT GUIDES

1. Leave an approximate 2" top margin or center the table vertically on the page, as directed.

2. Headings: Main heading: center, bold, caps, 14-point font, and then tap ENTER. Secondary heading: center, bold, 12-point font; capitalize main words. Center and bold all column headings. If styles are applied to main and secondary headings, adjust spacing as needed. The headings may also be placed in rows of the table.

3. Adjust column width attractively, and center the table horizontally.

4. Align text within the cells at the left. Align numbers at the right. Align decimal number of varying lengths at the decimal point.

5. When a table is within a document, the same amount of blank space should display before and after the table as between paragraphs.

FUNCTION REVIEW

81d

CREATE TABLES

INSERT/TABLES/TABLE

Tables can be created in several ways. This module reviews two of those ways—dragging across the table grid and using the Insert Table command.

To insert a table:

1. On the Insert tab, in the Tables group, click Table **①**.

2. Drag across the grid **②** to select the number of rows and columns desired; then click the left mouse button. -or-

3. Click the Insert Table command **③** to display the Insert Table dialog box **④** and use the up and down arrows to select the number of columns and rows **⑤**. Click OK **⑥**.

3x4 Table

Insert Table... **③**
Draw Table
Convert Text to Table...
Excel Spreadsheet
Quick Tables ▸

Insert Table **④**   ? ✕

Table size

Number of columns: 3   ▲▼

Number of rows: 4   ▲▼   **⑤**

AutoFit behavior

⦿ Fixed column width: Auto   ▲▼

◯ AutoFit to contents

◯ AutoFit to window

☐ Remember dimensions for new tables

⑥ OK   Cancel

43-d1

Continued

Summary

Effective speakers understand the importance of knowing the audience and developing a clear purpose in the beginning and maintaining that focus throughout the research, composition, and delivery of the presentation. The speaker's task will be much easier, and the audience will benefit as well.

Footnotes

[1]Samantha Vilella and Nathan T. Gunach, *Effective Presentations* (Indianapolis: Manchester Press, 2008), p. 38.

[2]Isabella Carrabbua, "The Purpose of the Purpose: A Clear Focus," *Contemporary Writers' Digest*, December 2008, p. 141.

43-d2

Title Page

1. Create a title page for the leftbound report prepared in *43-d1*. Use the Cover Page feature.
2. Key the following information:
   Document title: See *43-d1*.
   Document subtitle: **For Stoltman & Langston Associates, LLC**
   Author name: **John E. Swartsfager, Chief Training Officer**
3. Check and close the document. (*43-d2*).

43-d3

Leftbound Report

1. Open *38-d2* and format the document as a leftbound report.
2. Insert page numbers. Do not print the page number on the first page.
3. Add the last paragraph shown below.
4. Check and close the document. (*43-d3*)

Summary

Remember to plan your page layout with the three basic elements of effective page design. Always include sufficient white space to give an uncluttered appearance. Learn to add bold when emphasis is needed, and do consider your audience when choosing typestyles. Finally, use typestyles to add variety to your layout, but remember, no more than two typestyles in a document.

Table Mastery

LEARNING OUTCOMES

- Review tables.
- Edit and format tables.
- Perform calculations in tables.
- Change page and text orientation.
- Build keying skill.

LESSON 81   Table Review

WARMUP 81a

Key each line, striving for control. Repeat if desired.

alphabet	1	Jed quickly bought five or six pan pizzas after winning the game.
figures	2	The winning numbers for 12/08 are 19, 35, 46, 54, 90, 75, and 63.
fig/sym	3	I got a 10% discount ($38) on 2 invoices (#B*248736 & #E*596043).
fluency	4	Dick, Jake, and Ken paid for the right to fish from the big dock.

SKILL BUILDING

81b Timed Writing

1. Key one 1' timing on each paragraph, striving for speed.
2. Key one 3' writing on all paragraphs.

all letters

	gwam	1'	3'

A good day planner can simplify your life by giving order to   13   4
chaos. It will organize the details of your week and will also notify   27   9
you when you should be somewhere. Your planner will promptly remind   41   14
you of your many duties and responsibilities. Just store the names   54   18
and the addresses of all your important contacts, and it will quickly   68   23
retrieve them for you.   73   24

You can enjoy life more when you are organized. You will be able   14   29
to remember all your usual classes, quizzes, projects, and work   27   33
responsibilities. You can also expect to know where you need to go,   40   38
arrive promptly, and not miss any important events.   51   41

Electronic planners are called personal digital assistants.   13   46
These devices can serve all the purposes of an excellent day planner   27   50
and also let you send and receive e-mail. In addition, many of them   40   55
can share files with other software and some allow you to use the   54   59
Internet and can serve as a telephone as well.   63   62

```
1'  | 1 | 2 | 3 | 4 | 5 | 6 | 7 | 8 | 9 | 10 | 11 | 12 | 13 |
3'  |     1     |       2       |       3       |      4      |
```

Traditional Report

WARMUP 44a

Key each line, striving for control. Repeat if desired.

alphabet 1 Jim Ryan was able to liquefy frozen oxygen; he kept it very cold.

double letters 2 Aaron took accounting lessons at a community college last summer.

one-hand 3 Link agrees you'll get a reward only as you join nonunion racers.

easy 4 Hand Bob a bit of cocoa, a pan of cod, an apricot, and six clams.

| 1 | 2 | 3 | 4 | 5 | 6 | 7 | 8 | 9 | 10 | 11 | 12 | 13 |

SKILL BUILDING

44b Textbook Keying

1. Key each line once, concentrating on using good keying techniques; tap ENTER twice after each 3-line group.
2. Repeat if time permits.

d 5 do did dad sad faded daddy madder diddle deduced hydrated dredged

k 6 keys sake kicked karat kayak karate knock knuckle knick kilometer

d/k 7 The ten tired and dizzy kids thought the doorknob was the donkey.

w 8 we were who away whew snow windward waterway window webworm award

o 9 on to too onto solo oleo soil cook looked location emotion hollow

w/o 10 Those who know their own power and are committed will follow through.

b 11 be bib sub bear book bribe fiber bombard blueberry babble baboons

v 12 vet vat van viva have over avoid vapor valve seven vanish vanilla

b/v 13 Bo gave a very big beverage and seven coins to everybody bowling.

r 14 or rear rare roar saturate reassure rather northern surge quarrel

u 15 yours undue unity useful unique unusual value wound youth succumb

r/u 16 The truth of the matter is that only Ruth can run a rummage sale.

| 1 | 2 | 3 | 4 | 5 | 6 | 7 | 8 | 9 | 10 | 11 | 12 | 13 |

TIP

Keep hands and arms still as you reach up to the third row and down to the first row.

44c Timed Writing

1. Key a 1' timed writing; work to increase speed.
2. Key a 3' timed writing; work for control.

LA

all letters

	gwam	1'	3'
The leisure activities you choose make up your life style and, to	13	4	37
a great extent, show your personality. For example, if your daily	26	9	41
activities are people oriented, you may balance this by spending your	40	13	46
free time alone. On the other hand, if you like being with people most	55	18	51
of the time, your socialization needs may be very high. At the other	68	23	55
end of the scale are people whose work is done alone and who also	82	27	60
enjoy spending free time alone. These people tend to be rather quiet	95	32	64
and reserved.		98	33	65

1' | 1 | 2 | 3 | 4 | 5 | 6 | 7 | 8 | 9 | 10 | 11 | 12 | 13 |
3' | 1 | 2 | 3 | 4 |

80-d3

Continued

Forms Design, Management, and Control

A recent survey of the forms used by Watson & Phillips, Inc. indicated that 65 percent of all forms were paper based, and only 26 percent were in electronic format. Forms were produced both internally and externally. However, the majority of the forms were created internally.[1] The following table shows the source of the forms used at that time.

Employee—Paper	26%
Company—Paper	35%
External—Paper	4%
Company—Electronic	17%
Employee—Electronic	9%

.5" left tab

6" leader tab

6.5" right tab

Single space

The bulk of the paper-based forms were created either by individual employees to simplify their work or as standard forms used throughout the company. These forms were targeted for conversion to electronic format.

Existing System

No centralized forms management or control system existed at the time of the study. The responsibility for managing each form rested with the individual who created it. The cost, quality, and effectiveness of forms that were in use varied widely. Many forms were poorly designed and were ineffective. An analysis of the forms indicated that a significant number of them could be put online. Taking this action would reduce the cost and increase the effectiveness of all forms used by Watson & Phillips, Inc.

New System

The Executive Committee approved the recommendation for the new system and authorized the consultant to develop the implementation plan.[2] The office manager was made responsible for the design, management, and control of all forms.

Footnote text

[1]Thomas J. Gilliand, *Forms Design, Management, and Control Report* (Portland: Hess and Glenn, Inc., 2009), p. 5.

[2]*Executive Committee Minutes: January 15, 2009* (Portland: Hess and Glenn, Inc., 2009), p. 10.

References

Executive Committee Minutes: January 15, 2009. Portland: Hess and Glenn, Inc., 2009.

Gilliand, Thomas J. *Forms Design, Management, and Control Report.* Portland: Hess and Glenn, Inc., 2009.

CHECKPOINT ➡ Congratulations! You have successfully completed the lessons in Module 12. To check your understanding and for more practice, complete the objective assessment and performance assessment located on the textbook website at www.collegekeyboarding.com.

REPORT FORMATS IN TRANSITION

With *Word 2007* and its new defaults, it is likely that two report formats may be used until all users transition to the new interface. The report keyed with *Word 2007* defaults includes the 1.15 spacing that is very readable and takes less space than double spacing; it is expected that few people in industry will use double spacing for reports. In recent years, however, double-spaced reports have been used primarily in academic settings and less in industry.

Study the two reports below to note the appearance of the report keyed in *Word 2007* with its defaults and a report keyed in the traditional format with *Word 2003* defaults.

Electronic Mail Guidelines

Electronic mail, a widely used communication channel, clearly has three major advantages—time effectiveness, distance effectiveness, and cost effectiveness. To reap full benefit from this popular and convenient communication medium, follow the basic guidelines regarding the creation and use of e-mail.

E-mail Composition

Although perceived as informal documents, e-mail messages are business records. Therefore, follow these effective communication guidelines. Write clear, concise sentences, avoiding clichés, redundancies, and wordiness. Break the message into logical paragraphs, sequencing in an appropriate order. White space is important in e-mail messages as well as printed documents, so be sure to add extra space between paragraphs.

Spell-check e-mail messages carefully, and verify punctuation and content accuracy. Do limit e-mail messages to one idea per message, and preferably limit to one screen. To ensure your e-mail message is opened, always include a subject line and compose a subject line that clearly defines the e-mail message.

E-mail Practices

Although many people are using e-mail, some do not use it as their preferred method of communication and may check it infrequently. To accomplish tasks more effectively, be aware of individuals' preferred channels of communication and use those channels. Understand that your preferred channel of communication is not always that of the person to whom you must communicate.

Consider an e-mail message the property of the sender, and forward only with permission. Some senders include a note in the signature line that reminds recipients not to forward e-mail without getting permission.

New Report Format

ELECTRONIC MAIL GUIDELINES

Electronic mail, a widely used communication channel, clearly has three major advantages—time effectiveness, distance effectiveness, and cost effectiveness. To reap full benefit from this popular and convenient communication medium, follow the basic guidelines regarding the creation and use of e-mail.

E-mail Composition

Although perceived as informal documents, e-mail messages are business records. Therefore, follow these effective communication guidelines: write clear, concise sentences; break the message into logical paragraphs; and add extra space between paragraphs. Proofread all e-mail messages carefully, and verify punctuation and content accuracy. Do limit e-mail messages to one idea per message, and preferably limit to one screen. Include a subject line that clearly defines the e-mail message.

E-mail Practices

Although many people are using e-mail, some do not use it as their preferred method of communication and may check it infrequently. To accomplish tasks more effectively, be aware of individuals' preferred channels of communication and use those channels. Consider an e-mail message the property of the sender, and forward only with permission. Some senders include a note in the signature line that reminds recipients not to forward e-mail without getting permission.

Traditional Report Format

80-d1

Leftbound Report with Table of Contents

BUSINESS

1. In the open document, convert the report to a leftbound report.
2. Convert the numbered items to square bullets.
3. Format the title, side, and paragraph headings with the appropriate styles.
4. Choose the MLA manuscript style. Insert the two citations where shown in the report. Use the citation shown below to create each source.
5. Edit the first citation (Levinson) to add page 51 as the location of the direct quote and to suppress the author's name.
6. Insert a next page section break at the beginning of the document. You will create the table of contents on this blank page later in step 9.
7. Insert the page number for the table of contents in section 1. Start numbering at the appropriate number.
8. Break the links to the header and footer in section 2, edit the footer as needed, and insert the page numbers for section 2. Start numbering at the appropriate number. Suppress the page number on page 1 of section 2.
9. Generate the table of contents on the blank page at the beginning of the report. Begin the title at 2" and format using Table Style 2.
10. Move the *Recommendations* section to display as the last section. Update the table of contents.
11. Generate the bibliography as the last page of the report.
12. Continue to the next document. (*80-d1*)

Citation data:

1 Journal Article—Marcus Thomas Levinson, "Benchmarking Internet Advertising," *The Small Business Journal*, Volume 10, Issue 5, 2009, pp. 49-58.

2 Book—Mary Stackhouse, *Website Development* (Chicago: Seiver, Inc., 2009), p. 88.

80-d2

Cover Page

1. In the open document, use the Cover Page feature to create a title page for the report created in *80-d1*. Choose the Motion style.
2. Key the following information:
   a. Year: Current
   b. Document Title: Refer to *80-d1*. Shrink the font to fit on one line.
   c. Author: Student's Name
   d. Company: **Pat's Place**
   e. Date: Current date
3. Continue to the next document. (*80-d2*)

80-d3

Traditional Report with Footnotes

1. Key the report shown on the following page as a traditional unbound report, double-spaced. Insert the two footnotes as shown in the report.
2. Key the reference page as the last page of the report. Insert page numbers at the top right on all pages except the first page.
3. Preview to ensure side headings are not left alone.
4. Check the test and close it. (*80-d3*)

TRADITIONAL REPORT FORMAT

The traditional report format is keyed using the *Word 2003* defaults. To restore these defaults, apply the *Word 2003* style, change the font to Times New Roman, and change the line spacing to double space for academic reports and single space for business reports. The changes needed for the traditional report format are explained below. Study the full-page illustration on the next page.

Style: *Word 2003* style

Font and font size: Times New Roman, 12 point

Spacing: Generally, educational reports are double spaced (DS) and business reports are single spaced (SS). Indent the first line of paragraphs 0.5" when the body of the report is double spaced. Begin paragraphs at the left margin when the report is single spaced, and double-space between paragraphs.

Enumerated items: Align bulleted or numbered items with the beginning of a paragraph. Single-space each item and double-space between items.

Title: Position at approximately 2". Center and key the title in uppercase, 14-point and bold.

Side heading: Bold

Footnote: Indent 0.5"; change font to Times New Roman and font size to 12 point.

APPLICATIONS

44-d1
Traditional Report

1. Change the style set to *Word 2003* and change the font to Times New Roman.
2. Key the model traditional unbound report on page 179.
3. Change the line spacing to double. Tap ENTER three times to position the title at about 2". Use default side margins.
4. Key the title in uppercase; tap ENTER. Select the title; then change the font size to 14-point bold and center-align the title. (**Tip:** Tapping ENTER before formatting the title prevents the format of the title from being applied to the body of the report.)
5. Check and close. (*44-d1*)

44-d2
Unbound Report

PRESENT

1. In the open document, convert this leftbound report to an unbound report.
2. Format title and side headings correctly. Position the title on the correct line.
3. Insert the following footnote at the end of the last paragraph just before the heading *Follow-up Activities*. Indent the footnote and change it to 12 point, Times New Roman font.

   [1]Emily Elizabeth Watson, *A Reference Guide for Presentation Skills* (San Francisco: The Liberty Press, 2008), p. 45.

4. Number the pages at the top right; do not print page number on the first page. Apply Keep with next if necessary to prevent headings from being alone at the bottom of the first page.
5. Check and close. (*44-d2*)

Assessment

Key each line, striving for control. Repeat if desired.

adjacent keys

1 Jamie quickly apologized for submitting the complex reviews late.

2 Where were Mario, Guy, and Luis going after the water polo class?

fig/sym

3 Jay paid Invoice #2846 ($3,017.35) and Invoice #7925 ($8,409.16).

4 I caught 20 halibut (69.5# average) and 37 trout (4.81# average).

| 1 | 2 | 3 | 4 | 5 | 6 | 7 | 8 | 9 | 10 | 11 | 12 | 13 |

SKILL BUILDING

80b Timed Writing
1. Key one 3' timed writing.
2. Key one 5' timed writing.

all letters

	gwam	3'	5'
Just what does it mean to be young and when is a person young?	4	3	49
To be young is perhaps a feeling or disposition, a particular manner	9	5	51
of looking at things and responding to them. To be young is never	13	8	54
a chronological period or time of life, although it might be a young	18	11	57
person examining some material with fascination and pleasure or	22	13	59
the composer Verdi in his eighties writing his best opera. To be	26	16	62
young might be a person "hanging ten" on a surfboard or swinging	31	18	64
to a musical composition. To be young might be Einstein in his	35	21	67
seventies still working with his field theory, sailing his boat,	39	24	70
or playing his cherished fiddle.	41	25	71
To be young is never the monopoly of youth. It flourishes	45	27	73
everywhere visionaries have stimulated our thinking or amazed us.	50	30	76
To be young in nature is quite desirable whether you are a young	54	32	78
person, a middle-aged person, or a chronologically old person. To	59	35	81
be young should be respected whether the beard is soft and curly	63	38	84
or firm and gray. To be young has no color; it seems often trans-	67	40	86
lucent with its own imaginative light. There is no generation	71	43	89
space between the young of any age because they see things as they	76	46	92
ought to be.	77	46	92

```
3' |      1      |      2      |      3      |      4      |
5' |        1        |        2        |        3        |
```

APPLICATIONS

80c
Assessment

➡ Continue

✓ Check

With Keyboarding Pro DELUXE: When you complete a document, proofread it, check the spelling, and preview for placement. When you are completely satisfied, click the Continue button to move to the next document. Click the Check button when you are ready to error-check the test. Review and/or print the document analysis results.

Without Keyboarding Pro DELUXE: Key the documents in sequence. When time has been called, proofread all documents again and identify errors.

Set DS
About 2" ← (Tap ENTER three times on DS.)

ELECTRONIC MAIL GUIDELINES ← Uppercase, 14-point Bold

Electronic mail, a widely used communication channel, clearly has three major advantages—time effectiveness, distance effectiveness, and cost effectiveness. To reap full benefit from this popular and convenient communication medium, follow the basic guidelines regarding the creation and use of e-mail.

Side heading bold → **E-mail Composition**

Although perceived as informal documents, e-mail messages are business records. Therefore, follow these effective communication guidelines: write clear, concise sentences; break the message into logical paragraphs; and add extra space between paragraphs. Proofread all e-mail messages carefully, and verify punctuation and content accuracy. Do limit e-mail messages to one idea per message, and preferably limit to one screen. Include a subject line that clearly defines the e-mail message.

E-mail Practices

Although many people are using e-mail, some do not use it as their preferred method of communication and may check it infrequently. To accomplish tasks more effectively, be aware of individuals' preferred channels of communication and use those channels. Consider an e-mail message the property of the sender, and forward only with permission. Some senders include a note in the signature line that reminds recipients not to forward e-mail without getting permission.

1"   1"

Verbatim minutes. The Annual Meeting will be recorded, and a verbatim transcript of the meeting will be prepared by the Corporate Secretary. Verbatim minutes are costly; ~~and~~ *therefore, they* will be used only for the Annual Meeting.

Action minutes. Action minutes, consisting of identifying information, *and* a brief summary of decisions made, and of key views expressed, will be used for most meetings. ③ The emphasis should be on decisions, assignment of responsibility, and action planned for the future.

Footnotes

[1]Cameron Maslin, cmaslin@ProdCon.com "Enhancing Productivity: The Moss Springs Company," April 13, 2009, e-mail to Patrick Demetrio (accessed April 15, 2009).

[2]*Moss Springs Company Policy Manual* (Chicago: Moss Springs Company, 2009), p. 42.

[3]Scott Altig, *Effective Meetings* (Philadelphia: Bay Publishing Co., 2009), p. 80.

References

Maslin, Cameron. cmaslin@ProdCon.com "Enhancing Productivity: The Moss Springs Company." April 13, 2009, e-mail to Patrick Demetrio (accessed April 15, 2009).

Moss Springs Company Policy Manual. Chicago: Moss Springs Company, 2009.

Altig, Scott. *Effective Meetings.* Philadelphia: Bay Publishing Co., 2009.

79-d2

Report with Citations

1. Open *79-d1*.
2. Delete the three footnotes and the reference page.
3. Insert MLA citations where each footnote was deleted. Refer to the footnotes above in *79-d1* and to the information below as you add the three new sources to this report.

   [1] Interview—Interviewee Cameron Maslin; interviewer Patrick Demetrio, April 13, 2009

   [2] Book

   [3] Book
4. On the last page of the report, generate a bibliography page. Position at 2" and format the title in Title style.
5. Check and close. (*79-d2*)

79-d3

Edit Citations and Bibliography

1. Open *79-d2*. Change the manuscript style to APA.
2. Delete the first citation (Maslin) from the current document and from the master list of sources.
3. Edit the *Moss Springs Company Policy Manual* citation by adding **p. 15** as the page number of the quote. Update the bibliography.
4. Check and close. (*79-d3*)

Hunter McWhirter, Vice President, has requested that you format a reference page using the traditional format for a report needed for a meeting today.

1. In a new blank document, change to *Word 2003* style and change font to Times New Roman. Key the references shown below in appropriate hanging indent format.

2. Format the title appropriately in the traditional format. Change left margin for a leftbound report.

3. Check and close. (*44-d3*)

References

Duran, Delane. *New Markets for the 21st Century*. 7th ed. Boston: Serendipity Press, 2008.

Grantham, Connor. gconnor@mail.com "My Concerns About the Market." August 8, 2008, e-mail to Alexandra Sarnowska (accessed August 12, 2008).

Townsel, Gabriel. "World Events and the Market." *Marketplace Today*. Fall 2008. http://www.mt.com/worldevents.htm (accessed October 23, 2008).

Westberry, Anna Maria and Margarita Cruz. "How to Invest in Today's Markets." *Market World*. March 20, 2008, 103-108.

44-d4

Edit Leftbound Report

1. Open *44-d2*. Read this report carefully for content.

2. In the first paragraph of the *Delivering Presentations* section, tap ENTER before the last sentence that begins "The speaker must be energetic and must project the voice." Move your insertion point to the end of that sentence.

3. Search the Internet for information about using the voice effectively when delivering an oral presentation.

4. Compose a short paragraph that adds more meaningful information to this paragraph. Be sure to paraphrase your research. If you choose to lift words, phrases, or entire sentences, key quotation marks around the direct lift. If you quote more than four lines, indent the quotation.

5. Insert a footnote at the end of the paragraph. Use the three examples below to assist you in formatting your footnote correctly.

6. Check and close the document. (*44-d4*)

Website

[1]Lori Guo-Patterson, "Top Ten Athletes," *The Sports Journal*, Spring 2008, http://www.tsj.edu/athletes/topten.htm (accessed June 25, 2008).

Website (No Author)

[1]"Delivery Skills," The Speech Clinic, February 2008, http://www.speechclinic/delivery.htm (accessed December 1, 2009).

Online Journal, Magazine, or Newspaper

[1]Missy Watson, "Technology Helps," *Hopper Business Journal*, Fall 2008, http://www.hbj.edu/technologyhelps.htm (accessed May 26, 2009).

Annual Meeting

The following quote from the <u>Moss Spring Company Policy Manual</u> *italic* contains the policy for the documentation of the Annual Meeting: *stet*
The annual Meeting of the Moss Springs Company shall be held within 3 *sp* months of the end of the fiscal year. The Corporate Secretary shall mail to all who are eligible to attend the meeting a notice and agenda ~~thirty~~ 30 days prior to the meeting. The Corporate Secretary shall prepare a verbatim record of the meeting and provide each member of the Board of Directors with a copy of the minutes within two weeks of the meeting. The minutes shall be a part of the permanent records of the Moss Springs Company. ②

Other Meetings

Meetings ~~other than the annual meeting~~ will be held at the discretion of the Board of Directors and the appropriate company managers. Documentation for regular and "called" meetings of the Board ~~as~~ is described in the following paragraphs.

Support Documents

The Senior Management Committee required that an agenda be distributed prior to all formal meetings of committees and of staff at the departmental level or higher. Minutes must be prepared and distributed to all participants after the meeting.

Minutes

The Administrative Manager developed the following procedures to ~~to~~ implement the policy on maintaining ~~appropriate~~ minutes. The Senior Management Committee ~~met and~~ approved these procedures for immediate implementation.

Agenda

The agenda should contain the date, time, and place of the meeting. It also should contain a listing of all topics to be discussed during the meeting. Distribution of the agenda should allow adequate time for ~~participants to~~ prepare for the meeting. *stet*

continued

LESSON 45

Assessment

WARMUP 45a

Key each line, striving for control. Repeat if desired.

one-hand sentences

1 In regard to desert oil wastes, Jill referred only minimum cases.
2 Carra agrees you'll get a reward only as you join nonunion races.
3 Few beavers, as far as I'm aware, feast on cedar trees in Kokomo.
4 Johnny, after a few stewed eggs, ate a plump, pink onion at noon.
5 A plump, aged monk served a few million beggars a milky beverage.

| 1 | 2 | 3 | 4 | 5 | 6 | 7 | 8 | 9 | 10 | 11 | 12 | 13 |

SKILL BUILDING

45b Timed Writing

1. Key a 1' timed writing on each paragraph; work to increase speed.
2. Key a 3' timed writing on both paragraphs.

all letters

	gwam	1'	3'
How is a hobby different from a business? A very common way		12	4
to describe the difference between the hobby and the business is		25	8
that the hobby is done for fun, and the business is done as work		38	13
which enables people to earn their living. Does that mean that		51	17
people do not have fun at work or that people do not work with their		65	22
hobbies? Many people would not agree with that description.		77	26
Some people begin work on a hobby just for fun, but then they		12	30
realize it has the potential to be a business. They soon find out		26	34
that others enjoy the hobby as well and would expect to pay for		39	39
the products or services the hobby requires. Many quite successful		52	43
businesses begin as hobbies. Some of them are small, and some grow		66	48
to be large operations.		72	49

1' | 1 | 2 | 3 | 4 | 5 | 6 | 7 | 8 | 9 | 10 | 11 | 12 | 13 |
3' | 1 | | 2 | | 3 | | 4 |

APPLICATIONS

45c

Assessment

→ Continue

✓ Check

With *Keyboarding Pro DELUXE*: When you complete a document, proofread it, check the spelling, and preview for placement. When you are completely satisfied, click the Continue button to move to the next document. Click the Check button when you are ready to error-check the test. Review and/or print the document analysis results.

Without *Keyboarding Pro DELUXE*: Key the documents in sequence. When time has been called, proofread all documents again and identify errors.

SKILL BUILDING

79a Textbook Keying
Key each line, striving for
control. Repeat if desired.

1st/2nd
fingers

3rd/4th
fingers

1 dirt nut fun drum try buy been curt very hunt bunt rent cent jump
2 We think Julio may give Ruth a ring Sunday if she will accept it.
3 My name is Geoffrey, but I very much prefer Jeff on this nametag.
4 was pill look zoom loop west low loose quiz walk saw wax box zeal
5 Paul Velasquez was at a popular plaza quilt shop when he saw Sal.
6 Sal was at a Palawan zoo; he was also at Wuxi Plaza for six days.

| 1 | 2 | 3 | 4 | 5 | 6 | 7 | 8 | 9 | 10 | 11 | 12 | 13 |

APPLICATIONS

79-d1

**Leftbound Report with
Table of Contents and
Reference Page**

1. Key the leftbound report on pages 362–364.

2. Format the title and the side headings with the appropriate styles learned in this module.

3. Insert the three footnotes, as indicated in the report. The footnote text is on page 364. Remove e-mail hyperlinks. Tap ENTER once between footnotes.

4. Prepare the reference page at the end of the report. The reference text is on page 364. Arrange the references in alphabetical order and format in hanging indent style.

5. Insert a next page section break at the beginning of the document. You will create the table of contents on this blank page in step 9.

6. Position the insertion point in section 1 and insert page numbers formatted as small Roman numerals centered at the bottom of the page. Start numbering at page ii.

7. From the Navigation Group, click Next Section. Break the link between the footer in the first section and the second section. Delete the page number at the bottom center.

8. From the Navigation Group, click Go to Header. Break the link between the header in the first section and the second section. Insert Arabic numbers at the top right. Select Different First Page so that a page number will not print on the first page of the report. Start numbering at page 1.

9. Generate the table of contents on the blank page at the beginning of the report. Begin the title at 2" and apply Automatic Table 2 style.

10. Check and close. (79-d1)

Meeting Documentation Guides

The procedures used to prepare support documents for meetings in the Moss Springs Company were reviewed during the productivity analysis that was completed. The type of support documents used, and the way in which they were prepared varied widely through out the company. The primary document used were meeting notices, agendas, handouts, visualaids, and minutes. The following guides were compiled on the basis of the productivity review.

1. Key the leftbound report shown below in the new report format, using *Word 2007* defaults.

2. Insert footnotes as shown in the report. Indent the long quotation appropriately.

3. Number the pages at the top right; do not print the page number on the first page.

4. Key the references on a separate reference page at the end of the report.

5. Continue to next document. *(45-d1)*

Copyright Law in the Internet Age

Copyright owners continue to face copyright challenges as technology advances more rapidly than ever before. History shows us that copyright infringements occur at the introduction of each new invention or emerging technology. Examples include the phonograph and tape recorder and mimeograph and copy machines. Today, the Internet age provides users the ease of copying and distributing electronic files via the Internet.

Copyright owners of content published on the Web, photographers who view their photographs on Web pages, and recording artists whose music is downloaded from the Internet are only a few examples of copyright issues resulting from the Internet age. Compounding the issue is that many Internet users may not be aware they are violating copyright law. The following list shows actions taken daily that are considered copyright infringements:

- Copying content from a Web page and pasting it into documents
- Reproducing multiple copies of a journal article that were printed from an online journal
- Distributing presentation handouts that contain cartoon characters or other graphics copied from a Web page
- Presenting originally designed electronic presentations that contain graphics, sound and video clips, and/or photographs copied from a Web page
- Duplicating and distributing copies of music downloaded from the Web

Copyright Laws

To avoid copyright infringement, the Internet user must be knowledgeable about copyright law. Two important laws include The Copyright Law of 1976 and the Digital Millennium Copyright Act, which was enacted in 1998 to update the copyright law for the digital age. Morgan explains that under the Copyright Law of 1976:

> Original works are protected by copyright at the very moment that they are first originated—printed, drawn, captured, or saved to a digital storage area. The copyright protection is automatic when the original work is first established in the real medium of expression.[1]

continued

78-d3

Reference Page

1. Open *78-d2*. On a new page at the end of the report, prepare the reference page.
2. Format the title appropriately in the traditional format.
3. Key the references shown below and format in the hanging indent style.
4. Check and close. (*78-d3*)

References

Jackson, Matthew and Jennifer F. Jensen. *Listening Is an Essential Skill for the 21st Century.* New York: New York Press, 2008.

Simpson, Warren and Chien Lee. "Beware of Distractions." *Speaking Guide for Today's Executive.* January 2009, 93-95.

Williams, Janet. "Learning to Listen Effectively." *The Journal of Nonverbal Communication.* December 2008, 33–37.

78-d4

Traditional Table of Contents with Section Break

1. Open *78-d3*. Read all the directions before you begin so that you understand that you must insert a section break first, number pages in section 1, edit numbering in section 2, and key a table of contents.
2. Insert a next page section break at the beginning of the document. In step 9 below you will key the table of contents, but first you must number the pages correctly.
3. Position the insertion point in section 1. Insert page numbers formatted as small Roman numerals at the bottom center of the page. Start numbering at page ii.
4. In the Navigation group, click on Next Section, which takes you to the footer of section 2. Click Link to Previous to break the link between the footer in the first section and the second section. Delete the page number at the bottom center.
5. In the Navigation group, click Go to Header to move to the header section of section 2. You have already numbered the pages in this section, but you must change the format to begin numbering this section at 1. Note that Different First Page is selected so that a number does not print on the first page.
6. Check the page numbering on sections 1 and 2.
7. On the blank page at the beginning of the document, key the table of contents for this report. Refer to the illustration on page 331 if necessary.
8. Key the title **Table of Contents** at the center; format in uppercase, bold, and 14-point font; double-space the contents.
9. Set the following tabs:

   Left tab: 0.5" to indent for the paragraph heading

   Leader tab: 5.5" for the dot leaders

   Right tab: 6.0" for the page number
10. Key the side headings at the left margin. Tap TAB and key the paragraph headings indented ½" from the left margin. After keying the heading, tap TAB to display the dot leaders; tap TAB again to move to the right tab. Key the page number. Key **References** as the last side heading.
11. Check and close. (*78-d4*)

Note: If styles are applied to the headings, the Table of Contents feature automatically generates a table of contents.

45-d1

Continued

With an understanding of the copyright laws, users now realize that materials placed on a website may be copyrighted and are not available for downloading or copying and pasting into other documents. Sound advice is always to seek permission from the original copyright owner before using the material. Purchasing royalty-free content is another excellent way to avoid any question of copyright infringement.

Technology

Understanding the copyright laws and awareness of all types of copyrighted material are important as copyright owners fight against infringement. Interestingly, technology is and will continue to be a key player in the policing of copyright offenders. Weatherford shares the following ways technology is currently being used:

- Locking up data by disabling the printing function and removing the cut, copy, and paste functions
- Placing digital watermarks on an image that identify the source
- Requiring a password from the copyright owner for users to gain access to copyrighted material[2]

Summary

Awareness of copyright laws and the various copyright infringements—especially in light of possibilities available through the Internet—is very important in combating violations. Additionally, individuals must realize that technology will continue to be an effective tool in policing copyright violators.

Footnotes

[1]Allison Morgan, "Know the Copyright Law," *Digital Journal*, February 2008, p. 21.

[2]John E. Weatherford, "Technology Aids in Stopping Copyright Offenders," *Hopper Business Journal*, Fall 2008, http://www.hbj.edu/technologyaids.htm (accessed December 26, 2008).

References

Morgan, Allison. "Know the Copyright Law." *Digital Journal*. February 2008, 20-25.

Weatherford, John E. "Technology Aids in Stopping Copyright Offenders." *Hopper Business Journal*. Fall 2008. http://www.hbj.edu/technologyaids.htm (accessed December 26, 2008).

Poor Listening Habits

The poor listening habits presented below by Williams (2008) are quite common among listeners. Being aware of the most common poor listening habits will aid in overcoming them.

- Pretending to listen is easy to do. By nodding, saying yes, and looking directly at the speaker, listeners can fake listening.

- On the other hand, not looking at the speaker also results in poor listening as facial expressions and gestures are not communicated to the listener.

- A listener's commitment to recording detailed notes often results in poor listening or overlistening.

- Judgments by the listener about the speaker or the topic result in poor listening.

- Rushing the speaker causes the speaker to think the listener's time is being wasted.

- Interrupting the speaker is rude and does not enhance listening.

- Showing interest in something other than the conversation and allowing any distractions to obtain the listener's attention result in poor listening.

Summary

Understanding that listening is not easy is a first step in becoming a better listener. Identifying individual habits that do not enhance effective listening is the next step. The first session of the Listening Skills Training Program will focus on poor listening habits.

45-d2

1. Create a title page for the leftbound report prepared in *45-d1*. Use the Cover Page feature.
2. Key the following information:

   Document title: See title *45-d1*.

   Document subtitle: **For Design Department**

   Author name: **Student's Name, Information Technology Manager**
3. Continue to next document. (*45-d2*)

45-d3

Traditional Report

1. Rekey the report prepared in *45-d1*, stopping after the first bulleted list. Format in the traditional report format; double-space. Assume the report is an unbound report.
2. Single-space the bulleted items; double-space between the items.
3. Check the test and close. (*45-d3*)

CHECKPOINT → Congratulations! You have successfully completed the lessons in Module 5. To check your understanding and for more practice, complete the objective assessment and performance assessment located on the textbook website at www.collegekeyboarding.com.

Title at 2"

BARRIERS TO EFFECTIVE LISTENING

In the initial phase of study of customer service operations, Fleming Communications, Inc. determined that listening is the communication task that our customer representatives spend almost 50 percent of their time doing. This report is the first in a series of reports. The purpose of this report is to explain a major barrier to effective listening and to present poor listening habits.

Side heading

Issues in Listening

Contrary to common belief, listening is not an easy task. Two issues to consider are the rate that listeners can process words and barriers to listening.

Rate. Studies show that listeners can recognize words at a rate of approximately five times faster than the rate at which speakers can speak. A very important question to consider is at what rate does the mind process these words? With the mind processing information at over 1,000 words per minute, the listener is challenged to listen actively (Jackson and Jensen, 2008).

Paragraph heading

Listening barriers. Listeners are also confronted with various other barriers to effective listening. These might include assumptions already made about the topic, about the speaker, about what the speaker will say, or about the specific setting. All of these assumptions will lead the listener to tune out what the speaker is actually saying. Another barrier to listening may be simply fatigue—the listener is too tired or perhaps too hungry or too busy to listen. Distractions often influence the listener's ability to be an active listener. These annoyances may be loud noises near the speaker or a room that is too cold or too warm (Simpson and Lee, 2009).

The final and important step in producing a document is proofreading. Error-free documents send the message the organization is detail-oriented and competent. Apply these procedures when producing any document.

1. Check spelling using the Spelling feature.
2. Proofread the document on the screen. Be alert for words that are spelled correctly but are misused, such as *you/your*, *in/on*, *of/on*, *the/then*, etc.
3. Check the document for necessary parts for correctness; be sure special features are present if needed—for example, in a letter, check for the enclosure or copy notation.
4. View the document on screen to check placement. Save and print.

These additional steps will make you a better proofreader:

5. Try to allow some time between writing a document and proofreading it.
6. If you are reading a document that has been keyed from a written draft, place the two documents next to each other and use guides to proofread the keyed document line by line against the original.
7. Proofread numbers aloud or with another person.

Proofreading for consistency is another important part of preparing documents. Consistency in style or tone, usage, facts, and format conveys an impression of care and attention to detail that reflects well on the writer and his or her organization. In contrast, lack of consistency gives an impression of carelessness and inattention to detail. Lack of consistency also makes documents more difficult to read and understand.

Proofreading statistical copy is extremely important. As you proofread, double-check numbers whenever possible. For example, verify dates against a calendar and check computations with a calculator. Remember these tips for proofreading numbers.

- Read numbers in groups. For example, the telephone number 618-555-0123 can be read in three parts: **six-one-eight**, **five five-five**, **zero-one-two-three**.
- Read numbers aloud.
- Proofread numbers with a partner.

DRILL 1

PROOFREADING

PROOF-IT

1. Print the data file.
2. Use proofreaders' marks to mark corrections. The letter contains nine mistakes in formatting, capitalization, number use, spelling, and keying.
3. Revise the letter and format it correctly.
4. Preview, check, and close. (*proofreading-drill1*)

Traditional Report Format

The traditional report format is keyed using the *Word 2003* defaults. To restore these defaults, apply the *Word 2003* style, change the font to Times New Roman, and change the line spacing to double space for academic reports and single space for business reports. Study the full-page illustration on the next page.

Style: *Word 2003*

Font and font size: Times New Roman, 12 point

Spacing: Generally, educational reports are double-spaced and business reports are single-spaced. Tap TAB to indent paragraphs 0.5" when the body of the report is double-spaced. Begin the paragraphs at the left margin when the report is single-spaced, and double-space between paragraphs.

Enumerated items: Align bulleted or numbered items with the beginning of a paragraph. Single-space each item and double-space between items.

Title: Position at approximately 2". Center, in uppercase, 14 point, and bold.

Side headings: Bold, 12 point, capitalize main words

Paragraph headings: Tab to 0.5", bold, capitalize first word, and end with a period.

Page numbers: Times New Roman

Footnote: Indent 0.5"; change font to Times New Roman and font size to 12 point.

APPLICATIONS

78-d1
Traditional Report

1. Key the model traditional unbound report on pages 359–360.
2. Change the style set to *Word 2003* (**Home/Styles/Change Styles**).
3. Change the font to Times New Roman.
4. Change the line spacing to double. Tap ENTER three times to position the title at about 2".
5. Key the title in uppercase; tap ENTER once. Select the title; then change the font size to 14-point bold and center-align it. (**Tip:** Tapping ENTER before formatting the title prevents the format of the heading from being applied to the body of the report.)
6. Insert page numbers at top right except on first page. Change font to Times New Roman.
7. Check and close. (*78-d1*)

78-d2
Edit Report

1. Open *78-d1* and convert this unbound report to a leftbound report.
2. Delete the internal citations and change to footnotes. Indent the footnotes; change to 12-point, Times New Roman font. Check and close. (*78-d2*)

   [1]Matthew Jackson and Jennifer F. Jensen, *Listening Is an Essential Skill for the 21st Century* (New York: New York Press, 2008), p. 103.

   [2]Thomas Simpson and Chien Lee, "Beware of Distractions," *Speaking Guide for Today's Executive*, January 2009, p. 95.

   [3]Janet Williams, "Learning to Listen Effectively," *The Journal of Nonverbal Communication*, December 2008, p. 34.

DRILL 2

PROOFREADING AND EDITING

1. Key the drill, making all necessary corrections.
2. Preview, check, and close. (*proofreading-drill2*)

First impressions does count, and you never get a second chance to make a good first impression. This statement applys too both documents and people. The minute you walk in to a room you are judged by you appearance, your facial expressions, and the way you present your self. As soon as a document is opened, it is judged by it's appearance and the way it is presented. First impressions are often lasting impressions therefore you should strive to make a positive first impression for yourself and for the documents you prepare. Learn to manage your image and the image of your documents.

DRILL 3

PROOFREADING FOR CONSISTENCY

LINGER

1. Proofread the letter for consistency in usage, facts, and format (block letter style).
2. Verify information against the price list below. Make corrections. Use today's date for the letter and your name for the writer's.
3. Preview, check, and close. (*proofreading-drill3*)

COMPUTERS AND PRINTERS		
Product	**Manufacturer**	**Price**
Workstation 2010	**Chimera**	**$2,779**
550MHz processor, 19" monitor, 64GB RAM, 9.1GB hard drive, 7 x 24 dedicated workstation, 40X variable CD-ROM drive		
Amina Optima Notebook	**Finn**	**2,199**
1.86GHz processor, 17" XGA active matrix display, 2GB RAM, 100GB hard drive, latest Capstone Office Suite, combo 24x/10x/24x CD-RW and 8x DVD-ROM drives		
Winger Laser Printer	**Primat**	**399**
1200 dpi, 250-sheet input tray, 27 ppm		
Ink Jet Color Printer	**Primat**	**299**
9600 x 2400 dpi, 100-sheet input tray, 24 ppm, up to 16 million colors		
AZ Printer/Copier/Scanner	**Ventura**	**499**
1200 dpi, 150-sheet input tray, 22 ppm, scans directly to e-mail, integrated desktop software for organizing scanned documents, OCR software for text editing		

REPORT FORMATS IN TRANSITION

With *Word 2007* and its new defaults, it is likely that two report formats may be used until all users transition to the new software. The report keyed with *Word 2007* defaults includes the 1.15 spacing that is very readable and takes less space than double spacing; it is expected that few people in industry will use double spacing for reports. In recent years, however, double-spaced reports have been used primarily in academic settings and less in industry.

Study the two reports below to note the appearance of the report keyed in *Word 2007* with its defaults and the report keyed in the traditional format with *Word 2003* defaults.

Electronic Mail Guidelines

Electronic mail, a widely used communication channel, clearly has three major advantages—time effectiveness, distance effectiveness, and cost effectiveness. To reap full benefit from this popular and convenient communication medium, follow the basic guidelines regarding the creation and use of e-mail.

E-mail Composition

Although perceived as informal documents, e-mail messages are business records. Therefore, follow these effective communication guidelines. Write clear, concise sentences, avoiding clichés, redundancies, and wordiness. Break the message into logical paragraphs, sequencing in an appropriate order. White space is important in e-mail messages as well as printed documents, so be sure to add extra space between paragraphs.

Spell-check e-mail messages carefully, and verify punctuation and content accuracy. Do limit e-mail messages to one idea per message, and preferably limit to one screen. To ensure your e-mail message is opened, always include a subject line and compose a subject line that clearly defines the e-mail message.

E-mail Practices

Although many people are using e-mail, some do not use it as their preferred method of communication and may check it infrequently. To accomplish tasks more effectively, be aware of individuals' preferred channels of communication and use those channels. Understand that your preferred channel of communication is not always that of the person to whom you must communicate.

Consider an e-mail message the property of the sender, and forward only with permission. Some senders include a note in the signature line that reminds recipients not to forward e-mail without getting permission.

New Report Format

ELECTRONIC MAIL GUIDELINES

Electronic mail, a widely used communication channel, clearly has three major advantages—time effectiveness, distance effectiveness, and cost effectiveness. To reap full benefit from this popular and convenient communication medium, follow the basic guidelines regarding the creation and use of e-mail.

E-mail Composition

Although perceived as informal documents, e-mail messages are business records. Therefore, follow these effective communication guidelines: write clear, concise sentences; break the message into logical paragraphs; and add extra space between paragraphs. Proofread all e-mail messages carefully, and verify punctuation and content accuracy. Do limit e-mail messages to one idea per message, and preferably limit to one screen. Include a subject line that clearly defines the e-mail message.

E-mail Practices

Although many people are using e-mail, some do not use it as their preferred method of communication and may check it infrequently. To accomplish tasks more effectively, be aware of individuals' preferred channels of communication and use those channels. Consider an e-mail message the property of the sender, and forward only with permission. Some senders include a note in the signature line that reminds recipients not to forward e-mail without getting permission.

Traditional Report Format

Table Essentials

LEARNING OUTCOMES

- Create tables.
- Change table structure.
- Format tables.
- Incorporate tables within documents.
- Build keying speed and accuracy.

LESSON 46 ▸ Create Tables

WARMUP 46a

Key each line, striving for control. Repeat if desired.

alphabet	1	Jim Ryan was able to liquefy frozen oxygen; he kept it very cold.
figures	2	Flight 483 left Troy at 9:57 a.m., arriving in Reno at 12:06 p.m.
direct reaches	3	My brother served as an umpire on that bright June day, no doubt.
easy	4	Ana's sorority works with vigor for the goals of the civic corps.

| 1 | 2 | 3 | 4 | 5 | 6 | 7 | 8 | 9 | 10 | 11 | 12 | 13 |

SKILL BUILDING

46b Timed Writing

1. Key a 3' timed writing, working for speed.
2. Key a 3' timed writing, working for control.

all letters

	gwam	3'
The most important element of a business is its clientele. It is	4	61
for this reason that most organizations adopt the slogan that the	9	65
customer is always right. The saying is not to be taken literally, but	13	70
in spirit.	14	71
Patrons will continuously use your business if you provide a	18	75
quality product and good customer service. The product you sell must	23	79
be high quality and long lasting. The product must perform as you	27	84
claim. The environment and surroundings must be safe and clean.	32	88
Customers expect you to be well groomed and neatly dressed.	36	92
They expect you to know your products and services and to be	40	96
dependable. When you tell a customer you will do something, you must	44	101
perform. Patrons expect you to help them willingly and quickly. Add	49	105
a personal touch by greeting clientele by name, but be cautious about	54	110
conducting business on a first-name basis.	56	113

3' | 1 | 2 | 3 | 4 |

78a Textbook Keying
Key each line, striving for control. DS between groups. Repeat if desired.

i	1	sit in said did dirk city did fin its lit iris wit hit ilk simmer
e	2	gem ewe men eke ever me le hen cede key led fen eye be pen leader
i/e	3	pie lei piece feign mein feint neigh lie reign die veil vein diem
i/e	4	Either Marie or Liem tried to receive eight pieces of cookie pie.
w	5	new jaw awe win we was awe away hew saw flaw law wan pew wit wavy
o	6	to onto rot job coho sox box oboe wok roe out oil dot tote oriole
w/o	7	ow wows how won worn now woe wool mow row work cow woke flows low
w/o	8	Women won't want to work now; we are worn out after woeful worry.
s	9	sans is ants sons has sun spas his six bus asps skis its spy sobs
l	10	el let la alp lot lilt led elk lab old lily fly lip ilk loll milk
s/l	11	also slow else sly false slaw sells slag sails sly sled slip slam
s/l	12	Slater tells us Elsie is also slightly slow to slip off to sleep.

| 1 | 2 | 3 | 4 | 5 | 6 | 7 | 8 | 9 | 10 | 11 | 12 | 13 |

COMMUNICATION ✳

78b

You have learned the importance of formatting reports correctly and citing references appropriately. Equally important is selecting the correct word choice when producing a credible report.

1. Key the following sentences selecting the correct word shown in parentheses. Use the Research tool (Review/Proofing/Research) or the Thesaurus (Review/Proofing/Thesaurus) if help is needed.
2. Check and close. (78b)

1. The data (is, are) reported in the appendix of the report.
2. The recommendation was based on four (criteria, criterion) studied by the committee.
3. The graphic selected for the article in the newsletter must (complement, compliment) the content of the story.
4. The number of credit hours (is, are) reported on the annual report.
5. Insert a number on every page (accept, except) the first one.
6. The review committee has studied the proposal and asked the subcommittee to research the matter (farther, further).
7. The (principal, principle) focus of this research study is to determine the relationship (among, between) the two variables.
8. Dr. Watson cautioned the committee, "Don't (lose, loose) sight of the real issue here."
9. (Their, There, They're) required to submit (their, there, they're) manuscripts to the FTP site by noon tomorrow.
10. (Fewer, Less) than half the budget had been spent by the end of the second quarter.

NEW FUNCTIONS

46c

TABLES FEATURE

The Tables feature makes it easy to present data and graphics in a *Word* document. Aligning text, numbers, and graphics in a *Word* document can be tedious if you only use tabs and spaces. A table will help you align columns and rows of text and numbers with ease.

Tables: Columns and rows of data—either alphabetic, numeric, or both.

Column: Vertical list of information labeled alphabetically from left to right ❶.

Row: Horizontal list of information labeled numerically from top to bottom ❷.

Cell: An intersection of a column and a row ❸. Each cell has its own address consisting of the column letter and the row number (cell A1).

Use Show/Hide to display end-of-cell markers in each cell ❹ and end-of-row markers at the end of each row ❺. End-of-cell and end-of-row markers are useful when editing tables. Use Print Layout View to display the Table Move handle in the upper left of the table ❻. Drag the Table Move handle to move the table to a different location in the document. The Sizing handle in the lower right of the table can be used to make the table larger or smaller ❼.

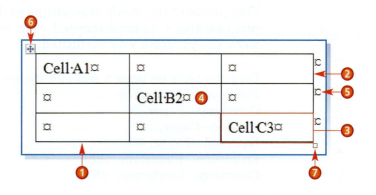

CREATE TABLES

INSERT/TABLES/TABLE

Tables are inserted into existing documents or new documents. Begin creating a table by clicking the Insert tab ❶ to display the Insert ribbon. Locate the Tables group ❷. The **Table button** ❸ contains options for creating various types of tables; you will use several of the options in this module.

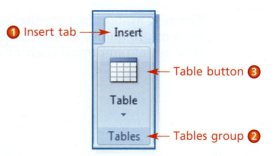

77-d2

Continued

9. Position the insertion point on the blank page left for the table of contents (not in the header section). Generate the table of contents using the Automatic Table 2. Position the title at approximately 2" and apply Title style.

10. Preview, check, and close. (77-*d2*)

Forms Inventory

A perpetual forms inventory system was designed and maintained online for all company-wide forms. Employees were encouraged to add their individual or departmental forms to the inventory system so that they could be shared with others.

Goal of the System

The goal of the system was to convert 70 to 75 percent of the forms to an electronic format within a three-year time period. This goal was considered to be ambitious because a wide range of computers were used in the various departments, and some departments did not have access to the central network. During this same time frame, the company planned to upgrade computers and make the network available to all employees except warehouse and delivery personnel.

Follow-Up Study

This phase of the study was authorized to determine the effectiveness of the program that was implemented. The following chart shows the progress made since the program was instituted.

Copy the table on page 1 and edit the percentages as follows:
Employee—Paper, 8%
Company—Paper, 5%
Vendor—Paper, 3%
External—Paper, 4%
Employee—Electronic, 32%
Company—Electronic, 48%

Results

Currently, 80 percent of all forms are in electronic format, and 20 percent are paper-based. The four forms that are currently purchased from vendors are being redesigned so that they can be made available electronically. The remaining paper-based forms are used primarily by warehouse and delivery personnel. However, the technology committee has recommended providing these employees with handheld computers to perform their work. As soon as this recommendation is implemented, the forms they use can be converted to electronic format.

The new system has resulted in a 20 percent cost savings over the previous system. In addition, more than 80 percent of the employees indicated that the new system improved their efficiency and effectiveness.

Several methods can be used to create a table. If you are creating a small table with just a few columns and rows, it may be easier to use the Table menu. If you are creating a more complex table, you will want to use the Insert Table command.

To create a table using the Table menu:

INSERT/TABLES/TABLE

1. Click the insertion point at the position where the table is to be inserted. Click the Insert tab to display the Tables group.
2. Click the Table button, and then under Insert Table, drag to select the number of columns and rows needed for the table.
3. Click the left mouse button to display the table in the document.

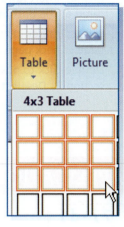

To create a table using the Insert Table command:

INSERT/TABLES/TABLE

1. Click the insertion point where the table is to be inserted.
2. In the Tables group on the Insert tab, click the Table button.
3. Click the Insert Table command ❶ to display the Insert Table dialog box.
4. Insert the number of columns by keying the number or using the spin buttons ❷.
5. Insert the number of rows by keying the number or using the spin buttons ❸; then click OK ❹. The table displays with the insertion point in the first cell, cell A1.
6. Key the text in cell A1; tap TAB to move to the next cell.

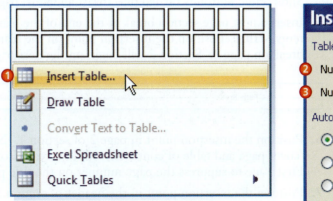

1. Open *77-drill1*. This document includes two sections of a report.
2. Position the insertion point on page 2 of section 1—the memo. Insert lowercase Roman numeral page numbers centered at the bottom of the page.
3. Select Different First Page to suppress numbers on the first page. Check page numbers in section 1.
4. Double-click to position the insertion point in the header of section 2. Deselect Different First Page.

5. Break the link between the headers of the two sections.
6. Click Go to Footer. Break the link between the footers of the two sections. Delete the page number in the footer of section 2.
7. Click Go to Header. Insert Arabic numeral page numbers at the top right. Start numbering at page 1. Select Different First Page to suppress numbers on the first page.
8. Check page numbers in section 2.
9. Check and close. (*77-drill2*)

APPLICATIONS

77-d1

Title Page

1. In a new document, create a title page using the Cover Page feature. Choose the Alphabet style from the Built-In gallery.
2. Key **Forms Design and Management** as the document title. Key **Hess and Glenn, Inc.** as the document subtitle.
3. Select the current date as the document date.
4. Key your name as the author of the report. Key **Consultant** as your title.
5. Check and close. (*77-d1*)

77-d2

Report with Preliminary Pages

FORMS

1. Open *77-d1*.
2. Position the insertion point on page 2. Insert the data file *forms*.
3. Key the remainder of the report on the next page below the file you inserted. Format the title and the side headings appropriately.
4. Insert a blank page after the cover page for the table of contents. **Hint:** Position the insertion point immediately after the Page Break marker on the title page. Be sure the Show/Hide button is turned on. Insert a manual page break.
5. Insert a next page section break at the end of the blank page left for the table of contents. **Hint:** Position the insertion point on the blank page immediately after the page break on page 2. Section 2 will begin on the next page.

---------Page Break--------- ·Section Break (Next Page)· ·

6. Position the insertion point in page 2 of section 1. Number the preliminary pages (cover page and table of contents) with lowercase Roman numerals. Select Different First Page to suppress the page number on the title page.
7. Position the insertion point in the header of section 2. Deselect Different First Page. Break the links between the header for both sections. Go to the footer of section 2. Break the link between the footers for both sections. Delete the page number in the section 2 footer.
8. Go to the header of section 2 and number the pages of the report with Arabic numerals beginning with page 1. Click Different First Page to suppress the page number on the first page of the report.

TABLES TOOLS

Table Tools

Design   Layout

When the insertion point is clicked in a table cell, additional tabs are added to the right of the Ribbon. A **Design** tab and a **Layout** tab are added under Table Tools. Click the Design tab to display features that allow you to change the appearance of the table. The Layout tab contains features that allow you to alter the table structure.

TIP

Remember to proofread and preview each document as a SOP. You will not be reminded to do this.

MOVE WITHIN A TABLE

The insertion point displays in cell A1 when a table is created. Tap the TAB key to move to the next cell, or simply use the mouse to click in a cell. Refer to the table below as you learn to key text in a table.

Tap or Press	Movement
TAB	To move to the next cell. If the insertion point is in the last cell, tapping TAB will add a new row.
SHIFT + TAB	To move to the previous cell.
ENTER	To increase the height of the row. If you tap ENTER by mistake, tap BACKSPACE to delete the line.

KEYBOARDING PRO DELUXE See References/Word commands/Lesson 46

DRILL 1   CREATE TABLE

1. Create a three-column, four-row table using the Table menu.

2. Turn on Show/Hide and notice the marker at the end of each cell and each row.

3. Use Print Layout View to see the Table Move handle and the Sizing handle.

4. Drag the Table Move handle down the page. This moves the table. Drag the handle back to the original position.

5. Close the table without saving.

6. Create a four-column, four-row table using the Insert Table command.

7. Move to cell C1. Move to cell B3.

8. Move to cell B1 and tap ENTER. Delete the ¶ to restore the size of the cell.

9. Move to cell D4 and tap TAB; this added a row to the bottom of the table. Close the table without saving it.

To break the links in section 2:

5. Position the insertion point in the header section of section 2 and double-click. The header displays with labels as shown below. Note the Same as Previous label at the right. **Note:** If the report has a First Page Header—Section 1, deselect Different First Page in the Options group to remove First Page Header in section 2.

Header -Section 2-   Same as Previous

6. In the Navigation group, click the Link to Previous button to break the link for the header. Note the Go to Header button is dimmed, meaning the insertion point is in the header. (Section 1 did not have a header; in section 2 you want to add a header.)

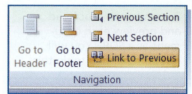

7. In the Navigation group, click Go to Footer to move to the footer of section 2. Click the Link to Previous button to break the link for the footer. At this point there should be no links to headers or footers in section 2.

8. Delete the page number that appears in the Footer box. (Section 1 had a footer with a centered lowercase Roman numeral; section 2 will not have a page number.)

Footer -Section 2-

4

To insert page numbers in section 2:

9. In the Navigation group, click Go to Header.

10. In the Header and Footer group, click Page Number.

11. Format the page numbers as Arabic numerals. Start the page number at 1.

12. Insert the page number at the top right of the page.

13. From the Options group, click Different First Page to suppress the page numbers on the first page.

14. Check the page numbers in section 2. No number should appear on page 1; a page number should display at the top right of the remaining pages.

SELECTING PORTIONS OF A TABLE

TABLE TOOLS/LAYOUT/TABLE/SELECT

If you wish to apply a format such as bold, alignment, or italics to the table, you must first select the table. Likewise, to format a specific row, column, or cell, you must select the table parts and then apply the format.

The **Select** button, found in the Table group of the Layout tab under Table Tools, makes it easy for you to select portions of a table or the entire table. Click the insertion point in the cell of the table; then click the Select button and choose Select Cell to select only the cell the insertion point is in. Choosing Select Row or Select Column will highlight the entire row or column that contains the cell. Choose Select Table to highlight the entire table.

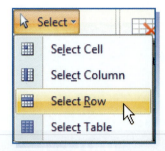

The mouse can also be used to select the entire table or portions of a table.

To select	Move the insertion point:
Entire table	Over the table and click the Table Move handle in the upper left of the table. (**Option:** Table Tools, Select, Select Table) To move the table, drag the Table Move handle to a new location.
Column	To the top of the column until a solid down arrow appears; click the left mouse button.
Row	To the left area just outside the table until the pointer turns to an open arrow (⇗), then click the left mouse button.

Note: You can also select rows and columns by selecting a cell, column, or row, and dragging across or down.

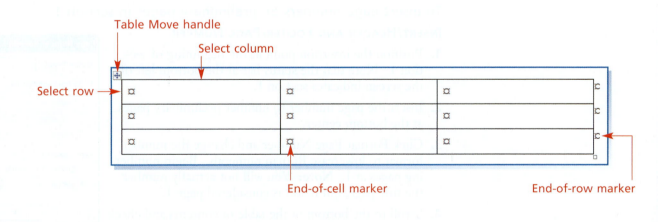

Table Move handle

Select column

Select row

End-of-cell marker

End-of-row marker

In Draft View, section breaks appear as a dotted line with the type of break indicated. *Word* displays the current section number on the status bar.

Section Break (Continuous)
Section Break (Next Page)
Section Break (Even Page)
Section Break (Odd Page)

Refer to the status line to determine the section in which your insertion point is located. If you do not see the section number, place the insertion point on the status bar and right-click. Click Section.

Section: 1   Page: 1 of 5   At: 2"

DRILL 1   SECTION BREAKS   SECTIONS

1. In the open document, insert a next page section break after the table of contents. Do not edit the name field.
2. Change to Print Layout View.
3. Check that the table of contents and the first page of the report begin at approximately 2". You will number the pages and update the table of contents in the next drill.
4. Check and close. *(77-drill1)*

INSERT PAGE NUMBERS AND BREAK LINK BETWEEN SECTIONS

INSERT/HEADER & FOOTER/PAGE NUMBER

After learning to insert section breaks, you are ready to learn to insert page numbers with appropriate format in section 1, break the link between sections 1 and 2, and then insert the appropriate format for section 2. It is important that you follow this order exactly as shown.

To insert page numbers on preliminary pages in section 1:

INSERT/HEADER AND FOOTER/PAGE NUMBER

1. Position the insertion point at the beginning of section 1. Note that the status bar at the bottom left of the screen indicates section 1.

2. Insert the page number to number preliminary pages at the bottom center.

3. Click Format Page Number and change the number format to lowercase Roman numerals. Begin numbering pages at 1. **Note:** You will not actually number the title page, but it still is considered page 1.

4. Scroll to the bottom of the table of contents and check the page number in section 1.

Page Number Format   ? ×

Number format: | 1, 2, 3, ...   ▼ |

☐ Include chapter number

Chapter starts with style: | Heading 1   ▼ |

Use separator: | - (hyphen)   ▼ |

Examples: 1-1, 1-A

Page numbering
○ Continue from previous section
◉ Start at: | 1   ⬍ |

OK   Cancel

Footer -Section 1-

ii

1. Center-align and key the main heading in bold; tap ENTER.
2. Change the alignment to left and turn bold off.
3. Create a three-column, four-row table.
4. Key the table shown below.
5. Select row 1; then bold and center-align the column headings. Row 1 is called the **header row** because it identifies the content in each column.
6. Check and close. (*46-drill2*)

COLLEGE SPORTS PROGRAM

Fall Events	Winter Events	Spring Events
Football	Basketball	Golf
Soccer	Gymnastics	Baseball
Volleyball	Swimming	Softball

APPLICATIONS

46-d1

Create Table

1. Key the main heading using center alignment, bold, and uppercase. Tap ENTER, change the alignment to left, and turn bold off.
2. Create the table shown below.
3. Select row 1. Bold and center-align the column headings. Center-align cells C2–C7.
4. Center the table vertically on the page (Page Layout/Page Setup dialog box launcher/Layout tab).
5. Check and close. (*46-d1*)

TIP

Remember to select cells before applying formatting commands.

KEY CONTACTS FOR BUILDING PROJECT

Contact	Title	Telephone Number
Lara G. Kim	Architect	420-555-0176
James C. Weatherwax	Contractor	317-555-0190
Kkatere Shadab	Site Supervisor	513-555-0164
Joanna B. Breckenridge	Interior Designer	624-555-0137
Loriana Gonzalez	Project Consultant	502-555-0126
Mei Liang Pong	Engineer	812-555-0171

SECTIONS

PAGE LAYOUT/PAGE SETUP/BREAKS

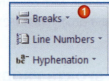

Often long documents such as reports are formatted in sections so that different formats may be applied on the same page or on different pages using section breaks. Normally, the preliminary pages of a report are numbered at the bottom center with lowercase Roman numerals. The pages in the body of a report are numbered in the upper right with Arabic numerals. For convenience, you will want to save the report as one file and not two or more.

To use different page numbers formats within the same document, you must format the preliminary pages as one section and the remainder of the report as another section. *Word* continues to use the same format for page numbers in a new section as it did in the previous section until you first break the link or connection between the sections.

Section 1

Title Page	Letter of Transmittal	Table of Contents
	ii	iii

Section 2
(Break link before changing page format)

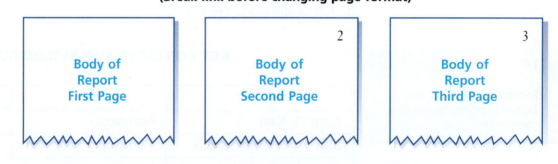

Body of Report First Page	Body of Report Second Page	Body of Report Third Page
	2	3

To enter a section break:

1. On the Page Layout tab, in the Page Setup group, click Breaks ❶.

2. From the Section Breaks category, click the desired section break ❷.

   Next Page: Begins a new page at the point the section break is entered.

   Continuous: Begins a new section on the same page.

   Even Page: Begins a new section on the next even-numbered page.

   Odd Page: Begins a new section on the next odd-numbered page.

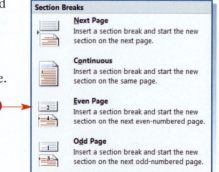

46-d2

Table with Formatting

1. Key the main heading using uppercase, center alignment, and bold; tap ENTER. Key the secondary heading using bold. Capitalize each word; tap ENTER. Change the alignment to left and turn bold off.
2. Create the table and key the information in the cells.
3. Select row 1. Bold and center-align the column headings. Center-align cells A2–A6. Right-align cells C2–C6.
4. Center the table vertically on the page.
5. Check and close. (46-d2)

PERSONAL COMPUTER ACCESSORIES
Inventory as of December 31, 20--

Stock Number	Description	Units Available
JGC2144	4mm Transporter	5,745,000
JGC9516	DLT/TK 20-pack Transporter	19,034,100
TMA3252	Mobile Base Storage System	3,972,155
CDS4971	Casa Multimedia Storage	9,734,250
LGT8920	Optical Keyboard and Mouse	10,457

46-d3

Table with Proofreaders' Marks

1. Create a three-column, four-row table. Key the text in the table.
2. Place the cursor in cell C4; tap the TAB key to create another blank row. Key the last row.
3. Center table vertically on the page. Check and close. (46-d3)

POMMERY SPRINGS PROJECT STATUS *Center and Bold*

Job	Description	Date Completed
Road work	Building and grading	February 10, 20--
Drain	Adding french drain	February 25, 20--
Lot prep *aration*	Clearing and leveling	March 12, 20--
Pond	Adding silt fence	March 15, 20-- *(add row)*

Report with Sections

WARMUP 77a

Key each line, striving for control. Repeat if necessary.

1 Oak Road; Ninth Blvd; Union Avenue; Main Court; High Circle

shift 2 Wade and Jeff; Randy and Paul; Carl and Nan; Teresa and Jane

3 Mr. and Mrs. Brian Nunn's grandson is Andrew Michael Quincy.

4 Keep your fingers curved.

5 Keep your eyes on the copy.

ENTER 6 Use quick and snappy keystrokes.

7 Tap Enter without pausing.

| 1 | 2 | 3 | 4 | 5 | 6 | 7 | 8 | 9 | 10 | 11 | 12 | 13 |

SKILL BUILDING

77b Textbook Keying

1. Key each line, concentrating on good keying techniques. Tap ENTER twice after each 2-line group.
2. Repeat if time permits.

3rd row
8 query were pure wipe wept you tort twirp report rip tire weep tip

9 Perry required two types of paper, a protractor, and four rulers.

3rd/home
10 we tattle wayward pepper rattle eloped require your yellow queasy

11 Patty wrote poetry, took art, and worked two jobs this past year.

1st/3rd
12 minimum box zip zinc bomb ripen corner mine cure woven zoo winner

13 Merv and Robert were to turn a valve to terminate the water flow.

| 1 | 2 | 3 | 4 | 5 | 6 | 7 | 8 | 9 | 10 | 11 | 12 | 13 |

77c Timed Writing
Key two 3' timings for control.

all letters

	gwam	3'	5'

As you read copy for keyboarding, try to read at least a word   4 | 2 | 44
or, better still, a word group ahead of your actual keyboarding   8 | 5 | 46
point. In this way, you will be able to recognize the keystroking   13 | 8 | 49
pattern needed as you learn to keyboard balanced-hand, one-hand,   17 | 10 | 51
or combination word sequences. The adjustments you make in your   22 | 13 | 54
speed will result in the variable rhythm pattern needed for expert   26 | 16 | 57
keyboarding. It is easy to read copy correctly for keyboarding   30 | 18 | 59
if you concentrate on the copy.   32 | 19 | 60

When you first try to read copy properly for keyboarding, you   36 | 22 | 63
may make more errors, but as you learn to concentrate on the copy   41 | 25 | 66
being read and begin to anticipate the keystroking pattern needed,   45 | 27 | 68
your errors will go down and your keyboarding speed will grow. If   50 | 30 | 71
you want to increase your keyboarding speed and reduce your errors,   54 | 33 | 74
you must make the effort to improve during each and every practice   59 | 35 | 76
session. If you will work to refine your techniques and to give a   63 | 38 | 79
specific purpose to all your practice activities, you can make the   68 | 41 | 82
improvement.   69 | 41 | 82

3' | 1 | 2 | 3 | 4 |
5' | 1 | 2 | 3 |

46-d4

1. Center the main heading in uppercase and bold; tap ENTER. Key the secondary heading in bold and center it. Capitalize each word; tap ENTER.
2. Use the Insert Table dialog box to create the table shown below. Key the text in the table and center column heads.
3. Center the table vertically on the page.
4. Check and close. (*46-d4*)

OFFICIAL BIRDS AND FLOWERS
For Selected States

State	Official Bird	Official Flower
Alaska	Willow ptarmigan	Forget-me-not
Arkansas	Mockingbird	Apple blossom
California	California valley quail	Golden poppy
Connecticut	American robin	Mountain laurel
Delaware	Blue hen chicken	Peach blossom
Georgia	Brown thrasher	Cherokee rose
Idaho	Mountain bluebird	Syringe
Illinois	Cardinal	Native violet
Louisiana	Eastern brown pelican	Magnolia
Maryland	Baltimore oriole	Black-eyed Susan
Massachusetts	Chickadee	Mayflower
Nebraska	Western meadowlark	Goldenrod
New Jersey	Eastern goldfinch	Purple violet
New Mexico	Roadrunner	Yucca
North Carolina	Cardinal	Dogwood

2. Interview
Wright, Dona (Interviewee)
Nurse Practitioner
Young, Dean (Interviewer)
November 4, 2009.

3. Journal Article
Sanchez, Rosa
"Did You Get Your Water Today?" (Title)
Nutrition Journal (Journal Name)
May 2009
pp. 58-60

4. Document from Web site:
Kwon, Chien
"What Should I Weigh?" (Name of Web Page)
Medical Notes (Name of Web Site)
May 2009
http://www.doctorsandnurseshi-energy.com/whatshouldiweigh.html
Accessed July 23, 2009.

76-d2

Change Manuscript Style

1. Open *76-d1*.

2. Change the manuscript to MLA.

3. Delete the Baker citation from the master list. Add a space before each citation if necessary.

4. Check and close. (*76-d2*)

76-d3

Copy Citations and Compose Report

1. Select APA as the manuscript style and copy the Wright citation from the master list to the current list.

2. Key the text below. Format the main heading appropriately.

3. Move the Wright citation to display after *Ms. Wright* at the beginning of the second sentence. Edit the citation to suppress the author's name. Suppress the title as well.

4. Search the Internet to list at least five food substitutions for high-calorie food choice and list at least five easy ways to increase daily physical activity. One example is given for you. Reference your sources in the body of this report.

5. Create a bibliography page. Check and close. (*76-d3*)

DISCOVER

Move Citation—Click on the citation to select it.

Click on the move handle in the upper-left corner of citation and drag to new location.

Interview with Dona Wright

On March 2, 20--, I met with Dona Wright, nurse practitioner with the Foundation Nutrition Center in (Student's Home Town). Ms. Wright suggested beginning my weight management program by (1) reviewing my food choices and substituting high-calorie choices with lower-calorie choices and (2) listing ways to increase my daily physical activity (Wright citation). After researching possible substitutions and ways to increase physical activity, I agree to do the following things:

Replace High-Calorie Food Choice	Substitute with Low-Calorie Choice
Regular soda	Diet soda
Increase Physical Activity	
Park away from the front door of the office and shopping mall.	

LESSON 47

Enhance Table Appearance

WARMUP 47a

Key each line, striving for control. Repeat if desired.

alphabet	1	Dixie Vaughn acquired that prize job with a firm just like yours.
figures	2	By May 15 do this: Call Ext. 4390; order 472 clips and 168 pens.
easy/figures	3	The 29 girls kept 38 bushels of corn and 59 bushels of rich yams.
easy	4	The members paid half of the endowment, and their firm paid half.

| 1 | 2 | 3 | 4 | 5 | 6 | 7 | 8 | 9 | 10 | 11 | 12 | 13 |

SKILL BUILDING

47b Textbook Keying

1. Key the drill, concentrating on good keying techniques.
2. Repeat the drill if time permits.

1/2 fingers

5 Take the Paz exit; make a right turn; then the street veers left.
6 Stop by and see the amateur videos of Zoe at six o'clock tonight.
7 We made an excellent pizza with leftover bread, cheese, and beef.

Home row

8 Dallas shall ask Sal to sell fake flash fads; Sal sells all fads.
9 A small fast salad is all Kallas had; Dallas adds a dash of salt.
10 Dallas saw all flasks fall; alas Dad adds a fast fake hall flask.

Third row

11 We used thirty pails of yellow powder; Wesley threw the rest out.
12 I should go to the store with Paul to get eggs for the apple pie.
13 Did you see the request for Sy to take the test with your sister?

47c Timed Writing

1. Key a 3' timed writing, working for speed.
2. Key a 3' timed writing, working for control.

	gwam	1'	3'
Little things do contribute a lot to success in keying.	11	4	35
Take our work attitude, for example. It's a little thing; yet	24	8	40
it can make quite a lot of difference. Demonstrating patience	36	12	44
with a job or a problem, rather than pressing much too hard for a	50	17	48
desired payoff, often brings better results than we expected.	63	21	53
Other "little things," such as wrist and finger position, how we	76	25	57
sit, size and location of copy, and lights, have meaning for	88	29	61
any person who wants to key well.	95	32	63

1' | 1 | 2 | 3 | 4 | 5 | 6 | 7 | 8 | 9 | 10 | 11 | 12 | 13 |
3' | 1 | 2 | 3 | 4 |

76-d1

Continued

Selecting the proper food and beverages is only one part of a healthy diet. The quantity consumed and the manner in which foods are prepared are equally important. A person's diet should be planned carefully to maintain a desirable weight for the body size. Obesity increases the risk of many diseases. Being underweight can also create problems.

Foods should also be prepared in a manner that does not add fat to the food. Baking, steaming, poaching, roasting, and cooking in a microwave are the best ways to prepare foods.

Wise food choices are important for a healthy diet. Many health-conscious individuals have learned to make the following substitutions for foods that are high in fat and calories (Citation 2).

- Diet soda for regular soda
- Skim, 1%, or 2% milk for whole milk (begin with 2% and work down to skim milk)
- Egg whites for whole egg
- Low-fat cheese for full-fat cheese

Drinks. The body needs a significant amount of fluids. The daily minimum of water is eight glasses per day. Rosa Sanchez (Citation 3), a well-known nutritionist, states, "Increase the minimum requirement of water when exercising briskly, when weather temperatures are hot, and when dieting to burn fat." Consider creative ways to consume the daily requirement of water, such as drinking water at all meals, keeping a measured container of water in your work area, and substituting water for a snack.

If alcoholic beverages are consumed, they should be consumed in moderation. Alcoholic beverages are high in calories and low in food value. In addition, excessive drinking can lead to major health problems.

Weight Guides

A person's body frame helps to determine the desirable weight for that person. Desirable weight for a person with a small frame is less than for a person with an average or large frame. For example, the desirable weight for a 6'0" male with a large frame is 164-184 pounds, while weight for a 6'0" male with a medium frame is 154-170. On the other hand, the desirable weight for a 5'5" female with a medium frame is 116-130 and a female with a small frame is 111-119 (Citation 4). Desirable weights based on body frame size are helpful to guide individuals in healthy body weight.

Summary

Health-conscious individuals make wise choices daily related to foods and drinks realizing that health issues can become problematic. Maintaining the desirable weight level for the size frame is equally important.

Data for APA Citations

1. Journal Article
Livingston, Steven
"A Study of Diseases Related to Diet,"
Medical Journal
2009
Volume 47, Issue 2
pp. 51-69.

ADJUST COLUMN WIDTH

Tables extend from margin to margin when they are created, regardless of the width of the data in the columns. Some tables, however, would be more attractive and easier to read if the columns were narrower. Column widths can be changed manually using the mouse or automatically using AutoFit. Using the mouse enables you to adjust the widths as you like. Once you change the width of a table, you will need to center it horizontally.

Column width ⎯⎯⎯⎯⎯⎯⎯⎯⎯

Column marker ⎯⎯⎯⎯⎯⎯

Point to the column border and hold down the left mouse button to display the dotted line.

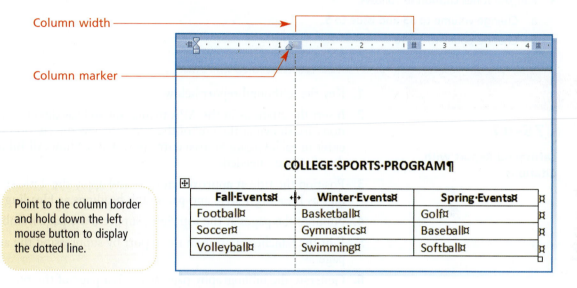

COLLEGE·SPORTS·PROGRAM¶

Fall·Events¤	Winter·Events¤	Spring·Events¤	¤
Football¤	Basketball¤	Golf¤	¤
Soccer¤	Gymnastics¤	Baseball¤	¤
Volleyball¤	Swimming¤	Softball¤	¤

To adjust column widths using the mouse:

1. Point to the column border that needs adjusting.

2. When the pointer changes to ✛, hold down the left mouse button and drag the border to the left to make the column narrower or to the right to make the column wider.

3. Adjust the column widths attractively. Leave approximately 0.5" to .75" between the longest line and the border. Use the Horizontal Ruler as a guide.

4. The widths of the columns can be displayed by pointing to the column marker on the ruler, holding down the ALT key, and clicking the left mouse button.

To center table horizontally on the page:

TABLE TOOLS/LAYOUT/TABLE PROPERTIES/TABLE TAB/CENTER ALIGNMENT

1. Click in a table cell.

2. Click the Layout tab.

3. From the Table group, click the Table Properties button. The Table Properties dialog box displays.

4. From the Table tab, select Center Alignment.

KEYBOARDING PRO DELUXE See References/Word commands/Lesson 47

1. In the open document, edit the Brantley citation as follows:

   a. Change city to **Portland**.

   b. Change year to **2009**.

2. Click Close and if prompted, click Yes to update both the master list and the current list.

3. Edit the Jones citation as follows:

   a. Change volume to **55** and issue to **5**.

   b. Change pages to **11-16**.

4. Close and if prompted, agree to update both the master list and the current list.

5. Generate the bibliography and format appropriately.

6. Check and close. (*76-drill5*)

APPLICATIONS

76-d1

Leftbound Report with Citations

1. Key the leftbound report below.

2. Insert the citations in the APA manuscipt style as directed in the text below. The citations are shown at the end of the text. Review the citation to determine which data to enter in each Create Source entry box. Click Show All Bibliography Fields if additional data fields are needed.

3. Position the title at approximately 2" and apply the Title style. Format the side headings as Heading 1 style and paragraph headings as Heading 2 style.

4. Number the pages at the top right; suppress the page number on the first page.

5. Edit the Sanchez citation in the report by suppressing the author's name and adding page 59.

6. Generate the bibliography page as the last page of the report. Position the title at approximately 2"; apply the Title style. Format the reference list as a hanging indent.

7. Edit the Kwon source. Change *Medical Notes* to **Nutrition Notes**. Click Yes to update the master list and the current list.

8. Edit the Sanchez source. Insert volume number 10 and issue 1. Click Yes to update the master list and the current list. Update the bibliography page. Format the reference list as a hanging indent.

9. Check and close. (*76-d1*)

Title → **Nutrition Guides for Good Health**

Good health is a high priority for most people. Yet many individuals know relatively little about nutrition and make dietary choices that are detrimental to their health. Studies show that at least one-third of all cancer and heart attack deaths are directly related to diet (Citation 1). This report presents valuable guides to eating and drinking as well as weight guides.

Side heading → **Guides for Eating and Drinking**

Diet consists of both the foods and beverages consumed daily. The foods and beverages consumed should be selected carefully to ensure good nutrition as well as healthy guides for preparing and making wise food choices.

Paragraph heading → **Food.** A wide variety of foods should be eaten each day since no one food contains all of the nutrients needed. Foods that are rich in vitamins and high in dietary fiber should be eaten daily. Fruits, vegetables, and whole-grain breads are particularly good sources of vitamins and fiber.

A good diet also avoids harmful foods. Sodium, saturated fat, high-fat dairy products, salt, and sugar should be eaten in moderation.

1. Open *46-drill2*.
2. Display the widths of the columns by pointing to the ruler, holding down the ALT key, and clicking the left mouse button.

3. Use the mouse to adjust column width. Leave approximately 0.5" to .75" between the longest line and the border in each column.
4. Center the table horizontally on the page. Check and close. (*47-drill1*)

NEW FUNCTIONS

47e

TABLE STYLES

Design

Microsoft Word has preformatted table styles that you can use to make your tables more attractive. The styles contain a combination of font attributes, color, shading, and borders to enhance the appearance of the table.

Under Table Tools, click the Design tab to access the Table Styles group ❶. As you move the mouse over each style, you will also see your table formatted in that style. A tab also displays with the name of the style. Additional styles display when you click the More button ❷.

To apply Table Styles:

TABLE TOOLS/DESIGN/TABLE STYLES

1. Display the table on the screen. Click the insertion point in the body of the table to display the Table Tools tabs.
2. Click the Design tab to display the Table Styles group.
3. Move the mouse over each table style until you find the desired style. View more styles by clicking the More arrow; then use the scroll bar to view the available styles.
4. Click the style to apply it to the table.
5. Click the Layout tab. From the Table group, select Properties and recenter the table on the page.

1. Open *47-drill1*. Click in the table.
2. Click the Design tab. Apply the Colorful List – Accent 1 style to the table.

3. Click the Layout tab; then select Properties. Recenter the table horizontally on the page.
4. Check and close. (*47-drill2*)

To edit a citation source:

1. From the Source Manager dialog box, select from the master list the citation to be edited **1**.

2. Click Edit **2**.

Source Manager

Search: [   ]   Sort by Author ▼

Sources available in:
Master List   Browse...   Current List

Baker, Marshall; High School Athletic Records (2007)   Copy ->
Brantley, Austin; Knowledge of the Copyright Law Goes a Long Way (2   Delete
Devaul, Payton (2008)
Jones, Benjamin (2009)   Edit...   **2**

1   New...

                                              ✓ cited source
                                              ? placeholder source

Preview (APA):

Citation: (Brantley, 2009)

Bibliography Entry:
Brantley, A. (2009). *Knowledge of the Copyright Law Goes a Long Way.* Portland: Jones Press.

                                                            Close

3. The Edit Source dialog box displays. Key the edits **3**.

Edit Source

Type of Source   Book ▼
Bibliography Fields for APA

   * Author   Brantley, Austin   Edit
              ☐ Corporate Author [   ]
   * Title   Knowledge of the Copyright Law Goes a Long Way
   * Year   2009
   * City   Portland **3**
      State/Province [   ]
      Country/Region [   ]
   * Publisher   Jones Press
      Editor   [   ]   Edit
      Volume   [   ]
      Number of Volumes [   ]
      Translator   Edit

4 ☑ Show All Bibliography Fields   * Recommended Field   **5**
Tag name   Example: IV
Bra09   OK   Cancel

4. Click Show All Bibliography Fields **4** if more fields are needed.

5. Click OK **5**. Click Close **6**. A *Microsoft Word* prompt automatically displays. Click Yes **7** to update both the master list and the current list with these changes.

Microsoft Office Word

⚠ This source exists in your master list and current document. Do you want to update both lists with these changes?

6   Yes   No   Cancel

TABLE FORMAT GUIDES

1. Position the table (or main heading) at about 2", or center the table vertically on the page.

2. Headings: Main heading: center, bold, uppercase, 14-point font; and then tap ENTER. Secondary heading: center, bold, 12-point font; capitalize each word. Center and bold all column headings. If styles are applied to main and secondary headings, adjust spacing as needed.

3. Adjust column width attractively, and center the table horizontally.

4. Align text within the cells at the left. Align numbers at the right. Align decimal number of varying lengths at the decimal point.

5. When a table is within a document, the same amount of blank space should display before and after the table as between paragraphs.

APPLICATIONS

47-d1
Create Table and Apply Style

1. Key the table below. Format the main heading appropriately. Adjust column width and center column heads.

2. Right-align column C. Apply Medium Grid 1 - Accent 6 table style.

3. Center the table vertically and horizontally on the page.

4. Check and close. (47-d1)

MAJOR METROPOLITAN AREAS OF CANADA

City	Province	Population
Toronto	Ontario	5,427,250
Montreal	Quebec	3,921,375
Vancouver	British Columbia	2,285,750
Ottawa	Ontario	1,893,987
Winnipeg	Manitoba	685,957
Quebec	Quebec	1,097,982
Hamilton	Ontario	757,250

47-d2
Applying Communication Knowledge

1. Key **NUMBER EXPRESSION** as the main heading. Key **Times and Dates** as the secondary heading. Format the headings appropriately.

2. Key the table on the next page. Do not adjust column width.

3. Column A contains guidelines for using figures and words when keying dates and times. Key the examples in column B to comply with the guidelines.

4. Apply Medium Shading 1 - Accent 2 table style. The table style will bold the text in column A.

5. Apply italics to column B. Bold column heads. Center the table on the page horizontally and vertically.

6. Check and close. (47-d2)

5. At the appropriate place in the document, click the Insert Citation button. At the top of the drop-down menu ⑤, choose the reference that you just copied to the current document.

⑤	**Guo-Patterson** Top Ten High School Athletes, (2007)
📖	Add New Source...
📑	Add New Placeholder...
🔍	Search Libraries...

To delete a citation from the master source:

1. From the Source Manager dialog box, select the reference to be deleted from the master list ①.

2. Click Delete ②. The source does not display in the master list of sources and cannot be used in later manuscripts.

Source Manager

Search: [   ]   Sort by Author [▾]

Sources available in:
Master List   Browse...   Current List

Baker, Marshall; High School Athletic Records (2007)   Copy ->   ✔Baker, Marshall; High School Athletic Records (2007)
Devaul, Payton (2008)   ✔Devaul, Payton (2008)
Guo-Patterson, Lori; Top Ten Athletes (2008)   ①   Delete   ✔Guo-Patterson, Lori; Top Ten Athletes (2008)
                                                          ②
                                                           Edit...

                                                           New...

                                                          ✔ cited source
                                                          ? placeholder source

Preview (MLA):

Citation: (Guo-Patterson)

Bibliography Entry:
Guo-Patterson, Lori. "Top Ten Athletes." Spring 2008. The Sports Journal. 25 June 2008

                                                                        Close   ③

3. Click Close ③.

Note: If you wish the source to be deleted from the current list, delete the citation in the document first and then delete it in the Source Manager dialog box. See page 344 for review.

DRILL 4	**COPY AND DELETE CITATIONS FROM THE MASTER LIST**

1. In a new document, copy the Baker, Devaul, and Guo-Patterson sources in the master list.

2. Rekey the paragraph in Drill 1 using APA manuscript style. Insert the three citations by choosing the sources that have already been keyed.

3. Delete the Guo-Patterson source from the master list only.

4. Generate the bibliography and format appropriately.

5. Check and close. (*76-drill4*)

General Guidelines	Example
Use words for numbers that precede o'clock.	Mail pickup is at 11 and 2 o'clock. I need to be home by 6 o'clock.
Use figures for times with a.m. or p.m. and days when they follow the month.	The store closes at nine p.m. Tarian was born on February 23, 2007. Classes begin on August 23, 2008.
Use ordinals for the day when it precedes the month.	The next Board of Directors meeting will be held on the tenth of August. Taxes are due on the fifteenth of April.

47-d3

Text Table

1. Create a two-column, ten-row table. Key the table using wordwrap.
2. Drag the left border of the table to make column A narrower.
3. Apply the Colorful List - Accent 5 style. Center the table horizontally.
4. Bold column heads and change the main heading to 14-point font.
5. Center the table on the page.
6. Check and close. (*47-d3*)

MACKINNON'S CLASSES OF EXPERT SYSTEMS

Class	Area of Classification
Configuration	Assemble proper components of a modern expert computer system in the proper way.
Diagnosis	Expert system infers underlying problems based on observed evidence.
Instruction	Intelligent teaching so that an inquirer can ask *why*, *how*, and *what if* questions just as if a human were teaching.
Interpretation	Expert system explains observed data.
Monitoring	Ability to compare observed data to expected data to judge performance.
Planning	Devise actions to produce a desired outcome.
Prognosis	Ability to predict the outcome of any given situation.
Remedy	Prescribe treatment for a given problem.
Control	Regulate a process. May require interpretation, diagnosis, monitoring, planning, prognosis, and remedies.

5. In the document bibliography, click Update Citations and Bibliography ⑦. Check that the citation does not appear in the updated bibliography.

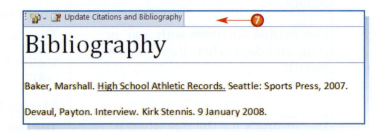

DRILL 3   DELETE CITATION AND UPDATE BIBLIOGRAPHY

1. Open *76-drill1*. Delete the second citation.
2. Click on Manage Sources and delete from the current list.

3. In the bibliography of the document, click Update Citations and Bibliography.
4. Check and close. (*76-drill3*)

MANAGE SOURCES

REFERENCES/CITATIONS & BIBLIOGRAPHY/MANAGE SOURCES

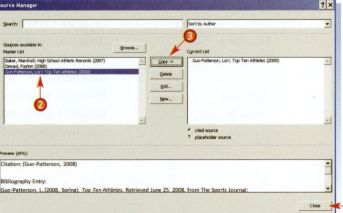

Writers working on various manuscripts will find it helpful to use the Source Manager. The Source Manager maintains a master list of all references keyed in *Word 2007*. Using this list, the writer may copy references from the master list to the current list (new document), delete sources from the master list, and edit sources in the master list.

To copy a citation from the master list:

1. On the References tab, in the Citations and Bibliography group, click Manage Sources ①. The Source Manager dialog box displays.

2. Select the reference to be copied in the master list on the left side of the Source Manager ②.

3. Click Copy ③. Note the reference now displays in the Current List on the right side of the dialog box.

4. Click Close ④.

LESSON 48 ▶ Change Table Structure

WARMUP 48a

Key each line, striving for control. Repeat if desired.

alphabet	1	Jacqueline quickly moved up front and seized the big pile of wax.
1st/2nd fingers	2	I went to the baseball game to see Ginger hit the first home run.
3rd row	3	I should go to the store with Paul to get eggs for the apple pie.
balanced hand	4	Did the neighbor and his visitor roam down to the town for clams?

SKILL BUILDING

48b Textbook Keying
1. Key the drill, concentrating on good keying techniques.
2. Repeat the drill if time permits.

direct reaches	5	June and my brother, Bradly, received advice from junior umpires.
	6	My bright brother received minimum reward for serving many years.
adjacent reaches	7	Clio and Trey were sad that very few voters were there last week.
	8	Western attire was very popular at the massive auction last week.
double letters	9	Tommie Bennett will go to a meeting in Dallas tomorrow afternoon.
	10	Lee will meet Joanne at the swimming pool after accounting class.

NEW FUNCTIONS

48c

CHANGE TABLE STRUCTURE

Table Tools
Design Layout

Word makes it easy to alter the structure of an existing table. Columns, rows, and cells can easily be inserted or deleted in a table. Cells can be joined or merged horizontally or vertically to make the table more attractive and easier to read.

Changes to a table structure are made in the Layout ribbon under Table Tools.

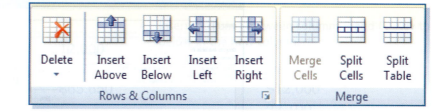

1. Key the paragraph shown below. Insert the MLA citations as indicated in the paragraph. The data for the three citations are shown in the three Create Source dialog boxes below.

2. Edit the Baker citation to add page 56 as the page where this reference appeared in this reference. Note the citation in the report displays (*Baker 56*).

3. At the end of the document, insert a manual page break. Position the insertion point at 2" and create the bibliography page.

4. Select the title *Bibliography* and apply the Title style.

5. Select the list of references and format as a hanging indent.

6. Check and close. (*76-drill1*)

Payton set the school record for points in a game—50 (Citation 1). He holds six statewide records. This makes him one of the top ten athletes in the school's history (Citation 2). He expects to receive a basketball scholarship at an outstanding university (Citation 3).

Citation 1: Book

Create Source

Type of Source: Book

Bibliography Fields for MLA

Author: Baker, Marshall
☐ Corporate Author
Title: High School Athletic Records
Year: 2007
City: Seattle
Publisher: Sports Press

Citation 2: Document from Website

Create Source

Type of Source: Document From Web site

Bibliography Fields for MLA

Author: Guo-Patterson, Lori
☐ Corporate Author
Name of Web Page: Top Ten Athletes
Name of Web Site: The Sports Journal
Year: 2008
Month: Spring
Day:
Year Accessed: 2008
Month Accessed: June
Day Accessed: 25
URL: http://www.tsj.edu/athletes.topten.htm

Citation 3: Interview

Create Source

Type of Source: Interview

Bibliography Fields for MLA

Interviewee: Devaul, Payton
Title:
Interviewer: Stennis, Kirk
Year: 2008
Month: January
Day: 9

MERGE AND SPLIT CELLS

Merging is the process of combining two or more table cells located in the same row or column into a single cell. Cells can be joined horizontally or vertically. For example, you can merge several cells horizontally to create a table heading that spans several columns. A cell or several selected cells can be divided into multiple cells and columns by using the Split Cells feature.

To merge cells:

TABLE TOOLS/LAYOUT/MERGE/MERGE CELLS

1. Select the cells that are to be merged.
2. Under Table Tools, click the Layout tab. Then click Merge Cells in the Merge group.

To split cells:

TABLE TOOLS/LAYOUT/MERGE/SPLIT CELLS

1. Click in the cell that is to be divided into multiple cells. If multiple cells are to be split, select the cells.
2. Under Table Tools, click the Layout tab. Then click Split Cells in the Merge group.
3. Enter the number of columns or rows that the selected cells are to be split into.

DRILL 2   INSERT COLUMNS AND ROWS

1. Create a two-column, five-row table.
2. Merge the cells in row 1. Key the main heading shown on the next page in 14-point font, uppercase; center and bold it.
3. Center **Course Name** in cell B1. Center **Enrollment Figures** in cell B2. Bold row 2.
4. Select cells B3–B5; split these cells into two columns and three rows.
5. Center and bold **Undergraduates** in cell B3. Center and bold **Graduates** in cell B4.
6. Select cells A2 and A3; merge the cells. In the Alignment group, click the Align Center button to center *Course Name*.
7. Key the table. Adjust column width.
8. Center the table vertically and horizontally on the page.
9. Check and close. (48-drill2)

FINAL SEAT COUNT		
	Enrollment Figures	
Course Name	**Undergraduates**	**Graduates**
English Reading and Composition	12,875	97
Medical Microbiology	782	1,052

To insert citations:

REFERENCES/CITATIONS & BIBLIOGRAPHY/INSERT CITATION

1. Switch to Print Layout View if you are working in a different view.

2. Position the insertion point in the document where the reference is to be inserted.

3. On the References tab, in the Citations & Bibliography group, click the down arrow in the Style box ❶. Select the desired style, e.g., APA, Chicago, MLA, etc. This example will illustrate the MLA style.

4. Click Insert Citation ❷. From the drop-down list, select Add New Source ❸. The Create Source dialog box displays.

5. Click the down arrow in the Type of Source box ❹. Select one of the choices, e.g., book, journal article, etc. The following example illustrates the book type.

6. Key the fields that are displayed from your type of source choice ❺. Click OK.

7. Note the report text when the citation has been created. To edit the citation, click on the citation and then click the down arrow ❻.

8. Select Edit Citation from the drop-down list ❼. The Edit Citation dialog box displays.

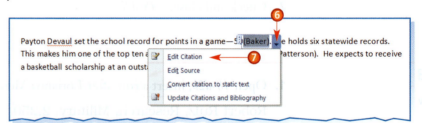

9. Make the needed corrections to the current citation ❽, e.g., add 56 as the page number where a direct quotation was lifted. Click OK ❾.

48-d4

Table with Merge Cells

1. Create a six-column, ten-row table. Merge the cells in rows 1 and 2 as needed.
2. Key the main heading in 14-point font, bold, uppercase.
3. Center the table vertically. Check and close. (*48-d4*)

CANADA GEOGRAPHICAL INFORMATION					
Key Islands		Key Mountains		Key Lakes	
Island	**Sq. Miles**	**Mountain**	**Height**	**Lake**	**Sq. Miles**
Baffin	195,928	Logan	19,524	Superior	31,700
Victoria	83,897	St. Elias	18,008	Huron	23,000
Ellesmere	75,767	Lucania	17,147	Great Bear	12,095
Newfoundland	42,031	Fairweather	15,300	Great Slave	11,030
Banks	27,038	Waddington	13,104	Erie	9,910
Devon	21,331	Robson	12,972	Winnipeg	9,416
Melville	16,274	Columbia	12,294	Ontario	7,540

WORKPLACE SUCCESS

Staying Fit on the Job

© IMAGE100/JUPITERIMAGES

People often say that they do not exercise because they are stuck at the office most of the day and do not have time. Daily exercise is important; even a little exercise is better than no exercise at all. Exercise and movement is not only good for the heart, but also good for your bones and joints.

Here are some suggestions on how you can incorporate exercise into your workday:

- Park farther away—whether you take the bus, train, or car for your morning commute—than you need to. Steps add up and pounds go down.

- Use the stairs instead of the elevator. If the stairs are too much for you, then try a combination of stairs and elevator.

- Get up and walk to deliver a message or document rather than make a phone call or send an e-mail down the hall.

- Take a break each hour to stand, stretch, and walk around.

75-d2
Title Page

1. Create a title page for the report created in *75-d1*; use the Cover Page feature. Choose the Motion style from the Built-In style gallery.
2. Key the following information:
   a. Year: Current
   b. Document Title: Refer to *75-d1*.
   c. Author: **Jason J. Dailey**
   d. Company: **Dailey & Dailey Associates**
   e. Date: Current date
3. Check and close. (*75-d2*)

75-d3
Document with Footnotes

CHECKLIST

1. In the open document, insert the following explanatory footnotes to this administration checklist. Be sure to add a blank line between footnotes.
   a. 18 computers[1]

      [1]All computers are installed with the *Vista* operating system and *Office 2007*.
   b. Door prize—Joey's Steak House Gift Certificate[2]

      [2] Instructors must pick up the gift certificate from Mary Katherine Morgan, Office 208.
2. Check and close. (*75-d3*)

75-d4
Report with Endnotes

WORKSTATION

1. In the open document, insert the same footnotes you keyed in *75-d1* as endnotes. Refer to your *75-d1* solution to guide you in the placement of the endnotes.
2. Tap ENTER four times at the end of the last endnote. Key the reference page appropriately.
3. Check and close. (*75-d4*)

CHANGE ROW HEIGHT AND CENTER TEXT VERTICALLY IN CELL

The height of a row can be increased to draw more attention to a specific row. In Lesson 48, you learned to merge cells in the first row and place the main heading in the row. Greater emphasis can be placed on that row by increasing the row height. You can also increase the row height for an entire table. This will make the table more attractive and easier to read.

The default settings align text at the top of the cell. After increasing row height, you will want to center the text vertically in the cells to enhance the appearance of your table.

To change row height and center text vertically in cell:
TABLE TOOLS/LAYOUT/CELL SIZE/TABLE ROW HEIGHT

1. Click the insertion point in the cell in which the height will be altered.
2. Under Table Tools, click the Layout tab.
3. Increase or decrease the cell height by clicking the spin arrows in the Table Row Height box ❶.
4. Click the appropriate Center alignment button in the Alignment group ❷ to center the text vertically in the cell or row.

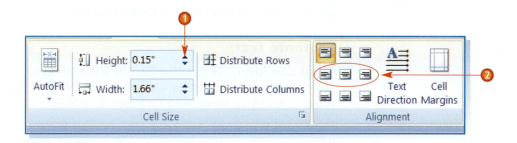

Note: You can also increase row height by dragging the top or bottom border of the row away from the text.

KEYBOARDING PRO DELUXE   See References/Word commands/Lesson 49

DRILL 2	CHANGE ROW HEIGHT	ESTIMATES

1. Double-click the word *Estimates* in the page header. Replace *Estimates* with your name.
2. Replace the words *Prerecorded Document* with **49-drill2**.
3. Under Header & Footer Tools, on the Design tab, in the Close group, click Close Header & Footer.
4. Insert a row above row 1. Merge the cells in the new row 1.

5. Cut the main heading and paste it in the new row 1. Apply Heading 1 style; change spacing before and after paragraph to 0.
6. Change the height of row 1 to .4".
7. Click the Align Center button to center the text vertically in the row. Center the table vertically on the page.
8. Check and close. (*49-drill2*)

TIP

When e-mail Internet addresses appear in a printed report, remove the hyperlink (right-click the hyperlink; then click Remove Hyperlink).

TIP

Keyboarding Pro DELUXE: Insert the data file from the CD in the back of this text.

Position Yourself Properly

Preventing tired wrists and hands is really a matter of taking charge of your posture and computer work environment. Awkward posture while keying and failure to change your keying or sitting position can add to wear and tear on your wrists and hands.

Hand position. Keep your wrists and hands straight. When you work with straight wrists and fingers, the nerves, muscles, and tendons stay relaxed and comfortable. Therefore, they are less likely to develop the strains and pains that are often associated with keying.

Insert file injuries; format like the rest of the report.

6. Do you tilt your neck backward to see the computer screen? (No)

7. Do you take two 5-minute breaks and one 15-minute break in the morning and afternoon? (Yes)

8. Do you vary your activities to break the repetitive motion? (Yes)

9. Do you drink plenty of water to lubricate your joints? (Yes)

For each of your responses that do not match the desired response, please accept the challenge today to correct the undesired practice and avoid computer-related stress injuries.

Footnote text:

[1]Alan Stockton, "Repetitive Strain Injuries Costs Businesses Billions," *The Human Resource Journal*, January 10, 2008, http://www.hsj.com/rsiinjuries.html (accessed October 2, 2009).

[2]Malcolm Winston, *Are Your Hands and Wrists Comfortable When Computing?* (Houston, TX: Jones Insurance Company, 2009), p. 53.

[3]Andres Allen Ortiz, "Ergonomics in Today's Workplace," *Ergonomics News Reporter*, March 2009, p. 46.

References text:

Stockton, Alan. "Repetitive Strain Injuries Costs Businesses Billions." *The Human Resource Journal*. January 10, 2008. http://www.hsj.com/rsiinjuries.html (accessed October 2, 2009).

Winston, Malcolm. *Are Your Hands and Wrists Comfortable When Computing?* Houston, TX: Jones Insurance Company, 2009.

Ortiz, Andres Allen. "Ergonomics in Today's Workplace." *Ergonomics News Reporter*. March 2009, 46-49.

REMOVE TABLE BORDERS

 The Table feature allows text and data to be easily aligned in columns and rows. There may be times when you need to use the Table feature, but may not want the "boxed in" look that tables create. You can remove some or all of the borders to give a table a more "open" look.

To remove table borders:

TABLE TOOLS/DESIGN/TABLE STYLES/NO BORDER

1. Click the table move handle to select the entire table.
2. Click the Borders drop list arrow in the Table Tools Design tab.
3. Click No Border to remove the table gridlines.

⊞	Bottom Border
⊞	Top Border
⊞	Left Border
⊞	Right Border
⊞	No Border
⊞	All Borders
⊞	Outside Borders
⊞	Inside Borders

DRILL 3   **REMOVE TABLE BORDERS**   ESTIMATES

1. In the header, replace the word *Estimates* with your name.
2. Replace the words *Prerecorded Document* with **49-drill3a**.
3. Under Header & Footer Tools, on the Design tab, in the Close group, click Close Header & Footer.
4. Click the Table Move handle to select the entire table.
5. Remove all borders in the table. Center the table vertically on the page and print. (*49-drill3a*)
6. Change the drill number in the header to *49-drill3b*. Click the Table Move handle to select the entire table. From the Borders drop-list menu, choose Inside Borders.
7. Check and close. (*49-drill3b*)

---

1. In the open document, apply the appropriate styles to the title and the side headings. Apply Heading 2 style to the paragraph headings. **Hint:** Select the paragraph heading; then apply the style.

2. Position the insertion point in the blank page at the top of this report and generate a table of contents using the Automatic Table 1.

3. Position the title at about 2", and apply Title style. Tap ENTER above the title to reposition it at about 2".

4. Check to ensure that page numbers are correct in the table of contents and close. (*74-drill1*)

Note: You will not number the preliminary pages in this drill until you learn to insert section breaks in Lesson 77.

UPDATE TABLE OF CONTENTS

A table of contents can be modified after it has been created. Changes can be made manually using standard editing procedures, or *Word* can update the table of contents.

To update a table of contents:

1. At the top of the generated table of contents, click Update Table ❶. The Update Table of Contents dialog box displays.

2. Select Update page numbers only or Update entire table ❷ and click OK.

Update Table of Contents

Word is updating the table of contents. Select one of the following options:

○ Update page numbers only
○ Update entire table

OK   Cancel

1. In the open document, make the following revisions to the report.

   a. Select the *Market Analysis* section on page 1 of the report. Also be sure to select the three paragraphs with paragraph headings. Move this section to page 2 of the report just before the side heading *Developers*. This section is now on page 2 of the report.

   b. In the paragraph heading *Small Businesses*, change *Businesses* to lowercase.

2. Position the insertion point in the table of contents.

3. Update the entire table of contents.

4. Verify that the page numbers were updated and the capitalization error was corrected.

5. Do not edit the memo. Check and close. (*74-drill2*)

DOCUMENT DESIGN

74c

TABLE OF CONTENTS

A table of contents contains a list of headings in a document along with the page number on which each heading appears. The table of contents is easily created using the Table of Contents feature. Study the format of the table of contents that is generated automatically by *Word*.

Position title at about 2"

Table of Contents ← Title style

DOCUMENT DESIGN   DOCUMENT D

Assessment

alphabet 1 Jacob Kazlowski and five experienced rugby players quit the team.

figures 2 E-mail account #82-4 is the account for telephone (714) 555-0108.

double letters 3 Anne will meet with the committee at noon to discuss a new issue.

easy 4 The men may pay my neighbor for the work he did in the cornfield.

| 1 | 2 | 3 | 4 | 5 | 6 | 7 | 8 | 9 | 10 | 11 | 12 | 13 |

SKILL BUILDING

51b Timed Writing
Take two 5' timed writings.

	gwam	3'	5'

Whether any company can succeed depends on how well it fits into the economic system. Success rests on certain key factors that are put in line by a management team that has set goals for the company and has enough good judgment to recognize how best to reach these goals. Because of competition, only the best-organized companies get to the top.

(3' / 5' gwam: 4/2, 9/5, 13/8, 17/10, 21/13, 23/14)

A commercial enterprise is formed for a specific purpose: that purpose is usually to equip others, or consumers, with whatever they cannot equip themselves. Unless there is only one provider, a consumer will search for a company that returns the most value in terms of price; and a relationship with such a company, once set up, can endure for many years.

(3' / 5' gwam: 27/16, 32/19, 36/22, 41/24, 45/27, 47/28)

Thus our system assures that the businesses that manage to survive are those that have been able to combine successfully an excellent product with a low price and the best service—all in a place that is convenient for the buyers. With no intrusion from outside forces, the buyer and the seller benefit both themselves and each other.

(3' / 5' gwam: 51/31, 55/33, 60/36, 64/39, 69/41, 69/42)

3' | 1 | 2 | 3 | 4 |
5' | 1 | 2 | 3 |

APPLICATIONS

51c

Assessment

→ Continue

✓ Check

With *Keyboarding Pro DELUXE*: When you complete a document, proofread it, check the spelling, and preview for placement. When you are completely satisfied, click the Continue button to move to the next document. Click the Check button when you are ready to error-check the test. Review and/or print the document analysis results.

Without *Keyboarding Pro DELUXE*: Key the documents in sequence. When time has been called, proofread all documents again and identify errors.

Report with Title and Reference Page

WARMUP 73a

Key each line, striving for control. Repeat if necessary.

direct reaches
1 June and my brother, Bradly, received advice from junior umpires.
2 My bright brother received minimum reward for serving many years.

adjacent reaches
3 Clio and Trey were sad that very few voters were there last week.
4 Western attire was very popular at the massive auction last week.

double letters
5 Tommie Bennett will go to a meeting in Dallas tomorrow afternoon.
6 Lee will meet Joanne at the swimming pool after accounting class.

| 1 | 2 | 3 | 4 | 5 | 6 | 7 | 8 | 9 | 10 | 11 | 12 | 13 |

FUNCTION REVIEW

73b

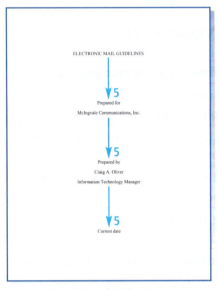

Traditional Title Page

COVER PAGE

INSERT/PAGES/COVER PAGE

Reports often include a cover or title page that identifies the report to the reader. As the name implies, the cover page is positioned on top of the report and provides an attractive cover for the report.

Word offers the Cover Page feature, which inserts a fully formatted cover page. You may choose from a variety of attractively formatted covers. Study the illustration of a cover page created using the Cover Page feature below. Remember, this only illustrates one specific style; you have many others from which to choose.

A traditional title page is illustrated at the left if a more traditional appearance is desired.

To create a cover page:

1. From the Insert tab, on the Pages group, click Cover Page ❶. A gallery of cover pages displays.

2. Click the scroll arrows to determine the desired style ❷.

3. Select the desired style ❸. The cover page opens as a *Word* document.

4. Select *Type the document title* ❹ and key the report title. Repeat for all other items located in the template. **Note:** A blank page follows the cover page for keying the report.

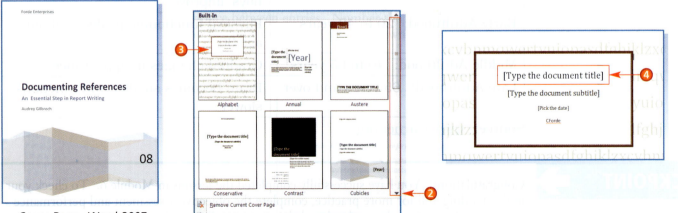

Cover Page, *Word 2007*

SUBJECT/VERB AGREEMENT

USE A SINGULAR VERB

1. With a **singular subject**. (The singular forms of *to be* include: am, is, was. Common errors with *to be* are: you was, we was, they was.)

> She monitors employee morale.
> You are a very energetic worker.
> A split keyboard is in great demand.

2. With most **indefinite pronouns**: *another, anybody, anything, everything, each, either, neither, one, everyone, anyone, nobody*.

> Each of the candidates has raised a considerable amount of money.
> Everyone is eager to read the author's newest novel.
> Neither of the boys is able to attend.

3. With singular subjects joined by *or/nor, either/or, neither/nor*.

> Neither your grammar nor punctuation is correct.
> Either Jody or Jan has your favorite CD.
> John or Connie has volunteered to chaperone the field trip.

4. With a **collective noun** (*family, choir, herd, faculty, jury, committee*) that acts as one unit.

> The jury has reached a decision.
> The council is in an emergency session.
> But:
> The faculty have their assignments. (Each has his/her own assignments.)

5. With words or phrases that express **periods of time**, **weights**, **measurements**, or **amounts of money**.

> Fifteen dollars is what he earned.
> Two-thirds of the money has been submitted to the treasurer.
> One hundred pounds is too much.

USE A PLURAL VERB

6. With a **plural subject**.

> The students sell computer supplies for their annual fundraiser.
> They are among the top-ranked teams in the nation.

7. With **compound (two or more) subjects** joined by *and*.

> Headaches and backaches are common worker complaints.
> Hard work and determination were two qualities listed by the references.

8. With *some, all, most, none, several, few, both, many*, and *any* when they refer to more than one of the items.

> All of my friends have seen the movie.
> Some of the teams have won two or more games.

APPLICATIONS

72-d1
Unbound Report

1. Key the model unbound report on pp. 323–324. Position the title at approximately 2" from the top of the page.

2. Format the headings as follows:
   Title: Title style
   Side headings: Heading 1 style
   Paragraph headings: Heading 2 style

3. Insert a page number at the top right; suppress the page number on the first page.

4. Apply the Keep with next feature to any side headings left alone at the bottom of the first page.

5. Check and close. (*72-d1*)

72-d2
Leftbound Report

1. Open *72-d1*.

2. Change the margins to convert this unbound report to a leftbound report.

3. Check and close. (*72-d2*)

WORKPLACE SUCCESS

What Is Your Listening Grade?

© DIGITAL VISION / GETTY IMAGES

Isn't it interesting that students are not required to complete a course in listening when 80 percent of our time each day is spent listening? To perform well in organizations, a keen listening skill is essential. Evaluate yourself on the following areas and start today working on a listening improvement plan in those areas. Search for excellent listening quizzes to assist you.

BODY LANGUAGE:

Do you … sit with your arms closed?
stand with your hand on the door as you listen to someone?
doodle while listening or play with a pen or some other object?
look at your watch while others are talking?
continue checking your e-mail while listening to someone on the phone or someone face to face?

MINDSET

Do you … think you already know what the speaker has to say?
think the speaker is wasting your time?
tune out anything boring? or too long?
disregard anything being said if you do not agree with it?
judge the speaker before he/she begins to speak?

RESPONSES TO THE SPEAKER

Do you … finish the speaker's sentence because you know what he/she is going to say?
think about what you will say while the speaker is talking?
interrupt the speaker so you can start talking sooner?
look ridiculous sometimes when you respond in a manner that tells others that you were not listening?

DRILL 1

SUBJECT-VERB AGREEMENT

SUBJECTVERB1

1. Review the rules and examples on the previous page.
2. Follow the specific directions provided in the data file.
3. Preview, check, and print. (*subjectverb-drill1*)

DRILL 2

SUBJECT-VERB AGREEMENT

SUBJECTVERB2

1. Follow the specific directions provided in the data file.
2. Preview, check, and print. (*subjectverb-drill2*)

DRILL 3

SUBJECT/VERB AND CAPITALIZATION

1. Key the ten sentences at the right, choosing the correct verb and applying the correct capitalization.
2. Preview, check, and print. (*subjectverb-drill3*)

1. both of the curies (was/were) nobel prize winners.
2. each of the directors in the sales department (has/have) given us approval.
3. mr. and mrs. thomas funderburk, jr. (was/were) married on november 23, 1936.
4. my sister and her college roommates (plan/plans) to tour london and paris this summer.
5. our new information manager (suggest/suggests) the following salutation when using an attention line: ladies and gentlemen.
6. the body language expert (place/places) his hand on his cheek as he says, "touch your hand to your chin."
7. the japanese child (enjoy/enjoys) the american food her hosts (serve/serves) her.
8. all of the candidates (was/were) invited to the debate at boston college.
9. the final exam (cover/covers) chapters 1-5.
10. turn south onto interstate 20; then take exit 56 to bossier city.

DRILL 4

EDITING SKILLS

1. Key the paragraphs.
2. Correct all errors in grammar and capitalization.
3. Preview, check, and close. (*editing-drill4*)

This past week I visited the facilities of the magnolia conference center in isle of palms, south carolina, as you requested. bob bremmerton, group manager, was my host for the visit.

magnolia offers many advantages for our leadership training conference. The prices are reasonable; the facilities is excellent; the location is suitable. In addition to the beachfront location, tennis and golf packages are part of the group price.

5. Rushing the speaker causes the speaker to think the listener's time is being wasted.
6. Interrupting the speaker is rude and does not enhance listening.
7. Showing interest in something other than the conversation and allowing any distractions to obtain the listener's attention result in poor listening.

Summary

Understanding that listening is not easy is a first step in becoming a better listener. Identifying individual habits that do not enhance effective listening is the next step. The first session of the Listening Skills Training Program will focus on poor listening habits.

Editing Essentials

LEARNING OUTCOMES

- Build keying skill.
- Build editing skills.
- Edit letters.
- Edit memos and e-mail.
- Edit tables and reports.

LESSON 52 · Editing Essentials

WARMUP 52a

Key each line, striving for control. Repeat if desired.

alphabet	1	Jim Daley gave us, in that box, a prize he won for his quick car.
figures	2	At 7 a.m., I open Rooms 18, 29, and 30; I lock Rooms 4, 5, and 6.
adjacent reaches	3	As Louis said, few questioned the points asserted by the porters.
easy	4	Did he vow to fight for the right to work as the Orlando auditor?

| 1 | 2 | 3 | 4 | 5 | 6 | 7 | 8 | 9 | 10 | 11 | 12 | 13 |

SKILL BUILDING

52b Textbook Keying

1. Key each line once, concentrating on good keying techniques; tap ENTER twice after each 3-line group.
2. Repeat the drill if time permits.

	5	James Carswell plans to visit Austin and New Orleans in December.
caps	6	Will Peter and Betsy go with Mark when he goes to Alaska in June?
	7	John Kenny wrote the book Innovation and Timing—Keys to Success.
	8	Jeanne arranges meeting room space in Massey Hall for committees.
double letters	9	Russell will attend to the bookkeeping issues tomorrow afternoon.
	10	Todd offered a free book with all assessment tools Lynette sells.
	11	Jane, a neighbor and a proficient auditor, may amend their audit.
balanced hand	12	Blanche and a neighbor may make an ornament for an antique chair.
	13	Claudia may visit the big island when they go to Orlando with us.

Barriers to Effective Listening

In the initial phase of study of customer service operations, Fleming Communications, Inc. determined that listening is the communication task that our customer representatives spend almost 50 percent of their time doing. This report is the first in a series of reports. The purpose of this report is to explain a major barrier to effective listening and to present poor listening habits.

Side heading / Heading 1

Issues in Listening

Contrary to common belief, listening is not an easy task. Two issues to consider are the rate that listeners can process words and barriers to listening.

Rate. Studies show that listeners can recognize words at a rate of approximately five times faster than the rate at which speakers can speak. A very important question to consider is at what rate does the mind process these words? With the mind processing information at over 1,000 words per minute, the listener is challenged to listen actively (Jackson and Jensen, 2008).

Paragraph heading / Heading 2

Listening barriers. Listeners are also confronted with various other barriers to effective listening. These might include assumptions already made about the topic, about the speaker, about what the speaker will say, or about the specific setting. All of these assumptions will lead the listener to tune out what the speaker is actually saying. Another barrier to listening may be simply fatigue—the listener is too tired or perhaps too hungry or too busy to listen. Distractions often influence the listener's ability to be an active listener. These annoyances may be loud noises near the speaker or a room that is too cold or too warm (Simpson and Lee, 2009).

Poor Listening Habits

The poor listening habits presented below by Williams (2008) are quite common among listeners. Being aware of the most common poor listening habits will aid in overcoming them.

1. Pretending to listen is easy to do. By nodding, saying yes, and looking directly at the speaker, listeners can fake listening.
2. On the other hand, not looking at the speaker also results in poor listening as facial expressions and gestures are not communicated to the listener.
3. A listener's commitment to recording detailed notes often results in poor listening or overlistening.
4. Judgments by the listener about the speaker or the topic result in poor listening.

52c Timed Writings

1. Key a 1' timed writing on each paragraph, working for speed.
2. Key a 3' timed writing, working for control.

A

all letters

Time is a perplexing commodity. Frequently, we do not have   12 | 4 | 45
adequate time to do the things required; yet we all have exactly the   26 | 9 | 50
same amount of time. The way we utilize time differs greatly.   38 | 13 | 54

Seldom do we focus just on the quantity of time available because   13 | 17 | 58
it is beyond our control. Rather we tend to concentrate on the critical   28 | 22 | 63
things that must be accomplished in the time that is available.   40 | 26 | 67

Keep in mind that our efforts should be devoted primarily to   12 | 30 | 71
enhancing the quality of the activities that occupy our time. Time, the   27 | 35 | 76
most precious thing an individual spends, can never be regained once   41 | 40 | 81
it has been lost.   44 | 41 | 82

1' | 1 | 2 | 3 | 4 | 5 | 6 | 7 | 8 | 9 | 10 | 11 | 12 | 13
3' | 1 | 2 | 3 | 4

NEW FUNCTIONS

52d

SYMBOLS AND SPECIAL CHARACTERS

INSERT/SYMBOLS/SYMBOL

Symbols and special characters that are not on your keyboard can be inserted using the Symbol command. Different types of symbols can be inserted depending on the font selected. Some of the symbols are scientific or mathematical and are generally located on the Symbols font. Other symbols are decorative and are generally located on the Wingdings fonts.

To insert symbols:

1. Position the insertion point where the symbol is to be inserted.

2. Click the Symbols command ❶ to display a gallery of symbols ❷. If the symbol you want to insert is not shown on the Gallery, click More Symbols to display the Symbols dialog box.

3. Click on the Symbols tab to insert a symbol if it is not already selected ❸.

4. Select a Symbol font for mathematical or scientific symbols or a Wingdings font ❹ for decorative symbols.

5. Select the desired symbol ❺; then click Insert ❻ and close.

KEYBOARDING PRO DELUXE   See References/Word commands/Lesson 52

REPORT FORMAT—UNBOUND AND LEFTBOUND REPORTS

Lesson 72 reviews reports created with the *Word 2007* defaults. Study the full-page illustrations of a two-page unbound report shown on pages 323–324.

72e

Barriers to Effective Listening

In the initial phase of study of customer service operations, Fleming Communications, Inc. determined that listening is the communication task that our customer representatives spend almost 50 percent of their time doing. This report is the first in a series of reports. The purpose of this report is to explain a major barrier to effective listening and to present poor listening habits.

Issues in Listening

Contrary to common belief, listening is not an easy task. Two issues to consider are the rate that listeners can process words and barriers to listening.

Rate. Studies show that listeners can recognize words at a rate of approximately five times faster than the rate at which speakers can speak. A very important question to consider is at what rate does the mind process these words? With the mind processing information at over 1,000 words per minute, the listener is challenged to listen actively (Jackson and Jensen, 2008).

Listening barriers. Listeners are also confronted with various other barriers to effective listening. These might include assumptions already made about the topic, about the speaker, about what the speaker will say, or about the specific setting. All of these assumptions will lead the listener to tune out what the speaker is actually saying. Another barrier to listening may be simply fatigue—the listener is too tired or perhaps too hungry or too busy to listen. Distractions often influence the listener's ability to be an active listener. These annoyances may be loud noises near the speaker or a room that is too cold or too warm (Simpson and Lee, 2009).

Poor Listening Habits

The poor listening habits presented below by Williams (2008) are quite common among listeners. Being aware of the most common poor listening habits will aid in overcoming them.

1. Pretending to listen is easy to do. By nodding, saying yes, and looking directly at the speaker, listeners can fake listening.
2. On the other hand, not looking at the speaker also results in poor listening as facial expressions and gestures are not communicated to the listener.
3. A listener's commitment to recording detailed notes often results in poor listening or overlistening.
4. Judgments by the listener about the speaker or the topic result in poor listening.

2

5. Rushing the speaker causes the speaker to think the listener's time is being wasted.
6. Interrupting the speaker is rude and does not enhance listening.
7. Showing interest in something other than the conversation and allowing any distractions to obtain the listener's attention result in poor listening.

Summary

Understanding that listening is not easy is a first step in becoming a better listener. Identifying individual habits that do not enhance effective listening is the next step. The first session of the Listening Skills Training Program will focus on poor listening habits.

Margins: Use default side, top, and bottom margins in an unbound report. In a leftbound report, set the left margin at 1.5", allowing ½" binding.

Font size: Use the 11-point default font size.

Spacing: Use the default 1.15 line spacing for all reports.

Page numbers: Insert page numbers at the top right. Suppress the page number so that it does not print on the first page of the report. The number is automatically positioned ½" from the top edge of the paper.

Headings: Headings should reflect a hierarchy, with the title being the most important. To create this hierarchy, follow these guidelines:

Title: Tap ENTER to position the title about 2" from the top edge of the paper. Apply the Title style. Capitalize all main words.

Side heading: Key at the left margin; apply the Heading 1 style. Capitalize all main words. Use Keep with next feature when headings appear close to the bottom of the page to keep the side headings with at least two lines of the paragraph.

Paragraph heading: Key at the left margin. Capitalize the first word and follow the heading with a period. Apply the Heading 2 style.

Single lines: Avoid single lines at the top or bottom of page (called widow/orphan lines).

Enumerated items: Use default alignment for bulleted or numbered items. Tap ENTER once after each item.

SPECIAL CHARACTERS

INSERT/SYMBOLS/SYMBOL

Special characters are inserted from the Symbols dialog box. Examples of special characters include:

Em dash —   En dash –   Copyright ©   Trademark ™

1. Repeat steps 1 and 2 for inserting symbols. (Click Symbol command and then More Symbols on Gallery to display the Symbols dialog box.)
2. Select the Special Characters tab **1**.
3. Select the special character desired **2**.
4. Click Insert **3** and then close.

1. Key the following lines as a numbered list; do not include the text in parentheses.
2. Insert the symbols and special characters shown.
3. Check and close. *(52-drill1)*

Special Characters
1. Parker House—Best Dining (em dash)
2. Pages 13–25 (en dash)
3. July 20 (nonbreaking space)
4. Brighten your day with a smile and … (ellipsis)
5. Revise §2, ¶4. (Section 2, Paragraph 4)

Symbols
6. ☺ Have a nice day.
7. ⇨ Room 253
8. ✎ Sign here.
9. The size is 2 acres±.
10. The cost is 6€. (6 Euro)

OFFICE CLIPBOARD

HOME/CLIPBOARD/DIALOG BOX LAUNCHER

1 Clipboard   In Lesson 27, you worked with the commands from the Clipboard group. In this lesson, you will work with the Clipboard. Up to 24 segments of text or graphics that have been cut or copied can be stored on the Clipboard and then pasted individually or as a group into a document.

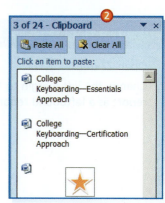

To use the Clipboard:

1. On the Home tab, click the Dialog Box Launcher **1** to display the Clipboard **2**. Each item that you cut or copy will display on the task pane.
2. To paste an item into a document **3**, click the item you want to paste and then click the down arrow and select Paste.

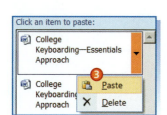

1. In the open document, apply the Keep with next feature to the side heading left alone at the bottom of the first page.

2. Verify that Widow/Orphan control is on (✓ appears in box).

3. Apply Title style to the title of the report.

4. Apply Heading 1 style to the two side headings.

5. Insert page numbers at the top right.

6. Suppress the page number on the first page.

7. Check that no side heading appears alone at the bottom of the page.

8. Check and close. (*72-drill1*)

MARGINS

PAGE LAYOUT/PAGE SETUP/MARGINS

Leftbound reports require a left margin of 1.5" to allow for the binding on the left. If you need to review setting margins, study the instructions below and complete Drill 2.

To change the margins:

1. From the Page Layout tab, in the Page Setup group, click Margins ❶. A gallery of margin settings display.

2. Click Custom Margins. The Page Setup dialog displays.

3. From the Margins tab, click the up or down arrows to increase or decrease the default settings ❷. **Note:** In the dialog box at the right, the left margin has been changed to 1.5".

4. Apply margins to the Whole document unless directed otherwise ❸.

5. Click OK. The margins you have just set will be saved in the margins gallery as the Last Custom Setting.

1. Open *72-drill1*.

2. Change the left margin to 1.5" to format this unbound report as a leftbound report.

3. Check and close. (*72-drill2*)

PASTE OPTIONS BUTTON

 The Paste Options button is a "smart tag" that appears when you paste an item from the Clipboard. It enables you to select the format you prefer to use.

To use the Paste option:

1. Point the mouse at the Paste Options button when it appears. Then select the down arrow **1**.

2. Select the desired option **2**. To format the text using the same format as the new document, click Match Destination Formatting. To format the text using the same format as the document from which the text was copied, click Keep Source Formatting.

- ○ Keep Source Formatting
- ◉ Match Destination Formatting **2**
- ○ Keep Text Only
- Set Default Paste...

DRILL 2   CLIPBOARD   EFFECTIVE PRES

1. In the open document, display formatting marks and the Clipboard.

2. Select the heading *Opening* and the paragraph that follows, and cut them.

3. Select the heading *Presentation Body* and the paragraph that follows, and cut them.

4. Select the heading *Closing* and the paragraph that follows, and cut them.

5. Place the insertion point on the line below the paragraph following the heading *Planning and Preparing Presentations*. Paste all items on the Clipboard at once.

6. Select the first sentence in the paragraph with the heading *Follow-up Activities* and cut it. Move the insertion point to the end of the paragraph.

7. On the Clipboard, click in the sentence you just cut and click the down arrow and select Paste. On the Paste Options button, choose Keep Source Formatting.

8. Add or delete extra spaces before or after sentences as necessary. Clear the Clipboard.

9. Preview and adjust line spacing if necessary.

10. Check and close. (*52-drill2*)

DRAG-AND-DROP EDITING

Another way to edit text is to use the mouse. With **drag and drop**, you can move or copy text using the mouse. To move copy, you must first select the text, then hold down the left mouse button, and drag the text to the desired location. The mouse pointer displays a rectangle indicating that copy is being moved. Release the mouse button to "drop" the text into the desired location.

Follow a similar procedure to copy (or duplicate) text. Hold down the left mouse button and the CTRL key, and drag the text to the desired location. A plus sign indicates the text is being copied.

DRILL 3   DRAG AND DROP   EFFECTIVE PRES

1. In the open document, use drag-and-drop editing to make the same changes you made in *52-drill2*.

2. Check and close. (*52-drill3*)

PAGE NUMBERS

INSERT/HEADER & FOOTER/PAGE NUMBER

 In Module 5, you learned to number pages in reports at the top right and to suppress the page number on the first page. If you need to review inserting page numbers at the top right, study the instructions below and complete Drill 1.

To insert page numbers:

1. On the Insert tab, in the Header & Footer group, click the down arrow on the Page Number button ①.

2. Click Top of Page ②. A gallery of page number styles displays.

3. Click the down scroll arrow to browse the various styles ③. Click Plain Number 3 from the gallery ④. The page number displays in the header position at the top right.

To remove the page number from the first page:

DESIGN/OPTIONS/DIFFERENT FIRST PAGE

On the Design tab, under Header & Footer Tools, in the Options group, click Different First Page ⑤. The page number does not display on the first page.

LINE AND PAGE BREAKS

HOME/PARAGRAPH/DIALOG BOX LAUNCHER

Widow/Orphan control prevents a single line of a paragraph from printing at the bottom or top of a page and is automatically turned on. **Keep with next** prevents a page break from occurring between two paragraphs. Use this feature to keep a side heading from being left alone at the bottom of a page. The Keep with next feature is turned on automatically when styles are applied to a side heading.

To use Keep with next:

1. Select the side heading and the paragraph that follows.

2. On the Home tab, in the Paragraph group, click the Paragraph Dialog Box Launcher.

3. From the Line and Page Breaks tab ①, select Keep with next ②.

4. Click OK. The side heading moves to the next page.

FIND AND REPLACE

HOME/EDITING/FIND AND REPLACE

① **Find**—locates text, formatting, footnotes, graphics, page breaks, and other items within a document. When text is located, it is highlighted.

② **Replace**—finds text, formatting, or other items within a document and replaces them with different text, formatting, or other items. Replaced text will have the same capitalization that the original text had.

To find text:

1. Click Find **①** and key the text you wish to locate in the Find what box **③**.
2. Click Find Next **④** to find the next occurrence of the text.

To replace text:

1. On the Home tab, click Replace **②** in the Editing group.
2. Key the text you wish to locate in the Find what box **③**.
3. Key the replacement text in the Replace with box **⑤**.
4. Click Find Next **④** to find the next occurrence of the text. Click Replace **⑥** to replace one occurrence or click Replace All **⑦** to replace all occurrences of the text.

DRILL 4   **FIND AND REPLACE**   RESTRUCTURE

1. In the open document, find the word *restructuring* the first place it appears.
2. Find the second and third occurrences of *restructuring*.
3. Find *Workgroup A* and replace with *Team A*.

4. Note that the letter is formatted using the traditional *Word 2003* style, but the letter format is inconsistent. Edit the document so that the letter is formatted correctly as a block-style letter.
5. Check and close. (*52-drill4*)

72c Timed Writing

Key two 3' timings for control.

all letters

What characterizes the life of an entrepreneur? Those who have never owned their own businesses may think owning a business means being your own boss, setting your own hours, and making a lot of money. Those who have run their own businesses are quick to report that owning a business may be exciting and challenging, but it also requires hard work, long hours, and personal sacrifice. A good idea is not the only prerequisite for a successful business. A little luck even helps.

Many small businesses are operated as businesses from the initial stages. However, some small businesses that turn out to be successful are just hobbies in the early stages. The entrepreneur has a job and uses the income from it to support the hobby. When the hobby begins to require more and more time, the entrepreneur has to choose between the job and the hobby. The decision is usually based on finances. If enough money can be made from the hobby or can be obtained from another source, the hobby is turned into a business.

	3'	5'
	4	2	23
	8	5	46
	13	8	48
	17	10	51
	21	13	54
	26	15	56
	30	18	59
	32	19	60
	36	22	63
	41	24	65
	45	27	68
	49	29	70
	53	32	73
	57	34	75
	62	37	78
	66	39	80
	66	41	82

3' | 1 | 2 | 3 | 4
5' | 1 | 2 | 3

FUNCTION REVIEW

72d

STYLES

HOME/STYLES/QUICK STYLES

The Styles feature enables you to apply a group of formats automatically to a document. A new *Word* document opens with approximately 18 styles attached to it. In Module 5 you used styles to format report headings. Apply the Title style to the report title and the Heading 1 style to the side headings. If you need to review applying styles, study the instructions below and complete Drill 1.

To apply paragraph styles:

1. Select the text to which you want to apply a style.
2. On the Home tab, in the Styles group ❶, choose a desired style shown in the Quick Styles gallery ❷.
3. If the desired style does not display, click the More button ❸ to expand the Quick Styles gallery.
4. Select the desired style from the expanded list of styles ❹.

AaBbCcD	AaBbC(	AaBbCc	AaBbCcI
¶ Normal	Heading 1	Heading 2	Heading 3
AaBbCcL	AaBbCcL	AaBbCcD	AaBbCcD
Heading 4	Emphasis	Strong	¶ Block Text
AaB	AaBbCcI	AaBbCcD	AABBCCDL
Title	Subtitle	Subtle Emp...	Intense Em...
AaBbCcD	AaBbCcD	AABBCCDL	AABBCCDL
Quote	Intense Qu...	Subtle Refe...	Intense Ref...
AABBCCDL	AaBbCcD		
Book Title	¶ List Parag...		

CUSTOMIZE QUICK ACCESS TOOLBAR

In Lesson 27, you learned to use the Quick Access toolbar as a shortcut for saving documents and for the Undo and Redo commands. The Quick Access toolbar can be customized to add other functions that you use frequently.

To customize the Quick Access toolbar:

1. On the Quick Access toolbar, click the down arrow to display the Customize Quick Access Toolbar dialog box.

2. Click the desired command that you wish to add to the Quick Access toolbar. Note that the default commands Save, Undo, and Redo are already on the toolbar.

3. If you clicked New, Open, Quick Print, Print Preview, and Spelling and Grammar to add them to the toolbar, it would appear as shown below. Note you have to add one command at a time to the toolbar.

DRILL 5   CUSTOMIZE QUICK ACCESS TOOLBAR

1. Click the down arrow on the right side of the Quick Access toolbar.

2. Select New, Open, Quick Print, Print Preview, and Spelling & Grammar one at a time from the list of options available.

3. Check to see that the commands have been added to your Quick Access toolbar.

4. Open *52-drill2* using the Quick Access toolbar.

5. Key the paragraph shown below after the last paragraph in the document.

6. On the line below the last line on the document, key the drill name, *52-drill5*.

7. Use the Quick Access toolbar to check spelling and grammar, preview, and print the document.

8. Check and close. (*52-drill5*)

Follow-up activities vary depending on the type of presentation and the audience to whom the presentation is delivered. A presentation made within a company or to clients of a company is more likely to have follow-up activities other than questions and discussion than one made to an external audience. The follow-up activities required for an external audience such as members of a professional association are generally limited to questions and discussion.

Report Mastery

LEARNING OUTCOMES

- Format reports with cover page, table of contents, and reference page.
- Insert footnotes and endnotes.
- Prepare report using citations and bibliography features.
- Insert page numbers in report with preliminary pages.
- Format traditional report using *Word 2003* defaults.
- Improve keying speed and accuracy.

LESSON 72 — Review Report Formats

WARMUP 72a

Key each line, striving for control. Repeat if desired.

alphabet 1 Jamie quickly apologized for submitting the complex reviews late.

figures 2 Those 1,863 bars cost $27.05 each for a total cost of $50,394.15.

easy 3 I may go to the zoo or to see you if I do not go to the new pool.

easy 4 The men may be busy, but they go to the lake to work on the dock.

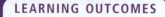
| 1 | 2 | 3 | 4 | 5 | 6 | 7 | 8 | 9 | 10 | 11 | 12 | 13 |

SKILL BUILDING

72b Textbook Keying
1. Key each line once, concentrating on good keying techniques. Tap ENTER twice after each 3-line group.
2. Repeat the drill if time permits.

b 5 be bib bribe bubble baby baboon bobble cobble bonbon bogie bobbin

n 6 no nun new none noon napkin nanny ninth nonsense nothing national

b/n 7 Benny and Nate have been told to begin with bends before running.

j 8 jet joy join joke jelly jacket jackel jewel rejoice judge jonquil

f 9 of fast fief fanfare fearful fifteen flora forefoot format buffer

j/f 10 Join Jon Fondren and his staff for a fun-filled five-day journey.

y 11 yes you your yield yokes yellow yesterday phyloid reply navy away

t 12 twin total trinket triplet title ticket token meant impact tattle

y/t 13 Tom, Timothy, and Tony are triplets; Yvonne and Yvette are twins.

| 1 | 2 | 3 | 4 | 5 | 6 | 7 | 8 | 9 | 10 | 11 | 12 | 13 |

THESAURUS

REVIEW/PROOFING/THESAURUS

The Thesaurus is a tool that enables you to look up words and replace them with synonyms, antonyms, or related words. Many words have several different meanings. It is important to select the appropriate meaning before replacing a word.

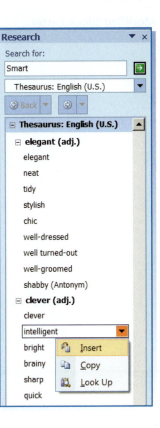

TIP

An alternative way to use the Thesaurus is to position the insertion point in a word and right-click the mouse. Select Synonyms and then the desired word or Thesaurus to display the Research task pane.

To use the Thesaurus:

1. Position the insertion point in the word you wish to replace.

2. In the Proofing group on the Review tab, click Thesaurus to display the Research task pane.

3. If more than one meaning displays, select the appropriate meaning. Note that synonyms are listed first and then antonyms for each meaning.

4. Hold the mouse over the desired synonym or antonym, click the down arrow, and then click Insert.

DRILL 6 — THESAURUS

1. Key the following words on separate lines:

   generous   data   smart   profit

2. Replace *generous* and *data* with synonyms.

3. Replace *smart* (meaning clever) with a synonym.

4. Key **smart** again (meaning elegant) on the next line and replace it with an antonym.

5. Replace *profit* with an antonym.

6. Check and close. (*52-drill6*)

COMMUNICATION ✳

52e
Applying Communication Knowledge

TEAM WRITING

1. Print a copy of the open document and use proofreaders' marks to edit it. Note that this is a very rough draft that is packed with 25 errors.

2. Correct all keying, spelling, grammar, capitalization, number usage, and word usage errors.

3. At about 2", add the title: **STRATEGIES FOR TEAM WRITING**; center it, use Cambria 14-point font, and apply bold.

4. For side headings, use Cambria 12-point font and apply bold.

5. Change the bullets on the ten steps to numbering.

6. Key your name below the last line of the document; right-align it.

7. Insert the date and time below your name using the format of your choice.

8. Use Full Screen Reading view to proofread the document.

9. Check the document. (*52e*)

71-d2

Modified Block Letter

1. Key the modified block letter with mixed punctuation using *Word 2003* style set in 12-point Times New Roman font. The letter is from **Michael Truong, President**.

2. Add the mailing notation **CONFIDENTIAL** and the subject line **Invitation to Honor Society**. Send a copy to **Dr. Zimiko Tayyar**. Provide the appropriate complimentary closing and other notations. Center vertically on the page.

3. Generate an envelope and add it to the file.

4. Continue to the next document. (*71-d2*)

words

January 30, 20-- | Miss Shea Patterson | 43 University Drive | Lacombe, LA	10
70445-2536 | Dear Shea	18

Congratulations! Because of your outstanding academic record and	32
leadership potential in your teaching profession, you have been selected	47
for membership in Pi Omega Pi, the honorary society for undergraduate	61
business education majors. Being selected for membership in Pi Omega	75
Pi is the highest honor that a student of business education can achieve.	89

A formal initiation ceremony will be held on Tuesday, February 13, at	103
4 p.m. in Room 252 of the T. S. McKinney Building. Please complete	117
the enclosed form and return it to me by Friday, February 9. A one-time	132
initiation fee of $40 is also due by the initiation.	142

Shea, I am delighted that you have been selected as a Pi Omega Pi member	156
and look forward to your initiation on February 13.	168

71-d3

Block Letter

1. Key the block letter with open punctuation. Supply necessary letter parts; center vertically.

2. Check the test and close it. (*71-d3*)

Ms. Audra Meaux \| 268 Marsalis Lane \| Hot Springs, AR 71913-1004

Our professional staff finalized the Technology Task Force report requesting approval of four major technology enhancements for K-14. A draft copy is enclosed for your review. Please make any corrections and return the draft to us within one week so that the final report can be prepared.

The report will be sent special delivery to each school board member no later than Monday. This deadline must be followed if the item is to appear on the November 15 agenda. If we do not hear from you within one week, we will assume that you accept the draft as submitted.

Audra, thank you for your willingness to serve on the Technology Task Force.

Ryan Messamore, NTA President

CHECKPOINT ➡

Congratulations! You have successfully completed the lessons in Module 11. To check your understanding and for more practice, complete the objective assessment and performance assessment located on the textbook website at www.collegekeyboarding.com.

52-d1

Edit Document

PUNCTUALITY

WORKPLACE SUCCESS

1. Select the first paragraph below the title and apply Times New Roman, 12-point font; change line spacing to double (2.0); indent paragraphs.

2. Remove extra space after the paragraph. Then use the Format Painter to copy that format to the next two paragraphs.

3. Center the title and apply Arial, 14-point bold font.

4. In the third sentence of the first paragraph, *Punctuality-Not Performance-Determines Outcome!*, change the hyphens to em dashes; then apply italic format. Delete the quotation marks.

5. In the sentence that follows, replace the commas around *and by all accounts one who was unbeatable and assured to repeat the title* with em dashes.

6. Move paragraph 3 between paragraphs 1 and 2.

7. Find *weak* and replace it with *lame*.

8. Add the following below the last paragraph: **©2008 by Student's Name**. Right-align this information.

9. Select the last sentence of the document and change the text color to red.

10. Center the page vertically.

11. Use Full Screen Reading view to proofread the document.

12. Check and close. (*52-d1*)

WORKPLACE SUCCESS

Building Credibility

© PHOTODISC BLUE/GETTY IMAGES

Very competent young people who have limited or no work experience often find it difficult to build credibility with managers and experienced employees. To bridge the credibility gap, they need to focus on four key factors:

1. **Expertise**—demonstrate in a confident manner the knowledge and skills they have acquired.

2. **Trust**—earn the respect and trust of managers and other employees by being honest and open. You must be believable. Use empathy and build rapport with colleagues.

3. **Consistency**—performing in a predictable, consistent manner gives managers and employees a feeling of comfort with the individual.

4. **Commitment**—managers and employees want to work with people who do what they say they will do and when they say they will do it. They trust people who understand the importance of punctuality and who will persevere until the job is done properly.

1. Key the two-page memo to **All Employees**, from **Allen Payne, Risk Manager**. The subject is **Reporting On-the-Job Injuries**. Use the current date. Create a header for the second page.

2. Assume the following documents are attached: Compensation Claim Form (DWC-1) & Notice of Potential Eligibility, Employee's Account of Injury, Report of First Aid, and Medical Authorization.

3. Continue to the next document. (*71-d1*)

As an employee of Franklin Industries, you are entitled to workers' compensation benefits if you sustain a work-related injury or illness. Copies of the forms that need to be filed are included in this packet.

If your injury is a reportable claim, you must complete the required forms in order to have your claim evaluated to receive benefits. If your injury requires continued treatments, prescription medications, or if you were unable to work at least one full day after the date of injury, it is considered to be a reportable claim. The completed forms must be returned to the Risk Management department within 48 hours of your injury. Signing these forms is not admission of liability, but enables us to investigate and pay benefits, if applicable.

Any delay in reporting a work-related injury/illness or in the filing of the claim forms may jeopardize your workers' compensation benefits or delay the processing of your claim. Upon receipt of the completed claim form, you will receive an acknowledgment copy of the form and a benefits letter. If you are in need of medical attention, you must obtain authorization for treatment from your manager and receive treatment at one of the following designated occupational medical facilities:

Please put these phone numbers on separate line.

Bon Ami Medical Group, Department of Occupational & Environmental Health Services

3980 North Euclid Avenue, Suite 250, Fullerton, CA 92835-4757 (Open 24 hrs, 7 days a week) 714-555-0111

St. Simon Industrial Medicine Center

5002 Orangewood Avenue, Garden Grove, CA 92841-3462 (Open 24 hrs, 7 days a week) 714-555-0190

First Response Medical Center

987 Orangethorpe Avenue, Suite 110, La Palma, CA 90623-0598 (Open 24 hrs, 7 days a week) 714-555-0120

If you have an Employee's Request for Pre-Designation of Physician form on file with the District office prior to your injury/illness, you may use your pre-designated physician for treatment of this work-related injury/illness. However, in the event of a life-threatening emergency, you will be directed to the closest emergency facility available. If you utilize your personal physician, you may wish to verify that the correct information is on file with this office. Otherwise, any unauthorized visits or charges incurred may ultimately be your responsibility.

The attached Authorization for the Release of Medical/Employment Records must be signed and returned to this office as it is required by your treating physician before medical information can be released to our workers' compensation administrator.

Please call me at 714-555-0131 or send an e-mail to apayne@franklin.com if you have questions or concerns regarding these forms, request for medical treatment, or any additional questions related to your injury. Your cooperation in promptly returning these forms is greatly appreciated.

LESSON 53

Edit Letters

WARMUP 53a

Key each line, striving for control. Repeat if desired.

alphabet	1	Jakob will save the money required for your next big cash prizes.
fig/sym	2	I saw Vera buy 13 7/8 yards of #240 cotton denim at $6.96 a yard.
3rd/4th	3	Zone 12 is impassable; quickly rope it off. Did you wax Zone 90?
easy	4	Did an auditor handle the formal audit of the firms for a profit?

| 1 | 2 | 3 | 4 | 5 | 6 | 7 | 8 | 9 | 10 | 11 | 12 | 13 |

SKILL BUILDING

53b Textbook Keying
1. Key the drill, concentrating on good keying techniques; tap ENTER twice after each 4-line group.
2. Repeat the drill if time permits.

1/2 fingers

5 Did bedlam erupt when they arrived after my speech ended quickly?
6 Joyce bought me a new bright red jacket for my birthday tomorrow.
7 Did Rebecca make the needlepoint cushion for the club room couch?
8 Much to the concern of our teacher, I did my homework on the bus.

3/4 fingers

9 Zam saw six small poodle puppies playing in the meadow last week.
10 Paxton saw a lazy lizard on the old wooden oar at Pawley's Plaza.
11 Zam Velasquez sells squid in six stores near the pool at the zoo.
12 Paul quizzed a shop owner about a patchwork quilt we saw in Waco.

all fingers

13 Jarvis Zackery played quarterback with six teams before retiring.
14 Jan Weitzel made grave errors, but he quickly fixed the problems.
15 Quinn Zack wrote just six poems and a short story before leaving.
16 Maxey Czajka will quit swimming because he performed very poorly.

53c Timed Writing
1. Key a 1' timed writing on each paragraph, working for speed.
2. Key a 3' timed writing, working for control.

all letters

| | gwam | 1' | 3' |

Have you ever thought about how you shake hands with 11 4 51
people? One of the early impressions you make on other individuals 24 8 56
is the way you greet them. Do you extend your hand immediately 37 12 60
as a friendly gesture, or do you defer until the other person takes 51 17 65
the initiative? 54 18 66

When you prepare for an interview or an important meeting, 12 22 70
it is very important for you to analyze the manner in which you 25 26 74
shake hands. You can be sure that the individual in charge will 37 30 78
examine the way in which you shake hands. Most people make a 50 35 82
quick judgment about you that can be either positive or negative. 63 39 87
To make that early impression a very favorable one, always use a 76 43 91
firm, professional handshake that is neither limp nor bone crushing. 90 48 95

| 1' | 1 | 2 | 3 | 4 | 5 | 6 | 7 | 8 | 9 | 10 | 11 | 12 | 13 |
| 3' | | 1 | | 2 | | 3 | | 4 | | | | | |

alphabet	1	Liz Page quickly found six major errors in the book she reviewed.
figures	2	Chapters 7, 18, 19, and 23 had 65 pages; the others had 40 pages.
space bar	3	Ty saw us as we got in a new car to go to the zoo; he did not go.
easy	4	Is the problem with the ancient chapel or the chapel at the lake?

| 1 | 2 | 3 | 4 | 5 | 6 | 7 | 8 | 9 | 10 | 11 | 12 | 13 |

SKILL BUILDING

71b Timed Writing
1. Key one 3' timed writing.
2. Key one 5' timed writing.

Average

	gwam	3'	5'
Eating is often the solution to any and all problems for many	4	3	35
people. Our society has been known to use food as a tranquilizer.	9	5	38
Many times if a child expresses unhappiness, someone will try	13	8	40
soothing the child with a cookie.	15	9	41
Food cravings may mean that a person is hungry. But for	20	12	44
emotional eaters, it may mean that they need something else. For	24	14	46
some people, it may be a sign of boredom, frustration, or loneliness.	29	17	49
It is important to understand the reason for eating and then try	33	20	52
confronting those issues.	35	21	53
You can control your eating by changing the way you do things.	39	24	56
Work on a hobby during commercials rather than going to get	43	26	58
something to eat. Special events do not need to be centered around	48	29	61
food. Celebrate a special occasion by going dancing rather than	52	31	63
going out for dinner.	54	32	64

| 3' | 1 | 2 | 3 | 4 |
| 5' | 1 | 2 | 3 |

APPLICATIONS

71c

Assessment

→ Continue

✓ Check

With *Keyboarding Pro DELUXE*: When you complete a document, proofread it, check the spelling, and preview for placement. When you are completely satisfied, click the Continue button to move to the next document. Click the Check button when you are ready to error-check the test. Review and/or print the document analysis results.

Without *Keyboarding Pro DELUXE*: Key the documents in sequence. When time has been called, proofread all documents again and identify errors.

COMMUNICATION ✳

53d
Composing and Editing

1. Compose a paragraph with at least two or three complete sentences to finish the three statements listed below.
2. Double-space the answers and indent each paragraph.
3. Print the paragraphs; use proofreaders' marks to edit the paragraphs carefully to improve your writing. Make the corrections.
4. Check and close. (*53d*)

TIP
Remember to proofread and preview each document as a SOP. You will not be reminded to do this.

1. **Currently, I live in** (name and describe the city, town, or area in which you live—indicate if it is a large city, small town, or rural area and provide other descriptive information about the locale).

2. **When friends from other locations come to visit me, the places I enjoy taking them are** (describe two or three places in your area that would be interesting to show to visitors).

3. **If I could pick one place in the United States to visit, it would be** (describe one place you would like to visit and explain why you would like to go there and what you would like to see and do while you are there).

APPLICATIONS ◖

53-d1
Letter from Rough Draft

1. Use *Word 2003* style, Times New Roman font, and *Word 2003* default margins; key the letter below making all corrections noted.
2. Use the current date, block style, and open punctuation; add an enclosure notation and center the page.
3. Check and close. (*53-d1*)

Ms. Karen Bradley
228 High Ridge Road
Irmo, SC 29063-4187

Dear Ms. Bradley

Thank you for giving Todd Travel associates the opportunity to plan and arrange an exciting vacation for you and your family. We are certain that this trip will be a memorable one for all of you ~~will remember~~. The Greek Isles are a ~~fun~~ delightful destination and you have selected outstanding pre- and post-cruise tours in Athens and Istanbul.

All of the travel arrangements have been confirmed stet, and a detailed itinerary and cruise brochure are enclosed. Please carefully review the itinerary to ensure ~~make certain~~ that we have followed all of your instructions correctly. If any changes need to be made, please call us ~~soon~~ within ten days.

Your travel documents will be sent to you 2 weeks prior to departure. Please let us know if we can provide additional information for you.

Sincerely

Jane R. Todd
President

70-d2

Personal Business Letter

1. Open the template you created in Drill 1, *70-drill1.dotx*. Key the letter in modified block style with mixed punctuation. Add a complimentary close; use your name in the signature line. (Reference initials are not required.)

2. Check and close. (*70-d2*)

January 5, 20-- | Mr. Hans Schliem | Chalet Landhaus Inn | 879 Highway 81 | New Glarus, WI 53574-2481 | Dear Mr. Schliem

This letter confirms that the Blackhawk High School class of 1980 will hold its 25-year class reunion at your hotel on June 20.

Please set aside a block of 12 rooms, each having two queen-size beds for the evening of June 20. You will hold these rooms at a rate of $100 until May 15.

We also confirmed these arrangements this morning:

- Reception will be set up in the patio area for approximately 60 guests to begin at 4 p.m.
- Our group will have sole access to the patio for the remainder of the evening.
- Dinner will be served on the patio at 7 p.m.

Your dinner suggestions sound excellent. I believe many in our class would enjoy the Swiss Cookout for $25 per person. It is my understanding that in order for you to prepare this dinner, we must confirm by June 10 that at least 40 persons will choose this entrée. If we do not have the required number, we will choose from a limited menu to include Filet Landhaus, Cordon Bleu, or Grilled Salmon.

Thank you very much, Mr. Schliem, for your help with the planning of this event. Also, you can plan on about 25 extra persons for the breakfast buffet on Sunday morning. You can reach me at 608-555-0169 if you have any questions.

70-d3

Create Personal Letterhead

Keyboarding Pro DELUXE: Exit and use *Word 2007* for this document and *70-d4*. Create your own personal letterhead. Follow the directions in *70-drill 1*. Save your letterhead as a template on a flash drive with a meaningful filename.

70-d4

Personal Letter

1. Key the letter below to your instructor in block letter style with open punctuation. Use your letterhead template created in *70-d3* and save as a *Word* document.

2. Check and close. (*70-d4*)

Additional templates are available on the Microsoft Office Online website. The New Document dialog box contains a link to the Microsoft Office Online templates. Follow the steps below to download a memo template onto your computer:

Move the enumerated items to the left margin.

1. Click the Office button, and then click New.
2. In the Templates pane under Microsoft Office Online, choose Memos. Memo templates from the Microsoft Office Online website display.
3. Click the memo template you want to use; then click Download. The template displays as a new document on your screen.
4. Click the Office button and then click Save As. In the left pane, click Trusted Templates, and in the Save the type box, choose Word Template.
5. Once the template is downloaded, it is saved on your computer. Access it by clicking the Office button, New, and then My templates. To use it, click the memo template and Create New.

53-d2

Letter

BRADY

1. Make the following edits in the open document:
   - Revise the letter so that it will be formatted correctly as a modified block letter; indent paragraphs; remove extra space after paragraph in the inside address and closing lines.
   - Search for the name *Debauche*; each time it appears, replace it with *DeBauche*.
   - Use the Thesaurus to find a synonym for *statistics*. Replace *statistics* with the second synonym listed.
   - Make the following correction in the first sentence of paragraph 2:

     Brad Swinton, our new vice president of marketing, indicated. . .
   - Cut the following sentence from paragraph 2:

     I hope this will not be a problem for you.
   - Center the page vertically.
2. Check and close. (*53-d2*)

53-d3

Letter

1. Open *53-d2* and reformat it as a block style letter.
2. Check and close. (*53-d3*)

53-d4

Letter

1. Prepare another letter for Ms. DeBauche using the same address, salutation, and closing lines that were used in *53-d3*. Note that this letter does not contain an enclosure.
2. Key the letter below in block style format with open punctuation using *Word 2007* defaults.
3. Decrease the indent on the numbered items to position them at the left margin.
4. Search for *section*, and replace it each time it appears with *phase*.
5. Use the Thesaurus to find a synonym for *prolific*. Select the first option.
6. Center the page vertically.
7. Check and close. (*53-d4*)

October 11, 20--

Our team completed its preliminary review of your proposal today. Overall, we are very pleased with the approach you have taken.

Please plan to provide the following information at our meeting on October 18:

1. Please provide a more detailed pricing plan. We would like to have each section of the project priced separately specifying hourly rate and expenses rather than the one total sum quoted.

2. How many hours do you estimate will be necessary to complete each section of the project? When would your firm be able to begin the project?

We look forward to a very prolific meeting on October 18.

70c

PERSONAL BUSINESS LETTER

Personal letters of a business nature are formatted on plain paper or personal letterhead. Personal business letters are appropriate when sending a letter of application, a follow-up letter after an interview, or whenever a degree of formality is desired. Personal business letters should not be prepared on a company's letterhead stationery. A personal business letter must include the individual's home address; it may also include a telephone number, e-mail address, or Web address. All other letter parts are the same as a business letter, including use of reference initials.

If personal business letterhead is not available, the sender's home address is positioned two lines immediately above the dateline. An example of the sender's address is shown below for both letterhead stationery and plain paper.

890 West 65 Street
Chicago, IL 53678-9832
Current date

Mr. Fred Barrington
3820 Hunting Hill Lane
McLean, VA 22102-3853

Dear Mr. Barrington

Personal letter on plain paper

Jennifer Morganhouse

890 West 65 Street, Chicago, IL 53678-9832, Jennifer.Morganhouse@Morganhouse.net

Current date

Mr. Fred Barrington
3820 Hunting Hill Lane
McLean, VA 22102-3853

Dear Mr. Barrington

Personal letterhead

APPLICATIONS

70-d1

Personal Business Letter

1. Open the template you created in Drill 1, *70-drill1.dotx*. Key the personal business letter in block style with open punctuation. Position the date two lines below the letterhead; add the appropriate salutation and your reference initials; notice that a transcript is being enclosed.

2. Check and close. (*70-d1*)

Ms. Assyia Farhang | First United Bank | 7285 Valley View | El Centro, CA 92243-1720

Thank you for interviewing me for the Administrative Assistant position that is available at First United Bank. I enjoyed meeting with you and your staff and learning more about the position.

I appreciate your taking the time to talk with me and to learn more about my qualifications and interest in the position. My three years of experience as an office assistant, coupled with the knowledge I have acquired in my studies as a Computer Information Systems major at Alpha College, have prepared me for this position. A copy of my transcript is enclosed.

I look forward to hearing from you. Please contact me if you need any additional information to consider my application.

Sincerely | Jennifer Morganhouse

LESSON 54 EDIT MEMOS AND E-MAIL

WARMUP 54a

Key each line, striving for control. Repeat if desired.

1 Sandra quickly gave the boy a major prize for his excellent work.
2 Invoice #758 for $294 is due 2/14/03 and #315 for $67 is due now.
3 Todd and Ann meet with a committee at noon to discuss all issues.
4 He may sign both of the forms for the amendment to the endowment.

| 1 | 2 | 3 | 4 | 5 | 6 | 7 | 8 | 9 | 10 | 11 | 12 | 13 |

SKILL BUILDING

54b Textbook Keying
1. Key the drill, concentrating on good keying techniques.
2. Repeat the drill if time permits.

5 Lou kicked the gray umbrella Fred gave me and broke it in pieces.
6 Cecilia jumped in the pool, kicked the side, and fractured a toe.
7 Bunny browsed in the library while June served the healthy lunch.

8 Teresa was there to operate the projection equipment on Saturday.
9 Walker sang three hymns, and Louisa taught everyone how to polka.
10 Guy and Teresa were going to buy ice cream after the polo match.

COMMUNICATION

54c
Composing and Editing

1. Use the information below to compose and send an e-mail to your instructor.
2. Use the subject line **Extra Credit Assignment**.
3. Read the second bulleted item carefully. Select one of the three topics, key the title of the topic on the first line of a new document, and apply Title style. Check and close. (*54c-attach*)
4. Proofread and edit the e-mail carefully before sending it.
5. Print a copy of your e-mail.

- Thank your instructor for providing the opportunity to complete an extra-credit assignment.

- Indicate which of the three topics available (E-Mail Etiquette, First Impressions Count, and Developing a Professional Attitude) you selected. Add a sentence indicating why you selected that topic for the three-page paper.

- Indicate that an electronic copy of your paper is attached to this e-mail and that a printed version has been placed in the appropriate assignment folder. Attach the file *54c-attach* to your e-mail.

INSERT HORIZONTAL LINE

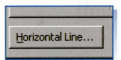

PAGE LAYOUT/PAGE BACKGROUND/PAGE BORDERS

A horizontal line is a type of graphic. *Word 2007* has a gallery of lines from which to choose.

To insert a horizontal line:

1. From the Page Layout tab, in Page Background group, click the Page Borders command.
2. On the Page Border tab, click Horizontal Line. Choose an appropriate style of line.

DRILL 1   CREATE LETTERHEAD TEMPLATE

Keyboarding Pro DELUXE users: Your document will be saved as a *Word* file rather than as a template.

1. In a blank document, create a personal letterhead for Jennifer Morganhouse. This will be saved as a template.
2. Key her name, tap ENTER twice, and key her address and other information on the next line. Tap ENTER twice to position the insertion point for the dateline.
3. Turn on Show Hide (¶), select the first ¶, and insert a horizontal line of your choice.
4. With ¶ displayed, format her name in Palatino, 16 point, left-aligned font; format the address in 10-point, right-aligned Calibri font. Delete the extra space above and below the horizontal line.

5. Check that the insertion point is positioned for the dateline. Select it and verify that the font is Calibri 11 point.
6. Check and close. (*70-drill1.dotx*)

Jennifer Morganhouse

¶ (Insert the horizontal line here)

890 West 65 Street, Chicago, IL 53678-9832, Jennifer.Morganhouse@Morganhouse.net

Jennifer Morganhouse

890 West 65 Street, Chicago, IL 53678-9832, Jennifer.Morganhouse@Morganhouse.net

---

DRILL 2   USE TEMPLATE

1. Open the morganhouse template (*70-drill1.dotx*) from your flash drive; remember to look for the extension *.dotx.* Your insertion point should be positioned about 2.3". Key the two paragraphs from the Workplace Success feature below. Use modified block style with open punctuation; add the closing lines.

Current date | Mr. Fred Barrington | 3820 Hunting Hill Lane | McLean, VA 22102-3853 | Dear Mr. Barrington

2. In the Save as type box, click the down arrow and choose *Word* Document. You do not want to save over the template.
3. Check and close. (*70-drill2*)

WORKPLACE SUCCESS

Letters

© DIGITAL VISION / GETTY IMAGES

Letters should be carefully planned. List all the points that need to be covered and make sure they relate to the main purpose of the letter. Letters need to be accurate and written in a timely manner. Business letters often have financial implications, so check to make sure that all stated facts are accurate.

Letters are a more formal means of communicating than are e-mails, text messages, or memos. Letters should be formal and factual, and at the same time be reader friendly. If the letter is part of a package, limit the cover letter to one page and relegate technical details to enclosed documents. Avoid language that is specific to gender, race, or religion in all business correspondence. For example, use words such as workforce rather than manpower and chairperson rather than chairman.

INTERNET ACTIVITY

54d

WORKPLACE SUCCESS

1. Use a search engine such as Google to find five articles that would help you as a relatively new employee learn more about building credibility. Use *building credibility* as keywords. Avoid articles that focus on building credibility for a business, brand, or product.

2. Select two articles that you found to be most helpful. Then do the following:
   - Key the name of the first article, the name of the author, and the Web address (URL). Apply left align and bold.
   - Write a paragraph pointing out at least two things in the article that made you believe it was helpful.
   - Write a second paragraph explaining why the article itself had credibility—why it was believable.

3. Follow the same procedure for the second article.

4. Proofread and edit your work carefully.

5. Check and close. (*54d*)

APPLICATIONS

54-d1

Memo

1. Key the memo below.

2. Position the heading at about 2".

3. Move paragraph 2 so that it will be the last paragraph.

4. Search for *NatureDesigns* and replace it with *NatureLink* each time it appears.

5. Use the Thesaurus to find another option for *wide-ranging* in the third sentence; select the first option.

6. Change the date in the memo from *November 10* to two weeks from today.

7. Check and close. (*54-d1*)

To: Richard M. Taylor | From: Dianne Gibson | Date: Current | Subject: Trail Design

Last week, Madilyn signed the contract for the trail design for Phase 1 of our Georgetown property. NatureDesigns was selected as the contractor. This firm was chosen because of its wide-ranging experience in selecting interpretative sites, designing trails, and installing boardwalks to protect wetlands and environmentally sensitive areas.

Please let me know if you plan to participate in the initial meeting with NatureDesigns.

The first onsite meeting is scheduled for November 10. We plan to meet at the main entrance at 10:30 a.m. to tour the property and review the procedures that NatureDesigns plans to use in designing the trails near the red cockaded woodpecker (RCW) habitat. Since RCW is an endangered species, we want to balance the desire of ecotourists to observe these birds and the need to protect them.

xx | c Bruce Diamond

Correspondence Review and Letter Template

WARMUP 70a

Key each line, striving for control. Repeat if desired.

alphabet 1 Maxwell paid just a quarter for a very big cookie at the new zoo.

fig/sym 2 Lunches for the 14 customers cost $77.37 ($67.28 × 15% = $10.09).

3rd/4th fingers 3 Quinn will oppose an opinion of Max about a jazzy pop show we saw.

easy 4 Angie, the neighbor, paid to go to the island and fish for smelt.

| 1 | 2 | 3 | 4 | 5 | 6 | 7 | 8 | 9 | 10 | 11 | 12 | 13 |

REVIEW FUNCTION

70b

SAVE AS TEMPLATE

MS OFFICE BUTTON/SAVE AS/WORD TEMPLATE

 A template is a set of predefined styles for a particular type of document. The purpose of a template is to reuse it whenever it is needed. *Word 2007* contains preformatted templates for letters, fax cover sheets, and other documents that anyone can use. Additional templates are also available on the Microsoft website. However, because documents are unique to organizations, companies and individuals often create their own templates. In this lesson, you will create your own personal letterhead and then save it as a template that you can use whenever you send a personal letter.

By default, templates are saved to the Trusted Templates folder within the program. In a classroom environment, your instructor may direct you to save templates you create to a flash drive or another location.

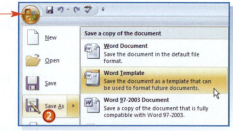

To save a document as a template:

1. Click the Office Button ❶ and then Save As ❷.

2. At the right side of the pane, select Word Template. The Save As dialog box displays.

3. *Save to flash drive*: Select My Computer and browse to the flash drive.

    Save to hard drive: By default, the software will save to the Trusted Templates folder ❸.

4. In the File name box, key an appropriate template name; for example, *my letterhead*. The extension *.dotx* is assigned automatically.

5. In the Save as type box, note that *Word Template* has been selected for you ❹. Click Save.

To use the template:

Saved to a flash drive: Click Open and browse to your flash drive. Click the down arrow next to Files of type and change to All Files. Look for the file with a .dotx extension.

Saved to hard drive: Click the Office button and select New. From the Templates pane (left pane), choose My Templates; browse to locate the desired template. Click OK.

TIP

Remember to insert a nonbreaking hyphen:

Insert tab/Symbol; then click More Symbols, and click the Special Characters tab and select nonbreaking hyphen.

Shortcut: CTRL + SHIFT + -

1. Key the memo below. Make all of the corrections noted by proofreaders' marks.
2. Send the memo to **David C. Kline** from **Carolyn M. Pastides**; use the current date and the subject **Economic Development Project**.
3. Search for *Department of Commerce* and replace it with *Board of Economic Development* each time it appears.
4. Check and close. (*54-d2*)

The meeting with ^several^ representatives of the department of commerce and the representatives ^of the Company^ being recruited to move ~~here~~ ^to this area^ provided a very interesting perspective on the changing approach of recruiting small, knowledge-based companies rather than large manufacturing operations. The company being recruited is a recent spin- ^nonbreaking hyphen^ off ~~form~~ ^of^ a research project at a major university. Its stage of development could best be described as developmental.

We signed non-disclosure forms, and the Department of Commerce provided us with ^a set of^ financials ~~provided~~ ^prepared^ by the company's auditor. However, the audit was not signed, and the management letter ~~was not~~ ^nor was^ included. I have requested that the CFO ^chief financial officer^ bring to the meeting tomorrow a complete copy of the audit and proformas for two years forward. My guess is that the audit will contain a "going concern" clause. The company currently has a stockholders' deficit of approximately $15,000,000 ^million^.

Unless ^additional^ financing is obtained, it is unlikely that the company can continue to operate. I ^also^ requested copies of contracts ~~are~~ ^or^ agreements that would support the revenue projections in the proformas.

The technology developed by the company is exciting, and the upside potential of the joint venture appears to be very good. ~~Documentation of prototype orders was provided.~~ Because of the risk involved in a company at this early stage of development, it is imperative that we do ~~a lot of~~ ^extensive^ due diligence before investing in this company.

69-d1
Traditional Block Letter

1. In a new document, change the style set to *Word 2003* style. Key the letter on the previous page in traditional block style with open punctuation. Change the font to Times New Roman.
2. Check and close. (*69-d1*)

69-d2
Traditional Modified Block Letter

1. Key the letter as a traditional modified block letter in 12-point Times New Roman font. Set a tab at 3.25" as usual. Use open punctuation.
2. Add a copy notation to the instructor named in the letter. Add other necessary letter parts. Check and close. (*69-d2*)

Dr. Ellen Gedney | Chairperson, Business Department | Harbor Community College | 9031 Bayside Drive | Fremont, CA 94538-3115

Sharon Schmidt was employed as an instructor in the Business Division from October 7, 1998, until her resignation, December 9, 2008. Ms. Schmidt taught word processing, office administration, and desktop publishing. She is highly knowledgeable in the computer field, and more importantly, she is gifted as an instructor.

The students' evaluations proved her abilities in the classroom; almost without exception, she received a superior rating in every category. Ms. Schmidt presented the curriculum to enable the least capable student to succeed, gain self-confidence, and demonstrate proficiency. Moreover, she displayed compassion for all her students, caring for their intellectual growth along with their psychological well-being.

Sharon demonstrates the professional ethics of an outstanding employee: punctuality, efficiency, competency, and sincerity. We regret her decision to relocate out of state because of family obligations. We wish her continued success at your college; she will surely be an asset to your school.

Laura Meathe | Vice President, Instruction

69-d3
Traditional Block Style

1. Key the letter in *67-d2* on page 301 using the *Word 2003* style. Change the font to Times New Roman. Make these changes:
   - Letter style: Modified block; omit the mailing notation.
   - Punctuation style: Open
   - Letter address: **Mr. Charles McCormick | 8762 Race Street | Cincinnati, OH 45297-9874.**
   - **Re: Order No. S4379**
2. Send a copy to **Steven Farrar**.
3. Check and close. (*69-d3*)

LESSON 55   Edit Tables and Reports

WARMUP 55a

Key each line, striving for control. Repeat if desired.

1 When Jorg moves away, quickly place five dozen gloves in the box.
2 Flight 372 leaves at 10:46 a.m. and arrives in Omaha at 9:58 p.m.
3 I obtain unusual services from a number of celebrated decorators.
4 She may sign an authentic name and title to amend this endowment.

| 1 | 2 | 3 | 4 | 5 | 6 | 7 | 8 | 9 | 10 | 11 | 12 | 13 |

SKILL BUILDING

55b   Textbook Keying

1. Key the drill, concentrating on good keying techniques; tap ENTER twice after each 2-line group.
2. Repeat the drill if time permits.

adjacent reaches
5 Teresa's choice is to use a free option that is quite easy to do.
6 Sergio was trying to avoid errors, but he still made quite a few.

direct reaches
7 Frederick lost my large, bright red golf umbrella on a sunny day.
8 Debra bought too much junk, but she found the prices to be great.

first row
9 Zack and Max became exercise advocates, but they ate many pizzas.
10 Max Mizel verbalized his excessive love for throwing curve balls.

home row
11 Ada Hall's class was at a lake in Dallas; Kala Klass had a salad.
12 Sally's glass flask was full of salt; Sal also saw a glass flask.

third row
13 Trey, a poet, wrote the quote for Peter; we were there with Trey.
14 Poppy hurt her eye at their pool; were you, Troy, or Peter there?

55c   Timed Writing
Key two 3' timed writings. Strive for control.

all letters

gwam   3'

	3'	

Reports are one of the best means by which busy executives   4 | 44
at any level of a business can keep well informed. The pertinent   8 | 48
data in reports can be used to solve a wide variety of problems   13 | 53
that arise, make any changes that may be required, analyze   17 | 57
results, and make precise, timely decisions.   20 | 60

The quality of the plans and decisions made on the basis of   24 | 64
the information found in reports depends in large measure on how   28 | 68
well the reports are produced. A good report is a thorough and   32 | 72
objective summary of all pertinent facts and figures. If reports   37 | 77
are not well produced, the firm will surely suffer.   40 | 80

3' | 1   2   3   4 |

Tap ENTER 6 times

Quality Collies

5775 Arondale Road, Bronx, NY 10466-8906

January 15, 20-- ↓4

Mr. Dean Nguyen
4221 Elma Lane
Bronx, NY 10466-1234

Dear Mr. Nguyen ↓2

Exquisite Quadruplet Puppies ↓2

Thank you for your interest in our dogs. As you know, there are two varieties of collies. The rough-coated collie and the smooth-coated collie both make excellent family pets. ↓2

Our kennel, Quality Collies, regularly has rough-coated collies available. We generally have smooth-coated puppies available only in the spring. ↓2

Enclosed is a photograph of our most recent litter. You will agree that these quadruplets are adorable. Contact our office 718-555-0198 Monday through Saturday to arrange a time for you to visit our kennel and see these exquisite puppies for yourself. ↓2

Sincerely ↓4

Sally Moss, Owner ↓2

xx ↓2

Enclosure

Traditional Letter Using Word 2003 Style Set

1. Key the report double spaced; apply Times New Roman 12-point font. Remove space after paragraphs.

2. Use approximately a 2" top margin; add the title: **FOUNDATION PROPERTY**; apply Arial 14-point bold format. Add side headings; apply Arial 14-point bold format.

3. Number the pages at the top right and suppress the page number on the first page.

4. Make the edits shown in the table. In addition, apply Arial 14-point format to the table title and Arial 12-point format to the column heads; add a row at the bottom of the table. Key in the three columns: **Total**, **$34,815,000**, and **100%**.

5. Proofread carefully and make corrections.

6. Check and close. (*55-d1*)

The Foundation owns both out-of-state and in-state property. However, the bulk of the property is located within South Carolina. Properties are acquired either by gift or purchase.

Insert side heading:
Out-of-State Property

Virtually all of the out-of-state property is acquired by gift. Occasionally, a parcel of undeveloped or developed land will be offered to the Foundation at a bargain price. The Foundation then sells the property as soon as it is feasible to do so and retains the profit. The total value of the out-of-state property is $2,145,000.

Insert side heading:
South Carolina Property

Some of the in-state property is purchased by the Foundation for future use. Other property is donated to the Foundation. Donated property may be retained for future use or sold. In-state property is divided into three regions—Coastal, Midlands, and Other. The following table shows the distribution of the property by region:

Property Location and Value *Bold*		
South Carolina Regions *Bold and Center headings*	Value of Property in~~Region~~	~~Percentage of~~ Total Property
Coastal Region *Set right*	$18,325,000	53%
Midlands Region *align tab*	12,650,000	*Center align* 36%
Other Regions—In-State *at 3.5"*	3,840,000	11%

The total value of the in-state property is $34,815,000. More than half of the property is located in the Coastal region. The next largest concentration is in the Midlands region. The property values are based on the appraisal price at the time of the acquisition. Most real estate professionals estimate that the current value is more than double the value shown in the table.

1. From the Home tab, in the Styles group, click Change Styles.
2. Choose Style Set ❶. Click *Word 2003* ❷. The line spacing is now 1.0; the space after paragraph is 0; the font size is 12.

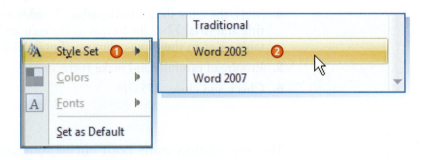

DOCUMENT DESIGN

FORMAT A TRADITIONAL LETTER

Because industry does not update software automatically when new versions become available, you will also want to know how to format a business letter using *Word 2003*. The parts of a letter are the same whether the letter is formatted in *Word 2003* style or using the defaults of *Word 2007*. Since the line spacing and spacing after paragraphs are different in the *Word 2003* style, the number of times you tap ENTER between letter parts will differ.

To format a traditional letter:

Style Changes: Apply the *Word 2003* style. Change the font to Times New Roman.

Dateline: Key the date at approximately 2" (tap ENTER six times) or center the page vertically.

Letter address: Three blank lines below the dateline (tap ENTER four times); no extra space is added between lines.

Salutation: Tap ENTER twice below the letter address.

Body: Tap ENTER twice below the salutation and begin the body. Single-space the body of the letter. Tap ENTER twice between paragraphs.

Complimentary close: Tap ENTER twice below the body.

Writer's name and title: Tap ENTER four times after the complimentary closing.

Reference initials, Enclosures, Copy notation: Tap ENTER twice between each.

55-d2

Report with Table

 LEPPARD

1. In the open document, change format to leftbound report.
2. Position title about 2" from the top of the page and apply Title style to both the first page and the Reference Page.
3. Use Heading 1 format for all side headings. Capitalize main words in all side headings.
4. Insert the following table where noted on the first page:

Capacity	Babcock	Leppard
Number of beds	184	385
Hospital utilization average daily census	94	326
Medicare utilization average daily census	53	104
Full-time equivalent	364	1,682

5. Format the title of Table 1 using Heading 2 and center it.
6. Use Table Design, Light List - Accent 1. Center column headings.
7. Insert a column to the left of *Babcock*; use the column heading *Juk*, and insert the following data in the column:

    165
    136
    60
    615

8. Replace each of the citations (example: Miguel, 2008, 6) in the report with the following footnotes:

    Isabella Miguel, *Hospital Growth Analysis* (Atlanta, 2008), p. 6.

    Andrew Glenn, *Metro Analysis Feasibility Study—Leppard Outpatient Center* (Atlanta, 2008), p. 8.

    Mark Gibson, "Outpatient Costs in the Southeast," *Health Care News*, January 2008, p. 36.

9. Use the Keep with Next feature to ensure that headings remain with the text that follows them and that the table is not separated from its title or divided on two pages.
10. Number the pages using a plain number at the top right side. Do not show the number on the first page.
11. Use Spelling and Grammar to check the document.
12. Proofread using Full Screen Reading view.
13. Check and close. (*55-d2*)

alphabet	1	Mixon plays great jazz with a quintet at a club five days a week.
fig/sym	2	Errors were found on page 389 (line #17) and page 460 (line #25).
direct reach	3	Brad and Cec had a great lunch and much fun with many youngsters.
easy	4	The city may pay for half of the maps, and Jake may pay for half.

| 1 | 2 | 3 | 4 | 5 | 6 | 7 | 8 | 9 | 10 | 11 | 12 | 13 |

SKILL BUILDING

69b Timed Writing

1. Key a 1' timing; work to increase speed.
2. Key a 3' timing.

	gwam	1'	3'
Technical, human, and conceptual skills are three types of	13	4	35
skills all supervisors are expected to have. The skills are quite	26	9	40
different, and they vary in importance depending on the level of the	40	13	44
supervisor in an organization. Technical skills refer to knowing how	54	18	49
to do the job. Human skills relate to working with people and getting	68	23	54
them to work as a team. Conceptual skills refer to the ability to	81	27	58
see the big picture as well as how all the parts fit together.	93	31	62

1' | 1 | 2 | 3 | 4 | 5 | 6 | 7 | 8 | 9 | 10 | 11 | 12 | 13 |
3' | 1 | 2 | 3 | 4 |

REVIEW FUNCTION

69c

CHANGE TO WORD 2003 STYLE SET

HOME/STYLES/CHANGE STYLES/STYLE SET/WORD 2003

You have been using the *Word 2007* defaults as you key documents. The default formats are stored in the *Normal* style set. The quickest and easiest way to key a letter in traditional format using *Word 2007* is to change to the *Word 2003* style set. The table below compares the two style sets. The biggest difference is the space after a paragraph or hard return. Extra spacing is not added automatically after a hard return.

Word 2007 Normal Style	Word 2003 Style
Calibri font	Calibri font
11-point font size	12-point font size
1.15 line spacing	1.0 line spacing
10-point spacing after paragraph	0 spacing after paragraph

Edit Documents

WARMUP 56a

Key each line, striving for control. Repeat if desired.

alphabet 1 Jacki might analyze the data by answering five complex questions.

figures 2 Memo 67 asks if the report on Bill 35-48 is due the 19th or 20th.

double letters 3 Aaron took accounting lessons at a community college last summer.

easy 4 Hand Bob a bit of cocoa, a pan of cod, an apricot, and six clams.

| 1 | 2 | 3 | 4 | 5 | 6 | 7 | 8 | 9 | 10 | 11 | 12 | 13 |

SKILL BUILDING

56b Textbook Keying

1. Key the drill, concentrating on good keying techniques; tap ENTER twice after each 2-line group.
2. Repeat the drill if time permits.

First row

5 Zam name bank man came exam cave band comb six mine vent back van

6 Zack came back excited; Max made a banner for a vacant zinc mine.

Home row

7 sad lass lag had gag laggard fax hulk salad sales flask glass has

8 Dallas Klass had a jello salad; Ada asked for a large salad also.

Third row

9 were pot toy pew wept you quit power quip peer tower or rope wire

10 Terry wrote Troy for help after a power tower guide wire was cut.

56c Timed Writing

Key two 3' timed writings. Strive for control.

all letters

	gwam	3'	5'
For many years, readers who had chosen a particular book had		4	2
just one question to answer: Do you want to purchase a hardcover		8	5
or a paperback book? It was assumed that books would be purchased		13	8
from a retail outlet, such as a bookstore. Currently, books are		17	10
being marketed and sold online. The book itself, however, is still		22	13
printed on paper.		23	14
With the technology that is on the market today, a third		27	16
alternative, the electronic or the so-called e-book, is emerging.		31	19
E-books are sold in digitized form. The book must be read from the		36	21
website on a computer or on a special device designed for reading		40	24
e-books. Many publishers are experimenting with electronic books,		45	27
but only a few well-known ones have moved into the e-book market		49	29
in a major way. Most e-book companies are small organizations that		54	32
are willing to take a risk to make a profit.		56	34
The cost of producing and selling books in digital form is		60	36
far less than it is in paper form. The result is that books		65	39
that appeal to small markets are now feasible in digital form. The		69	41
cost was too great in print form. Many publishers have two key		73	44
concerns about the e-book market. The first is that a large number		78	47
of readers still are not comfortable reading from electronic media		82	49
for long time periods. The second factor is that they worry about		87	52
copyright protection. Many are very aware of the problems the music		91	55
industry experienced in this area.		94	56

3'	1	2	3	4
5'	1		2	3

68-d2

Continued

Submission of Assignment

Submit this assignment in a three-ring folder—not a notebook. Label the outside of the folder with your name and the title *Library Research*.

Postmark your assignment no later than Monday, March 17. Submit the assignment to Linda T. Walters, 307 Springdale Drive, Ellisville, MS 39437-5736.

Additionally, post the electronic file to the drop box labeled *Library Research*. When naming your file, use one word. The drop box will be open only up to the deadline—**March 17** at 11 p.m.

Good luck on this project. I look forward to reading **your** outstanding research in these areas of electronic presentations. |xx| Attachment

---

68-d3

Two-Page Modified
Block Letter

 APPLICATION

1. Create the opening lines for a modified block letter with open punctuation. Include an attention line to the **Search Committee**. Letter address is **College of Education Search Committee | Lynn State University | 323 University Avenue | Albuquerque, NM 87105-1742**. Also create a subject line: **Subject: Assistant Professor of Curriculum Position**. Add the required letter parts.

2. Key the paragraphs below, beginning at the end of the data file.

3. Create a header for the second page; use **Search Committee** in the header.

4. Check and close. *(68-d3)*

In addition to supervising curriculum development during the past five years, I have been loaned to three other states to help with their curriculum development. Each assignment gave me the opportunity to use and expand my expertise in my field. These experiences in particular are significant when considering the knowledge base that I can bring to the classroom.

I also have classroom experience at the secondary level. After obtaining my bachelor's degree, I taught Business Education for Finton Public Schools. During the five years that I held this position, I taught for two years at Shadowland Community College. These invaluable experiences of developing curriculum for and teaching in both secondary and postsecondary schools will make it possible for me to personally guide the future teachers being trained by Lynn State University to a point where they are prepared to excel at whatever teaching level they seek.

I look forward to hearing from you to discuss your faculty needs. I can be reached at 505-555-0199 Monday through Friday. Your advertised position and my curriculum development certainly appear to be a good fit. | Sincerely | Betheny Isner | Enclosure

56-d1

Edit Memo

TRAIL DESIGN

1. In the open document, position the first line of the heading correctly. Search for *sights* and replace with *sites* each time it occurs.

2. Add bullets to the list of sites. Use a nonbreaking space with Phase 1 and Phase 2 to avoid the number from being placed on a separate line from Phase.

3. Make other edits shown and add reference initials.

4. Check and close. (*56-d1*)

To: Trail design task force

From: Dianne Gibson

Date: Current

Subject: Trail design

Thanks you for participating in the Trail Design meeting last week. We did *I think* make a tremendous amount of progress on this fun *exciting* project. Specific sights were designated for the components of phase one of the Environmental learning center *stet* complex and the first trail loop. Tentative sights were located *identified* for the phase two 2 components including the conference center.

Ken provides *d* us with a new lay out of the property showing the following sights that were designated during the visit.

Main Entrance *lc*
Parking lot *area*
Environmental Learning Center
General shelter *buildings*
Outdoor linear classroom *s*
First trail loop with key interpretative sights designated
Sustainability exhibit sights

Please review *the positioning of* these sights to make sure that the layout and documentation *both* interprets the groups wishes *decisions* properly. Once we recieve feed back from every one, Ken needs to *will* finalize the design documents.

Our timeframe requires us to have finalized concept documents within two weeks to turn over to the architects. The architects will develop the construction documents needed to obtain the necessary permits.

68-d1

Two-Page Modified Block Letter

LONG LETTER

1. Format the letter in modified block style and open punctuation. Correct the format and add required letter parts.

2. On the second page, insert the header **Ms. Jacqueline Santos, Page 2,** and the **Current date.** Do not display the header on the first page of the letter. Apply Keep lines together command to the last paragraph and the closing.

3. Check and close. (*68-d1*)

68-d2

Two-Page Memo

1. Key the memo. **TO**: Electronic Presentations Class. **FROM**: Linda T. Walters, Instructor. The **DATE**: January 16 **SUBJECT**: Library Research.

2. Bold the side headings. Add a second-page header using the recipient's name, the page number, and the date.

3. Check and close. (*68-d2*)

The library research assignment described in this memo comprises 10 percent of your total grade. Read the directions carefully, follow the format on the attached document, and mark the deadline on your calendar. If you have questions about this assignment, please call me at my office or e-mail me.

Assignment

Prepare a critical review of five recent (2008 to present) journal articles (not the popular press) related to the following electronic presentation issues. Discuss, summarize, and evaluate each article separately. Compare and contrast the information with other sources.

1. What design rules should be considered in creating electronic presentations?

2. What delivery skills are needed when using electronic presentations?

3. What copyright issues should be considered when creating electronic presentations?

4. What advanced features of PowerPoint are available to make a powerful electronic presentation?

5. What speaking skills are necessary when delivering a presentation (with or without visual aids)?

6. What helpful advice would be given to new presenters who will design their own presentations?

7. What resources are available to assist the presentation designer?

References and Citations

Please be sure to reference correctly all sources of information used for your report. All reports will be checked for plagiarism. The required format is attached. Be sure to read it carefully and follow it.

Use a combination of textbooks, journals, and the online databases at the University Library. Use websites cautiously. Beware that some sites are not scholarly but are simply someone's opinion. See the websites provided in the syllabus. List references in a single, alphabetized list. Examples of correct reference format are included in the attachment.

continued

Report with Table

 MASTER PLAN

1. In the open document, position title about 2" from top of page and apply Title format.
2. Format headings as noted in the copy below and ensure that they are not separated from the paragraphs that follow.
3. Open *55-d1*, copy the *Property Location and Value* table, and paste it after the second paragraph. Apply Medium Grid 3 – Accent 5 table design. Delete extra blank lines if any. Insert the following footnote so that the note reference mark is positioned after the word *Value* in the table title:

   [1]Property values are based on the appraised value at the time of acquisition.

4. Make all edits shown below. Add text shown in script to the document.
5. Prepare a cover page using the design of your choice.
6. Proofread. Ensure that you have made all edits and followed all instructions.
7. Check and close. (*56-d2*)

Master Plan for Properties

The Midlands University Foundation properties are categorized into four classifications: Coastal Property, Midlands Property, other in-state property, and out-of-state property. The Foundation acquires property either by purchasing it or by accepting gifts from donors desiring to support Midlands University.

Insert → *Generally, the Foundation retains coastal properties for research and environmental education purposes and properties in the Midlands area for future development and use by Midlands University. Usually, properties in the other two categories are held only if they are likely to appreciate significantly; otherwise, they are sold and the proceeds are used to support various University needs. Currently, the total value of the out-of-state property is $2,145,000.*

Insert table here.

Coastal Properties   *Heading 1*

                                                          seven
Currently the Foundation owns ~~a number of~~ different tracts of land in the Coastal Region valued at $18,325,000. Decisions on the future use of five of the tracts are pending. The master plan contains specific plans for only two of the tracts the Marshall tract and the Richardson tract.

                              em dash

68d

HEADERS

INSERT/HEADER & FOOTER/HEADER

A header is located in the top margin of a document. In a letter or memo, the header includes the name of the recipient, the page number, and the dateline each on a separate line. A header is placed on all pages, except the first.

To insert a header:

1. Click the insertion point at the top of page 1.

2. From the Insert tab, in the Header & Footer group, click Header. The style gallery displays. Choose the Blank style ❶.

3. Key the name of the recipient and tap ENTER.

4. Once a header or footer is inserted, a Header & Footer Tools Design tab displays. Click the Header & Footer Tools Design tab to display the Ribbon. Use the commands on this ribbon to complete the header.

5. Key **Page** followed by a space. Click the Page Number drop-list arrow and choose Current Position ❷. Choose the Plain Number style ❸. Tap ENTER.

6. Insert the date ❹ from the Ribbon; use the same format as page 1 of the letter or memo ❺.

7. In the Options group, select Different First Page to suppress the header on the first page ❻.

8. Click the Close Header and Footer button ❼.

EDIT HEADER

To edit a header, on the Insert menu, in the Header & Footer Group, click Header, and then click Edit Header. An alternate method is to double-click in the header section of the document. To move to the text of the memo, double-click in the memo—not the header.

To remove a header, on the Insert tab, in the Header & Footer Group, click Header, and then click Remove Header.

TIP

If you have trouble with the header appearing on both pages, delete and start over. Check that Different First Page is *not* checked before you begin. Then create the header and click Different First Page.

56-d2

Continued

The Marshall Tract   *Heading 2*

The Marshall tract consists of over 1,200 acres of environmentally sensitive coastal property. Approximately one-half of the tract consists of wetlands with a conservation and preservation easement on the property. A portion of the remaining property has endangered species, including the red cockaded woodpecker. An eagle nest has also been spotted on the property.

Insert   *The master plan calls for the retention of the property because of its potential for research and environmental education. The short-term plans call for the establishment of a system of nature trails and boardwalks and the development of a parking area for visitors. Long-term plans specify the design and construction of a research and learning center.*

The Richardson Tract   *Heading 2*

The Richardson tract consists of an entire barrier island that is used for research purposes. The property currently has a very basic research and education center. The gift agreement severely restricts development of facilities on the island; therefore, it is not likely to be highly developed at any point in the future.

Midlands Properties   *Heading 1*

The Midlands portfolio of property consists of more than sixty individual parcels of land. Approximately 60 percent of the land was purchased and 40 percent was received as gifts. The land is valued at $12,650,000.

The Wheeler Tract   *Heading 2*

A decision has been made to sell this property. Currently, the property is being surveyed and a new appraisal has been ordered. The property will be ~~put~~ placed on the market as soon as the survey and appraisal have been completed.

The Blossom Tract   *Heading 2*

The Foundation contracted to have infrastructure *work completed before turning the tract over to Midlands University for development.*

WARMUP 68a

Key each line, striving for control. Repeat if desired.

alphabet 1 Frances Zwanka exited very quietly just prior to the big seminar.

figures 2 Please call 235-9167 or 294-3678 before 10:45 a.m. on January 18.

adjacent reaches 3 Louis, Sadi, Art, and a few other people were going to a concert.

easy 4 Vivian may go with a neighbor or with me to work on an amendment.

| 1 | 2 | 3 | 4 | 5 | 6 | 7 | 8 | 9 | 10 | 11 | 12 | 13 |

SKILL BUILDING

68b Textbook Keying

1. Key each line once, concentrating on good keying techniques. Tap ENTER twice after each 3-line group.
2. Repeat if time permits.

5 to kite flat byte joyful hitter night vacuum tab yummy vague earn

first finger 6 Babbs hung a gorgeous hanging on the first floor by the fountain.

7 Annabelle gave her baby daughter big hugs and put her in the bed.

8 dike kind cider insider decided child creek cracked deadlock kite

second finger 9 Dicky screamed and cried as Mickey cracked the huge chicken eggs.

10 Tired divers tried to no avail to rescue the sinking cargo liner.

11 sap soap spots salsa poppy squares people wool swoosh assess pass

fourth finger 12 Sally knew pool, zymoscope, x-axis, wassail, Lallan, and swallow.

13 Palisade apologized to sloppy Wally for the lollipops and apples.

DOCUMENT DESIGN

68c

MULTIPLE-PAGE LETTERS AND MEMOS

Letters and memos that are more than one page in length require special layout considerations. Use letterhead paper or a memohead only for the first page. Use plain paper that matches the first page in quality and color for additional pages.

To format a multi-page letter or memo:

1. Format the first page of the letter and memo in the usual manner (see Lesson 64 or 65). When you key the document, overflow text will automatically move to the second page. Make sure that at least two lines of the paragraph being divided appear on each page. A 3-line paragraph cannot be divided between pages. To divide text attractively between pages, apply the Keep lines together command (Home/Paragraph/Line and Page Breaks).

2. On the second and following pages, use the default top margin (1").

3. Create a header for the second and following pages; suppress the header on the first page so that it does not print. A header includes the **recipient, page number,** and **dateline**. One blank line or hard return should follow the last line of the header.

alphabet 1 Max Biqua watched jet planes flying in the azure sky over a cove.

figures 2 Send 105 No. 4 nails and 67 No. 8 brads for my home at 329 Annet.

3rd row 3 We two were ready to type a report for our quiet trio of workers.

easy 4 Pamela owns a big bicycle; and, with it, she may visit the docks.

| 1 | 2 | 3 | 4 | 5 | 6 | 7 | 8 | 9 | 10 | 11 | 12 | 13 |

SKILL BUILDING

57b Timed Writing
Key two 3' timed writings. Strive for control.

all letters

	gwam	3'	5'

Voting is a very important part of being a good citizen. However, many young people who are eligible to vote choose not to do so. When asked to explain or justify their decision, many simply shrug their shoulders and reply that they have no particular reason for not voting. The explanation others frequently give is that they just did not get around to going to the voting polls.　　4 2 / 8 5 / 12 7 / 16 10 / 21 13 / 25 15

A good question to consider concerns ways that we can motivate young people to be good citizens and to go to the polls and to vote. Some people approach this topic by trying to determine how satisfied people who do not vote are with the performance of their elected officials. Unfortunately, those who choose not to vote are just as satisfied with their elected officials as are those who voted.　　29 18 / 34 21 / 39 23 / 43 26 / 48 29 / 52 31

One interesting phenomenon concerning voting relates to the job market. When the job market is strong, fewer young people vote than when the job market is very bad. They also tend to be less satisfied with their elected officials. Self-interest seems to be a powerful motivator. Unfortunately, those who do not choose to vote miss the point that it is in their best interest to be a good citizen.　　56 34 / 61 36 / 65 39 / 69 41 / 74 44 / 78 47 / 79 47

3' | 1 | 2 | 3 | 4 |
5' | 1 | 2 | 3 |

APPLICATIONS

57c

Assessment

→ Continue

✓ Check

With *Keyboarding Pro DELUXE*: When you complete a document, proofread it, check the spelling, and preview for placement. When you are completely satisfied, click the Continue button to move to the next document. Click the Check button when you are ready to error-check the test. Review and/or print the document analysis results.

Without *Keyboarding Pro DELUXE*: Key the documents in sequence. When time has been called, proofread all documents again and identify errors.

67-d4

Block Letter with Notations and Envelope

1. Format the letter in modified block style; use open punctuation. Center the letter on the page.

2. Add a subject line with the intern's name and a salutation. (Include the word *Subject*.)

3. Generate an envelope with the special notation. Check and close. (*67-d4*)

	words
Current date	CONFIDENTIAL	Merritt College	Attention Ms.	16
Internship Programs Louise Brown, Director	750 East Wolfe Rd. *Road*	Vienna, Wv	22
26105-0750	25

Thank you for the opportunity to participate as an 38
employer in your internship program. Paul Zieger *one of your technology majors,* worked 90 56
hours this summer; and was an excellent ~~edition~~ *addition* to our 67
department. His final project was a*n* interactive tutorial of 80
the Merritt College library. This tutorial provides an 91
electronic tour of the library, including the layout of the 103
library *its holdings,* and specific directions on locating certain materials. 119
¶ Paul has agreed to work for us part-time during the fall 130
semester. Our initial plans ~~is~~ *are* for him to work with faculty 143
in setting up and conduct*ing* private demonstrations for classes. 156
In addition, he will write a second tutorial for the graduate 168
library. ¶ *Please send another excellent intern next summer.* 181
Sincerely | Daniel E. Romano, Director | Library Services | xx 192

67-d5

Edit Letter and Create Envelope

1. Open *67-d4* and add a blind copy notation for the intern.

2. Create an envelope for the intern. The address is **619 West Main Street, Charleston, WV 25301-1916**.

3. Add the envelope to the document. **Note:** Create the envelope in the Envelopes and Labels dialog box. Click Change Document to add this new envelope to the document.

4. Check and close. (*67-d5*)

57-d1

Memo

1. Key the memo shown below.
2. TO: Planning Commission | FROM: Community Park Site Committee | Current date | SUBJECT: Community Park Site Assessment | Copy to Mayor Charles Morgan
3. Continue to next document. (*57-d1*)

TIP

Remember to proofread and preview each document before you move to the next one.

The Community Park Site Committee has completed its assessment of the potential sites for the new park. Our report is enclosed.

The Committee unanimously recommends that the Westlake site be used for the new park. The Woodcreek site was considered acceptable, but it is not as desirable as the Westlake site. The Southside site was the least desirable of the three sites.

Please contact us if you have any questions.

57-d2

Block Letter

1. Key the following letter; use the current date, block letter style, and your name as the signature.
2. Center the page.
3. Continue to next document. (*57-d2*)

Ms. Margaret C. Worthington
4957 Mt. Elon Church Road
Hopkins, SC 29061-9837

Dear Ms. Worthington

The Planning Commission has authorized me to contact you to discuss the possible purchase of the 120-acre site that we discussed with you for the new Community Park. When we spoke with you yesterday, you indicated that you would be available to meet with us any afternoon next week. If it is still convenient, we would like to meet with you on Wednesday afternoon at 2:00 at the site.

Earlier you indicated that you had a recent survey and an appraisal of the property. We would appreciate it if you could have those documents available for the meeting.

If this time is not convenient, please call my office and leave a message so that I may reschedule the meeting. We look forward to working with you.

Sincerely

67-d1

Modified Block Letter with Mixed Punctuation

1. Key the letter on the previous page using modified block format with mixed punctuation. Notice it includes an attention line, subject line, an enclosure, and a blind copy notation.
2. Center the letter vertically on the page.
3. Check and close. (*67-d1*)

67-d2

Modified Block Letter with Reference Notation and Envelope

1. Format the modified block letter and use mixed punctuation. Supply necessary letter parts. Center vertically.
2. Add the mailing notation **CERTIFIED** and the reference line **Re: Order No. S3835**.
3. Send a copy to **Eric Leiu**. Generate an envelope and add it to the document.
4. Check and close. (*67-d2*)

Current Date | Dr. Jeneve Dostorian, Instructor | Merritt College | 319 North Jackson Street | Jacksonville, FL 32256-0319

Your TIME+ personal manager software was shipped to you this morning by next-day air service. We realize that your time is valuable, and installing incorrect software is not a good use of your time. However, we are glad to learn that your students benefited from your demonstration of the software.

Easy-to-follow instructions for installing the new software over the current software are enclosed. You will also note on your copy of the invoice that you were billed originally for the TIME software. The TIME+ software is $99 more; however, we are pleased to provide it at no extra cost to you.

An additional bonus for choosing TIME+ is the monthly newsletter, *Managing Time with TIME+*. You should receive your first copy by the first of the month.

Sincerely, | Veronica Scrivner | Customer Service Manager

67-d3

Modified Block Letter with Special Features

GLOBAL

1. Format the open document as a modified block letter with mixed punctuation. Position the dateline at the appropriate position.
2. Read the letter and compose an appropriate subject line. Omit the word *Subject*.
3. Add an Enclosure notation.
4. Check and close. (*67-d3*)

Edit Report

 COMMUNITY PARK

TIP

Use Format Painter to copy heading format to other headings and paragraph formats to other paragraphs.

1. Make the following edits in the report.

2. Change the format from a leftbound report to an unbound report. Position the title at about 2", center it, and apply Arial 14-point bold format; convert to uppercase. Apply Arial 12-point bold format to side headings; ensure that headings are kept with the paragraphs below them. Remove space after the side headings.

3. Apply double spacing and 12-point Times New Roman to the first paragraph and remove extra space after the paragraph; copy format to other paragraphs. Insert page numbers at the top right; do not show on the first page.

4. Use Find and Replace to locate all occurrences of *theme* and replace it with *community* each time it occurs. Use uppercase and lowercase appropriately.

5. Add the following sentence to the end of the first paragraph in the document:

   The planning Commission also asked the Committee to recommend the most desirable location for the park.

6. Two paragraphs in the document need editing. Make the edits shown below:

   potential

   All members of the Committee visited the three sites selected—the

   em dash

   Westlake site, the Southside site, and the Woodcreek site to determine if

   the sites were both feasible and desirable for the location of the new

   comprehensive

   theme park. The Committee used the criteria developed by the planning

   in-depth   *summary*

   commission for the review of each site. A copy of the criteria is attached.;

   the complete document is posted on the Commission's website, www.planning commission.gov.

   A description of each site follows.

   All three sites met the size criteria and are within the cost projections of

   shown below details &

   the planning commission. The table on the next page shows the

   comparative costs of the sites when both land and the estimated cost of

   the infrastructure are considered. *The infrastructure cost estimates for all sites were prepared by J.M. Moore Engineering.*

   (Key the following table after this paragraph and before the heading *Other Factors*. Apply Black Medium Shading 2.)

Site Costs	*Center, bold, 14-point type*		
Cost Category	**Westlake**	**Southside**	**Woodcreek**
	Center column heads		
Land	$720,000	$630,000	$676,000
Infrastructure	175,000	210,000	180,000
Total	$805,000	$840000	$856,000

Left-align first column

7. Check the test and close. (*57-d3*)

CHECKPOINT ➡

Congratulations! You have successfully completed the lessons in Module 7. To check your understanding and for more practice, complete the objective assessment and performance assessment located on the textbook website at www.collegekeyboarding.com.

Monica A. Carter
Communication Consultant
100 Main Street
Clinton, MS 39056-0503

[2" or Center Page Vertically]

July 11, 20--

[Tab 3.25"]

Attention Office Manager
Professional Document Designs, Inc.
9345 Blackjack Boulevard
Kingwood, TX 77345-9345

Ladies and Gentlemen:

Modified Block Style Letters   [Subject line]

Modified block format differs from block format in that the date, complimentary close, and the writer's name and title are keyed at the center point.

Paragraphs may be blocked, as this letter illustrates, or they may be indented 0.5" from the left margin. We suggest using block paragraphs so that an additional tab setting is not needed.

We recommend that you use modified block style only for those customers who request it. Otherwise, we urge you to use block format, which is more efficient. Please refer to the model documents in the enclosed *Communication Experts Format Guide*.

Sincerely,

Monica A. Carter
Communication Consultant

xx

Enclosure

bc   Lyndon David, Account Manager   [(not printed on the addressee's copy)]

[Tab .5"]

Graphics Essentials

MODULE 8

LEARNING OUTCOMES

- Apply graphics and pictures to enhance document format.
- Insert and format columns in documents.
- Build keyboarding and production skills.

LESSON 58 — Basic Graphics

WARMUP 58a

Key each line, striving for control. Repeat if desired.

alphabet 1 Dave Cagney alphabetized items for next week's quarterly journal.
figures 2 Close Rooms 4, 18, and 20 from 3 until 9 on July 7; open Room 56.
easy/figures 3 Toy & Wurt's note for $635 (see our page 78) was paid October 29.
easy 4 The auditor is due by eight, and he may lend a hand to the panel.

| 1 | 2 | 3 | 4 | 5 | 6 | 7 | 8 | 9 | 10 | 11 | 12 | 13 |

SKILL BUILDING

58b Textbook Keying

1. Key the drill, concentrating on good keying techniques. Tap ENTER twice after each 4-line group.
2. Repeat the drill if time permits.

adjacent reaches
5 Sand castles are fun to build but are poor shelter in a downpour.
6 The Hoosiers scored three points in the fourth to avoid an upset.
7 Her articles are going to be reported in an edition of the paper.
8 Fewer people attend West Point to play polo than to join a choir.

one hand
9 A dazed beggar scattered after a red car swerved on a wet street.
10 Mimi feasts on milky eggs at noon after I feed Kipp plum dessert.
11 Mo started ragweed tests in a vacated garage after greeting Dave.
12 You debate Phil after I defeat John; rest up, you brave braggart!

balanced hand
13 Handiwork is busy work, but it's also a memento of a rich entity.
14 The hairy ape bit the fish, but the apricot and corn lay dormant.
15 Henry may dismantle an authentic antique auto for Zoe's sorority.
16 An Irish auditor quit work at the city and ambled to the fields.

LESSON 58 BASIC GRAPHICS

MODULE 8   244

DOCUMENT DESIGN

67d

MODIFIED BLOCK LETTER REVIEW

In the modified block letter style, the dateline, complimentary close, and the writer's name and title begin at the horizontal center of the page (3.25"). This is the only difference between the block and modified block style formats. Either open or mixed punctuation may be used with the modified block letter format.

Monica A. Carter
Communication Consultant
100 Main Street
Clinton, MS 39056-0503

July 11, 20--

Attention Office Manager
Professional Document Designs, Inc.
9345 Blackjack Boulevard
Kingwood, TX 77345-9345

Ladies and Gentlemen:

Modified Block Style Letters

Modified block format differs from block format in that the date, complimentary close, and the writer's name and title are keyed at the center point.

Paragraphs may be blocked, as this letters illustrates, or they may be indented 0.5" from the left margin. We suggest using block paragraphs so that an additional tab setting is not needed.

We recommend that you use modified block style only for those customers who request it. Otherwise, we urge you to use block format, which is more efficient. Please refer to the model documents in the enclosed *Communication Experts Format Guide.*

Sincerely,

Monica A. Carter
Communication Consultant

xx

Enclosure

bc Lyndon David, Account Manager

To format a modified block letter:

Begin by setting a left tab at the center of the page. Determine the center by subtracting the side margins from the center of the paper. Set a left tab at 3.25".

4.25" Center of the paper
−1.00" Margins
3.25" Set left tab

Tap TAB to position the dateline, complimentary close, and the writer's name and title.

Remove the extra spacing between the letter address and other short lines. Review the model modified block letter on the next page.

Note: If the letter has already been keyed and you are changing it to modified block format, select the entire document and then set the tab.

MAILING NOTATIONS

A mailing notation such as FACSIMILE, OVERNIGHT, CERTIFIED, SPECIAL DELIVERY, or REGISTERED provides a record of how the letter was sent. Other notations such as CONFIDENTIAL or PERSONAL indicate how the recipient should treat the letter.

Key special notations in uppercase at the left margin one line below the date. Tap ENTER once after the mailing notation. On the envelope, key notations that affect postage right-aligned below the stamp (about line 1.3"). Key envelope notations that pertain to the recipient below the return address.

April 2, 20-- ↓1

CONFIDENTIAL ↓1

Dr. Jose A. Barajas
Golden Triangle Clinic
P.O. Box 10984-4851
Tullahoma, TN 37388-1267 ↓1

Dear Dr. Barajas ↓1

December 14, 20-- ↓1

CERTIFIED ↓1

Attention Division 2
Clinard Security Services
207 Hollyhill Avenue
Downers Grove, IL 60515-0357 ↓1

Ladies and Gentlemen ↓1

Good plans typically are required to execute most tasks successfully. If a task is worth doing, it is worth investing the time that is necessary to plan it effectively. Many people are anxious to get started on a task and just begin before they have thought about the best way to organize it. In the long run, they frequently end up wasting time that could be spent more profitably on important projects that they might prefer to tackle.

	11
	25
	39
	53
	67
	79
	87

1' | 1 | 2 | 3 | 4 | 5 | 6 | 7 | 8 | 9 | 10 | 11 | 12 | 13 |

NEW FUNCTIONS

58d Graphics Elements

Clip art, pictures, and shapes are graphics elements that enhance documents such as announcements, invitations, reports, and newsletters. In this lesson, you will work with these graphics elements.

CLIP ART

INSERT/ILLUSTRATIONS/CLIP ART

Clip
Art

Clip art is a graphics file that includes illustrations (created by hand or by computer software).

Word 2007 (and other applications such as *Excel*, *PowerPoint*, and *Publisher*) provides a collection of pictures, clip art, and sounds that can be added to documents. Additional clips are available online. You can also add your own clips to the collection. The clips are organized into different collections to simplify finding appropriate clip art. The Clip Organizer adds keywords to enable you to search for various types of clip art. You also have the option of selecting the collection and viewing thumbnail sketches (small pictures) of the various clip art available in each category. Once clip art has been inserted into a document, you can size it, copy and paste it, wrap text around it, or drag it to other locations.

To insert a clip art:

INSERT/ILLUSTRATIONS/CLIP ART

1. On the Insert tab, in the Illustrations group, click Clip Art.
2. In the Clip Art task pane, key a word or phrase in the Search for text box that describes the clip art that you want to search for, such as *laptop* ❶.
3. In the Search in box ❷ click the down arrow and select Everywhere to search All Collections.
4. Click Go.
5. In the list of results, click the clip art ❸ to insert it in your document.

LESSON 67 | Modified Block Letter Format and Special Features

WARMUP 67a

Key each line, striving for control. Repeat if desired.

alphabet	1	Liz Bowhanon moved very quickly and just played exciting defense.
figures	2	I fed 285 cats, 406 dogs, 157 birds, and 39 rabbits at a shelter.
1st/2nd fingers	3	Jimmy or Vick sent my fur hat this summer, but I did not need it.
easy	4	An authentic ivory tusk may be key to the ancient island rituals.

COMMUNICATION

67b Composition

1. In a new document, key your name at the left margin. On the next line, insert the date using the Date and Time feature. Compose four short paragraphs that answer each of the following questions:

   • Why do business letters include the date at the beginning of the letter?

   • Why do companies require a standard or common style for business letters such as block format with open punctuation?

   • What personal letters will you be required to write in the months ahead?

   • How do you think this module on business correspondence will assist you in preparing those letters?

2. Edit and proofread the document carefully.

3. Check and close. (67b)

FUNCTION REVIEW

67c

TABS

HOME/PARAGRAPH/DIALOG BOX LAUNCHER

In this lesson you will set a left tab at 3.25" to format a modified block letter.

1. Click the Tab Alignment button at the far left of the Horizontal Ruler until it changes to the desired tab.

2. Click the Horizontal Ruler where you want to set a tab stop.

Tab Alignment button

To move a tab:

Select the text that will be affected and drag the tab to the new location. (If you do not select the text, only the tab that your cursor is on will be moved.)

To clear a tab:

Select the text affected and drag the tab off the Horizontal Ruler.

To set a precise tab:

1. From the Home tab, on the Paragraph group, click the Dialog Box Launcher.

2. In the Paragraph dialog box, click the Tabs button. The Tabs dialog box displays.

3. In the Tab stop position box ❶, key the measurement; click Set ❷ and OK.

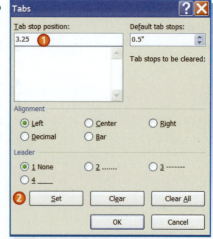

PICTURES

INSERT/ILLUSTRATIONS/PICTURES

Pictures can also be inserted into your documents. Pictures are photographs or other images created in a software other than *Word*. They may be located on the user's computer or another storage device.

To insert a picture:

INSERT/ILLUSTRATIONS/PICTURES

1. Click where you want to insert the picture.

2. On the Insert tab, in the Illustrations group, click Picture ❶.

3. Select the desired drive and folder. Click the desired picture to select it, and click Insert ❷.

> **TIP**
>
> Remember to proofread and preview each document as a SOP. You will not be reminded to do this.

Although inserted slightly differently, the steps for sizing and moving clip art and pictures are the same.

To size clip art or pictures:

1. Select the clip or picture.

2. Position your insertion point over one of the open circles ❷ around the edge of the image.

3. When the pointer turns to a double-headed arrow ❸, click and drag the image to your desired size. Drag the lower-right handle down and to the right to increase the size; drag it up and to the left to make the clip smaller.

> **TIP**
>
> You can drag the square handle on the sides of a clip to size the image, but you'll distort its size. Always drag a corner handle to maintain the clip's proportion.

To move a clip art or picture:

PICTURE TOOLS/FORMAT/ARRANGE/TEXT WRAPPING

1. Click to select the clip art to display the Picture Tools.

2. On the Format tab, in the Arrange group ❶, click the Text Wrapping command. Choose Tight (or one of the text-wrapping options) from the drop-down list.

3. Drag the shape to its new location.

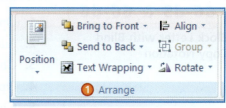

> **TIP**
>
> To move or "nudge" the shape in very small increments, hold down CTRL while you tap the Up Arrow, Down Arrow, Right Arrow, or Left Arrow keys.

66-d3

Block Letter with Attention and Reference Lines

TIP

Add special lines to letters as needed. You will not be reminded to add enclosure, attachment, or copy notations if the information is contained in the letter.

1. Key the letter in block style with open punctuation. Add a complimentary closing. Center the page vertically.
2. Key the flight information in a two-column, one-row table. Adjust column width and center the table horizontally.
3. Check and close. (*66-d3*)

	words
May 15, 20-- │Attention Frequent Flyer Service Center│Atlanta	14
International Airport│512 Airport Boulevard│Department 129│Atlanta, GA	27
30320-8441│ Re: #2521-70442│ Ladies and Gentlemen	43

	words
Please redeem an award of 30,000 miles from my frequent flyer account	57
#2521-70442. Award #D731 is being redeemed as a round-trip ticket	71
to Honolulu, Hawaii, with a departure on Thursday, August 15, and a	84
return on Monday, August 19, 20--. Flight information is listed below:	99

		words
Thursday, August 15	**Monday, August 19**	106
Depart Jackson, Mississippi	Depart Honolulu, Hawaii	116
7:10 a.m.	6:05 p.m.	120
Flight #5315	Flight #178	125

	words
Please mail a certificate to the business address listed on the letterhead.	140
Your agent, Azida Hamff, has instructed me to submit this certificate to	155
an airline agent by June 15 to receive my airline tickets. I will be sure	168
to follow these instructions and look forward to benefiting from my first	183
frequent flyer award.	189

	words
Frances Hamilton, Ph.D.│xx	194

66-d4

Reformat Letter

REFORMAT

1. In the open document, delete the first line of the letter address.
2. Send it to the attention of the Marketing Department. Insert the appropriate salutation.
3. Center the letter vertically on the page.
4. Key **Marketing Hightower Products at the Citrus Bowl** as the subject line.
5. Format in block style with open punctuation; insert missing letter parts, including the current date.
6. Check and close. (*66-d4*)

66-d5 & 66-d6

Block Letter with Blind Copy Notation

1. Open *66-d4*. Delete the second paragraph.
2. Add a copy notation to **John Fraser, Contract Manage**r.
3. Check and close. (*66-d5*)
4. Open *66-d5*. Add a blind copy notation to **Lisa Lopez, Legal Department**.
5. Check and close. (*66-d6*)

1. In a new document, search for *computers* in the clip art gallery. Insert a photo of a group of people working together. (If you can't find a photo such as this, insert a *computer* clip art of your choice into the document.)

2. Size the clip art to approximately 5 inches wide. Make sure you maintain its proportion. Use the Horizontal Ruler to guide you.

3. On the Picture Tools Format tab, in the Arrange group, choose Tight from the Text Wrapping command and choose Align Center from the Align command to move the photo to the center of the page near the top margin.

4. Check and close. (*58-drill1*)

1

SHAPES

INSERT/ILLUSTRATIONS/SHAPES

You can add one or more shapes to a document. Shapes are often combined to create a more complex drawing object. Available shapes include lines, basic geometric shapes, arrows, equation shapes, flowchart shapes, stars, banners, and callouts.

To add a shape to your document:

INSERT/ILLUSTRATIONS/SHAPES/SELECT SHAPE

1. On the Insert tab in the Illustrations group, click Shapes to display the Shapes gallery **1**.

2. Click the shape you want, click anywhere in the document, and then drag to place the shape.

TIP

To create a perfect square or circle (or constrain the dimensions of other shapes), press and hold SHIFT while you drag.

You can change the look of your shape by changing its fill or by adding effects, such as shadows, glows, reflections, soft edges, bevels, and three-dimensional (3-D) rotations to it. A **fill** is the interior of a shape. When you change the fill color of a shape, you can also add a texture, picture, or gradient to the fill. A **gradient** is a gradual progression of colors and shades, usually from one color to another color, or from one shade to another shade of the same color. A **3-D effect** adds depth to a shape. You can add a built-in combination of 3-D effects to your shape, or you can add individual effects.

To add or change a fill color:

DRAWING TOOLS/FORMAT/SHAPE STYLES/SHAPE FILL

1. Click the shape in which you want to add a fill.

2. In the Shape Styles group, click Shape Fill. Choose one of the Theme Colors, one of the Standard Colors, or click More Fill Colors to select the color that you want. To choose no color, click No Fill.

3. Click Shape Outline to change the Outline Weight or Color.

4. Click Shadow Effects or 3-D Effects to add shadow or 3-D effects.

66-d1

Block Letter with Subject Line and Copy Notation

1. Format the letter in block style with open punctuation. Include reference initials and Enclosures notation. Send a copy of the letter to the lead facilitator mentioned in it; align the name at the .5" tab position.

2. Position Chamber of Commerce immediately below writer's name.

3. Check and close. (66-d1)

Date: January 2, 20-- | Senator Alice Vinicki | 2459 Terrace Park Drive | Volusia, FL 30214-3852 | Dear Senator Vinicki | Subject: Volusia Community Goals Conference—January 30

Your positive response to deliver the keynote address at the Volusia Community Goals Conference on Saturday, January 30, was received with much excitement by the Goals Conference Planning Committee. Thank you, Senator Vinicki, for your commitment to this community effort. Mr. Roger Bourgeois, Director of the United Planning Institute, is the lead facilitator of the goals conference and will introduce you at the opening session beginning at 9 a.m. in the Vinicki Exhibit Hall of the Volusia Convention Center.

Hotel accommodations have been made for you at the Riverside Suites for Friday, January 29; confirmation is enclosed. Mr. Bourgeois and I will meet you at the hotel restaurant at 7:30 a.m. for breakfast and escort you to the convention center. A copy of the conference program and an outline of the issues to be discussed in the various breakout groups are also enclosed for your review.

We look forward to your address and to your being a key player in our goals conference.

Respectfully yours | Le-An Nguyen, President | Chamber of Commerce

66-d2

Block Letter with Subject Line

1. Format the letter in block style with open punctuation. Center the letter vertically.

2. Add an appropriate subject line. Check and close. (66-d2)

January 10, 20--	Ms. Denise McWhorter	HandPrints, Inc.		11
92 E. Cresswell Road	Selden, NY 11784	Dear Ms. McWhorter	24
Booth 24 your first choice had been reserved for you	35
for the annual craft fair on May 15-17. You booth was ex-	46
treme popular last year and we are very please to have you	59
participate in the fair again this year.	67
Our standard agreement from is inclosed. Please sign	78
the form and return it to us by April 15. Your booths will	90
have a large table and a minimum of two chair. If you need	102
any thing else for the booth please let us know prior to the	114
opening of the fair.	119
Sincerely	Jennifer A. Reed	President	xx	Enclosure	129

GROUPING SHAPES

Shapes or other objects are often grouped when they are used together. The objects are grouped so they can be moved as one item. They can also be ungrouped if you need to change the formatting of individual objects.

To group shapes or other objects:
DRAWING TOOLS/FORMAT/ARRANGE/GROUP

1. Select the objects you want to group by holding down SHIFT as you click each object.
2. Under Drawing Tools, on the Format tab, in the Arrange group, choose Group.
3. To ungroup an object, select the grouped objects. Under Drawing Tools, from the Format tab, in the Arrange group, click the down arrow on the Group command and select Ungroup.

To add text to a shape:
DRAWING TOOLS/FORMAT/INSERT SHAPES/EDIT TEXT button

Under Drawing Tools, from the Format tab, in the Insert Shapes group, click the Edit Text button. This allows you to add text to a shape or to edit text that is already in the shape.

TIP

You can also right-click the shape and choose Add Text.

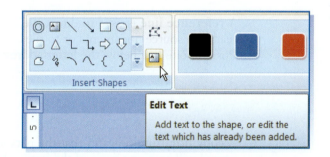

To delete a shape from your document:

Click the shape that you want to delete, and then tap DELETE.

KEYBOARDING PRO DELUXE See References/Word commands/Lesson 58

DRILL 2   **SHAPES**

1. In a new document, insert a rounded rectangle, right arrow, triangle, right arrow, and a circle as shown below.
2. Fill each shape with a color.

3. Select all shapes and group them.
4. Add the text as shown. (Hint: Tap ENTER before keying the text on the rounded rectangle and the circle. Use the Remove Space After Paragraph command if necessary to get the text to align properly.)
5. Check and close. (58-drill2)

DOCUMENT DESIGN

66c

SPECIAL LETTER PARTS

In addition to the standard business letter features, other special parts may be included, depending on the needs of the document. These special parts will cause the letter to move down the page. If you center the page vertically, preview the letter and check that sufficient space follows the letterhead.

An **attention line** directs a letter to a position or department within an organization. It is keyed as the first line of the letter address. Use *Ladies and Gentlemen* as the salutation with an attention line.

> Attention Accounting Department
> Chou Furniture Company
> 101 First Street
> Olympia, WA 99504-6480
>
> Ladies and Gentlemen

A **subject line** provides a short description of the purpose of the letter. It is placed between the salutation and the body of the letter. The subject line may be keyed using initial caps or uppercase. It may be preceded by the word *Subject*. Key it as shown here unless otherwise directed.

> Dear Mr. Perez:
>
> Subject: Projected Sales Figures
>
> The sales figures for the first quarter have been released.

A **reference line** is used to direct the reader to source documents or to files. Position one line below the letter address.

> 5000 Girard Avenue
> Minneapolis, MN 55405-4873
>
> Re: Policy FDW128
>
> Dear Mr. Woo

A **copy notation** indicates that the person named will receive a copy of the letter. Key the notation one line below the reference initials or enclosure notation (if there is one). Key **c** to indicate copy; then tap TAB and key the name(s). Key each name on a separate line (aligned at the .5" tab). Remove extra space between names.

> Kevin Almarzouk, President
>
> xx
>
> Enclosure
>
> c   Norman Elswick
>   Sheila Solari

A **postscript** is used to emphasize information. Tap ENTER after the last notation in the letter; then key the postscript. It is not necessary to begin with *PS*. Do not indent the postscript unless paragraphs of the letter are indented.

> Kevin Almarzouk, President
>
> xx
>
> Use modified block style for letters.

A **blind copy notation** indicates that a person(s) is receiving a copy of the letter without the addressee's knowledge. The notation appears on copies, but not on the original. Key the blind copy notation below all other notations. Align multiple recipients at the .5" tab. **Note:** E-mail messages containing attached letters may be addressed with blind copy recipients.

> Enclosure
>
> bc   Norman Elswick
>   Sheila Solari

PARAGRAPH BORDERS AND SHADING

PAGE LAYOUT/PAGE BACKGROUND/PAGE BORDERS

Page Borders

Borders and shading can be applied to paragraphs, pages, or selected text. Various line styles, weights, and colors can be applied to borders. Shading can be applied in a variety of colors and patterns.

> This paragraph illustrates a 3-D border with a 3-point purple line. The shading for the paragraph is Purple, Accent 4, 60%.

To apply a paragraph border:

PAGE LAYOUT/PAGE BACKGROUND/PAGE BORDERS/BORDERS

1. Click in the paragraph or select the text to be formatted with a border.
2. On the Page Layout tab, in the Page Background group, click Page Borders to display the Borders and Shading dialog box.
3. In the Borders and Shading dialog box, click the Borders tab.
4. Select the border setting, line style, color, and width; then click OK.

To apply shading:

PAGE LAYOUT/PAGE BACKGROUND/PAGE BORDERS/SHADING

1. Click in the paragraph or select the text to be formatted with a border.
2. On the Page Layout tab, in the Page Background group, click Page Borders.
3. Click the Shading tab.
4. Select the fill and pattern, and then click OK.

DRILL 3   BORDERS AND SHADING

1. Key the paragraph at the right.
2. Then apply a ½-point red, double-line box border and Dark Blue, Text 2, Lighter 60% shading.
3. Check and close. (58-drill3)

> This paragraph is formatted with a ½-point red, double-line box border and Dark Blue, Text 2, Lighter 60% shading.

Block Letter with Special Letter Parts

WARMUP 66a

Key each line, striving for control. Repeat if desired.

alphabet	1	The Lake View magazine of junior boxers may have clean equipment.
figures	2	She found 4,721 cats, 9,038 kittens, and 56 frightened bluebirds.
shift key	3	Mr. Paul Wilkes called Ms. Angie Pace on Friday, March 15 in OH.
double letters	4	Bill looked down the hall for a happy bookkeeper named Jill Mill.

| 1 | 2 | 3 | 4 | 5 | 6 | 7 | 8 | 9 | 10 | 11 | 12 | 13 |

COMMUNICATION

66b

PROOFREADING

1. Print the data file.
2. Compare the printed letter to the source copy shown below. Mark any errors using proofreaders' marks. (See *Reference Guide if necessary*.)
3. Key your corrections. Center the letter vertically.
4. Check and close. (*66b*)
5. Submit the marked copy and the corrected letter to your instructor.

January 23, 20--

Tap ENTER 2 times.

Ms. Audra Meaux
2689 Marsalis Lane
Hot Springs, AR 71913-0345

Dear Ms. Meaux

Thank you for agreeing to serve as Chair of the Hospitality Committee for the National Technology Association Convention on April 3-7 in Phoenix, Arizona.

The enclosed guidelines outline the responsibilities and timelines of the Hospitality Committee. Please read them carefully and call me at 602-555-0137 if you have any questions. You will need about 25 individuals to work with you on this committee. After you have organized this group, please mail me a complete roster including names, addresses, phone and fax numbers, and e-mail addresses.

Ms. Meaux, thank you for your professionalism and willingness to serve.

Sincerely

Tap ENTER 2 times.

Ryan Messamore
Vice President of Sales

xx

Enclosure

PAGE BORDERS

PAGE LAYOUT/PAGE BACKGROUND/PAGE BORDERS

Attractive page borders can also be added to pages using various line styles, weights, and colors.

To apply a page border:
PAGE LAYOUT/PAGE BACKGROUND/PAGE BORDERS

1. On the Page Layout tab, in the Page Background group, click Page Borders.
2. Make sure the Page Border tab is active on the Borders and Shading dialog box.
3. Choose the desired border setting, line style, line color, and line width; click OK.

DRILL 4   PAGE BORDERS

1. Open *58-drill3*.
2. Add a page border that is dark red and ½ point.

3. Check and close. (*58-drill4*)

APPLICATIONS

58-d1

Multiple-Page Manual with Picture and Page Border

 CLEANING MANUAL

CLEAN.JPG

1. In the open document, format both lines of the title in 28-point Cambria, bold, red.
2. Insert the picture *clean.jpg* from the data files between the title lines and the text at the bottom of page one.
3. Add the page border that looks like a house. (**Hint:** This is a custom border. On the Page Borders tab, in the Borders and Shading dialog box, click Custom and then click Art. Select the border that looks like houses.)
4. Check and close. (*58-d1*)

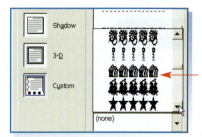

58-d2

One-Page Report with Clip Art and Shape

1. Key and format the title on the next page, **Trend Analysis Report**, using 36-point Arial font, bold, and Light Blue text color.
2. Create a subheading below the title by keying **Market Analysis** using Arial Black 20-point font and adding Light Blue shading to the paragraph.
3. Key the bulleted list. Click the Decrease Indent button to align the bullets at the left margin.
4. Search for clip art using the keyword **academic**, and add an appropriate piece of clip art centered below the five paragraphs.
5. Insert an Explosion 2 shape to the right of the clip art. Inside the shape, key **Key Market Trends** in 16-point Times New Roman font. Add a complementary fill color to the shape. If necessary, adjust the size of the shape so that the text fits properly.
6. At the bottom of the page, key **Understanding our community to prepare for our future!** in 18-point Brush Script MT font.
7. Check and close. (*58-d2*)

65-d3

Block Letter with Enclosure Notation

1. Format the letter in block style and open punctuation; center vertically. Send the letter to **Ms. Sylvia Gianchin, Redmon Publishers, 5280 Circle Point, Long Beach, CA 90840-0792**. Use the date **October 15, 20--**.

2. Add the appropriate letter parts and apply correct spacing. Do not include reference initials since you are both the originator and the typist. Align the enclosure notation at the default 1.0" tab.

3. Check and close. (*65-d3*)

The Foundation for Appalachian Studies will be having a seminar this spring entitled "Women of the Mountains." Elizabeth Chambers, author of *Rural Life in Modern Appalachia*, will be our keynote speaker, and we know that the attendees will be clamoring for her exciting book. Enclosed is our purchase order with shipping instructions for 100 copies.

If you have any questions regarding this order, please call me between 10 a.m. and 2 p.m. on Thursday or Friday. We will need these books delivered to the convention center during the first week of December. The center will be able to store them until the seminar, but they will not have storage space available before the first week in December.

Sincerely | Your Name, Coordinator | Enclosure: Purchase Order F6812

65-d4

Block Letter

1. Key the letter in block letter style to **Ms. Janna Skean | Cornet Services | 1592 Pullman Avenue, Cincinnati, OH 45230-1746**. The letter is from **Mr. Khalilah Kuar**. (Note use of personal title.) Center vertically and use open punctuation.

2. Correct the three errors in word choice in the message. (For example, *to* may be incorrectly keyed for *too*.)

3. Check and close. (*65-d4*)

¶ All form letters have been reviewed, revised, and approved for general use. You will receive a new copy within a few days of the correspondence manual.

Special thanks are do each of you for your help on this important project. The consultants were most complementary of the excellent corporation they received and of the quality of your suggestions for ~~improvement of~~ *improving* the letters.

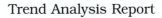

Trend Analysis Report

Market Analysis

- The population in the metropolitan area is growing both in the college's service area and in the demographic segments that represent the greatest market enrollment.

- The metropolitan area continues to add employment opportunities at a growth rate of 22 percent, but the area economy suffers from some of the same insecurities about the future as do other areas.

- Information technology is creating more customer potential and new demands for the delivery of coursework as well as generating new opportunities for competitors to enter this educational market.

- The pace of change is forcing people at all levels of the economy to learn new skills at the same time people are being asked to work harder—and sometimes hold more than one job.

- The new school improvement plan has not taken shape as quickly as anticipated, but a move toward mastering skills and testing for proficiencies—not rote knowledge—is gaining momentum.

WORKPLACE SUCCESS

Let's Do Lunch—Business Etiquette Around the World

Each culture has its own customs when it comes to social and business relations. While business lunches and dinners are common around the globe, they are handled differently in most countries. It is important to understand cultural etiquette when dining in order to avoid embarrassment to maximize your chances of business success.

In the U.S., it is customary to get down to business immediately. Yet this attitude may turn off clients from another country. Most Latin Americans, for example, prefer to be social over lunch before discussing business. You might be asked about your family, and you should reciprocate. Business lunches may last two or more hours. In Britain, a business lunch might occur at a local pub. Usually, there is less talk of family or personal life. The British are more formal, and so the talk is usually centered on business, economics, or politics. For the Japanese, lunch is traditionally the main meal of the day. Many Japanese enjoy slurping their noodles in order to make them cooler. Guests will never see a host paying the bill since it is always done discretely beforehand or after the lunch.

These examples provide a few tips when business is conducted at the international dining table. Take the time and learn the customs of other countries in order to build relationships and be an effective businessperson.

2"

Haas Pharmaceutical Supply Company

1010 Greenbrier Hill ✧ Ironton, OH 45638-1010

740.555.0112 ✧ Fax: 740.555.0111 ✧ www.HaasPharm.com

December 22, 20-- ↓2

Ms. Suba Patel
1228 North Oak Street   } ⟶ Remove Space After Paragraph
St. Albans, WV 25177-4900 ↓1

Dear Ms. Patel ↓1

All of the employees at Haas Pharmaceutical Supply are pleased that you are doing an internship at our company headquarters. One of your duties will be to assist Mr. Joseph Takaki in preparing the daily correspondence. We know that your training at Highview Community College has prepared you well for this task. ↓1

Remember that the correspondence our customers receive from us is one of the ways that they evaluate our effectiveness as a business. Our outgoing letters must be as perfect as we can make them in layout, content, grammar, and punctuation. Error-free communication will impress upon our customers that we have a company-wide commitment to excellence. ↓1

Enclosed is a sample company letter for your review. If you have any questions, contact me or your supervisor, Mr. Takaki. Again, we are glad to have you working in our organization. ↓1

Sincerely ↓2

Gerald Haas } ⟶ Remove Space After Paragraph
President ↓1

xx ↓1

Enclosure

Documents with Columns

WARMUP 59a

Key each line, striving for control. Repeat if desired.

alphabet	1	Jimmy Favorita realized that we must quit playing by six o'clock.
figure	2	Joell, in her 2001 truck, put 19 boxes in an annex at 3460 Marks.
double letters	3	Merriann was puzzled by a letter that followed a free book offer.
easy	4	Ana's sorority works with vigor for the goals of the civic corps.

| 1 | 2 | 3 | 4 | 5 | 6 | 7 | 8 | 9 | 10 | 11 | 12 | 13 |

SKILL BUILDING

59b Textbook Keying

1. Key the drill, concentrating on good keying techniques. Tap ENTER twice after each 2-line group.
2. Repeat the drill if time permits.

adjacent reaches	5	Is assessing potential important in a traditional career program?
	6	I saw her at an airport at a tropical resort leaving on a cruise.
direct reaches	7	Fred kicked a goal in every college soccer game in June and July.
	8	Ned used their sled on cold days and my kite on warm summer days.
double letters	9	Bobby Lott feels that the meeting at noon will be cancelled soon.
	10	Pattie and Tripp meet at the swimming pool after football drills.

59c Timed Writing

1. Key a 1' timing on each paragraph; work to increase speed.
2. Key a 3' timing on all paragraphs.

all letters

	gwam	1'	3'
Surrogate grandparents and pet therapy might not be the types	12	4	62
of terms that you expect to find in a medical journal, but they are	26	9	66
concepts that are quite popular with senior citizens. Two of the	39	13	71
most common problems experienced by senior citizens who do not live	53	18	75
with or near a family member are loneliness and the craving to feel	66	22	80
needed and loved.	70	23	81
Senior citizens who are healthy and who are stable mentally	12	27	85
often can have a high-quality relationship with deprived children	25	32	89
who do not have grandparents of their own. They often have time to	39	36	94
spare and the desire to give these needy children extra attention	52	41	98
and help with their schoolwork and other needs. At first, it may	65	45	103
seem that children gain the most from relationships with seniors.	79	50	107
However, it soon becomes evident that the surrogate grandparents	92	54	112
tend to benefit as much or even more than the children.	103	58	115

| 1' | 1 | 2 | 3 | 4 | 5 | 6 | 7 | 8 | 9 | 10 | 11 | 12 | 13 | 14 |
| 3' | | 1 | | | 2 | | | 3 | | | 4 | | |

PUNCTUATION STYLE

Letters may use either open punctuation or mixed punctuation. **Open punctuation** has no punctuation after the salutation or complimentary closing. **Mixed punctuation** adds a colon after the salutation and a comma after the complimentary closing.

Dear Mr. Jones Sincerely	Dear Mr. Jones: Sincerely,
Open Punctuation	**Mixed Punctuation**

APPLICATIONS

65-d1
Block Letter

1. Key the block letter on the next page with open punctuation. Position the dateline at approximately 2". Remove the extra space after the first two lines of the letter address. Change the *xx* to your first and last initials.
2. Generate an envelope and add it to the letter.
3. Check and close. (*65-d1*)

65-d2
Block Letter

1. Format the letter in block style with mixed punctuation; center it vertically on the page. Add your reference initials. Attach an envelope.
2. Check and close. (*65-d2*)

Current date ↓2

Ms. Alice Kumar
4723 Glacier Drive
Selden, NY 11784-4723

Dear Ms. Kumar:

Due to an unavoidable change in his schedule, Dr. Ibrahim Gadalla will be unavailable to see patients during the first week in November. Since your next regularly scheduled appointment is during this week, we would like to give you the opportunity to reschedule your appointment for a later date. If rescheduling your appointment is impossible, we will be glad to make arrangements for you to see one of the other physicians in the medical group.

We apologize for any inconvenience. Please call our office at 631-555-0102 as soon as possible to reschedule your appointment.

Sincerely, ↓2

Frederick Limerick
Office Manager

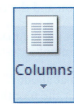
COLUMNS

PAGE LAYOUT/PAGE SETUP/COLUMNS

59d

Text may be formatted in multiple columns on a page to make it easier to read. A newsletter, for example, is usually formatted in columns. Typically, newsletters are written in an informal, conversational style and are formatted with **banners** (text that spans multiple columns), newspaper columns, graphic elements, and other text enhancements. In newspaper columns, text flows down one column and then to the top of the next column. A simple, uncluttered design with a significant amount of white space is recommended to enhance the readability of newsletters.

To create columns of equal width:

1. On the Page Layout tab, in the Page Setup group, click Columns .

2. Click to choose the desired number of columns ❷.

Column format may be applied before or after keying text. Generally, column formats are easier to apply after text has been keyed.

Occasionally, you may want certain text (such as a banner or headline) to span more than one column.

To format a banner:

1. Select the text to be included in the banner.

2. On the Page Layout tab, in the Page Setup group, click Columns.

3. Drag the number of columns to one and format the banner appropriately.

Balanced columns end at the same point on the page.

To balance columns:

1. Position the insertion point at the end of the text to be balanced.

2. Insert a Continuous section break (on the Page Layout tab, in the Page Setup group, click Breaks and click Continuous).

BUSINESS LETTER REVIEW

The block letter style is a common business letter format in which all letter parts begin at the left margin. The standard letter parts and the required spacing using the defaults of *Word 2007* are reviewed below. The model letter below and on page 292 illustrates **open punctuation**—no punctuation after the salutation and the complimentary closing.

Letterhead. Preprinted stationery that includes the company name, logo, address, and other optional information, such as a telephone number, e-mail, or Web address.

Dateline. Date the letter is prepared. Position at about 2" or center the page vertically. Begin at least .5" below the letterhead. Spell out the month; tap ENTER twice after the dateline.

Letter Address. The complete address of the recipient of the letter. Includes the personal title, first name, and last name of the recipient followed by the company name, street address, and city, state, and ZIP Code. Remove extra space after each line in the letter address except the last one.

Salutation. Include a courtesy title with the name, e.g., *Dear Mr. Nguyen, Dear Professor Glenn*. Use *Ladies and Gentlemen* when addressing a company. Tap ENTER once after the salutation.

Body. The message of the letter. Single-space the body and tap ENTER once after each paragraph.

Complimentary closing. Formal good bye. Capitalize only the first letter of the closing. Tap ENTER twice to allow space for the signature.

Writer's name and title. Key the first and last name of the sender. Include the sender's personal title (*Dr., Ms., Mrs., Mr.*) if the first name does not clearly indicate gender (e.g., *Ms. Liang Yuen*). Use a comma to separate the title if it is on the same line as the name. If two lines are used, remove the extra space between the writer's name and title.

Jeannette Kohn, President   or   *Jeannette Kohn*
                                          President

Reference initials. Key the typist's initials in lowercase letters. (Replace *xx* with your initials.)

Enclosure notation. Indicates that something is included in the envelope with the letter. If multiple enclosures are listed, set a tab at 1.0" and remove added space between lines.

Enclosures: *Print proofs*
                 Photo album

Space after paragraph was removed.

Tab 1.0"

At times, you will want to start a new column instead of letting the text flow naturally from one column to the next.

To force the starting of a new column:

1. Position the insertion point where the new column is to start.
2. On the Page Layout tab, in the Breaks group, click Column.

KEYBOARDING PRO DELUXE   See References/Word commands/Lesson 59

DRILL 1	SIMPLE COLUMNS	TRAINING

1. In the open file, on the Page Layout tab, in the Page Setup group, click Columns.

    a. Format the document in three equal-width columns. Preview the document.

    b. Change the columns to two balanced columns. Preview the document.

    c. Select *Productivity Enhancement Program*, click Columns and click One. Tap ENTER after the heading.

    d. Apply 20-point Arial Black font. Center-align the banner heading.

2. Add an appropriate clip art image related to "training" within the last paragraph. Change the text wrapping to Square, and align the graphic to the margin.

3. Check and close. (*59-drill1*)

WRAP TEXT AROUND GRAPHICS

When graphic elements are included in documents such as newsletters or reports, text usually wraps around the graphic.

To wrap text around graphics:

1. Select the graphic.
2. Under Drawing Tools, on the Format tab, in the Arrange group, choose Text Wrapping ❶.
3. Select the desired wrapping style ❷ (Square).
4. Click the desired alignment ❸ (Right), and then click OK.

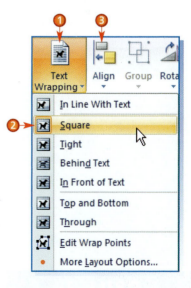

Block Letter and Envelope Review

Key each line, striving for control. Repeat if desired.

alphabet 1 The dizzy boxer's mad opponent jabbed quickly with his fat glove.

figures 2 I received 128 books, 7,349 magazines, and 560 newspapers yearly.

1st/2nd fingers 3 Prepare for the future by studying, working, and playing at home.

shift key 4 Mr. Sam Keatley gave the letters and memos to Ms. Charlene Jones.

| 1 | 2 | 3 | 4 | 5 | 6 | 7 | 8 | 9 | 10 | 11 | 12 | 13 |

FUNCTION REVIEW

65b

ENVELOPES

MAILINGS/CREATE/ENVELOPES

Word will automatically copy the letter address from the letter on the screen to the envelope. In the illustration below, the letter is displayed and then the software screen automatically displays the envelope address.

With the letter displayed on the screen, select the letter address. On the Mailings tab, in the Create group, click Envelopes. You can either print the envelope ❶ or choose Add to Document ❷ and print the envelope with the letter. Key the return address if it is not preprinted on the envelope,.

CENTER PAGE

PAGE LAYOUT/PAGE SETUP/DIALOG BOX LAUNCHER

1. On the Page Layout tab, in the Page Setup group, click the Dialog Box Launcher; click the Layout tab.

2. Click the down arrow in the Vertical alignment box and select Center ❶. Check the placement in Print Preview.

DRILL 1   ENVELOPE AND CENTER PAGE   BARRINGTON

1. Center the letter vertically. Check the placement of the letter in Print Preview.

2. Create an envelope and add it to the document.

3. Check and close. *(65-drill1)*

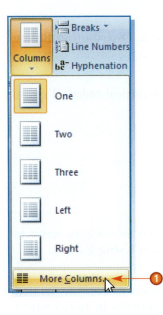

If you are creating multiple-column pages, you may want to add a vertical line between columns. Vertical lines help create order, move the eye up and down the page, and separate unrelated stories.

To insert a line between columns:

PAGE LAYOUT/PAGE SETUP/COLUMNS

1. On the Page Layout tab, in the Page Setup group, click Columns.
2. Choose More Columns ❶.
3. In the Columns dialog box, click Line between ❷ and click OK.

1. In the open document, balance the columns.
2. Change the Wrapping style of the graphic. If the graphic moves to the left column, drag it back so it is positioned above the *Integration* paragraph.
3. Check to see that the graphic is center-aligned.
4. Preview, check, and close the document when you are satisfied. (*59-drill2*)

INTERNET ACTIVITY 🌐

59e Search for Books

Search the Internet and locate at least five top-selling books about virtual teams. You will use these books in the next activity.

COMMUNICATION ✳

59f
Composing and Editing

Use proper bibliography style to list each book you found in *59e*. After each citation, use your own words to compose a short summary (1-2 sentences) for each book. A sample is provided below. Alphabetize the list by author. (*59f*)

Gladwell, Malcolm. *Blink: The Power of Thinking Without Thinking.* New York: Little Brown and Company, 2005.

This book discusses how individuals process information on a subconscious level in the blink of an instant. Gladwell states that most people can make better instant judgments by training their mind and senses to focus on the most relevant facts and that less input (as long as it is the right input) is better than more.

64-d4

Format Memo

MEMOS

1. In the open document, add a memo heading that is addressed to **Distribution Below** and is from **Mary Smith**. The subject is **Keying Memos**. Use the current date.
2. Key the reference initials and undo automatic capitalization.
3. Key the distribution list, and add your name to the list in alphabetical order. Tap TAB before keying the names. Remove extra space between lines.
4. Check and close. (*64-d4*)

Distribution List:
> **Amilee Ho**
> **Trina Parks**
> **Louis Young**

64-d5

E-mail

1. Key the e-mail message below to your instructor. **Note**: If you do not have access to e-mail, key the assignment in memo format. The subject line is **Using E-mail**.
2. If :) converts to a smiley face, undo it. Send the message. (*64-d5*)

E-mail has become one of the most popular forms of communication. In order to protect the privacy of your e-mail, keep the following points in mind when choosing an appropriate e-mail password.

- Do not choose a password that is named after a family member or a pet or uses a birth date.
- Choose a combination of letters, numbers, and symbols; preferably, use UPPERCASE and lowercase letters, e.g., TLQ+2mr or Sm!le9.
- Do not share your password with anyone or write your password on paper and leave it near your computer.

Keep the following points in mind when composing e-mail.

- Do not use bold or italic or vary fonts.
- Do not use UPPERCASE for emphasis.
- Use emoticons or e-mail abbreviations with caution (e.g. :) for smile or BTW for by the way.)
- Write clear, concise messages that are free of spelling and grammatical errors.
- Do not send an e-mail in haste or anger. Think about the message carefully before clicking the Send button.

TIP

E-mail attachments are not limited to text files; they can be pictures, spreadsheets, or just about any type of file.

64-d6

E-mail Message Attachment

ACTIVITY

1. Send the e-mail message (or memo) to your instructor and one student in your class. The subject line is **Competitive Events Report**.
2. Attach the data file *activity*. Send the message. (*64-d6*)

I have completed the Activity Report required for this year's competitive events. The file *activity* is attached for your review. Please proofread the report and give a printed copy to Lupe Funes for inclusion in the national project notebook.

Remember, the reports must be postmarked by December 1.

64-d7

E-mail Message with Picture Attachment

GREAT WALL.JPG

1. Send the e-mail to yourself and your teacher. Add **Trip to China** as the subject.
2. Attach the picture file *great wall.jpg* from the data files. (*64-d7*)

My summer vacation included a trip to China. Most of my time was spent sightseeing in Shanghai and Beijing. Attached is a picture of the Great Wall of China. It was exciting to be able to climb on one of the great wonders of the world.

1. Key the newsletter below. Use .5" left and right margins.

2. Key the title, **Arena Update**, using Arial, 48 point, bold. Use 18-point Arial type for the internal headings.

3. Insert clip art files, as shown in the newsletter. You may substitute any appropriate clip art you find if you cannot find the same images. Wrap the text around the graphics.

4. Balance columns so they all end at about the same place.

5. Create a double-line page border that is dark red and 1½ point.

6. Check and close. (*59-d1*)

Arena Update

Arena Update

Get Your Shovels Ready!

The architects have put the final touches on the arena plans, and the groundbreaking has been scheduled for March 18. Put the date on your calendar and plan to be a part of this exciting time. The Groundbreaking Ceremony will begin at 5:00 at the new arena site. After the ceremony, you will join the architects in the practice facility for refreshments and an exciting visual presentation of the new arena. The party ends when we all join the Western Cougars as they take on the Central Lions for the final conference game.

Cornerstone Club Named

Robbie Holiday of the Cougars Club submitted the winning name for the new premium seating and club area of the new arena. Thanks to all of you who submitted suggestions for naming the new club. For his suggestion, which was selected from over 300 names submitted, Robbie has won season tickets for next year and the opportunity to make his seat selection first. The Cornerstone Club name was selected because members of our premium club play a crucial role in making our new arena a reality. Without the financial support of this group, we could not lay the first cornerstone of the arena.

Cornerstone Club members have first priority in selecting their seats for both basketball and hockey in a specially designated section of the new arena. This section provides outstanding seats for both basketball games and hockey matches. Club members also have access to the Cornerstone Club before the game, during halftime, and after the game. They also receive a parking pass for the lot immediately adjacent to the arena. If you would like more information about the Cornerstone Club and how you can become a charter member, call the Cougars Club office during regular business hours.

What View Would You Like?

Most of us would like to sit in our seats and try them out before we select them rather than look at a diagram of the seating in the new arena. Former Cougar players make it easy for you to select the perfect angle to watch the ball go in the basket. Mark McKay and Jeff Dunlap, using their patented Real View visualization software, make it possible for you to experience the exact view you will have from the seats you select. In fact, they encourage you to try several different views. Most of the early testers of the new seat selection software reported that they came in with their minds completely made up about the best seats in the house. However, after experiencing several different views with the Real View software, they changed their original seat location request.

64-d1

Memo with
Distribution List

1. Key the memo on the previous page.
2. Check and close. (*64-d1*)

64-d2

Memo

1. Key the memo to **Marvell Hodges**, from **Christina Hagberg, Coordinator**. Use **July 27, 20--** as the date and **August 8-9 Workshop** as the subject.
2. Check and close. (*64-d2*)

Over seventy-five teachers have preregistered to participate in the Electronic Presentation Workshop scheduled for August 8-9 at Ferguson Community College. We are very pleased with the overwhelming response to this offering.

The workshop will begin at 8 a.m. and conclude by 5 p.m. each day. Please come to Room T38 of the Continuing Education Building. You may make your housing reservation today by calling 601-555-0142. I look forward to your participating in this outstanding seminar.

64-d3

Memo with
Distribution List

1. Key the memo to **Mexican-American Cultural Committee—Distribution Below**, from **Pablo Gonzales, Human Resources**. Use **November 21, 20--** as the date and **Mexican-American Achievers** as the subject. Format enumerated items using the defaults. Key **Attachment** below your reference initials.
2. Key the following names in the distribution list: **Samuel Gibbs, Angela Sansing, Collin Sheridan, Joan Wang**. Remove the extra space between the lines.
3. Check and close. (*64-d3*)

Acme Technologies has traditionally nominated a deserving Mexican-American staff member to be honored as a Mexican-American Achiever. This career development program seeks to expose, educate, and enlighten young adults to various opportunities found in the corporate sector. Mara Pena and Lydia Valquez were former recipients for Acme Technologies. They have served as volunteer counselors, tutors, confidants, and advisors to youth.

Last year Acme sponsored an At Large participant chosen by the Youth in Business Association (YBA). This year we would like to nominate an Acme staff member.

The nominating criteria established by the YBA are as follows:

• A current Acme employee who has been employed for at least two years.
• An individual who is willing to volunteer at least one year of service to the program.
• An individual recently completing a special leadership role by representing our company on a community service project.

Please make your nomination on the attached form and forward it to Human Resources by **Friday, December 5, 20--**.

1. Key the text below.
2. Format the title in Cambria, 18 pt., bold; center it.
3. Create two columns of equal width; balance the columns so that both end at about the same point.
4. At the right of two of the numbered items, insert an appropriate graphic. Wrap text around the graphics using square wrapping and right alignment; size the graphics appropriately.
5. Check and close. (*59-d2*)

TIPS ON CULTURE AND CUSTOMS

North American business executives need knowledge of customs and practices of their international business partners. The following suggestions provide an important starting point for understanding other cultures.

1. Know the requirement of handshaking. Taking the extra moment to shake hands at every meeting and again on departure will reap benefits.
2. Establish friendship first if important for that culture. Being a friend may be important first; conducting business is secondary. Establish a friendship; show interest in the individual and the family. Learn people's names and pronounce them correctly in conversation.
3. Understand the meaning of time. Some cultures place more importance on family, personal, and church-related activities than on business activities. Accordingly, they have longer lunches and more holidays. Therefore, they place less importance on adherence to schedules and appointment times.
4. Understand rank. Protocol with regard to who takes precedence is important; i.e., seating at meetings, speaking, and walking through doorways. Do not interrupt anyone.
5. Know the attitudes of space. Some cultures consider 18 inches a comfortable distance between people; however, others prefer much less. Adjust to their space preferences. Do not move away, back up, or put up a barrier, such as standing behind a desk.
6. Understand the attitude of hospitality. Some cultures are generous with hospitality and expect the same in return. For example, when hosting a party, prepare a generous menu; finger foods may be considered "ungenerous."
7. Share their language appropriately. Although the business meeting may be conducted in English, speak the other language in social parts of the conversation. This courteous effort will be noted.

2" or tap Enter three times

TO: Environmental Planning and Protection Committee—Distribution Below ↓1

FROM: Richard M. Taylor ↓1

DATE: October 31, 20-- ↓1

SUBJECT: Trail Design ↓1

Last week, Madilyn signed the contract for the trail design for Phase I of our Georgetown property. NatureLink was selected as the contractor. This firm was chosen because of its extensive experience in selecting interpretative sites, designing trails, and installing boardwalks to protect wetlands and environmentally sensitive areas. ↓1

The first onsite meeting is scheduled for November 10. We will meet at the main entrance at 10:30 a.m. to tour the property and review the procedures that NatureLink plans to use in designing the trails near the red cockaded woodpecker (RCW) habitat. Since the RCW is an endangered species, we want to balance the desire of ecotourists to observe these birds and the need to protect them. ↓1

Please let me know if you plan to participate in the initial meeting with NatureLink. ↓1

xx ↓1 ← Typist's first and last initials

Distribution List:

    Paula Alvarez
    Jason Liu   Remove extra space
    Ericka Palmer
    Roberto Valenzuala

LESSON 60 | Assessment

WARMUP 60a

WARMUP 60a

Key each line, striving for control. Repeat if desired.

alphabet	1	Jayne Cox puzzled over workbooks that were required for geometry.
figures	2	Edit pages 308 and 415 in Book A; pages 17, 29, and 60 in Book B.
one hand	3	Plum trees on a hilly acre, in my opinion, create no vast estate.
easy	4	If they sign an entitlement, the town land is to go to the girls.

| 1 | 2 | 3 | 4 | 5 | 6 | 7 | 8 | 9 | 10 | 11 | 12 | 13 |

SKILL BUILDING

60b Timed Writing

1. Key two 3' timed writings. Strive for control.

A

all letters

	gwam	3'	5'
What is a college education worth today? If you asked that		4	2
question to a random sample of people, you would get a wide range of		9	5
responses. Many would respond that you cannot quantify the worth of		13	8
a bachelor's degree. They quickly stress that many factors other		18	11
than wages enhance the quality of life. They tend to focus on the		22	13
benefits of sciences and liberal arts and the appreciation they		26	16
develop for things that they would never have been exposed to if		31	18
they had not attended college.		33	20
Data show, though, that you can place a value on a college		37	22
education—at least in respect to wages earned. Less than twenty		41	25
years ago, a high school graduate earned only about fifty percent		45	27
of what a college graduate earned. Today, that number is quite		50	30
different. The gap between the wages of a college graduate and		54	32
the wages of a high school graduate has more than doubled in the		58	35
last twenty years.		59	36
The key factor in economic success is education. The new		63	38
jobs that pay high wages require more skills and a college degree.		68	41
Fortunately, many high school students do recognize the value of		72	43
getting a degree. Far more high school graduates are going to		76	46
college than ever before. They know that the best jobs are jobs		81	48
for knowledge workers and those jobs require a high level of skill.		85	51

3'	1	2	3	4
5'	1		2	3

APPLICATIONS

60c

Assessment

→ Continue

✓ Check

With *Keyboarding Pro DELUXE*: When you complete a document, proofread it, check the spelling, and preview for placement. When you are completely satisfied, click the Continue button to move to the next document. Click the Check button when you are ready to error-check the test. Review and/or print the document analysis results.

Without *Keyboarding Pro DELUXE*: Key the documents in sequence. When time has been called, proofread all documents again and identify errors.

Dateline: Begin the dateline at about 2" as shown on the status line. If the vertical page position is not displayed at the bottom left of your status bar, right-click on the status bar and click Vertical Page Position.

Use the Date and Time feature to insert the date. Use the Month, day, year format; do not select Update automatically.

Reference Initials: To format reference initials in lowercase, click the AutoCorrect Options tag below your initials and choose Undo Automatic Capitalization.

E-MAIL REVIEW

Memorandums sent electronically are called e-mail. The header of an e-mail message is prepared by filling in the appropriate boxes, such as recipient's e-mail address and the subject line. The sender's name and the date are added automatically by the software.

Using e-mail requires an e-mail program, an e-mail address, and access to the Internet. If you cannot meet these requirements, format all e-mail in this text as memos.

Address e-mail carefully. Key and check the address of the recipient ❶ and supply a subject line. Add the e-mail address of anyone who should receive a copy of the e-mail. Supply a specific subject line ❷.

Format the body of an e-mail single space; tap the ENTER key to add space between paragraphs. Do not indent paragraphs. Limit the use of bold, italic, and uppercase. For business use, avoid abbreviations and emoticons (e.g., BTW for by the way or ;) for wink). Single-space the body of an e-mail. Double-space between paragraphs.

Attach electronic documents to an e-mail message using the attachment feature of the e-mail program. Distribution of electronic documents via e-mail is a common business practice. The attached file can then be opened and edited by the recipient. To attach a file, click the Attach Files ❸ or other appropriate button to locate the file. (A window will open to search for the file. When you locate the file, click the filename. Click Insert, Open, or Attach to attach the document; procedures will vary from one e-mail program to another.)

Keyboarding Pro DELUXE users: Key all e-mails as memos.

1. Key the newsletter below.
2. Format the document using two equal columns.
3. Create a heading using Comic Sans MS font, 18 point, and blue text color.
4. Create a paragraph border around the last paragraph. Choose White, Background 1, Darker 15% shading, 3-point solid dark red shadow border.
5. Create a triple-line box page border that is dark red and ½ point.
6. Insert an appropriate clip art in the second column.
7. Insert the rectangle and arrow shapes as shown below. Fill and group the shapes. Move the shapes below the columns.
8. Preview and proofread the document.
9. Check the test and close. (*60-d1*)

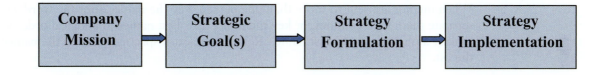

Strategic Planning Review

The last Board meeting involved reviewing the strategic planning for DataNet, Inc. The meeting began with an examination of the current mission statement, "Delivering the best-in-class integrated mobile and Internet solutions specifically tailored to meet our customers' business needs." To achieve this mission, DataNet has established a strategic goal of expanding and developing its international operations. More specifically, DataNet has the strategic goal of developing its business in the world's most populous country with more than 1 billion people, China.

DataNet conducted an extensive environmental analysis and organizational scan during the past year. This scanning inside the firm helped DataNet document its strengths and weaknesses. The external examination of the environment identified threats and opportunities DataNet faces. For example, DataNet's mission statement focuses on its strength of delivering a superior product as well as service. New leadership at many ranks in the company may be viewed as a potential weakness.

continued

64c

MEMORANDUMS

Memorandums and e-mails are two of the most widely used forms of informal written communication. Memorandums, often referred to as memos, are used for correspondence within an organization. Memos are generally prepared on plain paper and sent in plain or interoffice envelopes. Refer to the full-page model on page 286.

TO: Environmental Planning and Protection Committee—Distribution Below

FROM: Richard M. Taylor

DATE: October 31, 20--

SUBJECT: Trail Design

Last week, Madilyn signed the contract for the trail design for Phase I of our Georgetown property. NatureLink was selected as the contractor. This firm was chosen because of its extensive experience in selecting interpretative sites, designing trails, and installing boardwalks to protect wetlands and environmentally sensitive areas.

The first onsite meeting is scheduled for November 10. We will meet at the main entrance at 10:30 a.m. to tour the property and review the procedures that NatureLink plans to use in designing the trails near the red cockaded woodpecker (RCW) habitat. Since the RCW is an endangered species, we want to balance the desire of ecotourists to observe these birds and the need to protect them.

Please let me know if you plan to participate in the initial meeting with NatureLink.

xx

Distribution List:
    Paula Alvarez
    Jason Liu
    Ericka Palmer
    Roberto Valenzuala

To format a memo:

1. Tap ENTER three times to position the first line of the heading at about 2".

2. Format the memo heading in bold and uppercase. Tap TAB twice after *TO* and then either once or twice to align the remaining headings.

3. Tap ENTER once after each line of the heading, after each paragraph, reference initials, etc.

4. Single-space (1.15 default spacing) the body of the memo.

5. Key reference initials one line below the body of the memo.

6. Key the enclosure or attachment notation one line below the reference initials.

7. Key the copy notation one line below the enclosure notation or one line below the reference initials if no enclosure notation is needed.

DISTRIBUTION

When memos are sent to more than one person, key the names after the word *TO* and separate them with commas, or key them in a list. List names in a logical order such as rank or alphabetically by last name. Remove the extra spacing between the names in the list.

TO: Maxine Cagiano, Benjamin Morgan or **TO:** Maxine Cagiano
                                                            Benjamin Morgan
                                                            Cynthia Yost

When the memo is being sent to several people, use a distribution list.

1. After the heading *TO*, key a reference to a distribution list at the end of the memo. Example: **TO:** Steering Committee Members—Distribution Below.

2. At the end of the memo, key **Distribution List** or the name of the group (for example, *Project Managers*) followed by a colon.

3. Tap TAB and key each name on a separate line. Remove the extra spacing between the list of names.

Distribution List:
    Maxine Cagiano
    Heather Lewis
    Benjamin Morgan
    Naomi Peyton
    Cynthia Yost

In addition, DataNet recognizes the international opportunity that exists in China. Yet major competitive threats exist, and DataNet must closely examine its competition before entering a new international market.

Formulation of a strategy to achieve DataNet's goals involves concentrating its efforts on major affluent coastal cities like Shanghai. Recently, DataNet executives visited with top Chinese Communist Party officials in Huainan and discussed investing in that city, including building a factory there.

Competition for business remains intense with Chinese technology companies as well as other international conglomerate vendors. Yet DataNet has reformulated its strategy and is doubling its efforts to achieve its goals. Successful implementation of its strategy within the next two years will improve DataNet's market share both domestically as well as internationally.

CHECKPOINT

Congratulations! You have successfully completed the lessons in Module 8. To check your understanding and for more practice, complete the objective assessment and performance assessment located on the textbook website at www.collegekeyboarding.com.

Letter and Memo Mastery

LEARNING OUTCOMES

- Create e-mail and format interoffice memos.
- Format block and modified block letters with special features.
- Format traditional letters.
- Use letter template.
- Improve keyboarding skills.

LESSON 64 ▶ Memos and E-mail

WARMUP 64a

Key each line, striving for control. Repeat if desired.

alphabet	1	Judging by that quick quiz quality, were my extra videos helpful?
1st/2nd fingers	2	Using a good browser to connect to the Internet will please Benny.
fig/sym	3	Their new garden (10' wide x 23' long) will cost 48% of $13,695.72.
long words	4	Expect physiological or psychological reactions to unusual works.

| 1 | 2 | 3 | 4 | 5 | 6 | 7 | 8 | 9 | 10 | 11 | 12 | 13 |

SKILL BUILDING

64b Timed Writing

1. Key a 1' timing on each paragraph; work to increase speed.
2. Key a 3' timing on all paragraphs.

Average

	gwam	1'	3'
Do you ever "goof off" for an hour or more with a television		12	4
program or a visit on the telephone and realize later that you		25	8
haven't actually enjoyed your leisure? Each nagging little vision		38	13
of homework or chores to be completed always seems to result in		51	17
taking the edge off your pleasure. And then you must hurriedly		64	21
complete whatever you postponed. Why do so many people end up		76	25
rushing around in a frenzy, trying to meet their deadlines?		88	29
First, do not waste time feeling guilty. Check with your		12	33
friends who always seem ready for a good time but are also ready		25	38
for unexpected quizzes. Learn their secrets to managing time.		37	42
Knowing that there are sixty seconds in every minute and sixty		50	46
minutes in each hour, you can schedule your activities into the		63	50
time available. Second, learn to set priorities. You can achieve		76	55
your plans and enjoy your leisure as well.		85	58

| 1' | 1 | 2 | 3 | 4 | 5 | 6 | 7 | 8 | 9 | 10 | 11 | 12 | 13 |
| 3' | | 1 | | 2 | | | 3 | | | 4 | | | |

Grupo Azteca

LEARNING OUTCOMES

- Apply keying, formatting, and word processing skills.
- Work independently and with few specific instructions.

GRUPO AZTECA

Grupo Azteca is a Latino music conglomerate located in Mexico City. As an administrative assistant, you will prepare a number of documents using many of the formatting and word processing skills you have learned throughout Lessons 26 to 60.

Document 1

Memo

1. Prepare this memo.
2. Search for Hispanic; replace with Latino.
3. Check and close. (*mod9-d1*)

TIP

Remember to proofread and preview each document as a SOP. You will not be reminded to do this.

TO: Ricardo Sanchez | **FROM:**   Student's Name
SUBJECT: Telephone Interviews | **DATE:**   Current date

With the Hispanic population of the United States surging recently and the growth projected to continue for many years to come, Grupo Azteca has positioned itself to become a major player in the Spanish-language music market. A detailed consumer survey to be concluded by the Grupo Azteca marketing team will show specific areas of focus that will be important to Grupo Azteca.

"It is essential for Grupo Azteca to identify our best customers and most important genres if we want to break into this exploding music market," stated Vice President of Marketing Marita Norales. "What we will learn from this research will drive our business plan over the coming years." The understanding of customer preferences and buying patterns has been a major factor in Grupo Azteca's success in traditional genres, and is judged to be even more important as Grupo Azteca begins to focus on Spanish-language music.

Norales and her marketing team plan to survey 1200 purchasers of Spanish-language music. Five hundred will be contacted by phone after making purchases at large chain stores, while the remainder will be surveyed in person in smaller music stores and at Spanish-language concerts. Respondents will come from major metropolitan areas in the Southwest, southern Florida, as well as New York City and Chicago. All interviewers will be Spanish-English bilingual to ensure all consumers' replies are correctly understood and recorded.

63-d1

Continued

Demand for services is also high. Food preparation and catering businesses focus on pickup and delivery services. All food and beverages are catered for a small, but growing portion of tailgates. Setup and clean up services are also in high demand. Fans often spend more than $500 per tailgate.

Property Ventures

Many tailgates have moved from parking lots to other locations. Some teams make nearby grassy areas available to fans to set up tailgates. In some cases, the spaces can be reserved for a fee. In other cases, they are available on a first come first served basis. In many cases, entrepreneurs will arrive early and set up tents, flags, chairs, tables, and decorations to reserve those spaces. Food and beverages are often catered to those reserved areas.

Real estate developers soon saw the opportunity to move the tailgate to much more sophisticated venues. A number of creative options were made available to fans.

Parking Areas with Shelters

These areas are set up as condominium parking areas in which fans purchase a parking space as well as access to a sheltered place that provides facilities and entertainment. Some provide all food; others provide open shelters with a band and restroom facilities, but the tailgate still occurs on the owner's parking space. Costs vary depending on the location, but $30,000 plus an annual regime fee per parking space is very common.

Condominiums

Although many sporting venues are located in areas that would not be considered a typical residential area, large condominiums complexes have been built and sold to sporting fans. They are used primarily for hosting guests and for entertainment at the sporting events. Prices typically range from $150,000 to more than a million dollars.

Unique Tailgate Places

Many developments located at or near sporting venues are unique. They range from athletic clubs owned by members to an abandoned railroad track that hosts about 40 cabooses which have been turned into party places. They typically have an entertainment room, a small kitchen, and a bathroom. The top deck is covered with a canopy for additional partying space. These units can be purchased for $200,000 or more.

The bottom line is that tailgating has become a big and profitable business. In many cases, the amount of profit is dependent on the success of the team. However, in other cases, these ventures remain profitable even when the team is having a losing season.

CHECKPOINT →

Congratulations! You have successfully completed the lessons in Module 10. To check your understanding and for more practice, complete the objective assessment and performance assessment located on the textbook website at www.collegekeyboarding.com.

Document 2

Invitation

1. Key and format this document attractively.
2. Use a 20-point font for the title and add a special text effect.
3. Use a different font size for the subtitle. Use a fancy bullet for the bulleted list.
4. Check and close. (*mod9-d2*)

Grupo Azteca Presents
A Festival of Spanish Music

This festival is an unprecedented journey into the musical glories of Seville's Golden Age. Leading exponents of Spanish early music—from Spain, Britain and Morocco—perform in a variety of beautiful historic buildings. Carefully planned with regard to pace, balance, musical type and architecture, the experience is enhanced with talks, dinners, optional visits and the company of like-minded fellow participants.

The festival is planned and administered by Martín Randall Music Management, and admission is available exclusively through Grupo Azteca.

The festival package includes the following:

- Admission to seven concerts, all of which are private.
- Accommodations for five nights. You choose from a range of six carefully selected city-centre hotels. The choice of hotel determines the price you pay.
- Flights between the United States and Spain with British Airways and Iberia. *(There is a price reduction if you make your own arrangements for getting to Seville.)*
- Three dinners (with wine), all breakfasts, and interval drinks.
- Coach travel between the airport and your hotel, and on a few occasions within Seville.
- Lectures on the music and short talks on other aspects of Sevillian history and culture.
- All tips and taxes.
- The assistance in Spain of a team of Spanish-speaking festival staff.
- Practical and cultural information and a detailed program booklet.

Contact Alberto Gonzalez at +52 555 351 5500.

Bosque de Duraznos
No. 61, 4° Piso
Bosques de las Lomas
11700, D.F.
Mexico

Document 3

Table

1. Search the Internet for "Billboard top Latin albums."
2. Once the top ten albums are located, listen to some of them if possible to expose yourself to some of these songs with which you might not be familiar.
3. Create a table similar to the one below.
4. Format the table attractively.
5. Check and close. (*mod9-d3*)

Top Latin Albums			
Artist Name	**Album Name**	**Position This Week**	**Position Last Week**

63-d1

Rough-Draft Document

1. Key the document shown below; make the corrections in the two paragraphs with the proofreaders' marks.
2. Apply Equity Theme. Position the title at about 2" and apply Title style. ☀ Shrink the font to 24 points so that it will fit on one line.
3. Use square bullets and capitalize each item (Sentence case).
4. Apply Heading 1 style to the first three side headings and Heading 2 style to the last three.
5. Preview, proofread, and adjust spacing if necessary.
6. Check and close. (*63-d1*)

☀ **DISCOVER**

Document Themes
Page Layout/Themes/Themes

On the Page Layout tab, in the Themes group, click Themes and select the desired theme.

Tailgating—An Entrepreneurial Perspective

Most people view tailgating as a social event that occurs in parking lots prior to and after sporting events. Tailgating began at college football games when people had to arrive early in order to get a parking space. They brought food and beverages to consume while waiting for the football game to begin. The popularity of tailgating skyrocketed and expanded to numerous other sporting events at the college, professional, and high school levels. In addition, the amount of time spent tailgating extended significantly. Tailgating also became popular at concerts and other outdoor events.

Early Entrepreneurial Ventures

College students were some of the early entrepreneurs who saw an opportunity to make ~~a significant amount of~~ money assisting fans with the preparation and set up of extensive tailgates. They realized that *out-of-town* fans ~~who flew in for games~~ wanted these experiences, but it was difficult for them to make *all of* the arrangements. *for a tailgate* These entrepreneurial students arranged for rental items and provided services including *;place on separate lines; delete commas; apply bullets.* tents, tables, chairs, food, beverages, setup services ~~and~~ cleanup services. In the process, they made a substantial profit. Affluent local fans soon found these services to be attractive, and the businesses grew.

Supply and Services Ventures

As tailgating became more sophisticated, the demand for supplies increased significantly and numerous businesses cropped up. Typical supplies available *Apply bullets* include flags, pennants, tents, chairs with logos, paper products, food service items, tubs, coolers, umbrellas, portable grills, ~~and~~ novelty items. The best selling items are those with officially licensed logos of the team. *The second best selling items are those in team colors.*

continued

1. Key the letter using the block letter style and open punctuation.
2. Check and close. (*mod9-d4*)

Current Date | Mr. Jorge Bustos, Chairman of the Board | Grupo Azteca | Hamburgo 195 | Colonia Juarez | Mexico, D.F., Mexico 03100

Dear Mr. Bustos

Under the direction of Vice President Marita Norales, the marketing division of Grupo Azteca has just concluded a survey of 1200 consumers of Spanish-language music. Consumers in major metropolitan areas throughout the United States were contacted both in person and over the phone.

Results showed that the majority of music purchasers were between 15 and 24 years of age, and that among this group 30 percent of consumers made 70 percent of purchases. This closely mirrors results of polls of non-Spanish-language music consumers. Consumers in this age group indicated preference for the Latin Pop (62%) and Latin Hip-Hop (22%) subgenres above all other choices. As Ms. Norales predicted, this detailed marketing survey has provided Grupo Azteca with a focus for growth over the coming years.

Our survey results showed a major disparity in response to the question, "Are you satisfied with the Spanish-language music selection available?" Over 80 percent of respondents who mostly purchased their Spanish-language music at smaller retailers answered "Very Satisfied" or "Mostly Satisfied." Among consumers who mostly purchased their Spanish-language music at larger chain retailers, this number dropped to only 31 percent. We therefore suggest a strategy of aggressively placing Grupo Azteca products in large chain retailers.

Total sales of Spanish-language music have grown at least 15 percent in each of the last four years. With the detailed customer preference data we have compiled, Grupo Azteca is well positioned to become a leader in this exploding market.

Sincerely | Your Name | Administrative Assistant

Edit and Format Rough-Draft Documents

WARMUP 63a

Key each line, striving for control. Repeat if desired.

alphabet	1	We analyzed why my quick proxy fight was not over the objectives.
figures	2	Follow players number 18, 92, 40, and 57 to room 36 for more fun.
shift key	3	Mr. Jeff Smith called Ms. Helene Snow on Monday, April 15, in NY.
easy	4	He puts half the money he earns into the boxes and half in banks.

| 1 | 2 | 3 | 4 | 5 | 6 | 7 | 8 | 9 | 10 | 11 | 12 | 13 |

SKILL BUILDING

63b Textbook Keying
1. Key each line once, concentrating on good keying techniques. Tap ENTER twice after each 2-line group.
2. Repeat the drill if time permits.

home row	5	A lad has been hard at work all day; Sal and Dallas had to help.
	6	Sally and Jill also had Les Fasladd fill the large salad dishes.
3rd row	7	Take Wes to the plane to see if Patty is ready for a quick tour.
	8	Ray and Roy took a trip to walk with two pretty twins in Queens.
1st row	9	Vic and Ben came to show Manny the excellent new victory banner.
	10	Benny is excited about the new banners that help bring in money.
right hand	11	Start grading the tests before the exercises for Ted and Saddie.
	12	Dale and Dave are trading recipes for salsa, salads, and cookies.
left hand	13	Pay Kip for the many long hours he put in joining the old lines.
	14	Jill likes how my mom opens up her home to many homeless people.

| 1 | 2 | 3 | 4 | 5 | 6 | 7 | 8 | 9 | 10 | 11 | 12 | 13 |

63c Timed Writings
Key two 3' writings; strive for control.

A

all letters

	gwam	3'	5'

If you wish to advance in your career, you must learn how to make good decisions. You can develop decision-making skills by learning to follow six basic steps. The first three steps help you to see the problem. They are identifying the problem, analyzing the problem to find causes and consequences, and making sure you define the goals that your solution must meet.

Now you are ready to solve the problem with the last three steps. They include finding alternative solutions to the problem, analyzing each of the alternatives carefully to locate the best solution, and putting the best solution into action. Once you have implemented a plan of action, check to make sure that it meets all of your objectives. If it does not, then determine if the problem is with the solution or with the way it is being implemented. Always keep all options open.

gwam values:
4 | 2 | 37
8 | 5 | 39
13 | 8 | 42
17 | 10 | 44
21 | 13 | 47
25 | 15 | 49
29 | 17 | 52
33 | 20 | 54
37 | 22 | 57
41 | 25 | 59
46 | 27 | 62
50 | 30 | 64
54 | 33 | 67
57 | 34 | 69

3' | 1 | 2 | 3 | 4
5' | 1 | 2 | 3

1. In the open document, add the main title, **Eighth Annual Folk Festival**. Format the title in 14-point center and bold.
2. Format the main body of the newsletter for two columns. Balance the columns.
3. Search for a clip art related to "Hispanic" and insert it flush left in the first paragraph. Search for a clip art related to "guitar" and insert it flush right in the last paragraph of the newsletter. Set the position of the first clip art to Middle Left. Set the position of the second clip art to Top Right. Change the wrapping style for each of the clip art images to Tight.
4. Check and close. (*mod9-d5*)

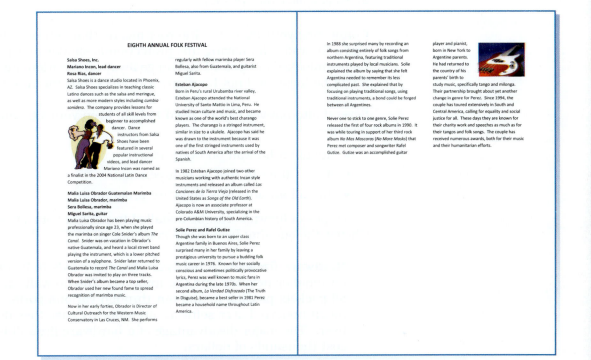

Document 6

Unbound Report

GLOBALIZATION

1. In the open document, key the title **GLOBALIZATION** and position the title at approximately 2 inches. Apply the Title style.
2. Add page numbers in the upper-right hand corner on all pages except the first. Choose Plain Number 3 style.
3. Add bullets for the items below paragraph 5 (beginning with Political and ending with Recreational).
4. Apply Heading 1 style to the side headings.
5. Insert the following footnote in paragraph 5 within the sentence where you see [1].

   [1]Makayla Record, "The Blue Riband of the North Atlantic: Westbound and Eastbound Crossings," *The GreatShips Journal*, April 3, 2009, http://www.greatships.org/globalization.htm (accessed May 2, 2009).

6. Check and close. (*mod9-d6*)

Document 7

Cover Page

1. Create a title page for the report prepared in Document 6. Use the Cover Page feature.
2. Key the following information:
   Document title: **Globalization**
   Document subtitle: **In the 21st Century**
   Author name: **Student's Name**
3. Check and close. (*mod9-doc7*)

1. Key the paragraphs below. Add the title **Protect Your Computer**; position it at about 2" and use Title style. Use square bullets for the bulleted items.
2. Find *PC* and replace it with *computer* each time it occurs. Match case on the replacement.
3. Apply Justify format to all paragraphs except the bulleted items.
4. Key your name below the last paragraph and right-align it. Insert the date directly below your name.
5. Check and close. (*62-d2*)

Connecting your PC to the Internet means that you need to have antivirus software and a firewall. Not having this protection is similar to leaving the front door of your home unlocked or open when you go away on vacation, just inviting anyone in. You might be lucky and not have any intruders, but the risk still exists.

Several alternatives can be used to help keep your PC safe and protected. They include:

- Install a firewall on every PC.
- Use a firewall that is bidirectional.
- Install an antivirus software program.

Two types of firewalls can be installed to provide your PC with adequate protection. Choose the one that best meets your needs.

1. **Hardware firewall.** A hardware firewall needs to be installed between the terminal or network and the Internet. The firewall can be set to block or allow all packets passing in and out through various ports. Hardware firewalls are much preferred over software firewalls because they do not impede the end user. The major disadvantage of a hardware firewall is the cost; it can easily cost thousands of dollars.

2. **Software firewall.** A software firewall is much less expensive and often can be downloaded from the Internet free of charge. Software firewalls are often loaded on computers used in the home and in small businesses.

If you choose the software firewall, you must install the updates and patches that are provided on a regular basis. Updating is extremely important with the virus software, as new viruses are created frequently.

2 Internet Activities

▶ **Activity 3**

EXPLORE SEARCH ENGINES

To find information on the World Wide Web (WWW), the best place to start is often a search engine. Search engines are used to locate specific information. Just a few examples of search engines are AltaVista, Excite, Google, Ask, Lycos, and Yahoo.

 To go to a search engine, click the Search button on your Web browser. (Browsers vary.)

DRILL

1. Go to the search engines on your browser. Click on the first search engine. Browse the hyperlinks available such as Maps, People Finder, News, Weather, Stock Quotes, Sports, Games, etc. Click each search engine and explore the hyperlinks.

2. Conduct the following search using Dogpile, a multithreaded search engine that searches multiple databases;

   a. Open the website for Dogpile (http://www.dogpile.com).

   b. In the Search entry box, key the keywords **American Psychological Association** publications; click Go Fetch.

3. Pick two of the following topics and search for each using more than one search engine. Look over the first ten results you get from each search. Which search engine gave you the greatest number of promising results for each topic?

   aerobics   antivirus software   interview techniques

   career change   college financing   dress for success

4. Key your findings in a report.

5. Check and close. (*ia2-a3-drill*)

▶ **Activity 4**

SEARCH YELLOW PAGES

Searching the Yellow Pages for information on businesses and services is commonplace, both in business and at home. Let your computer do the searching for you the next time.

DRILL

1. Open the search engine dogpile.com. Click Yellow Pages.

2. Determine a city that you would like to visit. Assume you will need overnight accommodations. Use the Yellow Pages to find a listing of hotels in this city.

3. Your best friend lives in (*you provide the city*); you want to send him/her flowers. Find a listing of florists in this city.

4. You create a third scenario and find listings.

5. Key your findings in a report.

6. Check and close. (*ia2-a4-drill*)

62d Draft Report

COMMITMENT

WORKPLACE SUCCESS

1. Print the open document.
2. Proofread the document carefully and locate the 10 errors in it. Use proofreaders' marks to indicate the errors.
3. Correct the errors.
4. Position the title at 2" and apply Title style.
5. Key your name below the last paragraph and right-align it.
6. Insert the date below your name using standard business format (e.g., January 3, 2009). Remove space after your name.
7. Check and close. (*62d*)

APPLICATIONS

62-d1

Composition

WORKPLACE SUCCESS

1. Read the *Workplace Success* information on self-management at the bottom of this page. Setting goals for yourself is one of the first skills that you must master. Once you have set goals, you must be able to monitor your progress in reaching them.
2. Use a search engine and search the Internet for tips in setting goals for yourself. Find five tips on setting goals that you would recommend to your classmates.
3. Use the title **Tips for Setting Goals**. Then write five tips with a sentence or two explaining each one. Use numbering for the five tips.
4. Edit your work carefully and format it as a short report using the style of your choice.
5. Check and close. (*62-d1*)

WORKPLACE SUCCESS

Self-Management

© BLEND IMAGES / JUPITER IMAGES

A simple definition of self-management is telling yourself what to do rather than waiting to be told what to do by someone else. People who are self-managed make many of the daily decisions that affect their lives. Just declaring that you will become self-managed does not work. Self-management skills must be developed.

Self-management is a concept that has worked very well in the medical world with patients who have chronic diseases. Patients learn how to deal with the pain and hassles of the disease, the appropriate use of their medications, and how to manage other factors such as exercise and nutrition, and how to evaluate new treatments. They learn to rely on themselves rather than on medical professionals to manage the disease.

Today, self-management is being applied to management and education. It is especially important in career management. Managers find that employees who are self-managed are very low maintenance employees and typically are very high performers. Companies are very willing to invest in training those employees.

▶ Activity 5

SEARCH SAVVY

Ready to sharpen your searching skills? Here are some tips:

- Choose search terms carefully. Use the most specific words, and put the most important and unique terms first.
- Use phrases when possible (in most search engines, anything inside quotation marks).
- When a word must appear in the search results, tag it as mandatory (in many search engines, a + before the word).
- Use Boolean logic in search engines to reduce off-target hits.
- Explore the Help feature of your search engine.
- If your top 25 to 50 hits aren't on point, rephrase your search or try a different search engine.

DRILL

Test the tips listed above and your searching savvy by searching on three topics that interest you. For example, you might want to search for major league baseball statistics. You could start your search using *baseball* as a search term. You also could search using *baseball statistics* to narrow the results. But to quickly get exactly what you want, you could search using *major league baseball statistics*.

▶ Activity 6

HOMEWORK HELPER

The Internet is a wonderful tool to help you do your homework. At your fingertips are dictionaries, encyclopedias, tutors, museums, laboratories, magazines, newspapers, books, and many other resources.

DRILL

Visit these websites to complete the following tasks.

1. http://www.m-w.com — Find the definition of piscine.
2. http://www.howstuffworks.com — Print an article on how batteries work.
3. http://www.vote-smart.org — Examine the voting record of one of your state senators. Print information showing how the senator voted on two bills that interest you.
4. http://www.ajr.org — Print a story from a newspaper in another state.
5. http://memory.loc.gov — Print a primary source for an American history topic.
6. http://www.consumerworld.org — Search for recalls. Then do a further search for automobile recalls. Determine whether anyone you know has one of these vehicles.

WARMUP 62a

Key each line, striving for control. Repeat if desired.

alphabet	1	With zeal the boy quickly jumped over the x-ray, avoiding a fall.
figures	2	Invoice #13579 for $24.80 will be released on or before 06/15/08.
adjacent reaches	3	Were we going to open the voice track before we check any others?
easy	4	I will call you this week to see if you can act in our new plays.

| 1 | 2 | 3 | 4 | 5 | 6 | 7 | 8 | 9 | 10 | 11 | 12 | 13 |

SKILL BUILDING

62b Textbook Keying

1. Key each line once, concentrating on good keying techniques. Tap ENTER twice after each 2-line group.
2. Repeat the drill if time permits.

az	5	Zen and Ozzie zealously played the anthem in the Aztec Jazz band.
	6	Batz went to Phoenix, Arizona, to take a math quiz he had missed.
by	7	Boyd drove by the Blue Bayou to bypass the roadblocks at the Bay.
	8	By daybreak, Mary will stop by to bake a birthday cake for Jayne.
cx	9	Please carry the X-ray from exit C to exit X for Cece and Xavier.
	10	Carol can meet Xian at the exit doors following the movie Exodus.
dw	11	Don walked the dog at dawn when he dwelled in his downtown condo.
	12	Did Dwight drive Wendy to the new drive-in or the new drive-thru?
figures	13	The 12 teams spent $3,489.00 on groceries for the 567 boy scouts.
	14	Judy's 13 puzzles had 60,789 pieces, but 524 pieces were missing.

| 1 | 2 | 3 | 4 | 5 | 6 | 7 | 8 | 9 | 10 | 11 | 12 | 13 |

62c Timed Writing

1. Key two 1' writings, working for speed.
2. Key one 3' writing at your control rate.

all letters

	gwam	1'	3'
One of the most important skills needed for success on the	12	4	42
job is listening. However, this is a skill that takes hours of	25	8	46
practice. You can maximize your effectiveness by learning and	37	12	50
using techniques for effective listening. People can listen two	50	17	55
or three times faster than they can talk. Use the difference be-	63	21	59
tween the rate at which a person speaks and the rate at which you	76	25	63
can listen to review what the person has said and to identify the	89	30	68
main ideas communicated. This active style of listening helps	102	34	72
you avoid the tendency to tune in and out of a conversation.	114	38	76

| 1' | 1 | 2 | 3 | 4 | 5 | 6 | 7 | 8 | 9 | 10 | 11 | 12 | 13 | 14 |
| 3' | | 1 | | 2 | | 3 | | 4 | |

Level

3

MASTERING DOCUMENT DESIGN

LEARNING OUTCOMES

Document Design Skills

- To format business correspondence with special features.
- To enhance report formats with elements that add structure, provide a consistent image, and increase readability.
- To format tables, forms, and financial documents.

Word Processing Skills

- To apply the basic word processing functions.

Communication Skills

- To produce error-free documents and apply language arts skills.

Keyboarding

- To improve keyboarding speed and accuracy.

61-d1

Document with Table

1. Key the document, making the corrections noted in the table.
2. Add the title **New Computer Lab Hours**. Position it at about 2" and apply Title style.

State budget cuts and reduction of revenue to our district require that the computer lab, located on the first floor of the Business/CIS building, reduce the number of hours of operation. The new lab hours will be effective beginning Monday, May 1.

Day	Hours
Monday	9:00 a.m. to 8:00 p.m.
Tuesday	10:00 a.m. to 9:00 p.m.
Wednesday	8:30 a.m. to 7:30 p.m.
Thursday	*10* ~~5~~:00 a.m. to 3:~~3~~0 p.m. *9:00*
Friday/~~Saturday~~	~~Closed~~ *9:00 a.m. to 3:00 p.m.*
~~Sunday~~	~~Closed~~ *Delete row*

Please announce the new lab hours to all your students so that they can adjust their schedules accordingly. The new hours will be posted on the lab doors and on the sign-in terminals.

3. Search for *lab* and replace with *laboratory*.
4. Apply table format Medium Shading 2 - Accent 1; center the table.
5. Check and close. (*61-d1*)

61-d2

Landscape Document for Posting

1. Use the title and the information from the table in *61-d1* to prepare a document to post. Format the document with 36-point bold, Cambria. Center the heading. Use Landscape orientation.
2. Key the days at the left margin and set a right-align tab at 9.0" for the hours. Omit headings. Center the page vertically.
3. Check and close. (*61-d2*)

61-d3

Document with Proofreaders' Marks

1. Use Wide margins and key the copy below. Make the changes shown.
2. Position the title **Self-Management and Online Education** at 2". Use Title style.
3. Check and close. (*61-d3*)

WORKPLACE SUCCESS

Instructors with experience teaching ~~distance education~~ *online* courses know that the students who are most successful in these programs are *those who are* self-managed. A program without direct supervision requires that students *assume both* ~~take~~ responsibility *new ¶* and accountability for their success. Self-monitoring is *a critical* part of the process. *Two key* ~~Some of the~~ personal attributes required for effective self-management are initiative and commitment. Self-monitoring requires *you to* accepting the consequences of your own actions.

KEYBOARDING PRO DELUXE **SKILL BUILDING/TECHNIQUE BUILDER**

DRILL 15

KEYSTROKING PATTERNS
Key each line once for fluency;
DS between groups.

3rd row

1 it we or us opo pop you rut rip wit pea lea wet pit were quiet
2 pew tie toe per rep hope pour quip rope your pout tore rip quirk

Home row

3 ha has kid lad led last wash lash gaff jade fads half sash haggle
4 as dad had add leg jug lads hall lass fast deal fall leafs dashes

1st row

5 ax ban man zinc clan bank calm lamb vain amaze bronze back buzzer
6 ax sax can bam zag cab mad fax vans buzz caves knack waxen banana

KEYBOARDING PRO DELUXE **TIMED WRITINGS**

Standard Plan for Guided Writing Procedures

1. Take a 1' writing on paragraph 1. Note your *gwam*.
2. Add four words to your 1' *gwam* to determine your goal rate.
3. Set the timer for 1' and the Timer option to beep every 15".
4. From the table below, select from Column 4 the speed nearest your goal rate. Note the ¼' point at the left of that speed. Place a check mark at each ¼' goal.
5. Take two 1' guided writings on paragraphs 1 and 2 striving to meet your ¼' goal.

A
all letters

1. Take a 1' writing on each paragraph.
2. Take one 3' or one 5' writing on both paragraphs.

Optional: Practice as a guided writing.

		gwam	
1/4'	**1/2'**	**3/4'**	**1'**
8	16	24	32
9	18	27	36
10	20	30	40
11	22	33	44
12	24	36	48
13	26	39	52
14	28	41	56
15	30	45	60
16	32	48	64
17	34	51	68
18	36	54	72

Writing 28

gwam 3' | 5'

Who is a professional? The word can be defined in many ways. Some may think of a professional as someone who is in an exempt job category in an organization. To others the word can denote something quite different; being a professional denotes an attitude that requires thinking of your position as a career, not just a job. A professional exerts influence over her or his job and takes pride in the work accomplished.

Many individuals who remain in the same positions for a long time characterize themselves as being in dead-end positions. Others who remain in positions for a long time consider themselves to be in a profession. A profession is a career to which you are willing to devote a lifetime. How you view your profession is up to you.

	3'	5'
	4	2	32
	8	5	35
	12	7	37
	17	10	40
	21	13	43
	25	15	45
	28	17	47
	32	19	49
	36	22	52
	40	24	54
	45	27	57
	49	29	59
	50	30	60

3' | 1 2 3 4
5' | 1 2 3

61c Textbook Keying

1. Key each line once, concentrating on good keying techniques. Tap ENTER twice after each 3-line group.
2. Repeat the drill if time permits.

1st finger
5   fog the turn for yet gun bright got gut nor just fun you give Bob
6   burns turn fern fight found girl granny from Juan hunt minute him
7   The brave boy found his neighbor giving Juan taffy to go hunting.

2nd finger
8   ice ore keep kind kitten echo dickens chicken I kneel nick icicle
9   Pat saw pop swap pizza with Adam as he zipped past the pool hall.
10 Ike etched kittens, chickens, and icicles on Dee's knee with ink.

4th finger
11 swap zone we poll was lap pa asp zap wad sap saw wax papa sow wow
12 as pax own sass is well all pan will ax sew pot Paul few loop Pam
13 Debra averages six fewer servings of sweet dessert during Easter.

left hand
14 beware greatest feet effects gag faster bazaar assess drawers ads
15 grease estate carafe awarded exerted get careers agrees beads ear
16 In my opinion, today anyone can play pool or Monopoly with Jimmy.

right hand
17 pill nylon million puppy uphill yoyo ninny opinion lion polio mum
18 Jimmy minimum pupil holly imply kinky monopoly pool union you ohm
19 Their neighbor's mangy dog and lame duck slept by a box of rocks.

balanced hand
20 coalfield ape fishbowl disorient ivory giant leprosy neurotic may
21 problem rogue whale theory ornament quench mandible jangle mentor
22 Their big naughty dog would torment us and ambush the wheelchair.

| 1 | 2 | 3 | 4 | 5 | 6 | 7 | 8 | 9 | 10 | 11 | 12 | 13 |

COMMUNICATION

61d

1. Key the procedures shown at the right.
2. Use Title style for the title. Shrink the font so the title will fit on one line.
3. Check and close. (61d)

STANDARD PROCEDURES FOR FINALIZING A DOCUMENT

1. Use Spelling and Grammar to check the document when you have completed it.
2. Proofread the document on screen to make sure it makes sense.
3. Preview the document and check the format and overall appearance.
4. Print the document.
5. Compare the document to the source copy (textbook), and check to see that text has not been omitted or added. Revise, print, and check the document.
6. Non-*Keyboarding Pro DELUXE* Users: Create a new folder for each module (*Module 10*) and save each document you key with the name of the drill or application. Examples include *61d, 62-d2,* and *63-d1.*

DRILL 16

KEYBOARDING TECHNIQUE
Key each line once for fluency;
DS between groups.

1st
1 Zam and six lazy men visited Cecil and Bunn at a bank convention.
2 Zane, much to the concern of Bev and six men, visited their zone.

2nd
3 Jill said she wished that she had fed Dale's dog a lot less food.
4 Jake Hall sold the glass flask at a Dallas "half-off" glass sale.

3rd
5 Did either Peter or Trey quip that reporters were out to get you?
6 Either Trey or Peter tried to work with a top-quality pewter toy.

4th
7 18465 97354 12093 87541 09378 34579 74629 45834 28174 11221 27211
8 02574 29765 39821 07623 17659 20495 39481 10374 32765 77545 22213

KEYBOARDING PRO DELUXE   **TIMED WRITINGS**

Writing 29

gwam 3' 5'

A
all letters

1. Take three 1' writings on each ¶.
2. Take one 5' writing or two 3' writings. Proofread; circle errors; determine gwam.

Option: Practice as a guided writing.

			gwam
1/4'	1/2'	3/4'	1'
8	16	24	32
9	18	27	36
10	20	30	40
11	22	33	44
12	24	36	48
13	26	39	52
14	28	41	56
15	30	45	60
16	32	48	64
17	34	51	68
18	36	54	72

Students, for decades, have secured part-time jobs to help pay for college expenses. Today, more students are gainfully employed while they are in college than ever before. Many of them are employed because their financial situation requires that they earn money. Earnings from jobs go to pay for tuition, books, living costs, and other necessities. Some work so that they can own cars or buy luxury items; others seek jobs to gain skills or to build their vitas. These students are aware that many organizations prefer to hire a person who has had some type of work experience than one who has had none.

Students often ask if the work experience has to be in exactly the same field. Obviously, the more closely related the experience, the better it is. However, the old adage, anything beats nothing, applies. Regardless of the types of jobs students have, they can demonstrate that they get to work regularly and on time, they have good human relations skills, they are organized and can manage time effectively, and they produce good results. All of these factors are very critical to employers. The bottom line is that employers like to use what you have done in the past as a predictor of what you will do in the future.

Editing

LEARNING OUTCOMES

- Apply text and paragraph formats.
- Apply page layout commands.
- Improve editing skills.
- Improve keyboarding skill.

LESSON 61 — Edit Basic Documents

WARMUP 61a

Key each line, striving for control. Repeat if desired.

alphabet	1	Quickly quiz veterans for kinds of whims and big jig experiences.
figures	2	Why add 17%, 26%, and 47%, when others (380, 95) will do as well?
adjacent	3	Miss too many meetings called for noon and you will need to call.
easy	4	Do you see the new dog and cats that play in the yard each night?

| 1 | 2 | 3 | 4 | 5 | 6 | 7 | 8 | 9 | 10 | 11 | 12 | 13 |

SKILL BUILDING

61b Timed Writing

1. Key a 1' writing on each paragraph. Work to increase speed.
2. Key a 3' timing on both paragraphs.

all letters

	gwam	1'	3'
Most men and women in executive positions accept travel as		13	4	53
a part of corporate life. At the same time, executives try to keep		26	9	57
time spent on the road to a minimum. Top management often		38	13	61
supports the efforts to reduce travel time as long as effectiveness		51	17	66
is not jeopardized. The primary reason for support is that it is		64	21	70
quite expensive for executives to travel.		73	24	73
One of the major factors that makes it hard to cut back on		13	28	77
travel time is the need for face-to-face contact. Technology		25	33	81
cannot replace face-to-face contact, but it does offer some		37	37	85
helpful tools that enable managers to interact with customers in		50	41	90
remote areas in an effective manner. Video conferences,		61	45	93
webcasts, and podcasts are a few of these very helpful tools.		74	49	97

| 1' | 1 | 2 | 3 | 4 | 5 | 6 | 7 | 8 | 9 | 10 | 11 | 12 | 13 |
| 3' | | 1 | | 2 | | 3 | | 4 | |

DRILL 17

NUMBER REACHES
Key each line once at a comfortable rate; practice difficult lines.

1 My staff of 11 worked 11 hours a day from May 11 to June 11.
2 Her flight, PW 222, lands at 2:22 p.m. on Thursday, June 22.
3 We 3, part of the 333rd Corps, marched 33 miles on August 3.
4 Car 444 took Route 4 east to Route 44, then 4 miles to Aden.
5 The 55 wagons traveled 555 miles in '55; only 5 had trouble.
6 Put 6 beside 6; result 66. Then, add one more 6 to get 666.
7 She sold 7,777 copies of Record 77, Schubert's 7th Symphony.
8 In '88, it took 8 men and 8 women 8 days to travel 88 miles.
9 The 9 teams, 9 girls and 9 boys, depart on Bus 999 at 9 a.m.
10 Million has six zeros; as, 000,000. Ten has but one; as, 0.

| 1 | 2 | 3 | 4 | 5 | 6 | 7 | 8 | 9 | 10 | 11 | 12 | 13 |

all letters

Writing 30

gwam 3' | 5'

	3'	5'
Planning, organizing, and controlling are three of the	4	2	65

Planning, organizing, and controlling are three of the functions that are familiar to all sorts of firms. Because these functions are basic to the managerial practices of a business, they form the very core of its daily operations. Good managerial procedures, of course, do not just occur by accident. They must be set into motion by people. Thus, a person who plans to enter the job market, especially in an office position, should study all of the elements of good management in order to apply those principles to her or his work.

Leadership is another very important skill for a person to develop. Leaders are needed at all levels in a business to plan, organize, and control the operations of a firm. A person who is in a key position of leadership usually is expected to initiate ideas as well as to carry out the goals of a business. Office workers who have developed the qualities of leadership are more apt to be promoted than those without such skills. While leadership may come naturally for some people, it can be learned as well as be improved with practice.

Attitude is an extremely important personality trait that is a big contributor to success in one's day-to-day activities. Usually a person with a good attitude is open-minded to the ideas of others and is able to relate with others because he or she has an interest in people. Thus, one's attitude on the job often makes a great difference in whether work gets done and done right. Because teamwork is a part of many jobs, developing a good attitude toward work, people, and life seems logical.

gwam markers (3' / 5'):
```
4   2  65
8   5  68
12  7  71
17 10  73
21 13  76
25 15  78
30 18  81
34 20  83
36 22  85
40 24  87
44 26  89
48 29  92
52 31  95
57 34  97
61 37 100
65 39 102
70 42 105
72 43 106
76 46 109
80 48 111
85 51 114
89 53 117
93 56 119
97 58 122
101 61 124
105 63 126
```

3' | 1 | 2 | 3 | 4 |
5' | 1 | 2 | 3 |

DRILL 19

OPPOSITE HAND REACHES
Key at a controlled rate; concentrate on the reaches.

1 yj my say may yes rye yarn eye lye yap any relay young berry
y/t 2 tf at it let the vat tap item town toast right little attire
3 Yesterday a young youth typed a cat story on the typewriter.

4 bf but job fibs orb bow able bear habit boast rabbit brother
b/n 5 nj not and one now fun next pony month notice runner quicken
6 A number of neighbors banked on bunking in the brown cabins.

7 gag go gee god rig gun log gong cog gig agog gage going gang
g/h 8 huh oh hen the hex ash her hash ah hush shah hutch hand ache
9 Hush; Greg hears rough sounds. Has Hugh laughed or coughed?

10 row or rid air rap par rye rear ark jar rip nor are right or
r/u 11 cut us auk out tutu sun husk but fun cub gun nut mud tug hug
12 Ryan is sure you should pour your food from an urn or cruet.

| 1 | 2 | 3 | 4 | 5 | 6 | 7 | 8 | 9 | 10 | 11 | 12 |

Writing 33

all letters

gwam 3' | 5'

Most people think traveling is fun because they associate   4 | 2
travel with exciting vacations. People who have to travel as   8 | 5
part of their jobs have a very different view of travel. They   12 | 7
are more prone to view business travel as a hassle than a plea-   16 | 10
sure. Business travelers often have to work under less than   21 | 12
ideal circumstances. While they are away from the office, regu-   25 | 15
lar work tends to pile up; and they often return to find stacks   29 | 17
of work waiting for them. Many business travelers learn to uti-   33 | 20
lize wisely the waiting time that is a part of most travel.   37 | 22

A successful business trip requires careful planning. The   41 | 25
typical business traveler tends to think of a trip as a success   45 | 27
if two conditions are met. The business goals must be achieved,   50 | 30
and the trip must be totally free of headaches. The person mak-   54 | 32
ing the trip has to worry about achieving the business goals, but   58 | 35
a good travel agent can relieve the traveler of many of the wor-   63 | 38
ries of making travel arrangements. A good checklist can help to   67 | 40
ensure that all the personal items as well as business items   71 | 43
needed for the trip will be handy when they are needed.   75 | 45

3' | 1 | 2 | 3 | 4 |
5' | 1 | 2 | 3 |

DRILL 18

IMPROVE RESPONSE PATTERNS
Key each line once; DS between 4-line groups; work at a controlled rate; repeat drill.

direct reaches: reaches with the same finger; keep hands quiet

1 brand much cent numb cease bright music brief jump special carved
2 create mumps zany mystic curve mummy any checks brag brunch after
3 Bradley broke his left thumb after lunch on a great hunting trip.
4 After having mumps, Cecil once saw June excel in a funny musical.

adjacent reaches: keep fingers curved and upright

5 were junior sad yuletide trees polo very join safe property tweed
6 tree trio trickle tripod quit excess was free easy million option
7 Gwen and Sumio are going to be quite popular at the Western Club.
8 Fred said we were going to join the guys for polo this afternoon.

double letters: strike keys rapidly

9 dill seem pool attic miss carry dragged kidded layoff lapped buzz
10 commend accuse inner rubber cheer commission football jazz popper
11 Tammy called to see if she can borrow my accounting book at noon.
12 Lynnette will meet with the bookseller soon to discuss the issue.

all letters

Writing 31

	gwam	3'	5'

Working at home is not exactly a new phenomenon, but the con- 12 | 2 | 47
cept is growing quite rapidly. For many years, people have worked 26 | 5 | 50
at home. In most instances, they were self-employed and operated 39 | 8 | 52
a business from their homes. Today, the people who work at home 52 | 10 | 55
fit into a variety of categories. Some own their own businesses; 65 | 13 | 58
others bring extra work home after the workday ends. A key change 79 | 16 | 60
is the large group of people who are employed by huge organizations 92 | 18 | 63
but who work out of home offices. These employees are in jobs that 106 | 21 | 66
include sales, creative, technical, and a host of other categories. 120 | 24 | 69

The real change that has occurred is not so much the numbers 12 | 26 | 71
of people who are working at home and the variety of jobs, but the 26 | 29 | 74
complex tools that are now available for doing the job. Technology 39 | 32 | 76
has truly made the difference. In many cases, clients and customers 53 | 35 | 79
are not even aware that they are dealing with individuals working 66 | 37 | 82
at home. Computers, printers, fax machines, telephone systems, 79 | 40 | 84
and other office equipment enable the worker in the home to function 93 | 42 | 87
in the same way as workers in a typical business office. 104 | 45 | 89

1'	1	2	3	4	5	6	7	8	9	10	11	12	13
5'		1			2			3					

A

all letters

Writing 32

gwam 3'

    Many small businesses fail. Surprisingly, though, many   4
people are still willing to take a chance on starting one of   8
their own. A person who is willing to take the risks necessary   12
to manage a business in order to receive the potential rewards is   17
called an entrepreneur. In a sense, such individuals are pio-   21
neers who enjoy each step on the way to achieving objectives that   25
they have determined to be important. This type of person has   29
had a profound impact on shaping our economy and our quality of   34
life.   34

    What does it take to start a business venture, and what   38
kinds of people make it work? Obviously, the desire to make   42
money and to be one's own boss are two basic incentives, but   40
these alone are not enough to guarantee success. Two qualifica-   50
tions common to most successful entrepreneurs, whatever field   54
they are in, are an attentiveness to detail and a knack for   58
solving day-to-day problems without losing sight of long-range   62
goals.   63

    While there is a high risk in organizing any new business,   67
the entrepreneur who is successful is seldom someone who could be   71
considered a gambler. Most gamblers expect to have the odds   75
against them. On the other hand, a clever businessperson sees to   80
it that the odds are as good as possible by getting all of the   84
facts and planning carefully before going ahead. Luck helps, to   88
be sure, but a new business enterprise depends far more on good   92
ideas and detailed plans.   94

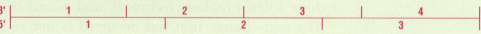

3' | 1 | 2 | 3 | 4 |
5' | 1 | 2 | 3 |

Reference Guide

Capitalization

1. First word of a sentence and of a direct quotation.
We were tolerating instead of managing diversity.
The speaker said, "We must value diversity, not merely recognize it."

2. Names of proper nouns—specific persons, places, or things.
Common nouns: continent, river, car, street
Proper nouns: Asia, Mississippi, Buick, State St.

3. Derivatives of proper nouns and geographical names.
American history   English accent
German food   Ohio Valley
Tampa, Florida   Mount Rushmore

4. A personal or professional title when it precedes the name or a title of high distinction without a name.
Lieutenant Kahn   Mayor Walsh
Doctor Welby   Mr. Ty Brooks
Dr. Frank Collins   Miss Tate
the President of the United States

5. Days of the week, months of the year, holidays, periods of history, and historic events.
Monday, June 8   Labor Day   Renaissance

6. Specific parts of the country but not compass points that show direction.
Midwest   the South   northwest of town

7. Family relationships when used with a person's name.
Aunt Helen   my dad   Uncle John

8. Noun preceding a figure except for common nouns such as line, page, and sentence.
Unit 1   Section 2   page 2   verse 7   line 2

9. First and main words of side headings, titles of books, and works of art. Do not capitalize words of four or fewer letters that are conjunctions, prepositions, or articles.
Computers in the News   Raiders of the Lost Ark

10. Names of organizations and specific departments within the writer's organization.
Girl Scouts   our Sales Department

Number Expression

General guidelines

1. Use words for numbers one through ten unless the numbers are in a category with related larger numbers that are expressed as figures.
He bought three acres of land. She took two acres.
She wrote 12 stories and 2 plays in the last 13 years.

2. Use words for approximate numbers or large round numbers that can be expressed as one or two words. Use numbers for round numbers in millions or higher with their word modifier.
We sent out about three hundred invitations.
She contributed $3 million dollars.

3. Use words for numbers that begin a sentence.
Six players were cut from the ten-member team.

4. Use figures for the larger of two adjacent numbers.
We shipped six 24-ton engines.

Times and dates

5. Use words for numbers that precede o'clock (stated or implied).
We shall meet from two until five o'clock.

6. Use figures for times with a.m. or p.m. and days when they follow the month.
Her appointment is for 2:15 p.m. on July 26, 2009.

7. Use ordinals for the day when it precedes the month.
The 10th of October is my anniversary.

Money, percentages, and fractions

8. Use figures for money amounts and percentages. Spell out cents and percent except in statistical copy.
The 16% discount saved me $145; Bill, 95 cents.

9. Use words for fractions unless the fractions appear in combination with whole numbers.
one-half of her lesson   5 1/2   18 3/4

Addresses

10. Use words for street names First through Tenth and figures for ordinals for streets above Tenth. Use figures for house numbers other than one. (If street name is a number, separate it from house number with a dash.)
One Lytle Place   Second Ave.   142—53rd St.

Use an apostrophe

1. To make most singular nouns and indefinite pronouns possessive (add **apostrophe** and **s**).

   computer + 's = computer's   Jess + 's = Jess's
   anyone's   one's   somebody's

2. To make a plural noun that does not end in s possessive (add **apostrophe** and **s**).

   women + 's = women's   men + 's = men's
   deer + 's = deer's   children + 's = children's

3. To make a plural noun that ends in s possessive. Add only the **apostrophe**.

   boys + ' = boys'   managers + ' = managers'

4. To make a compound noun possessive or to show joint possession. Add **apostrophe** and **s** to the last part of the hyphenated noun.

   son-in-law's   Rob and Gen's game

5. To form the plural of numbers and letters, add **apostrophe** and **s**. To show omission of letters or figures, add an **apostrophe** in place of the missing items.

   7's   A's   It's   add'l

Use a colon

1. To introduce a listing.

   The candidate's strengths were obvious: experience, community involvement, and forthrightness.

2. To introduce an explanatory statement.

   Then I knew we were in trouble: The item had not been scheduled.

Use a comma

1. After an introductory phrase or dependent clause.

   After much deliberation, the jury reached its decision.
   If you have good skills, you will find a job.

2. After words or phrases in a series.

   Mike is taking Greek, Latin III, and Chemistry II.

3. To set off nonessential or interrupting elements.

   Troy, the new man in MIS, will install the hard drive.
   He cannot get to the job, however, until next Friday.

4. To set off the date from the year and the city from the state.

   John, will you please reserve the center in Billings, Montana, for January 10, 2009.

5. To separate two or more parallel adjectives (adjectives could be separated by and instead of a comma).

   The loud, whining guitar could be heard above the rest.

6. Before the conjunction in a compound sentence. The comma may be omitted in a very short sentence.

   You must leave immediately, or you will miss your flight.
   We tested the software and they loved it.

7. Set off appositives and words of direct address.

   Karen, our team leader, represented us at the conference.
   Paul, have you ordered the CD-ROM drive?

Use a hyphen

1. To show end-of-line word division.

2. In many compound words—check a dictionary if unsure.
   - Two-word adjectives before a noun:
     two-car family
   - Compound numbers between twenty-one and ninety-nine.
   - Fractions and some proper nouns with prefixes/suffixes.
     two-thirds   ex-Governor   all-American

Use italic or underline

1. With titles of complete literary works.

   College Keyboarding   *Hunt for Red October*

2. To emphasize special words or phrases.

   What does *professional* mean?

Use a semicolon

1. To separate independent clauses in a compound sentence when the conjunction is omitted.

   Please review the information; give me a report by Tuesday.

2. To separate independent clauses when they are joined by conjunctive adverbs (*however, nevertheless, consequently, etc.*).

   The traffic was heavy; consequently, I was late.

3. To separate a series of elements that contain commas.

   The new officers are: Fran Pena, president; Harry Wong, treasurer; and Muriel Williams, secretary.

Use a dash

1. To show an abrupt change of thought.

   Invoice 76A—which is 10 days overdue—is for $670.

2. After a series to indicate a summarizing statement.

   Noisy fuel pump, worn rods, and failing brakes—for all these reasons I'm trading the car.

Use an exclamation point

After emphatic interjections or exclamatory sentences.

Terrific!   Hold it!   You bet!   What a great surprise!

Proofreading Procedures

Proofread documents so that they are free of errors. Error-free documents send the message that you are detail-oriented and a person capable of doing business. Apply these procedures after you key a document.

1. Use Spelling and Grammar to check the document.
2. Proofread the document on screen to be sure that it makes sense. Check for these types of errors:
   - Words, headings, and/or amounts omitted.
   - Extra words or lines not deleted during the editing stage.
   - Incorrect sequence of numbers in a list.
3. Preview the document on screen using the Print Preview feature. Check the vertical placement, presence of headers or footers, page numbers, and overall appearance.
4. Save the document again and print.
5. Check the printed document by comparing it to the source copy (textbook). Check all figures, names, and addresses against the source copy. Check that the document style has been applied consistently throughout.
6. If errors exist on the printed copy, revise the document, save, and print.
7. Verify the corrections and placement of the second printed copy.

Proofreaders' Marks

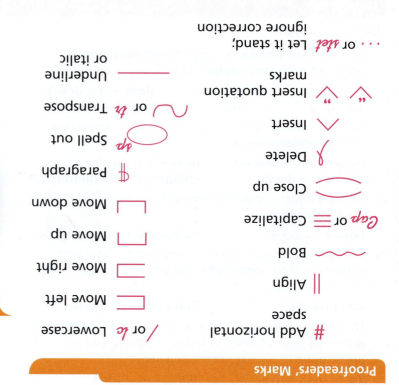

Cap or ≡	Capitalize	⋀	Insert
⌣	Close up	𝛾	Delete
⌢	Transpose *tr*	⌄⌄ ""	Insert quotation marks
sp	Spell out	· · · *stet*	Let it stand; ignore correction
#	Paragraph		Underline or italic
⊐	Move down		
⊓	Move up		
⊐	Move right		
⊏	Move left		
/ or *lc*	Lowercase		
#	Add horizontal space		
‖	Align		
∼	Bold		

Folding and Inserting Procedures

Large envelopes (No. 10, 9, 7¾)

Step 1   **Step 2**   **Step 3**

Step 1: With document face up, fold slightly less than 1/3 of sheet up toward top.

Step 2: Fold down top of sheet to within 1/2" of bottom fold.

Step 3: Insert document into envelope with last crease toward bottom of envelope.

Addressing Procedures

The Envelope feature inserts the delivery address automatically if a letter is displayed. Select the letter address and then create the envelope.

Business letters are usually mailed in envelopes that have the return address preprinted; return addresses are printed only for personal letters or when letterhead is not available. The default size of *Word* is a size 10 envelope (4¹/₈" by 9¹/₂"); other sizes are available using the Options feature.

An address must contain at least three lines; addresses of more than six lines should be avoided. The last line of an address must contain three items of information: (1) the city, (2) the state, and (3) the ZIP Code, preferably a 9-digit code.

Place mailing notations that affect postage (e.g., REGISTERED, CERTIFIED) below the stamp position (line 8); place other special notations (e.g., CONFIDENTIAL, PERSONAL) a DS below the return address.

IMAGE MAKERS
5131 Moss Springs Rd.
Columbia, SC 29209-4768

REGISTERED

Ms. Amy Vreede
Communications Limited
57 Santa Ynez Street
Santa Ana, CA 92708-1537

Formatting Decisions

Decisions regarding document formats require consideration of four elements: (1) attractiveness of the format, (2) readability of the format, (3) effective use of space on the page, and (4) efficiency in producing the format. Please note several formatting decisions made in this text regarding defaults in *Word 2007*.

Styles

Word 2007 offers a quick gallery of styles on the Home tab, and a gallery of cover pages. Using these styles results in efficient production of an attractive title page.

Default 1.15 Line Spacing

The new default line spacing of 1.15 in *Word 2007* provides readers with a more open and more readable copy.

Space after the Paragraph

The new default space after a paragraph in *Word 2007* is 10 points after the paragraph. This automatic spacing saves time and creates an attractive document.

In some situations, the additional 10 points of space after each paragraph consumes too much space and should be removed. For example, the layout is more attractive when the extra spacing is removed between the lines in the letter address or between the writer's name and title. Remove the extra space by clicking on options of the Line Spacing command.

Margins

The default margins for *Word 2007* are 1" top, bottom, left side, and right side. With *Word 2003*, many people simply used the default side margins of 1.25" for both unbound and leftbound reports. With the new side margin default of 1", additional space is needed for the binding of leftbound reports.

Fonts and Document Themes

Microsoft has provided five new true type fonts in *Office 2007* and a number of new document themes that incorporate color and a variety of fonts depending on the theme selected. Color printing has become increasing popular and more cost effective. Many documents presented in the text are based on the default document theme, *Office*, and uses the default heading font, Cambria, and the default body text font, Calibri, 11 point, black text. See the illustration below of the default headings and fonts.

Title (26 pt., Cambria, Bold, Color Text 2)

Subtitle (12 pt., Cambria, Italic, Color Accent 1)

Heading 1 (14 pt., Cambria, Bold, Color Accent 1)

Heading 2 (13 pt., Cambria, Bold, Color Accent 1)

Heading 3 (11 pt., Cambria, Bold, Color Accent 1)

Heading 4 (11 pt., Cambria, Bold, Italic, Color Accent 1)

The default body text is Calibri, 11 pt. color Black.

Default Document Theme: Office: Office

Letter Parts

Letterhead. Company name and address. May include other data.

Date. Date letter is mailed. Usually in month, day, year order. Position at 2" (3 hard returns).

Letter address. Address of the person who will receive the letter. Include personal title (*Mr., Ms., Dr.*); name, professional title, company, and address. In *Word 2007* remove the extra spacing in the letter address.

Salutation. Greeting. Corresponds to the first line of the letter address. Usually includes name and courtesy title; use *Ladies and Gentlemen* if letter is addressed to a company name.

Body. Message. Key in default 1.15 line spacing; tap ENTER once between paragraphs.

Complimentary close. Farewell, such as *Sincerely.*

Writer. Name and professional title. If the name and title are keyed on two lines, remove the extra spacing between the lines.

Initials. Identifies person who keyed the document (for example, *tr*). May include identification of writer (*ARB:tri*).

Enclosure. Copy is enclosed with the document. May specify contents. If more than one line is used, align at 1" and remove the extra spacing between the lines.

Copy notation. Indicates that a copy of the letter is being sent to person named. If more than one line is used, align at 0.5" and remove the extra spacing between the lines.

Note: To remove extra spacing between lines, click the down arrow on the Line Spacing command and select Remove Space After Paragraph.

Letter Placement

Length	Dateline position	Margins
Short: 1-2 ¶s	Center page	Default
Average: 3-4 ¶s	Center page or 2"	Default
Long: 4+ ¶s	2" (default + 3 hard returns)	Default

Block Letter (Open Punctuation)

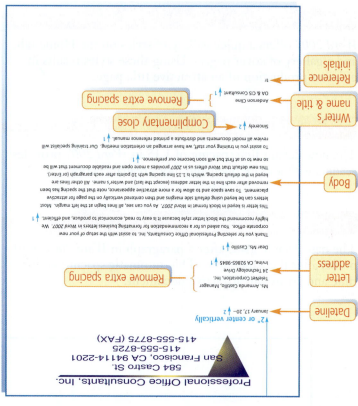

Professional Office Consultants, Inc.
584 Castro St.
San Francisco, CA 94114-2201
415-555-8725
415-555-8775 (FAX)

↓2 — January 17, 20—
2" or center vertically

Letter address (Remove extra spacing)
Ms. Armanda Castillo, Manager ↓1
Telenet Corporation, Inc.
24 Technology Drive
Irvine, CA 92865-9845 ↓1

Dear Ms. Castillo ↓1

Body
Thank you for selecting Professional Office Consultants, Inc., to assist with the setup of your new corporate office. You asked us for a recommendation for formatting business letters in Word 2007. We highly recommend the block letter style because it is easy to read, economical to produce, and efficient. ↓1

This letter is keyed in block format in Word 2007. As you can see, all lines begin at the left margin. Most letters can be keyed using default side margins and then centered vertically on the page for attractive placement. To save space and to allow for a more attractive appearance, note that the spacing has been removed after each line in the letter address (except the last) and writer's name. All other lines are keyed in the default spacing, which is 1.15 line spacing with 10 points after each paragraph (or Enter). This new default that Word offers us in 2007 provides a more open and readable document that will be so new to us at first but will soon become our preference. ↓1

To assist you in training your staff, we have arranged an orientation meeting. Our training specialist will review all model documents and distribute a printed reference manual. ↓1

Complimentary close
Sincerely ↓2

Writer's name & title (Remove extra spacing)
Anderson Cline
OA & CIS Consultant ↓1

Reference initials
tr

Modified Block Letter (Mixed Punctuation)

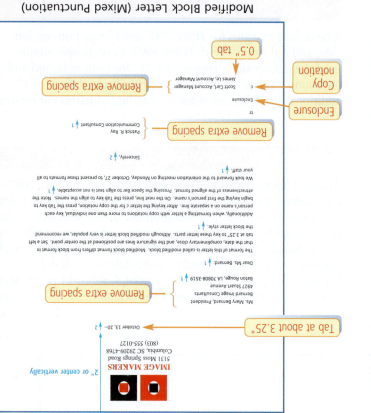

IMAGE MAKERS
5131 Moss Springs Road
Columbia, SC 29209-4768
(803) 555-0127
2" or center vertically

Tab at about 3.25" — October 13, 20— ↓2

Remove extra spacing
Ms. Mary Bernard, President
Bernard Image Consultants
4927 Stuart Avenue
Baton Rouge, LA 70808-3519 ↓1

Dear Ms. Bernard: ↓1

The format of this letter is called modified block. Modified block format differs from block format in that the date, complimentary close, and the signature lines are positioned at the center point. Set a left tab at 3.25" to key these letter parts. Although modified block letter is very popular, we recommend the block letter style. ↓1

Additionally, when formatting a letter with copy notations to more than one individual, key each person's name on a separate line. After keying the letter c for the copy notation, press the Tab key to begin keying the first person's name. On the next line, press the Tab key to align the names. Note the attractiveness of the aligned format. Pressing the Space Bar to align text is not acceptable. ↓1

We look forward to the orientation meeting on Monday, October 27, to present these formats to all your staff. ↓1

Sincerely, ↓2

Remove extra spacing
Patrick R. Ray
Communication Consultant ↓1

tr

Enclosure

Copy notation / 0.5" tab / Remove extra spacing
c   Scott Carl, Account Manager
    James Le, Account Manager

Envelope

IMAGE MAKERS
5131 Moss Springs Road
Columbia, SC 29209-4768

Ms. Mary Bernard, President
Bernard Image Consultants
4927 Stuart Avenue
Baton Rouge, LA 70808-3519

Tap ENTER 3 times

2"

August 15, 20--

CONFIDENTIAL

Ms. Louise Brown, Director
Merritt College
750 East Wolfe Road
Vienna, WV 26105-0750

Dear Ms. Brown:

Thank you for the opportunity to participate as an employer in your internship program. Paul Zieger, one of your technology majors, worked 90 hours this summer and was an excellent addition to our department. His final project was an interactive tutorial of the Merritt College Library. This tutorial provides an electronic tour of the library, including the layout of the library, its holdings, and specific directions on locating certain materials.

Paul has agreed to work part-time for us during the fall semester. Our initial plans are for him to work with faculty in setting up and conducting private demonstrations for classes. In addition, he will write a second tutorial for the graduate library.

Please send another excellent intern next summer.

Sincerely

Daniel E. Romano, Director
Library Services

xx

bc   Paul Zieg

Please take a few

CONFIDENTIAL

Attention Ms. Louise Brown, Director
Merritt College
750 East Wolfe Road
Vienna, WV 26105-0750

Envelope with mailing notation

Business letter with special features

Special letter parts/features

Attention line. Directs the letter to a specific title or person within the company. Positioned as the first line of letter address; the salutation is *Ladies and Gentlemen*.

Company name. Company name of the sender is keyed in ALL CAPS below the complimentary close.

Enumerations. Hanging indent format; position at left margin in a block format.

Mailing notation. Provides record of how the letter was sent (FACSIMILE, CERTIFIED, REGISTERED) or how the letter should be treated by the receiver (CONFIDENTIAL). Position below date.

Postscript. Used to emphasize information: One line below last line of copy.

Reference line. Directs the reader to a source document such as an invoice. One line below letter address.

Return address. Sender's address in a personal business letter. The return address may by keyed immediately above the date or personal letterhead stationery may be used as shown at the left.

Second-page heading. Addressee's name, page number, date arranged in block format in the header. Second sheet is plain paper of the same quality as letterhead.

Subject line. Indicates topic of the letter; below salutation at left margin. It may be keyed in ALL CAPS or cap-and-lowercase.

March 15, 20--

Attention Customer Service Department
Amazon Fashion Mart
4385 Felton Drive
Hays, KS 67601-2863

Ladies and Gentlemen

Fall Fashion Campaign

The demand for two of the items that were sent last week was

Attention line/Subject line

March 15, 20--

CERTIFIED MAIL

Mr. John West, Buyer
Tatnal Music Center
4385 Dove Avenue
Rigby, ID 83442-1244

Re: Order No. R-3855

Dear Mr. West

The items that you ordered last week were sent by overnight

Mailing notation/Reference line

Mr. Jason Artis
Page 2
April 2, 20--

Header position

You will need to perform the following steps:

1. Review the sample projects and proposed guidelines.
2. Determine the specific responsibilities of the project manager and put these in writing.

Thank you, Mr. Artis, for your cooperation. It is always a pleasure working with you.

Sincerely

Second-page heading
Enumerated items (hanging indent format)

Sincerely

Ray Mathias, President

xx

The cashmere sweaters will be shipped by air to you just as soon as our stock is replenished. Your will find them well worth the wait.

Postscript

Standard Memo

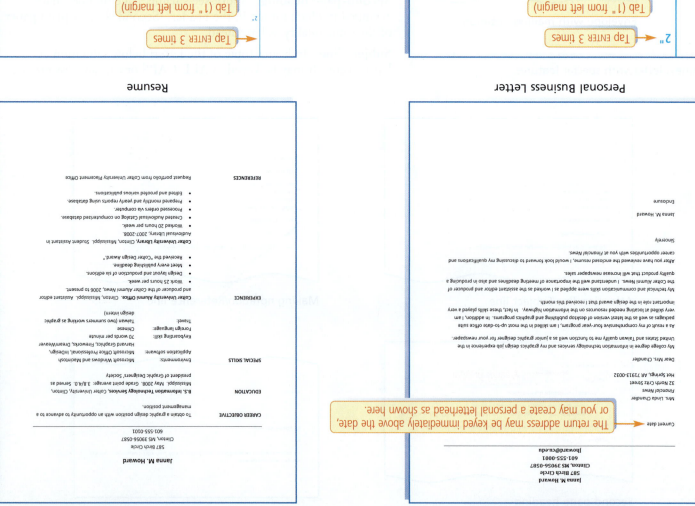

Tap ENTER 3 times → 2"

TO: *Tab (1" from left margin)* Executive Committee
FROM: Colleen Marshall
DATE: November 8, 20--
SUBJECT: Site Selection

Please be prepared to make a final decision on the site for next year's Leadership Training Conference. Our staff reviewed the students' suggestions and have added a few of their own. The following information may be helpful as you make your decision.

1. New York and San Francisco have been eliminated from consideration because of cost factors.
2. New Orleans is now open for consideration. New Orleans has tremendous appeal to students.
3. Charleston, San Antonio, and Tampa were suggested by students as very desirable locations for the conference.

Site selection will be the first item of business at our meeting next Wednesday. I am attaching various hotel brochures for each site.

xx
Attachments

Standard Memo with Distribution List

Tap ENTER 3 times → 2"

TO: *Tab (1" from left margin)* Team Leaders
FROM: Form Paragraph Task Force
DATE: November 9, 20--
SUBJECT: Initial Meetings with Task Force

The task force assigned the responsibility for developing form paragraphs to use in key departments of our company plans to work in your department beginning two weeks from today. Please assign two representatives from your department to coordinate the work with us.

The procedure that the Executive Committee asked us to follow is to collect samples of typical correspondence, meet with departmental representatives to collect additional information, and then to prepare a draft of the form paragraphs for review. After we receive your feedback on the draft copy, we will schedule a meeting to finalize the paragraphs.

Mathew Refern has been assigned as the task force coordinator for your department. Please direct all communication about the project to him.

xx
Distribution List
Nestor Garcia, Claims
Roberta Layman, Underwriting — *Remove extra spacing*
Rosa Romero, Agency Services
Diana Wang, Business Services

Personal Business Letter

Janna M. Howard
587 Birch Circle
Clinton, MS 39056-0587
601-555-0001
Jhoward@cu.edu

The return address may be keyed immediately above the date, or you may create a personal letterhead as shown here.

Current date

Mrs. Linda Chandler
Financial News
32 North Critz Street
Hot Springs, AR 71913-0032

Dear Mrs. Chandler

My college degree in information technology services and my graphics design job experience in the United States and Taiwan qualify me to function well as a junior graphic designer for your newspaper.

As a result of my comprehensive four-year program, I am skilled in the most up-to-date office suite packages as well as the latest version of desktop publishing and graphics programs. In addition, I am very skilled at locating needed resources on the information highway. In fact, these skills played a very important role in the design award that I received this month.

My technical and communication skills were applied as I worked as the assistant editor and producer of the Colter Alumni News. I understand well the importance of meeting deadlines and also in producing a quality product that will increase newspaper sales.

After you have reviewed the enclosed resume, I would look forward to discussing my qualifications and career opportunities with you at Financial News.

Sincerely

Janna M. Howard

Enclosure

Resume

Janna M. Howard
587 Birch Circle
Clinton, MS 39056-0587
601-555-0101

CAREER OBJECTIVE To obtain a graphic design position with an opportunity to advance to a management position.

EDUCATION B.S. Information Technology Services, Colter University, Clinton, Mississippi, May 2008. Grade point average: 3.8/4.0. Served as president of Graphic Designers' Society

SPECIAL SKILLS
Environments: Microsoft Windows and Macintosh
Application software: Microsoft Office Professional, InDesign, Harvard Graphics, Fireworks, DreamWeaver
Keyboarding skill: 70 words per minute
Foreign language: Chinese
Travel: Taiwan (two summers working as graphic design intern)

EXPERIENCE Colter University Alumni Office, Clinton, Mississippi. Assistant editor and producer of the Colter Alumni News, 2006 to present.
• Work 25 hours per week.
• Design layout and production of six editions.
• Meet every publishing deadline.
• Received the "Colter Design Award."

Colter University Library, Clinton, Mississippi. Student Assistant in Audiovisual Library, 2007-2008.
• Worked 20 hours per week.
• Created Audiovisual Catalog on computerized database.
• Processed orders via computer.
• Prepared monthly and yearly reports using database.
• Edited and proofed various publications.

REFERENCES Request portfolio from Colter University Placement Office

Standard Unbound Report

Margins: Tap ENTER three times to begin first page of report and reference page at 2"; default 1" for succeeding pages; *Side* 1"; *Bottom* 1".

Spacing: Default 1.15 line spacing; paragraphs blocked. Tap ENTER once between paragraphs.

Page numbers: Second and subsequent pages are numbered at top right of the page. One blank line follows the page number.

Titles: Title style. Main words capitalized.

Side headings: Heading 1 style. Main words capitalized.

Report Documentation

Internal citations: Provides source of information within report. Includes the author's surname, publication date, and page number (Bruce, 2008, 129). Generate with citation command.

Footnotes: References cited in a report are often indicated within the text by a superscript number (. . . story.[1]) and a corresponding footnote with full information at the bottom of the same page where the reference was cited.

Bibliography or references: Lists all references, whether quoted or not, in alphabetical order by authors' names. References are positioned at 2" on a separate, numbered page. Generated automatically with citation command.

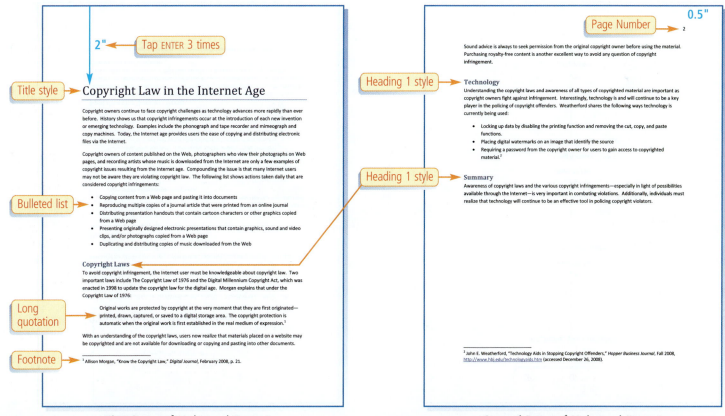

Reference Page

First Page of Unbound Report

Second Page of Unbound Report

Title Page Using Cover Feature

ghjklzxcvbnmqwertyuiopasdfghjklzxc
uiopasdfghjklzxcvbnmqwertyuiopasdf
vbnmqwertyuiopasdfghjklzxcvbnmrty
ghjklzxcvbnmqwertyuiopasdfghjklzxc
uiopasdfghjklzxcvbnmqwertyuiopasdf
mqwertyuiopasdfghjklzxcvbnmqwerty
klzxcvbnmqwertyuiopasdfghjklzxcvbn
pasdfghjklzxcvbnmqwertyuiopasdfghj
wertyuiopasdfghjklzxcvbnmqwertyuio
cvbnmq
dfghjklzx
tyuiopas
nmqwer
jklzxcvbnmqwertyuiopasdfghjklzxcvb
opasdfghjklzxcvbnmqwertyuiopasdfgh
qwertyuiopasdfghjklzxcvbnmqwertyui

Credible and Acceptable Reporting
for All Management Employees
9/23/2009
by Dana Olmstead, Division Manager

Table of Contents

Tap ENTER 3 times → 2"

Title style → Table of Contents

ii

Leftbound Report with Styles and Long Quotation

Tap ENTER 3 times → 2"

Title style → **Trends for Business Dress**

Casual dress in the workplace has become widely accepted. According to a national study conducted by Schoenholtz & Associates, a majority of companies surveyed allowed employees to dress casually one day a week, usually Fridays (Tartt, 2005, 23). The trend continued to climb as shown by the 2006 survey by Schoenholtz & Associates. Fifty-eight percent of office workers surveyed were allowed to dress casually at work every day, and 92 percent of the offices allowed employees to dress casually occasionally (Surphin, 2007, 10).

Heading 1 style → **Decline in Trend**

Internal citation → The trend to dress casually may be shifting, states Susan Monaghan (2008, 34):

Long quotation → Although a large number of companies are allowing casual attire every day or only on Fridays, a current survey revealed a decline of 10 percent in 2008 when compared to the same survey conducted in 2007. Some experts predict the new trend for business dress codes will be a dress up day every week.

What accounts for this decline in companies permitting casual dress? Several reasons may include:

Numbered list →
1. Confusion of what business casual is with employees slipping into dressing too casually (work jeans, faded tee-shirts, old sneakers, and improperly fitting clothing).
2. Casual dress does not portray the adopted corporate image of the company.
3. Employees are realizing that promotion decisions are affected by a professional appearance.

Heading 1 style → **Guidelines for Business Dress**

Companies are employing image consultants to teach employees what is appropriate business casual and to plan the best business attire to project the corporate image. Erica Gilreath (2008), the author of *Casual Dress*, a guidebook on business casual, provides excellent advice on how to dress casually and still command the power needed for business success. She offers the following advice to professionals:

Bulleted list → • Do not wear any clothing that is designed for recreational or sports activities, e.g., cargo pants or pants with elastic waist.

Traditional Title Page

Center the page vertically →

ELECTRONIC MAIL GUIDELINES

↕

Reported for

↕

Mcingvale Communications, Inc.

↕

Reported by

↕

Craig A. Oliver

Information Technology Manager

↕

Current date

Electronic Mail

Electronic mail (or e-mail) requires an e-mail program, an e-mail address, and access to the Internet. Address e-mail carefully. Key and check the address of the recipient and always supply a subject line.

Format the body of an e-mail SS; DS between paragraphs. Do not indent paragraphs. Limit the use of bold, italics, and uppercase. For business use, avoid abbreviations and emoticons (e.g., ;- for wink or BTW for by the way).

E-mail Etiquette

1. Create a meaningful subject line that is tailored to the specific content. Limit e-mail to one topic.

2. Get to the point quickly; the most important message should appear in the first paragraph.

3. Capitalize only to highlight proper nouns—do not use uppercase for emphasis.

4. Keep paragraphs focused and short. Use bullets for emphasis.

5. Be clear on the response you are expecting from the reader.

6. Include a signature that automatically includes your full name and contact information so that a recipient may follow up by telephone or fax.

7. Use file attachments to send detailed information; keep e-mail brief.

8. Check spelling and grammar before sending an e-mail. Read your message carefully before sending.

9. Assume the good intentions of the sender when reading or responding to others.

10. Consider talking to the receiver in person or by telephone if communication seems tense or unclear.

11. Do not forward a chain message.

12. Use company e-mail for company business. Companies have the right to monitor business e-mail accounts.

13. Respond to e-mails you receive within 24 hours if possible.

Table Format Guides

1. Position the table about 2" or center the table vertically on the page.

2. If the title/main heading is keyed outside the table, center, bold, and use 14-point font; for the secondary heading, center, bold, 12-point font; capitalize main words. Center and bold column headings.

3. Generally, key the title as part of the table so that if it is inserted within another document, the entire table is inserted.

4. Adjust column widths attractively; center the table horizontally.

5. Align text within the cells at the left; align numbers at the right; align decimals of varying lengths at the decimal.

6. When a table is within a document, leave one line above and below the table (same as between paragraphs).

OUTPATIENT PROSPECTIVE PAYMENT SYSTEM Unadjusted National Medicare Reimbursement				
Description	**Code**		**Insurance**	
	CPT	**APC**	**Medicare**	**Coinsurance**
Immobilization	77341	0303	71.08	69.28
Basic Dosimetry	77300	0304	388.52	498.26
Daily IMRT Treatment	60174	0302	7,625.19	8,662.14
Continuing Physics	77336	0311	270.48	253.26

Note the table style may vary.

SUMMARY OF COMMANDS

Commands	Path
Adjust Column Width	Ruler/Column Marker/Drag to appropriate position
Autofit Table	Table Tools/Layout/Cell Size/Autofit
Automatic Current Date	Key 4 characters/Enter
Bibliography	References/Citations & Bibliography/Bibliography
Bookmark	Insert/Links/Bookmark
Borders in Tables	Table Tools/Design/Table Styles/Borders
Bullets and Numbering	Home/Paragraph/Bullets or Numbering
Cell Alignment in Tables	Table Tools/Layout/Alignment
Cell Height and Width	Table Tools/Layout/Cell Size
Center Page	Page Layout/Page Setup/Dialog Box Launcher/ Layout tab/Vertical Alignment/Center
Center Table Horizontally	Click in table/Layout/Table/Properties/ Center Alignment
Change Row Height and Center Text	Click in cell/Table Tools/Layout/Cell Size/ Alignment
Change Styles	Home/Styles/Change Styles/Style Set
Change Table Structure	Click in table/Table Tools/Layout/Insert or delete rows or columns

Commands	Path	
Citation	References/Citations & Bibliography/Insert Citation	
Clip Art	Insert/Illustrations/Clip Art	
Clipboard	Home/Clipboard	
Clipboard Group: Cut, Copy, and Paste	Home/Clipboard/Click Cut, Copy, or Paste	
Clipboard Group: Format Painter	Home/Clipboard/Format Painter	
Close Document	Office Button/Close or Close button at top right of screen	
Columns	Page Layout/Page Setup/Columns	
Cover Page	Insert/Pages/Cover Page	
Create a Template	Office Button/Save As/Word Template	
Create Columns	Page Layout/Page Setup/Columns	
Crop Picture	Picture Tools/Format/Size/Crop	
Customize Quick Access Toolbar	Quick Access Toolbar/Click down arrow/ Click each command to be added	
Date and Time	Insert/Text/Date and Time	
Decimal Tab in Table	Select Column/Click Tab Alignment/Decimal Tab/Click appropriate position on Ruler	
Display Section in Status Bar	Right-click Status Bar/Section	

Commands	Path
Document Themes	Page Layout/Themes/Themes
Drop Cap	Insert/Text/Drop Cap
Edit Recipient List	Mailings/Start Mail Merge/Edit Recipient List
Endnotes	References/Footnotes/Insert Endnote
Envelopes	Mailings/Create/Envelopes
Exit Word	Office button/Exit Word
Find and Replace	Home/Editing/Find or Replace
Footnotes	References/Footnotes/Insert Footnote
Format Endnotes	References/Footnotes/Footnotes Dialog Box Launcher
Formulas in Table	Layout/Data/Formula
Hanging Indent	Ruler/Hanging Indent marker
Headers	Insert/Header & Footer/Header
Help	Click Help button

Commands	Path
Increase Indent	Home/Paragraph/Increase Indent
Indent	Page Layout/Paragraph/Indent
Insert and Delete Rows and Columns	Table Tools/Layout/Rows & Columns
Insert File	Insert/Text/Object/Text from File
Insert Table	Insert/Tables/Table
Insert Text from File	Insert/Text/Object/Text from File
Line and Page Breaks	Home/Paragraph/Dialog Box Launcher/Line and Page Breaks tab
Line Between Columns	Page Layout/Page Setup/Columns/More Columns/Line Between
Line Spacing	Home/Paragraph/Line spacing
Mail Merge	Mailings/Start Mail Merge/Start Mail Merge
Manage Sources	References/Citations & Bibliography/Manage Sources
Margins	Page Layout/Page Setup/Margins
Merge and Split Cells	Click in or select cells/Table Tools/Layout/Merge or Split Cells
Merge Envelopes	Mailings/Start Mail Merge/Start Mail Merge/Select Recipients
Merge Labels	Mailings/Start Mail Merge/Start Mail Merge/Select Recipients

Commands	Path
Merge or Split Cells	Table Tools/Layout/Merge or Split
Mini Toolbar	Appears when text is selected
Move Clip Art	Picture Tools/Format/Arrange/Text Wrapping
Normal Style (default)	Home/Styles/Normal
Open New Document, Open Existing Document	Office Button/New or Open; then locate the file
Page Borders	Page Layout/Page Background/Page Borders
Page Break	Insert/Pages/Page Break
Page Numbers	Insert/Header & Footer/Page Number
Page Orientation	Page Layout/Page Setup/Orientation
Paragraph Borders and Shading	Select paragraph/Page Layout/Page Background/Page Borders/Borders and Shading
Paragraph Formats	Home/Paragraph/Click desired command
Paragraph Formats: Alignment—Align Text Left, Center, Align Text Right, and Justify	Home/Paragraph/Click desired alignment
Paragraph Formats: Show/Hide	Home/Paragraph/Show/Hide
Paste Function	Layout/Data/Formula/Paste Function

Commands	Path
Paste Options Button	Home/Clipboard/Paste/Paste Options Button
Picture from File	Insert/Illustrations/Picture
Picture Styles	Picture Tools/Format/Picture Styles
Quick Access Toolbar	Upper-left corner of screen/Use down arrow to customize
Quick Print, Print, and Print Preview	Office Button/Print/Print Preview, Print, or Quick Print
Quick Styles	Home/Styles/Quick Styles
Remove Page Number on First Page	Design/Options/Different First Page
Remove Space After Paragraph	Home/Paragraph/Line spacing
Remove Table Borders	Select table/TableTools/Design/Borders/No Border
Save and Save As	Office Button/Save or Save As
Save as *Word* Template	Office button/Save As/Word Template
Section Breaks	Page Layout/Page Setup/Breaks
Select Portions of Table	Click in table/Table Tools/Layout/Select

Commands	Path	
Shading in Tables	Table Tools/Design/Table Styles/Shading	
Shapes	Insert/Illustrations/Shapes	
Size Clip Art	Picture Tools/Format/Size/Height	
Size Clip Art	Select Lower-Right or Lower-Left Handle/Drag to appropriate size	
Slider: Zoom in or out	Click Slider/move left or right to zoom in or out	
SmartArt	Insert/Illustrations/SmartArt	
Sort and Filter Records	Mailings/Start Mail Merge/Edit Recipient List/Sort	
Special Characters	Insert/Symbols/Symbol/More Symbols/Special Characters	
Spelling and Grammar	Review/Proofing/Spelling & Grammar	
Styles	Home/Styles/Quick Styles	
Symbols	Insert/Symbols/Symbol/More Symbols/Symbol	
Table of Contents	References/Table of Contents/Table of Contents	
Table Properties	Table Tools/Layout/Table/Properties	

Commands	Path
Table Styles	Click in table/Table Tools/Design
Table Tools	Insert/Tables/Table; click in Table/Table Tools
Tabs	View Ruler/Tab Alignment Button/ Click on Horizontal Ruler
Tabs in Table	Ruler/Tab
Templates	Office button/New/Installed Templates
Text Direction in Table	Table Tools/Layout/Alignment/Text Direction
Text Formats: Font, Font Size, Grow Font, Shrink Font, Bold, Italic, Underline, Text Highlight Color, and Font Color	Home/Font/Click desired text format command
Text Wrapping	Picture Tools/Format/Arrange/Text Wrapping
Thesaurus	Review/Proofing/Thesaurus
Underline Tab	Home/Paragraph/Paragraph Dialog Box Launcher/Tabs
Undo Automatic Capitalization	AutoCorrect Options/Undo Automatic Capitalization
Update Table of Content	References/Table of Contents/Update Table of Contents
Vertical Page Position	Right-click Status Bar/Vertical Page Position
View Ruler	Click View Ruler button

Commands	Path	
Views	Select view buttons on status bar	
Watermark	Page layout/Page Background/Watermark	
WordArt	Insert/Text/WordArt	
Wrap Text Around Graphic	Select graphic/Format/Arrange/Text Wrapping	

INDEX